SAGE
vantage

Praise for

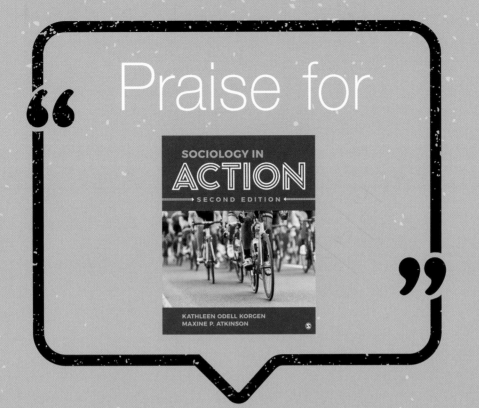

SOCIOLOGY IN ACTION

SECOND EDITION

KATHLEEN ODELL KORGEN
MAXINE P. ATKINSON

"The chapters are short, concise, and easily consumable for the undergraduate student. The authors are **VERY CLEAR** about what they want to cover. This text also has **GREAT ACTIVITIES** to go along with each chapter."

—Tabitha Ingle
Georgia State University

"What attracted me was the fact that I had to put together an online class, and *Sociology in Action* already had a package for that. They had **EVERYTHING** — discussion, activities—beyond what a regular text offers."

— Chandra Ward
University of Tennessee-Chattanooga

"I had been using [an OER] text, which was free. However, this book is **SO MUCH BETTER** in terms of content. It is well written, provides examples similar to ones I use, provides good thinking activities, and is **INCLUSIVE** of gender, race, and other identities."

—Melissa Bamford
The University of Memphis

"The associated coursepack for Canvas is incredible. I was able to add links to the relevant e-book chapters directly into my Canvas course modules. Students have really liked the additional video and audio content. In short, **I LOVE IT**."

—Edward Colin Ruggero
Community College of Philadelphia

Sara Miller McCune founded SAGE Publishing in 1965 to support the dissemination of usable knowledge and educate a global community. SAGE publishes more than 1000 journals and over 600 new books each year, spanning a wide range of subject areas. Our growing selection of library products includes archives, data, case studies and video. SAGE remains majority owned by our founder and after her lifetime will become owned by a charitable trust that secures the company's continued independence.

Los Angeles | London | New Delhi | Singapore | Washington DC | Melbourne

SOCIOLOGY IN
ACTION
SECOND EDITION

SOCIOLOGY IN ACTION

SECOND EDITION

KATHLEEN ODELL KORGEN

William Paterson University

MAXINE P. ATKINSON

North Carolina State University

Los Angeles | London | New Delhi
Singapore | Washington DC | Melbourne

FOR INFORMATION:

SAGE Publications, Inc.
2455 Teller Road
Thousand Oaks, California 91320
E-mail: order@sagepub.com

SAGE Publications Ltd.
1 Oliver's Yard
55 City Road
London EC1Y 1SP
United Kingdom

SAGE Publications India Pvt. Ltd.
B 1/I 1 Mohan Cooperative Industrial Area
Mathura Road, New Delhi 110 044
India

SAGE Publications Asia-Pacific Pte. Ltd.
18 Cross Street #10-10/11/12
China Square Central
Singapore 048423

Acquisitions Editor: Jeff Lasser
Content Development Editor: Tara Slagle
Editorial Assistant: Tiara Beatty
Production Editor: Tracy Buyan
Copy Editor: Jim Kelly
Typesetter: C&M Digitals (P) Ltd.
Proofreader: Alison Syring
Indexer: Kathy Paparchontis
Cover Designer: Gail Buschman
Marketing Manager: Will Walter

Printed in Canada

ISBN (pbk): 978-1-5443-5641-9
ISBN (loose-leaf): 978-1-0718-0228-1

This book is printed on acid-free paper.

20 21 22 23 24 10 9 8 7 6 5 4 3 2 1

BRIEF CONTENTS

DETAILED CONTENTS

©iStockphoto.com/foto-select

Chapter 3. Using Research Methods   36

Mikaila Mariel Lemonik Arthur and Amanda M. Jungels

Robert K. Chin/Alamy Stock Photo

Chapter 5. Understanding Socialization and Interaction 76
Amy Sodaro

©iStockphoto.com/ferrantraite

Chapter 6. Identifying Deviant Behavior 96
Rena C. Zito

©iStockphoto.com/SelectStock

Chapter 11. Understanding Institutions: Family 210
Carissa Froyum

BUSINESS GOVERNMENT SUPPORT

iStockphoto.com/kate_sept2004

Chapter 13. Experiencing Health, Illness, and Medical Care   258
Amy Irby-Shasanmi

Chapter 14. Understanding Institutions: Religion   278
Andrea N. Hunt

©Bill Pugliano/Stringer/Getty Images

AP Photo/Erik McGregor

PREFACE

If you, like us, have found yourself searching for activities to bring into your classroom and engage your introductory sociology students, you know why we wrote this book. We knew we couldn't be alone in our quest to get students to do more than read the text—we want them to *do* sociology, to understand and apply the terms and concepts they read about and realize them in the real world. Over the course of writing and refining the manuscript, as well as reading the reviews of instructors excited to see activities many of us have been cobbling together over the years now residing within a textbook, we became even more convinced that our approach is one that offers instructors material for how they want to teach and offers students the foundational content they need in sociology, as well as engaging activities that will help them *do* sociology. The overwhelmingly enthusiastic response to the first edition provided further evidence that this is a book that can help all sociology instructors get their students excited about sociology and what they can do with it.

Sociology in Action puts all the tools instructors need to create an active learning course into one student-friendly text. Active learning teaching techniques increase student learning, retention, and engagement with course material, but they also require more creative effort than traditional lectures. No other sociology textbook works to ease this load by providing full coverage of introductory content *and* active learning exercises fully integrated into the text (with clear instructions on how to use and assess them available through the instructor resources). *Sociology in Action* provides instructors of small, medium, large, and online introductory courses with the material they need to create learning experiences for their students, including creative, hands-on, data-analytic, and community learning activities.

A group of gifted instructors who use active learning techniques in their own classrooms has written the book's chapters. The contributors, focusing on their respective areas of expertise, expertly weave together content material, active learning exercises, discussion questions, real-world examples of sociologists in action, and information on careers that use sociology. Together, we have created a book that requires students to *do* sociology as they learn it and creates a bridge between the classroom and the larger social world.

Organization and Features

The clear organizational style of each chapter helps students follow the logic of the text and concentrate on the main ideas presented. Each chapter opens with focal learning questions, and each major section ends with review questions to remind students of the emphasis in the presented material. In addition, the chapters contain an analysis of subject matter from both *major theoretical perspectives* and, where appropriate, *middle-range theories*. Chapters close with conclusions, and end-of-chapter resources include lists of key terms and summaries that address the focal learning questions. The active learning activities and *Consider This* marginal questions throughout each chapter help create a student-centered class that engages student interest.

The book's rich pedagogy supports active learning and engagement throughout each chapter.

- *Learning Questions* start off every chapter, introducing students to the focus of the chapter and preparing them for the material it covers. These questions are tied to the learning objectives provided in the instructor resources. Each main section of the chapter addresses a learning question.

- *Check Your Understanding* questions appear at the end of every major section in a chapter, providing students with an opportunity to pause in their reading and ensure that they comprehend and retain what they've just read.

- *Doing Sociology* activities appear multiple times in each chapter. These active learning exercises enable students to apply the sociological concepts, theories, methods, and so on covered in the text. Each chapter contains a variety of exercises so that instructors can use them in class, online, or as assignments conducted outside of class. Reference the *Doing Sociology* activities and the clear instructions on how to carry them out—and on how they relate to the chapter objectives—in the Activity Guide available through the book's instructor resources. Additional exercises can be found in the digital resources accompanying the text.

- **Consider This** questions are designed to spark deep thinking as well as classroom discussions.

- **Sociologists in Action** boxes feature a student or professional "sociologist in action" doing public sociology related to the material covered in the chapter. This feature provides examples of how sociology can be used to make a positive impact on society.

- **Key Terms** appear in boldface type where they are substantially discussed for the first time and are compiled in a list with page numbers at the end of their respective chapters. Corresponding definitions can be found in the Glossary.

- Every chapter concludes with a **Chapter Summary** that restates the learning questions presented at the start of the chapter and gives answers to them. This provides an important way for students to refresh their understanding of the material and retain what they've learned.

In addition, as appropriate, chapters include information on careers that relate to the chapter content. This allows students to recognize, even during their first sociology course, the wide variety of career options a sociology degree provides.

What's New in the Second Edition

After using *Sociology in Action* ourselves—and hearing from many instructors who also used it—we worked to make it even more useful for instructors and interesting for students. Key changes and additions we made include the following:

- More *Doing Sociology* exercises that take a short time in class.

- Adding *Doing Sociology* exercises that use SAGE Stats to allow students to access and use statistical information created from more than 400,000 government and nongovernment data sets.

- Creating two new chapters: "Experiencing Health, Illness, and Medical Care" and "Understanding Institutions: Politics and the Economy."

- Using an even more applied and student-friendly approach in our writing.

- Expanding the "Understanding Socialization" chapter to "Understanding Socialization and Interaction," with a new section on groups, organizations, and bureaucracies.

- Making better connections between theories and the rest of the chapter narratives by using only perspectives and midrange theories that relate directly to the subject matter.

- Adding new *Doing Sociology* exercises, *Consider This* questions, and *Sociologists in Action* features (each now including a discussion question).

- Thoroughly updating all chapters without adding to their length, including new or updated topics (in addition to the new chapters), such as

  o the causes and ramifications of the 2016 election;

  o the latest issues facing the LGBT community, people of color, immigrants and refugees, and the shrinking middle class;

  o student loan debt;

  o class inequality;

  o climate change;

  o sexuality;

  o sexual harassment;

  o power and who writes history;

  o a more thorough explanation of racism and its systemic components;

  o the connections among social position, place and health, and life expectancy; and

  o the relationship between public education and democracy.

Digital Resources

We know how important good resources can be in the teaching of sociology. Our goal is to create resources that both support and enhance the book's themes and features. SAGE edge offers a robust online environment featuring an impressive array of tools and resources for review, study, and further exploration, keeping both instructors and students on the cutting edge of teaching and learning. SAGE edge content is open access and available on demand. Learning and teaching have never been easier! We gratefully acknowledge Sarah Calabi, Rachel Lovis, Rob Freeland, and Megan Glancy.

⑤SAGE vantage™

Engage, Learn, Soar with **SAGE vantage**, an intuitive digital platform that delivers *Sociology in Action* textbook content in a learning experience carefully designed to ignite student engagement and drive critical thinking. With evidence-based instructional design at the core, **SAGE vantage** creates more time for engaged learning and empowered teaching, keeping the classroom where it belongs—in your hands.

Easy to access across mobile, desktop, and tablet devices, **SAGE vantage** enables students to engage with the material you choose, learn by applying knowledge, and soar with confidence by performing better in your course.

Highlights Include:

- *eReading Experience.* Makes it easy for students to study wherever they are—students can take notes, highlight content, look up definitions, and more!

- *Pedagogical Scaffolding.* Builds on core concepts, moving students from basic understanding to mastery.

- *Confidence Builder.* Offers frequent knowledge checks, applied-learning multimedia tools, and chapter tests with focused feedback to assure students know key concepts.

- *Time-saving Flexibility.* Feeds auto-graded assignments to your gradebook, with real-time insight into student and class performance.

- *Quality Content.* Written by expert authors and teachers, content is not sacrificed for technical features.

- *Honest Value.* Affordable access to easy-to-use, quality learning tools students will appreciate.

Favorite SAGE vantage Features:

- 3-step course setup is so fast you can complete it in minutes!

- Control over assignments, content selection, due dates, and grading empowers you to teach your way.

- Quality content authored by the experts you trust.

- eReading experience makes it easy to learn and study by presenting content in easy-to-digest segments featuring note-taking, highlighting, definition look-up, and more.

- LMS integration provides single sign-on with streamlined grading capabilities and course management tools.

- Auto-graded assignments include:

  o formative knowledge checks for each major section of the text that quickly reinforce what students have read and ensure they stay on track;

  o dynamic, hands-on multimedia activities that tie real world examples and motivate students to read, prepare for class;

  o summative chapter tests that reinforce important themes; and

  o helpful hints and feedback (provided with all assignments) that offer context and explain why an answer is correct or incorrect, allowing students to study more effectively.

- Compelling polling questions bring concepts to life and drive meaningful comprehension and classroom discussion.

- Short-answer questions provide application and reflection opportunities connected to key concepts.

- Instructor reports track student activity and provide analytics so you can adapt instruction as needed.

- A student dashboard offers easy access to grades, so students know exactly where they stand in your course and where they might improve.

- Honest value gives students access to quality content and learning tools at a price they will appreciate.

⑤SAGE coursepacks

Our content tailored to your LMS
sagepub.com/coursepacks

The **SAGE coursepack** for *Sociology in Action* makes it easy to import our quality instructor materials and student resources into your school's learning management system (LMS), such as Blackboard, Canvas, Brightspace by D2L, or Moodle. Intuitive and simple to use, **SAGE coursepack** allows you to integrate only the content you need, with minimal effort, and requires no access code. Don't use an LMS platform? You can still access many of the online resources for *Sociology in Action* via the **SAGE edge** site.

Available SAGE content through the coursepack includes:

- Pedagogically robust assessment tools that foster review, practice, and critical thinking and offer a more complete way to measure student engagement, including:

  - Diagnostic chapter quizzes that identify opportunities for improvement, track student progress, and ensure mastery of key learning objectives

  - Test banks built on Bloom's taxonomy that provide a diverse range of test items

  - Activity and quiz options that allow you to choose only the assignments and tests you want

  - Instructions that are given on how to use and integrate the comprehensive assessments and resources provided

  - An Activity Guide that details all activities from the print book, as well as supplementary exercises, the learning objectives they address, and notes to instructors

  - Editable, chapter-specific PowerPoint slides that offer flexibility when creating multimedia lectures, so you don't have to start from scratch but you can customize to your exact needs

⑤SAGE edge™

http://edge.sagepub.com/korgen2e

SAGE edge is a robust online environment featuring an impressive array of tools and resources for review, study, and further exploration, keeping both instructors and students on the cutting edge of teaching and learning. SAGE edge content is open access and available on demand. Learning and teaching has never been easier!

SAGE edge for Students at **http://edge.sagepub.com/ korgen2e** provides a personalized approach to help students accomplish their coursework goals in an easy-to-use learning environment.

- Learning objectives reinforce the most important material

- Mobile-friendly flashcards that strengthen understanding of key terms and concepts and make it easy to maximize your study time, anywhere, anytime

- Mobile-friendly practice quizzes that allow you to assess how much you've learned and where you need to focus your attention

- An MCAT Guide that maps chapter content to sociology standards on the MCAT test and

connects you with free online MCAT study-and-review websites.

SAGE edge for Instructors at http://edge.sagepub .com/korgen2e supports teaching by making it easy to integrate quality content and create a rich learning environment for students.

- The **Test bank**, built on Bloom's taxonomy (with Bloom's cognitive domain and difficulty level noted for each question), is created specifically for this text.

- **Sample course syllabi** provide suggested models for structuring your course.

- Editable, chapter-specific **PowerPoint® slides** offer complete flexibility for creating a multimedia presentation for the course, so you don't have to start from scratch but can customize to your exact needs.

- **Lecture notes** feature comprehensive chapter outlines and learning objectives.

- A set of all the **graphics from the text**, including all the maps, tables, and figures in PowerPoint and JPG formats, are provided for class presentations.

SAGE Premium Video

Sociology in Action offers premium video, available exclusively in the **SAGE vantage** digital option, produced and curated spefor this text, to boost comprehension and bolster analysis.

Acknowledgments

We would like to acknowledge the many people who worked with us on *Sociology in Action*. Our thanks, first and foremost, go to the contributors who wrote the chapters and helped us create an active learning introductory sociology course in one text. Their exceptional ability to use active learning in the classroom has impressed and inspired us. We appreciate their willingness to share what they do so well and to collaborate with us on *Sociology in Action*.

The two of us would also like to extend our gratitude to the wonderful people at SAGE for their tremendous work on this project. Acquisitions editor Jeff Lasser believed in the need for this text, brought us together, and is the chief reason this book (and the entire *Sociology in Action* series) became a reality. Tara Slagle, our content development editor, provided her great expertise in helping us shape this book. Jim Kelly made sure the book was copyedited beautifully, while production editor Tracy Buyan engineered the transformation of the manuscript into real book pages. Editorial assistant Tiara Beatty managed to keep everything on track and moving forward throughout this long process.

We are also deeply indebted to the following reviewers who offered their keen insights and suggestions.

First edition reviewers:

Deborah A. Abowitz, Bucknell University

Rebecca Barrett-Fox, Arkansas State University

Chastity Blankenship, Florida Southern College

Mark Braun, State University of New York Cobleskill

Joslyn Brenton, Ithaca College

Jess Butler, Butler University

Linda Carson, Lander University

Susan Claxton, Georgia Highlands College

Steven Dashiell, Towson University

Jeffrey Debies-Carl, University of New Haven

Richard G. Ellefritz, Oklahoma State University

Sarah Epplen, Minnesota State University, Mankato

Michael W. Feeley, South Suburban College

Lisa George, Portland Community College

Danielle Giffort, St. Louis College of Pharmacy

Laura Fitzwater Gonzales, Pacific Lutheran University

Belisa Gonzalez, Ithaca College

Roderick Graham, Old Dominion University

Wendi Hadd, John Abbott College

Anita Harker, Whatcom Community College

Jodi A. Henderson-Ross, University of Akron–Wayne College

William Housel, Northwestern Louisiana State University

Aaron Howell, Farmingdale State College

Suzanne S. Hudd, Quinnipiac University

Peter Kaufman, State University of New York New Paltz

Michele Lee Kozimor-King, Elizabethtown College

Andrea Krieg, Lewis University

Ashley Lumpkin, John Tyler Community College

Lori Lundell, Purdue University

Elizabeth Lyman, Radford University

Sara F. Mason, University of North Georgia

Naomi McCool, Chaffey College

Cassandra McDade, Tidewater Community College

Stephanie Medley-Rath, Indiana University Kokomo

Marian J. Moore, Owens Community College

Madeline H. Moran, Lehman College, City University of New York

Jonathan Ortiz, Concordia University

Doris Price, Houston Community College

Barbara Prince, Bowling Green State University

Carolyn Read, Copiah Lincoln Junior College

Nicole Rosen, Pennsylvania State Behrend

Matthew Schoene, Albion College

Naomi Simmons, Newberry College

Chelsea Starr, Eastern New Mexico University

Melissa Swauger, Indiana University of Pennsylvania

Lori Waite, Tennessee Wesleyan University

Jeremy White, Pikes Peak Community College

Joshua Wimberly, Spring Hill College

Susan Wortmann, Nebraska Wesleyan University

Kassia Wosick, El Camino College

Mariah Jade Zimpfer, Sam Houston State University

John F. Zipp, University of Akron

Second edition reviewers:

Melissa Bamford, The University of Memphis

Terrie A. Becerra, East Central University

Stephanie L. Bradley, Radford University

Janice Crede, College of St. Scholastica

Máel Embser-Herbert, Hamline University

Tabitha Ingle, Georgia State University

Jamie L. Gusrang, Community College of Philadelphia

Kendra Jason, University of North Carolina at Charlotte

Joy Kadowaki, University of Dayton

Jeffrey Lentz, University of North Georgia

Ying Ma, Austin Peay State University

Kenjuana McCray, Fayetteville Technical Community College

Matthew McLeskey, University at Buffalo, SUNY

Lori Peek, University of Colorado Boulder

Edward Colin Ruggero, Community College of Philadelphia

Chandra Ward, University of Tennessee at Chattanooga

Finally, we offer our great thanks to our families for their support and patience as we devoted so much of our time to *Sociology in Action*.

—Kathleen Odell Korgen and Maxine P. Atkinson

ABOUT THE AUTHORS

 **Kathleen Odell Korgen**, PhD, is a professor of sociology at William Paterson University in Wayne, New Jersey. Her primary areas of specialization are teaching sociology, racial identity, and race relations. She has received William Paterson University's awards for Excellence in Scholarship/Creative Expression and for Excellence in Teaching.

 **Maxine P. Atkinson**, PhD, is a professor of sociology at North Carolina State University in Raleigh. Her primary area of specialization is the scholarship of teaching and learning. She has received the American Sociological Association's Distinguished Contributions to Teaching Award and the University of North Carolina Board of Governors' Award for Excellence in Teaching.

ABOUT THE CONTRIBUTORS

Mikaila Mariel Lemonik Arthur teaches research methods and other sociology courses at Rhode Island College. Her research focuses on the sociology of higher education. Prior publications include *Student Activism and Curricular Change in Higher Education* (2011) and journal articles on organizational change in higher education, social networks among colleges and universities, and the long-term outcomes of Rhode Island's comprehensive college graduates, as well as on teaching and learning in sociology.

Wendy M. Christensen received her PhD from the University of Wisconsin–Madison and is an associate professor of sociology at William Paterson University in New Jersey. Her research focuses on how inequalities (race, class, and gender) shape political participation. She has published articles on the political participation of mothers of U.S. military members, as well as the intersections of military recruitment campaigns and race, class, and gender. Her forthcoming book, *Our Families Your Freedom: How Military Mothers Support and Challenge the U.S. War on Terrorism*, examines how mothers of service members negotiate the politics of support through recruitment, deployment, and postdeployment health care. She is currently collecting data for a new research project on community political organizing and voter participation.

Sandra Enos, PhD, serves as an associate professor of sociology at Bryant University. She earned a PhD from the University of Connecticut after a long career in public service. She is the author of *Mothering from the Inside: Parenting in a Women's Prison* (2001), *Service-Learning and Social Entrepreneurship in Higher Education: A Pedagogy of Social Change* (2015), and chapters in books and articles on women and mass incarceration, the history of child welfare, pedagogy in sociology, and higher education reform.

Carissa Froyum is a professor of sociology at the University of Northern Iowa. Her research focuses on the roles emotions and identity play in reproducing inequalities. She is the coeditor of *Inside Social Life, Creating and Contesting Inequalities* and the forthcoming *Handbook of the Sociology of Gender* (with Barbara Risman and William Scarborough).

Melissa S. Fry is the director of the Applied Research and Education Center and an associate professor of sociology at Indiana University Southeast. Dr. Fry's research has included work on poverty, education (early childhood through higher education), homelessness, systems thinking for community development, government contracting with nonprofits, work supports for low-income families, the impact of the coal industry in central Appalachia, and payday lending. Dr. Fry's broad research agenda is to better understand how public policies are both shaped by and, in turn, shape social inequality and how nonprofit organizations manage the tensions among their missions, government contracts, and the interests of private philanthropies in their efforts to build resilient communities. Prior to joining the Indiana University Southeast faculty in 2011, Dr. Fry was a research and policy associate at the Mountain Association for Community Economic Development in Berea, Kentucky.

Andrea N. Hunt, PhD, is an associate professor of sociology at the University of North Alabama. Her teaching focuses on diverse families, race and ethnicity, gender, and social justice. Her research in the scholarship of teaching and learning focuses on gender bias in instructor evaluations, the role of academic advising in student retention, mentoring undergraduate research, and learning experiences that promote information literacy and cultural competency. Dr. Hunt has facilitated numerous workshops on academic advising for diverse student populations, preparing high school students for college, best practices for online learning, and techniques for teaching about social inequality. Her research has been featured in *Teaching Sociology*, the *International Journal for the Scholarship of Teaching and Learning*, the *Journal of Effective Teaching*, *Mentoring and Tutoring: Partnership in Learning*, and *Innovative Higher Education*. All of her teaching, research, and service are centered on empowering students and faculty for success.

Amy Irby-Shasanmi is an assistant professor of sociology at the University of West Georgia. Her research focuses on mental health, health disparities, chronic illness, and disabilities. She regularly teaches courses on all of these subjects in her department, as well as Introduction to Social Problems.

Amanda M. Jungels is a senior assistant director for faculty programs and services in the Center for Teaching and Learning at Columbia University. She earned her PhD from the Department of Sociology at Georgia State University, where she was a recipient of the Jacqueline Boles Teaching Fellowship and Teaching Associate Award. Her current work focuses on faculty and educational development, emphasizing inclusive teaching practices and pedagogy.

John Chung-En Liu is an assistant professor of sociology at Occidental College. He received his PhD in sociology from the University of Wisconsin–Madison, holds a joint master's degree in economics and environmental management from Yale University, and has a bachelor's degree in chemical engineering from National Taiwan University. His main research projects include a wide array of topics about climate change, including the construction of carbon markets, climate change skepticism, and climate change in higher education curriculums. He has research experiences in the United States, the European Union, China, Taiwan, and India.

Kathleen S. Lowney was a professor of sociology at Valdosta State University until May 2018, when she retired. Most of her published work falls under three broad research topics: the sociology of new religious movements, especially teen Satanism; media's role in the construction of social problems claims, such as her article on kudzu as a social problem and her book *Baring Our Souls: TV Talk Shows and the Religion of Recovery* (1999); and the scholarship of teaching and learning. She and Dr. Maxine Atkinson wrote *In the Trenches: Teaching and Learning Sociology* (2016) to help sociology teachers discover innovative ways to communicate the discipline we love to students. She has received several teaching awards at her university, from the University System of Georgia, and from the American Sociological Association.

David E. Rohall is the department head of the Sociology and Anthropology Department at Missouri State University. Prior to coming to Missouri State, he received the Distinguished Faculty Lecturer Award in 2014 for his teaching and research in sociology from Western Illinois University, where he taught for 11 years.

Amy Sodaro is an associate professor of sociology at the Borough of Manhattan Community College/City University of New York. She holds a BA in drama and classics from Tufts University and an MA and a PhD in sociology from the New School for Social Research. Her research interests include sociology of culture, memory, museums, and gender. She is the author of *Exhibiting Atrocity: Memorial Museums and the Politics of Past Violence* (2018) and a coeditor of *Memory and the Future: Transnational Politics, Ethics and Culture* (2010); *Museums and Sites of Persuasion: Memory, Politics and Human Rights* (forthcoming); and a special issue of *Women's Studies Quarterly*, "At Sea" (2017).

Richard A. Zdan is a member of the sociology faculty at Rider University. His current teaching and research interests are in the areas of political and community sociology and civic engagement. Recently, he spearheaded a revision of the Rider Sociology Department's introductory course for readoption as a part of the university's revised general education core curriculum. He is currently collecting data for a research project on the role played by funeral directors in local communities.

Rena C. Zito is an assistant professor of sociology at Elon University. She received her doctorate in sociology from North Carolina State University. Her research focuses primarily on family processes in the production of crime and delinquency. Specifically, her work uses a life-course perspective to examine how family structure histories and family formation shape gender processes, adolescent role exits, and law violation.

To all instructors and students who put sociology into action.

CHAPTER 1

TRAINING YOUR SOCIOLOGICAL EYE

Kathleen Odell Korgen

Looking at this picture of Grand Central Station in New York City from a sociological perspective can help us see how people both shape and are shaped by the cities in which they reside.

©iStockphoto.com/foto-select

1.1 What is sociology?

1.2 What do the sociological eye and the sociological imagination allow you to do?

1.3 What key aspects of sociology make it a social *science*?

1.4 How can you tell the difference between a good generalization and a stereotype?

1.5 What are the core commitments of sociology?

1.6 How can sociology benefit both individuals and society?

Have you ever wanted to know why more women than men graduate from college today? Why college tuition is so expensive? What you can do to improve your chances of landing a desirable job after college? Why the number of hate groups in the United States has increased by 30 percent since 2000? What types of jobs will be most available when you graduate? Why people vote for certain political candidates (or do not vote at all)? How you can make a positive impact on society? If so, you have chosen the right subject! Sociology can help you answer all these questions—and raise some new ones.

What Is Sociology?

So, what is sociology? **Sociology** is the scientific study of society, including how individuals both *shape* and *are shaped by* society. Notice in this definition that people are active beings, shapers of society, but they are also affected by society. It's important to remember that society influences us in myriad ways—how we think, what we notice, what we believe to be true, how we see ourselves, and so on. But it is simultaneously vital to realize that we help shape the society in which we live. This duality is at the heart of sociology and our daily lives—whether we are aware of it or not.

Shaping and Being Shaped by Society

The life of Malala Yousafzai, the youngest Nobel Prize winner in history, provides an excellent example of this duality. No one can deny that Malala is an extraordinary young woman. Her personal bravery and selflessness are awe inspiring. Just nine months after she was shot in the head by the Taliban for publicly promoting education for girls in Pakistan, Malala declared in an address to the United Nations Youth Assembly that "one child, one teacher, one book, and one pen, can change the world" (https://www.youtube.com/watch?v=3rNhZu3ttIU). Her organization, the Malala Fund, has provided the means for many other girls to gain an education. Clearly, Malala has shown the power of an individual to influence society.

Malala, however, just like the rest of us, is a product of her society. Imagine if, instead of growing up in the Swat Valley of Pakistan during the time of the Taliban, she grew up in the suburbs of New Jersey. Her life would have been very different. She would not have been shot by the Taliban, and she would not have created the Malala Fund. Indeed, the Malala raised in New Jersey may not have even been aware that girls in many areas of the world face violence for going to school. Sociology helps us understand

Malala Yousafzai was shot in the head and, later, awarded the Nobel Peace Prize for her work promoting education for girls. Her life helps us see how we both shape and are shaped by our societies.

Nigel Waldron/Getty Images Entertainment/Getty Images

HOW I GOT ACTIVE IN SOCIOLOGY

KATHLEEN ODELL KORGEN

I slept most of the way through the SOC 101 course I took in college. The professor lectured, and we took notes (or not).

That SOC 101 course was the last sociology class I took until I found a sociology graduate program in social justice and social economy that encouraged sociologists to put sociological tools into action. In that program, I learned that sociology could show me how I can change society. As a researcher, I have worked on issues related to race relations and racial identity, evaluated social justice efforts and

sociology programs, and helped create introductory textbooks that get students to *do* sociology as they learn it.

As a sociology teacher, I want students to know—right away—all that sociology offers them—and society. A major part of my work has been to help students use sociological tools to make a positive impact on society. In my classes, from SOC 101 to Public Sociology and Civic Engagement, students don't just learn about sociology—they become sociologists in action.

the impact of society on us and how we can work with others, as Malala is doing now, to solve the social issues facing our societies.

CONSIDER THIS

How have the time period and the nation in which you live influenced your life? How might your life be different if you lived during a different time period or in another nation?

The Origins and Current Uses of Sociology

Sociology developed out of the need to understand and address social issues. The roots of sociology are based in efforts to understand and to help control the impact of major societal changes. In the eighteenth and nineteenth centuries, in Europe and the United States, organized people challenged monarchies and the dominance of religion. The Industrial Revolution dramatically changed where people lived and how they worked. Social change occurred everywhere, and philosophers and scientists offered new answers to life's questions. Many began to believe science could help leaders understand and shape society. Auguste Comte (1798–1857), the French philosopher who gave sociology its name, envisioned that sociology would be the "queen science" that could help steer society safely through great changes.

Today, sociologists help us understand and address challenges like economic inequality, environmental racism, sexism, the social dimensions of global climate

change, war, terrorism, and so on. Sociologists work in a variety of settings, including colleges and universities, nonprofit organizations (e.g., environmental groups, public health programs, and community-based organizations), government, marketing, sales, social services, and the human resources departments of businesses and nonprofit organizations. People in every profession benefit from sociological training, and employers value employees with sociological skills.

A survey of hiring managers commissioned by the Association of American Colleges and Universities (2018) reveals that students who study sociology tend to gain precisely the skills employers seek. For example,

- 84 percent look for critical thinking and analytical skills in prospective hires,

- 85 percent noted that they seek employees who are proactive and can provide both ideas and solutions, and

- 87 percent look to hire people who can work well in teams and apply knowledge in real-world settings.

In this course alone, you will have the opportunity to learn *and use* many of these skills. In most sociology undergraduate programs, you can gain and use all of them!

Check Your Understanding

- What is sociology?
- What is the duality at the heart of sociology?
- Out of what need did sociology develop?
- In what types of settings do sociologists work?

HOW CAN SOCIOLOGY BOOST YOUR CAREER?

In this activity, you will consider the ways sociology can be a benefit in any workplace.

No matter what your major or what you intend to do after graduation, sociology can help you. Sociology is useful in any organization and any professional field. Gaining a sociological perspective will enable you to better understand how society, organizations, and groups work; interact effectively with people of different genders, sexual orientations, ages, races, cultures, and economic classes; make and use connections with other people and organizations; and recognize and address issues of inequality and privilege.

Write your answers to the following questions:

1. What career do you plan on pursuing? If you are not sure yet, think of any profession with which you are familiar (e.g., lawyer, marketing director, police officer, entrepreneur, Wall Street banker, environmental activist, social worker, teacher).

2. How can gaining a sociological perspective help you to succeed in that career?

Changing How You View the World

1.2   What do the sociological eye and the sociological imagination allow you to do?

This sociology course will help you develop your sociological eye and your sociological imagination. Together, they allow you to notice and make sense of social patterns in ways that enable you to understand how society works—and to help influence it.

The Sociological Eye

A **sociological eye** enables you to see what others may not notice. It allows you to peer beneath the surface of a situation and discern social patterns (Collins 1998). For example, there is a woman academic who conducts evaluations of various academic departments every year. Often, she does so as part of a team. She has noticed that whenever she is paired with a man, the clients always look at the man when speaking to them both. As a sociologist, she knows that what she is experiencing is gender bias. In general, both men and women tend to defer to men and pay more attention to them, particularly in business settings.

Once you start paying attention to gender patterns (e.g., who talks more in classes or meetings, who interrupts whom) or racial patterns (e.g., who eats lunch with whom in the cafeteria, what student organizations tend to attract specific racial groups, who is more likely to be stopped by the police), you won't be able to stop noticing them. Noticing these patterns can make you more aware of how your campus and the larger society work. Once you have this awareness, you can then take steps to change these patterns—if you so choose. The woman we referred to earlier, for example, now often prepares herself to talk more (and more authoritatively) when paired with

You can use your sociological eye to notice racial, gender, and social status patterns in the cafeteria scenes in the classic film *Mean Girls*—and in most real-life cafeterias.

A. F. Archive/Alamy

SHOWING OFF YOUR SOCIOLOGICAL EYE

With a group of classmates or individually, choose an image from a book cover, an ad for a movie or a product in a magazine, or an album cover that depicts a scene that requires a sociological eye to fully comprehend.

After doing so, write your answers to the following questions:

1. What message does this image portray?

2. How does your analysis of the image demonstrate that you have a sociological eye?

3. How might you use your sociological eye to better understand a scene from life on your campus?

Be prepared to share your answers and determine the similarities between yours and your classmates'.

---

a man and teaches others to make an effort to pay as much attention to women as to men. You will learn more about *why* we tend to pay more attention to men in Chapter 8!

CONSIDER THIS

Why do you think we need a sociological eye to notice some social patterns? Why aren't social patterns obvious to everyone all the time?

The Sociological Imagination

Once you develop your sociological eye, you can also expand your **sociological imagination**, the ability to connect what is happening in your own life and in the lives of other individuals to social patterns in the larger society. In doing so, you can differentiate between a personal problem and a social problem that requires a societal solution. For example, you may be having a difficult time paying for college. This is a challenge for many individuals. You may address it by taking out loans (and more loans), working while going to school, transferring to a more affordable school, and so forth. So far, these are all individual responses to the problem of high tuition. Looking at the problem with a sociological eye, however, can help you see that this is not just a hardship for a few individuals but part of a social pattern. Many college students across the United States face the same issue, and to address it effectively, we need to make changes on the societal, rather than just the individual, level.

As Figures 1.1 and 1.2 show, the cost of college has increased dramatically over the past decade. Consequently, approximately 70 percent of college graduates accept student loans. As students reach the debt limit allowed by federal loan programs ($31,000 for

dependent students and $57,500 for independent students), parents have borrowed more money to pay for their children's college education. Debt among associate degree students has also risen, reaching $18,501 in 2015–2016 (Kantrowitz 2018).

Once you begin to look at the high cost of college as a societal issue, you can investigate its causes. You can then work with other students and families across the nation to press elected officials to develop state and national solutions to this societal problem.

C. Wright Mills (1959, 1) developed the concept of the sociological imagination to describe how our individual lives relate to social forces. The sociological imagination gives us the ability to recognize the relationship between our own biographies and the society in which we live. Mills explained the impact of society on individuals this way:

When a society is industrialized, a peasant becomes a worker; a feudal lord is liquidated or becomes a businessman. . . . When wars happen, an insurance salesperson becomes a rocket launcher; a store clerk, a radar operator; a wife or husband lives alone; a child grows up without a parent. . . . Neither the life of an individual nor the history of a society can be understood without understanding both.

Our lives are shaped by the societies in which we live. Yet we can also help shape those societies. If a few thousand people in the United States voted a different way in 2016, Hillary Clinton would have become president. On a more personal level, your experience in this class depends a lot on how your professor chooses to teach it. Your behavior will also influence it. Imagine how different this class will be for everyone if you choose to prepare for each class and actively participate or if you choose to blow off the reading

▼ FIGURE 1.1

▼ FIGURE 1.1

Average Student Loan Debt at Graduation for Bachelor's Degree Recipients

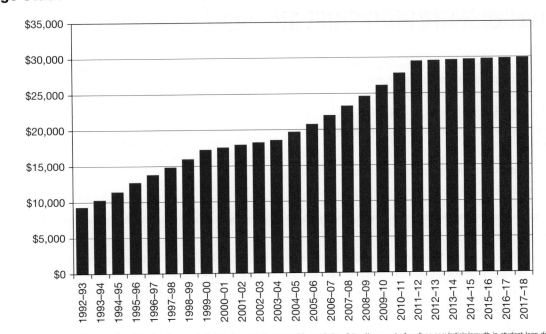

▼ FIGURE 1.2

Average Student Loan Debt at Graduation for Bachelor's Degree Recipients, 2015–2016

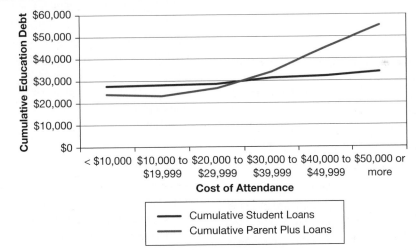

and groan every time one of your classmates says anything. Individuals choose how to behave within their social environments—and those choices affect the environments.

The Fallacy of the Individualist Perspective.

We often forget, however, that our choices are limited. In the United States today, the myth that we, as individuals, determine our own lives permeates society. From this *individualist*

perspective, whether we succeed or fail depends primarily on our own efforts. For example, you have probably heard of the saying that in the United States, anyone who works hard enough can "make it." A sociological eye quickly sees that this individualist perspective is flawed. Some people have fewer hurdles and more opportunities in life than others. For example, take two students with the same level of innate intelligence. Both work hard, but

DISTINGUISHING INDIVIDUAL AND SOCIAL PROBLEMS

In this exercise you will use your sociological imagination to distinguish between an individual problem and a social problem.

Briefly describe, in writing, two major problems a friend or a family member has experienced. Then, answer the following questions:

1. Are they personal problems or social problems?

2. Why do you categorize each the way you did?

Choose one of the social problems (or come up with one, if you did not think of one already) and explain why it should be addressed on the societal, rather than just the individual, level. Be prepared to share your work with your class.

---

one goes to a school that offers many AP courses, where students are expected and encouraged to apply to selective colleges. The other student goes to a school with few AP courses, where teachers and administrators focus on preventing kids from dropping out of high school rather than on getting them into selective colleges. Chances are, the second student may not even be aware of all the schools to which the first student applies. The two students' chances of "making it" are not the same—no matter how hard they both work.

CONSIDER THIS

How would you address a lack of affordable healthy food for low-income people (a) from an individualist perspective and (b) using your sociological imagination? Which would be more effective for the most people?

The sociological eye gives us the ability to recognize the impact society has on us and how the individualist perspective works to prevent people from noticing that impact. Having a sociological eye, therefore, gives us advantages over those who cannot yet see societal forces and recognize social patterns. Those blind to the influence of society are unknowingly shaped by it. Those with a sociological eye—and therefore a sociological imagination—recognize the impact society has on them *and* how they can work most effectively to shape society.

Check Your Understanding

- What does a sociological eye allow you to do?
- What can you do with a sociological imagination?

- According to C. Wright Mills, what do you need to understand the life of an individual?
- How does the sociological eye help us to see the fallacy of the individualist perspective in the United States?

Sociology as a Social Science

1.3 What key aspects of sociology make it a social *science*?

Sociology is a social science, a scientific discipline that studies how society works. As social scientists, sociologists follow rules to make sure our research is transparent and replicable and that others can confirm or refute our findings. For example, as we seek to better understand how society operates, sociologists use theories and the scientific research process to formulate research questions and collect and analyze data.

Theoretical Perspectives

Theoretical perspectives are paradigms, or ways of viewing the world. They help us make sense of the social patterns we observe, and they determine the questions we ask. Each perspective has its own foci and asks different questions about the social world. Some ask questions about social order and cohesion (e.g., How do the various parts of society work together?), some ask questions about problems in society (e.g., Why is there inequality?), and some ask questions about the ways we see ourselves in relation to others (e.g., How do our interactions with others influence how we see ourselves?). You will learn more about the most important theoretical perspectives sociologists use in Chapter 2 and about topic-specific (middle-range) theories that fall under their respective umbrellas throughout the book.

The Scientific Research Process

To understand how society operates and to test our perspectives and theories about how society works, sociologists must collect and analyze data. We do so in systematic ways that we clearly describe and offer for critique from other social scientists and the general public. The purpose of sociological research is to constantly learn more about how society works. Doing so in open, systematic ways allows others to replicate our research process and to support our conclusions or reveal flaws in our data-gathering process and findings. Together, we gain a better, scientifically sound understanding of our society.

Sometimes, our findings are unexpected. For example, a sociologist who uses a theoretical lens that focuses on inequality and group conflict may be surprised to learn that a corporation she is studying has a high level of camaraderie and evidence of strong teamwork among workers at all status levels. If our findings consistently diverge from our theoretical explanations, we need to adjust out theories accordingly. Sociologists are in the business of creating useful theories on the basis of good generalizations.

Check Your Understanding

- What makes sociology a social science?
- How do sociologists use theoretical perspectives and theories?
- Why do sociologists collect data in open, systematic ways?

Differentiating between Good Generalizations and Stereotypes

1.4   How can you tell the difference between a good generalization and a stereotype?

Has anyone said to you that "you shouldn't generalize"? That was probably right after you made some disparaging remark about all the people from a particular town, all the movies starring a particular actor, or all roads in New Jersey. What you were doing (and they were right that you shouldn't) was stereotyping or making a *bad* generalization. Sociologists generalize all the time as they recognize and point out social patterns in society.

Does this guy look like someone who just wants to crunch numbers all weekend? The movie *Harold and Kumar Go to White Castle* put a spotlight on some racial stereotypes about Asian Americans.

AF Archive/Alamy Stock Photo

However, we aim to make good generalizations and avoid stereotyping. Good **generalizations** are statements, backed by evidence, used to describe groups of people or things in overall terms, with the understanding that there can always be exceptions.

Stereotypes

Stereotypes are predetermined ideas about particular groups of people (e.g., all Irish are drunks, all Asians are good at math) based on hearsay or personal experience and held regardless of contrary evidence. Often used to promote or excuse discriminatory treatment, stereotypes can spark irrational fear or favor. Some may be closer to the truth than others, but none are based on solid evidence. Stereotypes are bad generalizations.

Movies and television shows can both expose and promote stereotypes. For example, in one scene in the film *Harold and Kumar Go to White Castle*, the White, male boss hands Harold, a Korean American, a bunch of his work—so he can start his weekend early. The boss holds a stereotype of Asians that makes him think Harold (and all other Asians) "live for" crunching numbers. Of course, however, movie viewers know that work is the last thing Harold wants to do that weekend. On the other hand, in most movies, East Asian characters tend to be either sidekicks to the White stars or villains. How many shows can you name that feature a young Korean or Chinese American girl as the glasses-wearing, nerdy friend of the main White character (e.g., *Gilmore Girls, Gossip Girl, Awkward*)?

STEREOTYPES AND GENERALIZATIONS ABOUT COLLEGE STUDENTS

In this exercise, you will examine the differences between stereotypes and good generalizations. Your instructor will assign you to groups of four. Together, answer the following questions. You may be asked to share your responses with the rest of the class.

1. Explain the difference between a stereotype and a generalization.

2. List three stereotypes you have heard describing the characteristics of students at your own school.

3. Go to your college or university's web site. Compare the stereotypes you had heard about with data you found on the web site. Can you confirm any of the stereotypes you had?

4. Using information on the web site, create some valid generalizations about the students at your school.

5. Can you generalize to *all* college students on the basis of the data about students at your school? Why or why not?

6. How does this research help you distinguish between a stereotype and a good generalization?

Good Generalizations

Good generalizations, unlike stereotypes, are based on social scientific research. For example, one common stereotype is that women are "chatty Cathys" and talk incessantly. A good generalization, on the contrary, is that in mixed-sex conversations, men tend to talk and interrupt more than women. Women ask more questions than men and tend to work harder at fostering conversation, but it is men who tend to dominate verbal interactions (Gamble and Gamble 2015).

Did you notice how the generalizations in the paragraph above are phrased? Unlike the stereotype about "chatty Cathys," they describe what social scientists have found about speaking patterns without denigrating one sex or the other. Good generalizations are used to describe rather than judge groups of people.

Good generalizations must change when new data counter them. For example, the generalization that "most people in the United States oppose same-sex marriage" was once true but no longer qualifies as a good generalization. As our generalizations change with new data, so do our research questions. For example, we may now want to ask, What led to the change in attitudes toward same-sex marriage? And will this acceptance of same-sex marriage also lead to national legislation to protect lesbian, gay, bisexual, and transgendered people from discrimination?

Check Your Understanding

- On what are stereotypes based?
- How do sociologists create good generalizations?
- How does new information affect (a) stereotypes and (b) good generalizations?
- For what purpose do sociologists use generalizations?

The Obligations of Sociology

> 1.5   What are the core commitments of sociology?

The earliest sociologists used sociology to find ways to understand and improve society. In 1896, Albion Small, the founder of the first accredited department of sociology in the United States (at the University of Chicago), implored his fellow sociologists to do so with these words:

> I would have American scholars, especially in the social sciences, declare their independence of do-nothing traditions. I would have them repeal the law of custom which bars marriage of thought with action. I would have them become more profoundly and sympathetically scholarly by enriching the wisdom which comes from knowing with the larger wisdom which comes from doing. . . . May American scholarship never so narrow itself to the interests of scholars that it shall forfeit its primacy among the interests of men! (Small 1896, 564, 583)

W. E. B. Du Bois, one of the founders of sociology, used sociological tools to show how society works and to fight racism.

Underwood Archives/Archive Photos/Getty Images

Jane Addams
Hulton Archive/Getty Images

W. E. B. Du Bois, one of the key founders of sociology, whom many White sociologists of his era ignored because of their racism, needed no prodding. An African American, Harvard-trained scholar, Du Bois faced rejection when applying for tenured faculty positions at White colleges and universities because of his race. Undaunted, he spent his career leading research studies at Atlanta University, writing prolifically, and organizing civil rights efforts.

Throughout his long career, Du Bois carried out a combination of research and activism, achieving groundbreaking work in both areas. In the late nineteenth century, Du Bois conducted the first large-scale, empirical sociological research in the United States, with the clear goal of refuting racist ideas about African Americans (Morris 2015). Later, he helped found the National Association for the Advancement of Colored People (NAACP) and tirelessly promoted civil rights for African Americans.

Jane Addams, the cofounder of the settlement house movement in the United States and one of the other major early sociologists, worked with—and helped inspire—Du Bois. Just as Du Bois faced racism, however, Addams had to deal with sexism. Although Addams and her colleagues carried out numerous community research projects while living and working with low-income people in poor, urban neighborhoods, they also faced discrimination and did not receive the recognition they deserved.

The research Addams and her colleagues conducted helped guide that of Du Bois and many of the male faculty at the University of Chicago in the late 1800s and early 1900s (Deegan 1988). It also helped create such social goods as child labor laws, a juvenile court system, safer conditions for workers, and mandatory schooling for children. Addams cofounded both the NAACP (along with Du Bois, among others) and the American Civil Liberties Union.

The Two Core Commitments

In the spirit of Addams, Du Bois, and Small, Randall Collins (1998) has described two **core commitments** of sociology. The first core commitment of sociology is to *use the sociological eye* to observe social patterns. The second requires noticing patterns of injustice and *taking action* to challenge those patterns. Collins and the sociologists who have authored this book believe that sociology should be used to make a positive impact on society. If you have developed a sociological eye, you are obligated to use it for the good of society. For example, if we perceive that in more than half of the states in the United States, it is still legal to fire people on the basis of their

SUICIDE RATES AND THE SOCIOLOGICAL IMAGINATION

Suicide is one of the most personal and intimate of matters. But a sociological eye looks for larger social forces and patterns that influence individual lives and personal decisions.

In this online activity, you will explore data from the U.S. Department of Health and Human Services in order to examine how suicide rates vary from state to state.

─────────────

*Requires the Vantage version of *Sociology in Action*.

▼ FIGURE 1.3

Age-Adjusted Death Rate by Suicide (State), 2015

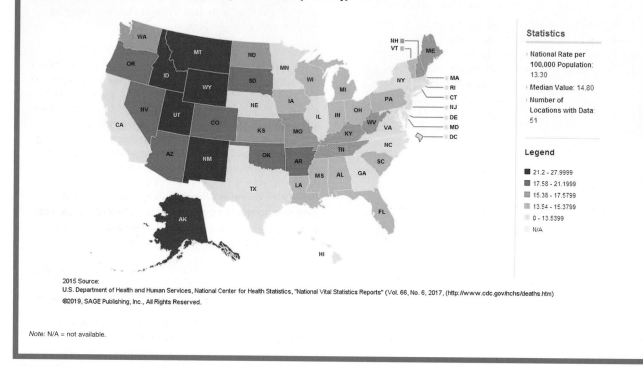

Statistics

› National Rate per 100,000 Population: 13.30

› Median Value: 14.80

› Number of Locations with Data: 51

Legend

■ 21.2 - 27.9999
■ 17.58 - 21.1999
■ 15.38 - 17.5799
■ 13.54 - 15.3799
□ 0 - 13.5399
□ N/A

2015 Source:
U.S. Department of Health and Human Services, National Center for Health Statistics, "National Vital Statistics Reports" (Vol. 66, No. 6, 2017, (http://www.cdc.gov/nchs/deaths.htm)

©2019, SAGE Publishing, Inc., All Rights Reserved.

Note: N/A = not available.

─────────────

sexual orientation (in nonreligious institutions as well as in religious organizations), we should work to address that injustice.

Check Your Understanding

- For what purpose did the earliest sociologists use sociology?

- Why did W. E. B. Du Bois conduct large-scale empirical research in the United States?

- What were some of the ways Jane Addams used sociological research to help create social goods?

- What are the two core commitments of sociology?

The Benefits of Sociology

> 1.6 How can sociology benefit both individuals and society?

Developing a sociological eye and gaining a sociological perspective will benefit both you and society. You will notice social patterns that many others cannot see. Even if these patterns are unpleasant (sexism, racism, ableism, etc.), noticing and understanding them will help you develop ways of dealing with them in your own life. Forewarned is forearmed. You can also see patterns that you can proactively use to your advantage (e.g., what careers will be most in demand soon, how to gain social capital useful in the job market). Through gaining a

THE CLOTHESLINE PROJECT

WILLIAM EDMUNDSON

I helped lead the Clothesline Project on Virginia Wesleyan College's campus. I was able to do so through Dr. Alison Marganski's Family Violence: Causes, Consequences, and Responses course. The Clothesline Project is a community education campaign on the issue of violence against women—see www .clotheslineproject.info (note that our class also extended this to include other forms and types of family violence to be more inclusive of other victimization experiences).

Part of my contribution to the Clothesline Project were "Myth versus Facts" bookmarks; one focused on the victim while another focused on the abuser, and both displayed common myths with corresponding facts as well as local resources available both on and off campus. My classmates and I distributed them to students, staff, and faculty who stopped by the weeklong event to make a T-shirt to support the project. Through creating and distributing the bookmarks, I educated myself as well as others to recognize myths about domestic violence and to replace them with the facts they serve to mask.

Throughout our class, my classmates and I learned of the need for education with respect to family violence, including violence against women. The Clothesline Project enabled those directly affected by such violence to tell their stories through T-shirts they created and provided a form for the community to learn more about—and take a stand against—domestic violence. One victim both created a shirt and came into our class to share her story. Additional course-related activities included advertising the event, running the T-shirt creation table, and displaying the created T-shirts at the end of the event.

Toward the end of the project, our class took all of the almost 100 T-shirts created during the weeklong event and hung them up across a walkway on campus. Hanging up the shirts served to both raise awareness and provide a medium for participants' voices to be heard. The strategic placement of these shirts allowed the entire campus community to gain exposure to the messages created by the participants.

My experience as a leader in the Clothesline Project taught me the extent of planning and networking required for such community outreach events. As a class, we were able to form connections with local organizations, such as the Samaritan House and the YWCA, whose members also distributed materials at the event. Hosting the Clothesline Project provided me with valuable organizing experience and helped me to create valuable networks with local organizations for potential volunteering positions, internships, or even jobs in the future. Perhaps the most important lesson I learned from the Clothesline Project was just how big of a role I could play in educating Virginia Wesleyan College about societal issues from a sociological perspective.

Discussion Question: How does William show that using sociological tools to make a positive impact on your community can benefit you, as well as your community?

William Edmundson is a criminal justice major at Virginia Wesleyan College in Norfolk, Virginia.

sociological perspective, you will learn how to act more effectively in groups and with members of different cultures. You will also gain the ability to collect, analyze, and explain information and to influence your society.

CONSIDER THIS

Can you see yourself fulfilling the two core commitments of sociology in response to a particular issue? If yes, both or only one? Why? If not, why not? Do you think most of your peers would be able and willing to do so? Why?

The last points concerning what you, personally, will gain from a sociological perspective relate to how sociology can help you contribute to society. Just knowing how society operates and how individuals are both shaped by and shapers of society can make you a more effective member of your community. You can learn how to work with others to improve your campus, workplace, neighborhood, and society. As seen in the above Sociologists in Action box, William Edmundson provides an excellent example of how sociology students can use sociological tools to benefit both individuals and society.

Sociology and Democracy

In democratic societies, it is particularly important for citizens who vote in elections to understand how society works and to develop the ability to notice social patterns. It is also vital that they be able to understand the difference between good information and fake news. Can you tell what news to trust? Checking to see if the data described in a news source were gained through the scientific research process and knowing how to tell the difference between good generalizations and stereotypes will help you discern real news from fake news.

Fake news became increasingly common during the 2016 presidential campaign. One piece, "BREAKING: 'Tens of Thousands' of Fraudulent Clinton Votes Found in Ohio Warehouse," was shared more than 6 million times on social media before the election. Cameron Harris, a recent college graduate, created a fake news site, ChristianTimesNewspaper.com, and included a picture of some ballot boxes in a warehouse (no one could tell that the warehouse was in England, not Ohio) to make his story appear "real" to viewers, who were unaware of the need to look into the veracity of the news source or the information described in the story (Shane 2017). The completely fabricated story took off. It's hard to know how much this one story influenced the election, but it was far from the only fake news story sweeping across social media before Americans went to vote (you may remember "Pizzagate," one of the more famous of the fake news stories leading up the election) (Fisher, Cox, and Hermann 2016).

The same people who believed and promoted fake news stories like "Pizzagate" show up at Trump rallies with "Q" (for QAnon) signs, indicating their allegiance to "an interactive conspiracy community" that views President Trump as a hero battling "anti-American saboteurs who have taken over government, industry, media and various other institutions of public life." Alarmingly, this "paranoid worldview has crossed over from the internet into the real world several times . . . On more than one occasion, people believed to be followers of QAnon have shown up—sometimes with weapons— in places that the character told them were somehow connected to anti-Trump conspiracies." In April 2018, the app QDrops was one of the ten most downloaded paid apps in the Apple Store. In this dark world, baseless conspiracy theories are facts, and facts are "fake news" propagated by the news media, which President Trump describes as "the enemy of the American people"

(Bank, Stack, and Victor 2018; Brooks 2018). Today, a sociologically informed public is more necessary than ever for a democratic society.

CONSIDER THIS

Give an example of how you can use sociology to understand how society works and to help shape society.

Sociology and Careers

Finally, as noted earlier, sociological knowledge is useful in any career you can imagine—including teaching, business management, politics, human resources, medical administration, social work, nonprofit management, and marketing. For example, to be effective, social workers need to understand the populations they serve and the structural and cultural forces affecting them. A marketer must have the research skills to learn what appeals to different groups and how to advertise to each most persuasively. Managers need cultural competency to create a motivated and engaged workforce. From knowing what job to apply for, what degree you need to gain it, and how to conduct yourself in the workplace to advance, sociological skills can help you succeed in the workforce. In each of the chapters that follow, take note of the sociological skills you gain and in what professions you might use them.

Check Your Understanding

- How can sociology benefit individuals?
- How can sociology benefit society, particularly democratic societies?
- How might you use sociology in your career?

Conclusion

In this introductory chapter, you learned that sociology, the scientific study of society, provides myriad benefits to both individuals and society. We now turn to how sociologists make sense of how society operates by looking at the different major sociological perspectives. As you will see, each perspective views the world in distinct ways. As you read the chapter, think about which perspective(s) make the most sense to you.

REVIEW

1.1 What is sociology?

Sociology is the scientific study of society, including how individuals both *shape* and *are shaped by* society.

1.2 What do the sociological eye and the sociological imagination allow you to do?

A sociological eye enables you to see what others may not notice. It allows you to peer beneath the surface of a situation and discern social patterns. The sociological imagination gives you the ability to connect what is happening in your own life and in the lives of others to social patterns in the larger society.

1.3 What key aspects of sociology make it a social *science*?

Sociologists use theories and the scientific research process to formulate research questions and collect and analyze data to better understand how society operates.

1.4 How can you tell the difference between a good generalization and a stereotype?

Good generalizations, unlike stereotypes, are based on social scientific research, used to describe rather than judge groups, and change or are discarded with new information.

1.5 What are the core commitments of sociology?

The first of the two core commitments is to use the sociological eye to observe social patterns. The second commitment requires us to notice patterns of injustice and take action to challenge those patterns. Sociology should be used to make a positive impact on society.

1.6 How can sociology benefit both individuals and society?

Through gaining a sociological perspective, you will learn to notice and deal with patterns others do not recognize; act more effectively in groups and with members of different cultures; collect, analyze, and explain information; and influence your society.

Sociological knowledge is useful in any career you can imagine.

In democratic societies, it is particularly important for citizens to develop the ability to notice social patterns and how to tell the difference between good generalizations and stereotypes.

KEY TERMS

core commitments   11

generalizations   9

sociological eye   5

sociological imagination   6

sociology   3

stereotypes   9

CHAPTER 2

UNDERSTANDING THEORY

Kathleen S. Lowney

We all have perspectives or ways of seeing the world, but few of us are aware of alternative points of view.
© iStockphoto.com/Simon Dannhauer

2.1 Why and how do sociologists use theoretical perspectives?

 2.2 What is structural functionalism?

 2.3 What is a conflict perspective?

 2.4 What is symbolic interaction?

 2.5 How do structural functionalism, conflict perspectives, and symbolic interaction work together to help us get a more complete view of reality?

What Is Theory?

2.1 Why and how do sociologists use theoretical perspectives?

Children often will try on another person's glasses. Sometimes they will see worse—things look out of focus and fuzzy—but other times, they will see better. Imagining theory as a pair of glasses we put on to look at the social world can be a helpful metaphor. A theory can help us see some aspects of society more clearly, while obscuring others.

Sociologists develop and use **theories**, explanations for various social patterns within society. Groups of theories that share much in common are what sociologists call **theoretical perspectives**. This chapter focuses on the three main theoretical perspectives in sociology—structural functionalism, conflict theory, and symbolic interaction—and how each of them "sees" or explains the social world.

Check Your Understanding

- What is theory?
- What is the difference between a theory and a theoretical perspective?

Understanding the Structural Functionalist Perspective

2.2 What is structural functionalism?

The view of modern societies as consisting of interdependent parts working together for the good of the whole is known as **structural functionalism**. Individuals work for the larger society's interests, rather than their own, because of social solidarity, or the moral order of society. Families, religion, education, and other institutions teach individuals to help society function smoothly.

Durkheim and Types of Societies

Émile Durkheim, writing in the early 1900s, examined social solidarity throughout history. In smaller, preindustrial societies, social solidarity derived from the similarity of its members, what Durkheim referred to as mechanical solidarity. Most did similar types of labor (working the land) and had similar beliefs (based on religion).

As societies evolved, science gained predominance over religion, and jobs became differentiated during the industrial era, a different type of solidarity, an organic solidarity, formed. These societies operated more like a living organism, with various parts, each specializing in only certain tasks but dependent on the others for survival (e.g., the circulatory system and the digestive system perform different functions, but if one does not do its job, the other will not survive). Durkheim argued that for a society based on organic solidarity to be "healthy" (i.e., in social harmony and in order), all the "parts" of the society had to be working well together, in an interconnected way, just as in a human body. Thus, sociologists who use this theoretical perspective tend to focus on social harmony and social order. They often overlook issues such as conflict and inequality. Instead, structural functionalists emphasize the role of the major social institutions and how they help provide stability to society.

Social Institutions

What are **social institutions**? They are sets of statuses and roles focused around one central aspect of society (think of social institutions as similar to the different organ systems in a human body). A status is the position a person occupies in a particular institution. For example, you occupy the status position of college student. But you are also a son or daughter, a former high school student, and a member of many other groups. So, you have multiple status positions. A role is composed of the many behaviors that go into occupying

HOW I GOT ACTIVE IN SOCIOLOGY

KATHLEEN S. LOWNEY

I went to college knowing that I wanted to study religion. But then I took Introduction to Sociology—799 other students and me (yes, the course had 800 students!)—and I was hooked. Learning about structure, agency, and sociological theories gave me a language and intellectual framework to see the social world that I still use today. So on the third day of that first quarter of college, I added sociology as another major. The questions that consume me still focus on the intersection of religion and sociology, be they about the new religion I studied for my doctoral dissertation or for the past nineteen years when I have studied adolescent Satanism. I welcome each of you to the study of the academic discipline that I love.

a status. So, part of your role as a college student is to come to class on time and prepared. If sociologists were to examine the educational institution as a whole, they would have a macro-level focus. If, however, they were to look at how you and your friends fill the role of college students, they would be working at the **micro level of analysis**.

The statuses individuals occupy and the roles they play come together to form the unique social structure of a group, an organization, an institution, or a society. Once the group becomes large enough, social institutions form around accomplishing the tasks central to the survival of the group. Thus, while social institutions are made up of individuals fulfilling their roles, they are much more than these individuals—they are societal in nature. When sociologists examine large-scale social processes, like institutions, they use a **macro level of analysis**.

Structural functionalists note that there are seven primary social institutions: family, religion, economy, education, government, health care, and media. These seven institutions cover nearly all the major aspects of a modern society. Each social institution fulfills tasks on behalf of society. Structural functionalism calls these tasks functions. There are two types of functions. Let's talk about them one at a time.

Manifest Functions. The obvious, stated reasons that a social institution exists are known as **manifest functions**. Structural functionalists maintain that manifest functions of each institution fulfill necessary tasks in society. For example, let's look at the social institution of the family. One function the family performs is to encourage individuals to procreate—to have children. Otherwise, a society would likely die after one generation, wouldn't it? So, a manifest function of the family institution in any society is reproduction. But institutions can have more than one manifest function. Families are also responsible for raising and instructing their children. For example, families teach children the cultural norms (rules for behavior) and values of their particular society, a process known as socialization.

Consider education as a social institution. What tasks does the education institution do for society? It teaches those in school the knowledge that society says is important to know to become a contributing adult member of that society. In the United States today, that includes grammar, spelling, mathematics, U.S. and world history, and basic computer skills.

Latent Functions. Manifest functions are only the first type of function structural functionalists use to

Studying is an important part of your role as a student.
©iStockphoto.com/vm

examine the social world. They also use latent functions. **Latent functions** are good or useful things that a social institution does but are not the institution's reason for existing.

Let's return to the family institution for a moment. We know that its manifest function is to reproduce and then socialize children, so that the society can continue indefinitely into the future. But family as a social institution supports the society in many other ways. Families help the economic institution, for example, when they purchase food or school supplies or pay rent or buy a house. Helping the economy is a good thing, but it is not a family's core function.

CONSIDER THIS

What might be some latent functions of the educational institution?

Latent functions almost always link to a second social institution (e.g., both family and education support the economic institution). These connections between one social institution and another build the social harmony structural functionalists see when they look at society.

Sometimes behavioral patterns have unintended negative consequences, called **dysfunctions**. For example, the United States built the interstate highway system to move people and products more quickly from location to location, which helps the economic institution. But that good idea also led to an increase in air pollution (a dysfunction) because more people purchased cars and chose to drive, because highways made it so much easier to get to and from places in a car.

Seeing the Social World Using Structural Functionalism

Structural functionalism is a macro-theoretical perspective. It looks at society as a whole and focuses on the institutions, rather than individuals, within it. When they put on structural functionalism's glasses, sociologists view society from a distance and look for social order and harmony.

In looking at the big picture of society, functionalist sociologists focus less on discrete individuals and their daily lives and interactions with one another and more on social institutions and how they fit together to build social harmony and stability. So, for example, structural functionalists study the institution of the family, not individual families, to learn how social institutions function to meet societal needs. Although particular families may not fulfill

each of the functions, as a social institution, the family can and must carry out certain functions in order for society to function smoothly. By concentrating on social institutions, structural functionalism rises above the unique ways millions of families go about their daily lives of cooking, taking out the garbage, cleaning up after each other, loving one another, raising children, and so on to focus on the vital role society assigns to the institution of family—to birth and then socialize children.

Using the structural functionalist lens, sociologists see that social institutions construct stability and order. In large part, this is because several institutions (e.g., family, religion, education) cooperate to socialize each of us into adhering to the same set of cultural norms and values. Thus, American drivers stay on the right side of the road, we stop at stop signs, we more or less follow the speed limit, and so on. We also don't rob banks or commit murder. Put differently, most citizens of a society are "good" people who follow the social norms.

Curbing Violations of Social Norms. But what about an individual who chooses to act against those shared cultural norms? How does structural functionalism see that person? First and foremost, that person—for whatever reason—is violating social norms. Perhaps that person's parents failed to properly teach their children society's norms. Or the person may know the norms but consider them unfair (see Chapter 6). Or perhaps the person might simply be selfish and putting her or his needs ahead of what is best for society.

So, let's talk about a bank robber for a moment. He or she should have learned from family, teachers, and perhaps religious leaders that robbing a bank is not socially acceptable behavior. But despite those socializing messages, the person still chose to rob a bank. The person has stepped outside of the moral order of the community and must be punished (once caught, of course). But why? Why is punishment needed? Structural functionalist theorists believe that punishment is required for at least two reasons. First, accepting one's punishment is a step in the rehabilitation and resocialization process of the individual back into the community (if deemed possible). Second, structural functionalist theorists, building on the sociological work of Émile Durkheim, also worry that without punishment, "bad" behavior will spread like an epidemic in the community. If you were a customer in the bank and saw the bank robber get a bunch of money and never get caught, you might try to get away with something

MANIFEST AND LATENT FUNCTIONS OF INSTITUTIONS

In this exercise, you will identify the manifest and latent functions of the seven social institutions.

Sociologists recognize seven key social institutions. Each institution has both manifest and latent functions. Think of at least one manifest and one latent function of each institution, then complete the following table.

Social Institution	Manifest Function(s)	Latent Function(s)
Economy		
Education		
Family		
Government		
Health care/medicine		
Media		
Religion		

bad too. And then a third person might see you do that act of unpunished bad behavior and do something else, and so on. Soon, the social order will have broken down completely. So structural functionalists note the importance of punishing the deviant individual to "head off" future deviant acts—not only by that person but by others in the society who might use that person as a role model.

Social Change. Given this background, you can begin to predict how structural functionalist theorists view social change. What is social change? Sociologists see change happening when there are large-scale, macro, structural shifts in society or institutions within one or more societies. Functionalists, because they see harmony deriving from the stable functioning of institutions and cooperation among them, are not sure that social change is necessarily a good thing. Change in one institution rips apart the social harmony and equilibrium between it and the other institutions and requires a long time for the other social institutions to "catch up" and to reestablish social equilibrium. So, theorists using a structural functionalist perspective would argue that if change is needed at all, it should be done very slowly so as not to upset the equilibrium that undergirds the society and makes it strong.

We avoid accidents in traffic circles by following the norms for their use.
©iStockphoto.com/pro6x7

What Doesn't Structural Functionalism See?

Can rapid social change and the disharmony that comes along with it ever be a good thing for society to experience? Structural functionalist theorists would argue that no, it wouldn't—indeed couldn't—be a good thing. But think about that more deeply and use your sociological imagination.

Imagine we could go back in time to the mid-1940s, just after World War II ended. Pick nearly any town in the United States; what was it like? Let's just focus on one social institution—economics. Most likely, many men were just returning from fighting overseas, and many women were still in the paid workforce. During the war, more women entered the paid labor force as men went off to fight. As the war ended, many men came back home and wanted, even needed, their jobs back. Some women wanted to go back to working primarily in the home, but others didn't. Of course, some—those widowed by the war, for instance—had to keep working to pay the family's bills. Many women were upset when they were urged to leave the labor force and return home to have babies and keep house. They resented the fact that their job opportunities were once again limited to just a few fields, such as nursing and education.

How would functionalists evaluate this situation? Although they might not support the sex discrimination clearly evident in the labor force, they would want slow, incremental change to occur, because they could see how immediate gender equality in the workplace would create upheaval in the labor force. So, they might have argued for the benefits of many women's returning to unpaid labor while also advocating for public discussions and education about the possible merits of changing laws and regulations that discriminated against women in the workforce.

But another way of thinking about slow, gradual social change is that it would allow continued discrimination. Structural functionalism, by focusing on the need for social order and harmony, can overlook times in the life of the society when rapid social change—even if it may lead to some social chaos—is the just thing to do.

During World War II, women worked in formerly male-dominated jobs like these in the Douglas Aircraft factory in California.

Using Structural Functionalism to Analyze the Case of the Meitiv Family

We will now make use of the structural functionalist perspective to examine an incident that hit the news in 2015: the case of Danielle and Alexander Meitiv; their two children, Rafi, age ten, and Dvora, age six; the Montgomery County, Maryland, police; and Child Protective Services (CPS) of Maryland (for more about this case, including video, check out the sources at the end of the chapter). On December 20, 2014, the Meitiv children were at a local park at 5 p.m. and started to walk the one mile back to their house, alone. Three blocks from their destination, police stopped the children, put them in their squad car, and brought them to police headquarters. Later that night, they were placed in the custody of CPS. The Meitivs did get their children back later that evening but were told that they were under investigation by CPS. Asked why they let their children walk the one mile from the park to their home, they stated that "children learn self-reliance by being allowed to make choices, build independence and progressively experience the world on their own" (St. George 2015c, paragraph 16). Almost two months later, CPS completed its investigation, with a finding of "unsubstantiated child abuse" (St. George 2015c, paragraph 1). But the case was far from over.

Just a few months later, the parents dropped both children off at another park at 4 p.m. and told them to be home by 6 p.m. At 4:58 p.m., a man walking his dog called local police about two unsupervised children in the park. The man did not approach or talk with the children before placing the call. Police detained both children again, taking them immediately to CPS, where they were held without being allowed to contact their parents for more than five hours. CPS launched another investigation of their parents, questioning their ability to protect and parent their children correctly.

Why might the Meitiv parents allow their children to walk home alone? Are they just bad parents, too lazy to take proper care of them? No. The Meitivs practice what is called "free-range parenting," a parenting philosophy that encourages parents to allow children to grow up independently, with a minimum of adult supervision, appropriate to the age of the children. Free-range parents feel that today, U.S. society prevents children from learning to be truly self-sufficient.

Let's analyze the situation at this point. From a structural functionalist perspective, the manifest functions of the family as a social institution are to reproduce and then socialize the children to accept and follow the prevailing values in society. Obviously, the Meitivs have children, so their family has met that first manifest function. Where this example gets murky is when we shift our attention to the second manifest function.

The United States as a society values individualism and independence, and therefore parents are expected to teach their children to be self-reliant and independent. The devil's in the details, though. *How* should they teach them independence and at *what* age? Are children aged six and ten too young to be walking alone on a moderately busy street? Is it abuse or neglect if a parent teaches this particular instance of self-reliance "too soon" (i.e., at a time when many in society feel it is inappropriate)? And should parents who do so be judged "bad parents" by authorities—in this case, law enforcement and CPS?

This second investigation by CPS ended with "neglect 'ruled out'" (St. George 2015a, paragraphs 1, 7), and the case was closed. A spokesperson for Maryland's Department of Human Resources (to which CPS reports) added that "a child playing outside or walking unsupervised does not meet the criteria for a CPS response absent specific information supporting the conclusion that the child has been harmed or is at substantial risk of harm if they continue to be unsupervised" (St. George 2015a, paragraph 10).

Notice how this case shows the interrelatedness of social institutions (e.g., family and government), which is at the core of structural functionalism. Those using a structural functionalist perspective likely would leave unquestioned the assumption that family, law enforcement, and CPS all had a duty to be concerned about children in general and the Meitivs' two children in particular. Each agency's duty and, therefore, their employees' behavior were grounded in its manifest function.

Structural functionalists would likely argue that today, in a populous community like Montgomery

Alexander Meitiv, right, prepares dinner with the help of his daughter, Dvora, and son, Rafi. The Meitivs' "free-range parenting" led to their facing charges of child neglect.

Bonnie Jo Mount/The Washington Post/Getty Images

County, Maryland, most parents would not allow a six-year-old to play unsupervised and walk back home at night, even in the company of a ten-year-old sibling. If this *is* the value consensus, then law enforcement and CPS's decisions to take the children into custody and investigate their home life could be easily justified as correct. CPS's initial review was meant to teach the Meitivs how to better parent their children and, simultaneously, to reinforce proper parenting behaviors to all who live in the county.

CONSIDER THIS

Be a structural functionalist. What evidence in society can you find to illustrate that there is a consensus on how parents should raise children in the United States today?

Could other sociologists look at the story of what happened to the Meitiv family and reach different sociological conclusions? Let's turn next to the other macro-sociological theoretical perspective—conflict—and look at how sociologists using that perspective see social reality. Then we'll return to the Meitiv family as our example.

Check Your Understanding

- What do structural functionalists see as the role of institutions in society?
- Why do structural functionalists want social change to happen slowly?
- What social institutions were involved in the Meitiv incidents?
- Can you retell the story of the Meitiv family using the structural functionalist concepts of social institutions and manifest function?

Understanding the Conflict Theoretical Perspective

2.3   What is a conflict perspective?

Sociologists using the second macro-theoretical perspective, the **conflict perspective**, view society very differently than those looking at it from a functionalist perspective. Instead of seeing society as groups of institutions working together for the good of the whole, conflict theorists believe that society is composed of groups competing for power.

Karl Marx and Advanced Capitalism

Karl Marx, the founder of the conflict perspective, believed that there were ten stages of societal development, but he was most concerned with the last three stages. Given that, we'll start with stage 8, advanced capitalism. Marx held that advanced capitalism is an economic system based on the pursuit of maximum profit. Capitalism divides people into two major categories and a third, smaller group. There are the bourgeoisie, the rich owners of the **means of production** (the technology and materials needed to produce products, such as factories), and the proletariat, the poor workers (in the factories, etc.). The perpetually unemployed constitute the third group, the lumpenproletariat.

The advanced capitalism of Marx's time was a far cry from what we know capitalism to be today in the United States. Because there were no labor laws and it was so much cheaper to hire children than adults, the labor force included many children. There were no inspectors making sure that the workplace was safe, so many among the proletariat were injured. There was no worker's compensation insurance either, so injured members of the proletariat faced a difficult choice: show up and work despite the injury (but face the wrath of the owner for working slower) or quit work to heal—and starve. Wages were incredibly low because the bourgeoisie could use the ever growing pool of the lumpenproletariat as a stick over any worker who dared ask for a raise. Such a worker would be fired, as it was very easy to find a member of the lumpenproletariat who would work for the original wage (or an even lower one).

False Consciousness. For Marx and like-minded individuals of the time period, the exploitation of the proletariat by the bourgeoisie was a bit puzzling at first. Why didn't the proletariat realize how economically exploited they were under advanced capitalism and, for instance, stop showing up for work? Surely that would bring down the capitalist system.

Marx theorized that the workers were in a state of **false consciousness**. They collectively and individually did not understand that they and the owners had different self-interests. They were, he argued, misled to believe that what was good for the owner also benefited them. They believed that, if they just worked hard every day, they too might become members of the bourgeoisie. The media of the day, the religious institution, and the political institution all promulgated this: a good worker, in time, could "strike it rich" and get in on the many advantages of capitalism. But that was not going to happen for most of the proletariat; they lived on subsistence wages while the factory owner lived in a huge home, profiting from the proletariat's hard work. Yet their false consciousness kept them from seeing the reality of their lives—as members of the proletariat, they were compelled to work in a factory, sewing button after button for sixteen hours a day, for the rest of their lives. Was this really what life should be, Marx asked?

Alienation. No, it was not. The human race had what Marx called species being—the unique potential to imagine and then create what we imagine. Humans can sketch fantastically intricate designs and then make them become real in the world. No other animal can do that. But the proletariat were prevented from living up to their species being by the very nature of the capitalist exploitation they endured. They lived in a state of **alienation** that left them laboring for others and separated from what they created. Their monotonous jobs were small and repetitious; they often never even knew what the finished product of their labor looked like. Worse yet, they couldn't afford the products they were making.

Karl Marx and Socialism

Marx felt that the proletariat could move from false consciousness to **true consciousness** if they came to grips with the depths of their exploitation by the bourgeoisie and the capitalist system they controlled. He believed that his writing, along with that of others, would "wake them up" from their state of alienated false consciousness and lead them to bring about change in their society.

Marx predicted that when the proletarian revolution began, society would move from the eighth stage of societal development, advanced capitalism, into the ninth stage, socialism. This ninth stage was a sort of "working it out" stage of social change. Economically, things would be more just than under capitalism but not yet truly equal. In socialism, children would be off the factory floors and sent to free public schools while able-bodied adults would work. The state would take over the means of production from the bourgeoisie through imposing a heavy progressive income tax on all adult citizens. This tax would economically hurt only the bourgeoisie (although many in that group were expected to die in the revolution). A proletariat worker, with almost no income, would not have to pay much. Also, new inheritance laws would ensure that rich families would no

longer be able to pass money, property, and other expensive goods down to the next generation of their families. After a bourgeoisie died, the socialist government would "inherit" the rest of their money and goods and redistribute it to the citizens.

Socialism, Marx predicted, would last a few generations. He felt that the values of capitalism, such as support for the accumulation of wealth in the hands of just a few, the acquisition of goods as a sign of high status, and so forth, would take a while to die out. It might take a generation or two with people who had grown up only under socialism as an economic system before society would be ready for the tenth stage of social development: communism.

CONSIDER THIS

If you were alive when Marx was and you were a wealthy owner of a factory who'd been planning to pass down your wealth to your children, what would you think of Marx's new economic system called socialism? Why? And how would you feel as a member of the proletariat?

Karl Marx and Communism

Marx believed that after a few generations of socialism as an economic system, some of the key social institutions, such as the political and economic systems, would no longer be needed and would disappear. Under **communism**, all citizens would be equal and, at long last, able to fulfill their species being. Each person could contemplate and then go create. There would be no social classes under communism because every person would make the same wage for work done. Marx's vision of communism never became a reality, not even in nations that refer to themselves as communist.

All of these stages of social change are economic ones, and Marx is often called an economic determinist. The social institution that was the base of the society, for him, was always the economy. He believed that as the economy changed from advanced capitalism to socialism and ultimately to communism, the other six social institutions would necessarily change and adapt.

From Marx to the Conflict Perspective

Marx's theory became the intellectual foundation for our second macro-theoretical perspective: the conflict perspective. Expanding upon Marx's analysis, conflict theorists recognize many ways in which social rewards are unequally distributed (e.g., race, ethnicity, gender, sex, sexual orientation, citizenship status, age, ability or disability). They talk about the haves—those individuals and social institutions that gain access to more of society's scarce rewards—and the have-nots—those unable to get even their fair share of social rewards because of their category membership.

Seeing the Social World Using the Conflict Perspective

Again, conflict is a macro-theoretical perspective; it analyzes society as a whole. But whereas structural functionalist theorists examine society and see social order and harmony, conflict theorists see something completely different. They see oppression: the haves holding the have-nots back to maintain their own elevated status.

Conflict theorists notice patterns of inequitable distribution of resources and rewards. They would note which groups in society have the most power and representation in the major institutions in society (e.g., who are our government and religious leaders, media owners, school board members, and sports team owners?). Sociologists using this perspective would also note how the structure of society perpetuates inequality by placing hurdles in front of some groups but not others. For example, as mentioned in Chapter 1, the cost of tuition has led many students into debt. Why? Whom does this benefit and whom does it hurt?

Many conflict theorists aren't satisfied with merely recognizing such inequalities; they go that next step and suggest ways that they and others can reduce, if not completely eliminate, the oppression that they observe. Like Marx, sociologists who take a conflict perspective advocate social change to help the have-nots in society to gain more of society's rewards. And unlike most structural functionalists, who want social change to be slow and gradual so as not to upset the social harmony between social institutions, conflict theorists believe that social change to alleviate social injustice should be done rapidly. For conflict thinkers, slow, gradual social change is merely another term for continued oppression. They want to help the have-nots—now.

What Doesn't Conflict See?

The conflict perspective is so laser focused on oppression and making life better for the have-nots that it can overlook moments when society is going along fairly well. By concerning itself primarily with injustices and oppression, conflict can overlook times of societal harmony and equilibrium. Moreover, conflict theorists do not always acknowledge how disruptive and harmful change can be—for the have-nots as well as the haves.

Theories under the Umbrella of the Conflict Perspective

The conflict perspective, although unified in the focus on oppression and efforts to combat it, contains many types of conflict theories within it. For example, feminist conflict theorists argue that men as a category of people have greater access to social rewards than women (see Chapter 8). Critical race theorists focus on the social construction of race and the White-dominated racial hierarchy (see Chapter 9). All conflict theorists, however, build on Marx's insight that some individuals and groups have more resources and rewards than others do and that this is unjust.

Disability scholars frequently use the conflict perspective to analyze how modern Western societies create the built environment (the architecture of public and private spaces) in ways that work for the able-bodied but not for people living with disabilities. Why, for example, cannot every entrance to a building include a ramp? A few decades ago, few buildings had ramps for people using wheelchairs. Today, often only one entrance is "made accessible." Notice that the language used implies that creating accessibility is an "extra," something that must be added to a structure rather than an organic part of every building. With that kind of a mind-set, it becomes easy to see that "normal bodies" are the standard against which all others are judged. Those of us with disabilities then are somehow lesser, deviant people and less deserving of access. As you can see, the fundamental assumption of the modern conflict theoretical perspective is still rooted in Marx's insight: the social rewards of society are not equally shared.

Using the Conflict Perspective to Understand the Meitiv Family

Now turn your attention back to the Meitiv family, who advocated free-range parenting, an approach to parenting that encourages teaching children to be independent and autonomous from an early age. How might the conflict perspective analyze what happened to them? Recall the conflict perspective's basic assumption: different categories of people get different social rewards on the basis of their location in the social structure. In the family's interactions with law enforcement and CPS, you can see a power imbalance right away.

CONFLICT THEORY AND STUDENT ATHLETES

In this activity you will apply conflict theory to analyzing pay for student athletes.

Under NCAA regulations, student athletes can neither be paid nor profit in any way, including through their images, likenesses, or autographs. Think about the different groups who are associated with college basketball and football at your school. In addition to the student athletes, there are the coaches, student fans, and others who are spectators at the games. Using conflict theory, consider the costs, resources, and rewards that are involved with

college basketball and football. Write your answers to the following questions: (1) Are those costs, resources, and rewards fairly distributed? (2) Should student athletes be paid? Also consider that the great majority of football and basketball programs take more money to run than they bring in, and these costs are partially paid with student fees (https://www.acenet.edu/news-room/Pages/Myth-College-Sports-Are-a-Cash-Cow2.aspx). Be prepared to discuss these two questions in small groups and/or report back to the class.

An anonymous person placed a call to the police—without even talking to the children in question. Recall that the police and CPS detained the children before any investigation occurred. True, law enforcement and CPS workers were simply performing their jobs, but they represented the state and all its power. The Meitiv parents, in contrast, had little or no power. Indeed, Alexander Meitiv had to listen to the police lecture him on the dangers of the modern world when the police returned the children after the first incident (St. George 2015a). Educated people (Alexander is a theoretical physicist, Danielle a climate science

consultant) discovered that they had not—at least in that moment—either the power or the freedom to decide how to raise their own offspring. And who had even less power in this situation? The children. Their feelings were ignored throughout the bureaucratic wrangling.

Now imagine the story playing out a bit differently. The family in question did not have an intact set of two parents but instead was led by a single parent. A poor, single parent. A poor, single parent of color working several jobs to make ends meet. Do you think that—at each step of the Meitivs' story—this poor single parent of color would have been treated the same way as the Meitivs were? Would he or she have gotten the kids back the night of the first "walking alone" incident? Still gotten the kids back after the second incident of their walking alone? Had neglect "ruled out" after the second incident? Had enough money to possibly sue CPS and law enforcement? In fact, would anyone even have called law enforcement if they had seen two children of color walking alone? Or if there had been a call, might it have been less about concern for the children's *safety* and more about "what are those kids up to" (i.e., someone worried about what possible criminal behavior they might be about to do)?

Nine-year-old Regina Harrell's mother was arrested and lost custody of Regina for almost three weeks because she allowed Regina to play in a park a block away from where she was working at a McDonald's.

AP Photo/Jeffrey Collins

Consider the 2014 South Carolina case involving Debra Harrell, a forty-six-year-old African American woman, and her nine-year-old daughter Regina. Debra worked at a McDonald's and, lacking other childcare options, often had to bring her child with her. The girl would usually sit in the restaurant until her mother was done working, but on three days that summer, Debra allowed her child to play in a popular park about a mile away. On the third day, a parent of another child at the park asked Regina where her parents were. Alarmed when Regina told her that her mom was working, the parent called the police. The police then arrested Debra on the charge of felony child neglect and placed Regina in foster care. Debra was released on $5,000 bail, but Regina remained in foster care for seventeen days before being returned to her mother. Debra's arrest also meant that she lost her job (until media coverage pressured the local McDonald's to take her back) (CBS News 2014; Friedersdorf 2014; Reese 2014).

As tense as the Meitiv situation was, their race, education levels, and social class likely buffered them from the full power of CPS and the police, whereas families of color living in poor neighborhoods, who, like Debra Harrell, cannot afford to hire a private attorney, are often denied those opportunities to quickly "fix" the situation.

Check Your Understanding

- According to Marx, why are the proletariat in a state of false consciousness in advanced capitalism?

- How does a society move from advanced capitalism to socialism, according to Marx?

- Can you explain the difference between socialism and communism?

- What are the conceptual differences between the terms *bourgeoisie* and *proletariat* and *haves* and *have-nots*? Can you correctly use these terms?

- What are two examples of conflict theories that fall under umbrella of the conflict perspective?

Understanding the Symbolic Interactionist Perspective

2.4   What is symbolic interaction?

Macro-theoretical perspectives let sociologists see the big picture (the macro unit of analysis) of what is happening in the entire society, be it order and harmony (structural functionalism) or oppression (conflict). These theoretical lenses, however, miss something vital to the study of people in groups: interaction between individuals—the micro level. **Symbolic interaction** provides that theoretical balance for sociology. As the micro-theoretical perspective, it asks questions macro perspectives do not. For example, we can use it to examine how any one person develops a **self**—a sense of our place in society and who we are in relationship to others. It helps us study how meaning comes to be constructed and shared by a group of people. Symbolic interactionists view society as a social construction, continually constructed and reconstructed by individuals through their use of shared symbols.

The Social Construction of Reality

Interactionist theorists study how **culture**—the way of life of a particular group of people—comes to be created. Individuals come together around one or more shared purposes and begin to interact. This interaction, over time, becomes routinized in various ways. So, for example, when the individuals first interact, they may create a common greeting. That greeting gets repeated every time they meet, and suddenly they have created a norm—an expectation about behavior. Now individuals *must* use this now standardized greeting or else be judged by the group as deviant. These creators of the greeting continue to use it, further normalizing it for their group. They will then teach new members (either born into the group or converts to it) the greeting and pass it along to the next generation.

In effect, the group constructs its culture. Culture includes norms and the symbols through which we communicate (e.g., language, numbers, gestures, and the meaning we attach to objects such as a nation's flag, a swastika, and a cross). Culture also consists of values, what we believe to be good or bad, and material objects the group creates to make life easier and meaningful. All of these are

USING DRAMATURGY THEORY TO ANALYZE A SOCIAL EVENT

In this activity, you will apply dramaturgy theory to a specific social event and discuss your answers with another student.

Dramaturgy theory can be helpful when examining all kinds of social interactions. Analyze a party you recently attended, your class, an athletic event, or some other social event using this theory.

1. Use dramaturgy theory to describe a social gathering from the ones above, being sure to identify all the component parts Goffman would use. Write your response.

2. Share your analysis with another student and be ready to report out to the entire class.

---

social constructions. This raises a significant sociological question: how does this socially constructed content (i.e., culture) get "inside" each person? Interactionists argue that it happens through the process of socialization, the sharing of culture from generation to generation.

Although we experience socialization throughout our lives, the most intense time for socialization is in childhood (what we often call **primary socialization**), so that will be our focus. George Herbert Mead and Charles Horton Cooley, the founders of the symbolic interactionist perspective, both emphasized the importance of the socialization process. You will learn more about their work in Chapter 5. In this chapter, we will focus on Cooley's contributions. Through his "looking glass self" theory, he described how a child develops a sense of self in three steps.

The Looking Glass Self Theory. A child's first step in developing a sense of self is to imagine how she appears to relevant others—her parents, siblings, grandparents, and so on. Cooley argued that it isn't possible to receive direct information about how others think or feel; instead, the child tries to put herself in the shoes of the other person and then contemplates what that other person is feeling about her. So, she might imagine, "I think my parents love me."

In the second step, the child reacts to the feedback the parents and others give about their perceptions toward the child. That feedback could be verbal (e.g., "I love you") or nonverbal (e.g., holding hands, hugging, smiling). What is important in this step, Cooley argued, is that the child is responding to what she feels the feedback means about her. The child perceives who she is (to others—and thus to herself) via feedback from others. These others are the social mirror that the child uses to develop a sense of self.

Finally, in the third step, the child integrates the first two into a coherent and unique sense of self. Interaction

with **primary groups** (small collections of people of which a person is a member, usually for life, and in which deep emotional ties develop, such as one's family of origin) shapes the child's sense of self. Others in effect become the "mirror" by which each person sees oneself.

Although socialization in childhood is foundational, Cooley would argue that socialization continues throughout a person's life. A new employee receives feedback from the boss and peers and integrates that feedback into a sense of self as a worker, for example.

Dramaturgy Theory. Interaction does not just focus on the construction of the self. Erving Goffman (1959) was a sociologist who said that life was like a play—a drama—in which we are all actors. He created dramaturgy theory to explain interaction among small groups by looking at the social actors (the individuals involved in the interaction), the social scripts the actors follow, and the props (material objects) the actors use to enhance their performances. Goffman also looked at the settings where interactions take place. Two of the key ones are the **front stage** (where the interaction takes place) and the **back stage** (where one prepares for the interaction).

According to Goffman, we each try to control the vibe we give off to others. Each of us uses **presentation of self** skills—shaping the physical, verbal, visual, and gestural messages that we give to others—to (try to) control their evaluations of us. This is what Goffman called impression management. Let's say some new friends you'd like to impress invite you to go to a football game, assuming you, like them, love the sport and this particular team. You have never gone to a football game or paid much attention to the sport, but you'd like to fit in with your friends. Your roommate helps you (back stage) dress appropriately by lending you her sweatshirt with the team's mascot emblazoned on

LANGUAGE AND SOCIAL CONSTRUCTION

In this exercise, you will consider the ways whereby groups of people construct language.

Language, both written and symbolic (think, for example, of our use of numerals in mathematics as a type of scientific language), is a social construction. It is different from place to place and group to group, including age groups. Are your grandparents fluent in emoji? Do they know what "That's the tea" means? Write your answers to the following questions:

1. What are some elements of the language you use that are age-specific? What words or symbols do you use that a member of an older generation is less likely to understand?

2. How does this help show that language is a social construction?

it and gives you a quick lesson on how football is played and the key players on the team. She also tells you that your friends may well expect you to eat and drink with them outside the stadium before the game.

You join your new friends outside the stadium (front stage). The pregame eating and drinking goes without a hitch, and your new friends tell you how happy they are to have found you, a fellow fan of their beloved team. All goes well until you get into the stadium and the game begins. Suddenly, everyone is shouting chants at the top of their lungs—except you. Your roommate forgot to fill you in on this part of the script!

Goffman's work helps us see that the world is a stage and we are all actors as we interact with one another. Like other theories under the symbolic interactionist perspective, dramaturgy allows us to understand why individuals behave differently in various social settings. In turn, this knowledge can help us navigate our social world successfully.

What Doesn't Symbolic Interaction See?

Recall that both macro-theoretical perspectives we have discussed allow us to examine the causes of social problems, how to solve them, and the rate of social change. Social problems and social change are macro-sociological concepts, but symbolic interaction is a micro-level theoretical perspective. We could use symbolic interaction to study the experience of a female cadet in a predominantly male military academy, but not to understand the institutional issues of gender inequality in the government, economy, and military that led to the academy's being predominantly male. By concentrating on how individuals become

socialized into the norms and values of their social group and thereby shape their sense of self, interaction focuses on different questions than the two macro-theoretical perspectives.

Social Constructionism. Some sociologists, frustrated with symbolic interaction's inability to study social problems, have combined it with conflict theory and created **social constructionism**. This theory begins with the social construction of reality, just as symbolic interaction does: every society creates norms, values, objects, and symbols it finds meaningful and useful. Social constructionists, however, also note that different categories or groups of people in the society get different rewards, as conflict theory states. Some have more, some have less. Social constructionists argue that this stratification—although felt in the world by individuals—is ultimately created and sustained through social systems, which must be made more just.

So, constructionists would argue that it is more important to study the *idea* of poverty than individual poor people (Best 2012). They focus on the constructed nature of every stratification system (e.g., wealth/poverty, race, sex/gender, age, the digital divide). In turn, they see the possibilities for change embedded in social interactions that can persuade particular audiences (e.g., Congress, the mayor, the local press). For example, if poverty is constructed as "something that will always be with us"—and everyone believes that to be true—then policy makers do not need to focus their time, energy, or efforts on reducing poverty. However, if poverty is constructed as something that we can—and should—eliminate, then policy makers will feel more pressure to create policies that work to minimize, if

COURAGEOUS CONVERSATIONS ABOUT RACE

CHELSEA MARTY

At Valdosta State University in Georgia, I was involved with a speaker series titled Courageous Conversations about Race (CCR). This series grew out of an effort to address racial tension present on our college campus. We wanted students, faculty, and other members of the community to feel open and safe enough to discuss racial topics and concepts that often go unmentioned. In the process, we hoped to create a campus environment more inclusive and appreciative of diversity.

While working with CCR, I eventually became a member of the organizing and planning team. I, along with my research partner and friend Ashlie Prain, created a student-led CCR series. This series featured students who gave presentations, panels, and performances that focused on racial issues. Topics included White supremacy, colorism, intersectionality, police brutality, and race and politics.

During one CCR, I presented on the research project "The Path of Our Narratives," which I conducted with Ashlie. Using narratives of racism encountered in childhoods, we discussed the early internalization of racism and racial stereotypes. We then connected the early socialization of such biases to systematic oppression and institutionalized racism.

My presentation and approach to working on this series are closely related to the sociological theory of social constructionism. Social constructionists focus on the social construction of reality and how interpretations and experiences shape our social structure. This is evident in my presentation, as I point out how childhood experiences of racism can be linked to the institutionalization of racism itself.

For example, in one narrative a young White girl shares her experience of being moved from a predominantly Black school to a predominantly White school. As a child, she was told that this move was for her own good and that she would make better friends and have better opportunities. Although this individual story may seem insignificant, it actually is indicative of the racial biases used to structure our school system. Such biases contribute to the segregation, underfunding, and lack of resources that severely damage the quality of education that marginalized groups in our society receive.

Additionally, the series as a whole reflected how social interpretations of race have influenced our actions, relationships, politics, and much more. Through an understanding of the theory of social constructionism, we can collectively work to recognize and dismantle racial biases and stereotypes.

Perhaps the most encouraging aspect of CCR is that, in addition to sparking conversation and promoting education, it inspires action and encourages community involvement. Several individuals from the community have taken on the responsibility of planning more talks and campaigns that address racial issues within our community, and I look forward to being a part of those efforts.

Discussion Question: How can understanding the theory of social constructionism help you recognize and dismantle racial biases and stereotypes?

Chelsea Marty was an undergraduate at Valdosta State who went on to get a master's degree in sociology and currently works as a program support specialist for a federal grant program called Upward Bound.

not eradicate, poverty. So too, how the press covers policy makers will shift on the basis of how poverty (or any other social problem) is socially constructed.

The social constructionist theory can be used to understand how our interactions can lead to a variety of societal issues and help address them. In the following Sociologists in Action, Chelsea Marty, an undergraduate at Valdosta State University, relates how she used social constructionism to understand how the internalization of racism and racial stereotypes can lead to systematic oppression and institutionalized racism. Chelsea also describes the steps she is taking to confront and tackle these social problems.

Using Symbolic Interaction to Understand the Meitiv Family

We now return to the Meitiv family one last time, to examine their situation through the lens of symbolic interaction. Danielle and Alexander Meitiv socialized their children by modeling appropriate behavior and incrementally giving them more responsibility. They then provided feedback to the children on their behavior. Part of that socialization process involved having the children walk together short distances. The parents followed behind the children, without their knowledge, to observe their behavior during these solo outings. What they saw led them to trust that their children could cope with any possibilities that might occur when they walked the mile home from school together. These successful outings boosted the children's self-concepts. Danielle described the reasoning behind their socialization methods, saying that "I think it's absolutely critical for their development—to learn responsibility, to experience the world, to gain confidence and competency" (St. George 2015b, paragraph 6).

> "We wouldn't have let them do it if we didn't think they were ready for it," Danielle said. She said her son and daughter have previously paired up for walks around the block, to a nearby 7-Eleven and to a library about three quarters of a mile away. "They have proven they are responsible," she said. "They've developed these skills." (St. George 2015b, paragraph 4)

But while the Meitiv parents felt that they were properly socializing their children, others did not see the children's behavior in the same way. They wondered if the children had enough life experience to cope with whatever might happen. When they went on longer walks, the children often carried a card the family had created, which read, "I am not lost. I am a free-range kid" (St. George 2015b, paragraph 11). Without that prop—a symbolic piece of information—the police officers who responded had little information to go on about who the children were and why they were out alone and therefore took them into protective custody.

As the family became caught up in the CPS legal system, Danielle claimed that these authority figures were attempting to socialize her children to be fearful, in contrast to the parents' view that the world, overall, was a safe place for children:

> My son told us that the social worker who questioned him asked, "What would you do if someone grabbed you?" and suggested that he tell us that he doesn't want to go off on his own anymore because it's dangerous and that there are "bad guys waiting to grab you." This is how adults teach children to be afraid even when they are not in danger. (Meitiv 2015, paragraph 7)

The Meitiv story spread as national media picked up the story, and more and more individuals began to weigh in publicly, writing comments on online news articles and other social media. Many parents supported the Meitivs, but others criticized their free-range parenting style. Their story showed that there are competing cultural understandings of what it means to be a child and to be a parent in U.S. culture.

A social movement in support of free-range parenting sprang up, leading to a petition to change Maryland's laws. Today, Maryland's laws remain the same, but the movement exists across the nation, and Utah became the first state to pass a "free-range parenting" law, in 2018. Utah's new law protects parents from charges of abuse for "permitting a child, whose basic needs are met and who is of sufficient age and maturity to avoid harm or unreasonable risk of harm, to engage in independent activities." These activities include "traveling to and from school, including by walking, running, or bicycling; traveling to and from nearby commercial or recreational facilities; and remaining at home unattended" (Utah State Legislature 2018, lines 316–22).

Full Theoretical Circle

2.5 How do structural functionalism, conflict perspectives, and symbolic interaction work together to help us get a more complete view of reality?

Each family creates, within reason, its own norms for how to raise children and implements those norms. But what do we mean by "within reason"? Society determines what is "reasonable"; it is socially constructed. Over time, certain behavioral patterns will become more commonplace in society and become the institutionalized version (in this case, of the family institution).

And now we have come full circle: a small group creates its own norms. Over time, some of those norms get shared among more members of the society as people interact, which is what symbolic interactionists study. These norms end up constructing sets of statuses and roles around key aspects of how society operates and creates social institutions. Once social institutions become routinized, they shape society and how individuals react to those social institutions, which structural functionalists analyze. And, inevitably, power differentials arise between the haves and the have-nots in social institutions and in the broader society, which sociologists using the conflict perspective study.

CONSIDER THIS

Describe your hometown using one of the theoretical perspectives described here. Which one will you use? Why? Do you see social harmony or social oppression? Are you interested in how small groups in society construct and then implement their values?

VIEWING THE SAME EDUCATION DATA FROM THREE DIFFERENT PERSPECTIVES

Sociological perspectives are different ways of "seeing" and thinking about the social world more broadly. They help us decide what questions we should ask about the social world.

In this online activity, you will examine data from the National Center for Education Statistics about a common social event—school homework—to consider how different theoretical perspectives can be applied to the same set of facts.

*Requires the Vantage version of *Sociology in Action*.

▼ FIGURE 2.1

Percent of Public School Eighth Graders Who Reported Spending 30 or More Minutes on Math Homework Each Day (State) (2000)

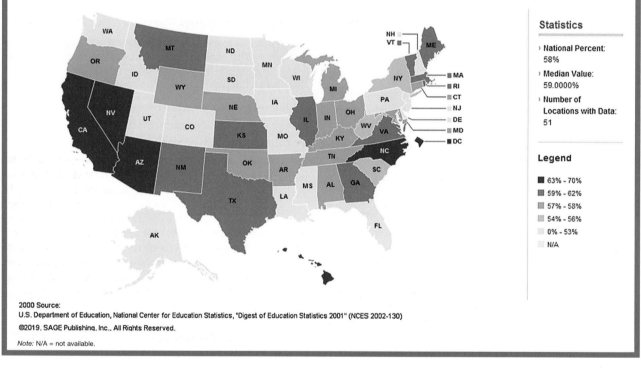

Statistics

› National Percent: 58%

› Median Value: 59.0000%

› Number of Locations with Data: 51

Legend

■ 63% - 70%
■ 59% - 62%
■ 57% - 58%
■ 54% - 56%
▢ 0% - 53%
▢ N/A

2000 Source:
U.S. Department of Education, National Center for Education Statistics, "Digest of Education Statistics 2001" (NCES 2002-130)

©2019. SAGE Publishing, Inc., All Rights Reserved.

Note: N/A = not available.

The theoretical perspectives we have discussed give us ways to analyze human behavior. Each perspective (and the many theories it encompasses) offers a unique viewpoint. None of them is the correct one; rather, each of the perspectives gives sociologists a particular lens with which to see human society. Structural functionalists focus on social order and institutions and agreement on the basic values that create and sustain that social order but tend not to notice conflict and inequality. Conflict theorists do just the opposite; they see social problems caused by oppression and injustices but overlook moments of order and social harmony. Neither structural functionalists nor conflict theorists deal with the behavior of small groups, leaving that to symbolic interactionists, who examine how groups create culture and pass it on to the next generation but ignore macro issues of power and control, social harmony, and balance.

Most likely one or more of these perspectives make better sense to you, and that is fine. Practice using all three of them as you look around your social world, however. You will see how you can focus on different angles of society with each.

Check Your Understanding

- Why is symbolic interaction a micro-level theoretical perspective?

- What do sociologists mean by "the self"?

- According to interactionists, how is society socially constructed?

- How can different groups of individuals see the same social problem differently? Can you give an original example of this?

Conclusion

Theoretical perspectives frame the social world for sociologists. They highlight some parts of human behavior and blur others. Many sociologists use the lenses of multiple theoretical perspectives to compensate for the theoretical oversights of each perspective. The theoretical language you have learned in this chapter will reemerge in many future chapters, because these are the main ways sociologists see human behavior. Chapter 3 will add to your sociological skill set by showing you the varied ways that sociologists collect data about the social world—to which we then apply theoretical perspectives and theories.

REVIEW

2.1 Why and how do sociologists use theoretical perspectives?

The three theoretical perspectives—structural functionalism, conflict, and symbolic interaction—help sociologists to examine the complexities of social life. They provide structure to the vast data that sociologists gather and allow us to find patterns in human behavior.

2.2 What is structural functionalism?

Structural functionalism is a macro-level theoretical perspective that helps us analyze an entire society and how its parts work together. Structural functionalists tend to see social harmony and social equilibrium, on the basis of the perceived smooth interactions of the seven social institutions. Structural functionalism is a "big-picture" way of viewing societies. Imagine a sociologist standing at a distance and looking at how society and its parts are working together.

2.3 What is a conflict perspective?

Conflict perspectives are macro-level perspectives that analyze entire societies. Whereas structural functionalist theorists examine society and see social order and harmony, conflict theorists see something completely different. They see inequality—the haves holding the have-nots back to maintain their own elevated status. Conflict theories focus on the oppression and injustice at work in society caused by the haves' excessive political, economic, and social power. Conflict thinkers advocate for rapid social change to give more social rewards to the have-nots.

2.4 What is symbolic interaction?

Symbolic interaction is a micro-level theoretical perspective that focuses on the individual or small groups rather than an entire society. Symbolic interactionists focus on how the self is constructed through socialization and how a group socially constructs norms and values that then govern the group's behaviors. Symbolic interaction helps us understand how individuals can shape, as well as be shaped by, society. It also helps us study how meaning comes to be constructed and shared by a group of people. Symbolic interactionists view society as a social construction, continually constructed and reconstructed by individuals through their use of shared symbols.

2.5 How do structural functionalism, conflict perspectives, and symbolic interaction work together to help us get a more complete view of reality?

Each of the major theoretical perspectives provides a different view of society. Structural functionalists focus on how the social institutions of society can work together to create and sustain social order but tend to overlook inequality and conflict. Conflict theorists focus on inequality and conflict but tend to overlook social order and consensus in society. Neither of these macro perspectives focuses on individuals and small groups in society. Symbolic interactionists use a micro lens to focus on how individuals and small groups work together to create and re-create society. In the process, they show how individuals develop a sense of self through socialization. Together, structural functionalism, conflict perspectives, and symbolic interaction give us a more complete view and understanding of how society works.

KEY TERMS

CHAPTER 3

USING RESEARCH METHODS

Mikaila Mariel Lemonik Arthur and Amanda M. Jungels

Nearly half of all Americans believe that immigrants increase crime in the United States, but in fact, immigrants are less likely to commit crimes than those born in the United States. Research allows us to distinguish fact from perception.

LEARNING QUESTIONS

3.1 Why do sociologists do research?

3.2 What are some of the different ways sociologists collect data?

3.3 How do sociologists analyze data?

3.4 What are the steps of the social scientific research process?

3.5 When are data from a sample generalizable to the larger population?

3.6 Why should you be able to recognize good (and bad) research and media claims?

According to a Gallup poll in 2019, 42 percent of Americans believe that immigration to the United States makes crime rates worse (Gallup 2019), and this belief is commonly repeated by media commentators and political figures. But is it true? Research over the past 20 years has shown that it is not (Adelman et al. 2017; Ewing, Martínez, and Rumbaut 2015). Immigrants are less likely to commit crime than those born in the United States. One study found that people born outside the United States were 45 percent less likely than those whose families had been in the United States for at least three generations to commit violent crimes (Sampson 2008). Furthermore, although immigrants often live in high-crime neighborhoods, as the proportion of immigrants in a neighborhood goes up, the level of property and violent crime actually declines (Adelman et al. 2017; Sampson 2008). Research indicates that immigration may *decrease* crime rates in metropolitan areas (Adelman et al. 2017)!

How do we know that this common perception that immigrants increase crime is incorrect? We know because researchers went out and systematically collected and analyzed data. Sometimes, research confirms what we expect to find, but in other cases, it shows that our assumptions were wrong. Correcting those misconceptions ensures that we better understand our world. It also helps us make better policy, business, and life decisions. For example, consider how a small business owner might change his or her perceptions of where to locate a new store on the basis of the research on immigration and crime.

What Is Research?

3.1 Why do sociologists do research?

We can define **research** as *the systematic process of data collection for the purpose of producing knowledge.* This means that when we do research, we collect data according to a careful plan and use those data to figure out something new about the world. This definition of research might seem different from the research you have been asked to do in the past. In high school, for example, many students complete research projects based entirely on sources found in the library or online. When carrying out such a project, you were a consumer of knowledge, a person who finds knowledge that already exists and uses it to enhance your understanding. But scientific research requires you to move beyond being only a consumer of knowledge and to become a producer of knowledge. Producers of knowledge do research to find out things we did not know previously. Prior sources are indeed important to this research process—but for sociologists, the use of prior sources is only one step in the journey to new knowledge, and it is data collection that is most essential.

Research must be **empirical** in nature. Empirical statements are statements that could hypothetically be proved true or false. In other words, they are statements of possible facts. These kinds of statements can be contrasted with **normative** statements, or statements with which you are expressing an opinion. These include statements that have words such as *should* in them, in which you state that the world would be better in certain circumstances, or in which you express a moral, ethical, or religious view. In other words, when we do research, we are trying to find out how the world actually is, not make an argument for how we wish the world would be. (Of course, once we do research and find out how the world is, we can use our findings to advocate for social change! But research itself is about the development of knowledge.)

The definition of research discussed above would apply to research in most physical, natural, and social science fields, but sociological research is distinct because it is social in nature. This means that sociological research is about groups, societies, and/or social interaction. In general, sociological research addresses patterns, comparisons, relationships, and meanings in social life. So, sociological research must involve people, organizations, or social systems. Where it involves people, it must involve aspects of those people's experiences that go beyond the biological or psychological. A simpler way to think about this is that sociological research must go beyond what is inside of people's heads.

HOW I GOT ACTIVE IN SOCIOLOGY

MIKAILA MARIEL LEMONIK ARTHUR

As a high school student, I wanted to be a writer of fiction, and I began college planning to study creative writing. My favorite pieces of fiction were stories that helped illuminate social dynamics—and I found that sociology provided a similar window into the social world. As I took more classes in sociology, I found that it provided me with better tools for investigating and writing about the social world than fiction. So I chose to major in sociology and go on to earn my PhD.

As a graduate student, I got the chance to teach various sociology courses and decided on a career in which I could do exciting sociological research *and* focus on teaching sociology to undergraduates. Today, I combine research and teaching while working in the Sociology Department at Rhode Island College, where I love introducing students to the process of sociological research and seeing them develop the skills to make new discoveries themselves and to bring the techniques they learn in college to their careers. I continue to use my sociological research and writing skills to illuminate the social institution of higher education and to contribute to debates about social policy.

AMANDA M. JUNGELS

I have always been interested in understanding why and how society operates the way that it does. Why do some people have more power than others? How is this power structured and maintained? How do those with less power learn to operate in, and rebel against, the current power structure? In high school and college, I took sociology, psychology, religion, and anthropology classes to try to understand this dynamic, and I found my home in sociology. Sociology encouraged me to understand how people, and the societies they live in, are the result of an interplay between their personal biographies—their choices, desires, and life circumstances—and the history of the society.

I attended graduate school in sociology with the goal of becoming a professor, and I was lucky enough to get extensive training and experience teaching undergraduate students in a variety of sociology classes. Today I work in the Center for Teaching and Learning at Columbia University, designing programs and services to help support faculty in their teaching, and I also teach research methods courses focusing on surveying and interviewing to graduate students at New York University's Wagner School of Public Service. In this way, I am able to combine my passions for teaching and for research and support students at the same time.

iStockphoto.com/PeopleImages

Why Do We Do Research?

As college students, you are likely very familiar with the rising costs of college and with the sacrifices today's students must make in order to attend college. Sara Goldrick-Rab is a sociologist who studies the lives of college students. Goldrick-Rab and her colleagues surveyed students to understand their financial situations, whether they were worried about their finances, and how today's college students make ends meet. Before we go any further, take a moment to think about a few questions:

1. Have you ever been upset or worried about not having enough money to pay for both daily living expenses and college expenses?

2. What percentage of college students do you think experience food insecurity (e.g., didn't have enough money to buy food, ate less than they should, or skipped eating entirely)?

3. Do you think all students at all types of colleges are equally likely to experience hunger or food insecurity?

Their study, which included 30,000 students at more than 120 two- and four-year colleges, found that more than half of students had some level of food insecurity, with the most common challenges being an inability to afford well-balanced and healthy meals or enough food and having to cut the size of meals or skip meals (Broton and Goldrick-Rab 2018). They also found that students at two-year colleges were more likely to experience food insecurity and hunger, though students in all types of institutions report experiences with hunger and food insecurity (Broton and Goldrick-Rab 2018; Andrews 2018). One study, conducted at the City University of New York, found that students who had poor or fair health, had incomes under $20,000 annually, worked more than 20 hours per week, or were Black or Hispanic were at greater risk for experiencing hunger (Andrews 2018).

Do these findings surprise you? Or are they consistent with what you expected? Either way, we do research to find out if our expectations about the world are accurate. Before Goldrick-Rab and her colleagues began conducting their research, very little was known about whether college students experienced hunger and, if they did, who was most likely to experience it. Without research like this, many people might have assumed the stereotype of a typical college student (someone in his or her early twenties who attends a four-year college full-time and doesn't have a job) was the reality and conclude that few, if any, college students experience financial or food insecurity. With this research, we are learning more about the real-life experiences of college students (40 percent of whom work in addition to going school and 25 percent of whom are parents), their needs, and how administrators and student organizations can support students (Andrews 2018).

Using Research Skills outside the Classroom

Although much of the research you will encounter as you continue your sociological education is conducted by academic researchers, the importance of research is not limited to the academic sphere. Indeed, an understanding of how to conduct and use research is a very marketable skill for college graduates looking for good jobs outside academia after they have completed their schooling. Research on students who complete college degrees in sociology finds that listing research-related skills on resumes helps students get jobs and that many students—even those working in fields that might seem unrelated to research—use their research skills at work (Senter, Spalter-Roth, and Van Vooren 2015).

Research skills are useful outside the workplace as well. Understanding research makes us better citizens and more effective consumers. In the modern world, we are surrounded by data of all kinds, and knowing how to interpret, think critically about, and use these data helps us make better choices. Let's consider a few examples.

CONSIDER THIS

What do you think the differences might be between decisions made on the basis of empirical research and those made without access to research? How might you decide whether to have knee surgery or physical therapy to recover from knee pain if you did not have access to empirical research? Or where to locate a new branch of your ice cream store chain? Or whether the state government should provide tuition-free college to students?

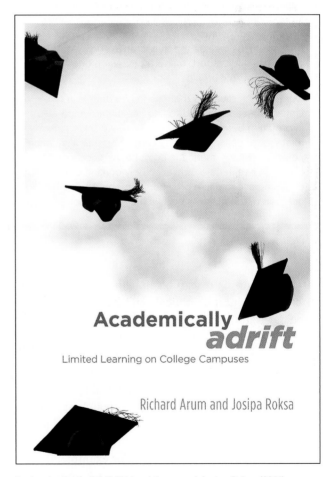

In *Academically Adrift*, Richard Arum and Josipa Roksa (2011) document that students spend less time studying than they did in the past. Not surprisingly, they also found that those who spend more time studying learn more.

Used with the permission of the University of Chicago Press

UNDERSTANDING HOW AMERICANS USE PRICE INFORMATION IN HEALTH CARE

DAVID SCHLEIFER

As part of a team, I worked on a project designed to understand whether, how, and why Americans seek and use price information in health care. This is an important question because individuals and families bear increasing responsibility for paying for their health care, not only because of growing insurance premiums but also because of increases in copayments, deductibles, and coinsurance.

To carry out this project, we first wrote a research proposal that included the study design and a budget. After it was funded by the Robert Wood Johnson Foundation, we carried out a multimethod data collection process, including interviews with experts working on health care price transparency, demographically diverse focus groups, and a nationally representative survey. We analyzed the interview notes and focus group transcripts, as well as the quantitative survey data, and wrote a full report, a shorter research brief, and a scholarly journal article.

Our research revealed that one in two people in the United States have tried to find health care price information before getting care, typically asking friends, relatives, or colleagues or by contacting their insurance company. Most Americans *do not* think price signals quality in health care, however; only one in five compared prices across multiple providers. Among those who compared, the majority believe they saved money.

Unfortunately, we also learned that most Americans are not aware that health care providers' and hospitals' prices can vary, which suggests a need to help people understand the extent of health care price variation. Projects like this show how sociological research can contribute to knowledge and inform policy and practice. Many Americans bear significant out-of-pocket costs for health care. Many personal bankruptcies are related to health care expenses. Our findings have helped elevate and amplify public perspectives on health care prices, thereby helping policy makers and other leaders understand the urgency of Americans' interest in price information and the obstacles they face in understanding it. I hope that our research contributes to broader efforts to reduce the burden of health care costs on individuals and families.

Discussion Question: When you go to the doctor, do you think about comparing prices before your appointment? Why or why not? In what other areas of your life where you are a consumer could sociological research help you make better choices?

David Schleifer is a senior research associate at Public Agenda, a nonprofit, nonpartisan organization in New York City. See https://nyshealthfoundation.org/resource/still-searching-how-people-use-health-care-price-information/.

Understanding research can help people make better choices about the political candidates they support. Candidates and elected officials often put forward policy proposals of various kinds, and there is usually research available that assesses the likely cost and impact of these proposals. At the federal level, some of this research is conducted by the Congressional Budget Office; in other circumstances, academic or policy researchers, such as David Schleifer, the sociologist in action featured in this chapter, write articles and reports that give guidance to policy makers and the public. For example, if your town wants to add parking meters to a busy commercial district, you might want to know whether this change would increase revenues to your town, if it would reduce spending at local businesses, and if it would increase the availability of parking as you consider whether to support or oppose such a change. Being able to comprehend the research that can answer these questions will help you figure out whether to support or try to stop the effort to add the parking meters.

You can use knowledge about research to assess the results of political polls and surveys to determine if they are accurate reflections of public sentiment. Understanding research can also help you judge the trustworthiness of information in the media.

In terms of your role as a consumer, understanding research can help you make better decisions about products and services to use and buy. For example, if you visit

REFLECTING ON SOCIOLOGY IN YOUR CAREER

In this exercise, you will explain, in your own words, the study of sociology and the value of sociological skills beyond the classroom.

Draft an email to a parent, a high school teacher, or another person from whom you have received support and guidance in the past to tell them that you are thinking about majoring or minoring in sociology in college. Although you may plan to focus your college education on other subjects, it is still worthwhile to think about the skills you can gain from sociology, both in this particular course and as part of a larger program of study. In your email, explain what sociology is as a discipline, as well as the potential career benefits of a sociology education. Pay special attention to how research methods training can be useful for a variety of careers. Be sure to mention at least one specific career you are interested in and describe how your sociology major can help you achieve success in it.

the doctor with a medical complaint and are prescribed a particular medication, you might want to know whether this medication is likely to be effective, how common its side effects are, and whether there are equally effective alternatives that are safer or less expensive. Learning about research will give you the skills to understand the evidence about your medication so that you can decide for yourself whether you want to ask the doctor for a different option. Similarly, when you choose to buy a house or rent an apartment, your research skills will allow you to investigate the characteristics of the neighborhoods you are considering without relying on a real estate agent's perceptions and priorities.

Using Research

As the examples above suggest, we, as a society, use the results of research in many different ways. To understand some of the different ways in which we use research, let's consider the distinction between **basic research** and **applied research**. Basic research is research directed at gaining fundamental knowledge about some issue. In contrast, applied research is research designed to produce results that are immediately useful in relation to some real-world situation. The results of applied research help us solve specific problems. However, basic research is just as important, and it lays the foundation for applied research by enabling the development of key ideas necessary for applied research that will be undertaken later.

It may be easier to understand this distinction by considering an example from biomedical science. For most of human history, people had little idea what caused illnesses, often assuming that "bad air" or spirits were responsible for disease. It was not until Antonie van

Leeuwenhoek, an inventor who developed advanced microscopes, was first able to view a bacterium in 1676 that researchers had any chance of understanding how bacteria related to disease (Porter 1976). Note that van Leeuwenhoek's research was not designed to enhance our ability to treat illnesses; he just wanted to understand more about the world around him. Alexander Fleming, on the other hand, was conducting applied research when he discovered the *Penicillium* mold, the basis for the first effective antibiotic, penicillin (Bennett and Chung 2001). Fleming had been a doctor in the British military service, and he carried out his research to find effective treatments for the infected wounds that killed so many soldiers in World War I. Thus, van Leeuwenhoek was conducting basic research, while Fleming was conducting applied research. To use a more sociological example, a researcher focused on understanding the relationship between poverty and educational attainment conducts basic research, while a researcher testing new interventions to boost academic performance in disadvantaged schools is practicing applied research.

Despite the importance of basic research to the later development of applied research, basic research is rarely economically profitable. Therefore, most basic research today is undertaken by academic researchers paid to teach as well as carry out research. Some academics conduct applied research, but you can find it in many other contexts as well, including nonprofit organizations, government agencies, market research firms, corporations developing new products and services, and many other entities. All these types of organizations hire researchers, including sociologists, to help develop suitable research projects, collect data, conduct data analysis, and interpret the results. Some

Sir Alexander Fleming discovered penicillin as he was trying to find treatments for infection. He was conducting applied research.

of these positions are even suitable for recent bachelor's degree graduates!

Check Your Understanding

- What do sociologists mean when they talk about research?

- Why do sociologists do research?

- How can understanding research methods be useful in your life outside of school?

- What is the difference between applied and basic research?

What Are Data and Where Do We Get Them?

3.2   What are some of the different ways sociologists collect data?

So far, you have learned that research is fundamentally based on the collection of **data**. So what are data, then? Basically, data are pieces of information, including facts, statistics, quotations, images, or any other kind of information you can think of. Note that *data* is the plural; if you want to talk about only one piece of data, you would say *datum*. Sociological researchers collect data in many different ways.

Asking Questions

The most common forms of data collection in sociology involve asking people to answer questions. This is because, as sociologists, we are interested in the ways people think about and experience their worlds, and what better way to find out than to ask them? Data collection involving asking questions can be conducted either through **surveys** or through **interviews**.

In a survey, the researcher develops a set of prewritten questions and asks respondents to answer these questions. Survey questions are often multiple choice. For example, we might ask people to state their opinions about a political policy, product, or religious teaching by giving them a list of answer choices such as "strongly agree, agree, neither agree nor disagree, disagree, strongly disagree." Or we might ask them to indicate the type of work they do by selecting from one of ten common categories, with the option of "other" for those who do not fit into any of the categories. Typically, surveys do not provide respondents with the opportunity to explain their answers at length, though they may include short open-ended questions to which respondents can provide a number or a short phrase for an answer (such as how many children they have, or the state or country in which they were born). Although survey data can be collected in a variety of ways, typically respondents answer questions over the phone, on paper, or on a web site.

Many researchers who rely on survey data do not go out and collect their own data. Some organizations conduct very large-scale surveys and make their data available to researchers for further analysis. For example, the General Social Survey has been collecting data on social and political opinion among Americans every other year since 1972 and makes its data freely available to researchers. Researchers also draw on data collected by government agencies such as the U.S. Census Bureau.

In contrast to surveys, interviews allow the researcher to develop a more nuanced and detailed understanding of what respondents think and believe. When conducting an interview, the researcher develops a list of questions to ask or topics to cover in the interview (called an interview guide). The researcher then talks with each respondent, usually in person but sometimes over the phone or using a video chat app. Interviews are usually conducted with a single respondent at a time, but interviewers can interview multiple people at once by using a focus group. Interviews allow more in-depth responses because researchers can ask follow-up questions, and interviewees can speak at length in response to questions and ask for clarification if they do not understand a question or think it does not apply to them. When researchers conduct any type of interview, they must take detailed notes, and they usually make audio recordings of the interviews and transcribe the recordings later to create an accurate written record.

Focus groups allow multiple people to be interviewed at once.
iStockphoto.com/HRAUN

Interviews are usually conducted with one person at a time.
iStockphoto.com/JackF

Observing and Interacting

Not all research can be conducted by asking questions. Sometimes, we need to see how individuals actually behave in the real world. For example, imagine that you wanted to understand how individuals go about solving problems in groups. You could ask your respondents to answer questions about the last time they solved a problem in a group, but they may not remember what happened, and their answers may not reflect the experiences of other people in the same group. If instead you watched the group as they tried to solve the problem, you would probably get a much more accurate understanding of the group process and dynamics. Therefore, many sociologists turn to methods in which they can watch people act and interact in real life.

Sometimes, researchers who want to watch people act and interact do so through **observation**, in which they simply

Participant-observation allows sociologists to observe action and interaction while participating with a group.

iStockphoto.com/FatCamera

observe as a spectator. More frequently, sociologists engage in **participant-observation**, in which they observe action and interaction while participating as part of the social context they are studying. To consider this difference, think about how a researcher studying friendship groups among first graders might collect data. A researcher conducting an observational study would find a good spot in the classroom and simply watch and listen. In contrast, a researcher using participant-observation would interact with the students in the class. Perhaps he or she would take on the role of a teaching assistant, chatting with small groups working on class projects, monitoring recess, and performing other classroom tasks, allowing a closer and more personal understanding of the social dynamics of the classroom.

Participant-observation is particularly likely to be found in **ethnography**, research that systematically studies how groups of people live and make meaning by understanding the group from its own point of view. When researchers conduct observational or ethnographic studies, their data consist of field notes, or a written record of what the researchers saw, heard, and experienced as they conducted the research.

Another way in which researchers can get a clear picture of how people act is by conducting an **experiment**. Experimental research is the cornerstone of some fields, such as psychology and biomedical sciences, but is much less common in sociology. In controlled laboratory experiments, researchers have control over the setting and interactions, so they can manipulate the conditions to test the effects of one particular circumstance. This requires an experimental group, which is exposed to some sort of treatment or

manipulation, and a **control group** that does not experience the treatment or manipulation. By comparing the two groups, the researcher can see exactly what the impact of the treatment or manipulation was.

Because sociologists are interested in the social world, most sociologists who do experiments carry out **field experiments**, conducted outside the lab, in the real world. In both types of experiments, the researcher manipulates certain conditions so that he or she can find out what happens when these conditions are changed. Consider the following example of a field experiment. Sociologist Devah Pager wanted to find out how having a criminal record affected job applicants' job prospects. She could have just studied formerly incarcerated people after their release from prison, but it might be that aspects of these individuals' experiences, personalities, and backgrounds—apart from their criminal records—were shaping their job market experiences. Instead, she hired four young actors and trained them to present themselves in very similar ways. Two were Black and two were White. She then sent them out to apply for entry-level jobs, alternating which testers claimed to have a criminal record and which did not (all other elements of their background were kept the same). Perhaps unsurprisingly, Pager found that having a criminal record made job candidates much less likely to get a call-back for a job interview. Her findings also revealed that Black job candidates were much less likely than White job candidates to get a call-back (Pager 2003). Indeed, Pager found that Whites *with* criminal records got called back at about the same rate as Blacks without criminal records, indicating that both race and a criminal record can affect a person's ability to get a job.

Looking at Documents

Sometimes, researchers use documents or other existing materials as the basis for their research. This type of research is particularly advantageous when researchers are interested in topics for which it would be very difficult to talk to people, such as questions about the past, or when researchers are interested in documents themselves, as in studies of the media.

Content analysis is one way researchers use documents to collect data. When conducting content analysis, researchers use texts—which may be written or

Researchers have special ethical duties to their respondents including getting informed consent.
iStockphoto.com/kate_sept2004

visual—and systematically categorize elements of those texts on the basis of a set of rules. Content analysis can involve counting elements of a text (e.g., how many girls and boys show up in children's books) or can involve more interpretive and relational elements (e.g., comparing the sexualization of women and men in advertisements).

Research Ethics

When collecting data, researchers need to pay careful attention to their ethical responsibilities. Some of these ethical responsibilities might seem obvious—for instance, it is unethical to make up data or to plagiarize other people's work. Researchers also have special ethical duties to the human subjects who participate in their research: they must minimize any risks of harm to the participants, and they have to make sure to get **informed consent** from each participant. Informed consent requires that the participants be told the purpose of the research, what they will be asked to do, and any risks prior to participating. Also, they must be given the chance to withdraw their participation at any time.

Any research receiving federal funding, which includes almost all research conducted at colleges and universities, and most other research involving human subjects must be reviewed by an **institutional review board** (IRB) to ensure that the rights of human subjects are properly protected. The IRB's intended role is to protect human subjects, not to comment on the importance of the research or the research design. When the risks to human subjects are substantial or procedures for obtaining informed consent are not sufficient, IRBs will require changes in the research design to ensure the protection of human subjects. For example, an IRB might require a researcher to develop a protocol to ensure that the names of respondents remain confidential. The IRB engages in even more care when reviewing research involving special populations that might be less able to exercise informed consent, including those younger than eighteen years and people who are imprisoned.

CONSIDER THIS

Imagine yourself as a participant in each of the kinds of research described above. How would your experience differ if you were a survey respondent or someone who was being observed? What kinds of data would your participation provide? What kinds of ethical guidelines would you want in place to protect you?

Check Your Understanding

- What are some of the different kinds of data sociologists use in their research?
- What are the ethical obligations of a sociologist conducting research?

Researchers may conduct *comparative-historical research* when it is not possible to actually speak with people or when documents provide pertinent information on a social issue.
iStockphoto.com/urbancow

What Do We Do with Data?

3.3   How do sociologists analyze data?

Once researchers have collected their data, they need to analyze them. **Data analysis** refers to the process of reducing the mass of raw data researchers have collected to a set of findings that provide the basis for making conclusions. There is a wide variety of different types of data analysis techniques, but most can be classified as either **qualitative methods** or **quantitative methods**. Quantitative methods rely on numbers, while qualitative methods rely primarily on things other than numbers, such as words and images. Some researchers use mixed-methods approaches that include elements of both qualitative and quantitative methods.

Qualitative Data Analysis

There are a variety of approaches to qualitative analysis. Thick description is an approach in which the researcher crafts a detailed narrative so that readers can see for themselves what a social context is really like and assess whether the data supports the researcher's conclusions. For example, in Matthew Desmond's (2016) Pulitzer Prize–winning book *Evicted: Poverty and Profit in the American City*, readers are taken along with Desmond as he spends time with tenants and landlords in poor urban neighborhoods at the height of the Great Recession, including observing evictions. The personal stories Desmond tells enable readers to understand the experiences of the people Desmond studied in a way that simply reporting the number of evictions could not convey. Qualitative researchers also use qualitative **coding**, applying descriptive labels to sections of text or images and then classifying them into categories or themes to denote patterns in the data. Other approaches to qualitative analysis involve developing maps, timelines, or other visual representations of the data.

Matthew Desmond, author of *Evicted: Poverty and Profit in the American City*.

Ray Chavez/Digital First Media/Mercury News via Getty Images

Quantitative Data Analysis

In quantitative data analysis, researchers use numbers to represent the data they collect. This approach is typical for survey data. When researchers conduct surveys, they assign a numerical code to each possible answer choice for every question. They then record the numerical codes, not the actual words of the answer choice. If you are familiar with spreadsheet software such as Microsoft Excel or Google Sheets, you will have a sense of what these data look like: each column represents a particular survey question and each row a particular respondent. Once researchers enter all their data, they can analyze them using the tools available in various statistical software packages, including Microsoft Excel or Google Sheets, but more frequently specialized software such as SPSS, SAS, Stata, or R.

Quantitative analysis techniques form the basis of the relatively new field of data science, an interdisciplinary field in which practitioners use various statistical and computational techniques to access, work with, and analyze large data sets in a variety of subject areas, including technology and social media, health care, finance, and government. Data scientists get advanced training in computer science, statistics, data analysis, and related fields and then apply this training to research questions, typically in applied research settings. Many analysts predict that data science will be a high-demand career field for years to come.

Check Your Understanding

- When sociologists carry out "data analysis," what are they doing?

- What is the difference between qualitative and quantitative data?

- What type of data to researchers in the new field of data analysis use?

UNDERSTANDING BASIC QUANTITATIVE ANALYSIS

In this activity, you will use a stacked column graph to perform basic data analysis.

Although most quantitative sociological research uses sophisticated computational and statistical techniques,

at their most basic level, such techniques originate in the relationship between different variables, as in Figure 3.1 (Goldrick-Rab et al. 2019).

▼ FIGURE 3.1

Employment Behavior by Basic Need Insecurity Status*

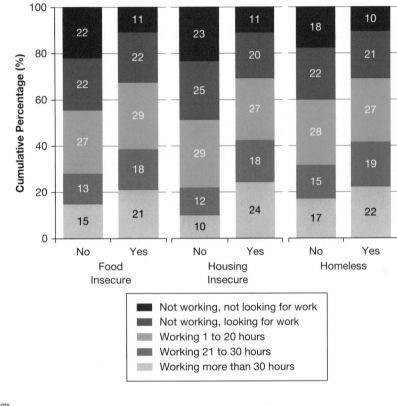

*Among CUNY survey respondents

Source: 2018 #RealCollege Survey.

Note: For more detail on how each measure of insecurity was constructed, see Appendix C. Cumulative percentage may not add up to 100 due to rounding error.

1. Looking at this graph, what do you think the relationship is between:

   - Food insecurity and the likelihood of working less than twenty hours a week?

   - Housing insecurity and the likelihood of working more than twenty hours a week?

   - Homelessness and the likelihood of working more than thirty hours a week?

2. How would you summarize the relationship between employment and food and housing insecurity?

USING RESEARCH DATA TO STUDY A PUBLIC HEALTH PROBLEM

By collecting data and analyzing trends and patterns, social scientists are better able to identify vulnerable populations and develop strategies to address social problems like the AIDS (acquired immunodeficiency syndrome) epidemic, caused by the human immunodeficiency virus (HIV). Although AIDS is a national epidemic, diagnoses of HIV infection are not evenly distributed across states or social groups.

In this online activity, you will observe patterns of AIDS deaths across the United States using data from the Centers for Disease Control and Prevention.

*Requires the Vantage version of *Sociology in Action*.

▼ FIGURE 3.2

Age-Adjusted Rate of Death from AIDS in the United States, 2017

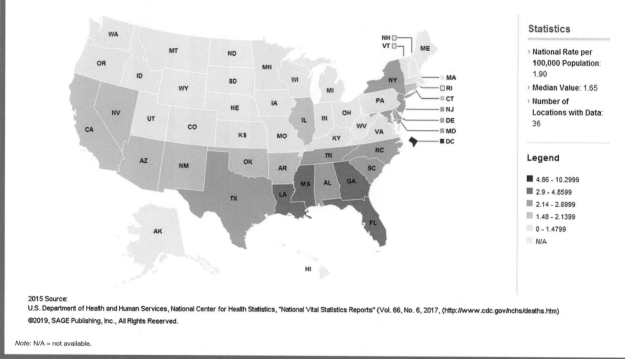

Statistics

› National Rate per 100,000 Population: 1.90
› Median Value: 1.65
› Number of Locations with Data: 36

Legend

- ■ 4.86 - 10.2999
- ■ 2.9 - 4.8599
- ▪ 2.14 - 2.8999
- ▫ 1.48 - 2.1399
- □ 0 - 1.4799
- □ N/A

2015 Source:
U.S. Department of Health and Human Services, National Center for Health Statistics, "National Vital Statistics Reports" (Vol. 66, No. 6, 2017, (http://www.cdc.gov/nchs/deaths.htm)
@2019, SAGE Publishing, Inc., All Rights Reserved.

Note: N/A = not available.

Getting Started Doing Research

3.4 What are the steps of the social scientific research process?

Now that you have a basic understanding of what sociological research is and how sociologists carry out research projects, let's think about some of the details researchers must consider as they design and develop their research projects. Researchers must first decide what they will study. Then they must figure out what sort of data they hope to collect and how they will measure the concepts and ideas they are interested in studying. They must decide whom they will include in their project and how they will find these respondents. And they must consider a variety of other issues important to ensuring that they conduct their project in a systematic and rigorous way consistent with the broadly held standards for sociological research.

Sociologists, like all other scientific researchers, use the **scientific method**, a systematic process that begins with the development of a research question through the collection, analysis, and reporting of data. In the scientific method, researchers begin by defining a research question. Next, they find out what is already known about their research question by reading prior scholarly literature on the topic, a process we call the **literature review**. On the basis of this prior literature, the researchers may develop one or more **hypotheses**, or predictions about what they expect to find in their research. Then, the researchers develop a research design and collect data according to this design. Once data collection is completed, the researchers analyze and interpret these data, submit them to review by other social scientists, and publish the results of the research project. These results then become part of the literature to be used by future researchers focused on this topic, making the scientific method a cyclical process.

As you can see in Figure 3.3, the first step in the scientific method is to figure out the research questions, what it is that the researchers plan to study. Researchers develop their research questions in various ways. Perhaps, as in many applied research projects, a supervisor or a client provides the research question. If researchers get to choose their own research questions, they might develop them on the basis of personal interests, experiences, or something they learned about in the course of taking sociology classes or conducting prior research.

Researchers use their research questions to select or develop a theory (or more than one theory) guiding their research. As discussed in the previous chapters, theories help sociologists notice and understand social patterns in society. Researchers also make use of theory when figuring out what data to collect and how to make sense of the data once they have them.

Researchers often conduct research to test theories, but they remain theories even if they have been tested and supported with data many times. When nonscientists hear the phrase "the theory of evolution" or "the theory of global climate change," they assume that these are untested ideas or speculation on the part of scientists. But to scientists, calling these ideas "theories" simply means that they are statements about relationships that explain patterns in data. The overwhelming majority of scientists today agree that research evidence confirms the existence of both evolution and climate change, but scientists still call these ideas theories.

CONSIDER THIS

How are sociological research and sociological theory connected? What contributions does each one make to what we know and what we do in sociology, and how are those contributions strengthened when we consider them together?

▼ FIGURE 3.3

The Steps in the Scientific Method

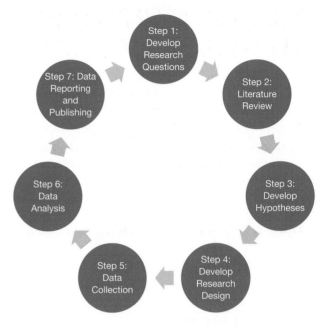

Check Your Understanding

- What is the scientific method?
- What are the first two steps of the scientific method?
- What is the role of theory in developing a research project?

Sampling and Measurement

3.5 When are data from a sample generalizable to the larger population?

Once researchers have figured out the basic parameters and design of their study, they must turn to the more detailed question of whom and what they are collecting data about. **Sampling** refers to the process of selecting respondents for inclusion in a research project. In most research studies, it would be impossible for researchers to talk to every single person who meets the criteria for participation in a study (called the **population**). For example, imagine you were conducting a study of sophomores at your college or university to understand why they choose to live on or off campus. If you go to a very small college, perhaps it would be possible to interview every single sophomore. But if you attend The Ohio State University, one of the largest schools in the country, you could not interview all of the more than 11,000 sophomores enrolled every year. Thus, you would need to select a sample of sophomores to participate in your study.

Samples can be either random or nonrandom. The research-specific definition of *random* is quite different from the way the term is used in ordinary language, in which it often means something like odd or unexpected. To researchers, **random** means that everyone has an equal chance of being included in a sample, and there is no bias or other factors shaping who is included. In random samples, everyone who meets the criteria for participation in a study has not only a chance but the *same* chance of being selected. For example, if you were conducting a random sample of sophomores at your college or university, all sophomores should have an equal chance of being selected; juniors, of course, would not. In general, in order to collect a random sample, you need a list of all the people who could be included in the study (e.g., a list of all the sophomores enrolled at your school).

Generalizability refers to whether it is possible to assume that the patterns and relationships observed among the sample in the research study would also hold true for the broader population. For research to be automatically generalizable, the participants must have been obtained via the use of a properly constructed random sample. This is because random samples give every member of the relevant population an equal chance to be selected into the sample, so there is nothing systematically different between those who participate and those who do not. This is important to understand because research findings can be generalized only to the population from which the sample was drawn. For example, let's say you wanted to conduct a random-sample survey of students living in the dorms at your college or university to understand their satisfaction with the living spaces. If you designed your sampling strategy properly and carried out the project without bias, you could generalize and assume that the results you find are consistent with the degree of student satisfaction among all students living in the dorms, even though you surveyed only a small subset of them. These results could not be generalized to students living off campus or to those living in dorms at other colleges and universities, though, because the sample was not drawn from these populations.

Nonrandom samples are used when a random sample is impossible or extremely impractical to obtain. Because you need a list of potential respondents to conduct a random sample, nonrandom samples tend to be used where such a list does not exist. As stated above, your college or university registrar could provide a list of all sophomores from which you could draw a sample. But if you wanted to conduct a study of students at your college or university who are currently dating someone living more than fifty miles away, you would not be able to get such a list. Researchers unable to attain random samples of respondents can still strive to ensure that their samples are **representative**, meaning that the people in their samples have characteristics typical of people in the broader population they seek to analyze. Although the results will not be automatically generalizable, if the sample is representative, the researchers can make the case that their findings provide a good representation of the overall population studied.

Biased samples, those that are neither random nor generalizable, can present a problem for researchers, especially when they try to apply their findings to the larger population. For example, imagine if, when you conducted your research on sophomores at your college, you inadvertently excluded students who commute to your campus. And say you used that research in a report to college administrators about the major concerns of sophomores so the administrators could make informed choices about how to make student life better. Your report would make it look as if issues related to timing of classes, availability of parking, and traffic levels—issues that affect commuter students more than those who live on campus—are not major concerns for sophomores (even if they *are* of concern to many sophomores—those you did not include in your sample). If the administrators act on the basis of your findings, they would do so without knowing all they should. This is an example of selection bias.

Other types of bias can result when researchers

- rely on people who volunteer themselves to participate (because they may be different from those who would not volunteer to participate),

- collect data from only one geographic region of the population (e.g., trying to study the population of residents of Massachusetts but collecting data from only people in Boston or trying to study all sociology majors at your school but collecting data from only sociology students you see in the hall outside your sociology class),

- have a high nonresponse rate (when a large portion of those selected to participate never respond or refuse to participate), or

- ask biased or leading questions that guide participants toward particular answers.

Roosevelt, Landon, and *Literary Digest*

An old story provides a powerful illustration of the impact sampling bias can have on the results of research. In 1936, during the height of the Great Depression, the magazine *Literary Digest* conducted a poll seeking to predict who would win that year's presidential election: Alfred Landon, the governor of Kansas, or the incumbent, Franklin Delano Roosevelt. The poll predicted that Landon would win easily, but if you remember your U.S. history, you'll know that Roosevelt won. Indeed, Landon ended up winning only two states, Vermont and Maine, while Roosevelt got the other forty-six (in 1936, Alaska and Hawaii were not yet states).

It turns out that the *Literary Digest* poll used a very biased sample. The magazine selected its respondents using telephone directories, lists of subscribers to *Literary Digest*, and registered automobile owners. Remember, this was during the Great Depression, and cars and phones were still new (and expensive) technologies, and not everyone could afford (or wanted) a subscription to *Literary Digest*. So, *Literary Digest* was sampling only well-off people, not those who were suffering the most from the Great Depression and composed most of the population. It is easy to see how their results came to be so incorrect given this biased sample.

CONSIDER THIS

Assume that you were designing a poll like the *Literary Digest* presidential poll for the next presidential election. What would you have to do to ensure that your sample was not biased? How might the method you use to contact potential respondents affect the extent to which your sample would be representative of the population?

Check Your Understanding

- Why do researchers use samples rather than simply studying everyone?
- How is the meaning of *random* different when discussing sampling in comparison with how you use it in regular conversation?
- What does it mean for research to be generalizable?
- How can bias occur in research, and how can it affect the results?

How Can You Recognize Good (and Bad) Research?

3.6 Why should you be able to recognize good (and bad) research and media claims?

When researchers carry out research projects, they strive to develop accurate and useful answers to their research questions. The decisions researchers make about research design can have important impacts on whether their projects ultimately meet these goals. In assessing the accuracy and usefulness of research projects, we assess whether the results and findings are reliable, valid, and (as discussed earlier in this chapter) generalizable. Research projects can achieve all these goals, none of them, or any one or two, so they must be considered separately.

Reliability refers to the extent to which research results are consistent, and consistency helps us understand whether the form of measurement in the research actually measures what we think it measures. There are a variety of different types of reliability, but all involve the question of whether repeating research measurements will produce the same results each time. For instance, if you ask the same person the same question on multiple days, will he or she understand and respond to the question in the same way? If you give students an exam with similar questions on multiple days, will they get the same general score? If the answers to these questions are no, the reliability of the research may be in question.

In contrast, **validity** refers to whether the research results are trustworthy. Your results might be reliable, but they also need to be correct. There are a variety of types of validity, but all involve the question of whether the measures and findings of a research study consistently measure the phenomena accurately. For instance, if a researcher wanted to measure your knowledge of sociology by asking you to sing your campus alma mater or fight song, this would not be valid. She or he would have to give you a properly designed sociology test instead. Many factors can affect validity, such as poorly developed measures or other researcher errors, such as using biased samples.

Many researchers and consumers of research find that what they are really interested in is understanding **causation**—whether a change in one phenomenon causes a change in another. It makes sense to be interested in causation. After all, if we could claim with certainty that a particular student behavior causes better grades, it would be easy for students to understand how to do better in classes! Alas, the real world is much too complicated for easy causal answers. It turns out that it is very difficult for researchers to demonstrate that a particular relationship is causal.

EVALUATING CLAIMS IN THE MEDIA AND IN RESEARCH

In this activity, you will practice the skills necessary to distinguish between real news and "fake news."

Candiru/Flickr/PD

Step 1: Look at the photo of the "Fukushima Nuclear Flowers" and answer the following question: Does this post provide strong evidence about the conditions near the Fukushima Daiichi power plant? Write your answer and your reasoning.

Step 2: Review your response and the thought process behind your answer to step 1, then write your answers to the following questions: Did you consider the source of this photo, the authority or credibility of the author/photographer, or where it was posted? Did you question whether this photograph is real rather than Photoshopped, whether it was really taken near the Fukushima Daiichi power plant, or whether the mutation in these flowers was caused by radiation or some other cause?

If you answered no to any of the questions in step 2, you are not alone. In 2016, researchers from Stanford University assessed young people's ability to use reasoning skills to determine the credibility of materials shared online (such as whether they could tell the difference between advertisements and news stories on a news organization's home page). When the researchers asked high school students to examine this photo and answer the same question you were asked, fewer than 20 percent wrote responses that questioned the source of the photo. Forty percent of students said that the post was strong evidence of the conditions near the plant because it was a photo. Finally, 25 percent of students said that the photo wasn't strong evidence, but only because it only showed one type of flower, rather than other plants or animals (Wineburg et al. 2016).

It can be difficult to assess the credibility of claims we read online, but it's increasingly important for us to be able to discern what is real and what is not, especially given the speed at which these claims can spread. One helpful tool, developed by librarians at Meriam Library at California State University, Chico, is called the CRAAP Test, and it poses questions you can use to evaluate claims, especially if you are wondering whether to cite the information in a paper for class (see http://www.csuchico.edu/lins/handouts/eval_websites.pdf to see the whole test).

Currency, or the timeliness of the information. Was the information posted recently, and has the information been revised or updated since it was first released?

Relevance, or the importance of the information. Who is the intended audience for the information, and does it answer the question you are asking?

Authority, or the source of the information. Who is the author(s), and where is the information published?

Accuracy, or the reliability and/or correctness of the information. Is the information supported by reliable and valid research that can be verified through other sources? Is the information presented in an unbiased way?

Purpose, or the reason the information exists. Is the purpose of the information to inform, entertain, persuade, or sell a product, and are these purposes clear and transparent? Does the author's point of view seem objective, or are there biases at play in the presentation of the information?

Step 3: Return to the photograph and the prompt at the beginning of this exercise. Write one question for each of the CRAAP categories that might help you think critically about images like this you see online. Which of these questions would have been most useful to have answered when you first encountered the image above?

DISTINGUISHING GOOD RESEARCH FROM BAD RESEARCH

In this exercise, you will generate ideas about how to distinguish good research from bad research.

Imagine you are a researcher who wants to know how many students at your school experience food insecurity. Think about the concepts of reliability, validity, and generalizability that you've learned about in this chapter, and consider how you would design your study to meet these criteria. How will you ensure that your research is reliable, valid, and generalizable? Write down answers to these questions:

1. Why does the reliability of research matter? How might the conclusions of your food insecurity research be incorrect if the research is not reliable?

2. Why does the validity of research matter? How might the conclusions of your food insecurity research be incorrect if the research is not valid?

3. Why does the level of generalizability of research matter? How might the conclusions of your food insecurity research be incorrect if the research is not generalizable?

Be prepared to share your answers.

Demonstrating causation requires researchers to meet three specific conditions. First, they must show that the supposed cause is associated with the supposed effect. This means that if a change in the cause occurs, a related change should be observed in the effect. Second, they must demonstrate that the cause comes before the effect. After all, if the cause does not come first, it cannot very well be the cause, right? Finally—and this is the hard part—the researchers must be able to eliminate all other possible alternative explanations for the effect. There are hundreds or thousands of possible explanations for most social phenomena, though, and in most cases, it is impossible to study more than a handful of these explanations at a time. Thus, researchers are often unable to definitively show that a relationship is causal.

CONSIDER THIS

Sociologists develop analyses and arguments on the basis of empirical research. How do these analyses and arguments differ from the types that nonsociologists make? For example, how does empirical research as a basis for analysis and argument differ from the use of anecdotes in regular interpersonal conversation? How is it different from the analysis and argument that you hear on TV news or talk radio? How does the term *research* as used in sociology differ from the way you might have used it when talking about a paper you wrote for a high school class?

One primary way researchers can demonstrate causation is when they conduct a controlled experiment, such as those conducted in a laboratory. Because researchers conducting controlled experiments have complete control over all aspects of the experimental context, they can ensure that the only difference between the experimental group and the control group is the one variable they are hoping to study. Thus, if a difference in results is observed between the two groups, it must be due to the manipulated variable and cannot be due to any other factor. Therefore, controlled experiments, when conducted carefully and properly, make it possible for researchers to assess causation.

Check Your Understanding

- Why is it important that research participants be representative of the broader population?
- Under what circumstances is it possible to generalize from research results?
- What is the difference between reliability and validity?
- Under what circumstances is it possible for researchers to demonstrate causal relationships in their research results?

Conclusion

This chapter has just been an introduction to sociological research, and there is so much more you can learn about collecting, analyzing, and using data and writing about the results. But even with this short introduction, you should now have a sense of how we can use sociological research methods to find out new things about the world around us. Empirical research allows us to test our assumptions about the world and find out what is really going on. These results form the basis of the body of knowledge in the discipline of sociology. Sociological research can also inform decision making by helping nonprofits, government agencies, and companies understand the issues important to them and the likely consequences of different choices.

As noted above, sociological research skills can open the doors to many career opportunities, including those in academia, the corporate world, government, and nonprofits. People with training in sociological research can work as research assistants, project managers, data analysts, data scientists, and a variety of other positions drawing on these skills. The research tools you gain in sociological research are useful for other kinds of research as well, including—to give just a few examples—research in the health sciences, marketing, public policy, and fund-raising. They can also help you in your personal life when you seek to make decisions about which political candidates and policy initiatives to support, where to live, what types of medical care to seek, and what products to buy.

As a college student, there are lots of ways to get involved in research. You can seek out research opportunities on campus, including opportunities to work with professors on their research projects as well as opportunities to develop and conduct your own research project. You can also look for internships and volunteer opportunities that draw on your growing research skills, such as helping a food pantry collect data on the people it serves or working with a government agency to clean up and use a data set on educational outcomes.

Research is the root of the discipline of sociology. When sociologists write about culture, socialization, deviant behavior, social inequality, social institutions, and social change (topics covered later in this book), they base their writing and their analyses on the findings of empirical research projects carried out according to the methods and procedures discussed in this chapter. Research is not just an important part of the process of doing sociology; it is part of what makes sociology *sociology*. Remember the definition of sociology in Chapter 1 ("Sociology is the scientific study of society . . .")? The word *scientific* in that definition refers to the fact that sociology requires careful, empirical, rigorous research to study its subject matter: society.

In this chapter, you learned how sociologists go about studying society. We now turn to an exploration of culture, an important factor shaping society and social experience. As you read the next chapter, as well as the others that follow, think about how sociological research methods have been used to develop the ideas and concepts you read about—and how you might use sociological research methods to find out more!

REVIEW

3.1 Why do sociologists do research?

Sociologists do research to understand how society works. Without research, all we would have to go on is our assumptions. Although our assumptions sometimes turn out to be correct, in many cases, the real data tell a different story. Thus, research is essential for understanding social behavior and how society works. And this knowledge can also help us make policy decisions, sell products, design solutions to social problems, and do other useful things.

Sociologists use research in a wide variety of career paths. For example, market researchers use interviewing, observation, and surveys to collect data about how people use products, what products they might be interested in buying, and which sorts of advertisements or promotions are most likely to encourage people to buy particular products. Law enforcement officers use interviewing and document analysis in the course of investigating crimes. They also collect quantitative data on crime rates in different areas of their city and at different times of day to develop better strategies for preventing and detecting crime and to schedule and organize patrol shifts. And health care researchers conduct survey and interview studies as part of their efforts to determine which kinds of treatments will help individuals and communities improve their health.

3.2 What are some of the different ways sociologists collect data?

Sociologists use a variety of techniques to collect data. Some of these methods involve talking to or interacting with people, including surveys, interviews, participant-observation, and experiments. Sociologists can also collect data through observation or by using existing documents. Sociologists often combine multiple methods of data collection in one project. Regardless of the methods they use, sociologists must conduct their research in accordance with ethical standards.

3.3 How do sociologists analyze data?

Sociologists use qualitative, quantitative, or mixed-methods approaches to analyze data. Qualitative approaches rely on words, images, and ideas, while quantitative approaches rely on statistical, numerical techniques.

3.4 What are the steps of the social scientific research process?

When researchers begin a research project, they must first develop a research question. They then look at the previously published research on the topic. On the basis of this prior literature, the researchers may develop one or more hypotheses, or predictions about what they expect to find in their research. Then, the researchers develop a research design and collect data according to this design. Once they complete data collection, the researchers analyze and interpret these data, review them with peers, and publish the results of the research project.

3.5 When are data from a sample generalizable to the larger population?

Data from a sample are generalizable to the larger population only when it is possible to assume that the patterns and relationships observed among the sample in the research study would also hold true for the broader population. For research to be generalizable, the participants must have been obtained via the use of a properly constructed random sample or from a representative sample.

3.6 Why should you be able to recognize good (and bad) research and media claims?

When sociologists look at the products of research, they often look at whether the research is reliable, valid, and generalizable to help understand whether the research is good or bad—and whether they should trust its findings. Similarly, when reviewing news articles or other claims online, it is important to think critically about the source of the information, as well as the timeliness, reliability, purpose, and accuracy of the information that is being presented.

KEY TERMS

applied research   41

basic research   41

causation   51

coding   46

content analysis   44

control group   44

data   42

data analysis   46

empirical   37

ethnography   44

experiment   44

field experiments   44

generalizability   50

hypotheses   49

informed consent   45

institutional review board   45

interviews   42

literature review   49

normative   37

observation   43

participant-observation   44

population   49

qualitative methods   46

quantitative methods   46

random   50

reliability   51

representative   50

research   37

sampling   49

scientific method   48

surveys   42

validity   51

CHAPTER 4

RECOGNIZING CULTURE

David E. Rohall

What cultural traditions can be found in your culture? What makes your society unique?
©iStockphoto.com/ferrantraite

4.1 What is culture?

4.2 What are some ways that the different elements of culture influence everyday life?

4.3 How do societal types relate to variations in culture?

4.4 How do changes to our culture shape our behaviors and ways of viewing the world?

4.5 In what ways can you use cultural capital to help both yourself and society?

Defining Culture

4.1 What is culture?

Here is a sociological riddle: what affects almost all your thoughts, feelings, and behaviors but cannot be seen or touched in its entirety? The answer is culture! Culture is the way of life of a particular group of people, including the characteristics that make it distinct from other groups. Technically, culture can take a physical form, but in this chapter we focus primarily on intangible forms of culture. **Nonmaterial culture** includes concepts such as norms, values and beliefs, symbols, and language. **Material culture** consists of artifacts ranging from tools to products designed for leisure, like flat-screen TVs or Xboxes. Material culture reflects the values and beliefs of the people who live in a culture.

Finding Culture

Take a few minutes to think about the physical items in your bedroom or living room. Note what these items are but also what they look like, the colors and placement of those items. What do these artifacts say about you? Consider what other people can learn about you simply by observing the types of things that you own.

If you have a lot of sports memorabilia, it probably says something about your appreciation of sports. But these artifacts also represent the culture in which you live. For example, if you are in North America, you are much more likely to have (American) football-related items than someone in South America, where people play and watch soccer (which they call football) rather than American football. Consider some other items. If you have a smartphone, a television, and a computer, these items reflect a way of life that did not exist 100 years ago and still does not

exist in some places in the world today. Although people in most places have started using these products, only some people—in some areas of the world—have access to the resources necessary to own and power all of them.

Let's go one step further: why do you own these items? You would probably say that you need these things, right? Smartphones keep us connected to other people, and computers are for work—and everyone watches television! You can easily argue that you cannot live without them. The truth is that a good number of people live without one or more of them, even in the United States, but the belief that these things are necessary reflects an important dimension of the study of human culture: the social construction of reality, the ways that people give meaning to the world around them through interaction with other people (Berger and Luckmann 1966).

CONSIDER THIS

Would you like to live and work in a country with a culture quite different from the one in which you were raised? Why?

Imagine you have a baseball you caught at a major league American baseball game. Even better, imagine this ball was caught during the World Series, the most important set of games of a given year. What would happen if that baseball were stolen? The absolute value of this baseball is probably around five American dollars. But its relative value, what you may be able to get by selling it on eBay, is much higher. Which one is the true value of the item? If you believe that it is worth a lot of money, its loss will cause you much more stress and concern than if you believe that it is only worth five dollars.

Things get more complicated when we consider how important the baseball is to you. You may never consider selling the ball because it has a lot of sentimental value, representing an important memory in your life. The loss of this baseball is likely to cause great stress and anxiety, not just because you lost a potential source of money but also because it symbolizes something important to you.

In any case, the ball has a lot of value because people give it value. You give it your own value as a cherished keepsake and the people around you value it for its association with a famous baseball game. Once a value is established, once we come to believe that it is real, we think, feel, and behave on the basis of that understanding rather than on any "objective" value that it has (e.g., on how much it costs to produce it).

HOW I GOT ACTIVE IN SOCIOLOGY

DAVID E. ROHALL

My first sociology textbook in college was coauthored by George Ritzer (famous for *The McDonaldization of Society*, among other books) at a much earlier stage in his career. It was from this book that I first learned about the sociological imagination. I started to see the ways social structure affects my day-to-day life and to help understand the thoughts, feelings, and behaviors of the people around me. I continue to use the sociological imagination as I study the nexus of the individual and society and how people develop their senses of self

within the cultures in which they live. I view my textbook, *Social Psychology: Sociological Perspectives* (3rd ed., 2014), as a repository of theory and research on the ways sociologists approach the study of social-psychological processes. My other research includes numerous projects that show how our membership in different subcultures affects how we think about the world. Together, I hope that this work reflects the importance of the sociological imagination for understanding our social world.

Constructing Culture

Sociologists see culture as socially constructed, created through interactions among people. For example, have you ever created a secret word or something that only you and a good friend or family member understood? Such a word may simply be a fun way of interacting with that person or a code to help you get out of a social situation. The key here is that this new language was created by you and the other person or persons (hence, socially constructed), and you use this new code to interact and convey what you mean to each other. The same process goes on in larger society, albeit on a much larger scale. We learn languages at home and later in classrooms, but even languages shared by a whole culture change as we add and drop words over time (e.g., the terms "gender nonconforming" and "garbage time" are new to the 2019 Merriam-Webster dictionary). We use words as symbols to describe our material goods, beliefs, values, hopes and fears, and every other aspect of our culture. In turn, they become part of our culture and indicate who we are as a people. What do you think the term *binge-watch* says about American culture?

We tend not to be aware of our culture and its influence on us until we find ourselves viewing it from a different cultural perspective, such as when we travel or read about another time or place. The view of life through our culturally tinted lens appears to be *the* rather than *a* version of reality (Berger and Luckmann 1966). This way of experiencing the world helps keep us grounded. Imagine if you constantly thought that all your values were relative and that other values might be just as good and useful. It would make it very difficult to have a coherent sense of the world or to create stable relationships. The rest of this chapter will outline the contents of culture and how we use it in our everyday lives.

Check Your Understanding

- What is culture?
- What is the difference between material and nonmaterial culture?
- How do artifacts represent the culture in which we live?
- What do sociologists mean when they say culture is socially constructed?
- When do we tend to notice our culture?

Identifying Elements of Culture

4.2 What are some ways that the different elements of culture influence everyday life?

Groundhog Day is a funny film from the 1990s that portrays a television weatherman who is stuck in time, repeating the same day over and over again. He does everything he can to break this cycle, but he cannot seem to get out of this rut. Consider your own life. What do you normally do each day? What sorts of things do you own to help you in your routines? How do you feel when you are taken out of this routine?

Patterns of behavior may appear to be rather mundane or even boring at times, but they provide a framework for making decisions in our lives. If we follow these routines too closely, we may lose some sense of spontaneity, but without routines, it is very difficult to coordinate activities with other people. If, at your job, you must work in tandem with another person to complete a task, what happens if one of you decides not to go to work? What would happen to one of your courses if the professor just showed up whenever she felt like it? Or only a few of the students tended to go to class? This section reviews the basic ways different cultures address the need to coordinate the lives of many different people. In doing so, we look at the various

DOING SOCIOLOGY 4.1

RINGS AND THE SOCIAL CONSTRUCTION OF REALITY

This exercise asks you to consider the message engagement rings send in American society and how that message is socially constructed.

In this chapter, you have just learned how members of a society give meaning to the objects around us. For example, consider how we view and make use of rings in our society.

Think about what comes to your mind when you see a ring with a diamond on it on the fourth finger of someone's left hand and then write your answers to the following questions:

1. What does the ring symbolize?

2. What was the gender of the person you imagined? Why?

3. What is it about our society that has led to that image?

4. Now, read the *New York Times* article "Men's Engagement Rings Proclaim, 'He's Taken'" (www.nytimes.com/2010/08/01/fashion/weddings/01FIELD.html) and answer question 3 again. Did the article influence your perspective on the topic? Why or why not?

5. How does this experience relate to the fact that we tend not to notice our culture and its influence on us until we find ourselves looking at it from a different cultural perspective?

---

elements of nonmaterial culture: norms, values and beliefs, and symbols and language.

Social Norms

Norms are expectations about the appropriate thoughts, feelings, and behaviors of people in a variety of situations. The key to this definition is that it involves *expectations* about thoughts, feelings, and behaviors. We may not be actually thinking, feeling, or behaving in ways that follow the norms of society, but we tend to try to appear as though we are. For example, how are you supposed to feel at a funeral? Perhaps you are tired and feel nothing at all, or you may even feel happy. You try to suppress those feelings so as not to offend the family of the deceased or simply to avoid the looks and sneers of people who believe that your feelings are inappropriate. You do not want to appear to be violating the norms of appropriate thoughts and behaviors at a funeral.

Consider almost anything you do in a given day, and you can probably determine the appropriate norms that go with each behavior. On what side of the sidewalk do you walk? What do you say when someone sneezes? How do you greet someone you do not know very well? There are hundreds or even thousands of things that we do each day, and most of them have some sort of norm that goes along with them. How do we learn all these norms? In many cases, we are instructed by our parents, teachers, and peers. In other cases, we simply learn norms by observing how other people act.

We do not have to know each person we interact with before we have an idea of how to interact with them appropriately. Throughout our lives, we develop a collective knowledge of people that we bring to each situation. This concept is called the **generalized other**, our perceptions of the attitudes of the whole community (Mead 1934). You can recognize the generalized other whenever you or someone else uses expressions such as "most people think . . ." or "no one does that!" These expressions imply that we know what most people think or feel about something when we have never actually asked or observed *most* people behaving in a given situation. We learn from those with whom we have interacted or from the media and project those ideas onto the rest of society. For example, think about the past few times you were introduced to someone for the first time. You probably did not ask them how much money they earn, what political party they voted for, or how old they are. Chances are, in that first encounter, you each knew how to speak to each other without saying something that would surprise or insult the other person. Your sense of the generalized other helps you to navigate such interactions smoothly.

Do you do everything that you are told to do? Consider a time at work or home when a supervisor or parent told you to do something. Did you do what was asked? Perhaps you completed the work but did not put a lot of time and energy into it as a sign of disapproval. Or maybe you ignored the task altogether. It is important to note that you do not have to follow norms! You have probably violated

Imagine the chaos in this class if the students violated a classroom folkway and did not wait to be called on before speaking!

Fredrick Kippe/Alamy Stock Photo

norms many times in your life. People have **agency**, or the ability to act and think independently of social constraints (Leming 2007; Musolf 2003; O'Brien 2015). Some norms are easier to ignore than others. **Mores** are widely held beliefs about what is considered moral and just behavior in society. In the United States, for example, mores include expectations that parents will feed their children and people will pay their taxes. When people violate mores, they threaten the stability of society, so governments create laws to enforce many mores. **Folkways** are rules of behavior for many routine interactions, which if violated might lead to annoyance but would not threaten society. Common folkways in the United States and other cultures include waiting in line when buying something at a store or raising your hand if you want to ask a question or make a comment in class.

There are more sanctions associated with breaking mores than folkways; you can go to prison for violating some mores (stealing, causing a fire, etc.), but folkway violations (interrupting someone, belching in public, etc.) may only lead to a disapproving look. Someone, somewhere, is breaking a norm right now, even, perhaps, in the face of very stern sanctions. Murder is considered one of the worst norm violations, yet murders occur every day, even though people may face prison or death if they are found guilty of killing another person. The important thing to remember is that whether individuals decide to follow or go against the social norms that exist in society, they still serve as a society's guideposts for our thoughts, feelings, and behaviors.

Status and Roles. In addition to norms, each society creates statuses and roles. *Status* refers to our relative position in society, while roles are the expectations about how people of a given status should think, feel, and behave. Status is about relative power and respect. Salaries reflect the value of positions most directly, with lawyers and doctors receiving more money for their time than, say, janitors. The roles of these three statuses also vary: doctors are expected to work with patients and lawyers with clients and janitors to clean. But statuses and roles can vary in each society. For example, consider the status position of primary and secondary teacher (see Figure 4.1). Teachers in China are considered on the same status level as doctors, while in France and Turkey, they have the same status level as nurses (Varkey GEMS Foundation 2018). Therefore, how teachers think, feel, and behave also varies across these societies. For example, Chinese teachers, reflecting their relatively high status in society, tend to act toward their students in a very hierarchical way, expecting complete attention and obedience from their students. What status do teachers have in your own country? How might this information help you to understand your relationship with teachers over the years?

Values and Beliefs

Values and beliefs are two other basic elements of culture. Sociologists define **values** as what a society holds to be desirable, good, and important. **Beliefs** are what we deem to be true. The two ideas overlap in that we believe certain values to be true; one could say that all values are beliefs, but not all beliefs are values. We may believe that honesty is the most important thing in a relationship (a value), but the idea that the Kansas City Royals are the best baseball team of all time is a belief, not a value. People hold on to their values and beliefs and will find any number of ways to prove them to be true.

So, what is important to you? What do you believe? Is religion very important to you? Civil rights? Are you pro-life or pro-choice? Consider where and how you developed those beliefs. Studies regularly show that beliefs relate to family upbringing; conservative adults typically come from conservative families, and liberal

Teacher Status Index, 2018

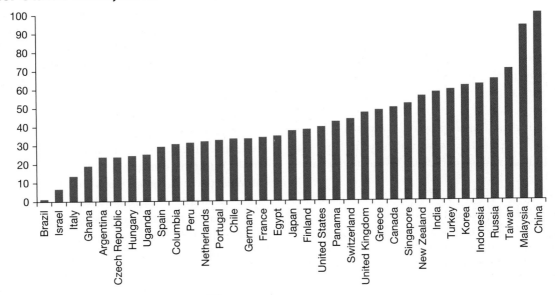

Source: 2018 Global Teacher Status Index, Varkey GEMS Foundation, September 2018.

adults tend to grow up in liberal families. The most obvious mechanism for transmitting beliefs is through observation and reinforcement. Conservative and liberal parents live their respective ideologies and teach their children that doing so is normal and good. However, other aspects of children's environment can affect beliefs and attitudes. For example, men who had sisters while growing up reported more conservative attitudes than men with brothers only (Healy and Malhotra 2013). Researchers traced these attitudes to the amount and type of housework the men did as children: boys with sisters did less housework associated with girls and women (e.g., washing dishes), which carried over into their adult gender roles. Using this framework, whether you believe in evolution or that God created the world in seven days, your beliefs reflect the culture in which you were raised and may be traced to the social construction of reality.

When it comes to culture, the society we grow up in provides "the box" when we use phrases such as "thinking outside of the box." For instance, research in the sociology of religion shows that the role of religion in the Netherlands has declined over the past sixty years on multiple levels (Kregting et al. 2018). In the 1960s, as education and income levels started to go up, people began to become less religious. At the same time, parents spent less time and attention teaching children religious practices and beliefs. This example helps show that whether we are aware of it or not, our society and its institutions (education, economy, family) influence our culture (e.g., values and beliefs) both directly and indirectly over time.

Using your generalized other, you will probably be able to come up with a short list of American values. Although you may have a different set of personal values, you can still understand where the larger culture stands on any number of issues. Approximately fifty years ago, sociologist Robin Williams (1970) developed the following list of American values:

- Individualism: a focus on the person rather than the group

- Achievement and success: a concentration on hard work and economic well-being

- Activity and work: an emphasis on appearing busy and hard-working

- Science and technology: a reliance on technological know-how

- Progress and material comfort: the use of science and technology to produce items designed to make life easier

- Efficiency and practicality: an emphasis on getting things done without wasting time

- Equality: a desire for greater equality in the distribution of wealth and income in the United States

- Morality and humanitarianism: the prominence of moral issues in the United States

- Freedom and liberty: a focus on individual freedom and the right to pursue wealth and property

- Racism and group superiority: the fact that there is a racial hierarchy in which some groups are valued more than others

Although these values may be relevant today, it is important to note that the list was published in 1970. Has American culture changed since then? What do you think?

Symbols and Language

A **symbol** is anything that has the same meaning for two or more people. Symbols can convey meaning to large numbers of people and instill both thoughts and emotions. Consider flags or national anthems. They can yield intense feelings of pride. For example, after a terrorist attack in Barcelona in 2017, thousands of residents, carrying flags and "I am not afraid" signs, took to the streets to show their unity and bravery in the face of terrorism (https://www.youtube.com/watch?v=YuJA4Lg7snE). Symbols can also produce negative feelings (e.g., the Nazi swastika). Although any two people may create their own set of symbols, what is interesting about symbols in society is how many can affect such large numbers of people at the same time!

Political leaders use symbols all the time. Consider the fact that both Republican and Democratic presidents—who have very different political ideologies—use the American flag when they give speeches in the United States. The flag is always placed on their right (your left as you look at them). They often start their speeches with "my fellow Americans" and end with something like "God bless

America." The use of these symbols gives presidents and other politicians the ability to invoke certain meanings and evoke certain sentiments among Americans. Those who hear these speeches feel a connection to the speaker because they share a common identity as Americans, a feeling that the speaker—like most Americans—is a religious person who respects God, the belief that God favors and blesses the United States. People from different cultures, however, would react differently to these same objects and phrases. They might feel indifference, puzzlement, or anger that Americans believe that God is on their side or bewilderment that someone would mention God in a political context, whereas others would find it very normal. Each culture creates its own set of symbols.

Language is a series of symbols used to communicate meaning among people. Language can occur in the form of written letters and words but also in the form of body language. We learn both types of language in school, through reading and from interacting with and listening to those around us. Language allows us to create levels of

President Trump hugs the flag at an American Conservative Union conference.

Tasos Katopodis/Pool via Bloomberg

All U.S. presidents—no matter their political ideology—use the flag as a symbol of their patriotism.

Jeff Kravitz/FilmMagic, Inc/Getty Images

DOING SOCIOLOGY 4.2

EXPLORING NORMS AND SYMBOLS IN SPORTS

In this exercise, you will examine the culture surrounding two sports.

There are norms and symbols associated with sports, both for players and for those watching the games. For example, baseball players regularly keep sunflower seeds in their mouths while they play (and spit them out!), and basketball fans try to distract opposing players attempting free throws by shaking things and making loud noises.

1. List as many norms and symbols associated with NFL football as you can.

2. Which ones relate to (a) individual teams and (b) football as a national sport?

3. What are the norms associated with national anthems at sporting events?

4. What does it mean when norms associated with these national symbols are not observed?

---

complexity in meaning that do not come from pictures or sounds alone because language, by definition, allows people to string together thoughts and feelings to create larger ideas with several dimensions. Consider some of the great works of literature and philosophy, which may include hundreds of pages of ideas or stories that all work together to convey a central theme. It is language that provides the tools to create such complex sets of meaning.

CONSIDER THIS

Write down a list of symbols that are important in American society today. What kinds of thoughts, emotions, and/or behaviors do these symbols tend to produce in Americans? How do they represent American culture?

The **Sapir-Whorf hypothesis**, also known as linguistic relativism, notes that language influences our understanding of reality above and beyond the meaning of its symbols (Sapir 1958). For example, a person from a culture with more words available to describe an object will be able to provide much more detail about it than someone from a culture with fewer words for the object. Not only do these additional words give people the ability to better describe people, objects, and experiences, but they also allow people to understand those things more fully. Consider wine tasting; there are many words and phrases professional wine tasters use to describe a wine, such as "full-bodied" or "full of tannins" or "acidic," or even that the wine has the flavor of a particular fruit, such as cherries or strawberries or even chocolate. If you have ever been to a winery, you know that it is very common for the

salesperson to encourage you to look for elements of the wine's flavor that you may not have been able to ascertain without being told.

Having access to words also gives people the ability to understand an object, a person, or a phenomenon in a much deeper way. Here is another way to look at it: have you ever been speechless, lacking the words to describe your thoughts or feelings in a situation? In some cases, this experience may simply reflect your emotional shock or that you have not learned the language available to explain what you are feeling. In other cases, however, it may reflect your culture's lack of words to describe what is happening.

Symbols and language are a vital part of the social construction of reality. Language is a framework of meaning that two or more people use to make decisions in everyday life. However, as noted earlier, languages, like all social constructions, change over time. We can modify meaning over time by adding new words or altering the meanings of existing ones. For example, the word *wicked* usually means "evil," but in New England, it can be used to replace the word *very* or *really* (e.g., "It is wicked cold today!"). *Bougie* and *bingeable* are two recently created words that have come into fashion throughout the United States. Often, technological inventions prompt the creation of new words. For example, you did not hear the word *sexting* before the invention of texting. In the next section, we will see the relationship between culture and societies at different stages of technological development.

Check Your Understanding

- How do patterns of behavior provide a framework that helps us make decisions?

- How do we learn how to behave appropriately in our society?

- Why are there more sanctions associated with breaking mores than folkways?

- What is the relationship between statuses and roles?

- Describe how your values and beliefs relate to the family and society in which you were raised.

- How do symbols and language help us to socially construct reality?

Typology of Societies

4.3   How do societal types relate to variations in culture?

Have you ever considered what you would be like if you were suddenly transplanted into a different country? If you are from Europe or the United States, you are more likely to find affiliation with the people in Japan and Canada than many other nations, simply because they share aspects of your lifestyle, including running water, electricity, smartphones, and so forth. These elements of material culture are a by-product, in part, of the level of technology in those societies and their economic development.

Gerhard Lenski (see Nolan and Lenski 2010) argued that technology is the driving force in the development of society and leads to different types of societies, from hunter-gatherer to postindustrial. Technological developments allow groups of people to increase in size. In turn, this population growth leads to cultural complexity and the development of subcultures that do not exist among groups with smaller populations. Let us look at the relationship between technology and culture among different types of societies.

Hunter-Gatherers

Groups defined as hunter-gatherers include people who use simple tools to gather available plants and to hunt animals. Although these groups were widespread more than 10,000 years ago, just a few groups of hunter-gatherers still exist today. These people are nomadic, and their food supply is limited to what is available to them at a given location.

Hunter-gatherers may be viewed as "presociety" in the sense that they lack the stability of place and time. That is, they must move from place to place to obtain the food and other supplies they need to live. As a result, they are unable to take many things with them. Imagine having to move every few months or years to a new location. How much could you take with you if you did not have access to cars and trucks to haul things? Perhaps you could load a few items on work animals, but these animals are quite expensive, and you probably would not have many of them, if any at all. The scope of your culture's artifacts is likely to be limited to those things that are portable and most useful to you. Although each hunter-gatherer group develops its own culture, most of the roles and norms of these groups relate to food production. These societies tend to be more egalitarian than modern societies as a result of their comparatively simple means of existence.

Horticultural/Pastoral Societies

With the development of hand tools and domestication of animals about 10,000 years ago, people were able to maintain basic sustenance in one geographic location, in what we call horticultural/pastoral societies. A few such societies still exist today, including the Yanomami, a group of about 35,000 people who live in more than 200 villages in the Amazon rainforest on the border of Venezuela and Brazil.

Although people in this type of society do not have much if any excess food stores, they can attain food without constantly moving, develop homes and common areas, and better care for the sick, the very young, and the aged. These changes allow populations to grow and people to begin the processes of specialization, in which people split up the work of community life. Some may raise cattle while others farm grain or develop tools. Specialization is also associated with the growth of inequality as some skills become more valued and thus more highly rewarded than others.

Living in this type of society does not allow a lot of free time, because people still have to work hard to meet basic needs. People generally do not have access to more than what they need for survival; there are no video game consoles, televisions, Internet, or even lamps to read by! Cultures in horticultural/pastoral societies focus on the community and survival rather than personal development or technology.

Agrarian Societies

Agrarian societies are extensions of horticultural and pastoral societies except in the size and scope of farming. Like horticultural/pastoral societies, agrarian societies raise crops and domestic animals, but their tools are more advanced, allowing much higher levels of production and a larger population. There is no precise time or place where agrarian societies started to appear in the world, but a common example is the Fertile Crescent (modern-day Iraq, Lebanon, Cyprus, Jordan, Israel, and Egypt) more than 8,000 years ago. Today, much of the world still lives in agrarian-type societies. According to the World Bank (2018), 45 percent of people live in primarily rural areas. Many of the countries of South America and Africa, for instance, rely on agriculture to sustain their economies.

The sport of polo, limited to those with access to horses and riding lessons, is a part of high culture.

Victor Hugo/Patrick McMullan/Getty Images

Baseball, which can be played by anyone with a little space, a stick, and a ball, is part of pop culture.

Mark Cunningham/Getty Images Sport/Getty Images

When societies gain more education and technology, they have better tools to grow and harvest food (e.g., irrigation systems and plows), which leads to the creation of more food than they need to eat. Those people with extra food can use it to trade for material goods; the possession of more material goods provides more money or capital to pay for other people to do work (e.g., paid labor or slaves), giving owners more time to devote to expanding their businesses, education, or even leisure activities.

Although every human society has rulers with lifestyles that differ from those of most people, the agrarian world ushered in a level of distance between the upper classes (both political and economic elites) reflected in the concepts of **high culture**, the culture of elites, and **popular culture**, culture that exists among common people in a society. In such societies we see the development of music, poetry, and playwriting paid for and consumed by elites in agrarian societies. High culture develops as wealthy planters develop hobbies like traveling and art collecting, which require lots of time and money. They use their excess money to pay skilled artisans to make things for them. With this infusion of money from the truly wealthy classes, a small group of skilled workers can participate in some aspects of high culture through education (Bourdieu 1984). Lenski's typology of society, as illustrated in Table 4.1, demonstrates the ways technological changes can affect the type of society that we live in.

Industrial and Postindustrial Societies

Industrial societies rely on the use of technology to produce goods as well as food. In terms of culture, this is important because of the sheer number of objects industrial

▼ TABLE 4.1

Lenski's Typology of Society

Society Type	Impacts on Lifestyle
Industrial	Very large populations, lots of diversity, growth of middle classes, and larger number of wealthy people
Agrarian	Larger, more diverse populations with excess food and resources among wealthier classes
Horticultural/pastoral	Small, stable populations with adequate food supply
Hunter-gatherer	Small population, low diversity, less stable food supply

processing can produce. As products like books, bicycles, and furniture become easier and cheaper to make, all classes have more access to these items, and the development of consumer cultures begins.

CONSIDER THIS

Consider your upbringing. In what class would you say that you grew up? How might that class position affect the types of music with which you are familiar or the sports you play or follow? Why do we associate the appreciation of the fine arts (e.g., opera) with rich people?

Industrial societies continue the process in which very wealthy people invest in art and other forms of culture for the sake of art itself. Art among the masses tends to be functional in nature, serving both to bring pleasure and to serve a purpose, like cars or furniture, which can be both beautiful and useful at the same time (Bourdieu 1984). Meanwhile, wealthy people can buy objects that serve no purpose but to produce a sense of joy or happiness. This sparks the growth of more obscure art as artists experiment with new art forms with the knowledge that there is a group of people who will have the desire—and the money—to purchase them. Art becomes a kind of game among people as they compete to find and obtain the most obscure works they can—ranging from NYC Garbage Cubes for $50 (Google it!) to Jeff Koons's *Balloon Dog (Orange)* that sold for $58.4 million in 2013 (Hahl, Zuckerman, and Kim 2017; Wetzler 2018)! There is enough wealth in society that musicians and other artists become wealthy merely from their creative work, while middle-class people participate in this process through education and enjoyment of some aspects of the art world online and through films, reprints or copies, and visiting libraries and museums.

Check Your Understanding

- According to Gerhard Lenski, what is the driving force in the development of society?

- How does an excess of food affect societies?

- What is the difference between high culture and popular culture?

Considering Cultural Variations

4.4   How do changes to our culture shape our behaviors and ways of viewing the world?

A country's culture, much like one's own personality, changes over time as populations experience technological growth, interact with other cultures, and face large-scale events such as famines, economic depressions, wars, tsunamis, or earthquakes. Such experiences can change the way of life and perceptions of the world for large groups of people at the same time. The unique conglomeration of events reflects generational differences. Consider the Baby Boom Generation, people born in the United States between 1946 and 1964. What do they have in common? They all experienced the Vietnam War (and the protests associated with it), the Cold War and arms race, the sexual revolution, and the assassination of Martin Luther King Jr., among other things.

Historical events can affect a people's cultural heritage even if they do not have a direct impact on all of the individuals in a given society. Think about events and inventions that have affected how members of your own generation act and view the world. How have terrorism, school shootings, global climate change, the invention of mobile phones, texting, and so on influenced you and your peers? Consider the 2017 shooting at a concert in Las Vegas, the deadliest mass shooting in U.S. history, and the Valentine's Day massacre at Marjory Stoneman Douglas High School in 2018, where seventeen students and faculty were killed by gunfire (CNN 2019). These horrific acts took the lives of many, wounded many more, and deeply affected people across the nation. A similar incident occurred in Australia in 1996, when twenty-eight-year-old Martin Bryant killed thirty-five people and wounded many more. This incident let to bipartisan support for stricter gun control laws in Australia.

Changes in law reflect changing norms and values as people try to put current conditions in the context of large-standing cultural values. In the United States, the desire to stop massacres conflicts with other cultural norms, specifically, some people's interpretation of the Second Amendment of the U.S. Constitution, which states, "A well regulated militia being necessary to the security of a free state, the right of the people to keep and bear arms shall not be infringed." How do people in the United States make stricter gun laws while trying to maintain their beliefs regarding the Second Amendment?

Subcultures and Multiculturalism

As noted earlier, there can be many different cultures within a country, reflecting the diversity of its population and the different locations from which people come and when they are born. If you live in a large city, you have probably interacted with people who reflect different cultures in their mannerisms or dress.

Subcultures are simply cultural groups that exist within another, larger culture. Members of subcultures accept many of the values and beliefs of the larger culture while maintaining some unique ways of life. Some of these subcultures reflect immigration patterns, as people from other cultures congregate into certain areas of a city, creating neighborhoods like Chinatown or Little Italy that reflect the different symbols, languages, and material cultures of the places from which they—or their ancestors—came. These neighborhoods take on elements of two different cultures, creating a new subculture. Other subcultures reflect ideologies or lifestyles such as the hip-hop and youth cultures. Members may have unique slang and different styles of dress or appearance than other people in the area.

To what subcultures do you belong? What are some of the rules, values, and artifacts that distinguish one of your subcultures? How do these aspects of your subculture give you a sense of belonging to this group and make your membership in it apparent to others?

How can subcultures exist if the role of culture is to build relationships among people, to give them a shared identity and help them relate to one another? The ideal of **multiculturalism** is that people respect differing cultures in a society and honor their unique contributions to a larger, "umbrella" culture that incorporates multiple subcultures. This ideal is often difficult to live out, because differences in cultures often lead to conflict among groups.

In cases in which one group in a society espouses rules, values, or beliefs that conflict with the mainstream culture, they become a **counterculture**. Today, in U.S. society, the Westborough Baptist Church, the Nation of Islam, the Catholic Worker Movement, the American Indian Movement, the Aryan Brotherhood, and the Amish are all examples of countercultural groups. Each of these groups opposes one or more of the basic tenets of U.S. culture outlined above. The Catholic Worker Movement, for instance, focuses on the ideals of communitarianism, a focus on the good of the community over the individual, which goes against the U.S. emphasis on individualism. Many people in this movement live in group homes and give up their personal possessions for the good of the group.

Although some countercultural groups exist peaceably within the larger society, as the Catholic Worker Movement does, others do not and threaten U.S. society in the form of domestic terrorism. The Federal Bureau of Investigation defines the Earth Liberation Front, for instance, as a domestic terrorist group because it espouses the destruction of private property as a way to stop businesses from exploiting the environment for profit.

Cultural Relativism and Global Culture

Franz Boas popularized the concept of **cultural relativism**, the idea that cultures cannot be ranked as better or worse than others. He was writing in the nineteenth century, a time when many social scientists believed that society was evolving much as species do. The model for this development included European countries as they transformed from agrarian to industrial societies. Boas's work initiated an intellectual movement to dispel the notion that hunter-gatherers or pastoral societies are less "advanced" than industrial nations; rather they are simply different. From this perspective, we cannot judge a people or their culture on the basis of the type of society they live in, and we should look at each culture as unique.

Although each society creates a unique culture, anthropologist George Murdock (1945) argued that there are some **cultural universals**, cultural practices that exist in most or all societies, such as social structures, tool making, art, song, dance, religious beliefs, rituals, families, a division of labor, and politics (Brown 1991). The implication of this work is that people naturally develop certain elements of culture no matter their unique histories or backgrounds; that is, they are part of the human way of doing things. Under this schema, all human groups do some of the same things, but each does them in (slightly or very) different ways. Consider how visitors from another planet might view the whole human race; they would see many of the

This 2017 picture of an Amish family in central Pennsylvania reveals some ways in which the Amish are part of a counterculture.

Volkan Furuncu/Anadolu Agency/Getty Images

The critics are raving...
the natives are restless...
and the laughter
is non-stop!

the GODS
must
be crazy

At last, a comedy everyone can laugh with!

WINNER
GRAND PRIZE
The Seventh
International Humor
Film Festival.

Jensen Farley Pictures, Inc. and CAT Film Productions present
XAO the bushman in THE GODS MUST BE CRAZY
with SANDRA PRINSLOO · MARIUS WEYERS · NIC DE JAGER as the Cuthure Playboy
MICHAEL THYS · LOUW VERWEY · KEN GAMPU · SIMON SABELA
STANFORD C. ALLEN Written and Directed by JAMIE UYS Executive Producer BOET TROSKIE

The Gods Must Be Crazy is a comedy film about a man who is first exposed to Western culture from a Coke bottle dropped from an airplane.
Everett Collection, Inc./Alamy Stock Photo

same types of things occurring in varying ways in every part of the world!

Cultural attributes can also spread throughout the world when some societies spread out and dominate others. The culture, both material and nonmaterial, of the nations that first became industrial and then postindustrial (the United States and those in Western Europe) has been introduced around the planet through colonization and the growth of capitalism. In the movie *The Gods Must Be Crazy*, an empty Coca-Cola bottle is dropped from an airplane onto the Kalahari Desert. The local people have very little contact with Western culture and try to understand the meaning of the event. At first, they view the event as a good thing but later decide that they must get rid of the bottle, leading to an adventure that serves as the basis for the rest of the movie. This comedy highlights the ways Western countries can affect other parts of the world without consciously trying to do so. Of course, there are also conscious attempts to spread Western values around the world, notably the importance of democracy and freedom, two American values that affect U.S. foreign policy decisions. Table 4.2 reveals some of the ways cultural traits can overlap and differ across societies.

Check Your Understanding

- How can technological growth, interactions with other cultures, and severe events such as such as famine, economic depressions, war, tsunamis, or earthquakes change a country's culture?

- What is the ideal of multiculturalism?

- Explain the difference between a subculture and a counterculture.

- What are some cultural universals that exist today?

- How has U.S. and Western European culture been introduced around the planet?

▼ TABLE 4.2

Similarities and Differences in World Values

	Germany (%)	India (%)	Iraq (%)	United States (%)
Importance of family (percentage very or rather important)	95.5	93.7	99.3	98.2
Negative attitudes toward homosexuality[a] (percentage who listed homosexuals as people they would not like to have as neighbors)	22.4	42.1	80.3	20.4
I see myself as a world citizen (percentage who see themselves as world citizens)	60.0	82.3	54.0	67.4

Source: World Values Survey, Wave 2010–2014 (http://www.worldvaluessurvey.org).

a. Percentage of respondents who mentioned this as a response to the question "On this list are various groups of people. Could you please mention any that you would **not** like to have as neighbors? Homosexuals" (emphasis added).

DOING SOCIOLOGY 4.3

GLOBAL CULTURE IN THE SOCIOLOGICAL EYE

In this assignment, you will explore values across cultures. You will start by comparing values in two different cultures chosen as examples and then compare at least two other cultures of your choosing.

1. Go to the web site of the World Values Survey (http://www.worldvaluessurvey.org).

2. Pick "Data & Documentation" from the menu on the left, then "Online Analysis" from the submenu.

3. Pick the most recent years of the survey and choose China and Sweden. Click "Next." Choose "V6 Important in life: Leisure time" and click on the "Show" button.

You should then see the total distribution of results for that question on the survey followed by the findings from each country. We can see that in the case of China and Sweden, 69.8 percent of Chinese people say that leisure is very or rather important to them compared with 94.9 percent of Swedes.

Choose two other countries and another variable that interests you. Predict how similar or different the countries are *before* you click on the "Show" button. Write your predictions. How did you guess the countries might be similar or different? Now, click on the "Show" button. Record your results.

Reflect on what your findings say about the people who live in the countries you analyzed, and write your answers to the following questions:

1. In the example of the value placed on leisure in China and Sweden, what social forces may influence these cultural differences? What makes you think so?

2. How about the countries you chose to compare, were your predictions accurate, or nearly so? On what basis did you make your predictions? What social forces may influence these cultural differences or similarities?

The Power of Culture

4.5 In what ways can you use cultural capital to help both yourself and society?

You have heard the expression that knowledge is power, right? In the case of culture, this is very true. Culture is a tool kit for us to use in our day-to-day lives. Having the right cultural tools can help us interact with others effectively and gain what we seek (Swidler 1986). For example, before you go on a job interview, it makes sense to learn all you can about what your prospective employer expects of employees in terms of behaviors, attitudes, styles of dress, and so on, and display that culture during the interview. These dynamics have infiltrated online cultures, as people must learn the appropriate "netiquette" for interacting with people in different forums ranging from social networks and gaming sites to professional associations (Faucher 2018).

This cultural knowledge can help you advance in both personal (e.g., number of "likes") and professional arenas. Consider the number of politicians and celebrities—and students—who got into trouble for saying offensive things or posting images that conflict with the values of the general public. For example, Harvard rescinded the acceptance decisions for ten members of its class of 2021 after they posted obscene comments on a Harvard Facebook site for accepted students (Kamenetz, Lattimore, and Depenbrock 2017). In 2018 ABC canceled the updated *Roseanne* show because of an offensive tweet from Roseanne Barr. Knowing culture in all its mediums is important to navigating social life in the age of social media.

Cultural Capital and Social Intelligence

You have also surely heard of the expression "it takes money to make money." An extension of this idea is that it takes capital to make capital. Capital is your assets, anything you own. Capital can take many forms, including fiscal capital (money) and intellectual capital, which can include skills or knowledge for which other people are willing to pay. **Cultural capital** is a type of capital related to education, style, appearance, and dress that promotes social mobility (Bourdieu and Passeron 1990).

Wealthier families with fiscal capital can provide their children with an elite education, travel, music

THE DIFFERING POWER OF IMAGERY

Image from the *Chronicle of Higher Education.*

Julia Wall/Raleigh News & Observer/TNS via Getty Images

In this activity, you will consider the power of an image and compare its meanings.

This is an image of a toppled "Silent Sam"—a monument to fallen Confederate soldiers on the campus of the University of North Carolina–Chapel Hill. Although clearly designed as an homage to the Confederacy when it was erected in 1913, it lost favor among modern students, who forcibly took it down in 2018.

Consider these questions, write your answers, and be prepared to discuss them.

1. What does this monument symbolize? Does it mean the same thing to everyone in the United States? What do you think it means to African Americans?

2. Do you think that the "vandalism" was appropriate or not? Why? Would everyone agree that it was indeed an act of "vandalism"?

3. What does the incident tell us about U.S. culture?

---

lessons, fine dining, language immersion programs, and so forth so that they can develop cultural capital as they grow up. In turn, cultural capital can help us gain employment and fiscal capital as we learn to interact effectively with powerful members of society (Mark 2003). Many businesses today need employees who speak multiple languages, can interact effectively with people of diverse cultures, and know what will sell (and how to sell it) in different areas of the world. We can use these forms of capital for both our own personal gain and in efforts to help shape society.

Cultural capital provides the information people use when deciding if others are part of their group. In the case of elites, knowing how to tie a necktie properly or selecting appropriate clothing to wear at different events (e.g., polo or wine tasting) signals that a person belongs there (or not). It works the other way around as well; wealthy people trying to gain access to working-class environments face similar obstacles. The difference, here, is that wealthier people have access to more fiscal capital, hence access to personal and business loans and job markets, among other things. Being able to interact with people with high status has implications for our ability to grow wealth over time.

CONSIDER THIS

List three ways we use culture in our everyday lives. Think about the types of clothing you wear in different social situations (e.g., work and home), the types of activities you engage in, and the material objects you have access to (e.g., automobiles vs. public transportation). How might you use this knowledge if you lived in a country with a culture quite different from the one in which you were raised?

Social Intelligence. Psychologist Daniel Goleman popularized the expression "social intelligence" in the 1990s (Goleman 2006). **Social intelligence** is our ability to understand social relationships and get along with others. This ability requires cultural capital. People with social intelligence know the appropriate cultural cues in their society (a sign of cultural capital) *and* can accurately read the cues given off by others. Those with high levels of social intelligence have great social skills and work well with others. They can read a room and know just what to say—and when.

DOING SOCIOLOGY 4.5

ASSESSING CULTURAL CAPITAL AND SOCIAL INTELLIGENCE

In this activity, you will use online quizzes to assess your own social intelligence and then consider how your skills may help or hurt you in your future career.

How well do you understand the cultural cues around you? We (often) unconsciously share our thoughts and feelings using cultural cues such as smiling to indicate happiness and raised eyebrows to represent shock or fear or surprise. It is possible to assess how well you "read" cultural cues, or the extent of your social intelligence.

Visit the following web sites and take the quizzes provided, which will rate how well you are able read the people around you:

- http://greatergood.berkeley.edu/ei_quiz/#15
- http://socialintelligence.labinthewild.org/mite/

Write a one- to two-page essay describing some of your career goals and how the findings of either of the two tests may have an impact on those goals. For instance, if you plan to work in the area of law or medicine, how might a high or low score affect your success in that career? If you believe that low scores on the quizzes will have a negative impact, discuss ways that you might increase your abilities in these areas.

An extreme example of the use of cultural and social intelligence comes from the literary classic *The Great Gatsby*. The main character, Jay Gatsby, uses his knowledge of how to interact effectively with wealthy people (and the fortune he earned illegally) to fake being a member of American elite society. He makes use of fiscal capital to buy expensive things and host lavish parties, cultural capital to know and emulate how the wealthy live, and social intelligence to manipulate people's perception of him.

Culture and Identity

Cultural capital and social intelligence are housed in us through our social identities. Social identities are the unique set of statuses, roles, and traits that each of us has. As noted earlier, each society creates a unique set of statuses and roles; there are fathers, nurses, teachers, drifters, and children, each with their own relative power and prestige in a given society and each with a set of expectations about how to act in those positions that we have defined as roles. We develop our identities on the basis of the statuses and roles available to us. It is important to know that we rarely accept all the cultural expectations associated with a given role in a culture. Rather, we incorporate elements of culture with our own individual way of doing things. A "good" college student in the United States may go to class, take notes, and do well on exams, but "good" students may approach studying differently on the basis of personal

traits (e.g., how much sleep they need or how fast they can read). It is this synergy between our culture (expectations for being a good student in society) and individual traits (our unique personality or lifestyle) that makes our identity unique.

Social identity also gives us the power to change ourselves and society. If culture is part of our identity, we can change our identity by taking on new elements of culture and exposing ourselves to new cultures. Living for a time in other countries exposes us to new ways of thinking about the world and teaches us new norms, symbols, and languages. We do not have to go to other countries to get this experience, however. Simply visiting a new neighborhood or an organization for new immigrants can yield similar results. Likewise, spending time at a shelter for homeless people or at the opera or other high-culture events can give us a different perspective on society—and our place in it.

CONSIDER THIS

Social identity includes the ways that we bring the cultures from our group affiliations into our sense of self. How might this process be positive for individuals? How might it divide people in everyday interactions?

How do you want to influence your culture? You may want to start small and be sure to work with other interested

SPANISH-SPEAKING U.S. HOUSEHOLDS

The languages we speak are perhaps the most distinctive features of the cultures we live in. Although English and Spanish are the two most common languages spoken in United States, the Census Bureau reports that at least 350 different languages are spoken in U.S. homes.

In this online activity, you will learn about the U.S. population that speaks Spanish at home, using data from the Census Bureau's American Community Survey.

*Requires the Vantage version of *Sociology in Action*.

▼ FIGURE 4.2

Percentage of U.S. Population Speaking Spanish at Home, 2017

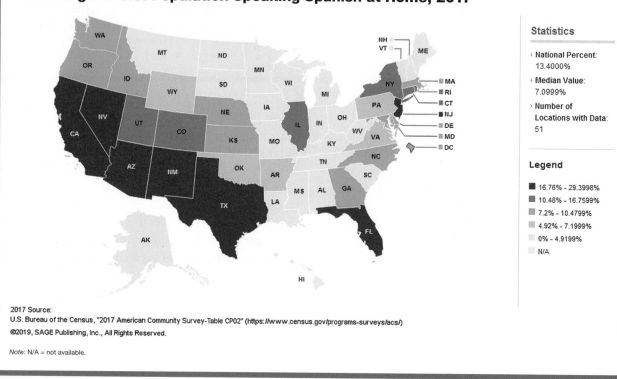

Statistics

› National Percent:
13.4000%

› Median Value:
7.0999%

› Number of Locations with Data:
51

Legend

■ 16.76% - 29.3998%
■ 10.48% - 16.7599%
■ 7.2% - 10.4799%
■ 4.92% - 7.1999%
□ 0% - 4.9199%
■ N/A

2017 Source:
U.S. Bureau of the Census, "2017 American Community Survey-Table CP02" (https://www.census.gov/programs-surveys/acs/)
©2019, SAGE Publishing, Inc., All Rights Reserved.

Note: N/A = not available.

members of your community. In the Sociologists in Action box, Lyle Foster and Tim Knapp, two public sociologists, describe how they initiated a project to memorialize and bring to light the important events that affected African Americans in Springfield, a small city in Missouri.

Efforts to change culture can occur at almost any level. Consider how Sabrina Fernandez, student body president of Marjory Stoneman Douglas High School, the Florida school where seventeen people were killed in a mass shooting, and many of her classmates helped create the #NeverAgain movement for stricter gun laws in the United States (Cottle 2018). In just its first year, it led to the passage of fifty new laws across the United States restricting access to guns (Vasilogambros 2018). These students show that people can work together to change the larger culture under the right circumstances and with a lot of work!

Check Your Understanding

- In what ways can the right cultural tools help you during a job interview?

- How is cultural capital related to social mobility?

- What is social intelligence, and how does it relate to the development of cultural capital?

- What makes up our social identities?

- How might removing or displaying a cultural symbol change society?

SOCIOLOGISTS IN ACTION

USING PUBLIC SOCIOLOGY TO CHANGE LOCAL CULTURE

LYLE FOSTER AND TIM KNAPP

Lyle Foster
Courtesy of Missouri State University

Tim Knapp
Courtesy of Missouri State University

We have been engaged in a multiyear research project centered on the history of the African American community in Springfield, Missouri. We are particularly interested in the unique history of the region compared with other Midwest cities that have much larger African American communities. The project, titled "The Journey Continues," includes a community history booklet and oral interviews of local residents sharing their experiences growing up in the Ozarks (the interviews are available online via the Missouri State University library and the local National Public Radio station, KSMU).

Finding that we were learning about many historical experiences no longer known to most people in the area led us to the idea of an African American Heritage Trail. We wrote a proposal, formed a planning committee of local residents, and invited the city, the park district, and community organizations to collaborate with us. They immediately supported the idea.

In the summer of 2018, we installed the first marker at Silver Spring Park, a park created for the Black community in Springfield more than 100 years ago. The trail will consist of 24 sites with historical markers. Each marker contains several paragraphs recognizing the history of the location and describing its contribution to the region's African American community. Together, the historic sites will form a trail system connecting existing greenways. An app connects viewers to a web site featuring a trail map, photos, archival materials, and video content that provides descriptions of the various locations.

The trail and web site make a number of significant contributions to the region, including preservation of the historical accuracy and integrity of the African American community's past and present, promotion of healing and appreciation for the experience of the African American community in the region, establishment of an important cornerstone toward efforts for diversity and inclusion, and providing a source of pride for the unique and important accomplishments of the African American community in the city and county.

This project reflects the goals of the public sociology program that we are a part of and should have a long-lasting positive impact on our local culture and community.

Discussion Question: What might be some historical experiences no longer known to most people in the United States (or some other nation)? How can losing knowledge of history affect various members of society—and the whole society?

Lyle Q. Foster is assistant professor of sociology and Tim Knapp is professor emeritus in the Sociology and Anthropology Department at Missouri State University in Springfield.

CONSIDER THIS

Are you now or can you see yourself becoming part of the #NeverAgain movement? Many students in Parkland, Florida, where the movement started, come from highly educated, affluent families. How do you think your participation in such a movement may be related to your background in some way (e.g., your upbringing or local culture)?

Conclusion

Culture shapes our lives and our society. We may not be able to literally see or touch culture, but with a sociological eye, we can recognize it and learn to use it. In the next chapter, we examine socialization, the process through which we learn how we fit in society and how to interact with others. As you will see, the culture in which we live influences the socialization process and all the key actors in it. We cannot escape culture, but once we are aware of it, we can use it to influence our individual lives and our society.

REVIEW

4.1 What is culture?

Culture refers to the characteristics of a group or society that make it distinct from other groups and societies. Nonmaterial culture includes concepts such as norms, values and beliefs, symbols, and language. Material culture consists of artifacts ranging from tools to products designed for leisure like flat-screen TVs and Xboxes. These things reflect the values and beliefs of the people who live in a culture.

4.2 What are some ways that the different elements of culture influence everyday life?

Patterns of behavior, guided by our culture, provide a framework for making decisions in our lives. The key elements of a culture—norms, values and beliefs, symbols, and language—help shape our everyday lives.

Norms (expectations about the appropriate thoughts, feelings, and behaviors of people in a variety of situations) guide our interactions. Our beliefs and values shape our understanding of the world and how we act in it. We communicate through the use of symbols, which can convey meaning to large numbers of people. The language we use is a series of symbols. The multicultural ideal respects differing cultures in a society and honors their unique contributions to the larger culture.

4.3 How do societal types relate to variations in culture?

Gerhard Lenski (see Nolan and Lenski 2010) argued that technology is the driving force in the development of society and leads to different types of societies and cultures. Technological developments allow groups of people to increase in size, and this population growth leads to cultural complexity that does not

exist among groups with smaller populations. For example, with the invention of more advanced tools to harvest crops and raise more animals, agrarian societies were able to support larger numbers of people and to develop high culture (the culture of the elites).

4.4 How do changes to our culture shape our behaviors and ways of viewing the world?

A country's culture changes over time as its population experiences the impact of technological growth, interactions with other cultures, and severe events such as such as famine, economic depressions, war, tsunamis, or earthquakes. For example, school shootings and other acts of terrorism, global climate change, the invention of mobile phones, texting, and so on have affected the behaviors and perspectives of young adults today. These events also can create and influence subcultures, cultures that exist within another larger culture that accept many of the values and beliefs of the larger culture while maintaining some unique ways of life. They can also lead to the creation of countercultures, groups in a society that espouse rules, values, or beliefs that conflict with the larger umbrella culture of the society.

4.5 In what ways can you use cultural capital to help both yourself and society?

Culture is a tool kit for us to use in our day-to-day lives. Having the right cultural tools can help us interact with others effectively and gain what we seek. Cultural capital is knowledge related to education, style, appearance, and dress that promotes social mobility (Bourdieu and Passeron 1990). Cultural capital can help us gain access to powerful arenas of society. We can use these connections and our cultural knowledge for both our own personal gain and in efforts to help shape society.

KEY TERMS

agency 60	generalized other 59	norms 59
beliefs 60	high culture 65	popular culture 65
counterculture 67	language 62	Sapir-Whorf hypothesis 63
cultural capital 69	material culture 57	social intelligence 70
cultural relativism 67	mores 60	subcultures 66
cultural universals 67	multiculturalism 67	symbol 62
folkways 60	nonmaterial culture 57	values 60

CHAPTER 5

UNDERSTANDING SOCIALIZATION AND INTERACTION

Amy Sodaro

How many of the ordinary things we do every day are taught to us by others?
©iStockphoto.com/SelectStock

LEARNING QUESTIONS

5.1 What is socialization?

5.2 According to George Herbert Mead, how does an individual develop a social self?

5.3 What are the key agents of socialization?

5.4 What is gender socialization?

5.5 What are status, social roles, and identity?

5.6 How can groups, formal organizations, and bureaucracies benefit individuals and societies?

5.7 How do sociologists describe and analyze social interaction?

What Is Socialization?

5.1   What is socialization?

Think about what you did this morning. Probably you woke up to an alarm clock that you set last night to ensure that you would be on time for your classes or other obligations. When you got out of bed, you probably followed some kind of morning routine, such as taking a shower, brushing your teeth, getting dressed, and eating breakfast. For each of these activities, you may not have realized it, but you were following norms determined not by you but by your culture and society. You were not born knowing that you need to shower every day and brush your teeth to stay clean, or that you should wear clothes to go to class and eat cereal for breakfast. These are things that you learned through your interactions with others.

From the time you were an infant, your family, peers, and others have taught you what you need to know to live in your society, such as how to keep yourself clean, what kinds of foods are typically eaten for breakfast and how, and the importance of being on time for your classes and other obligations. Imagine that you were born in a village in the highlands of Peru or 200 years ago. Your morning routine would be quite different!

You know what to do to start your day because you have undergone the process of **socialization**; that is, you have learned, through social interaction, how to follow the social norms and expectations of your society. In Chapter 4, you learned about how culture structures our lives within society, establishing norms and social patterns that we are expected to adhere to, but we are not born knowing how to fit into our culture. Through the process of socialization, individuals become functioning members of their society.

Socialization is part of a larger process of **social reproduction**, in which a society's norms and values are passed on from generation to generation. Societies have continuity over time because individuals learn and internalize the values and norms of their society and pass them on to future generations. Values and norms of societies do change over time. Perhaps one of the first things you did today was check your phone for social media updates, certainly not something your grandmother did as part of her daily routine! And 200 years ago, few people bathed daily. But many structural components of societies remain the same from one generation to the next—such as the organization of our days around family and work obligations and the expectation that you must get dressed to begin your day. These are some of the social norms that have been passed down to you from your parents, grandparents, and great-grandparents.

Socialization begins the moment babies are born. Everything from the names they receive, to the blankets they snuggle in, to the hospitals where they are born, and the homes where they reside is part of their socialization. It is a process that continues throughout the life course, or the various stages of one's life, from birth to death.

In different periods of life, individuals undergo new and different processes of socialization and **resocialization**, whereby they learn to adapt to new social norms and values. For example, when a young adult first moves out of her parents' home, she must learn how to perform a new social role: that of an adult living independently who must shop, cook, clean, manage money, and pay her own bills. This role requires learning new skills and new norms and disengaging from old norms that were appropriate when living as a dependent child. Becoming an adult involves learning a whole new role set and associated norms.

CONSIDER THIS

Can you think of a resocialization process you have undergone?

Nature versus Nurture

Most of us cannot remember far enough back to recall when we first began to acquire the skills we need to live in society. We learn things like language, how to walk and feed ourselves, and basic hygiene when we are very young

HOW I GOT ACTIVE IN SOCIOLOGY

AMY SODARO

I was a latecomer to sociology. Astonishingly, although I had a lifelong interest in culture and society, I made it through my undergraduate degree with two majors—drama and classics—and not one sociology course. I was working in New York City as a costume designer when the terror attacks of September 11, 2001, occurred. Watching the towers fall convinced me that I didn't have a sufficient framework or vocabulary for understanding the complexity of contemporary society, so I enrolled in an interdisciplinary master's program at the New School for Social Research in New York. I took my first sociology course there and realized that sociology provides the conceptual framework I had been looking for to merge my interests in culture, politics, and society and make sense of the world around me. Both my PhD studies and my current research focus on the sociology of culture, with an emphasis on how societies remember and come to terms with violence. I currently teach sociology just a few blocks away from the World Trade Center site, at the Borough of Manhattan Community College, where I strive to demonstrate to students the value and importance of developing a sociological perspective.

children and internalize these skills to the point where they feel like a natural part of who we are. Occasionally, however, children are discovered who did not undergo a "normal" process of socialization. They can help us to understand just how much we learn through our social interactions and how socialization cannot occur in social isolation.

In 1970, a young girl was found who had spent more than ten years of her life in almost complete isolation. Genie, as she was called, is one of a handful of examples of feral—or wild—children. Feral children live in isolation and do not have the opportunity to interact with others and become socialized. Genie had spent most of her life alone in a locked room and did not know how to talk, use the toilet, or feed herself. She didn't know how to interact with others and in many ways behaved like an infant when she was found. Throughout history, there have been a handful of examples of children like Genie who were not socialized through regular human interaction. Their cases intrigue scientists looking to understand how much of who we are comes from **nature**—that is, biology—or **nurture**, our cultural and social learning. Sociologists are more interested in understanding the impact of culture and learning, or nurture, on individuals. Feral children remind us just how much our social interactions with others in the process of socialization shape us.

Check Your Understanding

- What is socialization?
- When does socialization occur?
- What is social reproduction?

- What is resocialization?
- How do we know that social interaction is necessary for socialization?

Understanding Theories of Socialization

> 5.2 According to George Herbert Mead, how does an individual develop a social self?

Sociologists have a deep interest in understanding why humans are the way we are. Although sociologists are not interested in any one particular individual, they are interested in individuals as they are situated in and shaped by society. It is therefore important for sociologists to understand how, through socialization, individuals develop into social beings capable of navigating the many demands of social life.

Because socialization is focused on the individual, sociological understanding of it is shaped by the micro-level symbolic interactionist approach, particularly the work of its founder, George Herbert Mead (1863–1931). In Chapter 2, you learned about symbolic interaction as a theoretical approach that focuses on the ways in which we construct meaning through our social interactions. Mead (1964) argued that it is through these symbolic interactions with others that we develop into social beings.

Mead's Theory of Childhood Development

As you read in Chapter 2, Mead was influenced by Charles Horton Cooley's concept of the looking glass self, which is a way of seeing yourself the way you think others see you.

DOING SOCIOLOGY 5.1

FERAL CHILDREN AND SOCIALIZATION

In this activity, you will watch a documentary about Genie, a feral child, and answer questions about her socialization.

Watch the first ten minutes of the documentary *Genie: Secret of the Wild Child* (http://topdocumentaryfilms .com/genie-secret-wild-child/) and write your answers to the following questions:

1. What sorts of things did Genie not know how to do because she was kept in isolation and did not undergo a "normal" socialization process?

2. What can a "wild child" like Genie teach us about socialization and human development?

3. What do such feral children reveal to us about the importance of nurture when considering the age-old debate of nature versus nurture?

Cooley believed that we adjust our behavior and selves according to how we imagine others perceive and judge us. Think about taking a "selfie": when you snap a photo of yourself, you see yourself as you think others will see you, imagine their response, and adjust your appearance and expression accordingly. Taking a selfie is an example of your looking glass self. George Herbert Mead similarly saw the self as shaped by others through our social interactions.

Like Cooley, Mead believed that we are not born with a sense of self but rather learn **self-consciousness** through our social interactions. Self-consciousness is an individual's awareness of how others see her. The individual develops a sense of self through the reactions and attitudes of others. For example, babies are born completely unaware that they are individuals distinct from those individuals and things around them. This awareness is something that develops as babies grow into toddlers and interact with those around them.

Mead was particularly interested in the role of play in the development of children's self-awareness. He maintained that children begin to develop into social beings who are aware of themselves as distinct individuals through what he termed **taking the role of the other**: that is, imitating those around them. Have you ever noticed a young child pushing a baby doll in a toy stroller? Or a toddler making mud "pies" in the sandbox?

Children imitate the adults they observe, especially those of the same gender.
©iStockphoto.com/tirc83

These children are imitating the grown-ups they see around them. As toddlers get older, they begin to put themselves in others' positions in imagined scenarios like playing doctor or school. Although this may seem to be merely child's play, Mead viewed it as an extremely important step toward developing a social self. In taking the role of the other, children begin to see themselves the way others see them while also starting to understand that they are separate individuals distinct from those around them and capable of compelling particular reactions from others.

As children get older, their play becomes more sophisticated, and they begin to play organized games. Mead uses the example of baseball to describe the importance of these games in the further development of the social self. Through imitation, children put themselves in the shoes of a specific and particular other and begin to see themselves the way others see them. In organized games like baseball, individuals must be able to imagine and anticipate the actions of *all* of the other players. A shortstop needs to understand the role of the pitcher and catcher, as well as the other fielders and the batter. Furthermore, there are rules that all players must follow for the game to work, and they all must agree upon the goal. What emerges in this kind of play is not the specific other of imitation but what Mead describes as the generalized other: an other that represents the whole community of players and ultimately of society. Just as young children gain an understanding of what it means to perform the role of a specific other, like a parent or teacher, older children engaged in organized games develop an understanding of the larger rules, norms, and values of the society in which they live. This leads to the emergence of a self that responds not only to individual reactions but also to the norms and expectations of society.

What develops in these play and games stages is what Mead refers to as the "me," which differs from the "I." The "I" is the self's unsocialized impulses and attitudes that respond to the reactions and attitudes of others in a creative and active way. But the "me," the part of the self that has internalized the generalized reactions and attitudes of other members of society (the generalized other), often censors and hold back the "I." The "me" is the side of our self that follows the norms and expectations of society and works to control our behavior accordingly.

CONSIDER THIS

How does a game like hide and seek teach children about the generalized other? What societal expectations does one learn in a game like hide and seek?

Check Your Understanding

- What is Cooley's looking glass self?
- According to Mead, how do children develop a social self?
- What is the generalized other?
- What does Mead mean by the "I" versus the "me"?

Agents of Socialization

5.3   What are the key agents of socialization?

People, groups, institutions, and social contexts that contribute to our socialization are known as **agents of socialization**. We encounter different agents of socialization as we move through the life course. Primary socialization occurs from the time we are born to when we start school. During this time, we learn things like language and other foundational skills for life in society; at this point, the family is the primary agent of socialization. However, as we age, we move through many different social groups and contexts that shape us, such as sports teams or clubs, schools, religious organizations, and neighborhoods. Some of us may join the military, a highly powerful agent of socialization that has its own distinct set of norms and expectations, and each of us will move through more than one workplace, in which we will encounter distinct processes of socialization and resocialization. Socialization is a lifelong process and central to our experiences as social beings.

Family

Because family is generally the first agent of socialization and interaction with family is so intense in the years from infancy through childhood, family is the most influential agent of socialization. Although family structures vary widely in cultures and societies around the globe, most infants and children undergo significant socialization by their families.

In the Western world, the nuclear family predominates, meaning that children are usually raised by a mother, a father, and perhaps siblings. Throughout history and around the globe, extended families of grandparents, aunts, uncles, and cousins may be more typical family structures in which socialization occurs. And in today's world, family structures are rapidly changing; for example, one in three children in the United States today lives with an unmarried parent (Livingston 2018)—and a growing number of children are being raised by same-sex couples (Goldberg and Conron 2018); you'll learn more about the family in Chapter 11. No matter the family formation, family is an extremely important agent of socialization.

External social structures and forces influence socialization within families. Historically, the family one was born into determined one's position in life. Although today there is more opportunity for social mobility, one's social class still greatly influences how families socialize children. Sociologist Annette Lareau (2002) conducted a now classic study of the impact of social class on socialization, finding that children in lower income families were more likely to "hang out," play, and watch television in their free time, than middle-class children whose free time was structured with various extracurricular activities. A similar difference is reflected today in a newly emerging digital divide in U.S. society, with tweens and teens from lower income families spending significantly more time with media (two hours and forty-five minutes more) than their higher income peers (Common Sense Media 2018, 27). With growing worries about the impact of screen time on young people's mental and physical health, performance in school, and general well-being, this gap is important; whereas some parts of the country are embracing technology for children (even creating entirely online preschools), many middle-class and upper-class families are trying to ban screen time for their children entirely (Bowles 2018). In Chapter 7, you will learn more about economic inequality, but we can begin to see how economic inequality shapes the process of socialization and is, in turn, reproduced through socialization.

Families are the most influential agents of socialization regardless of the family's social class or structure. The sitcom *Modern Family* portrays evolving ideas of family structure.

Bob D'Amico/Disney ABC Television Group/Getty Images

We learn many essential things about our culture and society from our families, and their influence on us lasts a lifetime. Families teach us not only foundational skills like language and how to feed and dress ourselves but also the values, beliefs, and social norms that will shape us throughout our life course. We learn about gender roles and expectations by observing what our mothers and fathers and our brothers and sisters do and how they behave (Halpern and Perry-Jenkins 2016). For example, we might see our mothers cook, clean, and care for the children, while our fathers take out the trash, mow the lawn, and go off to work, reinforcing traditional expectations about gender roles, which we'll learn more about in Chapter 8. As individuals get older, they encounter different agents of socialization that may reinforce or challenge the things that they have learned from their families.

School

School is a significant agent of socialization; in America, most children begin school by the age of five, if not before, and spend much of the next thirteen years in school, with the majority then going on to college. In school, students not only learn academic content, such as reading, writing, mathematics, science, social studies, and so on, but also important norms and values. Through this "hidden curriculum," children learn how to interact with authority figures who are not their parents (teachers and administrators) and their **peers** (others in their age group). They also learn many rules and norms that are particular to the school context but can carry over into other settings, such as being quiet, raising one's hand to speak, following instructions, obeying authority figures, not cheating, and working with others (Jackson 1968). Schools also teach students about cultural values. For example, in this country, most students recite the Pledge of Allegiance each day before class, reinforcing their "allegiance" to American culture and values. In fact, many would argue that socialization is school's most important function in society (Parsons 1959; Gatto 2017).

Various social factors influence children's experiences of socialization in schools. Educational psychologist Katherine Wentzel (2005), for example, found that students who are socially accepted and enjoy a "popular" status are more successful academically. Strong ties to peers from kindergarten through high school are linked to greater motivation in school and higher academic performance (Wentzel and Muenks 2016). This probably doesn't surprise you as you think about your own experience in elementary, middle, and high school, when fitting in with your peers was so very important. But other social factors, such as social class, race and ethnicity, skin color, and gender, also affect one's experience in school. For example, data from the U.S. Department of

HOW MANY CHILDREN ARE BEING RAISED BY GRANDPARENTS?

Family members are the first and most influential agents of socialization. In the United States, the nuclear family, consisting of a mother, a father, and perhaps siblings, is the predominant family structure. But families are changing and are increasingly headed by single parents, same-sex couples, and even grandparents.

In this online activity, you will examine the number of children raised by grandparents, using data from the Census Bureau's American Community Survey.

*Requires the Vantage version of *Sociology in Action*.

▼ FIGURE 5.1

Grandchildren Living with Grandparent Responsible for Their Care (Metro), 2017

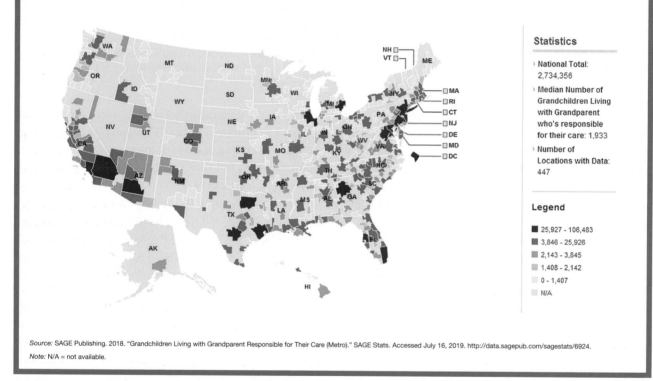

Statistics

> National Total: 2,734,356

> Median Number of Grandchildren Living with Grandparent who's responsible for their care: 1,933

> Number of Locations with Data: 447

Legend

■ 25,927 – 106,483
■ 3,846 – 25,926
■ 2,143 – 3,845
■ 1,408 – 2,142
□ 0 – 1,407
■ N/A

Source: SAGE Publishing. 2018. "Grandchildren Living with Grandparent Responsible for Their Care (Metro)." SAGE Stats. Accessed July 16, 2019. http://data.sagepub.com/sagestats/6924.

Note: N/A = not available.

Education in 2014 show that Black girls were suspended at a rate of 12 percent in comparison with a suspension rate of just 2 percent for White girls (Wun 2016). Other recent studies showed that not only are Black students more likely to be suspended than White students, but Black students with darker skin tones were two times more likely to be suspended than White classmates, though this was not the case for Black classmates with lighter skin tones (Blake et al. 2017). Likewise, Black students with dark skin tones have lower grade point averages than White students and Black students with lighter skin tones (Thompson and McDonald 2016, 101). Thus, the color of a child's skin may play a role in determining whether she learns to like school and feels a sense of

safety and belonging in the classroom or views school as a place where she does not belong or cannot succeed because she is perceived to be a troublemaker. In Chapter 9, you will learn about the impact of race on individuals and society and how racial inequalities are structured into social institutions like schools, affecting the experiences and socialization of students.

CONSIDER THIS

What are some elements of your high school's "hidden curriculum"? Other than academics, what sorts of things did you learn in high school?

Peers

As children get older, they spend more time with their peers and less time with their families. Peers, then, become an increasingly important agent of socialization that can both reinforce and challenge what children have learned from the family. In school—and for many children today this can begin with preschool or daycare at age two or younger—children spend their days surrounded by other children of the same age, interacting with them both inside and outside the classroom. Peers become extremely powerful agents of socialization. You have, no doubt, heard the term **peer pressure**. Peers often expect conformity to a set of particular social norms relating to appearance, behavior, language, and so on. Accordingly, young people, surrounded by peers in school, often face pressure to conform to the norms accepted by their classmates.

Much of the sociological research on peers and socialization involves deviant behaviors, or behaviors that go against society's norms, which you will learn more about in Chapter 6. A recent study, for example, found that adolescents associated with delinquent peers were more likely to be both bullies and victims of bullying (Cho and Lee 2018). Another recent study showed that middle school students were more likely to engage in homophobic teasing if their friends were doing the same thing (Merrin et al. 2017).

Peers are critical agents of socialization at various stages in the life course and can challenge the kinds of norms and values learned from families, teachers, and administrators. Peers expose us to new cultures, norms, values, and beliefs, some of which may manifest in deviant behaviors, but many of which can increase our acceptance and understanding of diversity and multiculturalism. For example, the Pew Research Center (2017) has found that 74 percent of Millennials (the generation born after 1981) support same-sex marriage, a proportion much higher than Generation X (65 percent) and Baby Boomers (56 percent).

Media

Media are an increasingly influential agent of socialization. Books, radio, and television have long been influential social forces, but today we live in an "information age" in which we have unprecedented access

Video games are a socializing agent that, depending on the game, can have either positive or negative impacts on behavior.
©iStockphoto.com/dangrytsku

to media, much of them conveniently and constantly accessible on our smartphones and tablets. According to Nielson's (2018) "Total Audience Report," American adults spend more than 11 hours each day consuming various forms of media; another report found that 45 percent of teens said that they use the Internet "almost constantly," while another 44 percent said that they go online several times a day (Anderson and Jiang 2018). We live in a media-saturated society and are very much shaped by this constant stream of images and information. Every movie we watch, magazine we flip through, or text we read contains messages that contribute to the ongoing shaping of our values and norms.

The huge recent increase in media consumption (see Figure 5.2) has led to many questions about how it is influencing society, especially young people. Recent studies have shown a link between screen time and symptoms of attention-deficit/hyperactivity disorder (Chatterjee 2018) and between media consumption and depression and anxiety (Heid 2018). And since long before the creation of the Internet and iPhones, studies have tried to determine the effect of violent media on children and young adults. For example, a 1956 study by Alberta Siegel found that four-year-olds who watched *Woody Woodpecker* cartoons, in which said woodpecker frequently violently pecks those around him, later behaved more aggressively than four-year-olds who had watched the relatively peaceful *Little Red Hen*. In 1968, communications scholar George Gerbner established the Cultural Indicators research project at the Annenberg School of Communication at the University of Pennsylvania to determine how television

FIGURE 5.2

Media Consumption by Adults, 2018

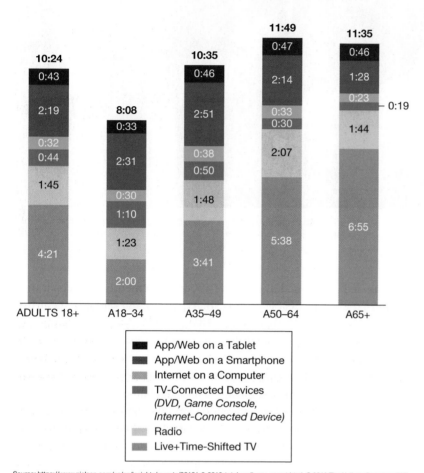

Daily Hours: Minutes of Usage
Based on Total U.S. Population

Legend:
- App/Web on a Tablet
- App/Web on a Smartphone
- Internet on a Computer
- TV-Connected Devices (DVD, Game Console, Internet-Connected Device)
- Radio
- Live+Time-Shifted TV

Note: Q2 = second quarter.

How have the media served as an agent of your socialization? Think, for example, of one of your favorite movies when you were younger. What did that movie teach you about social and cultural norms, values, and beliefs? Have any of those norms, values, and beliefs been challenged as you have grown older?

Recent studies have looked at new forms of media, especially video games, to try to determine whether and to what extent they are linked to violent real-life acts. Most studies find that there is a link between violent media and later aggression and violence (e.g., Calvert et al. 2017; Gabbiadini et al. 2016; Hasan et al. 2018). However, most scholars agree that there is no one cause that can explain why someone becomes violent. And on the other side, scholars have found positive effects of video games, including greater empathy (Harrington and O'Connell 2016) and increased cooperation, even while playing violent video games (Adachi et al. 2016). What all scholars agree on, however, is that media are an extremely powerful agent of socialization to which individuals are exposed more and more.

shapes viewers' perceptions of the world. The project's analysis of thousands of hours of television programming led Gerbner to argue that television creates "mean world syndrome," leading people to believe the world is more dangerous than it actually is. With young people exposed to so much media today, much of them depicting violence—an estimated 60 percent of all televisions shows contain acts of violence, including children's Saturday morning cartoons, which have on average 16.7 violent acts per hour (Scharrer 2018)—these questions have become pressing, especially in the wake of mass violence committed by young people, such as mass shootings at Sandy Hook Elementary School in Newtown, Connecticut; Emanuel African Methodist Episcopal Church in Charleston, South Carolina; and Marjory Stoneman Douglas High School in Parkland, Florida.

Agents of Socialization for Adults

Although socialization may be most intense in our early years, we never stop being socialized. As individuals move into adulthood, they encounter new agents of socialization and have to unlearn some of their old norms and values. For example, for most people in cultures around the world, work is an important social context in which we spend much of our time. Before industrialization, most people did not work outside of their homes; they farmed or had trades in or very near their homes. Today that has changed, and most of us spend our workday in a different location, surrounded by people who are not our family and sometimes not even friends. Many Americans begin working when they are teenagers and continue to work for most of their lives.

Each new workplace constitutes a new set of agents of socialization, including bosses, colleagues, clients or customers, and others. In the workplace, individuals are expected to perform particular social roles and adhere to a slightly different set of social norms and values than what they might follow at home or in other contexts. For example, someone with tattoos covering her arms may need to wear long sleeves to work. A gay man or woman might pretend to be straight to avoid discrimination in the workplace. As of 2019, twenty-eight states do not have laws explicitly prohibiting discrimination on the basis of sexual orientation (Movement Advancement Project 2019).

The Netflix show *Orange Is the New Black* has taught many of us that a total institution, like a prison, has its own routines, values, and norms.

Pictorial Press Ltd/Alamy Stock Photo

Total Institutions. Many people will at some point find themselves in what is known as a **total institution**, an institution that is closed to external influences in which a group of people live together, following a strictly structured routine (Goffman 1961). In a total institution, our sleep, work, and play all occur within the confines of one institution—rather than in different locations—under a single authority that oversees and administers these activities.

CONSIDER THIS

Describe how at least two different agents of socialization influenced your decision to attend college.

One example of a total institution is prison. According to the U.S. Bureau of Justice Statistics, in 2016, a total of 1,506,800 adults were incarcerated in state and federal prisons (Carson 2018). Each of these prisoners had to undergo resocialization upon entering prison, learning new norms to which they must adhere and new values. For example, prisoners must dress alike; eat, wake up, and sleep at the same time; and follow the orders of prison guards. At the same time, they must stop following the norms that structure life as a free individual, like getting up when they want to, eating what and when they wish, and following

their former daily routines. They also must give up old values, like autonomy and their relationships with family and friends, and embrace new values, like keeping to oneself, defending oneself when challenged, and not "snitching." Prisoners also learn a new language—prison slang—to communicate in this new social context.

Another total institution is the military, especially basic training or "boot camp." Military recruits live, eat, and train together, following a strict schedule and rules that guide practically every moment of their lives. They must wear uniforms and shave their heads, march in line and chant together, and leave behind civilian concerns in the face of an all-encompassing basic training experience. They are resocialized to follow the norms and expectations of this new and total institution, changing from a civilian to a soldier.

Check Your Understanding

- What are agents of socialization?

- What are some of the most important agents of socialization and what do we learn from each?

- Why are the media an increasingly powerful agent of socialization? What kinds of things do they teach individuals?

- What are total institutions? How do they resocialize adults?

FROM ANOTHER PLANET

In this exercise, you will analyze the messages about gender conveyed in a magazine.

Imagine that you are from another planet and know nothing about gender expectations in American society. Pick an American magazine and examine it for clues about what is required of women and men in this society. Spend some time looking at your magazine's depiction of men and women as a reference to learn your new culture, then answer the following questions:

1. What are men expected to be like in American society? How should they look, dress, behave, and so on?

2. What are women expected to be like in American society? How should they look, dress, behave, and so on?

Gender Socialization

5.4   What is gender socialization?

Just as we learn the general norms and expectations of our society, we also learn the particular expectations of society when it comes to gender. Learning gender identity and roles through socialization is known as gender socialization. From birth—or arguably even as early as the sex of a baby is known—individuals are assigned gender roles and socialized through various socializing agents to perform these roles. From the way parents decorate a nursery and to how they dress their babies and how people interact with them, gender socialization is an ongoing process of learning the social expectations of males and females in one's society and culture.

In one classic study, new mothers were observed to behave differently with a baby depending on whether the child was presented to them as a boy or a girl. Although the women all reported that they did not treat their own babies differently on the basis of their sex, they smiled more at the baby in the study if told it was a girl and held her closer to them. They were more likely to hold the boy away from them and to offer him a toy train to play with, rather than a doll (Will, Self, and Datan 1976). Although the baby was only six months old, clear gendered patterns in interaction emerged among these mothers, although they were unaware of them.

These subtle differences in how boys and girls are treated as babies are reinforced through other social agents over the life course; you'll learn much more about gender socialization in Chapter 8. Throughout the process of socialization, gendered messages and expectations are all around us. Think, for example, about the kinds of toys children play with. How do "girl" toys versus "boy" toys help demonstrate what it means to be female or male in our society? Recall some of your favorite books or movies as a child: how did they help you understand what it means to be a boy or girl or man or woman? Think about the media that you consume today. What music, sports, movies, or other icons do you follow, and what do you learn from them about gender? Each different agent of socialization we encounter teaches us something about the expectations of us regarding gender.

CONSIDER THIS

Think back on your experience with gender socialization. How did it affect how you learned your gender role?

In Chapter 8, you will learn much more about gender and sexuality. Gender socialization affects all aspects of both men's and women's lives, sometimes in seemingly trivial ways that can actually have a big impact. For example, a group of sociology students at William Paterson University in New Jersey noticed that because individuals are socialized to believe that menstruation is a private issue that should not be publicly discussed, many low-income women do not have access to a fundamental necessity: feminine hygiene products. These Sociologists in Action decided to do something about this to help women have a "happy period."

Check Your Understanding

- What is gender socialization?
- Why is gender socialization important?
- What is an example of gender socialization?

SOCIOLOGISTS IN ACTION

"HELPING WOMEN HAVE A HAPPY PERIOD"

ANGELO R. MILORDO, SHANEY LARA, PETER FALCICHIO, AND CASSANDRA SUNDSTROM-SMITH

As part of our class requirement for our Public Sociology and Civic Engagement class, we were required to complete a total of twenty hours of volunteer work at Oasis, a "haven for women and children," in Paterson, New Jersey. Oasis provides low-income women and children with a variety of services, including GED, English as a second language, and job training courses; after-school and summer youth programs; meals; food bags; and clothing. While volunteering at Oasis, we used our sociological eye and observed that the women were receiving food, clothes, shoes, an education, and diapers for their babies. However, we noticed a need that Oasis was unable to meet: feminine products for the low-income women the organization serves.

Every woman, regardless of race, social class, or any other social category, menstruates throughout much of her life. We tend, however, not to talk about it. Through our socialization process, most of us learn that menstruation is solely a women's issue and a matter not to be discussed in public—and certainly never with men. This contributes to many poor women's having a difficult time gaining access to sanitary pads and tampons.

This relative silence around menstruation has also contributed to the taxation of such goods in most states and raising their price, even though they are necessary and not luxury items. One of YouTube's star interviewers, Ingrid Nilsen, asked President Barack Obama in a live YouTube interview, "Why are menstrual products being taxed?" Obama said that he had had no idea that this "tampon tax" was in place. However, he believes it exists "because men were making the laws when those taxes were passed." Even the president of the United States,

who has two daughters and a wife, did not realize these products are taxed (see https://www.youtube.com/watch?v=8c2Ro54Alkk)!

In response to the need we noticed at Oasis, we decided to organize a drive called "Helping Women Have a Happy Period." The goal was to collect as many sanitary pads and tampons as possible for the women of Oasis. We created colorful boxes and fliers and collected the feminine products from everyone who was willing to donate on our campus. Throughout this process, we noticed that the women who donated were much more uncomfortable when approached by the men in our group than by the women. This is related to our socialization to treat menstrual cycles as private matters that women should only discuss among themselves. Women who donated quickly threw their pads and tampons into our donation box, embarrassed to be seen with these products in front of men. Shaney publicized our efforts on social media, and she is still receiving donations that she continues to give to Oasis. Through our efforts, we brought to light issues rarely discussed in public, collected hundreds of donations for the women of Oasis—and helped many women have happier periods!

Discussion Question: Would you feel comfortable running a sanitary pads and tampons drive at your school? Why? How did your key socializing agents (e.g., family, peers, school) affect your comfort level when discussing menstruation?

Angelo R. Milordo, Shaney Lara, Peter Falcichio, and Cassandra Sundstrom-Smith are undergraduate students at William Paterson University in Wayne, New Jersey.

Status, Social Roles, and Identity

> 5.5   What are status, social roles, and identity?

Through the different agents of socialization, individuals learn the various social expectations of them in the different social statuses and social roles they occupy throughout their lives. As you will recall from earlier chapters, status is one's position relative to others in society, while social roles are the expectations others

have of us in particular status positions in terms of how we act, behave, dress, and so on.

Just as we perform distinct gender roles, as we move through our daily lives, we perform a range of other social roles that hold social expectations of us in terms of the norms we follow, how we dress and appear, the language we use, and how we behave. For example, let's imagine a day in the life of an imaginary college student, Maria. Maria wakes up and is a roommate to the girls she lives with. On her way to class, she stops and buys a coffee and a muffin, and is a customer to the cashier.

In class, she plays the role of student; after class, she meets a group of students to work on a project, performing the role of a classmate. She meets some friends for lunch, playing the role of friend. After lunch, she goes to her job at the campus bookstore and is an employee to her boss, a colleague to her coworkers, and a retail assistant to the customers. Later on, she calls her parents, playing the role of daughter, and perhaps after that she goes out dancing as a friend. In each of these roles, Maria faces different expectations: she would not behave in class the way she behaves around her friends, just as she would not talk to customers in the bookstore the way she talks to her parents. At work, she might have to wear a uniform that she would not wear when she goes dancing with her friends. In each of these roles, Maria has a different status as well: when she is in the classroom as a student, she has a lower status than she has when she is with her friends, and she dresses, speaks, and acts accordingly.

Although it may sound exhausting (and sometimes is!) to perform so many social roles, each of us does this on a daily basis and usually moves seamlessly from one role and status to another. And while you might imagine that with your friends or family you are able to be your "true" self, you are still performing a role when you are with them. For each social context in which we find ourselves, there is a different set of social expectations of us in terms of our attitudes and behaviors.

Our social roles and statuses are not always compatible and comfortable. Sometimes we experience competing demands within a particular social role and status, or what is known as **role strain**. Maria may experience role strain in her role as a college student when she is required to do a sociology presentation on the same day that she has a physics exam. The demands of her role as a student to prepare for her presentation coincide with the expectations of her to study hard for her physics exam. These competing demands of her college student role result in a strain placed on Maria that is probably familiar to you!

Alternatively, when our different social roles conflict with one another, we experience **role conflict**. Now imagine that Maria's younger sister is home sick from school and there is no one to stay home with her except Maria, who must miss class to do so. In this case, Maria's role of student conflicts with her sister role; there is no way she can fulfill both roles at the same time. Although our roles have relatively clear expectations of us, this does not mean that they always fit together in a way that is comfortable, and we must constantly negotiate our social roles and statuses.

CONSIDER THIS

List five social roles you perform in your daily life. What are the expectations of you in these roles in terms of how you behave, the norms you follow, the language you use, the way you dress, and so on? Have you experienced role strain in any of these roles? What about role conflict between two or more of them?

Identity

Through the process of socialization, we learn about our culture and society but also develop our distinct identities. **Identity** generally refers to the characteristics by which we are known. Some of the key sources of identity are factors determined by society, such as gender, social class, race, ethnicity, and so forth. These are social categories to which we belong that shape our social identity, that is, the identity that others ascribe to us. Think of the many ways others might describe you: a student, an athlete, a woman, a man, a daughter, a son, a father, a mother, and so on. Each of us has multifaceted social identities others assign to us. We also each have our

Working parents must constantly negotiate their social roles to minimize role conflict.
©iStockphoto.com/Geber86

own understanding of who we are—**self-identity**—that is shaped by our interactions with others. Through individual agency and the social and symbolic world that individuals move through, identity is constantly shaped, reshaped, and negotiated through our interactions with others.

Check Your Understanding

- What are social roles?
- What is social status?
- How do role strain and role conflict differ? What are some examples of each?
- What is the difference between social identity and self-identity?

Groups, Organizations, and Bureaucracies

> 5.6 How can groups, formal organizations, and bureaucracies benefit individuals and societies?

With whom do you interact? You probably can't answer that question without thinking about the groups you belong to—your classes, teams, religious organizations, workplace colleagues, study groups, and so on. A **group** is any set of two or more people with whom you share a sense of belonging, purpose, and identity.

Types of Groups

Throughout our lives, we become part of primary and secondary groups. Primary groups (e.g., family, close friends) tend to be smaller, more intimate, and longer lasting than other, secondary groups. Secondary groups are less personal, and some last just a short period of time (e.g., students assigned a class project, a party planning committee, a workers' union).

The Power of Groups: Formal Organizations and Bureaucracies

Working in a group can help us accomplish tasks that would be much harder (e.g., studying for a final, painting a house) or impossible (e.g., raising a barn, moving a large refrigerator) to accomplish alone. Have you ever seen a one-person barn raising?

Formal organizations allow us to accomplish even larger tasks (e.g., giving local youth opportunities to play organized soccer, educating a nation's children, selling goods to customers all over the world, providing medical care for a region of the country). Youth soccer leagues, education systems, multinational corporations, and hospitals

are examples of **formal organizations**—planned secondary groups created to achieve a goal. Formal organizations follow a plan for dividing power, assign members to fill specific responsibilities, and have a system to replace individuals. For example, a soccer league divides power among the commissioner, coaches, assistant coaches, referees, and players. Each member of the league has set duties they must fulfill and rules to follow. If a referee gets caught letting her friends get away with fouling members of an opposing team, the commissioner will fire her and go through the (planned) process of filling her position with a new person.

As formal organizations grow and become more complex, they tend to become bureaucracies. Organizations that have the characteristics of an **ideal bureaucracy** are formal organizations designed to complete complex tasks rationally and with maximum efficiency. They have a standard set of rules that all employees must follow, a clear hierarchy of status positions with specific roles assigned to each, employees hired on the basis of their qualifications, and workers who interact impersonally with one another as they focus on carrying out their responsibilities as efficiently as possible (Weber [1947] 2012).

The media tends to portray bureaucracies as inefficient and cumbersome—and poorly run ones often fit this image. However, imagine trying to run a large formal organization like a university without such a system. Professors might teach only the courses they love to teach, deans might hire people on the basis of friendships rather than qualifications, department administrators might have to bribe custodians to clean their departments. It would be mayhem! Bureaucracies are vital components of almost all large formal organizations.

Our groups and our roles in them also affect how others view us, how we see ourselves, and how we behave. How might people view you differently depending on your status position at work, among your close friends, in your family? How would your status in these groups affect your image of yourself? What would you do to maintain or raise your status in a group?

Think about the last time you missed a joke but joined the laughter after it. You were acting as you thought you should, as a member of your group. As you will see below, different groups lead us to act in different ways.

Check Your Understanding

- What is a group?
- What are formal organizations?

- When formal organizations grow and become more complex, what do they tend to become?

- What are the components of an ideal bureaucracy?

- Why do complex societies need bureaucracies?

Social Interaction

5.7 How do sociologists describe and analyze social interaction?

"All the world's a stage, And all the men and women merely players; They have their exits and entrances, And one man in his time plays many parts." Well before sociologists began to analyze individuals' **social interactions**, or the way individuals behave and react in the presence of other people, Shakespeare penned this enduring description of the theatrical nature of human life. Almost four hundred years later, a Canadian American sociologist, Erving Goffman, built upon this insight and developed a dramaturgical approach to analyzing and explaining social interaction. As you learned in Chapter 2's discussion of the symbolic interactionist theoretical approach, Goffman used the metaphor of theater to describe how our social lives are a kind of performance. We each play different roles as we move throughout social lives, performing for different audiences on various "stages," just as Shakespeare suggested. Goffman is considered the pioneer of the study of social interaction in everyday contexts, or microsociology, and his work gives us tremendous insight into the sociological significance of our everyday behaviors and social interactions.

Social interaction is the basis for our lives within society. As we have seen, it is through social interaction that we develop a sense of self and undergo the socialization that allows us to live in society. Our everyday lives are made up of meaningful interactions with people we care about very much but also seemingly insignificant interactions: buying a cup of coffee, holding the door for someone, nodding at an acquaintance in passing, riding an elevator, and so on. Goffman believed that all moments in which we engage with others socially, no matter how fleeting, are fundamental to our lives as social beings.

Goffman argued that in social interactions, we use cues and clues from the individuals and objects around us to make meaning of what is going on, or to define the situation. As individuals, we become socialized into particular expectations about social interactions and use this knowledge to make sense of our social lives. In the way that we define the situation, we are also innovative and shape our own reality through the meanings we make of social interactions. Goffman focused much of his career on understanding why we act in the way we do in everyday situations.

Performances and Impression Management

In his book *The Presentation of Self in Everyday Life*, Goffman (1959) developed his theatrical metaphor to describe how individuals' social lives consist of a series of performances of social roles for different observers, or audiences. Like Cooley and Mead, Goffman believed that individuals are very attuned to and concerned about how others see them. So, in their performance of different social roles, they work hard to make sure that others see them the way they want to be seen. Because we construct reality in our social interactions, it is very important that when we perform particular social roles others believe that we are what we claim to be. For example, when you are performing the social role of student in the classroom, you are (hopefully!) working to make sure that your professor believes that you are, in fact, a good student: you come to class on time with your textbook, notebook and pen, or laptop; you raise your hand when you wish to speak; you make eye contact with your professor and nod along with what he or she is saying; and you take notes to show that you are following the class discussion (even if you are actually just doodling in your notebook!).

What you are doing when you perform this role of student is what Goffman termed *impression management*. Through impression management you present yourself the way you want others to see you. As a student, you take on a set of social expectations of your behavior and attitudes, and when you perform the role of student, you work hard to give off the right impression to your professor and classmates. As Goffman (1959, 208) would say, you are "successfully staging a character."

In each performance, there is what Goffman (1959, 22) referred to as the **front**, or the "expressive equipment" the individual uses to define the situation and convince others of the sincerity of his or her performance. The front consists of the setting, appearance, and manner of the context in which a particular performance occurs. To continue the example of the social role of student, the **setting** for the performance of student is generally a classroom, which is equipped with all of the necessary items for students' learning: desks, chairs, blackboards, screens and projectors, and the many "props" used by a student, such as backpacks, notebooks, textbooks, pens and pencils, and so on. As noted before,

IMPRESSION MANAGEMENT ON SOCIAL MEDIA

In this activity, you will conduct a content analysis of Facebook or Instagram to determine how users engage in impression management on social media. If you do not use social media, your instructor will give you an alternative assignment.

Goffman formulated his theories of social interaction before the age of the Internet and social media. Social media sites like Facebook dramatically change the ways in which individuals are able to use impression management to ensure that people see them the way they want to be seen.

1. Select three people you follow on Instagram or are friends with on Facebook.

2. Analyze their profile photos by asking the following questions: What does the photo depict? If it is a person, what is he or she doing? What is he or she wearing? If it is not a person, what is it? Where? What impression of your friend does the photo create?

3. Next, review the last ten posts of each person. What are the posts about?

4. Create categories to help you classify the posts (e.g., politics, everyday life, accomplishments, vacations or other outings). If any posts are of photos, analyze the photo in the way that you did the profile picture.

5. Once you have coded the status updates, write a one- to two-page sociological analysis of how each individual uses impression management on Facebook.

these elements of setting are necessary for an individual to perform the role of student convincingly: a student who comes to class without a notebook and pen or computer will likely be perceived by his or her professor and classmates as unprepared.

Appearance consists of everything from dress to age, sex, and race or ethnicity, to nonverbal forms of communication like body language and gestures. For example, a student wearing the school colors and sitting up straight and attentive in the front row of the classroom will convey a very different impression to those around her than one slumped in the back row with a baseball cap pulled low over her face. Appearance and setting work in conjunction with **manner**, or the attitude conveyed by an individual in his or her particular social role. And it is through this combined front that an individual seeks to influence the perception others have of her.

CONSIDER THIS

Have you ever interviewed for a job? How did you engage in impression management to try to get hired? What about using impression management on a first date? What are some other examples of how you use impression management in your everyday life?

Regions: Front Stage and Back Stage

Goffman's dramaturgical approach to describing our social lives goes further, to argue that there are also different regions in which we perform our interactions. The front stage is where we actively perform our roles, using impression management to compel a certain reaction from our audience. The back stage, on the other hand, is where we are "out of character" and no longer have to put on a performance.

In performing your role as student, you are front stage when you are in class. You are acting out the role of student for your audience (your professor and classmates), raising your hand to answer questions, taking notes, and nodding along as the professor speaks. You are putting on a show to convince those around you that you are an excellent student who is fulfilling society's expectations of you as student. Perhaps, however, you pulled an all-nighter studying for your chemistry exam last night and did not prepare for class at all and are mostly trying to stay awake. As soon as you leave class, you might rush home and fall into bed, texting a good friend that you just fudged your way through sociology class. This is your back-stage region, where you no longer have to put on a show.

It is important that we keep these regions separate in our social lives. For example, as a student, you might be embarrassed, or your grade might be affected, if it is obvious you are unprepared for class. It's often even more important in the workplace to keep front stage and back stage separate. For example, if you work in a restaurant or retail store, you are probably told that "the customer is always right." This means that you need to be polite even if the customer is nasty to you. You may wish to be rude back to him or her, and you might vent your frustrations to colleagues, but if your back-stage attitude toward the customer comes out when you are front stage, you may very well be fired.

Goffman constructed his theories on social interaction before the Internet and social media dramatically altered the ways in which we interact. Although maintaining a separation between front stage and back stage in face-to-face interaction often seems very straightforward, it is more difficult to do in online interactions. For example, have you ever accidentally "replied all" on an email that you intended to send just to the sender? Or sent a text message to the wrong person?

New online forms of interaction often make it more difficult for us to keep track of which region we are in and for whom we are performing. For example, in November 2018 a photograph was anonymously posted on Twitter of a group of male high school students from Baraboo High School in Wisconsin doing a Nazi salute. The photo went viral, and there was a media storm of criticism of the boys and school (Caron 2018). Although ultimately the students were not punished, this kind of blurring of "front"-stage and "back"-stage behavior can have serious repercussions for the actors involved. That same month, photos were posted on an Idaho school district's Facebook page of teachers and staff dressed in stereotypical Mexican costumes, like sombreros, ponchos, and large mustaches, standing behind a cardboard border "wall" touting "Make America Great Again." When these photos went viral and created a similar outcry, fourteen staff members were placed on administrative leave (Mervosh 2018). In both cases, the individuals (large groups of them!) failed to realize that this "back-stage" behavior becomes front stage when circulated on social media.

CONSIDER THIS

How do you maintain the distinction between the front-stage and back-stage regions in your online social media interactions, such as on Facebook or Instagram?

Ethnomethodology

Harold Garfinkel was another sociologist who focused his work on seemingly unimportant everyday social interactions. He gave the most basic, trivial, everyday occurrences the kind of attention "usually accorded extraordinary events" (Garfinkel 1967, 1). To do this, he created a field of study that he called **ethnomethodology**, the study of the "ethno" (meaning ordinary or everyday) methods people use to make sense of their social interactions.

Garfinkel's focus was on language and the simplistic small talk that makes up many of our basic interactions with others. He argued that language is not as simple as it may seem. Take, for example, the question "What's up?" If you are from this country, you probably know just what is meant by this question (something like "What is happening with you right now?") and what kind of response is expected (e.g., "Not much"). However, for someone who is not from here and does not know the social context and background in which this question is being asked, this is a very confusing question, the answer to which is not at all clear: perhaps "the sky" or "the ceiling"?

Garfinkel conducted a series of experiments to help understand this complexity of language and the norms that dictate our everyday interactions through language. He enlisted his college students to carry out experiments with friends and acquaintances in which they would pretend to not understand the conventions of small talk and instead push their conversation partners to be more specific and precise in what they were asking. Here is one example of an experiment (Garfinkel 1967, 44); S is the friend of E, the student experimenter:

S: How are you?

E: How am I in regard to what? My health, my finances, my school work, my peace of mind, my . . .?

S: [Red in the face and suddenly out of control.] Look! I was just trying to be polite. Frankly I don't give a damn how you are.

Garfinkel and his students found that breaking the conventions of everyday small talk made people deeply uncomfortable and upset. We rely on others understanding our expectations when it comes to common verbal interactions, and it is unsettling and frustrating when these expectations are broken. Think of how annoying it is when you've politely asked someone "How are you?" as a form of small talk and you get their whole life story! Smooth navigation of such daily interactions requires shared cultural assumptions about how these interactions should proceed.

Check Your Understanding

- What is Goffman's dramaturgical approach?
- What is impression management and why do we use it?
- What is the difference between front stage and back stage?
- What does Goffman refer to as the "front"?
- What is ethnomethodology? Why do people get upset when the rules of small talk are broken?

Conclusion

Through our interactions and the process of socialization, we learn how to act within our society and culture. This means that we are very much shaped by the place and time in which we are born and raised. This should call to mind C. Wright Mills's concept of the sociological imagination and how individual lives are influenced by society and history.

Our social lives are structured by larger social and cultural patterns and norms that we learn through socialization. In each social context we find ourselves, we perform a different social role, based on the social expectations others have of us in that role. In these social interactions, we make meaning and construct the reality of our social lives. At the same time, however, there are limits to socialization and the social structures that pattern our behavior. Individuals, as you know, have free will and can make choices that breach or challenge social norms and expectations. Individuals can change the culture they live in, resisting the norms and values they were socialized to accept and instead creating social change. Thus, although socialization is a powerful phenomenon, you are not entirely a product of your culture but can also be an agent of change. You'll learn more about deviance, or breaking social norms, in the next chapter.

REVIEW

5.1 What is socialization?

Socialization is the social process through which individuals learn the norms of the culture and society that they live in. Through the process of socialization, individuals become functioning members of their society. It is a lifelong process that begins when we are born and continues through our many stages. As we age, we may undergo resocialization as we enter different social contexts and learn new sets of social norms and expectations. Socialization contributes to social reproduction, the continuation of a society's culture across generations.

5.2 According to George Herbert Mead, how does an individual develop a social self?

Mead's theory of child development was inspired by another social psychologist, Charles Cooley, who argued that individuals develop a sense of self, what he termed the looking glass self, by imagining how others see us. Mead similarly believed that individuals develop into social beings through their interactions with others. This begins when very young children engage in what Mead called taking the role of the other, or imitating those around them, putting themselves in someone else's shoes and seeing what kind of reaction they get. As they get older and engage in more organized games, like sports, they develop an understanding of the generalized other that represents society as a whole, with all of its norms and values.

5.3 What are the key agents of socialization?

Socialization occurs with individuals and within groups and social contexts, which are referred to as agents of socialization. Family is the primary agent of socialization, because it is generally the first group and sometimes only group an individual is exposed to in his or her earliest years. From our families, we learn many fundamental skills for life in society, such as language and how to feed and dress ourselves, as well as many other norms and values. As we age, we encounter different agents of socialization like peers, schools, the media, work, and so on, learning from each different norms and values. Some adults end up in total institutions, where they must be resocialized into an entirely new culture and context.

5.4 What is gender socialization?

An extremely important aspect of socialization is learning gender roles and identity. Gender socialization begins the moment a baby is born (or that baby's sex is determined), when that individual is assigned a gender role and socialized to perform that role. Gender socialization is an ongoing process of learning the social expectations of males and females in one's society and culture.

5.5 What are status, social roles, and identity?

Throughout the process of socialization, individuals develop an individual identity and learn the various social expectations that come with the different social statuses and social roles that they occupy throughout their lives. Status is one's position relative to others in society, while social roles are the expectations others have of us in particular statuses and positions. Identity is the characteristics by which we are known. Through individual agency and the social and symbolic world that we move through, our identity is constantly shaped, reshaped, and negotiated through our interactions with others.

5.6 How can groups, formal organizations, and bureaucracies benefit individuals and societies?

Groups give us a sense of identity and allow us to complete tasks that are difficult or impossible to do alone. We create planned groups called formal organizations (e.g., a youth soccer league, regional hospitals, multinational organizations, public school systems) to help us achieve complex goals in a deliberate way. Bureaucracies allow formal organizations to carry out multilayered tasks rationally and efficiently.

5.7 How do sociologists describe and analyze social interaction?

Sociologists Erving Goffman and Harold Garfinkel both believed that our everyday interactions with others were important to analyze sociologically because this kind of microsociology gives us great insight into our experiences as social beings. Goffman used a dramaturgical approach to argue that individuals' social lives are a series of performances; we use impression management to perform our social roles in a way that compels others to see us the way we want to be seen. Garfinkel was especially concerned with how individuals make sense of what others say and do in everyday interactions. He created ethnomethodology as a field that could study how regular people make sense of the interactions that structure our social lives.

KEY TERMS

agents of socialization 80

appearance 91

ethnomethodology 92

formal organization 89

front 90

group 89

ideal bureaucracy 89

identity 88

manner 91

nature 78

nurture 78

peer pressure 83

peers 81

resocialization 77

role conflict 88

role strain 88

self-consciousness 79

self-identity 89

setting 90

social interactions 90

social reproduction 77

socialization 77

taking the role of the other 79

total institution 85

CHAPTER 6

IDENTIFYING DEVIANT BEHAVIOR

Rena C. Zito

How do you know a deviant act when you see one? What can be deviant in one place and time can seem perfectly normal in another.

iStockphoto.com/chameleonseye

LEARNING **QUESTIONS**

6.1 How do we define what is deviant, and what do sociological theories suggest about the causes of deviant behavior, including crime?

6.2 How do individual-level theories of deviance differ from structural-level theories of deviance?

6.3 What are the social processes involved in creating social norms?

6.4 How do individuals manage deviant identities?

Defining Deviance

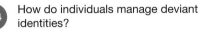

6.1 How do we define what is deviant, and what do sociological theories suggest about the causes of deviant behavior, including crime?

Think about and jot down five acts you consider to be "deviant." Now rank those five acts from 1 (least deviant of the five acts) to 5 (most deviant of the five acts). What guided your rankings? Perhaps you considered how unusual the acts were (is this a typical behavior or something that rarely occurs?), the societal reactions to them (would onlookers call the police or simply laugh?), or the harm they produce (was anyone injured or were some people just offended?). You have just shown that you have your own sense of what makes a behavior deviant. But is your personal understanding of deviance reflected in sociological definitions? That depends. There are many approaches to the conceptualization of deviance. The word *conceptualization* refers to how we define a concept, like deviance, so that researchers can measure it. If we are interested in studying deviance from a sociological perspective, we must first figure out how to conceptualize deviance.

First, we must consider what can be deviant. Sociologists argue that it is not just behaviors that can be deviant but also conditions and beliefs. For example, medical conditions, such as a facial disfigurement or having a feared disease like leprosy or AIDS, can be considered deviant. And subscribing to beliefs that are out of sync with the broader culture's belief system, such as believing that humans are alien life forms that will return to their home planet upon death, can also be considered deviant. But why are some behaviors, conditions, and beliefs considered deviant? The answer depends on the definition, or approach, used.

Approaches to Defining Deviance

The central question when conceptualizing deviance is, Deviance from what? There are statistical, legalistic, and normative approaches to defining deviance.

The Statistical Approach. If, when you ranked the five deviant acts you came up with, your rankings depended on how unusual the behaviors are, then you were using a **statistical approach** to the definition of deviance. Statistics are about probability and likelihood. Therefore, the statistical approach treats as deviant anything that is statistically unusual or anything that has a low probability or likelihood. It is about deviance from what is usual or common. When people defend their behavior by saying "everyone does it" (say, when "fudging" on their taxes or driving recklessly or drinking excessively), they are invoking a statistical conceptualization of deviance. But consider that the average twenty-year-old woman in the United States is five feet, four inches tall, with fewer than 5 percent under five feet, zero inches, and fewer than 5 percent over five feet, nine inches (Centers for Disease Control and Prevention 2000). Using a statistical approach, we would say that a six-foot-tall twenty-year-old woman is deviant. But being tall does not meet the criteria most sociologists use to determine what is and isn't deviant. Instead, most approaches are about deviance from social norms.

Social Norms. As we discussed in Chapter 4, social norms are rules of behavior that tell us what is and isn't acceptable in a given culture. Sociologists identify three types of norms: folkways, mores, and laws (Sumner 1907). Folkways are the rules that guide everyday behavior, and responses to violation are mild. Think about the person who speaks too loudly in a library or uses a urinal directly next to another person when there are other options. They have violated folkways. Mores (pronounced "mor-ays") are more serious rules that carry moral weight and, when violated, evoke harsher responses. Let's imagine that our rude library patron exposed himself or herself sexually to other library visitors. Laws, when violated, can result in formal punishments, as they are rules formalized by the state. Unsurprisingly, many mores (e.g., against killing, stealing, and exposing one's sexual organs in public spaces) are codified in law.

The Legalistic Approach. If your rankings of the so-called deviant acts in Doing Sociology 6.1 depended on whether the behavior was illegal, then you were using a **legalistic approach** to defining deviance. In this approach, any violation of the law is necessarily deviant.

RENA C. ZITO

As a young person, I saw adolescence as a kind of identity toy store where I could play with new, offbeat personas and see if I liked them, keeping the parts that felt right and discarding the rest. I also loved acting and improv, which was like wandering through the identity toy store in overdrive. Being able to manipulate how others perceived me, to create my own reality, felt like magic. This is probably why I fell in love with sociology while learning about symbolic interaction at the University of Rhode Island. I'd found my intellectual home. I double-majored in sociology and psychology and decided to pursue a PhD in sociology at North Carolina State University.

I have taught criminology, family sociology, and quantitative methods at Elon University and other institutions for a decade now, developing courses like Gender and Crime and heading our criminal justice studies program. I still get just as excited about the learning process as I did when I was newly on the other side of it. But I'm still learning all the time, too, as I conduct research on families, adolescents, and criminal behavior.

Therefore, shoplifting would be considered deviant, but your professor wearing a Halloween costume to work (not on Halloween) would not, as the latter would be a violation of a folkway but not a law.

This approach requires us to distinguish between crime, sin, and poor taste (Smith and Pollack 1976). Crimes are violations of the law, such as assault, kidnapping, theft, or murder. Sins are deviant acts, conditions, or beliefs that violate religious or moral prohibitions, many of which are not subject to legal regulation, such as promiscuity or eating food deemed impure by one's religion. Sins are violations of mores, not folkways or laws. Behaviors, conditions, or beliefs in poor taste are violations of customs or etiquette, such as picking one's nose in public or wearing a bikini as classroom attire. Folkways indicate what is and is not in poor taste in a given culture. The legalistic approach considers only crime as deviant.

The Normative Approach. If, in your rankings, you considered what would evoke a disapproving response from others, then you were using a **normative approach**. Unlike the legalistic view of deviance, the normative approach considers violations of any norms—folkways, mores, or laws. And unlike in the statistical approach, behaviors, conditions, and beliefs need not be statistically unusual to be deviant in this perspective. Rather, the collective disapproving response, or sanctions, they garner is sufficient for making them deviant.

Sanctions. When people break rules they face **sanctions**, which are punishments or penalties. Sanctions can range from benign, informal penalties, such as being ignored or gossiped about, to serious, formal punishment, such as imprisonment or execution. Who is imposing the sanction determines whether the sanction is informal or formal. *Formal sanctions* are enacted by official agents of the state, such as local law enforcement, Child Protective Services, or the Drug Enforcement Administration. *Informal sanctions* come from nonofficial sources, including friends, family members, and strangers.

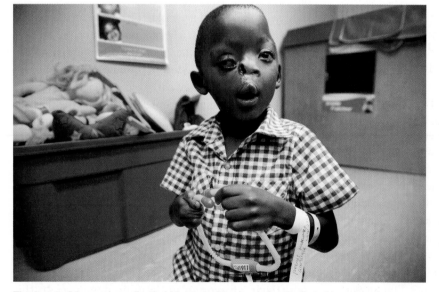

This boy, in Johannesburg, South Africa, is waiting to receive the first of two surgeries. Without the surgeries, he would face life with a deviant stigma because of his facial features.

Mary-Ann Palmer/Foto24/Gallo Images/Getty Images

DOING SOCIOLOGY 6.1

DEVIANCE IN THE ASHLEY MADISON HACK

In this exercise, you will consider the layers of potentially deviant behavior involved in identifying users of a web site intended to facilitate extramarital affairs.

AshleyMadison.com was a dating web site, but unlike other dating sites, this one was for married people seeking to have extramarital affairs. In July 2015, a group of hackers calling themselves "The Impact Team" stole the Ashley Madison user data and later released users' personally identifying information, including email addresses. Outcomes of the data breach included public shaming of users, extortion attempts, potentially serious legal consequences (e.g., 1,200 users had email addresses from Saudi Arabia, where infidelity can result in capital punishment), and even several suicides of publicly humiliated users.

The AshleyMadison.com data breach entailed multiple forms of so-called deviance: the theft and public release of the information by "The Impact Team," the marital infidelity (intended or actual) of the site's users, and the suicides that resulted.

With a partner or individually, write your answers to the following questions:

1. Which of these three do you consider the most deviant, and why?

2. Do you reject the label of "deviant" for any of these behaviors? Why or why not?

3. Considering both legal punishments and personal repercussions, who was likely punished most severely—the web site operators, the web site users, or the hackers? How would you match the severity of the punishment with the severity of the deviance? Explain.

Assumptions about Social Reality and Perspectives on Deviance

Defining deviance requires that we make assumptions about social reality. What is good and acceptable in the social world (i.e., what we ought to do, value, and believe) is either the result of social interactions and the meanings we collectively decide upon or is objectively real, irrespective of the definitions we agree upon. Consider our offending library patron. Is sexually exposing oneself in a library deviant because we, as members of society, consider it to be unacceptable? If so, that would mean that in another cultural setting, such behavior could be nondeviant. Or is deviance part of the inherent character of the act, such that exposing oneself in public is deviant regardless of cultural circumstances? If you subscribe to the first perspective, as many sociologists do, then you are making relativist assumptions. The second perspective reflects absolutist assumptions.

Relativist Perspective. According to those who maintain a **relativist perspective**, behaviors, conditions, and beliefs are deviant only to the extent that cultures regard them as deviant. Deviance is not an inherent characteristic of an act but, rather, is the result of social construction. Social construction, as we saw in Chapter 4, is the creation of the social world through interaction and the shared understandings that emerge from interaction.

For example, money (or gold or beads or whatever is used for trade in a society) has no inherent value. Instead, it becomes valuable because we define it as valuable in interaction with others. Behaviors (or conditions or beliefs), like money, have meaning because we ascribe meaning to them. Exposing oneself in a library and joining a dating web site for married people are deviant acts to the extent that we collectively regard these acts as deviant and react to them with disapproval. Thus, in this view, deviance is subjective, or relative.

Absolutist Perspective. The **absolutist perspective**, in contrast, states that some behaviors, conditions, and beliefs are inherently, objectively deviant. Deviance is part of their nature. Even if we do not treat them as deviant, they remain deviant. For example, if we were to regard marriage among first cousins as inherently deviant and unacceptable, then the acceptance of such marriages in many societies throughout the world—about one in ten marriages worldwide are between first or second cousins—would not change the deviance of the act (Kershaw 2009). The definition of first-cousin marriage as deviant, in this example, is absolute rather than relative to the culture in which it develops (or fails to develop).

Research Approaches versus Individual Morality. Most deviance scholars use a relativist lens when studying human behavior. That is, they put aside—or attempt to

APPLYING STATISTICAL, LEGALISTIC, AND NORMATIVE APPROACHES

In this exercise, you will compare and contrast statistical, legalistic, and normative approaches to understanding deviance.

Individually or in groups of three or four, think about and write down some behaviors, conditions, and beliefs that fit the following criteria:

- Deviant using a statistical approach but not a legalistic approach

- Deviant using a normative approach but not a statistical approach

- Deviant using all of the approaches

Write your responses to the following questions:

1. Which of the approaches best captures your own understanding of what constitutes deviance? Why do you think that approach is best?

2. Which of the deviant acts involved in the Ashley Madison hack (see Doing Sociology 6.1) meet the criteria for the statistical, legalistic, and normative approaches?

put aside—their own feelings and biases so that they can understand behaviors, conditions, and beliefs from the perspective of so-called deviants. For example, Vanessa Panfil (2017) spent time with and interviewed gay gang members in Ohio. She recounted the daily lives, illicit behavior, relationships, and identities of the men she studied in her book *The Gang's All Queer: The Lives of Gay Gang Members*. She did not pass judgment on her research participants or engage in ethnocentrism. Ethnocentrism occurs when people evaluate other cultures on the basis of the standards of their own culture. Instead, Panfil understood her participants from the perspective of the subcultures in which they lived.

CONSIDER THIS

Imagine a world without any deviance—what would that look like?

Using a relativist lens in research does not mean that sociologists do not have strong moral positions about the behaviors, conditions, and beliefs they study. For example, in the research for his book *The Stickup Kids*, about armed robbers and torturers, sociologist Randol Contreras (2012) uses a relativist lens while recognizing his own moral opposition to his research participants' violent behaviors and racist and sexist attitudes. Taking an absolutist moral stance as an individual—for instance, by opposing gender

inequality or violations of human rights—does not preclude using a relativist perspective in research.

Conflict/Critical Perspective. The conflict perspective (also known as the critical perspective) on deviance is a subtype of the relativist approach. Like all relativist perspectives, the conflict perspective regards deviance as socially constructed. It stands apart in that it emphasizes the role of social power in determining who and what is considered deviant. In this view, the label of "deviant" (and "criminal") is wielded as a weapon against the vulnerable in society and used to preserve and increase the social, economic, and political dominance of powerful groups. Conflict thinkers ask, Who benefits from this definition? For instance, in their now-classic text *The Rich Get Richer and the Poor Get Prison*, Jeffrey Reiman and Paul Leighton (2017) argue that the legal system operates as a carnival mirror that distorts the threats that face us, treating the minor deviance of the poor (e.g., illicit drug use and petty theft) as serious crimes and the harmful deviance of the wealthy (e.g., unsafe workplaces, environmental crimes, and corporate fraud) as minor wrongdoings. Theirs is a critical perspective.

"Nuts, Sluts, and Perverts" or "Deviant Heroes"?

What is in a name? The word *deviant* conjures up images of the outcast, the sexual psychopath, the persons and practices on the fringes of society. In 1972, sociologist Alexander Liazos argued forcefully against a "sociology of deviance." Attempting to humanize

DEVIANTS OR DEVIANT HEROES?

In this exercise, you will apply concepts in the sociology of deviance to NFL players who protest racial injustice by kneeling during the national anthem.

On August 14, 2016, San Francisco 49ers player Colin Kaepernick sat down during the national anthem in protest, stating, "I am not going to stand up to show pride in a flag for a country that oppresses Black people and people of color." Since then, about 200 NFL players have joined Kaepernick in kneeling or sitting during the anthem in protest.

Write your answers to the following questions. Be prepared to share your responses with your classmates.

1. What kind of social norms are the kneeling NFL players violating? What kinds of social norms are they challenging through their protest?

2. What would a relativist likely claim about the NFL protests? What about a proponent of the conflict perspective?

3. Public responses to the kneeling NFL players are deeply divided. Why do you think that is? Use the term "social construction" in your answer.

4. What other modern-day social movement participants are regarded as "deviant heroes" by some and just "deviants" by others?

---

so-called deviants—Liazos used the phrase "nuts, sluts, and perverts" to identify those of greatest interest to sociologists at the time—and to demonstrate that deviance and conformity are products of shared conditions. He argued that the creation of a sociology of deviance necessitates treating deviance as distinct from other behavior. Sociologists had, it seemed, created the very conditions they sought to abolish—stigmatizing those who do not conform to social norms. The solution? Liazos favored discontinuing the use of the term *deviant*, suggesting instead *victimization*, *persecution*, and *oppression*, which he believed better characterized the experiences of those on the fringes. What do you think? Should this chapter have a different title? If so, what should it be?

Sociologists have also argued that deviance is a requirement for social change (Wolf and Zuckerman 2012). Unjust and harmful social conditions will continue unless people challenge them by breaking the rules. Take, for instance, the Greensboro Four, a group of four African American college students who, in 1960, refused to leave a Woolworth's "Whites only" lunch counter until they were served. Their behavior was deviant in the Jim Crow South. Positive social change required their deviance. Can you think of any examples of "deviant heroes" today?

Check Your Understanding

- What are the three types of norms?
- What are the differences and similarities between the statistical, legalistic, and normative approaches to defining deviance?
- What are the differences between the relativist perspective, the absolutist perspective, and the conflict/critical perspective?
- Why is the "sociology of deviance" a controversial idea?

Origins of the Sociology of Deviance

6.2 How do individual-level theories of deviance differ from structural-level theories of deviance?

Think about the last time you heard about a mass shooting, a bank robbery, or the suicide of a celebrity. Or perhaps think about the last time you saw a stranger dressed or acting unusually. You may have wondered, Why do some people violate norms? And why do other people conform to them? Sociology has addressed these questions since its inception several centuries ago.

Early Perspectives in the Sociology of Deviance and Crime

Many early thinkers focused on biological abnormalities as the root causes of crime and deviance. For instance, nineteenth-century criminologist Cesare Lombroso and his contemporaries believed some people were "born criminals," with innate criminal tendencies, a perspective that has been thoroughly discredited (Lombroso 1876). Émile Durkheim, often regarded as a founder of sociology, transformed the scientific study of deviance in the late nineteenth century. Unlike Lombroso, Durkheim (1964 [1895],

The whipping of Quakers in Puritan Boston in the 1670s.

1951 [1897]) offered a theory of deviance that showed how deviance can benefit society and explained variation in rates of deviance across places, groups, and time periods. Rather than answer the question "Why do some individuals engage in deviance?" theorists like Durkheim seek to answer the question "Why do some places, groups, or time periods experience more deviance than others?"

Durkheim's Sociological Theory of Suicide. In the summer of 2018, fashion designer Kate Spade and celebrity chef and TV personality Anthony Bourdain committed suicide. In the weeks that followed, headlines proclaimed various possible causes of the suicides, including struggles with depression. Like those headlines, most of us gravitate to individual-level explanations when we think about suicide. We consider the effects of a person's mental illness, health problems, money troubles, or relationship woes. Durkheim's (1951 [1897]) classic book *Suicide*, in contrast, implores its readers to consider how the organization of societies gives rise to, or inhibits, suicide. He noted that some countries had consistently high rates of suicide and others had consistently low rates of suicide. This led Durkheim to conclude that characteristics of societies—namely, their ability to regulate behavior and foster social solidarity—mattered for deviance, including suicide.

Durkheim argued that norms become unclear and fail to constrain deviant behavior in the face of rapid social changes. He called this condition anomie. **Anomie** is a state in which a society's norms fail to regulate behavior. In anomic societies, the bond between the individual and the community breaks down, and society loses its moral force as personal and societal standards of behavior fail to align.

Let's put Anthony Bourdain's tragic suicide in sociological perspective. Bourdain, as a White, sixty-one-year-old man, was part of a demographic group with one of the highest rates of suicide in the United States. Examine Figure 6.1 and consider the following: How might Durkheim make sense of the high level of suicide among older White men in the United States? For instance, do older White men tend to be less connected to family life or religious institutions than younger White men or Black and Hispanic people?

Durkheim and the Normality of Crime. Durkheim's ideas about anomie were part of his larger structural functionalist perspective on human societies. Structural functionalism (also called functionalism) claims that all social activity, including crime and deviance, should be understood in terms of what it contributes to society, as we read about in Chapter 2. The very fact of its existence must mean, from the functionalist perspective, that it provides some necessary, positive function for society. Unsurprisingly, then, Durkheim argued that crime and deviance were normal and necessary aspects of human societies.

Durkheim points out that all societies, in all time periods, define some behaviors as deviant or criminal and that a society without crime is impossible. To understand this, Durkheim suggests that we imagine a society of saints. Everyone is, by our standards, exceptionally well behaved. No one steals or fights or paints graffiti. But there will still be behaviors that are regarded and punished as crime. Crime might be raising one's voice or speaking out of turn. The definition of crime will look different from our standards, but there must be *something* that is criminal, because crime serves a necessary function for society. If it didn't, crime would not exist in all societies. The purpose of punishment, therefore, is not to reduce crime (we need it!). Instead, it is to assert our shared values (Durkheim 1964 [1895]).

Suicide Death Rates by Age, Sex, and Race/Ethnicity, 2014

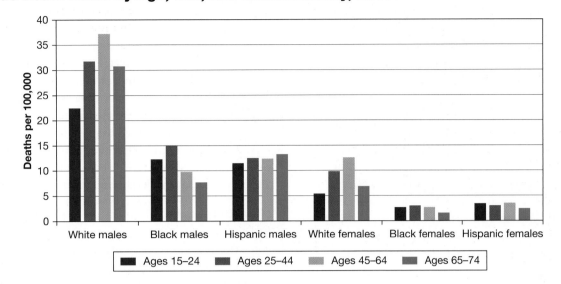

Source: Curtin, Warner, and Hedegaard, "Suicide Rates for Females and Males by Race and Ethnicity: United States, 1999 and 2014," Centers for Disease Control and Prevention, April 2016.

Note: Death rates per 100,000 resident population.

CONSIDER THIS

By coming together to punish deviants, we make visible the moral boundaries of our community. In what ways might social media serve the same function as the public square did in the past for the control of deviants and the expression of collective anger? In what ways might it fail to make us aware of our moral boundaries?

According to Durkheim's functionalist view, when deviance increases, the bar for being defined as "deviant" rises. Once deviant behaviors become normative or are at least no longer criminalized. Consider the contemporary example of cohabitation, or couples living together while unmarried. This formerly deviant and even sometimes criminal behavior—it was once illegal for unmarried couples to rent a room together in many states in the United States—is now, for many couples in the United States, a normal stage in romantic relationships. Or consider the legalization of recreational marijuana use in multiple U.S. states from Durkheim's perspective. Can you think of other examples of deviance being redefined?

Check Your Understanding

- What is the difference between individual-level and structural-level theories of deviance?

- What was Durkheim's perspective on suicide, and how did it differ from individual-level explanations of suicide?

- What is the functionalist perspective on crime and deviance?

Creating Deviance

6.3 What are the social processes involved in creating social norms?

Deviance is social. It cannot exist without a shared notion of what is deemed unacceptable or abnormal. The origins of those shared notions are the focus of this section: Just how do we come to define some behaviors, conditions, or beliefs as deviant? In other words, how is deviance socially constructed?

Moral Entrepreneurship

In some instances, individuals or groups, called **moral entrepreneurs,** actively seek to change norms to align with their own moral worldview (Becker [1963] 1973), often while taking part in social movements, which are the focus of Chapter 16. It may help to think about the meaning of the word *entrepreneur*: an organizer or operator of a business enterprise who, through risk and initiative, seeks to make a profit. A moral entrepreneur is in the business of manufacturing public morality. The profit is the widespread change in norms and the enforcement of them. Consider, for example, the antialcohol crusaders of the pre-Prohibition era in the United States. Temperance groups of the nineteenth and early twentieth centuries sought to change the norms surrounding drinking through religious and family-centered appeals as well as through the lobbying efforts that ultimately resulted in the Eighteenth Amendment, which prohibited the manufacture, transport, and sale of alcohol (ratified in 1920 and repealed in 1933). The Anti-Saloon League and the Women's Christian Temperance Union, antialcohol movements, were moral entrepreneurs.

Rule Creators and Rule Enforcers.

Moral entrepreneurs comprise both rule creators and rule enforcers. Rule creators campaign to have their definition of deviance taken seriously. They seek to transform private troubles into public issues through the creation of new norms. Once new rules are created, rule enforcers seek to ensure that the rules are not violated. The role of enforcer is not limited to formal agents of control, such as police and judges. Anyone can be a rule enforcer. This can include parents, neighbors, teachers, employers, or anyone else who imposes sanctions on rule violators.

Creating Public Morality.

Creating public morality requires two steps: generating awareness (or claims making) and moral conversion (Spector and Kitsuse 1977). To illustrate this social process, let's use an example: imagine you are a moral entrepreneur who is concerned with teenagers texting one another sexually explicit photographs of themselves (or "sexting").

Generating awareness involves multiple tasks. First, you need to provide danger messages: "Something must be done, and it must be done now! Your child could be next! And these images will haunt them for the rest of their lives!" Danger messages like these move people to action.

Next, you will need testimonials from "experts" who support your position. Your experts might include child psychologists or high school teachers who have discovered sexts on students' phones. Then you will need to provide data in a compelling (and potentially misleading) way. For example, note that the rate of sexting has increased astronomically over the past ten years (but fail to mention that smartphone ownership and texting have also increased during that time period). Not all data provided by moral

entrepreneurs are necessarily misleading, though. You may also note the percentage of teenagers who report sending or receiving sexts in national surveys. You will then need to highlight unambiguous cases that evoke an emotional response and have no moral gray area. For example, you might highlight the case of a non–sexually active, honor roll student who was pressured into sending a sexually explicit photo that was then plastered all over the web, causing the student to commit suicide. Some claims making also includes the presentation of a syndrome, or the idea that the offending behavior is pathological, akin to a sickness in need of a cure. You could, for instance, present teenage sexting as an addiction requiring intervention.

Moral Conversion.

Once the problem has been identified and awareness generated, moral entrepreneurs must convert people to their position. Moral conversion has three primary components. First, media attention must be sought. Public demonstrations, boycotts, and marches are useful for attracting coverage. Second, moral entrepreneurs must seek endorsements from respected public figures, typically nonexperts. Third, they must form coalitions, or partnerships, with powerful groups with shared interests, such as political organizations, religious groups, or professional associations. For your antisexting moral entrepreneurship, you might organize demonstrations at political events, obtain the support of a famous parent (such as an actress who plays a beloved sitcom mother and also has her own teenage children), and gain the support of the National Campaign to Prevent Teen Pregnancy and the organization Focus on the Family.

Moral Panic

Successful moral entrepreneurship can sometimes lead to a moral panic. A **moral panic** is an exaggerated, widespread fear regarding the collapse of public morality. Those blamed for the collapse and therefore treated as threats to the social order are called **folk devils** (Cohen 1972). Folk devils become the target of the public's anxieties about contemporary social life and the future, and they are blamed for a host of social problems. In a moral panic, the fear of a folk devil is out of proportion to its actual threat to society, even when the folk devil does, in some measure, contribute to some social problems. In some cases, folk devils are falsely blamed or even entirely imaginary.

In October 2018, U.S. news outlets began reporting on a "migrant caravan" composed of several thousand Central Americans—primarily from Honduras—who were making the 2,500-mile trek, on foot, to the United States to escape violence in their home countries. This

Moral entrepreneurs worked to establish the Eighteenth Amendment, which prohibited the manufacture and sale of alcohol in the United States until its repeal in 1933.

group of asylum seekers took on the characteristics of a folk devil, becoming a vehicle for public anxieties regarding crime, jobs, and the future of the middle class. Although those anxieties are certainly real, the blame is misplaced, with immigrants operating as scapegoats for these very real social problems. For example, a large body of criminological research on crime and immigration—including undocumented immigration—demonstrates that, controlling for other predictors of crime such as poverty, concentrations of first-generation immigrants have either no effect on crime rates or even reduce crime (Ousey and Kubrin 2018).

Examining drug scares, or moral panics focused on substances (e.g., alcohol, marijuana, cocaine), Craig Reinarman (1994) identifies what he calls "key ingredients" of any full-scale scare. Although his focus was on drugs, we can observe how these ingredients constitute many other kinds of moral panics. For example, the crack cocaine drug scare of the 1980s included many of the ingredients listed in Table 6.1: people were using crack cocaine (kernel of truth); there was a great deal of media attention given to the "crack epidemic," particularly focusing on so-called crack babies born to addicted women (media magnification); politicians focused their attention on crack, passing legislation that provided harsh penalties for even low levels of possession (politico-moral entrepreneurs); crack was portrayed as a drug solely of the Black urban underclass despite use across demographic groups (linking to a "dangerous class"); and crack markets and crack use were blamed for entrenched urban poverty rather than seen as the result of poverty (scapegoating for public problems).

Medicalization of Deviance

The modern era has seen a transformation in the social construction of deviance. Many behaviors, conditions,

Reinarman's Key Ingredients in a Drug Scare

Ingredient	Description
Kernel of truth	Drug use is occurring, providing some foundation for claims that the behavior is problematic.
Media magnification	Sensationalized media accounts create "routinization of caricature" wherein extreme cases are presented as typical.
Politico-moral entrepreneurs	Individuals or groups, often including political elites, take on the cause of changing behavior and laws.
Professional interest groups	Professional groups (e.g., the American Medical Association, law enforcement agencies) vie for "ownership" of the drug problem so that they may get to define its solution.
Historical context of conflict	Social context must be fertile for a scare, with mounting anxieties (e.g., about the economy, culture, politics) making the public receptive to defining certain people as "problems."
Linking to a "dangerous class"	The scare is not about the drug itself but, rather, the persons said to use the drug. Drug use will be defined as a "problem" (and a moral panic ensues) to the extent that it is associated with a group perceived as threatening.
Scapegoating for an array of public problems	The drug is blamed for a host of social problems that already existed and that are often only indirectly related to drug use.

and beliefs once attributed to the deviant's evil character, or "badness," are now constructed as due to pathology of the mind, or "madness." The transition from badness to madness is also referred to as the **medicalization of deviance**. What was once evidence of sin is now evidence of sickness, and sickness can be treated. This can be seen in the growth of the American Psychological Association's fifth edition of the *Diagnostic and Statistical Manual of Mental Disorders* (*DSM*). The most recent edition contains more than 300 disorders, described in the 947-page text, including "exhibitionistic disorder" (exposing one's genitals to others to gain sexual satisfaction), "kleptomania" (compulsive stealing), and "female sexual interest/arousal disorder" (inability to attain or maintain sexual arousal). In contrast, the first edition of the *DSM*, published in 1952, was less than 150 pages in length and contained just 106 disorders. Although the growth in the *DSM* may simply reflect a more nuanced understanding of mental health conditions, it is clear that many human experiences that differ from the norm are now diagnosable.

CONSIDER THIS

What do you think led to the medicalization of deviance and the movement away from a "badness" orientation and toward a "madness" orientation? What are the social consequences—good and bad—of the medicalization of deviance?

Labeling Perspective

So far, this section has addressed how behaviors, conditions, and beliefs are socially constructed as deviant. This next portion will describe how certain individuals (or groups) come to be regarded as deviant through a process of **labeling**. The labeling perspective has its roots in symbolic interaction.

As seen in earlier chapters, symbolic interaction posits that human action is driven by the meanings that individuals ascribe to people, objects, and interactions. The meanings themselves are the result of social interaction and are subject to change. Consider, for example, a young man standing outside a convenience store. He is there to register voters. But a passerby, seeing the young man's well-worn clothing and unkempt appearance, assumes that he is there to panhandle and averts her eyes and picks up her pace to avoid interaction. Her behavior is driven by the meaning she has ascribed to his appearance. His behavior, in response, will result from the meaning he attaches to her avoidance behavior. Symbolic interactionists argue that sociologists should examine how people experience the social world, including how their interactions create—and are the result of—interpretations that are attached to symbols (i.e., people, objects, and interactions).

Labeling theory emphasizes the power of definitions. Who is defined, or labeled, as deviant is the result of a social process in which others react as though the person is deviant. Although deviant labeling may be related to rule-violating behavior, it is the *reaction* rather than the behavior itself that produces the label of deviant. Following this logic, no actual rule-violating behavior is necessary for the deviant label to be applied. The man outside the convenience store is a deviant because of the woman's reaction, not because of any behavior or belief he may hold. Moreover, labels have the power to transform people. He who is treated as deviant becomes deviant.

The Thomas Theorem. Labeling theory relies on the logic of the Thomas theorem: "If men define situations as real, they are real in their consequences" (Thomas and Thomas 1928, 572). Franklin Tannenbaum (1938), an early labeling theorist, referred to this as the "dramatization of evil." Tannenbaum's focus was on youth behavior. He argued that police reactions to the ordinary rule-breaking behaviors of adolescents construct them as deviant or "bad." The social interplay of the adolescent and the police (the drama) is what creates the "evil," not the act itself. For instance, imagine two friends who get into an argument at school that leads to shoving and then punches being thrown. Are these just teenagers blowing off steam or are they criminals committing assault? It depends on whether they end up in the principal's office or the backseat of a police cruiser. And where they end up depends on how school authorities and the police already view them—"good kids" get the principal's office, "bad kids" get the police cruiser. Deviant labeling thus operates as a kind of self-fulfilling prophecy wherein it "sets in motion several mechanisms which conspire to shape the person in the image people have of him" (Becker [1963] 1973). The definition makes it so.

Primary and Secondary Deviance. Edwin Lemert (1951) elaborated on Tannenbaum's ideas, discerning between primary and secondary deviance. **Primary deviance** is rule breaking in which individuals engage in the absence of a deviant label. They do not regard themselves as deviant, nor—so far—do others. A great deal of primary deviance goes undetected. But sometimes it is identified and reacted to as deviant. Further rule-breaking behavior that occurs as a result of a deviant label is called **secondary deviance**.

To illustrate, let's imagine there are two people attending a party. Both get behind the wheel after drinking too much.

Because of their social location, poor Black and Hispanic youth are more likely to be perceived (and treated) as deviant than wealthier, White youth.

Michael Matthews—Police Images/Alamy Stock Photo

Both cause accidents involving other drivers who are badly injured. Person A drives away from the scene and is not caught. Person B cannot drive away from the scene because his car is badly damaged in the collision. Person B is arrested and ultimately pleads guilty to felony DUI with injury. As a result, person B is sentenced to twelve months in state prison and now has a felony record. The drunk driving that led to the label of "felon" for person B (and didn't for person A) was primary deviance. According to the labeling perspective, the "felon" label will increase the risk that person B will go on to engage in other criminal acts, or secondary deviance. Person A, in comparison, avoided a deviant label that would increase her likelihood of future rule breaking.

Official and Informal Labels and Stigmas. The label of "felon" in the example above is an official label. *Official labels* are labels applied by an authority, such as the state (e.g., felon, delinquent, sex offender), the military (e.g., dishonorably discharged), a school (e.g., truant), or a hospital (e.g., mentally ill, HIV positive). Official labels, because they are documented by recognized authorities, are difficult to shed and have important consequences for obtaining resources, such as jobs and housing. *Informal labels*, in contrast, occur when a person has been deemed deviant by family members, teachers, coworkers, or neighbors. Both official and informal labels are stigmatizing. **Stigma** is a mark of disgrace and interactions that communicate that one is disgraced, dishonorable, or otherwise deviant.

The stigmatizing reactions of both official authorities and everyday people matter for secondary deviance

CREATING A MORE JUST SOCIETY FOR ALL

SARAH SHANNON

I sometimes like to tell students that the best job I ever got with my sociology degree was cleaning toilets. Usually there's some nervous laughter while they wait for the punchline. My first job after my BA was at a home health agency, where my main task was supervising child protective visits between parents and their children in foster care, but I also filled out my hours doing housekeeping for other agency clients. This brought me into daily contact with some of society's most stigmatized people—parents accused of abusing or neglecting their children and people with serious mental health challenges. This job was the beginning of "sociology in action" for me.

Later I worked for an employment services agency helping people with criminal records find jobs. My clients' records ranged from minor drug offenses to more serious convictions, such as sex offenses. I was floored by the seemingly insurmountable obstacles put in front of people who were earnestly trying to reintegrate into society. Even my clients with very minor records could not get an interview, much less a job. Once I returned to graduate school, initially for a master of social work degree and ultimately a PhD in sociology, there was no doubt that I wanted to study these kinds of issues and help improve public policy and reduce stigma.

Along with collaborators similarly dedicated to doing research that is relevant and accessible to the public, I have worked on a range of projects focused on how the criminal justice and social welfare systems affect social inequality. For example, despite the fact that you can easily find out anyone's criminal history with a few keystrokes on Google, we don't know exactly how many people in the United States have criminal records. One of my collaborative projects has been to estimate the number of people who have ever been to prison (about 7.6 million) and who have ever been convicted of a felony (nearly 20 million). We regularly receive requests from the media and policy makers asking for these numbers, especially as they relate to employment and voting (in some states, you cannot vote if you have a felony conviction).

I am also studying how young adults navigate reentering their communities after spending time away in various institutions, including prison but also other places like mental health treatment and the military. This qualitative study reveals in depth just how hard these transitions can be and how individuals struggle to form identities and forge "successes" for themselves despite the stigma and barriers they face. In another project, I am working with collaborators in seven other states to uncover how states use monetary sanctions (fines, fees, etc.) to fund their criminal justice systems, often at the expense of their poorest citizens. Taken together, these research projects allow me to make an impact by creating knowledge that students, academics, and the broader public can use to make sense of our social systems and, hopefully, create a more just society for us all.

Discussion Question: Dr. Shannon writes that even her "clients with very minor records could not get an interview, much less a job." What are the ramifications of this for clients, their families, their communities, and society?

Sarah Shannon is an assistant professor of sociology at the University of Georgia.

because they can lead to role engulfment. **Role engulfment** occurs when the deviant role takes over people's other social roles because others relate to them in response to their "spoiled identities" (Goffman 1963). For example, if a person has a felony record, like person B in the DUI example above, then others may, to the extent that they know about the spoiled identity, relate to that person on the basis of his felon status, including landlords who won't rent to him, employers who won't hire him, and men or women who won't date him. In some instances, the deviant label—or spoiled identity—becomes a **master status**, or the primary status by which others interact with a person. Labels such as "sex offender" and "murderer" are particularly likely to become master statuses because of the extent of the stigma assigned to them.

Although early labeling theorists focused primarily on the impact of stigma on a person's view of himself or herself, contemporary theorists note that there are other reasons that stigmatizing labeling matters, including the creation of structural barriers to conventional life (e.g., the inability to get a job) and involvement in a deviant subculture that celebrates or at least tolerates spoiled identities.

DOING SOCIOLOGY 6.4

THE STIGMA OF OVERDOSE VIDEOS

In this activity, you will apply labeling theory concepts to what you read in a *New York Times* article titled "How Do You Recover after Millions Have Watched You Overdose?"

First, read the article found here: https://www.nytimes.com/2018/12/11/us/overdoses-youtube-opioids-drugs.html (or search "NY Times How Do You Recover after Millions Have Watched You Overdose?").

Then, in a one-page paper, answer the following questions:

1. What would a labeling theorist say about the impact of overdose videos on the people featured in those videos? Use the concepts of stigma, role engulfment, and master status in your answer. Use specific examples from the *New York Times* article.

2. One expert quoted in the article remarked, "The intent [of overdose videos] is not to help these people. The intent is to use them as an object lesson by scapegoating them." Sociologists similarly note that "folk devils" operate as scapegoats for social problems. On the basis of what you've read about moral panics and folk devils, do you think that individuals addicted to opioids are contemporary folk devils? Why or why not?

Social Position and Labeling. Social location—where one resides in a system of social stratification—is central in the labeling perspective. The power to define others as deviant and to resist having the label applied to oneself is linked to social position. Those with greater power—for example, politicians, professionals, and other members of the upper middle and upper classes—are better able to resist deviant labeling, even when their behavior does not differ from that of the less powerful "deviant."

Comparing the results of two sociological works allows us to see the effects of social location. In his book *Punished*, Victor Rios (2012) describes the "youth control complex" that characterizes the daily lives of low-income Black and Latino teenage boys in Oakland, California. In the boys' social world, the mundane misbehavior of adolescence (e.g., fighting, talking back to teachers) is treated as serious crime in need of criminal justice intervention. The boys are viewed by teachers, police, and business owners as potential criminals who must be managed, and there are few second chances for boys caught breaking the rules. The boys—marginalized economically, educationally, and racially and ethnically—were defined as a problem as soon as puberty hit and sometimes even before.

Scott Jacques and Richard Wright's (2015) *Code of the Suburb* examines a different group of teenage boys: White, middle-class drug dealers in a suburb of Atlanta, Georgia. Unlike the boys in *Punished*, the boys in *Code of the Suburb* are largely ignored by law enforcement, are regarded as upstanding young men, and experience few negative consequences of their lawbreaking behavior. Their privileges of wealth, race, and place enable them to resist detection and, when detected, stigmatizing labeling. In this chapter's Sociologists in Action, Sarah Shannon similarly studies the impact of stigmatizing labels on marginalized groups.

Howard Becker's Typology of Deviance. Howard Becker ([1963] 1973) refers to those labeled as deviant or criminal despite the absence of any actual deviant or criminal behavior as the "falsely accused." Marginalized, or relatively powerless, members of society are at greatest risk for being falsely accused, although certainly it can happen to others, such as the operators of the McMartin Preschool, who were falsely accused of satanic ritual abuse in the 1980s. As Table 6.2 notes, Becker described those who engage in deviance or crime as "pure deviants," as the label is a true reflection of their actions. The drug dealers in *Code of the Suburb* were what Becker called "secret deviants," because they avoided detection and labeling. Conformists, in contrast, do not engage in deviance behavior and are not labeled (we might also conceive of conformists as "pure nondeviants").

▼ TABLE 6.2

Becker's Typology of Deviance

	Deviant Behavior	Conforming Behavior
Labeled deviant	Pure deviant	Falsely accused
Not labeled deviant	Secret deviant	Conformist

WHICH STATES INCARCERATE THE MOST PEOPLE?

The United States has the highest incarceration rate of any nation on earth. There are 2.2 million people in our nation's prisons and jails, a number that has increased by more than 400 percent since 1980. In this online activity, you will consider how incarceration depends on place

and time by exploring state prison data from the U.S. Department of Justice.

*Requires the Vantage version of *Sociology in Action*.

▼ FIGURE 6.2

State Prisoner Imprisonment Rate, 2016

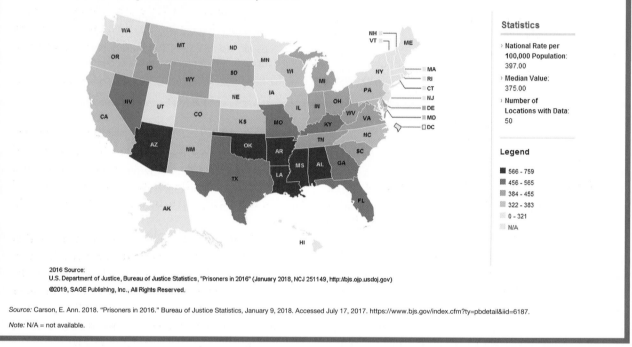

Statistics

› National Rate per 100,000 Population: 397.00
› Median Value: 375.00
› Number of Locations with Data: 50

Legend

■ 566 - 759
■ 456 - 565
■ 384 - 455
■ 322 - 383
□ 0 - 321
□ N/A

2016 Source:
U.S. Department of Justice, Bureau of Justice Statistics, "Prisoners in 2016" (January 2018, NCJ 251149, http://bjs.ojp.usdoj.gov)
@2019, SAGE Publishing, Inc., All Rights Reserved.

Source: Carson, E. Ann. 2018. "Prisoners in 2016." Bureau of Justice Statistics, January 9, 2018. Accessed July 17, 2017. https://www.bjs.gov/index.cfm?ty=pbdetail&iid=6187.

Note: N/A = not available.

CONSIDER THIS

Let's say that we accept that deviance is socially constructed, and therefore, behavior is deviant only to the extent that we react to it (or label it) as deviant. How then can there be secret deviance? Does the notion of secret deviance require us to take an absolutist stance on deviance? Why or why not?

Check Your Understanding

- What is moral entrepreneurship, and how do moral entrepreneurs generate awareness and convert others to their cause?

- Why do moral panics occur, and what are folk devils?

- What are the central claims of labeling theory (including symbolic interactionist assumptions, primary vs. secondary deviance, role engulfment, and master statuses)?

Managing Deviant Identities

6.4 How do individuals manage deviant identities?

Have you ever done something that violated your own code of ethics, such as stealing, cheating on a partner, or cheating on a test? If you have, then you have probably also sought to minimize the deviance of your act, either for yourself or for others. Perhaps you convinced yourself that you had no other choice, that you only did it because you had been drinking, or that it wasn't that big of a deal. You may have sought to justify or excuse your behavior using techniques of neutralization.

Techniques of Neutralization

Justifications and excuses allow rule violators to minimize, or neutralize, their deviance. Sociologists posit that to do "bad" while maintaining a sense of one's self as a "good" person, people must neutralize, or minimize, their deviance (Sykes and Matza 1957; Matza 2010). The strategies deviants use to maintain a positive self-concept, or **techniques of neutralization**, include the following:

1. **Denial of responsibility:** Offenders claim that they are not to blame. They may claim to be victims of circumstance or that the act was accidental or that they were subject to pressures beyond their control (e.g., alcohol or peer pressure). Denial of responsibility redefines the deviant as not culpable, reducing both social stigma and the feeling that one has failed oneself morally.

2. **Denial of injury:** Offenders say that they have not done anything wrong because either the act produced little or no harm or their intentions were not to inflict harm. This is a typical neutralization technique among those who engage in "victimless" offenses, such as drug use, as well as among those who can frame their behavior as victimless, even if another person is affected (e.g., auto thieves who use cars to "joyride," later returning them).

3. **Denial of victim:** Offenders acknowledge that their actions are harmful but refuse to acknowledge a legitimate victim. This can happen in two ways: either the offender claims that the victim deserved what happened, such as in cases of retaliatory violence, or the victim is unknown, abstract, or otherwise absent, such as in cases of fraud in which offenders never interact with and may not even know the names of their victims. In the former, the victim is denied status as a victim (i.e., "they had it coming"). In the latter, the victim is not visible and therefore is less of a burden on the offender's conscience.

4. **Condemning the condemners:** Offenders direct attention to those who judge them rather than their own behavior, claiming that those who condemn their actions have no right to do so because they are "hypocrites, deviants in disguise, or impelled by personal spite" (Sykes and Matza 1957, 668).

5. **Appeal to higher loyalties:** Offenders claim that the act was necessary to meet the moral obligations of a group even if it means violating another set of rules, such as laws. There are multiple, competing loyalties in the offender's life—to obey the law, to help friends, to assist coworkers, and so on. In this claim, the offender states that the loyalties to one group (e.g., to one's fraternity or to one's children) are more important—or higher—than the duty to obey the law or some other set of rules (e.g., religious prohibitions).

In their book *Identity Thieves*, Copes and Vieraitis (2012) describe the ways incarcerated identity thieves manage their spoiled identities. These offenders ranged from small-scale credit card thieves to mortgage fraudsters netting millions in illegal profits. They excused and justified their actions by denying injury, denying the victim, and appealing to higher loyalties. Examine the following quotations from the identity thieves they interviewed and see if you can identify the techniques of neutralization.

Danny: I mean, like, real identity theft, man I can't do that. Intentionally screw someone over—it's not right to me. So I couldn't do that. But corporations, banks, police departments, the government? Oh, yeah, let's go get 'em. Because that's the way they treat you, you know what I'm saying. If they done screwed me over, screw them! (p. 50)

Abbey: I did it for my son. I thought if I had money and I was able to live, have a nice place to live, and not have to worry about a car payment, I could just start a new life and that life is for him. . . . I just wanted my son to be happy and loved. (p. 52)

Dustin: With credit cards if you notify them that your credit cards were missing then [victims are] not liable. . . . The bank is gonna be insured, so the bank is gonna get their money back. The consumer is not gonna be hurt. Nobody really loses but the insurance companies. It's not taking from an individual per se, like a burglary. (p. 48)

Stigma Management

Techniques of neutralization allow individuals to minimize the deviance of their acts and maintain a positive self-concept, thereby avoiding a deviant identity. Once an identity has become spoiled, people can use strategies to reduce the stigma they receive as a result of their deviant condition, such as having an official deviant label, an unusual physical appearance, a physical or mental health condition, or uncommon gender or sexual identity. Stigma management strategies, or methods of reducing deviant stigma and maintaining a positive identity, differ depending on whether the stigma experienced is visible or invisible. Visible stigmas are those that are immediately apparent in face-to-face interaction (e.g., facial disfigurement or physical disabilities), whereas invisible stigmas can be hidden (e.g., sexual orientation, religious identities, or mental illness).

Managing Visible Stigmas. Managing visible stigmas involves **compensatory strategies**, in which individuals attempt to offset the deviance that is ascribed to them or make others more comfortable with their stigma. Compensatory strategies include acknowledgment, individuating information, and increased positivity. *Acknowledgment* occurs when a stigmatized person directly addresses his or her stigma in an attempt to relieve the tension in interaction. *Individuating information* involves revealing information about oneself to diminish the likelihood that the person with whom they are interacting will rely on stereotypical ideas about their status. *Increased positivity* is a kind of emotion work—or management of feelings, typically to preserve relationships—in which a stigmatized person intentionally tries to become more likable to counter the negative impact of stigma.

> ### CONSIDER THIS
>
> Think of a time you attempted to manage stigma, either visible or invisible. Did you use compensatory strategies, passing, or revealing? If so, were your efforts successful? Why or why not?

Managing Invisible Stigmas. Those whose identities may be spoiled as a result of invisible stigma have more options for managing their deviant identities, falling into two broad categories: passing and revealing. Passing involves attempts at presenting oneself as a member of a nonstigmatized group. Sociologists describe several forms of passing, including fabrication and concealment. *Fabrication* involves the presentation of a false identity. For example, in time periods, regions, and subcultural groups in which gay men, lesbians, and bisexuals are stigmatized and labeled deviant, fabrication may take the form of crafting a false heterosexual social identity at work. Unlike fabrication, *concealment* does not involve deception; rather, it involves taking steps to keep one's stigmatized identity hidden. For instance, in a study of dominatrices (a type of sex worker), Levey and Pinsky (2015) describe the strategies those who work in this sex industry used to hide their profession from friends and family. For instance, some used their second job as a "cover story" for how they made a living.

Revealing is a stigma management technique that intentionally and strategically makes the invisible stigma visible, including signaling, normalizing, and differentiating. *Signaling* is a revealing strategy that does not involve direct disclosure but instead relies on subtle or cryptic indications of one's deviant status. For instance, mentioning needing to pick up one's Prozac refill is a subtle signal of one's mental health status. Others seek to directly disclose their stigma but frame it for others as normal, called *normalizing.* An example would be a person who discusses his or her HIV status as though it were no different from any other nonstigmatized medical condition. *Differentiating* involves direct disclosure with the goal of differentiating oneself from the nonstigmatized group. In emphasizing differences, the revealer challenges others' perceptions and rejects stigmatizing labeling. It is a reclamation of one's identity. An example would be a transgender man who, while able to pass as biologically male from birth, chooses instead to identify as transgender in the workplace in the hope that the institution will become more inclusive of transgender workers and clients.

> ### CONSIDER THIS
>
> Think back to how you imagined the world would look without any deviance. How would you answer that question now?

Check Your Understanding

- What are the distinctions among the five techniques of neutralization, and what do they accomplish for individuals with deviant identities?
- What are some stigma management strategies for those with visible stigmas?
- What are some stigma management strategies for those with invisible stigmas?

Conclusion

Sociologists regard deviance as any behaviors, conditions, or beliefs that violate norms (i.e., folkways, mores, and laws) and/or are penalized with stigmatizing sanctions, consistent with a relativistic, social constructionist view of the social world. Sociologists focus on how the organization of societies (i.e., social structure) and individuals' relative positions within their societies shape the likelihood of deviant behavior and social responses to it. In addition, sociologists detail the processes whereby behaviors, conditions, beliefs, and individuals come to be defined as deviant, as well as the strategies used by individuals seeking to reduce deviant stigma and reclaim a nondeviant identity. The next chapter will continue to explore how the social world can constrain behavior and shape life outcomes, with a focus on economic inequality.

REVIEW

6.1 How do we define what is deviant, and what do sociological theories suggest about the causes of deviant behavior, including crime?

Deviance includes behaviors, conditions, or beliefs that violate norms and/or incur stigmatizing sanctions. Sociologists distinguish between statistical, legalistic, and normative approaches. The approach used depends on one's assumptions about the nature of deviance, including absolutist assumptions, relativist/social constructionist assumptions, and conflict/critical assumptions.

6.2 How do individual-level theories of deviance differ from structural-level theories of deviance?

Sociologists seek to explain why some individuals engage in more deviance than others (individual-level explanations) and why rates of deviance are higher in some regions, in some time periods, or for some groups than others (structural-level explanations). The earliest sociological explanations of deviance posited that every society has some form of deviance, and that deviance is necessary and functional for society. They also noted, however, that anomie—or normlessness—gives rise to dysfunctional levels of deviance.

6.3 What are the social processes involved in creating social norms?

Moral entrepreneurs create norms (and deviance) by actively campaigning for social change. Some moral entrepreneur campaigns produce moral panics in which the public regards the newly deviant behavior, condition, or belief as a threat to public morality. Those deemed responsible become folk devils. Social norms are then maintained by stigmatizing rule violators and labeling them as deviant.

6.4 How do individuals manage deviant identities?

Those who are labeled deviant or risk being labeled deviant engage in techniques of neutralization that enable them to maintain and project a positive self-concept. Those who have stigmatized statuses manage stigma in interaction with others through compensatory strategies (with visible stigmas) and passing or reveal strategies (with invisible stigmas).

KEY TERMS

absolutist perspective 99

anomie 102

compensatory strategies 112

folk devils 104

labeling 106

legalistic approach 97

master status 108

medicalization of deviance 106

moral entrepreneurs 103

moral panic 104

normative approach 98

primary deviance 107

relativist perspective 99

role engulfment 108

sanctions 98

secondary deviance 107

statistical approach 97

stigma 107

techniques of neutralization 111

CHAPTER 7

CONFRONTING ECONOMIC INEQUALITY

Sandra Enos

Why do some jobs pay so much more than others? Does everyone who works full-time deserve a living wage?

Marjorie Kamys Cotera/Bob Daemmrich Photography/Alamy Stock Photo

7.1 What is the difference between income and wealth?

7.2 How do major sociological theories explain income inequality?

7.3 What is social stratification and how does it work in society?

7.4 How do we distinguish social classes in the United States?

7.5 How has social mobility changed in the United States?

7.6 What are the impacts of class position on education, health, and other social outcomes?

7.7 What programs might address income inequality?

What Is Economic Inequality?

> **7.1** What is the difference between income and wealth?

What kind of car do you drive? Do you have enough funds for a car? The lifestyles that people in a society can afford differ according to their place on the economic ladder of society. This unequal distribution of economic resources (e.g., income and wealth) is known as **economic inequality**.

Economic inequality exists in every society. The extent and reasons for that inequality vary from society to society, however. Sociologists look at the reasons why. Why do some people seem to reap great benefits from work while others struggle to make ends meet? Are these differences the result of varying degrees of talent or hard work or luck? Are men and women, White people and people of color, native-born and immigrant members of society equally represented among the rich and the middle class and the poor? Or do we see some other patterns here?

CONSIDER THIS

On the basis of your own experience and observations, which is more important to attain a good career with a high salary—parental income and the quality of the schools you attend or individual motivation and determination? Why?

Although we focus on economic inequality in this chapter, as you know from discussions of intersectionality in previous chapters, economic inequality relates to and is influenced by other forms of inequality, such as those based on gender, race, and sexual orientation. Sociology gives us the tools to examine why these patterns occur and how they relate to our own experiences.

Measuring Inequality

When we talk about economic inequality, we usually are discussing income and wealth. **Income** is money received in exchange for services or investments, such as a paycheck, stock return, or Social Security benefits. **Wealth**, on the other hand, is the worth of your assets (e.g., savings accounts, houses, cars, and investment portfolios holding stocks and bonds) minus your debts.

Income Inequality. No doubt you already know that relatively few people reap large salaries. When we look at what people earn, we expect that those with good educations and special, in-demand skills will earn more than those

Economic inequality is represented, in part, by the houses we live in and whether we can afford to own our homes.
MBI/Alamy Stock Photo

SANDRA ENOS

I often joke that I have wanted to be a sociologist since I was five years old, and that statement is mainly true. As the first student in my family to graduate from high school, I was deeply aware early on in my life that life chances were not equally distributed in our society. My small town's population was made up of a diverse group of European immigrants and their children—Italians, French Canadians, Poles, Portuguese, Germans, and others. I was intrigued by the cultural differences among these groups. I didn't discover sociology until my junior year of college, but it was love at first reading. It lit up my curiosity and opened up my world.

After earning a BA in sociology, I spent a year as a VISTA volunteer in rural Alabama, then went on to Brown University for a master's in sociology. I subsequently made a career in public service, working in child welfare, corrections, policy work, and higher education reform. After a nearly twenty-five-year break in my education, I earned a PhD in sociology and have been teaching for twenty years. My long career applying sociology to real-world problems helps me make sociology real and important for students.

with less education and fewer valuable skills. People with great responsibilities also should earn more than others, right? For example, the president of the United States earns five times as much as the average employee of the federal government.

The president of the United States does not earn the highest income in the nation, however. Among the highest paid workers in our society are the CEOs of major corporations. Compared with the average worker, how much more do you think a CEO earns? Five times as much? Fifty? One hundred? In fact, CEOs in the United States earn more than 312 times the average nonsupervisory worker in their firms. Figure 7.1 shows how this ratio changed from 1965 to 2017. In 1965, CEOs made 20 times the average worker. In the 1990s, as more companies compensated CEOs in stocks, as well as cash, the ratio increased dramatically (Mishel and Schieder 2017). This change in compensation also made many CEOs personally invested in the stock value of the company and focused on short-term, rather than long-term, profits (Bower and Paine 2017).

In examining income inequality, we can also consider how various classes of individuals are doing in the economy. As the economy cycles through good times and bad, how are people at the top, in the middle, and at the bottom

doing? In Figure 7.2, we can see that from 1970 to 2016, the earnings of those at the top increased much more than those in the middle and lower classes. The incomes of those in the top 10 percent of earners grew by 73 percent, while the earnings of those at the bottom rose by just under half that (36 percent). The middle earners saw their income increase by somewhat more than those at the bottom but much less than those at the top (44 percent) (DeSilver 2018).

▼ FIGURE 7.1

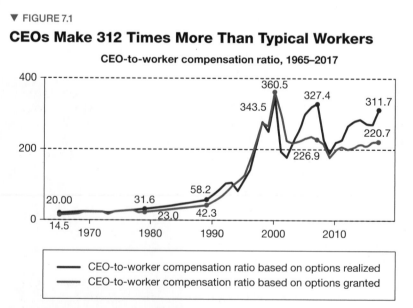

CEOs Make 312 Times More Than Typical Workers

CEO-to-worker compensation ratio, 1965–2017

— CEO-to-worker compensation ratio based on options realized
— CEO-to-worker compensation ratio based on options granted

Source: Mishel, Lawrence, and Jessica Schieder. 2018. "CEO Compensation Surged in 2017." Economic Policy Institute. https://www.epi.org/files/pdf/152123.pdf (accessed October 18, 2018).

Notes: CEO annual compensation is computed using the "options realized" and "options granted" compensation series for CEOs at the top 350 U.S. firms ranked by sales. The "options realized" series includes salary, bonus, restricted stock grants, options realized, and long-term incentive payouts. The "options granted" series includes salary, bonus, restricted stock grants, options granted, and long-term incentive payouts. Projected value for 2017 is based on the change in CEO pay as measured from June 2016 to June 2017 applied to the full-year 2016 value. Projections for compensation based on options. granted and options realized are calculated separately. "Typical worker" compensation is the average annual compensation of the workers in the key industry of the firms in the sample.

Nationally, Incomes Near the Top Are Rising at Twice the Rate of Incomes near the Bottom

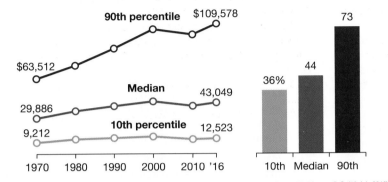

Incomes at selected percentiles (in 2016 dollars)

% change in income from 1970 to 2016, by percentile

90th percentile $109,578

$63,512

Median 43,049

29,886

10th percentile 12,523

9,212

1970 1980 1990 2000 2010 '16

73

36% 44

10th Median 90th

Source: "Income Inequality in the U.S. Is Rising Most Rapidly among Asians." Pew Research Center, Washington, D.C. (12 July 2018) https://www.pewsocialtrends.org/2018/07/12/income-inequality-in-the-u-s-is-rising-most-rapidly-among-asians/.

Note: Income is adjusted for household size and inflation. See Methodology for details.

Wealth Inequality. To really understand economic inequality, we need to look at wealth as well as income. It stands to reason that one cannot accumulate substantial wealth without a good income. After all, if you have meager earnings, there is little chance that you will have money left over to save for a house or to invest in the stock market. When individuals and families have assets that they inherit or that their parents can share with them, they have an advantage over families with little household wealth.

The wealth gap in the United States is even more significant than the income gap, as shown in Figure 7.3. This figure divides up all the wealth in the United States as if it constituted 100 slices of pie. You can see that the top 20 percent of the population holds nearly 90 percent of all the nation's wealth, or ninety slices of pie. Meanwhile, the middle 20 percent has just two slices, and the poorest 40 percent get no pie at all, having zero or negative wealth (debt) (Ingraham 2017; Wolff 2017).

How does income inequality in the United States compare with that in other postindustrial nations? As see in Figure 7.4, compared with other economically advanced nations, the United States ranks first on a measure of economic inequality called the Gini coefficient (Kochkar and Cilluffo

2018). This measures how much income would need to be distributed to have a completely equal society—the higher the coefficient, the more economic inequality.

CONSIDER THIS

What would it be like to live in a society with no inequality at all compared with one in which there are sharp differences between the rich and the poor?

Why? What has led to this increasing economic inequality in the United States over the past several decades? Some factors include changes in technology, globalization, the declining power of unions, tax policies favoring the wealthy, the erosion of social safety nets (e.g., access to welfare, public housing, food assistance), and the increasing costs of college (DeSilver 2018). Inequality also leads

▼ FIGURE 7.3

Actual Pie Distribution

Top 20% 90 slices of pie

avg. net worth: $3.0 million

Second 20% 8 slices of pie

avg. net worth: $273,600

Middle 20% 2 slices of pie

avg. net worth: $81,700

Fourth 20% 0 slices of pie

avg. net worth: –$8,900*

Bottom 20% –1 slices of pie

avg. net worth: –$8,900*

*Average net worth figure for fourth and bottom 20% categories are for the entire bottom 40%

Sources: Ingraham, Christopher. "The richest 1 percent now owns more of the country's wealth than at any time in the past 50 years." *The Washington Post*, December 6, 2017; data from Woolf, Edward N. 2017. "Household wealth trends in the United States, 1962 to 2016: Has middle class wealth recovered?" National Bureau of Economic Research. November. https://www.nber.org/papers/w24085.

EXPLORING THE CONCENTRATION OF WEALTH

In this exercise, you will watch a short video about the Gilded Age in the United States.

1. As part of the *American Experience* series from PBS, this video showcases a time in American history when the economy was booming and the United States was emerging as an economic superpower. Take notes as you watch this video and read the accompanying article: http://time.com/5122375/american-inequality-gilded-age/. One of the rich individuals attending the gala ball mentioned in the video states that "We own America . . . and we intend to keep it

if we can." What do you think he meant by that statement?

2. Describe at least two similarities and two differences between the United States during the Gilded Age and today.

3. One of the speakers in the video posed the question, "Are we two nations, the poor and the wealthy? Or, are we one nation where everyone has a chance to succeed?" Given current economic inequality, how would you answer that question?

4. How can studying the Gilded Age help policy makers in the United States today?

▼ FIGURE 7.4

Among G-7 Countries, Inequality Is Highest in the United States

Gini coefficient of income inequality, latest year available

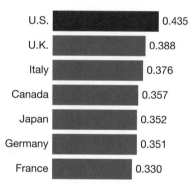

U.S.	0.435
U.K.	0.388
Italy	0.376
Canada	0.357
Japan	0.352
Germany	0.351
France	0.330

Source: "Income Inequality in the U.S. Is Rising Most Rapidly among Asians." Pew Research Center, Washington, D.C. (12 July 2018) https://www.pewsocialtrends.org/2018/07/12/income-inequality-in-the-u-s-is-rising-most-rapidly-among-asians/.

Note: Estimates are based on gross income, before taxes. Data for Japan are for 2012. Data for other countries are for either 2015 or 2016.

to further inequality as those at the bottom of the income ladder face declining opportunities for class mobility, greater segregation by income (which means more areas with low-quality schools and public services), increasing debt, and other negative health and social outcomes. Greater concentration of wealth at the top also means that the wealthy have more political influence and can shape legislation that benefits themselves at the expense of others (DeSilver 2018). Indeed, many people believe the economy is rigged in favor of the elite—the wealthy and politically connected (Pearlstein 2018).

Check Your Understanding

- Why are sociologists interested in inequality?
- How can we measure income inequality?
- What is the difference between wealth and income?
- Is income or wealth more concentrated?
- Why has economic inequality in the United States increased over the past several decades?

Meritocracy and the Functions of Inequality

7.2 How do major sociological theories explain income inequality?

Few of us would argue that we should all earn the same income no matter what we do or how we contribute (or not) to society. Most would suggest that some inequality is essential and productive for a society like ours. People who study hard, earn degrees, and work at demanding jobs should earn more than those who choose to slack off. Following this line of reasoning, as we discussed in Chapter 2, structural functionalists suggest that inequality is functional for society (Davis and Moore 1945). Our economic system should recognize and reward those who are talented and do the work that a society needs.

From the structural functionalist perspective, we need inequality to make sure that positions serving essential functions—caring for the sick, teaching children, disposing of trash, managing companies, ensuring public

DOING SOCIOLOGY 7.2

GRADE DISTRIBUTIONS AND INEQUALITY IN EDUCATIONAL MOTIVATION

In this activity, you will assess the impact of inequality across various grade distribution patterns.

How much inequality is good for teaching and learning? Suppose there are twenty-five students in a class.

Imagine that you could know ahead of time what the grade distributions were going to be in a class before you took it. Which of these six options would you choose?

Grade	Option 1	Option 2	Option 3	Option 4	Option 5	Option 6
A	1	5	5	5	2	
B	2	5	20	5	3	
C	3	5			15	25
D	7	5		10	3	
F	12	5		5	2	

Write your answers to the following questions:

1. Which distribution would most encourage you to work hard? Why?

2. Which distribution seems the worst to you? Why?

3. If you had to design your ideal distribution system, what would it look like? Describe the merits and potential downsides of your system and why you think it would be the best possible system of distributing grades.

---

safety, and much more—are filled. The positions most important to the functioning of society garner the greatest rewards in terms of income and prestige. Such a society is a **meritocracy**.

In a meritocracy, those with the most talent rise to the top and are appropriately rewarded for their contributions. In some societies, advancement comes through inherited offices or corruption, but meritocracies reward excellence rather than family relations or other influences. In meritocracies, income reflects the contribution of the social role to the larger society. For example, in a meritocracy, doctors earn more than nurses because they have more responsibility and have invested more years in their education. Likewise, teachers earn more than custodians because they have more training and because they fulfill important roles related to educating children. In a meritocracy, those with the ability to become key contributors to society, like doctors and teachers, should be guided toward those careers and given the training they need to succeed in them.

CONSIDER THIS

Is the United States a meritocracy? Do all children in U.S. society have an equal chance to develop their skills and talents? Do leaders always recognize merit and reward it accordingly?

If hard work and merit determine rewards, however, how do we explain the fact that in the United States, on average, full-time working women earn less than full-time working men? Also, a child may work very hard and excel in his public school, but if that school is of low quality, that child's effort may not be rewarded in the same way as that of a child who has the advantage of attending a high-quality school (with highly qualified teachers, many advanced course options, extracurricular activities, tutoring assistance, etc.). The theory of meritocracy assumes a level playing field, which in many cases is simply not the case (Stewart 2018).

One of America's most cherished myths is that anyone who works hard can become economically successful.

Blend Images/Alamy Stock Photo

Marx and Weber on Inequality

As we learned in Chapter 2, Karl Marx (Marx, Engels, and Bender 1988), the founder of the conflict perspective, saw things very differently from structural functionalists. He argued that the distribution of rewards is based on social class—not merit. Marx pointed out that throughout history, there have always been two classes—the owners of the means of production (bourgeoisie) and those who work for them (proletariat).

According to Marx, control of the means of production—how the economy creates goods and services for consumption and trade—is key to wealth. Economic inequality is a consequence of the fact that the interests of the bourgeoisie (to make profit by lowering costs and keeping wages low) and the interests of the proletariat (to make a good living) are incompatible. The bourgeoisie make a profit by employing the proletariat at wages lower than the true value of their labor. Marx predicted that the proletariat would eventually rise up against the bourgeoisie in a revolution.

Marx also wrote, however, that the bourgeoisie may fool the proletariat into accepting a high level of economic inequality. If the wealthy control the media and cultural messages, they may be able to convince the workers that the economic system is just and that the wealthy and the poor deserve their fates. A powerful ideology, or set of beliefs, about how wealth is created may convince the workers to support policies that benefit the bourgeoisie. For example, if they are convinced that the wealthy deserve their riches (and that if they work hard enough, they can be wealthy,

too), they might support policies that would lower taxes on the wealthy and cut programs that benefit low-income households. When members of a class embrace values that work against their own interests, they have developed what Marx called a false consciousness.

Max Weber (Weber, Gerth, and Mills 1958) expanded on some of Marx's ideas about classes. For Weber, class position is not just about whether you own capital but also about your own "human capital" (skill sets) and social status. Weber pointed out that skilled workers can demand more money from the owners of production than unskilled laborers. They also have a higher standing in society. Weber suggested that three traits determine **socioeconomic status** or social standing: class, status (or prestige), and party (e.g. a person's position in a political party). In this understanding of social class, we consider how much someone may earn in a job, the esteem in which others hold that position, and the power their political position exerts. In some cases, all these elements align. A doctor may earn a large salary, be held in high regard, and be able to exert her political influence over others. On the other hand, a drug dealer may earn lots of money and may be quite a powerful figure to those who work for him, but he may have little prestige or influence in general society.

Check Your Understanding

- How does structural functionalism explain economic inequality?
- How does Marx's theory explain economic inequality?
- Why might the proletariat support policies that support the bourgeoisie at their own expense?
- According to Weber, what is the basis of economic inequality?

Understanding Social Stratification

7.3   What is social stratification and how does it work in society?

The way valuable goods and desired intangibles (like social status and prestige) are distributed in society is known as **social stratification**. It is hard to imagine a gathering of humans not organized according to some hierarchy, whether based on physical strength, birthright, race, gender, or some other variable. Likewise, every society has some form of social stratification created and maintained through **structured inequalities**, advantages and disadvantages built into the social institutions of a society (e.g., education, religion, family).

Systems of Stratification

Various systems of stratification exist, from the most confining to those that allow some movement across divisions. The most rigid form of stratification is slavery, in which individuals own other individuals as property and have the legal right to dispense with that property as they wish. Slavery is now against the law in every nation but still exists in most areas of the world (e.g., children sold to pay off family debts, women and children forced into the sex trafficking trade) (Free the Slaves 2019).

In an **estate** system, there is very limited social mobility, but those with the least standing, the serfs or peasantry, have more freedom than slaves. In this system, laws distribute power and rights on the basis of social standing. For example, the right to vote might be restricted to those holding property. The clergy, the nobility, and commoners each have their respective rights—each person has his place in the social order and, with few exceptions, assume the social position held by his parents. Estate systems were prevalent in Europe and in much of Asia until the 1800s.

More stringent than the estate form of social stratification, **caste** systems are rigid systems that confine individuals to social groups for their lifetimes, assigning to them specific roles in a society with tight rules over the relationships among castes. Examples of caste systems exist in South Asia, in nations like India, where four main castes are in place. Members of the lowest caste, the Dalits, are restricted from occupations that require purity and confined to jobs like cremating corpses and dealing with human waste.

In **class-based** systems, like the United States, members of a given social class share a common economic status and lifestyle. For example, members of the middle class can afford to live in moderately priced houses, take annual vacations, and send their children to college. Class systems offer more mobility than other forms of stratification, and individuals in a class-based system may move up or down the economic ladder.

In India, the Dalit, or the "untouchables," are on the lowest rung of the Hindu caste system of stratification.

Bloomberg/Bloomberg/Getty Images

Check Your Understanding

- What is social stratification?
- What is the most rigid form of stratification?
- How do class- and caste-based systems of stratification differ from each other?

Examining the Class System

7.4 How do we distinguish social classes in the United States?

Social class refers to distinctions among groups of people based on income, occupation, and education. Most scholars have settled upon five distinct social classes: the upper, upper middle, middle, lower/working, and lowest. These constitute quintiles (fifths) that allow us to categorize each class in terms of income, wealth, and life chances (opportunities for class advancement).

As Table 7.1 shows, the U.S. Census Bureau breaks down the nation's population into the five quintiles by household income. In 2017, the richest 20 percent of households earned annual incomes of $121,018 or more, taking in about half (51.1 percent) of all the income in the United States. Meanwhile the poorest 40 percent of households took home just 11.3 percent of the total income (Fontenot, Semega, and Kollar 2018).

In Figure 7.5, which tracks the share of national income from 1980 to 2016, we can see that the top 1 percent of earners in the United States obtained a much larger percentage of the nation's income over those years.

Income by Quintile

	Percentage of Total U.S. Income	Median Income	Income Range
Top 5 percent	22.6	$345.539	More than $225,252
Highest quintile	51.5	$196,127	More than $121,018
Fourth quintile	22.9	$89,502	$74,870 to $121,018
Third quintile	14.2	$56,904	$45,601 to $74,869
Second quintile	8.2	$33,622	$24,003 to $45,600
Lowest quintile	3.1	$13,095	Less than $24,002

Source: Fontenot, Kayla, Jessica Semega, and Melissa Kollar. 2018. U.S. Census Bureau, Current Population Reports, P60-263. Income and poverty in the United States, 2017, U.S. Government Printing Office, Washington, D.C., 2018.

▼ FIGURE 7.5

Share of National Income

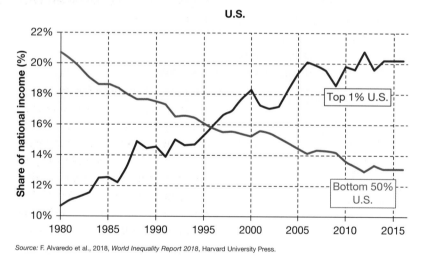

Source: F. Alvaredo et al., 2018, World Inequality Report 2018, Harvard University Press.

▼ TABLE 7.2

Average Adjusted Gross Income by Percentile, 2016

Earners	Top 1 Percent	Top 0.1 Percent	Top 0.01 Percent	Top 0.001 Percent
Minimum income	$1,421,735	$6,859,762	$32,713,039	$145,446,416

Source: US Internal Revenue Service, 2018.

Meanwhile, the share of income held by the bottom 50 percent of the population declined from just over 20 percent to 12 percent (Alvaredo et al. 2018).

Dramatic levels of economic inequality exist even among the top 1 percent of earners. For example, Table 7.2 shows the dramatic differences among the average incomes of the top 1 percent, 0.1 percent, 0.01 percent, and 0.001 percent of earners. Imagine how those with incomes of $1,421,735 feel about being lumped together with people making $145,446,416 a year (or vice versa).

Wealth inequality, always more concentrated than income inequality, is even more stark. Just three individuals—Bill Gates, founder of Microsoft and well-known philanthropist; Jeff Bezos, founder and CEO of Amazon; and Warren Buffett, CEO of Berkshire Hathaway—hold more wealth ($250 billion) than the 160 million people in the United States on the bottom half of the economic ladder. This sharp increase in the concentration of wealth has created a small number of extremely wealthy families that can pass on their riches to succeeding generations, creating, some predict, an American aristocracy (Collins and Hoxie 2018).

The Upper Class

Among the upper class, tools to maintain social status include residential enclaves, exclusive private schools, and clubs with invitation-only admission policies. This creates a bubble in which children are not exposed to members of other social classes but instead provided a well-supervised and carefully monitored socialization experience solely among their peers. Expensive vacations, education, and leisure activities guarantee that children will interact only with children like themselves. Together, this constitutes the **social class reproduction** process, through which members of the upper class ensure that their children maintain their status. Children from lower income groups receive far fewer supports, and their families have less political power to advocate for changes to policies that would enhance their opportunities.

At the top of the class ladder are the power elite, members of the corporate community that dominate politics in Washington. These individuals share membership in the same closed clubs,

Melinda Gates and Bill Gates, the founder of Microsoft, are members of the power elite who influence policies all over the world.

fotopress/Getty Images

Charles and David Koch (pictured with the opera singer Samuel Ramey) use their position in the power elite to advocate for lower taxes and limiting the role of government in the United States.

PATRICK MCMULLAN/Patrick McMullan via Getty Images

This picture, taken in New York City, helps capture economic inequality in the United States today. Note that the women seem to completely ignore the homeless person right next to them as they talk to each other.

Ulrich Baumgarten via Getty Images

circulate among luxury resorts, and attend the same elite schools. The power elite supports a range of institutions, like foundations and think tanks, that advance their ideas and influence policy makers and voters. They have power and influence over government decisions affecting every facet of U.S. life, including health care, education, tax policy, and regulation of industries (Domhoff 2018).

The Middle Class

Among American core beliefs is the strong assertion that the middle class serves as the center of the nation's economic power and prestige. A large middle class provides opportunities for class mobility and provides enough wealth to fuel consumption, savings, and investments in housing and education. Today, however, growing inequality has led to fewer people in the middle class.

The Working Class and the Poor

Those at the bottom half of the income structure face challenges in meeting living expenses each month. Four in ten adults faced with an unexpected expense would have to sell their possessions or borrow the money (if they could) in order to pay it. More than one-fifth of people in the United States cannot pay their monthly bills for food, housing, transportation, and other necessary expenses. More than one in four has gone without health care because of a lack of funds (Board of Governors of the Federal Reserve System 2018).

According to the federal government, as of 2018, individuals earning less than $12,140 a year or families of three earning less than $25,980 were living in poverty. The poverty level is used to assess need and determine eligibility for programs like TANF (Temporary Assistance to Needy Families), SNAP (Supplemental Nutrition Assistance Program; formerly known as food stamps), and school lunch programs.

ARE YOU IN THE MIDDLE CLASS?

In this exercise, you will examine you own social class.

Go to http://www.pewresearch.org/fact-tank/2018/09/06/are-you-in-the-american-middle-class/ and follow the directions in step 1. Use your family's household if you are still living at home with your parents or guardians, and choose the closest metropolitan area to your home. Compare your metropolitan area with the United States. How are they similar or different? Write your answers.

Complete step 2 using your individual characteristics. Recalculate income using one level of education lower than the one you have or plan to have. How does education affect income? Return to your original characteristics and recalculate for another—race/ethnicity. Which variable influenced income the most, education or race/ethnicity? Write your answers.

Another 20 percent of households, those whose members work at manual, low-skill jobs, in so-called blue-collar occupations with annual incomes between $24,003 and $45,600, are classified as working class. The low wages earned by the working class mean that they must devote long hours to work. Children in these families may join the workforce early so they can contribute to household income.

Poverty, homelessness, and hunger also affect many college students. As Figure 7.6 reveals, almost half of all college students do not have enough healthy food to eat, and more than half lack stable housing. Thirty-five percent of respondents from four-year schools and 40 percent of those from two-year schools report skipping or cutting the size of meals because of a lack of money for food (Goldrick-Rab et al. 2019)

CONSIDER THIS

Would a middle-class person feel relatively wealthy or relatively poor at your school? Why?

Culture of Poverty Theory and Policies toward the Poor. Are you living in poverty? Most Americans have been or will be in poverty. Nearly 60 percent of Americans live through at least one year of poverty, and 75 percent experience near poverty, earning just 150 percent of the poverty level. Mark Rank and Thomas A. Hirschl created a tool that predicts your chances of falling into poverty. Their economic risk calculator (https://confrontingpoverty.org/poverty-risk-calculator/) considers race, education, and marital status to forecast the likelihood that individuals will experience poverty in the next five, ten, or fifteen years.

Oscar Lewis coined the term **culture of poverty** in 1959 to describe the beliefs, attitudes, and values that characterize those living in poverty and distinguish them from more productive members of society. He found that conditions of poverty and deprivation create cultural responses geared to survival. The poor find themselves in networks of mutual support and obligation with other poor people, which allow them to survive under severe economic constraints but also make it nearly impossible to move out of poverty. For example, seeing school

▼ FIGURE 7.6

Highlights from the #RealCollege Survey

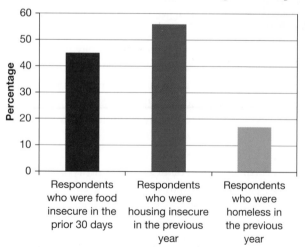

Source: Data from Goldrick-Rab, Sara, Christine Baker-Smith, Vanessa Coca, Elizabeth Looker and Tiffani Williams. April 2019. "College and University Basic Needs Insecurity: A National #RealCollege Survey Report."

as pointless because no one around you has gone to college will likely lead you to follow the culture of poverty norm of slacking off in school and dropping out before graduating. The culture of poverty thesis suggests that the poor could move out of poverty if they changed their attitudes and worked harder.

As Figure 7.7 reveals, most people in the United States do not believe in the culture of poverty thesis. However, there is a marked political divide, with far more Republicans than Democrats maintaining that poverty and wealth result from individual effort rather than societal forces. Meanwhile, many government policies rely on the ideas behind the culture of poverty. Welfare reform, shaped in the 1990s by proponents of the culture of poverty, frayed the safety net, particularly for single adults without children. In some states, individuals may lose their eligibility for SNAP after being on the program just a few months.

Check Your Understanding

- What is social class?
- How do scholars distinguish social classes from one another?
- How many people in the United States experience poverty or near poverty during their lifetimes?
- How many college students are food insecure?
- To what does the term "culture of poverty" refer?
- How have theories on the culture of poverty influenced policies toward the poor?

Mobility within and across Generations

7.5 How has social mobility changed in the United States?

Mobility is the movement between social classes in a society. Individuals may experience **upward mobility**, when they climb up the economic ladder, or **downward mobility**, when their class position falls. An individual may start out as a member of a working-class family, earn a college education, and secure a place in the middle class. We would refer to that as upward mobility. **Intergenerational mobility** is a change in social class from one generation to the next. A person from a poor family who graduates from college and gains employment as an accountant and a middle-class salary provides an example of this type of class mobility.

It is interesting to examine how the United States, known as the land of opportunity, compares with other nations in terms of economic mobility. Research conducted by the Organisation for Economic Co-operation and Development ranks nations by the number of generations it would take to move from the bottom 10 percent to the average (mean) income in society. As you can see in Figure 7.8, the United States is in the middle of the pack. Compared with countries like Denmark, Sweden, Finland, and Norway, where individuals at the bottom can advance to the middle class in two or three generations, it tends to take individuals in the United States five generations to achieve the same mobility. Meanwhile, it would take residents of nations like India and China even longer (Organisation for Economic Co-operation and Development 2018).

▼ FIGURE 7.7

Political Divide on Beliefs about the Rich and Poor

Republicans are far more likely than Democrats to say people are rich because they worked harder – and that people are poor because of a lack of effort

In your opinion, which generally has more to do with . . . (%)

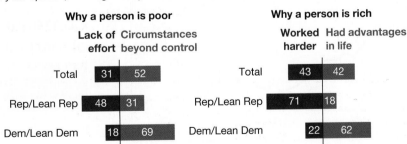

Source: Dunn, Amina. "Partisans are divided over the fairness of the U.S. economy—and why people are rich or poor." Pew Research Center, Washington, D.C. (4 October 2018). https://www.pewresearch .org/fact-tank/2018/10/04/partisans-are-divided-over-the-fairness-of-the-u-s-economy-and-why-people-are-rich-or-poor/.

Note: Don't know responses not shown.

Income Mobility across Generations

Source: OECD. 2018. "A broken social elevator? How to promote social mobility." http://www.oecd.org/social/broken-elevator-how-to-promote-social-mobility-9789264301085-en.htm.

▼ FIGURE 7.9

The Fading American Dream?

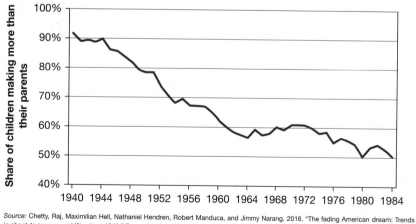

Source: Chetty, Raj, Maximilian Hell, Nathaniel Hendren, Robert Manduca, and Jimmy Narang. 2016. "The fading American dream: Trends in absolute income mobility since 1940." December. http://www.nber.org/papers/w22910.pdf (accessed September 10, 2018).

Changes in the Economy

As you can see, the society in which you live affects your ability to move up the social class ladder. **Structural mobility** occurs when changes in a society's institutions lead to upward or downward mobility for whole classes or groups of people. For example, with more advanced technology and globalization, U.S. workers compete for jobs with people in other nations, unions have lost power, automation has increased, and people with just a high school education have lost most avenues to the middle class. Today, most young adults must go to school longer, continually acquire new skills, and, in many cases, take on debt to attain a lifestyle similar to that of their parents. As shown in Figure 7.9, whereas more than 90 percent of people born in 1940 made more money than their parents, just 50 percent of those born in 1984 have higher incomes than their parents.

Check Your Understanding

- What are upward and downward mobility?

- What is intergenerational mobility?

- How does the United States compare with other nations in terms of intergenerational mobility?

- What is structural mobility, and how does it affect individual mobility?

Consequences of Inequality

7.6 What are the impacts of class position on education, health, and other social outcomes?

Economic inequality relates to other forms of social inequality. For example, economic inequality influences (and is influenced by) the type of education you receive and where you live. Economic inequality can even affect how long you live!

Education

If you ask most people in the United States about the best way to get ahead, they will say that getting a good education is the surest ticket to a good job. We know, however, that there is an achievement gap between wealthy students and those at the bottom of the economic pyramid. Test scores for wealthy students are better than those of middle-class students, which are higher than those of students from low-income families (Owens 2018). As you will see in Chapter 12, children who live in higher income communities tend to go to better resourced schools and to graduate from college at much higher rates than other students.

Contingent workers, like this Lyft driver, cannot count on consistent work hours or a steady paycheck.
Kelly Sullivan/Getty Images Entertainment/Getty Images

CONSIDER THIS

Think about the high school you attended. Did most students go to college? Could you observe rankings within your high school by social class? If you compare your high school with those attended by the students enrolled in this class with you, what do you find? What does this tell us about the relationship between high quality schooling and social class?

Summer enrichment activities, like these girls are experiencing, are common among members of high-income families but relatively rare among children from families with low incomes.
Enigma/Alamy Stock Photo

The major reasons many college students fail to earn their degrees include the high costs of tuition; the stresses of managing work, family obligations, and academic demands; poor advising; and lack of adequate preparation for college-level academic work (Marcus 2018). Approximately 30 percent of students who take out college loans fail to complete their degrees, which means that they carry debt for attending college but do not benefit from the added earnings that come with a college degree (Steele and Williams 2016). Some will never be able to pay what they owe on their student loans. The 44 million people in the United States with student loans owe a total of $15 trillion (Friedman 2018).

Housing

Increasing rental and home prices, decreases in tax-supported housing assistance programs, policies that favor homeowners over renters, concentration of ownership

DOING SOCIOLOGY 7.4

CONSIDERING THE IMPACT OF NEIGHBORHOODS ON INEQUALITY

In this exercise, you will reflect on the impact of neighborhoods on your chance of success.

Individually or with a partner, consider the impact of the neighborhoods in which you were raised on your life chances. Respond to the following questions.

- What kind of jobs did the primary breadwinners in your neighborhood have?

- Did both parents work outside the home?

- Did most of the adults in your neighborhood go to college?

- What was your school like. Was it public or private? Did you have advanced classes? Were students expected to go to college?

- Given these experiences, how did growing up in your neighborhood affect your life chances?

---

among landlords, and a decline in public housing have contributed to historically high housing costs (Desmond 2018). Young adults face particularly difficult housing challenges. Since 2000, rent and home prices have increased, respectively, 71 percent and 61 percent, but income for Millennials has increased just 31 percent. About 8 percent of (nonstudent) Millennials count on help from parents to pay their rent, and another 15 percent live with their parents because of high housing costs (Carter 2018).

When people fall short on their rent, they often face eviction, leading them into deeper poverty. They may lose security deposits attached to their old leases and incur expenses as they secure temporary housing. Many then find themselves homeless and without enough funds to pay security deposits and rent for new apartments.

Where children grow up matters. When children grow up in better neighborhoods and out of concentrated poverty, their social class outcomes as adults are much better (Badger and Bui 2018). They earn higher incomes than those children who remained in poorer neighborhoods (Chyn 2016). They also have much lower rates of imprisonment. Just a short distance can make the difference between

being incarcerated and staying out of prison. For example, the incarceration rates of Black men in the Watts and Compton neighborhoods of Los Angeles—less than three miles apart—differ dramatically. With a 44 percent incarceration rate in Watts, Black men in that neighborhood are more than 7 times as likely to face incarceration as those living in Compton, which has just over a 6 percent incarceration rate for Black men (Chetty et al. 2018).

A June 18, 2017, snapshot of a slum in Kolkata, India. Almost one in four people across the world live on less than $3.20 a day.

Debajyoti Chakraborty/NurPhoto/Getty Images

Total 1 Percent National Income Share

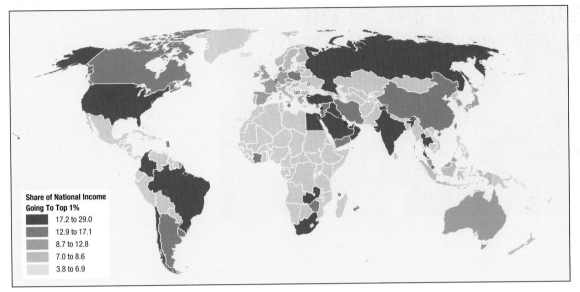

Source: WID.world (2018).

Life Expectancy

As we discuss more in Chapter 13, social class affects health and life spans. Quality of neighborhoods, rather than geography, is key. For example, in St. Paul, Minnesota, the average life expectancy for those who live in the poor neighborhood on the east side of St. Paul's Rondo neighborhood is sixty-five years. In the lower part of the wealthy Historic Hill neighborhood, just a fifteen-minute walk away, residents tend to live eighty-six years. In short, the more money you have, the safer and healthier your environment tends to be, and the more likely you are to live a long, healthy life.

Global Inequality

Looking at data compiled by the World Bank (2018a), we can see that stratification exists among, as well as within, nations. There are high-income (like the United States and Canada), upper-middle-income (like Mexico and Brazil), lower-middle-income (like Cambodia and India), and lower-income (like Haiti and Niger) countries. We can also see that inequality is a global phenomenon. Using the standard of the U.S. dollar, nearly half of the world's population (46 percent) lives on less than $5.50 a day. Nearly a quarter (23 percent) lives on less than $3.20 a day, while nearly one in ten lives on less than $1.90 a day (World Bank 2018b). The richest 1 percent hold half of the world's wealth, a share that has increased from 42 percent in 2008 at the peak of the global financial crisis (Credit Suisse 2018).

As mentioned earlier, rates of economic inequality vary from nation to nation. As Figure 7.10 shows, the United States has higher rates than many other nations. If we want to look at why, we need to examine policies that affect structural mobility in various nations. As you can see from the map, when comparing how much income the top 1 percent of earners in each nation holds, European nations have relatively little inequality. We look at why next.

Check Your Understanding

- What is the relationship between income and educational achievement?
- How are poverty and homelessness related?
- What is the relationship between educational inequality and economic inequality?
- How is where you live related to your life expectancy?
- How is economic inequality a global phenomenon?

Addressing Inequality

7.7   What programs might address income inequality?

National and global policies can mitigate or increase inequality. During times of increasing inequality, leaders tend to face political pressure to enact policies to decrease inequality and help those suffering from it. Those who cannot respond effectively risk the public's wrath and demands for a change in leadership. After decades of increasing

President Trump greets supporters in Hershey, Pennsylvania, on November 4, 2016, two days before the 2016 presidential election.

Mark Makela/Getty Images News/Getty Images

President Trump's economic policies, however, tended to repeat President Ronald Reagan's "trickle down" policies, which threw gasoline on the economic inequality fire in the early 1980s. Reagan believed that cutting corporate taxes and weakening regulations on businesses would lead to greater investments in the United States and more jobs that would lead wealth to "trickle down" to workers. Instead, corporations took the no-strings-attached tax breaks and invested in nations with cheaper workforces, leading to rapid deindustrialization and fewer jobs and greater economic inequality in the United States.

inequality in the United States, political change came in the form of the election of Donald Trump as president in 2016. As automation and globalization created greater wealth for a few, while decreasing middle-class jobs for many, increasing numbers of voters felt abandoned by traditional political figures. Trump promised that "the forgotten men and women of our country will be forgotten no longer" and that he would to bring jobs back to the United States (Jackson and Stanglin 2017).

In his first two years in office, President Trump, with help from a Republican-led Congress, enacted a $2.3 trillion tax cut. He also imposed tariffs on goods from other nations, changed long-standing treaties on trade, and weakened regulations on business, the environment, and consumer protection. Most of the benefits went to corporations and the wealthy. As Figure 7.11 indicates, from the tax cut, on average, a family in the bottom fifth of the nation's income quintile received $60 in tax relief, those in the middle gained $900, the top 20 percent received a $7,640 break in taxes, and the top 1

▼ FIGURE 7.11

Average Benefit from Tax Bill

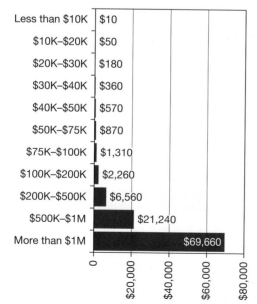

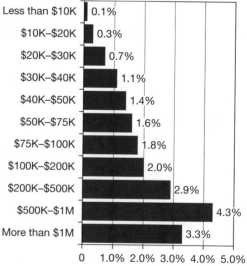

Source: Tax Policy Center

Credit: Danielle Kurtzleben & Katie Park/NPR

percent got a tax break of more than $50,000 (Tax Policy Center 2017). Some people ended up paying more in taxes (some taxes were raised as part of the tax deal). More than half of taxpayers have not seen any benefit from the tax break (Segarra 2018). Likewise, other Trump policies, such as tariffs and deregulation, have benefited some businesses at the expense of others, while hurting lower income people and the environment (which we discuss in Chapter 15).

In comparison with the United States, nations in the European Union have higher tax rates and more broad programs for social support, like free college, universal health, and job retraining. As seen in Figure 7.12, if nations adopt policies that mirror those of the United States, global income inequality will rise—the rich will get richer and the poor will get poorer. On the other hand, if they implement polices like those in the European Union, we can expect income inequality to decline. There will be less disparity in incomes across social classes, with better outcomes in education, health, public safety, and mobility. In other words, policies that influence structural mobility make real differences in economic inequality rates. Individuals can work very hard to succeed, but whether they make it depends largely on government policies (Alvaredo et al. 2018).

We can see evidence of the impact of government policies on economic inequality throughout the history of the United States. For example, policies under President Roosevelt's New Deal, enacted during the Great Depression in the 1930s (e.g., unemployment insurance, Social Security, the right of unions to bargain with employers, the Works Progress Administration, the federal

minimum age) established a safety net for the needy and put millions of people to work. In the early 1960s, social science research and the civil rights movement brought more public attention to high poverty rates. Almost one in four people (22.4 percent of the population) lived in poverty in 1960, and President Lyndon Johnson launched the War on Poverty to tackle this social problem. The programs carried out under the War on Poverty that began in the mid-1960s (e.g., Medicare, Medicaid, food stamps, the federal work study program, and Head Start) helped lead to a steep decline in poverty rates in the United States. By 1980, the poverty rate had dropped to one in eight (12 percent of the population) (Fontenot, Semega, and Kollar 2018).

The poverty rate has not declined for the past 40 years, however, and economic inequality has increased. As noted earlier, if we want to reduce both, it makes sense to look at how the United States might implement some policies similar to those in the European Union. We also need to examine the efficacy of other possible policies, such as raising the federal minimum wage or establishing a universal basic income. Data for both are now available, as many states and cities have already raised their minimum wages, and experiments with universal basic incomes have started to spread (in countries like Canada, Finland, and Spain) (Reynolds 2018). In 2019, the Democrat-led House of Representatives passed a bill to raise the minimum wage to $15 per hour, but the Republican-controlled Senate would not consider it (Stolberg and Smialek 2019).

Social scientists have a major role to play in policy-making efforts to reduce inequality. For example, the

▼ FIGURE 7.12

Rising Global Income Inequality Is Not Inevitable in the Future

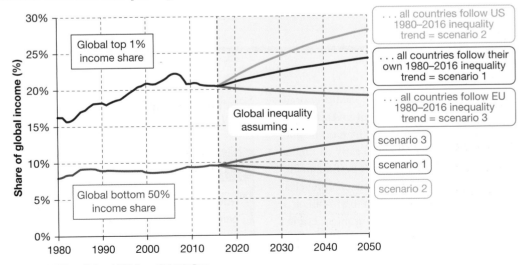

Source: F. Alvaredo et al., 2018, World Inequality Report 2018, Harvard University Press.

Note: EU = European Union.

HOW DO WE MEASURE INCOME INEQUALITY?

Levels of income inequality are often represented by the Gini index (also referred to as the Gini coefficient or ratio). It ranges from 0 to 1, where 0 indicates complete *equality* (everyone has the same income) and 1 indicates complete *inequality* (a single person has all the income). In real life, it ranges from .25 for Sweden at the low end to .63 for South Africa at the high end, with the United States somewhere in between with a Gini index of .45.

In this online activity, you will explore differences in income inequality among states, using data from the U.S. Census Bureau's American Community Survey.

*Requires the Vantage version of *Sociology in Action*.

▼ FIGURE 7.13

U.S. Income Inequality (Five-Year Average, 2013–2017)

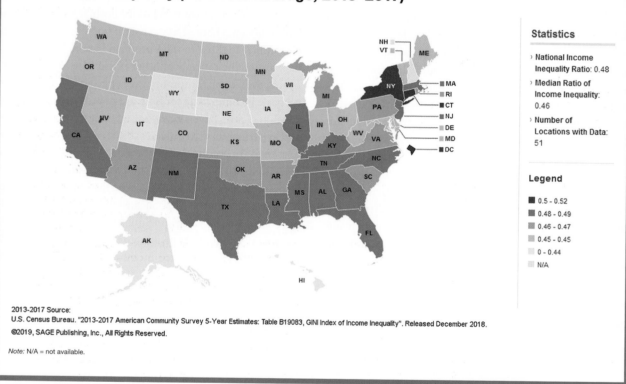

Statistics

› National Income Inequality Ratio: 0.48

› Median Ratio of Income Inequality: 0.46

› Number of Locations with Data: 51

Legend

- ■ 0.5 - 0.52
- ■ 0.48 - 0.49
- ■ 0.46 - 0.47
- ■ 0.45 - 0.45
- □ 0 - 0.44
- ■ N/A

2013-2017 Source:
U.S. Census Bureau. "2013-2017 American Community Survey 5-Year Estimates: Table B19083, GINI Index of Income Inequality". Released December 2018.
©2019, SAGE Publishing, Inc., All Rights Reserved.

Note: N/A = not available.

Bridgespan Group, a global nonprofit consulting organization, evaluated six ways in which an investment of $1 billion could significantly improve the lives of the poor and working poor. Such an investment in early childhood development would yield $5.5 billion to $11 billion in lifetime earnings. A similar investment in establishing clear pathways to careers would yield $7 billion to $15 billion in lifetime earnings. If put toward reducing incarceration and unintended pregnancies, the money would yield benefits three to eight times the initial investment (Murphy, Boyd, and Bielak 2016). Of course, for these or any policies to work, we need effective programs to implement them.

Sociologists like Brad Rose, this chapter's Sociologist in Action, design and evaluate such programs.

CONSIDER THIS

Now, having read this chapter, consider again whether parental income and the quality of schools you attend or individual motivation and determination are more important to attain a good career with a high salary. Why? Did your answers change from those you gave when answering this question at the beginning of the chapter? Why?

SOCIOLOGISTS IN ACTION

MAKING THE WORLD BETTER THROUGH PROGRAM EVALUATION

BRAD ROSE

Sociologists conduct program evaluations to determine the merit, worth, and effects of a program or initiative. They conduct applied, "real-world" research to answer questions such as the following: Is the program or initiative carried out effectively? What is the impact of the program? Should the program be continued or expanded? Should it be duplicated?

As an applied sociologist who conducts evaluations of a wide range of programs—from those serving homeless people to those assisting college and university faculty—my sociological education has helped me design and carry out evaluation research to determine the effectiveness of programs, initiatives, and policies. I have evaluated

1. the effectiveness of job training programs for homeless women;

2. a professional development program designed to help prepare preservice and in-service K–12 teachers to work with special-needs students;

3. a statewide AmeriCorps program that seeks to enhance the capacity of nonprofit organizations to serve their constituencies;

4. a federally funded national organization efforts to deliver technical assistance and training to state departments of education so that they are optimally positioned to meet the learning needs of deaf, blind, and otherwise disabled students;

5. a program that addresses the needs of first-generation, primarily minority, college students as they enter their first year of college;

6. a multisite after-school program for elementary school–aged students staffed by college and university students; and

7. a college's Urban Resource Institute's efforts to support the urban development of one of Massachusetts's small cities.

I have also conducted an evaluation of a national foundation's multicollege/university initiative to increase the number of minority students earning PhDs and pursuing academic careers in the arts and sciences. For this project and the others, my sociological training allowed me to design an effective evaluation strategy, collect appropriate information, analyze data, and provide critical analyses that helped my clients to strengthen their programs and initiatives.

During the minority PhD initiative evaluation, I gathered information that documented the program's achievements and challenges. For example, we looked at how many students the program has successfully shepherded through the PhD process and the difficulties involved in efforts to increase that number. On the basis of my findings, I made suggestions that could strengthen their ability to help more minority students earn PhDs.

My sociological understanding of organizations, the impact of social structure on opportunities, economic inequality, and poverty, race, and gender allows me, in all my evaluation work, to view the systemic rather than merely personal dimensions of the issues the programs and initiatives seek to address. In doing so, I am able to assist clients as they address many of the social challenges—from homelessness to the underrepresentation of minorities in higher education—that confront contemporary American society.

Discussion Question: Brad Rose writes that his sociological training allows him to "view the systemic rather than merely personal dimensions of the issues the programs and initiatives seek to address." Do you think he could effectively analyze social programs and initiatives without using a sociological perspective? Why? Can someone without a sociological perspective design and run a successful social program?

Brad Rose is an applied sociologist and president of Brad Rose Consulting, Inc. (www.bradroseconsulting.com), a program evaluation firm based in Boston.

Check Your Understanding

- How do the policies enacted under President Trump compare with those carried out under President Reagan?

- What are some European Union policies that lead to lower poverty rates?

- How has the United States reduced poverty in the past?

- What are some proposals scholars and policy advocates have made recently to reduce economic inequality in the United States?

Conclusion

Although social class serves as a key determinant of life chances and identity, class doesn't explain all aspects of inequality. The life chances of racial and ethnic minority group members, for example, are typically worse than those of Whites in the same social class. Also, women still tend to earn less than their male colleagues, and they suffer the effects of poverty to a greater degree than men because of discrimination and gendered family responsibilities. We will see in the following chapter how gender and sexuality play out in organizing social relationships.

Marchers demand an increase in the minimum wage to $15 an hour in Chicago on April 14, 2016. In 2019, the governor signed a bill to raise the minimum wage in Illinois to $15 per hour by 2025.

Scott Olson/Getty Images News/Getty Images

$SAGE edge™

Want a better grade? Get the tools you need to sharpen your study skills. Access practice quizzes, eFlashcards, video, and multimedia at **edge.sagepub.com/Korgen2e**

REVIEW

7.1 What is the difference between income and wealth?

Income is money received in exchange for services or investments, such as a paycheck, stock return, or Social Security benefits. Wealth, on the other hand, is the worth of your assets, like savings accounts, houses, cars, and investment portfolios, minus debts.

7.2 How do major sociological theories explain income inequality?

Structural functionalism posits that merit works to distribute goods and services so that social stratification mirrors the contributions individuals make to society. In contrast, conflict theory contends that the powerful manage the economy to benefit themselves, exploiting workers so that they can maximize profits.

7.3 What is social stratification and how does it work in society?

Social stratification refers to the ways in which valuable goods and desired intangibles like social status and prestige are distributed to different groups in society.

7.4 How do we distinguish social classes in the United States?

Social class refers to distinctions among groups of people based on income, occupation, and education. In the United States, we have five social classes: the upper, upper middle, middle, lower/working, and lowest.

7.5 How has social mobility changed in the United States?

Over the past fifty years, economic inequality in the United States has increased. Structural changes have transformed the labor force, making workers more contingent, shrinking the middle class, and narrowing the paths of mobility for more citizens.

7.6 What are the impacts of class position on education, health, and other social outcomes?

Those at the top of the social structure tend to enjoy better health, longer lives, better schools, higher educational achievement, safer neighborhoods, and more opportunities for mobility. Furthermore, they can pass along these advantages to their children.

7.7 What programs might address income inequality?

Policies and programs that enhance the wages and working conditions of low-wage workers and provide stronger support for education, health care, and alternatives to prison are promising approaches to reducing income inequality. In addition, raising taxes on the wealthiest Americans would reduce inequality and increase funds for social supports.

KEY TERMS

caste   121

class-based   121

culture of poverty   124

downward mobility   125

economic inequality   115

estates   121

income   115

intergenerational mobility   125

meritocracy   119

social class   121

social class reproduction   122

social stratification   120

socioeconomic status   120

structural mobility   126

structured inequalities   121

upward mobility   125

wealth   115

CHAPTER 8

CONSTRUCTING GENDER, SEX, AND SEXUALITY

Maxine P. Atkinson

How did you select the toys you played with when you were a child? Toys and childhood games are part of the gender socialization process.

8.1 What are the sociological definitions of sex, gender, intersex, and transgender?

8.2 How do sociologists understand gender through the three major theoretical perspectives and the theory that sees gender as a social structure?

8.3 How do we create our gender and sexual identities?

8.4 How does gender affect workforce experiences?

8.5 How have rates of sexual activity among young adults in the United States changed since the 1950s?

Defining Sex, Gender, Intersex, and Transgender

8.1 What are the sociological definitions of sex, gender, intersex, and transgender?

Asking someone who is old enough to be in college to define sex and gender may seem like a silly thing to do. After all, if there is anything a college student knows, it is the difference between sex and gender, right? Let's see. If someone asked you if you had ever had sex, you might answer "no" or "yes" or something like "it depends on what you mean." But if you were asked to designate your sex on a form, you would know what you were being asked—right? So, is sex a verb or a noun, an activity or a person? Not only is there a difference between sex and gender, the term *sex* is often used in at least two different ways.

How about gender? Are we all **cisgender** people whose gender identities correspond with the sex assigned to them at birth? Do all males see themselves as men? Do all females think of themselves as women? The terms *male* and *female* and *women* and *men* are crucial here because they designate the differences between sex and gender. **Sex** is a biological construct and is defined by our external genitalia, chromosomes, and internal reproductive organs. When we are born, someone, usually a physician or midwife, looks at our genitals and declares "It's a girl!" or "It's a boy!" They are announcing our sex, clearly declaring that we are either female or male. Most of us fit into one of these two categories, but as many as 1 in every 1,500 babies are born **intersex** (American Psychological Association n.d.), meaning that they are not clearly biologically male or female. Sometimes these biological characteristics result in ambiguous genitals, but other times, intersex conditions are evident only later in life (American Psychological Association n.d.).

Having a child neither clearly biologically male nor female can make many parents very uncomfortable, and some use surgery to assign their children to one sex or the other. It is easiest to surgically alter an intersex person's sex organs by making them female, and that is the most common practice (Fausto-Sterling 2000).

Do not confuse the term *intersex* with *transgender*. Transgender concerns identity and is thus a social construct. **Transgender** people identify as a gender other than the one assigned to them at birth. They may or may not choose to have surgery but do not typically present themselves in a way that is traditional for their assigned sex. Many transgender people (like all people) use hair and clothing styles as one of the ways they socially construct their gender. The term *cisgender* indicates a person who identifies as the gender that is consistent with the sex they were assigned at birth.

In this chapter, we focus on the importance of gender, how we learn our genders, and the impact of gender on our lives. Our **gender**, unlike sex, is a social concept and must be taught to us and continually created by us through interactions with others. This process varies across time and cultures as our assumptions about men and women change, but gender and gender identity, or the way we define ourselves as women or men, exist in some form or another in every society.

Of all the demographic groups to which we belong, perhaps none is more important than our gender. Gender has a tremendous impact on who we are, how others interact with us, and the opportunities we are granted or denied. That is a strong statement to make. How do we know that gender has that great an influence on us? How is gender reflected in our everyday lives? What impact does gender have on our life chances? These are all questions we will address in this chapter.

Check Your Understanding

- How do sociologists define sex, gender, intersex, and transgender?
- Which of the following terms refer to people's biological makeup: *sex, gender, intersex,* and *transgender*?

MAXINE P. ATKINSON

I graduated from a large state university, where I was happily memorizing my way through college and finding it easy, especially in the STEM (science, technology, engineering, and mathematics) courses. Then I took a sociology course at the suggestion of one of my friends. I learned how the rich get richer and how difficult it is to get out of poverty. I was determined to make a difference, even if it was only a very small one.

I am passionate about undergraduate education because I believe that higher education can be a mechanism for addressing issues of social justice and creating opportunities for social mobility rather than simply a mechanism for the privileged to pass on their advantage. My research focuses on methods of effective teaching and learning principles of sociology. I teach introductory classes, sociology of family and gender classes, and a graduate class titled Teaching Sociology. I focus a lot of my time and energy working with graduate students to advance their teaching skills, believing that we can harness the power of "doing sociology" to make a difference.

Using Theory to Understand Gender

> 8.2 How do sociologists understand gender through the three major theoretical perspectives and the theory that sees gender as a social structure?

In this section, we look at how the three major theoretical perspectives (structural functionalism, conflict theory, and symbolic interaction) and one theory (gender as a social structure) explain gender. Gender helps define who we are as individuals, but it also shapes the expectations others have of us and the social institutions in our societies. As our society changes, so do our understandings of gender. So, for example, structural functionalists' analysis of gender, which was dominant in the 1950s, appears out of date today.

Structural Functionalist Perspective

Structural functionalists typically equate sex and gender and see men and women as essentially different and complementary. Men play instrumental roles in society, being leaders and breadwinners, and women play expressive roles, supporting men and providing nurturance for children and the elderly. In this view, it is "natural" that only men would be authority figures in the family, presidents, governors, chief executive officers, priests, ministers, and rabbis. Women, on the other hand, are best suited to housework, taking care of children, and, if they work outside their homes, being nurses, teachers, and secretaries. Structural functionalists assume that these complementary roles contribute to order and stability in society and ignore the unfairness and inequalities inherent in this perspective. Very few sociologists now use this explanation of gender, but it was the dominant perspective from the 1940s into the 1960s.

Conflict Perspectives

Conflict theorists, like structural functionalists, focus on macro-level social structures that are a part of every society but see these social structures and their effect on us in very different ways than structural functionalists. Conflict theorists who study gender are referred to as feminist theorists and examine the seven institutions discussed in Chapter 2—family, religion, economy, education, government, health care, and media—and how they influence our lives through their unequal distribution of resources to each gender, the roles they assign to girls and boys and women and men, and the messages they convey.

We can see examples of the influence of institutions on gender and the inequalities created within them by looking at the family and religion. Every society has expectations for how men and women will behave as family members. In the United States, although gender roles have become somewhat more fluid, when people think of family roles for heterosexual married couples, most still think of husbands and fathers as the primary breadwinners and wives and mothers women as the primary caregivers. Although men have increased their time doing housework and childcare, women still do the bulk of household work. Fathers represent about 17 percent of all stay-at-home parents, but about a third of those say that the main reason they are home is because they cannot find jobs or they are physically unable to work (Livingston and Bialik 2018).

DISTINGUISHING TERMS

In this exercise, you will discuss the terms *sex*, *gender*, *intersex*, and *transgender*.

Write your answers to the following questions and be prepared to share your responses.

1. Why do you think it is important to distinguish between sex and gender?

2. Does your driver's license or another official document list your sex or your gender? What is the intent of these designations on this document? Should the document list sex, or is gender more appropriate? Why?

3. What are the options on the official document for those who are intersex or transgender?

Some religions allow only men to be clergy, the most powerful roles in any religion. The Roman Catholic Church is a good example of a religious institution with carefully scripted and differentiated roles for women and men. Women cannot become priests and certainly not considered candidates for pope! Likewise, Orthodox Jewish synagogues have only male rabbis, and some evangelical Protestant religions also prevent women from attaining leadership positions. As noted in Chapter 14, most religious leaders throughout history have been men. Conflict theorists who study inequality between men and women focus on how male dominance affects the unequal allocation of resources to women and men.

Symbolic Interactionist Perspective

Symbolic interactionists focus on the gender socialization lessons we learn as children, that is, how we define and present ourselves as boys and girls and, later in life, as men and women. Sociologists who study socialization see gender as socially created rather than biologically based but assume that gender is difficult to modify once we have learned it. This chapter presents several examples of gender socialization.

Symbolic interactionists who place emphasis on the ways we actively create our genders are referred to as social constructionists. These theorists argue that we create or "do" gender on the basis of what we think is appropriate for our "chosen"

gender in a given context (West and Zimmerman 1987). For example, those of us who identify as women create and re-create ourselves as women every day by the clothes we wear, our hairstyles, and, for many, makeup. Those who identify as men, likewise, create their gender identity by choice of clothing, hairstyle, and, usually, lack of makeup. We also create our gender by the way we talk, walk, carry our bodies, and use space.

These symbolic interactionists assume that gender is social, fluid, and, to some extent, chosen by individuals—but that choice is constrained by cultural norms. It is very hard not to follow the gender norms of our society, because the penalties can be harsh if we violate our culture's

Some religions, such as Greek Orthodox, still allow only men to hold leadership positions. This custom has worked to create and reinforce the notion of male superiority and inequality between men and women.
REUTERS/Eliana Aponte

Why are female breasts obscene while male breasts are not? Are there other body parts that are seen differently if they belong to men versus women?

Scott Metzger/Cartoonstock www.CartoonStock.com

rules about the definitions of masculinity and femininity. "Sissy" boys pay a high price, and girls who refuse to be soft and sweet also face penalties. Bullying often keeps children in their gendered place, and adults can be just as hard on other adults who violate gender norms. Men who do so risk being seen as weak or gay (as if there is something wrong with being gay). Strong women are often referred to as "bitches."

CONSIDER THIS

How would you explain this cartoon? Explain your reasoning.

Despite the costs of not following traditional gender norms, we can move toward gender equality by "undoing gender" (Deutsch 2007). That is, we can create social structures and practice interactional patterns that emphasize everyone's humanity. For example, we can create social policies that require employers to provide family leave for both men and women so that fathers and mothers can choose to share childrearing. These social policies are examples of social structure, and the choice fathers and mothers make to share childrearing is an example of social interaction.

A More Inclusive Theory: Gender as Social Structure

A recently developed theory provides us with an inclusive and overall view of how gender operates in our lives. Barbara Risman (2004) argues that gender should be studied as a social structure itself, just as we would study race or social class. She explains that instead of choosing one perspective on gender over another, we should make use of all of them as we seek to understand gendered behavior (Risman and Davis 2012). Her **gender as social structure** theory emphasizes that gender incorporates socialization, social interactions, and institutions and organizations and that these are all dimensions of every society's gender structure. We learn gender when we are children, but also as we interact with others over our lifetimes—resulting in structural (institutionalized) disadvantages for women.

This chapter provides many examples of how we learn our gender from our parents and various media, including books, movies, magazines, and social media. We also create our genders as we interact with our family members, teachers, and, very importantly, with our peers. Institutions are structured in ways that limit women's opportunities and advantage men. Occupations, schools, and even intimate relationships are settings that create unequal access to valued resources. In short, Risman reminds us that gender is not just about who we are as individuals but also about the societies in which we live. This chapter helps us understand gender as a social force created and reinforced through our individual interactions and through social organizations and institutions.

Check Your Understanding

- How do structural functionalists describe gender?
- How do people who use the conflict perspective describe gender?
- What do symbolic interactionists who are social constructionists emphasize about gender?
- How does the gender as a social structure theory use insights from the three major theoretical perspectives to understand gender?

WHICH IS MOST HELPFUL?

In this exercise you will apply the theoretical perspectives and gender as social structure theory to understanding gender.

Consider the three major theoretical perspectives and the theory of gender as a social structure. Which do you think is most helpful in understanding gender roles today? In your own words explain your choice. Be prepared to discuss this choice with a classmate.

Creating Gender and Sexual Identities, Recognizing Sexualities

8.3   How do we create our gender and sexual identities?

As you learned in Chapter 5, socialization is the process by which we learn to follow the norms and expectations of our society. **Gender socialization** is the process by which we learn to be a man or a woman in our particular place and time.

Starting Gender Socialization at Birth

We can see the importance society places on gender in many different ways. For example, from the moment we are born, others begin to construct our gender for us and teach us how to behave appropriately. Given ultrasound technology, a couple must decide if they want to know the sex of their unborn child and if they will share that information with others before the birth. No doubt they will be asked, again and again, if they know the sex of their child. Once they learn the sex, some expectant parents throw a "gender reveal" party to announce it and the assumed gender of their child. Why do you think people are so eager to know the sex of the baby? How are their images of and expectations for the child influenced by the words "It's a boy!" or "It's a girl!"? Why?

Imagine how you might feel if a person mistook your baby boy for a girl or vice versa. Does it matter? Have you seen people respond when someone assumes their child is a boy when she is a girl or vice versa? Most new parents make the sex of their babies very clear through how they dress their babies. We put bows on little girls' heads, even if they do not yet have hair—just to make sure it is clear to everyone that they are girls. Or have you ever encountered a baby dressed neutrally, perhaps in a simple green outfit?

What would you assume? How would you speak about the child to the parents?

Anyone who has ever tried to buy gender-neutral clothing for babies will tell you how difficult it is. Boys' clothing almost always comes in primary or vibrant colors and may have images of objects associated with masculinity, such as trucks or some masculine but cute male character like Mickey Mouse—never Minnie Mouse! Girls' clothing is usually pastel and more likely to have images of Bambi or dancers or some other soft and sweet image. Baby boys' and girls' booties are likely to have a bow for girls and a teddy bear for boys.

Recall that in Chapter 5, you read that parents not only dress their children differently on the basis of their sex but also treat them differently. Parents perceive much greater differences between male and female babies than actually exist and help create the differences that we see later in childhood and on into adulthood. For example, parents speak to their girl toddlers in a conversational style but are more likely to issue instructions to sons. Parents interact with sons in more aggressive and physical styles of play and are more likely to welcome gender nonconformity from their girls than their boys. Fathers, in particular, actively teach their boys how to be masculine and encourage heterosexuality well before their sons enter puberty (Gansen and Martin 2018).

CONSIDER THIS

Can you remember a time when you witnessed a male child or a teenager being ridiculed for "acting like a girl"? What had he done to prompt this ridicule? What were the consequences of this ridicule—how did it make the boy react? In your experience, are girls as likely to be ridiculed for "acting like a boy"? Why?

The first question that occurs to most of us when we hear of the birth of a child is "Is it a boy or a girl?" Lately, it has become popular to celebrate when we reveal babies' gender, before they are born, as in this episode of ABC's *Black-ish*.

Kelsey McNeal/Disney ABC Television Group/Getty Images

Gender Socialization through Children's Media

Our gender socialization does not end in infancy. We continue to get feedback on how we do gender throughout childhood (and beyond). Think about the gender ideas the media teach us every day. Advertisements, television and radio news, talk shows, magazines, and movies all instruct us on what a woman and a man should be and the consequences of not living up to these ideals (Gansen and Martin 2018). For example, in the popular children's television show *Paw Patrol*, viewers see the two female dogs (one pink and the other purple) behaving in stereotypically feminine ways (Gansen and Martin 2018). Children's books also communicate to girls and boys how they should behave and what they can expect to become. Many still emphasize male over female characters. For example, among the 100 most popular children's books of 2017 the best sellers *You Can't Take an Elephant on the Bus*, *The Koala Who Could*, and *There's a Monster in Your Bed* have no female characters (Ferguson 2018). However, there are now children's books written especially to help teach children gender equality, including twelve books published between 2015 and 2018 that specifically focus on powerful girls and sensitive boys (Ferguson 2018).

Learning Gender in School

Gender lessons are part of the hidden curriculum or the latent functions (see Chapter 2) of our schools. The hidden curriculum consists of the attitudes, behaviors, and values the educational system transmits outside the formal curriculum (see Chapter 12). In elementary school, when girls and boys are asked to line up separately or encouraged to compete against one another in classroom contests, the lesson is clear: Boys and girls are different.

In schools, children also learn that women nurture and men are in charge. Women make up 98 percent of preschool teachers and 80 percent of elementary and middle school teachers but only 68 percent of primary principals and 40 percent of middle school principals (Bureau of Labor Statistics 2018a). In high school, 58 percent of teachers are women, but 67 percent of principals are men (Taie and Goldring 2017). This pattern continues throughout most of our experiences with formal education. As you move higher up the prestige ladder in the institution of education, the more likely you are to see men. The majority of college professors are men (U.S. Department of Education 2018).

Peers, Gender Socialization, and Sexualities. Gender socialization continues during high school, and our peers are powerful agents of socialization. As noted earlier, the consequences of not sticking to our **gender scripts**, or expectations for behavior appropriate for our assigned genders, can be harsh. The way you walk, talk, and dress and the activities you choose all help create masculine or feminine images. Students who do not conform to stereotypical expectations are much more likely to be bullied. However, there is also a risk, especially for men, of hypermasculinity. Men who conform rigidly to masculinity norms are more likely to engage in risky behaviors, including drinking alcohol and smoking. We know less about hyperfeminine students, but the evidence we have suggests that they are more likely to be victims of sexual violence (Gordon et al. 2018).

C. J. Pascoe's (2007, 2011) now classic book *Dude, You're a Fag* describes the strict adherence to gender scripts boys must embrace and the penalty of failing to reject any stereotypical feminine behavior. Boys who dare to violate their gender scripts can pay a high social price. They must be stoic at all costs, hide any emotion other than anger, and be very careful to never show any physical affection for other men. If they violate this script, they will likely be

Changing Attitudes toward Same-Sex Marriage

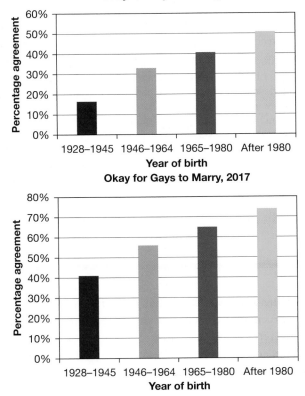

Sources: "5 facts about same-sex marriage." Pew Research Center, Washington, D.C. (26 June 2017) http://www.pewresearch.org/fact-tank/2017/06/26/same-sex-marriage/.

tarred with the label of a "fag." Although the term *fag* has been used to ridicule gay boys and men, Pascoe finds that it embodies far more than same-sex attraction and reaches to the core of what being a "man" is. Her research helps reveal the relationship between homophobia and the construction of masculinity. To be a "real man," you must be heterosexual. On the other hand, there is evidence that homophobia is declining. As seen in Figure 8.1, the acceptance of gay marriage has changed dramatically in the past two decades. In the United States, support for same-sex marriage increased from just 43 percent in 2001 to 62 percent in 2017. Today, a strong majority (74 percent) of Millennials support same-sex marriage (Pew Research Center 2017).

The Media and Gender, Sex, and Sexuality

As children grow older, media become an even more important part of their lives. Keeping up with the latest trends in music, apps, movies, and so on helps teens fit in with their classmates and gives them a sense of belonging with their peer group. It also teaches them how to create gender and sexual identities.

Sexuality refers to our emotional and physical attraction to a particular sex. The categories for sexualities include heterosexual/straight (attracted to a different sex), homosexual/gay/lesbian (attracted to members of one's own sex), bisexual (attracted to both sexes), and asexual (not attracted to either sex). You probably know the acronym LGBT (originally signifying lesbian, gay, bisexual, and transsexual people). As more non–heterosexual/straight people have gained recognition (e.g., those who are asexual and/or intersex), people began to add additional letters (e.g., LGBTQAI+ for lesbian, gay, bisexual, transgender, queer or questioning, intersex, and all other people who are not heterosexual/straight). Most people, however, now use the shorter LGBT when referring to everyone included under the longer and more cumbersome LGBTQAI+ label. This is what we do in this text.

Music, TV, and Movies. Music, television, and movies play a big role in the lives of teens and young adults and provide potent gender and sexuality lessons. Preadolescent boys learn gender lessons from television channels such as MTV, the Disney Chanel, and Nickelodeon. The more they watch these media outlets, the more likely they are to see men as sexually dominant and women as sexual objects whose value depends on their physical appearance (Rousseau, Rodgers, and Eggermont 2019).

In music videos, that lesson is reinforced; men are portrayed as aggressive and dominant, whereas women are sexually objectified and subservient (Gamble 2019). While hip-hop and rap are known for promoting violence against women, pop music, often heard by young teens, also markets violence. A third of pop songs, those that appear on the Billboard Hot 100, degrade women, presenting them as sex objects and/or depicting physical violence against women. For example, consider the lyrics of "Love the Way You Lie" by Eminem and Rihanna: "Throw 'em down, pin 'em, so lost in the moments, when you're in 'em . . . Sound like broken records, playin' over, but you promised her, Next time you'd show restraint, . . . but you lied again." The chorus is "I love the way you lie." Other songs also portray violent themes. "Wake Up Call" by Maroon 5 is about a man shooting his girlfriend's lover (Frisby and Behm-Morawitz 2019).

Popular films are also much more likely to portray women, rather than men, as sex objects in popular film. Among the top films of 2017, 28 percent showed women in sexy attire, but just 8 percent displayed men in such

GENDER AND SEXUALITY LESSONS IN MARVEL COMICS

In this exercise, you will explore gender and sexuality by examining Marvel Comics characters.

Using any Internet search engine, find at least two images of male and female Marvel Comics characters. Write descriptors for the male and female characters. How are your descriptors similar and how are they different? Write a brief paragraph answering these questions: What lessons do the comics teach about gender? What do you assume about their sexuality on the basis of their appearance? Why? Do you make different assumptions about the women's sexuality compared with the men's?

As Captain Marvel, Brie Larson plays one of the small but growing number of female superheroes.
© Marvel Studios/Entertainment Pictures

Best Actress winner Frances McDormand used her acceptance speech to put a spotlight on gender inequities in the movie industry.
Steve Granitz/WireImage

clothing. Moreover, 25 percent of women compared with 10 percent of men appeared at least partially undressed (Smith et al. 2018).

Recently, however, we have seen pushback against sexism in the media, particularly in movies. For example, in 2016, there was a female-led *Ghostbusters* reboot; in 2018, women starred in *Ocean's 8*, an *Ocean's Eleven* spinoff (Wetcher 2018); and 2019 gave us Brie Larson in the superhero blockbuster *Captain Marvel*. During the 2018 Academy Awards, many, including the host, Jimmy Kimmel, and Frances McDormand, winner of the Best Actress award, highlighted the social movements #MeToo and Time's Up (Rainey 2018). #MeToo shines a spotlight on sexual harassment, and Time's Up is a legal defense fund for sexual harassment victims.

News and Advertisements. It's easy to be unaware of the gender socialization we receive from the media. It happens continually, so it's a routine part of our lives. For example, men are much more likely to be newscasters than women, and news stories are much more likely to feature men than women. If you turn on a news show on a major network (ABC, NBC, or CBS), you are three times as likely to see a man as a woman reporting the news. On evening broadcasts, 63 percent of anchors are men, and in the print media, 59 percent of the bylines go to men (Women's Media Center 2019). The message, although often subtly delivered, is clear: Men are knowledgeable leaders to whom we should listen.

When the news takes a break, we see advertisements. Although there are exceptions, men are usually portrayed in ads as independent, in-charge, aggressive beings. Women are presented as very concerned about getting clothes clean and taking care of others or as sexually alluring. They tend to be thin and beautiful, like a Barbie Doll (Suggett 2019). The implicit—and sometimes explicit—message is that if you use a particular product you, too, will look like the gorgeous woman depicted in the ads. For example, Beyoncé stars in a sultry ad for the perfume Heat, wearing a very low-cut red dress, suggesting that if you use this perfume, you too will generate sexual "heat." The sexual imagery in these ads teaches sex roles for women and men and portrays sexual behavior and sexuality as crucial aspects of life that men and women must master to advance in society.

Beyoncé provides lessons on how to be sexually alluring in this perfume ad for Heat.
Jemal Countess/Getty Images Entertainment/Getty Images

Challenging Stereotypes. Advertisers, however, may also challenge existing gender and sexuality stereotypes. Budweiser remade ads from the 1950s and 1960s to reflect a 2019 reality. An ad that once showed a woman who served Budweiser to her husband to keep him happy now shows a woman with a group of beer-drinking women friends. The text changed from "And think of all the planning that goes into meals to make *him* contented!" to "She has it all. In fact, she's never been more fulfilled." The focus of these ads changed from a woman whose job it is to serve her husband to a woman who is enjoying her own life (Hidreley 2019).

Gillette, the maker of razors, directly responded to the #MeToo social movement with its ad challenging "toxic masculinity." The theme is "the best men can be" focusing on sexual harassment and encouraging men to be good fathers and role models. These messages promoting gender equality have received pushback. For example, Fox News labeled the Gillette ad "dishonest and insulting to men" (LaBella and Downey 2019), and thousands of "trolls" posted disparaging remarks about it online.

The Media, Sexuality, and Backlash. Other media forms have influenced attitudes toward members of the LGBT community. Shows that feature gay, bisexual, transgender, and questioning characters in a positive light help build empathy. Television shows like *Queer Eye, Glee, Modern Family, Gravity Falls, Orange Is the New Black*, and *Transparent* have helped shape many people's feelings toward LGBT people. In 2018, Fox 21 and FX Productions aired a new show titled *Pose*, which features the largest cast of transgender actors ever to be aired on TV. The show is set in New York City during the HIV/AIDS crisis. There is also a new Broadway musical titled *The Prom* that was featured in the 2018 Macy's Thanksgiving parade that included the first lesbian kiss in the parade's history, between Caitlin Kinnunen and Isabelle McCalla (Romano 2018).

The percentage of people in the United States characterizing themselves as LGBT increased from 3.5 percent in 2012 to 4.5 percent in 2017, with 5.1 percent of women and 3.9 percent of men identifying as LGBT (Newport 2018). Younger people (those born between 1980 and 1999) are about twice as likely to identify as LGBT as those from their parents' and grandparents' generations. Whereas only 1.4 percent of those born from 1913 to 1945 and 2.4 percent of those born between 1946 and 1964 do so, 8.1 percent of Millennials identify as LGBT. As seen in positive media portrayals, the legalization of same-sex marriage, and more people identifying as LGBT, gender and sexual norms have become less rigid (Bridges 2017).

On the other hand, the year after the 2016 election, the Federal Bureau of Investigation reported a 17 percent increase in hate crimes based on race, religion, disability, gender, and LGBT status (Human Rights Campaign 2018). The legal status of LGBT people is also an indicator of the extent to which they are accepted. In twenty-eight states, there are no state laws that protect LGBT people

Laverne Cox is a role model for transgender people and has helped make *Orange Is the New Black* highly successful.

Jason LeVeris/FilmMagic/Getty Images

The United States is not the only place where discrimination based on sexual orientation is legal. In six countries, having a same-sex relationship is punishable by *death*—Iran, Saudi Arabia, Yemen, Nigeria, Sudan, and Somalia—and death is one of the possible punishments in Mauritania, United Arab Emirates, Qatar, Pakistan, and Afghanistan (Mendos 2019). Thirty-five percent (seventy nations) of United Nations member states criminalize consensual same-sex acts. Figure 8.2 reveals the status of rights for gay people around the world.

Check Your Understanding

- How do we tend to treat girl and boy babies differently?
- Where do we get our ideas about how we should behave as boys and girls?
- What are some of the ways we learn gender and sexual identities at school and from our peers?
- What do the media teach us about gender and sexualities? What are current attitudes toward LGBT people, and how have the media influenced those attitudes?

Gender, Sexuality, and Work

8.4   How does gender affect workforce experiences?

Although they constitute almost half of all workers (as seen in Figure 8.3), women still face many inequalities based on their gender. **Gender segregation in the workplace**—the practice of labeling certain fields of employment as for

from discrimination in employment, housing, and public accommodations. That means that in more than half of our states, employers can fire workers, deny housing, and restrict which public restrooms people can use because of their sexual or gender identities (Williams Institute 2019).

▼ FIGURE 8.2
Gay Marriage around the World

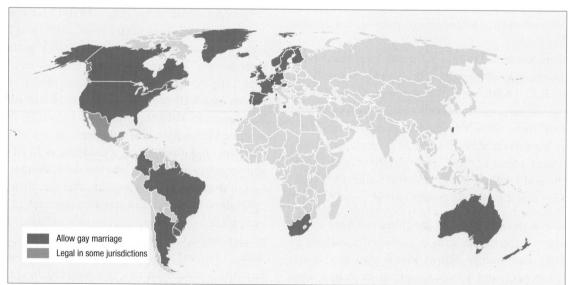

Allow gay marriage
Legal in some jurisdictions

Source: Adapted from Pew Research Center and Amnesty International.

▼ FIGURE 8.3

Labor Force Participation by Gender, 1972–2018

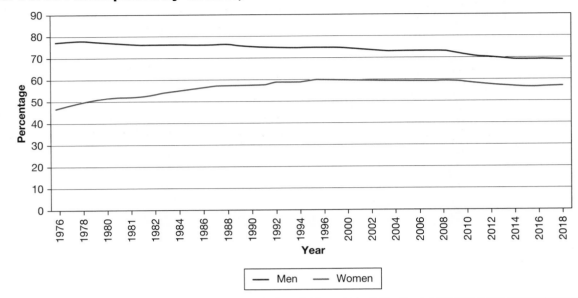

Source: Bureau of Labor Statistics. 2018b. "Labor Force Statistics from the Current Population Survey, U.S. Bureau of Labor Statistics, Household Data Annual Averages, Employment Status of the Civilian Noninstitutional Population 16 Years and Over by Sex, 1978 to Date." Accessed January 20, 2019. http://www.bls.gov/cps/cpsaat02.htm.

either men or women—has led to relatively few women in high-paying jobs. Many women also face a gender wage gap, earning less than men for the same work.

The U.S. labor force continues to be segregated by gender. There has been no significant change in the extent of gender segregation since the 1990s (Baker and Cornelson 2018). In order to have a gender-integrated labor force, more than 50 percent of men or women would have to change their occupations.

Nor have women made much progress in attaining high-status and high-paying jobs. They hold fewer than 20 percent of executive officer positions or seats on the boards of successful companies and fewer than 5 percent of *Fortune* 500 CEO positions (Wynn and Correll 2018). Women are more likely to hold lower paying positions that involve caretaking, and men dominate in higher paying jobs such as those in science and technology. For example, men hold 76 percent of all the jobs in computer, engineering, and physical science occupations and 85 percent of those in engineering architectures. Men are also overrepresented in skilled labor jobs (e.g., carpenters, plumbers, electricians),

▼ FIGURE 8.4

Percentage of Bachelor's Degrees Earned by Women

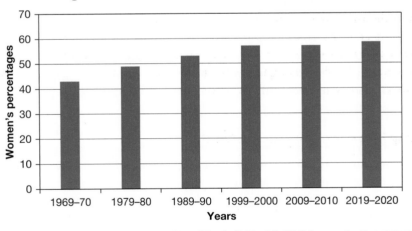

Source: National Center for Education Statistics. 2017. Digest of Education Statistics. Table 318.10. Degrees conferred by postsecondary institutions, by level of degree and sex of student: Selected years, 1869–70 through 2026–27. https://nces.ed.gov/programs/digest/d13/tables/dt13_318.10.asp. (accessed April 4, 2019).

Note: The figure for 2019 to 2020 is a projection.

and almost all construction jobs are held by men (Bureau of Labor Statistics 2018a).

Do differences in education or training explain why men and women are segregated in different professions? Figure 8.4 shows the percentage of bachelor's degrees earned by women. Notice that women have earned more college degrees than men for about forty years. Figure 8.5 reveals that more recently, women have also surpassed men in earning PhDs and professional degrees.

▼ FIGURE 8.5

Doctoral and Professional Degrees by Gender

**Number of Doctoral and Professional Degrees Conferred by Gender,
1969–1970 to 2019–2020**

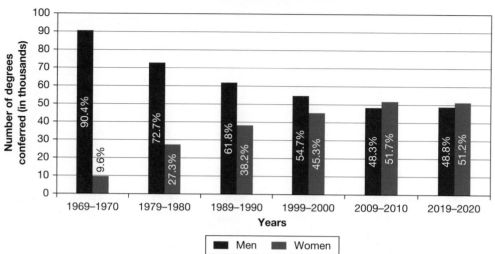

Source: National Center for Education Statistics, 2017; Russell Sage Foundation, https://www.russellsage.org/news/rise-women-seven-charts-showing-womens-rapid-gains-educational-achievement.

Note: Percentages include PhD, MD, EdD, DDS, and JD degrees. The figure for 2019 to 2020 is a projection.

CONSIDER THIS

Look at Figure 8.5. Does it surprise you that women's educational achievement is now higher than men's? Why do you think this has not resulted in women and men being more equally distributed in various occupations?

What types of degrees do men and women earn? For example, how many women major in science, technology, engineering, or math (STEM) and subsequently pursue careers that require this background—and tend to pay more than other professions? As seen in Figure 8.6, the percentage of female biological scientists and social scientists has increased, but those are the fields in which women have historically been more numerous. Other fields have remained relatively unchanged since the 1990s, and the number of computer and mathematical scientists has actually decreased. Engineering remains a heavily male dominated field, with only 15 percent of engineering jobs held by women (see Figure 8.6).

Gender socialization leads men into and women away from STEM fields. Women face stereotypes, a form of gender bias, that suggests that they are not as competent as men in these areas. Dr. Sarah Rugheimer (2018), an astronomer and astrobiologist at Harvard, maintains a web site with a bibliography of more than ninety-five articles that document gender bias in STEM. She cites articles that document faculty bias against female students, student bias against female instructors, and a gender pay gap among faculty in the sciences.

Among the research Rugheimer presents is a famous study of gender bias in STEM. Science professors at six major research universities were asked to evaluate applications for the position of laboratory manager. The applications were created by the researchers, who described identical skills and research backgrounds on every application. They then split the applications into two groups—one with the applicant's name listed as John and the other with the name listed as Jennifer. When the professors evaluated the applications, both women and men professors showed gender bias, rating John more highly than Jennifer. When asked to name a starting salary appropriate for the applicant, the professors were willing to offer an average of $30,328 to John but only $26,508 to Jennifer (Moss-Racusin et al. 2012). The researchers found that even trained scientists have gender bias! Scientists, like all people, are raised in societies with gender roles that work to confine men and women to certain behaviors and professions and result in gender inequality.

Gender segregation prevents some people from doing work they would be good at and would enjoy. That hurts both individuals and society as a whole. When we prevent

Women in Selected STEM Occupations, 1993–2018

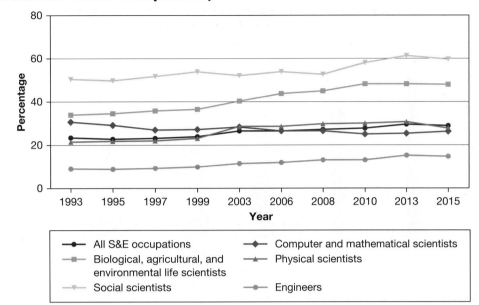

Source: National Science Board, Science and Engineering Indicators 2018. Figure 3-27 Women in S&E occupations: 1993–2015. https://www.nsf.gov/statistics/2018/nsb20181/report/sections/science-and-engineering-labor-force/women-and-minorities-in-the-s-e-workforce.

Note: S&E = science and engineering.

talented people from entering certain professions, we all lose. For our economy to be efficient and effective, we need the best match between talent, skills, and the work that needs to be done. Gender segregation keeps women out of many high-paying fields and limits everyone's freedom to choose the job for which they are most suited. Segregating our job choices by gender hurts our economy and contributes to the **gender wage gap**, that is, the difference between wages of men and women.

The Gender Wage Gap

Like gender segregation in the workforce, the gender wage gap has not decreased very much since the 1990s. As seen in Figure 8.7, women who work full-time earn on average between 80 and 83 cents for every dollar men earn (Bureau of Labor Statistics 2019). The gender wage gap varies by race and ethnicity, with Asian women earning 75 percent of what Asian men make and White women earning 82 percent of the wages of White men. The wage gap between Black women and Black men and Hispanic women and Hispanic men is somewhat smaller (with the women earning, respectively, 93 percent and 87 percent of the men's wages).

The Wage Gap and Segregation within Occupations

Occupational segregation within as well as across occupations contributes to the gender wage gap. For example,

for physicians, the specialties women and men choose influence the gender wage gap. In general, women are in the lowest paying and men in the highest paying medical specialties. In the class of 2013–2014, women made up 58 percent of the residents in family medicine, 75 percent of the residents in pediatrics, and 85 percent of the residents in obstetrics and gynecology. Men dominated in surgery (59 percent), anesthesiology (63 percent), and radiology (73 percent). Family practice physicians earned on average just under $200,000 a year, while many surgeons earned about $500,000 per year (Dill 2015).

The specialization choices male and female physicians make relate directly to male and female gender roles in society—and work to support them. Women are more likely to specialize in areas that allow them flexible hours and a family life, while men are more likely to have wives (with flexible hours) who can take care of them and their families (see Chapter 11). Moreover, areas of specialty are not the sole cause of the gender wage gap among physicians. The president of the American Medical Association notes that even within the same specialty, women tend to earn less than men (McAneny 2018).

One explanation for gender differences in salaries for attorneys, who tend to charge clients an hourly rate for their work, is the amount of time women and men spend in childcare, which takes away from the hours they can spend at work. As mentioned earlier, women do more work

Median Weekly Earnings, by Gender and Race/Ethnicity

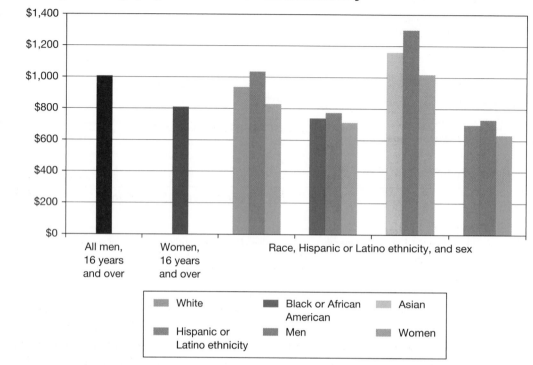

Source: Bureau of Labor Statistics. 2018a. "Labor Force Statistics from the Current Population Survey, Household Data Annual Averages, Employed persons by detailed occupation, sex, race an Hispanic or Latino ethnicity." https://www.bls.gov/cps/cpsaat11.htm (accessed March 19, 2019).

Note: People of Hispanic or Latino ethnicity may be of any race. Estimates for the race groups shown (White, Black or African American, and Asian) include Hispanics.

at home than men. Among employed men and women, men spend 1.23 hours a day while women spend 1.9 hours on household work (Bureau of Labor Statistics 2018a; see Chapter 11). Other explanations include requiring women to do "office housework," like taking notes in meetings, ordering meals for the firm, and providing comfort to colleagues having problems (Zraick 2018).

As we discuss more in Chapter 11, changes in workplace policies such as paid parental leave, flexible hours, and fewer work hours can address the gender wage gap and improve everyone's life. If each parent must take three months off (one at a time) when they have a child, more men would take time off, thereby negating part of the baby penalty mothers face. If workers set their own hours rather than work a standard shift, they can work around children's school hours and coordinate with spouses on childcare needs. A variety of U.S. companies have found that flexible work hour policies allow workers to be more successful on the job and at home (Laber-Warren 2018). Reducing work hours altogether would also benefit everyone and help reduce the gender gap. A New Zealand firm reduced its workweek to thirty-two hours over four days and found that workers were more productive during their time at work (Graham-McLay 2018). The federal

government can assist in this effort by making such family-friendly rules compulsory for places of work with more than fifty employees (as it does for other government-mandated workplace policies, such as the Family Leave Act).

Discrimination and the Wage Gap

Sometimes employers contribute to the wage gap by simply discriminating against women employees. Some pay men more than they pay women—even when they are doing the same job and have the same credentials. Although doing so is against the law, thanks to the Equal Pay Act of 1963, such discrimination persists.

Research on transgender men allows us a unique perspective on gender inequality in the workplace. Transgender men who began their jobs as women and then became men often gained authority and prestige at work even when they remained in the same job. Transgender men report that, upon their gender transition, they suddenly were assumed to know how to use electronics and set up computers and to know what they were talking about. Transgender men can clearly see that men succeed at higher rates than do women not because they are more skilled but because our culture perceives men as more competent than women (Tramontana 2017).

The Glass Ceiling

Many women experience a phenomenon known as the "glass ceiling." The **glass ceiling** is the unofficial barrier women and minorities face when trying to advance to the upper levels of an organization. The glass ceiling is called "glass" because it is invisible and not openly acknowledged. There are no formal rules that say that women cannot advance. However, when you bump up against it, it is as real as wood and plaster. And you can see it if you use your sociological eye. For example, if you were looking for evidence of a glass ceiling in a group of corporations, you would notice that the gap between the percentages of men and women increases from the managerial to vice presidential to CEO levels. One of the reasons so few women have higher level jobs is that candidates for these jobs are often recruited by word of mouth. In other words, it matters whom you know (Fernandez and Rubineau 2019). Women are less likely to have the strong professional networks that men have.

The glass ceiling becomes much stronger when women become parents. Some have even said that women who have children face a "maternal wall" (Williams 2013). Young women (ages twenty-five to thirty-four), on average, earn 90 cents for every dollar earned by men, but parenthood increases the gender wage gap. Thirty-nine percent of women compared with 24 percent of men take significant time off from work to care for a child or another family member. Slightly more than a quarter (27 percent) of women leave paid work completely to take care of their families (Brown and Patten 2017). Some would argue that mothers cannot even enter the room with the glass ceiling (Ferrante 2018)!

The glass ceiling (and the maternal wall) is more pronounced in some professions than in others. It is a particularly powerful impediment for women in *Fortune* 500

▼ FIGURE 8.8

Women CEOs in *Fortune* 500 Companies, 1995–2018

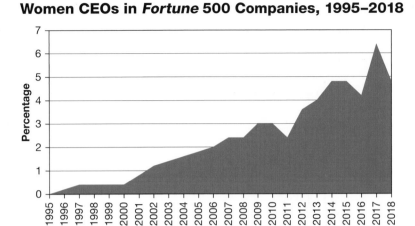

Source: "Women CEOs in Fortune 500 companies, 1995–2018." Pew Research Center, Washington, D.C. (14 January 2015). https://www.pewsocialtrends.org/chart/women-ceos-in-fortune-500-companies-1995-2014/.

Note: Prior to 2017, on the basis of the percentage of women CEOs at the time of the annual published *Fortune* 500 list. For 2017, share is as of the end of the first quarter.

companies, where few women have been able to break through. As Figure 8.8 reveals, in 2018, just 4.8 percent of all CEOs of *Fortune* 500 companies were women, down from a high of 6.4 percent in 2017 (Pew Research Center 2018).

Although women have not made much progress in obtaining leadership positions in *Fortune* 500 companies, they have made significant gains in U.S. politics, as seen in Figure 8.9 (next page). Women now constitute 23.4 percent of the members of the House of Representatives. A third of those won their seats

Few women break through the glass ceiling in their professions, and if they have children, women employees are likely to face a "maternal wall."
©iStockphoto.com/hudiemm

Number of Women in Congress Increases

The 116th Congress Represents the Biggest Jump in Women Members since the 1990s

Women member of Congress, by party

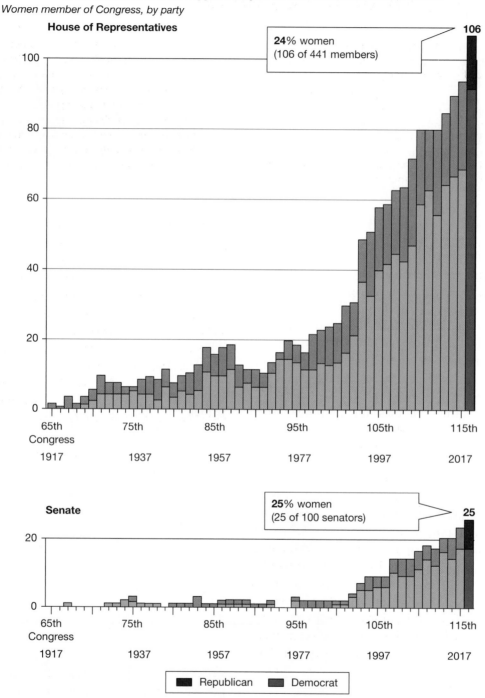

Sources: "A record number of women will be serving in the new Congress." Pew Research Center, Washington, D.C. (18 December 2018) https://www.pewresearch.org/fact-tank/2018/12/18/record-number-women-in-congress/.

in the 2018 midterm elections. Twenty-five percent of U.S. senators are now women, the largest percentage in history. There are far more Democratic than Republican women in Congress. Women make up 35 percent of all House Democrats and 8 percent of House Republicans. Thirty-six percent of Senate Democrats are women, and 15 percent of Senate Republicans are women. Of the newly elected Republican House members, only one is a woman (DeSilver 2018).

DOING SOCIOLOGY 8.4

WOMEN IN LEADERSHIP POSITIONS

In this exercise, you will look at data on leaders in politics, business, and education and propose a college curriculum to close the gender gap.

Look at the data on women in leadership positions in politics, business, and education presented by the Pew Research Center at https://www.pewsocialtrends.org/fact-sheet/the-data-on-women-leaders/.

1. Note the graph that most surprises you. Write any questions you have about the graph.

2. Individually or with a partner, propose a college curriculum that would help bridge the gap between men and women in at least one of the graphs. What classes would be required? What skills would need to be taught? Would it be important for women to be the professors in these classes? Who would take the classes? Would you assume that women would need to increase their skills, or would socializing men be more helpful?

CONSIDER THIS

After reading this chapter, how would you explain why, as of 2020, all U.S. presidents have been men?

Sexual Harassment

Recently, several high-profile cases put sexual harassment squarely in the public eye. Between October 5, 2017, and October 29, 2018, 205 prominent men and 3 women lost their jobs, or experienced other significant professional losses, because of allegations of sexual harassment at work and/or other forms of sexual misconduct, including having sex with a minor. Some face criminal charges. Many of those accused of sexual harassment worked in the media, including movie producer Harvey Weinstein and *Today Show* host Matt Lauer. Numerous politicians, primarily at the state level, lost their positions. A Supreme Court justice Brett Kavanaugh faced a public hearing on assault charges. Other well-known cases include Larry Nassar and R. Kelly. Nassar was the physician for the U.S. women's gymnastics team and a professor at Michigan State University. He is serving a life sentence for sexual abuse. R&B singer R. Kelly's long history of sexual abuse was highlighted in a Lifetime documentary in the winter of 2019, and he faces federal sex crime charges in both Chicago and New York (Carlsen et al. 2018; Meisner 2019).

CONSIDER THIS

What do you think of when you hear the phrase "sexual harassment"? Do you believe that the recent attention to sexual harassment and sexual abuse will help women in the workplace?

Sexual harassment is legally defined as verbal or physical harassment of a sexual nature when the harassment creates a hostile work environment or when the victim's advancement at work is affected (Equal Employment Opportunity Commission n.d.). About 5 million employees are harassed every year, but 99.8 percent never file charges, and of those who do, fewer than 1,500 go to court. A primary reason people do not file charges is that most employers retaliate against the victims by firing or demoting them. Almost two-thirds of those who file sexual harassment charges are fired. Although both men and women are sexually harassed, women are more likely to be victims, with an estimated 85 percent of all women harassed at some point during their careers (McCann, Tomaskovic-Devey, and Badgett 2018).

Check Your Understanding

- To what extent is the labor force segregated by gender?
- How large is the gender wage gap?
- What contributes to the gender wage gap?
- What is the glass ceiling?
- How prevalent is sexual harassment?

Gender and Intimate Relationships

8.5 How have rates of sexual activity among young adults in the United States changed since the 1950s?

Our most intimate relationships are also gendered. That is, women's and men's behavior in relationships and our attitudes toward our intimate lives differ by gender. Gender influences our private lives in everything, including how we conduct our romantic and sexual relationships. Barbara

PUBLIC SOCIOLOGY

BARBARA J. RISMAN

I was part of the women liberation movements in the 1970s as an undergraduate at Northwestern University. When the Equal Rights Amendment—a constitutional amendment passed by Congress in 1972—failed to be ratified by the states, I couldn't believe so many women voted against their own self-interest, against their own equality. I had to figure that out.

Sociology allowed me to put my two major commitments together: political activism and understanding why and how people do what they do.

One way I now combine my activism and scholarship is through public sociology, communicating sociological findings to the public. I have helped build the Council of Contemporary Families, a group that brings research and clinical expertise on families into the public realm. We communicate information available to social scientists and clinicians that the rest of the world does not yet know. For example, for the fiftieth anniversary of the *Moynihan Report*, we published a symposium on how policy has yet to address poverty in minority communities and how that affects families. Such symposia report what researchers have discovered and let us hold public debates about issues, even when we disagree.

Another way I combine my concern for public good with sociology is my work with the Scholars Strategy Network. We are a national group concerned with linking research with public policy. I co-chair the Chicagoland chapter. In the fall of 2019, our members wrote briefs about issues the city was facing and offered to meet with all the mayoral candidates, offering them those briefs and also the opportunity to meet other researchers in topics they cared about. Many of the candidates took us up on the offer, including the candidate who won, now Mayor Lori Lightfoot. We hope to continue to work with the city to introduce researchers to those policy makers working on social problems here in Chicago.

Another way I try to do public sociology is by publishing work I hope will be read outside classrooms. I publish op-eds on topics from open access to bathrooms, to whether Millennials are feminists (they are, and not just the women). I write a regular *Psychology Today* column titled "Gender Matters," because it does.

I feel strongly that spreading information from research is vital. It is up to us as activist-scholars to make sure what we know that might be useful for decision makers, and for our fellow citizens, gets into their hands.

Discussion Question: If researchers do not make their research public, where are we likely to get our information? Is it likely to be based on facts?

Barbara J. Risman is head of sociology at the University of Illinois at Chicago. Her latest book is Where the Millennials Will Take Us: A New Generation Wrestles with the Gender Structure *(Oxford University Press, 2018). She is coeditor (with Carissa Froyum and William Scarborough) of the* Handbook on the Sociology of Gender *(Springer, 2018) and editor of* Gender & Society.

Risman, our sociologist in action for this chapter, regularly writes about gender and intimate relationships in her *Psychology Today* column.

Romantic Relationships in Historical Context

Have you thought much about your ancestors' sex lives? You might think of your ancestors' romantic relationships as being sexually inhibited and rigidly defined by their genders. We tend to think of ourselves as being free to create our intimate relationships independent of gender norms and see ourselves as much more sexually liberated. Although the social structures under which we live our most private lives have changed, our romantic relationships are still remarkably gendered, and our ancestors were more sexually active than we might assume.

During the Colonial era, sexual activity was common outside marriage. About 33 percent of brides were pregnant before marriage (Godbeer 2004). During the Victorian age, middle-class girls were more carefully monitored than were those from the working class. The young women who worked in urban factories and department stores often lived away from their families in boarding houses and furnished rooms. They had more freedom from family oversight (Bailey 2004). During the early 1900s, dating became commonplace, and couples enjoyed even more distance from watchful eyes. By the 1950s and 1960s, going steady, or dating one person exclusively,

HOW SEXUALLY ACTIVE ARE HIGH SCHOOL STUDENTS?

Sexual norms have changed remarkably over the years. Although premarital sex is now more widely accepted than in previous periods, the number of sexually active teens is often smaller than many people might expect. Compared with teens born in the 1980s, teens today are less, not more, likely to have had sex.

In this online activity, you will examine how sexually active high school students are by state, using data from the Centers for Disease Control and Prevention's Youth Risk Behavior Surveillance System.

*Requires the Vantage version of *Sociology in Action*.

▼ FIGURE 8.10

Percentage of High School Students Sexually Active (State)

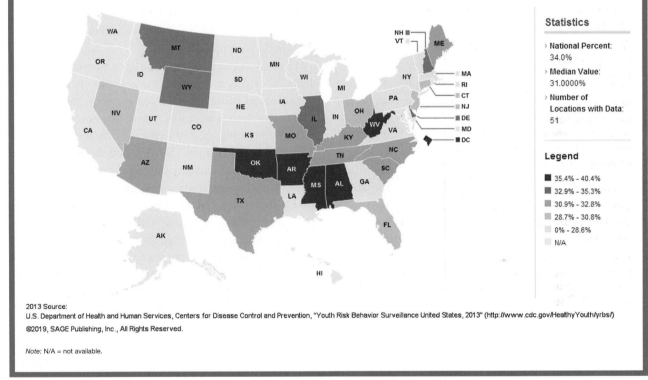

Statistics

› **National Percent:**
34.0%

› **Median Value:**
31.0000%

› **Number of Locations with Data:**
51

Legend

- ■ 35.4% – 40.4%
- ■ 32.9% – 35.3%
- ■ 30.9% – 32.8%
- ■ 28.7% – 30.8%
- ■ 0% – 28.6%
- ■ N/A

2013 Source:
U.S. Department of Health and Human Services, Centers for Disease Control and Prevention, "Youth Risk Behavior Surveillance United States, 2013" (http://www.cdc.gov/HealthyYouth/yrbs/)

©2019, SAGE Publishing, Inc., All Rights Reserved.

Note: N/A = not available.

was common, and more sexual intimacy was expected. During the decade of the 1950s, 70 percent of women and 60 percent of men reported being virgins at age eighteen, but by the 1980s, only about 50 percent of both women and men reported being virgins at age eighteen (Schwartz and Rutter 1998).

Recent data indicates that today's eighteen- to thirty-four-year-olds are less likely to be sexually active today than they have been in the past thirty years. In 1986 only 6 percent of men and women in this age group said that they had not had sex during the past year. By 2018, this number had risen to 23 percent. Remarkably,

the eighteen- to thirty-four-year-olds were less likely to be sexually active than any other age group except those over age sixty (Ingraham 2019)! This number is not surprising given that in 2018, more than half of eighteen- to thirty-four-year-olds report that they do not have a romantic partner (Bonos and Guskin 2019). Given that among people eighteen to thirty-four, 23 percent say that they have not had sex in the past year and 51 percent report not having a romantic partner, many of those who are sexually active must be having casual sex. Perhaps what we know about hooking up provides a partial explanation.

DOING SOCIOLOGY 8.6

ROMANTIC RELATIONSHIPS

The goal of this activity is to encourage you to think about the kind of intimate relationship you most value and consider how you developed those values. For example, you may know people who have the kind of relationship you want. The lyrics of a song may have helped you decide that some behaviors are not acceptable to you. Write your answers to the following questions.

What does a healthy romantic relationship look like? What personal characteristics do you most value? What kinds of behaviors would strengthen a relationship for you? What kind of behaviors would end a relationship with you? What sociological concepts or principles guide your answers to these questions? How did you learn the answers to these questions?

Hooking Up. Do college students on your campus date or just hook up? Several sociologists have examined the hookup culture on today's college campuses. In the most extensive study, more than 20,000 college students from twenty-one public and private colleges and universities provided researchers with information about their hookup behavior and attitudes in an online survey. These students were recruited primarily from sociology courses like the one you are in right now. The Online College Survey was conducted between 2005 and 2011 (England 2015).

Hooking up is a sexual encounter that happens between people who are not in a committed relationship. Often, hookups happen after meeting at a party or at a bar for the purposes of an intimate, no-strings-attached encounter. The hookup might entail only kissing or touching but could extend to sexual intercourse. When asked about their latest hookup experience, about 8 percent of men, compared with 3 percent of women, reported hooking up with a same-sex partner. A majority (68 percent) of the men who reported same-sex hookups identified as gay, while only 39 percent of the women who hooked up with other women said that they were gay or lesbian (Kuperberg and Walker 2018).

Hooking up is a common experience on today's residential college campuses, with estimates that range between 50 percent and 82 percent of all students reporting that they hooked up at least once while in college (Pham 2019; Risman 2019; England 2015; Kuperberg and Allison 2018). However, that does not mean that all college students are hooking up or even that the ones who do hook up do so on a regular basis. A slightly higher number of men report hooking up, and men are likely to have more hookups (Kuperberg and Allison 2018). Seniors report, on average, that they hooked up eight times over the course of

their college careers, and close to a third of all college students never hook up (Wade 2017).

Given how common hooking up is among college students, does this mean that college students now accept casual sex as being OK? To some extent, the answer is "yes," but there are limits. There are norms, or social rules, for hooking up, just as there were, and still are, for dating. Not surprisingly, there is a double standard based on gender. Men still tend to control the sexual experience, and women who engage in casual sex are viewed more negatively than men. Usually men gain social status, while women lose status. In hookup culture, women tend to pay a bigger emotional price than do men. Showing sentiment for a hookup partner can be viewed negatively for both men and women but is especially problematic for women (Wade 2017). As one student put it, "The two worst things that a boy can say to a girl is that she is fat or that she is clingy" (Wade 2017, 139).

Hookup culture has not led to the death of dating on campuses, however. Indeed, both men and women prefer dates over hookups, and both men and women wished they had better opportunities for long-term relationships. Many students choose hookups in hopes of their leading to long-term relationships, and many hookups do. Nor are college students today having sex at a younger age, with more partners or more often, than their parents. In fact, as noted above, college students and other young adults are having less sex than their parents did at their age (Kuperberg and Allison 2018; Wade 2017).

CONSIDER THIS

Do you think hooking up is a common occurrence on your campus? Why or why not?

Check Your Understanding

- Are unmarried teens today more or less likely to have had sex than those in other periods of our history?
- What is hooking up?
- How common is hooking up on college campuses today?

Conclusion

Gender is a socially constructed characteristic that is usually, but not always, consistent with the biological sex we are assigned at birth. The penalties for not abiding by the gender roles we learn in our homes, in our schools, and from our peers can be quite dramatic. Gender affects every part of our lives, including our opportunities in the labor force and our most intimate relationships. Knowing that it is a social construction gives us the ability to promote change in gender roles and to work for gender equality.

Race, another social construction that affects every aspect of our lives, is the focus of the next chapter. Like gender, it has become increasingly fluid over the past several years. Nonetheless, it remains a powerful force of inequality in society. As it does with gender, sociology gives us the tools to recognize and address societal issues related to race and ethnicity.

ⓢ SAGE edge™

Want a better grade? Get the tools you need to sharpen your study skills. Access practice quizzes, eFlashcards, video, and multimedia at **edge.sagepub.com/Korgen2e**

REVIEW

8.1 What are the sociological definitions of sex, gender, intersex, and transgender?

Sex is a biological construct that is defined by our external genitalia, chromosomes, and internal reproductive organs. Our gender, however, is a social concept, and we learn to be a woman or a man from interacting with others.

Intersex people are not clearly biologically male or female. In our culture, we are often very uncomfortable if our child is intersex, and some parents use surgery to assign their child to one sex or the other, usually female. Transgender is not a biological characteristic but rather an identity, a social construct. Transgender people see themselves as a gender other than the one assigned to them at birth and may or may not choose to have surgery.

8.2 How do sociologists understand gender through the three major theoretical perspectives and the theory that sees gender as a social structure?

Structural functionalists typically equate sex and gender and see men and women as essentially different and complementary. Men play instrumental roles in society, being leaders and breadwinners, and women play expressive roles, supporting men and providing nurturance for children and the elderly. This perspective ignores that assigning these roles results in gender inequity. Conflict theorists focus on the unequal distribution of resources between men and women and the inequality that results. Symbolic interactionists emphasize the social construction of gender and point out that gender is fluid and that we create and re-create our genders throughout our lifetimes. Gender as social structure theorists remind us that to understand gender, we should not simply pick and choose perspectives; rather, we must understand socialization, social interactions, and inequalities embedded within organizational structures. Gender reflects all of these dimensions of social life.

8.3 How do we create our gender and sexual identities?

We learn our gender and develop our sexual identities from the environment around us as we interact with others. We learn from the clothes we are given to wear, the toys that are chosen for us, the lessons taught by our teachers, our peers, and the media representations of men and women and we see and hear. Gender socialization is the process by which we learn to be a man or a woman in our particular place and time. Gender scripts are the expectations for behavior cultures assign to genders. Boys and men tend to have more narrowly defined gender scripts and face harsher reactions when they violate them.

8.4 How does gender affect workforce experiences?

Being a man or a woman affects our work lives in powerful ways. Gender segregation is the separation of men and women into different types of occupations. The gender wage gap is the difference between men's and women's wages. Men and women are often paid different salaries for the same job, and men generally have more opportunities for advancement than do women. Women often face a glass ceiling or a maternal wall, an invisible but real barrier that keeps women, especially working mothers, from advancing professionally. Most women in the workplace also face sexual harassment, verbal or physical harassment of a sexual nature when the harassment creates a hostile work environment or when the victim's advancement at work is affected. Most women who report it face punishment for doing so.

8.5 How have rates of sexual activity among young adults in the United States changed since the 1950s?

Between the 1950s and 1980s, the percentages of eighteen-year-old men and women who reported having sex jumped from 30 percent for women and 40 percent for men to 50 percent for both men and women. Recent data, however, indicate that today's young adults are less likely to be sexually active today than those in the 1980s. Whereas in 1986, 94 percent of men and women eighteen to thirty-four years of age said that they had had sex during the past year, that percentage had dropped to 77 percent by 2018.

KEY TERMS

CHAPTER 9

RECOGNIZING THE IMPORTANCE OF RACE

Kathleen Odell Korgen

If you want to understand society, you must acknowledge race and ethnicity—and the impact of these social constructions.
REUTERS/Stephanie Keith

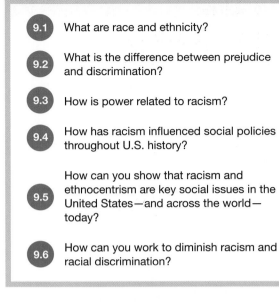

LEARNING QUESTIONS

9.1 What are race and ethnicity?

9.2 What is the difference between prejudice and discrimination?

9.3 How is power related to racism?

9.4 How has racism influenced social policies throughout U.S. history?

9.5 How can you show that racism and ethnocentrism are key social issues in the United States—and across the world— today?

9.6 How can you work to diminish racism and racial discrimination?

Defining Race and Ethnicity

9.1 What are race and ethnicity?

Ask a sociologist to define race and ethnicity, and you will probably want to pull up a chair. It may take a while, but the time will be well spent. Understanding race and ethnicity will help you understand society—and your experience in it.

Ethnicity can be explained much more easily than race. Members of an **ethnic group** share the same cultural heritage (e.g., language, nation of origin, and religion). There are various ethnic groups in the United States today, including African Americans, Jamaican Americans, Cuban Americans, Italian Americans, Irish Americans, and Chinese Americans. Diverse ethnic groups, with very different cultures, can fall under the same racial label (e.g., both Korean and Japanese Americans are considered Asian in the United States). Definitions of racial groups and how we place people into different racial groups have changed over the years.

Once thought of as based on biological or genetic differences among humans, race is now widely recognized as a social construction that varies over time and from society to society. Today, sociologists define a **race** as a group of people *perceived* to be distinct because of physical appearance (not genetic makeup). We tend to categorize people we meet into racial groups on the basis of their skin tone and facial features.

How people identify *themselves* racially may not match the perceptions of others, however. This is most often true for people with parents of different races. In 2015, among babies residing with both parents, one in seven had parents of different races (including Hispanic as a racial category) or at least one parent who self-classifies as multiracial (Livingston 2017). Today, how Americans of multiracial heritage identify racially (including whether they identify with more than one race or refuse any racial label) relates to a variety of social and minor genetic factors. These influencers include appearance (e.g., skin tone, facial features), ancestry, social class, location (where they live), the place they answer the question (e.g., school or home), and socialization (e.g., how their parents racially identify them) (Ignatiev 1995; Khanna 2013; Korgen 2010, 2016; LaBarrie 2017; Rockquemore and Brunsma 2008).

Distinguishing between race and ethnicity becomes complicated when dealing with Hispanic Americans— officially an ethnic group on the U.S. census. Although Hispanic Americans constitute an umbrella ethnic group and can be of any race, they tend to be treated as a distinct racial group. A combination of skin color, accent, and Spanish or English speech (characteristics that vary widely among the Hispanic population) largely determines the extent to which they face discrimination in the United States (Lopez, Gonzalez-Barrera, and Krogstad 2018; Rodriguez 2000).

Realizing the confusion, under the Obama administration the Census Bureau began to prepare to for possibly making "Hispanic, Latino, or Spanish" a category for both race and ethnicity. They also started to test a new "Middle Eastern or North African" racial category, separate from "White." Despite the racial and ethnic prejudice and discrimination many Arab Americans face, they are officially considered White. This makes it difficult to track and address discrimination aimed at this group. The Trump administration, however, has decided that the 2020 Census will use the 2010 racial and ethnic categories (White, Black or African American, American Indian or Alaska Native, Asian, and Native Hawaiian or Other Pacific Islander) (U.S. Census Bureau 2018).

CONSIDER THIS

Leading up to and during World War II, President Roosevelt turned back thousands of Jewish refugees seeking to enter the United States, because of fear that some of them were Nazi spies. It turns out that this fear was largely unfounded (Gross 2015, paragraph 5). Many of those rejected by the United States were put to death by the Nazis. What do you think you would have done, if you were president at the time? Why?

HOW I GOT ACTIVE IN SOCIOLOGY

KATHLEEN ODELL KORGEN

When I neared the midpoint in my PhD program and needed to identify a dissertation topic, my brother announced that I was soon to be an aunt. He, a White man, had married a Black woman, and they were going to have a baby boy! I started thinking about how my nephew's racial background would affect his life. To my dismay, I found that the existing research indicated that he would face all sorts of racial discrimination and live as a marginalized person, not fully accepted by either White or Black people. I had a sense, and certainly a hope, that society had changed and the research needed updating. I had found my dissertation topic.

It turns out that I was right. My nephew—and other members of his generation of mixed-race people—was not doomed to face a life of marginalization. That is not to say, however, that race no longer matters—it does. Race, a social construction, continues to affect our society and every institution and person in it. Recognizing that reality is the focus of this chapter.

Despite how individuals, institutions, and governments classify people, biologically speaking, the old saying "there is only one race—the human race" is true. We now know, thanks to the Human Genome Project, that there are more genetic differences *within* racial groups than between them. All humans share common ancestors and 99.9 percent of the same genetic makeup. Differences in "racial" appearance result from adaptations to different environmental conditions as humans spread across the world from their common origin in Africa (Jorde and Wooding 2004; Rutherford 2015; Smithsonian Institute 2016; see Figure 9.1).

The Social Construction of Race

To see how racial categories are socially rather than biologically constructed, one need only look at the U.S. census. For example, in the 1930 U.S. census, Mexican Americans were included under the category "Mexican." However, in 1940, they were placed under "White," "unless they appeared to census interviewers to be 'definitely Indian or of other Nonwhite races'" (Rodriguez 2000, 84). Today, they are asked to choose from the racial categories listed on the census form and then indicate that they are ethnically Hispanic/Mexican.

▼ FIGURE 9.1

Human Migration from Africa

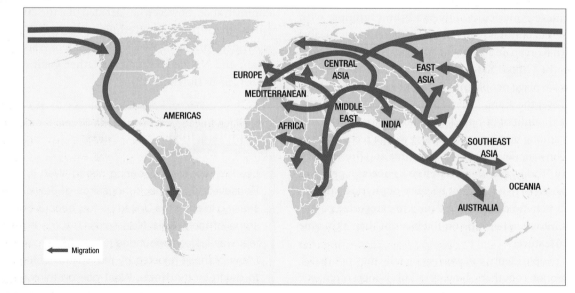

Source: Treat, Jason/National Geographic Creative.

SORTING PEOPLE BY RACE

In this exercise, you will attempt to place people into racial categories on the basis of their appearance.

As part of a documentary series, *RACE—The Power of an Illusion*, PBS created an online tool that allows you to sort a series of photographs of people by race and then check your answers against what those people marked on the U.S. census form.

Visit http://www.pbs.org/race/002_SortingPeople/002_00-home.htm and click "Begin Sorting" to get started. Once you have completed the activity, write your answers to the following questions:

1. Was it easy or difficult for you to place the people into the categories they selected on the U.S. census. Why?

2. Which of the people pictured might face racial discrimination in the United States today? Why?

3. Describe at least two things this exercise teaches us about racial and ethnic categorizations in the United States today.

Susie Guillory Phipps and the "One-Drop Rule." As noted earlier, today most people in the United States place people into racial categories on the basis of physical appearance, such as skin tone and facial features. In the past, however, heritage determined race. In the early twentieth century, as states began to codify practices of segregating the races, many states began to distinguish Whites and Blacks using the "one-drop rule," meaning that if you had any trace of Black racial heritage, you were Black. Starting with the 1930 U.S. census, census workers were instructed to categorize anyone with any "Negro" blood as Negro, and they continued to do so until individuals began to categorize themselves in 1970. The influence of the one-drop rule can be seen most clearly in that 1970 census, when there was not a noticeable drop-off in the number of people counted as Black even after individual heads of households, rather than census workers, began to identify themselves and their families racially. People of all races had been socialized to identify anyone with any trace of Black heritage as Black.

The state of Louisiana officially modified its one-drop rule, albeit just slightly, in 1970, when it passed a law that declared that anyone 1/32 or more Black (meaning that they had one Black great-great-great-grandparent) was Black (Harris 1983). The state had done so as a compromise during a closed session of the state legislature after a

After passage of the Act to Preserve Racial Integrity in 1924, all residents of Virginia were required to complete this form. Acts like these worked to uphold the "one-drop rule." The 2000 U.S. census was the first to allow respondents to identify with more than one race.
Library of Virginia

New Orleans lawyer had lobbied on behalf of a client with 1/32 Black lineage who wanted to be legally identified as White (Harris 1983). The rigidity of that 1970 law and of the "one-drop rule," in general, made headlines in the 1980s with the case of Susie Guillory Phipps.

In 1977, Phipps, a seemingly White homemaker married to a wealthy White man, applied for a passport for an upcoming trip her husband had planned for them. To her horror, she was told that she would not be granted the passport because she had indicated that her race was different from that listed on her birth certificate. Phipps learned that she had been classified as "colored" on her birth certificate.

Frightened at the thought of what his reaction might be if he found out her birth certificate identified her as colored, Phipps told her husband she couldn't travel because she was ill. She then proceeded (secretly at first, using her "wife allowance" and writing cashier's checks) to sue the state, asking it to change her race on her birth certificate. When she finally did tell her husband—after five years—he supported her efforts, arguing that she was White and that her birth certificate should indicate it.

Ultimately, Phipps lost. The state traced her lineage back 222 years and discovered that one of her great-great-great-great-grandmothers was a Black slave and that some more recent ancestors had some Black ancestry. The court determined that she was 3/32 Black and ruled against her request to change her official race on her birth certificate (Jaynes 1982; Harris 1983). Although the state of Louisiana repealed the 1/32 law in 1983, Phipps never won the right to change the race on her birth certificate. When the case landed before the Supreme Court in 1986, the Court refused to hear it, leaving the ruling against her in place.

Check Your Understanding

- What is race?
- What are ethnicity and ethnocentrism?
- What is the "one-drop rule"?
- How does the case of Susie Guillory Phipps illustrate the social construction of race?

The Repercussions of Race

9.2   What is the difference between prejudice and discrimination?

Just because race is a social construction does not mean that the repercussions of separating humans into racial groups are not real. When Phipps discovered that her "official" race was Black, she became physically ill and so scared about her husband's reaction at the news that she did not tell him for *five years*!

Even today, race still matters. Interracial marriages are on the rise (as we discuss below), but racial prejudice and discrimination remain issues in the United States and beyond. The racial group into which you are categorized by people in your society has profound implications on your life—and your life chances.

Prejudice, Stereotypes, and Discrimination

Members of both minority and dominant racial and ethnic groups face prejudicial attitudes and biased behavior that

Wealthier communities have more resources and better school facilities.

Cynthia Lindow/Alamy Stock Photo

affect every aspect of their lives—from the neighborhoods in which they reside to how long they can expect to live. **Prejudice**, irrational feelings toward members of a particular group, can lead to **discrimination**, unfair treatment of groups of people. As you will recall from Chapter 1, prejudice can stem from stereotypes, predetermined ideas about groups of people (e.g., all Irish are drunks, all Asians are good at math). Stereotypes are bad generalizations, passed on through hearsay or small samples and held regardless of evidence.

Just as many people confuse ethnicity and race, many also confuse racism with racial prejudice. **Racism** encompasses historical, cultural, institutional, and interpersonal dynamics *that create and maintain a racial hierarchy* that advantages Whites and hurts people of color. Although people of all races can hold racial stereotypes and be prejudiced toward and discriminate against individual members of racial groups, only members of dominant racial groups can be racist. Racism requires prejudice *and* institutional power. The very idea of race was an invention of White people designed to lend support to the notion that Whites are inherently superior to and should be granted more power and privilege than people of color (Crenshaw et al. 1995).

Inequality in school funding remains a persistent problem in public education in the United States.

AP Photo/Kamil Krzaczynski

CONSIDER THIS

Still unclear why only members of dominant racial groups can be racist? Look at the video "Aamer Rahman (Fear of a Brown Planet) - Reverse Racism," at https://www.youtube.com/watch?v=dw_mRaIHb-M&app=desktop&persist_app=1. How does it help explain the relationship between racism and institutional power?

Institutional Discrimination. Sometimes discrimination can occur without prejudice—or even intent. **Institutional discrimination**, which happens as a result of how institutions operate, can exist even if the people who run them do not feel negatively toward the group(s) hurt. For example, school funding that relies on local taxes may be based on the desire for community control of schools. The result, however, is that schools in poor communities, which are disproportionately attended by students of color, receive less funding than wealthier schools with more White students. The intent to discriminate many not be present; nonetheless, the discrimination (more money for wealthier and Whiter schools) and its negative repercussions exist.

CONSIDER THIS

Imagine you were born into a different racial group (or groups) than the one (or ones) into which you were born. What aspects of your life would be different now? Why?

Check Your Understanding

- Why does race matter—even if it is a social, rather than a biological, construction?
- What is a stereotype?
- Describe the difference between prejudice and discrimination.
- Why can members of racial minority groups be racially prejudiced but not racist?
- Give an example of how institutional racial discrimination can take place even without intent or racial prejudice.

Discrimination by the U.S. Government

9.3   How is power related to racism?

Often, however, racial discrimination comes with conscious intent. As White people spread across the land now known as the United States, they almost completely decimated the tens of millions of American Indians who resided there—portraying them as "savages" as they did. The history of the United States is full of examples of blatant racial prejudice and discrimination at both the individual and institutional levels. Indeed, they exist in the nation's founding documents as well as in legislation and court decisions throughout U.S. history.

The Constitution, the Compromise of 1877, and *Plessy v. Ferguson*

The Constitution of the United States acknowledged and supported slavery in the new nation. You may have heard of the **Three-Fifths Compromise**, which treated slaves as three-fifths of a person for purposes of representation in the House of Representatives and taxation. The Constitution also explicitly barred Congress from restricting the international slave trade until 1808 and declared that slaves who escaped to the North, if caught, must be returned to their masters in the South.

Slavery was finally abolished in 1865, after the Civil War, with the Thirteenth Amendment, but the federal government's efforts to protect the rights of Black people in the South were stopped with the **Hayes-Tilden Compromise of 1877**. The 1876 presidential election between Rutherford B. Hayes, the Republican (northern) presidential candidate, and Samuel J. Tilden, the Democratic (southern) presidential candidate, was deadlocked, with Tilden receiving more of the popular vote but neither receiving enough electoral votes to win the presidency. A committee in Congress assigned to break the impasse voted narrowly—the day before the new president was to take office—to give the election to Hayes.

With the *Plessy v. Ferguson* decision of 1896, the Supreme Court upheld racially segregated facilities, such as these water fountains in Oklahoma City, Oklahoma, in 1939.

The Democrats agreed to go along with the decision if Hayes promised to withdraw federal troops from the former Confederacy and allow Whites to once again dominate political power in the South. Hayes agreed, and Southern states began to establish Jim Crow laws that legally established a racially segregated society. The Supreme Court upheld these measures with the *Plessy v. Ferguson* decision in 1896, which ruled that "separate but equal" facilities were constitutional.

It was not until 1954 that the Supreme Court overruled *Plessy v. Ferguson* with its *Brown v. Board of Education* decision (King 2012). Even after that decision, interracial couples were not allowed to marry. It took another Supreme Court ruling, the *Loving v. Virginia* decision in 1967, to abolish state laws banning interracial marriage.

Immigration Legislation

Racism also influenced immigration legislation throughout the history of the United States. For example, Chinese and Japanese immigration were halted, respectively, through the **Chinese Exclusion Act of 1882** and the **Gentlemen's Agreement of 1907**. Then, a series of laws curtailed immigration of Southern and Eastern Europeans (at the time, they were considered "less than White"), culminating in the **Immigration Act of 1924**, which established 2 percent immigration quotas per nation, on the basis of the 1890 U.S. census (when relatively few Southern and Eastern Europeans were in the United States). So, for example, if there were 100,000 Italians residing in the United States in 1890, each year only 2,000 new migrants from Italy would be granted entry. A provision in the 1924

act also limited immigration to those eligible for citizenship. As Asian immigrants were not eligible for citizenship, it totally cut off immigration from Asia. (The Walter-McCarran Act in 1952 finally gave Asian Americans the right to citizenship.[1] Prior to that, Asian immigrants could not vote and lacked access to other rights restricted to citizens.)

In the late 1800s and early 1900s, Washington State and California passed laws aimed at Asian immigrants that prohibited noncitizens from owning land. In 1941, after Japan attacked Pearl Harbor and the United States joined World War II, more than 100,000 Japanese Americans who lived on the West Coast were forced into internment camps. In the process, they were forced to give up their businesses and most of their belongings—keeping only what they could carry (Spickard 2009; Torimoto 2017).

The racist immigration quotas remained in place until 1965, the height of the civil rights movement. The **Immigration Act of 1965** abolished national quotas (replacing them with quotas for the Eastern and Western Hemispheres) and did much to increase immigration and alter the racial makeup of the United States. The foreign-born population rose from 5.4 percent in 1970 (Gibson and Lennon 1999) to 13.5 percent in 2016 (López, Bialik, and Radford 2018). Figure 9.2 shows the dramatic shift in the makeup of the foreign born since the 1965 Immigration Act.

Racist restrictions on immigration came back into force with President Trump. The Muslim ban and the attempt to deter Central American families seeking refuge in the United States by separating refugee children from their parents provide two examples of discriminatory immigration policies enacted under the Trump administration. Facing an enormous public outcry against the family separation

---

1. There were some exceptions to Asian exclusion before 1952. In 1943, as China fought with the United States during World War II, President Roosevelt signed the Magnuson Act, which repealed the Chinese Exclusion Act, established an annual quota that allowed 105 Chinese immigrants to come to the United States per year, and granted Chinese immigrants the right to apply for citizenship. In 1946, the Luke-Cellar Act established a quota of 100 immigrants per year from India and the Philippines and allowed immigrants from those nations to apply for citizenship. And from 1924 to 1934, Filipinos were under the rule of the United States, so they were eligible to immigrate to the United States and become naturalized citizens.

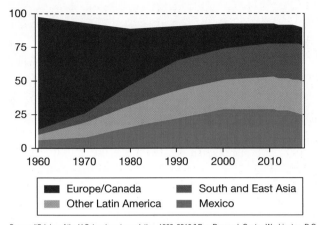

▼ FIGURE 9.2

Origins of the U.S. Immigrant Population, 1960–2016

% of foreign-born population residing in the U.S. who were born in . . .

Legend:
- Europe/Canada
- Other Latin America
- South and East Asia
- Mexico

Source: "Origins of the U.S. immigrant population, 1960–2016." Pew Research Center, Washington, D.C. (14 September 2018) http://www.pewhispanic.org/chart/immigrant-statistical-portrait-origins-of-the-u-s-immigrant-population/.

Note: "Other Latin America" includes Central America, South America, and the Caribbean.

policy, Trump rescinded it, but not before thousands of children were held in facilities away from their parents—and hundreds deported without them. After courts found the Trump travel ban unconstitutional (because it included only Muslim majority nations), President Trump changed the list of nations to include a couple of countries without many Muslims. In June 2018, in a five-to-four vote, the Supreme Court approved President Trump's order to ban most citizens from Iran, Libya, Syria, Yemen, Somalia, Chad, and North Korea from entering the United States and to increasing restrictions on Venezuelan and Iraqi citizens (Shear 2017). In a dissent, Justice Sonia Sotomayor noted the parallels between the Court's approval of the Trump travel ban and its 1944 decision that endorsed the detention of Japanese Americans during World War II. Sotomayor argued that both are "rooted in dangerous stereotypes about a particular group's supposed inability to assimilate and desire to harm the United States" (quoted in de Vogue 2018, paragraph 3).

Why Do People Immigrate, What Happens Once They Do, and Who Writes Our History?

What would make you leave family members, friends, your neighborhood, and your country? You probably would not do that lightly, would you? People tend not to leave their homes and move to another country without very compelling reasons.

A variety of "push" and "pull" factors drive immigration. Push forces include war, ethnic or political persecution, gang violence, economic depression, climate change, and so on. Receiving nations can pull immigrants to them with jobs, freedom, and safety. Immigration policies tend to be relatively open in peaceful and economic boom times and more restrictive during wars, political instability, and economic downturns.

CONSIDER THIS

If you visit the Statue of Liberty in New York Harbor, you can read these words by the poet Emma Lazarus:

> *Give me your tired, your poor,*
>
> *Your huddled masses yearning to breathe free,*
>
> *The wretched refuse of your teeming shore.*
>
> *Send these, the homeless, tempest-tost to me,*
>
> *I lift my lamp beside the golden door!*

What is your reaction when you read these words? Why? How closely do you think these words reflect the history of U.S. immigration—and current U.S. immigration policy? Why?

Assimilation and Conflict Perspectives. The first sociological theories that tried to explain what happens after immigrants reach a new land described a process of assimilation wherein the new arrivals (and their descendants) would gradually become a part of the dominant group. Robert Park's classic work in the early twentieth century described a four-step assimilation process:

1. Contact (when the groups meet)
2. Conflict (they compete for goods and power)
3. Accommodation (one group establishes dominance)
4. Assimilation (the minority groups embrace the ways of the dominant group and become accepted into it) (Desmond and Emirbayer 2009)

Although this describes the experience of some European immigrant groups, it does not apply to all racialized minority groups in the United States. For example, although Irish, Italians, and other Europeans were eventually able to "become White" and assimilate into the dominant culture and structure of U.S. society, Black Americans and many American Indians, Asian Americans, and Hispanic Americans were not (Ignatiev 1995).

The Statue of Liberty portrays one image of U.S. immigration policy, while history and current policies reveal another…

D Dipasupil/Getty Images Entertainment/Getty Images

A 2017 protest against President Trump's executive order to halt immigration from many predominantly Muslim nations.

REUTERS/Brian Snyder

W. E. B. Du Bois, a conflict theorist and contemporary of Park's, rejected Park's theory of assimilation, noting that it did not explain the experience of African Americans. A prolific writer, activist, and sociologist, Du Bois spent much of his life proving, through sociological studies, that the key factor behind the relatively low socioeconomic level of Black Americans was the discrimination they faced. Like Marx, he looked at the economic basis for racial hierarchies. In doing so, he described how capitalism produces a dominant group exploiting minority groups for private profit. Assimilation is not possible when the dominant institution sets groups against one another. Du Bois maintained that the only solution to such group conflict and exploitation is to overthrow the oppressive system, replacing it with one establishing public ownership of all resources and capital (Du Bois 1948, 1961).

Other conflict theorists describe the experience of American Indians, African Americans, and Hispanic Americans as **internal colonialism**, resulting from one ethnic or racial group (White Americans) subordinating and exploiting the resources of other racial and ethnic groups (Blauner 1972). As European powers established colonial empires across the world, taking the land and exploiting the labor of the local peoples, in the United States, both government and business leaders took land from Mexicans and American Indians and labor from African Americans. These leaders worked in tandem to create a capitalist society with a White-dominated racial hierarchy by killing or moving American Indians off their land, enslaving Africans, and annexing much of Mexico after the Mexican War.

Power and (Re)Writing History. Why don't we learn much about this history in our school textbooks? As Marx put it, the members of the dominant class "regulate the production and distribution of the ideas of their age" (Marx and Engels [1845] 1970). The false idea—still believed by many—that the Civil War was about states' rights rather than the defense of slavery provides one example of how power influences ideas.

In December 1860, four days after they voted to secede from the United States, South Carolina delegates made clear their reasons for leaving the union in a "Declaration of Immediate Causes." They declared that the election of Abraham Lincoln "represented the culmination of 'an increasing hostility on the part of the non-slaveholding States to the Institution of Slavery,' jeopardizing their property, their culture and their lives" (Kytle and Roberts 2018, 45). Shortly after the war ended, however, "a small group of white writers and editors…promoted a Lost Cause narrative that celebrated the Confederacy and disassociated it from slavery—a narrative they helped spread across the country" (Kytle and Roberts 2018, 13). The lost causers promoted two key ideas—the Civil War was not about slavery, *and* slavery had been a positive influence on African Americans (who should not have the same rights as Whites).

By the early 1900s these idea makers controlled the textbooks used in southern schools, leading countless children—of all races—to learn history from the lost-cause perspective. In South Carolina, for example, from 1917 to 1985, schoolchildren read a history book written by William Gilmore Simms, and later his granddaughter, that promoted the lost-cause narrative. A staunch defender of slavery, Simms was also a contributor to the 1852 book *The Pro-Slavery Argument, as Maintained by the Most Distinguished Writers of the Southern States* (Kytle and Roberts 2018).

DOING SOCIOLOGY 9.2

MAPS, HISTORY, AND POWER

In this exercise, you will look at how maps work to shape our understanding of history and to promote the perspective of dominant racial groups.

Go to the map at https://native-land.ca/ and look at both the territories and the different languages. Then, look at the current map of American Indian lands at https://www.bia.gov/sites/bia.gov/files/assets/bia/ots/webteam/pdf/idc1-028635.pdf and the map of the United States at https://geology.com/world/the-united-states-of-america-satellite-image.shtml

Then, write responses to the following questions:

1. The "Historical Primer" on the Native Land site points out that "as soon as lines were drawn on maps by European hands, indigenous [American Indian] place names, which are intricately connected with indigenous history, stories, and teachings, were replaced with English names, erasing indigenous presence from the lands" (Johnson n.d.). Do you agree? Why? What evidence supports your answer?

2. How does the Native Land site work to illustrate internal colonialism?

3. How has viewing these maps affected your understanding of the history of White and American Indian relations? Why?

Be prepared to share your responses.

Check Your Understanding

- How can you show that racial discrimination is evident through the founding documents of our nation and legislation and immigration policies throughout our history?

- Why do people immigrate?

- According to sociologists using Park's assimilation theory, what happens once two racial groups confront one another?

- Why did W. E. B. Du Bois disagree with Park's assimilation theory?

- According to conflict theorists, how are the historical experiences of American Indians, African Americans, and Hispanic Americans examples of internal colonialism?

- How is the lost-cause narrative an example of Marx's view that members of the ruling class "regulate the production and distribution of the ideas of their age"?

Racial and Ethnic Inequality Today

> 9.4   How has racism influenced social policies throughout U.S. history?

We can see the impact of historical and present-day racism in the United States by looking at how different racial groups are currently situated in some of the major social institutions—housing, the economy, education, the criminal justice system, health care, and government. Although much progress has been made in racial and ethnic relations in the United States, racial and ethnic inequality persists.

Housing

Have you ever tried to find an apartment to rent or a house to buy? Your experience may well depend on your race. Prior to passage of the Fair Housing Act of 1968, the reality of housing discrimination was much worse—and far more blatant. The Fair Housing Act prohibited discrimination by landlords, property owners, and financial institutions on the basis of race and national origin (except "owner-occupied buildings with no more than four units, single family housing sold or rented without the use of a broker, and housing operated by organizations and private clubs that limit occupancy to members") (FindLaw.com 2016, paragraph 3). Before 1968, racial discrimination in housing was commonplace—and backed by the federal government. In fact, the government used maps displaying "perceived investment risk," with affluent, White neighborhoods in green and Black neighborhoods in red, to determine what mortgages it would insure (or not). This "redlining," among other forms of housing discrimination, prevented Black people from benefiting, as White people did, from the explosion in homeownership after World War II (Swarns 2015). As discussed in Chapter 7, low historical rates of homeownership among Blacks are one of the drivers of wealth inequality.

Even though they are now prohibited by law, unofficial redlining practices persist. Today, although not explicitly refusing to give loans, many banks simply do not offer services in areas with high percentages of racial minorities—resulting in relatively few home loans for people of color. A study of 61 metropolitan areas shows that loan applicants of color "were turned away at significantly higher rates" than White applicants in many areas (Blacks in 48, Latinos in 25, Asians in 9, and American Indians in 3) (Glantz and Martinez 2018). Banks have also steered applicants of color to mortgages with higher rates. For example, in 2017, the city of Philadelphia sued Wells Fargo, accusing it of discriminating against Black and Hispanic people seeking home mortgages. The suit says that compared with Whites, the bank was nearly twice as likely to offer *equally qualified* Black and Hispanic applicants only high-cost mortgage loans. So, when Black and Latino home buyers can secure loans, they tend to have to pay more for them than similar White applicants (Marte 2017).

White home seekers tend to have advantages over racial minority prospective buyers at every stage of the home-buying process, from marketing to mortgage approval and appraisal (Korver-Glenn 2018). Homeownership is one of the primary means of attaining wealth in the United States, and racial and ethnic minorities consequently lag far behind White Americans in household wealth.

The Economy

Figure 9.3 shows the differences in wealth attainment among racial and ethnic groups in the United States. We described how racial discrimination in both the past and present influences people's abilities to obtain a home (and the wealth equity that comes with it). Income also plays a role in homeownership, as one must have an income to purchase a home. As Figure 9.4 indicates, income varies according to race and ethnicity.

Except for the very wealthy, income usually comes in the form of a job. The unemployment rate varies considerably by race and ethnicity. For instance, in the fourth quarter of 2018, the unemployment rate was 3.0 percent for Asian, 3.2 percent for White, 4.3 percent for Hispanic, and a notably higher 6.1 percent for Black people in the United States (Bureau of Labor Statistics 2017). Moreover, as Figure 9.5 shows, this gap has been consistent since the Bureau of Labor Statistics began to collect such data in the early 1970s (Federal Reserve Bank of St. Louis 2019).

We know that these differences in employment relate to both past and *current* practices of racial discrimination. A review of all known field experiments using job applicants of different races shows that "since 1989, whites receive on average 36% more callbacks than African Americans, and 24% more callbacks than Latinos." Moreover, this research shows that race-based hiring discrimination has remained constant, with no sign of improvement, over the three decades for Black applicants (Quillian et al. 2017, 10870). You can see a layperson's experiment with this type of employment discrimination by watching the much-viewed video "José Vs. Joe: Who Gets a Job?" (https://www.youtube.com/watch?v=PR7SG2C7IVU).

▼ FIGURE 9.3

Household Net Worth by Race

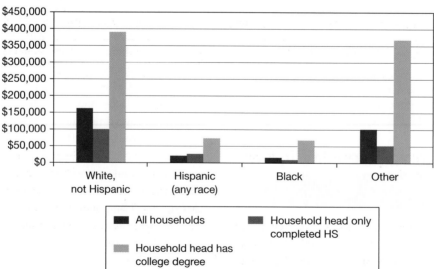

Source: Board of Governors of the Federal Reserve System, 2016 Survey of Consumer Finances, September 2017. Compiled by the Peter G. Peterson Foundation in "Income and Wealth in the United States: An Overview of Recent Data."

Note: HS = high school.

Real Median Household Income by Race and Hispanic Origin, 1967–2017

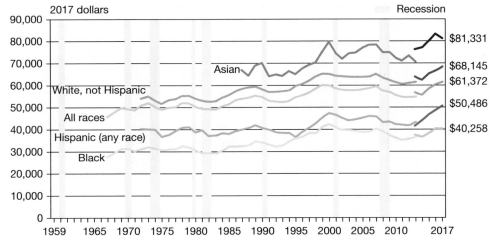

Source: U.S. Census Bureau.

Note: The data for 2013 and beyond reflect the implementation of the redesigned income questions. The data points are placed at the midpoints of the respective years. Median household income data are not available prior to 1967. For information on recessions, see Appendix A. For information on confidentiality protection, sampling error, nonsampling error, and definitions, see <www2.census.gov/programs-surveys/cps/techdocs/cpsmar18.pdf>.

▼ FIGURE 9.5

Unemployment Rates by Race, 1975–2017

Source: US Bureau of Labor Statistics, Unemployment Rate: Black or African American [LNS14000006], retrieved from FRED, Federal Reserve Bank of St. Louis; https://fred.stlouisfed.org/series/LNS14000006, June 2, 2019.

Racial and ethnic stereotypes tend to hurt applicants of color and help White applicants.

Education

Good jobs also usually require at least a college education. Educational experiences tend to vary widely along racial, ethnic, and class lines. These different school experiences (which you will learn more about in Chapter 12) play a role in racial and ethnic differences in high school and college graduation rates (as seen in Figures 9.6 and 9.7,

next page) and overall school experiences. For example, in public schools, whereas White students are twice as likely as American Indian students to take an Advanced Placement course, American Indian students are twice as likely to be suspended as White students (Green and Waldman 2018).

Criminal Justice System

Racial disparities are also evident in the criminal justice system—from arrests to sentencing and even selections of jury pools. Police are more likely to pull over, search, ticket,

Public High School Graduation Rates by Race and Ethnicity, 2016–2017

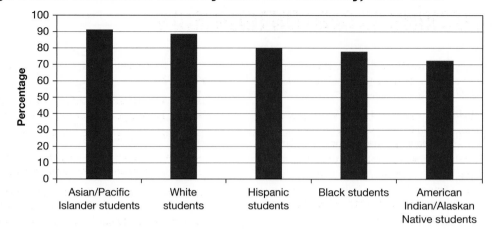

Source: US Department of Education, National Center for Education Statistics 2019. Public high school 4-year adjusted cohort graduation rate (ACGR), by race/ethnicity and selected demographic characteristics for the United States, the 50 states, and the District of Columbia: School year 2016–17.

Bachelor's Degree Attainment among Persons Age 25 and Older, by Race/Ethnicity, 2017

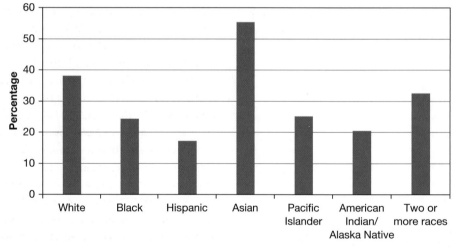

Source: National Center for Education Statistics. 2018. "Digest of Education Statistics 2017."

and arrest Black drivers than White drivers—and this is after controlling for location, age, and gender (Stanford Open Policing Project 2019). Even though Whites are as likely to use and sell drugs as Black people, Blacks are four times as likely to face arrest for drug charges (Federal Bureau of Investigation 2016). Blacks are also more likely to receive plea deals that include imprisonment. In addition, Blacks are 20 percent more likely than members of other races to be removed from a jury (Kahn and Kirk 2015).

As seen in Figure 9.8, Blacks and, to a lesser extent, Hispanics are overrepresented in U.S. prisons. Note that Whites are underrepresented in the prison population,

making up 30 percent of prisoners but 64 percent of the population (Gramlich 2018). A prison sentence has life-changing implications, with the formerly incarcerated facing discrimination in employment and housing and, in some states, denial of the right to vote (Ajunwa and Onwuachi-Willig 2018; Flake 2015; Domonoske 2016; National Conference of State Legislatures 2016).

The results of this discrimination in the criminal justice system are disproportionate numbers of Black and Hispanic families with absent and unemployed parents. People, particularly people of color, with prison records tend to have a much harder time finding jobs than those

RACE RELATIONS AS SEEN ON TELEVISION

In this exercise, you will watch a clip of the show *Black-ish* and answer questions about its perspective on race relations.

Black-ish, a hit television show on ABC, has projected race-related issues into living rooms across America. Watch this brief clip from a 2016 episode at https://sojo.net/articles/less-two-minutes-clip-blackish-explains-why-racism-america-isn-t-over (from the Sojourners article "In Less Than Two Minutes, This Clip from 'Black-ish' Explains Why Racism in America Isn't Over") and write answers to the following questions:

1. What issues discussed in this chapter does this clip raise?

2. Is the male character's perspective on race relations today positive or negative? Why?

3. Do you agree with his perspective? Why?

4. How do your own racial background and racial experiences influence your answer to question 3?

5. Do you agree with the title given to the clip by the authors of the article in which it is embedded that "everyone should see" this clip? Why or why not?

▼ FIGURE 9.8

Blacks and Hispanics Are Overrepresented in U.S. Prisons

Total U.S. adult population and U.S. prison population by race and Hispanic origin, 2016

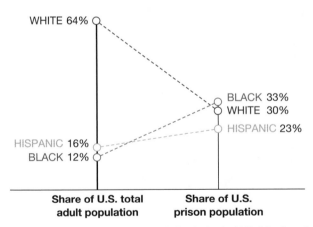

Source: "The gap between the number of blacks and whites in prison is shrinking." Pew Research Center, Washington, D.C. (30 April 2019) https://www.pewresearch.org/fact-tank/2019/04/30/shrinking-gap-between-number-of-blacks-and-whites-in-prison/.

Note: Whites and blacks include only those who are single-race, not Hispanic. Hispanics are of any race. Prison population is defined as inmates sentenced to more than a year in federal or state prison.

who have not been convicted of a crime (Ajunwa and Onwuachi-Willig 2018). "In the first full calendar year after their release, only 55 percent [of former prisoners] have any reported earnings. Among those with jobs, their median annual earnings is $10,090" (Looney and Turner 2018, 1).

Health Care

Racial minority groups also face various types of discrimination in health care. For example, Whites and Asians are more likely to have health insurance coverage than Blacks and Hispanics (National Center for Health Statistics 2018). Whites are also more likely than people of color to receive treatment for pain by doctors—in and out of emergency rooms. (Kennel 2018; Singhal, Tien, and Hsia 2016). Even among children, this disparity in pain relief treatment holds (Hewes et al. 2018)

Race-based discrimination in health care may be most clearly seen when looking at the experiences of Native Americans. Today, almost two out of three American Indians and Alaskan Natives receive health care through the federal government's Indian Health Service (IHS). However, the IHS provides services that are inadequate, often "dangerous," and sometimes "deadly." A congressional review of IHS health care revealed that it "is simply horrifying and completely unacceptable," according to Senator John Barrasso (R-Wy.), chair of the Senate Committee on Indian Affairs (Dovey 2016, paragraphs 1 and 3). For example, in 2017, inspectors from the Centers for Medicare and Medicaid Services noted many problems with the care given in the emergency room at the IHS hospital in Pine Ridge, South Dakota, with some resulting in unnecessary deaths (Siddons 2018). As you will learn more about in Chapter 13, institutional- and individual-level racial discrimination in health care causes unnecessary pain and premature deaths.

Government

You may be asking yourself, at this point, "Why hasn't our government done more to address racial and ethnic inequality?" One way of answering this question is to look at the racial and ethnic makeup of the U.S. government. Just as we saw in Chapter 8 that conditions for women employees improve when women are in high levels of management, our government tends to do more for racial minorities when there are more racial minority legislators in office. For example, increases in minority representation in state legislatures tend to lead to greater funding for districts with high minority enrollments. Other research indicates that Black and Hispanic legislators are more likely than White legislators to advocate for policies supported by many Blacks and Hispanics (Ueda 2008; Griffin 2014).

As Figure 9.9 reveals, the U.S. electorate is more diverse that ever. Still, however, relatively few people of color are elected to most high political offices. Reasons include

- racial gerrymandering—creating district lines that group the vast majority of minority voters into just a few districts, resulting in few minorities elected to office;

- a lack of the time and money needed to run for office, which restricts access to such endeavors to wealthier people (who tend to be White);

- the self-perpetuating lack of access to power and money that comes from not having ties to people already in political office; and

- historically low rates of voting among Hispanics and Asians (Wiltz 2015; Krogstad and Lopez 2017).

Today, all fifty governors in the United States are White, and 90 percent of U.S. senators are White. The 2018 midterm elections, however, saw many people of color voting in a midterm election for the first time. As seen in Figure 9.9, Hispanics were more than twice as likely and Blacks 50 percent more likely than Whites to say that they voted for the first time in a midterm election (Krogstad, Flores, and Lopes 2018). These voters helped bring greater racial and ethnic diversity to Congress, with the percentages of Black, Hispanic, Asian American, and American Indian/Native Americans increasing and that of Whites decreasing, as shown in Figure 9.10 (Panetta and Lee 2019).

▼ FIGURE 9.9

About a Quarter of Hispanic Voters Cast Ballots in a Midterm for the First Time This Election

% who say they voted for the first time in a midterm election

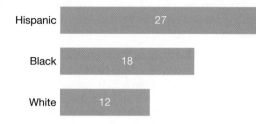

Hispanic 27
Black 18
White 12

Source: "Key takeaways about Latino voters in the 2018 midterm elections." Pew Research Center, Washington, D.C. (9 November 2018) https://www.pewresearch.org/fact-tank/2018/11/09/how-latinos-voted-in-2018-midterms/.

▼ FIGURE 9.10

Racial Makeup of the 116th Congress

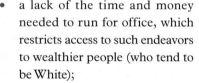

White

Black

Hispanic/Latino

Asian/Pacific Islander

Native American

RACE	BEFORE ELECTION	AFTER ELECTION	PERCENTAGE CHANGE
● Non-Hispanic White	328	319	↓ 2.7%
● African American	49	54	↑ 10.2%
● Hispanic/Latin American	41	42	↑ 2.4%
● Asian/Pacific Islander	13	15	↑ 15.4%
● Native American	2	4	↑ 100%

Source: Panetta, Grace, and Samantha Lee. 2019. "This Graphic Shows How Much More Diverse the House of Representatives Is Getting." *Business Insider*, January 12. Accessed February 2, 2019. https://www.businessinsider.com/changes-in-gender-racial-diversity-between-the-115th-and-116th-house-2018-12.

The diversity in Congress comes mostly from the Democratic side. Almost all Republican member of Congress—90 percent—are White. Among the newly elected members of the House of Representatives in 2019, 34 percent of the Democrats identified as people of color, compared with 2 percent of Republicans (Panetta and

People of Color Are Still Underrepresented in the 116th Congress

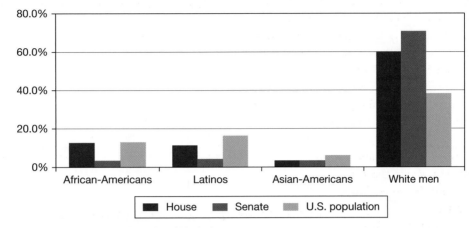

Representation in Congress

Despite gains in diversity, people of color are still underrepresented in the 116th Congress

Lee 2019). As Figure 9.11 indicates, Whites (and White men in particular) still retain a disproportionate share of elected positions in Congress.

Of course, justice for racial and ethnic minority groups need not require equitable representation across racial and ethnic groups in Congress. For example, there were no Black senators and only six Black representatives in Congress when that body passed—and a White president signed—the Voting Rights Act of 1965. As you will learn in Chapter 16, social movements can work outside institutions to create social change. Massive pressure from the civil rights movement and international politics effectively pushed White leaders to pass laws to address racial discrimination.

The civil rights movement was necessary, however, only because there were so few representatives of oppressed groups within the institutions that create and oversee the implementation of laws in the United States. These leaders had to be made aware of both the injustice of racial discrimination and the cost of perpetuating that injustice. As the great abolitionist Frederick Douglass (1857) said, "Power concedes nothing without a demand."

CONSIDER THIS

How aware were you of the extent of racial and ethnic inequality before reading this chapter? Why? What happens when the majority of people in a nation are unaware of the inequality that exists within it?

We have seen, as a group, Asian Americans tend to have lower unemployment rates and higher levels of education and income than other racial minority groups. Why?

Let's compare the situation of Hispanic and Asian Americans. Both the Hispanic and Asian American populations in the United States include people who have been in the United States for many generations, alongside first- and second-generation immigrant families. Both also contain many different subgroups with very different socioeconomic statuses. For example, third-generation Cuban Americans and first-generation Mexican Americans both fall under the Hispanic umbrella, but the former group includes more high-salaried, highly educated, and light-skinned members than the latter. This means that their socioeconomic status and experiences with racial and ethnic inequality differ markedly.

Likewise, the experience of Asian subgroups also varies widely. The majority of Asians who immigrated to the United States over the past few decades brought with them high levels of education and entered the United States legally to find greater economic opportunities than exist in their nations of origin. However, some Southeast Asian immigrants (such as war refugees from Vietnam, Cambodia, and Laos) came to the United States with little money or education. Today, other vulnerable Asians (such as young women from poor areas) are smuggled into the United States to work as indentured servants. Today, among all racial and ethnic groups, Asian Americans have the highest levels of inequality, as seen in Figure 9.12.

From lowest to highest: Income inequality in U.S. increased most among Asians from 1970 to 2016

Ratio of income at the 90th percentile to income at the 10th percentile

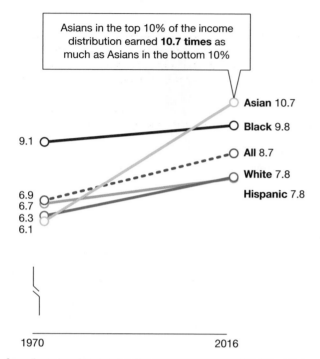

Source: "Income Inequality in the U.S. Is Rising Most Rapidly among Asians." Pew Research Center, Washington, D.C. (12 July 2018) https://www.pewsocialtrends.org/2018/07/12/income-inequality-in-the-u-s-is-rising-most-rapidly-among-asians/.

Note: Whites, blacks and Asians include only non-Hispanics and are single-race only in 2016. Hispanics are of any race. Asians include pacific Islanders. Income is adjusted for household size. See Methodology for details.

Despite these variations across subgroups, Asian immigrants to the United States as a whole tend to have more education than Hispanics. In 2017, among foreign-born workers age 25 and older, 81.2 percent of Mexicans and 74.6 percent of Central Americans had a high school diploma or less, and only 6.2 percent and 9.2 percent had a college degree. On the other hand, among Asian foreign-born workers, just 30.5 percent had a high school degree or less, and 52.1 percent were college graduates (Krogstad and Radford 2018).

One result of the disparity in education levels of the various immigrant groups is the difference in the positions they achieve in the U.S. workforce and in their subsequent socioeconomic status. Obtaining a college degree tends to lead to greater income, and foreign-born Asian workers make almost double what Hispanic foreign-born workers earn per week (Bureau of Labor Statistics 2018). Even highly educated native-born Asian Americans in high-salaried professional positions face discrimination, however. Many hit a glass ceiling that prevents them from advancing into management and CEO positions. In fact, among professional workers, Asians are less likely than any other racial or ethnic group to receive promotions to management positions. Meanwhile, White professionals are almost twice as likely as Asian Americans to gain such promotions (Gee and Peck 2018).

Check Your Understanding

- How can you show that racial and ethnic inequality exists in housing, the economy, and education institutions in the United States today?

- How can you show that racial and ethnic inequality exists in the criminal justice system and health care?

- How does the demographic makeup of elected officials reflect and help perpetuate racial and ethnic inequality in the United States?

- *Within* what racial or ethnic group is there the greatest level of economic inequality? Why?

- What are some reasons Asian Americans, as an umbrella racial group, have higher incomes than Hispanic Americans?

Racism and Ethnocentrism Globally

9.5   How can you show that racism and ethnocentrism are key social issues in the United States—and across the world—today?

Far from being a problem only in the United States, racism and ethnocentrism exist around the world. **Ethnocentrism** is the belief that one's own culture is superior to others. Europe's reaction to refugees from Syria provides a powerful example. Syria is a diverse nation, but most Syrians are ethnically Arab and Sunni Muslim. Millions of Syrians have fled the war-torn nation as refugees. The United States, during the Obama administration, agreed to take in just 110,000 Syrian refugees—but even that small number was met with a strong political backlash. President Trump's Muslim ban now bars Syrian refugees from entering the United States (Bradner and Barrett 2015; Valverde 2017). Most of the refugees are now in countries near Syria (Lebanon, Jordan, Turkey, Egypt, and Iraq), but more than a million have sought asylum status in Europe.

A backlash against the influx of refugees led some European nations to close their borders for the first time since agreeing in 1985 to allow people in the European Union (EU) to travel freely within union states (Syrianrefugees.eu 2016; Davis 2016). In June 2016,

MEASURING THE GROWTH OF THE ASIAN AMERICAN POPULATION

Although most of the global population is from Asia, U.S. policies often prevented Asians from immigrating to America, becoming citizens, and even owning land. With the removal of these barriers, Asian Americans have become a small but growing segment of the American population. Today, Asian Americans make up more than 5 percent, and the Census Bureau projects this number to nearly double by 2060.

In this online activity, you will explore the size of the Asian American population, how it has changed, and where it is most concentrated, using data from the U.S. Census Bureau's Population Estimates Program.

---

*Requires the Vantage version of *Sociology in Action*.

▼ FIGURE 9.13

Asian Population (State)

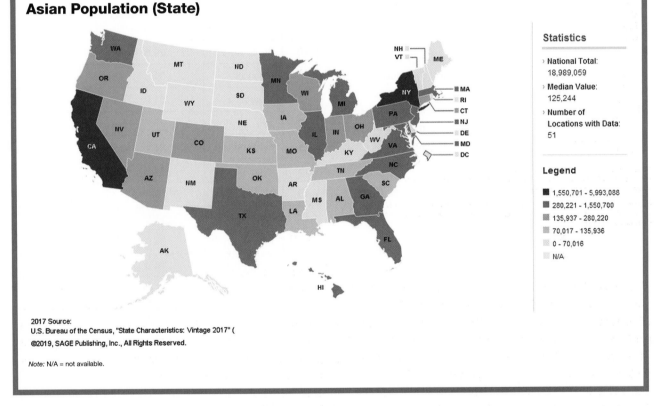

Statistics

› National Total:
18,989,059

› Median Value:
125,244

› Number of
Locations with Data:
51

Legend

■ 1,550,701 - 5,993,088
■ 280,221 - 1,550,700
■ 135,937 - 280,220
■ 70,017 - 135,936
▨ 0 - 70,016
▨ N/A

2017 Source:
U.S. Bureau of the Census, "State Characteristics: Vintage 2017" (

©2019, SAGE Publishing, Inc., All Rights Reserved.

Note: N/A = not available.

Britain voted to leave the EU, a referendum that was largely seen as a vote against the relatively open EU immigration policies (Zucchino 2016). Far-right, anti-immigrant parties have gained a greater share of the electorate in increasing numbers of European nations. A survey of Europeans by the Pew Research Center revealed that 38 percent want less immigration and 42 percent believe that "Islam is fundamentally incompatible with their national culture and values" (Pew Research Center 2018).

Negative views toward Muslim immigrants tend to relate to lower education levels, far-right political views, Christian identities, and lack of personal interaction with Muslims (Diamant 2018). For people in many European nations, the recent influx of immigrants is their first experience of cultural diversity. For example, the native-born population in Denmark has dropped from 97 percent in 1980 to 88 percent today (Zucchino 2016; Wike, Stokes, and Simmons 2016).

This picture shows Syrian refugees trying to cross the border into Greece on March 14, 2016. Three refugees had drowned while trying to cross that morning, but more kept trying, fearing the danger behind them more than the river or the ethnocentrism they might face in a new society.

REUTERS/Stoyan Nenov

▼ TABLE 9.1

Racism around the World

	Country	Percentage Who Don't Want Neighbors of Another Race	Percentage Who Witnessed Racist Behavior
1	India	43.6	64.3
2	Lebanon	36.3	64.4
3	Bahrain	31.1	85.7
4	Libya	54.0	33.5
5	Egypt	NA	39.7
6	Philippines	30.6	49.1
7	Kuwait	28.1	37.9
8	Palestine	44.0	32.0
9	South Africa	19.6	61.8
10	South Korea	29.6	36.5
11	Malaysia	31.3	34.4
12	Nigeria	21.0	42.5
13	Iraq	27.7	37.8
14	Kyrgyzstan	28.1	35.9
15	Ecuador	34.5	32.0
16	Algeria	19.8	41.0
17	Pakistan	14.5	48.8
18	Yemen	34.0	31.2
19	Hong Kong	18.8	40.4
20	Russia	17.0	38.5
21	Thailand	39.8	19.0
22	Cyprus	26.7	26.1
23	Turkey	33.8	19.1
24	Morocco	13.8	35.6
25	Japan	22.3	29.7

Source: Reprinted with permission from BusinessTech.

Note: NA = not available.

Animosity to racial and ethnic diversity exists far beyond Europe. A study analyzed data from sixty-one nations (including the United States) using respondents' answers to the following two questions: (1) whether they would like to have people from another race as neighbors and (2) how frequently racist behavior occurs in their neighborhood. Table 9.1 shows the twenty-five nations that scored highest in this measure of racism (on the basis of their average ranking after combining their rankings for each variable).

The Dangers of External Inequality and the Benefits of Diversity

Racial and ethnic discrimination has negative consequences for all members of a society. As discussed in earlier chapters, functionalists point out the interdependence of various parts of society. Durkheim stressed that individuals need to be socialized to work for the benefit of society rather than just their own individual interests. For society to function at its most effective, people must be allowed to do what they do best for the good of society. If, for example, one group of people are forced to work only as menial laborers, despite the fact that some of them might be more valuable to society as engineers or teachers, this can harm *all* of society. What if one of those menial laborers could have found a cure for cancer, if given the opportunity to gain the education and lab experience needed to do so?

Durkheim ([1892] 1997) divided social inequalities into *internal* (based on people's natural abilities) and *external* (those forced upon people). He argued that the existence of *external inequality* in an industrial society indicates that its institutions are not functioning properly. Because an industrial society needs all its members doing what they do best to function most effectively, external inequality—like racial discrimination—that

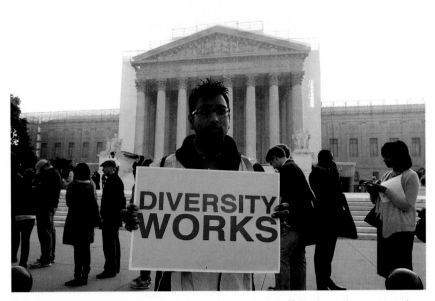

Many of the largest corporations in the United States support affirmative action programs in higher education, knowing that a diverse workforce is necessary in an increasingly multiracial and ethnic United States and in the global marketplace.

Mark Wilson/Getty Images News/Getty Images

prevents some people from using their innate talents damages all of society.

The same reasoning holds true for postindustrial societies. That is one reason many business leaders support affirmative action programs in higher education. Writing to the Supreme Court in support of such programs, more than sixty *Fortune* 500 companies pointed out that

the individuals who run and staff [our] corporations must be able to understand, learn from, collaborate with, and design products and services for clientele and associates from diverse racial, ethnic, and cultural backgrounds. American multinational corporations . . . are especially attuned to this concern because they serve not only the increasingly diverse population of the United States, but racially and ethnically diverse populations around the world. (Botsford et al. 2000, paragraph 14)

Reducing racial and ethnic inequality and promoting diversity efforts is not only the just thing to do—it also makes good business sense.

Diversity Programs That Work

Social science research can help us determine how best to promote diversity in organizations. It can also show us what does not work—like most of the diversity efforts

companies have used for the past few decades. For example, from 2003 to 2014, "the proportion of managers at U.S. commercial banks who were Hispanic rose from 4.7% in 2003 to [just] 5.7% . . . white women's representation dropped from 39% to 35%, and black men's [fell] from 2.5% to 2.3%" (Dobbin and Kalev 2016).

As indicated in Table 9.2, the standard practices of "diversity training to reduce bias on the job, hiring tests and performance ratings to limit it in recruitment and promotions, and grievance systems to give employees a way to challenge managers" have proved ineffective. Most (three-quarters) of diversity training programs are mandatory, leading to resentment and, often, increased rather than decreased prejudice against women and racial and ethnic minorities. Hiring tests are often used selectively and in a biased manner, working to *limit* rather than increase diversity in hires and promotions. Likewise, legalistic grievance systems tend to set up adversarial relations between supervisors and workers, leading to retaliation and *fewer* workers willing to challenge discrimination.

The good news is that we now know what diversity programs do work. Rather than using tactics that combine force and coercion, companies should ask managers to help address the problem, give them opportunities to work with people from minority groups, and promote transparent communication of the results of diversity efforts. These tactics lead to a positive cycle in which managers feel like they are part of an effort in which they are invested. As Table 9.3 shows, voluntary training, self-managed teams (which allow people in diverse roles to work together as equals), cross-training (which, like self-managed teams, increases exposure of people to different races and genders), college recruitment efforts targeting women and racial and ethnic minorities, mentoring programs, diversity task forces, and diversity managers increase diversity.

College recruitment programs provide a great example of a diversity effort that pays off. Research shows that managers become willing participants when they are asked to participate in a positive effort (e.g., "Help us find a greater

DOING SOCIOLOGY 9.5

THE WAITING GAME

What do you think happens to refugees who make it to the United States and request asylum? This exercise allows you to choose a story of an asylum seeker and experience what they go through. Go to https://projects.propublica.org/asylum/, choose a story, and begin playing "The Waiting Game." Then, answer the following questions:

1. Which story did you select to follow? Why?

2. Did you complete the story? If so, why? If not, when did you give up? Why? What does this experience tell you about what it is like to seek asylum in the United States?

Now, click on "How Asylum Works," and respond to the following questions:

1. Why was the U.S. asylum system originally created?

2. When was the system now in place created? Why was it created then?

3. Why have more refugees applied for asylum than originally anticipated?

4. On the basis of what you have read in this article, what steps would you suggest the United States take to revise its asylum system? Why?

▼ TABLE 9.2

Poor Returns on the Usual Diversity Programs

The three most popular interventions make firms less diverse, not more, because managers resist strong-arming. For instance, testing job applicants hurts women and minorities—but not because they perform poorly. Hiring managers don't always test everyone (White men often get a pass) and don't interpret results consistently.

% CHANGE OVER FIVE YEARS IN REPRESENTATION AMONG MANAGERS

Type of program	White		Black		Hispanic		Asian	
	Men	Women	Men	Women	Men	Women	Men	Women
Mandatory diversity training				−9.2			−4.5	−5.4
Job tests		−3.8	−10.2	−9.1	−6.7	−8.8		−9.3
Grievance systems		−2.7	−7.3	−4.8		−4.7	−11.3	−4.1

Source: Dobbin, Frank, and Alexandra Kaley. 2016. "Why Diversity Programs Fail." *Harvard Business Review*. July/August 2016. Retrieved May 14, 2018 (https://hbr.org/2016/07/why-diversity-programs-fail).

Notes: Authors' study of 829 midsize and large U.S. firms. The analysis isolated the effects of diversity programs from everything else going on in the companies and in the economy. Gray indicates no statistical certainty of a program's effect.

variety of promising employees!") and involvement is voluntary: "Managers who make college visits say they take their charge seriously. They are determined to come back with strong candidates from underrepresented groups—female engineers, for instance, or African-American management trainees. . . . Managers who were wishy-washy about diversity become converts" (Dobbin and Kalev 2016).

The results are remarkable. On average, companies that implement "a college recruitment program targeting female employees" see about a 10 percent increase in "white women, black women, Hispanic women, and Asian-American women in management." Similar programs that focus "on minority recruitment increase the proportion of black male managers by 8% and black female managers by 9%" (Dobbin and Kalev 2016).

Likewise, setting up diversity task forces, consisting of volunteer members who work to promote diversity throughout the organization, helps foster both accountability and a prodiversity culture. Mentoring programs that assign mentors and mentees to one another lead to increases in representation in management

Diversity Program That Get Results

Companies do a better job of increasing diversity when they forgo the control tactics and frame their efforts more positively. The most effective programs spark engagement, increase contact among different groups, or draw on people's strong desire to look good to others.

% CHANGE OVER FIVE YEARS IN REPRESENTATION AMONG MANAGERS

Type of program	White		Black		Hispanic		Asian	
	Men	Women	Men	Women	Men	Women	Men	Women
Voluntary training			+13.3		+9.1		+9.3	+12.6
Self-managed teams	−2.8	+5.6	+3.4	+3.9				+3.6
Cross-training	−1.4	+3.0	+2.7	+3.0	−3.9		+6.5	+4.1
College recruitment: women*	−2.0	+10.2	+7.9	+8.7		+10.0	+18.3	+8.6
College recruitment: minorities**			+7.7	+8.9				
Mentoring				+18.0	+9.1	+23.7	+18.0	+24.0
Diversity task forces	−3.3	+11.6	+8.7	+22.7	+12.0	+16.2	+30.2	+24.2
Diversity managers		+7.5	+17.0	+11.7		+18.2	+10.9	+13.6

*College recruitment targeting women turns recruiting managers into diversity champions, so it also helps boost the numbers for Black and Asian-American men.

**College recruitment targeting minorities often focuses on historically Black schools, which lifts the numbers of African-American men and women.

Source: Dobbin, Frank, and Alexandra Kaley. 2016. "Why Diversity Programs Fail." *Harvard Business Review*. July/August 2016. Retrieved May 14, 2018 (https://hbr.org/2016/07/why-diversity-programs-fail).

Notes: Authors' study of 829 midsize and large U.S. firms. The analysis isolated the effects of diversity programs from everything else going on in the companies and in the economy. Gray indicates no statistical certainty of a program's effect.

positions of "black, Hispanic, and Asian-American women, and Hispanic and Asian-American men, by 9% to 24%" (Dobbin and Kalev 2016). These results show that increasing diversity in U.S. businesses is indeed possible.

Check Your Understanding

- How does the animosity of many Europeans (and Americans) toward Muslim refugees exemplify ethnocentrism?

- Explain the difference between external and internal inequality, as described by Durkheim.

- How is racial discrimination an example of external inequality? Why is it harmful for society?

- Why do many business leaders support affirmative action programs on college campuses?

- Describe tactics businesses can use to promote diversity effectively in their organizations.

Responding (or Not) to Racism and Ethnocentrism Today

9.6 How can you work to diminish racism and racial discrimination?

As you will learn in more detail in Chapter 16, social movements that achieve their goals tend to face a backlash as those who lost power because of the success of the movement try to gain it back. This can be seen in reactions to the women's movement, the same-sex marriage movement, and the civil rights movement. After the successes of the civil rights movement, many people began to argue that racial discrimination was no longer a problem. This "color-blind" way of thinking gained further traction after the election of President Barack Obama, our first president of Black descent.

The Color-Blind Ideology and Racism Evasiveness

Young adults today grew up and were socialized in an era when the color-blind perspective on racial issues had tremendous influence over how people in the United States talked about (or avoided) issues of race. People who follow the **color-blind ideology**, or way of viewing race, maintain that if we ignore race and racial issues, racism will not exist. In reality, however, the color-blind ideology has worked to support, rather than reduce, racial inequality. Eduardo Bonilla-Silva describes four themes, or frames, of the color-blind perspective on race. He argues that each is used to justify or support the racial hierarchy in the United States today.

- *Abstract liberalism:* agreeing that everyone should have equal rights but opposing policies that will help achieve equality

- *Minimization:* believing that race does not matter anymore and that racism is no longer a problem

- *Naturalization:* maintaining that racist practices like segregation and opposition to interracial marriage are simply natural and part of human nature rather than based on racism

- *Culturalization:* arguing that it is their inferior culture that has hurt Black people rather than racism

Results of widespread use of the minimization frame have not been all negative, however. Since 1990, as the influence of the color-blind ideology permeated U.S. society, there has been a "dramatic" decrease in the percentage of non-Black people who would oppose a close family member marrying a Black person (Bialik 2017). Opposition to other types of racial and ethnic marriage has also declined, as seen in Figure 9.14. Today, one in six newlyweds are part of interracial marriages (when including Hispanic as a racial category) (Geiger and Livingston 2019).

The spread of the minimization frame has also had serious negative consequences. It has diminished efforts to address, or even discuss, racial discrimination. People in the United States (including Americans of color, to some degree) raised in the color-blind era grew up with the pervasive message that they should avoid talking about racial issues. Even noting someone's race could result in a negative sanction—maybe even an accusation of being racist for doing so. Does this sound familiar to you?

▼ FIGURE 9.14

Non-Blacks Opposing a Relative Marrying a Black Person

Dramatic dive in share of non-Blacks who would oppose a relative marrying a Black person

% saying they would be very or somewhat opposed to a close relative marrying someone who is _____ among U.S. adults who are not that race or ethnicity

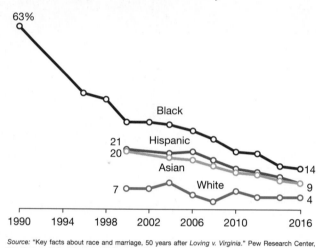

Source: "Key facts about race and marriage, 50 years after *Loving v. Virginia*." Pew Research Center, Washington, D.C. (12 June 2017) https://www.pewresearch.org/fact-tank/2017/06/12/key-facts-about-race-and-marriage-50-years-after-loving-v-virginia/.

Note: Because of changes in question wording, the universe of non-Blacks prior to 2000 includes anyone who reported a race other than Black; in 2000 and later, the universe of non-Blacks includes those who did not identify as single-race, non-Hispanic Blacks (and so may include Hispanic Blacks and multiracial Blacks).

Ironically, these color-blind ways of thinking, despite boosting interracial marriage rates, led not to the decline of racism but to **racism evasiveness**—ignoring issues of racism. Not talking about race does not reduce racism in a society with an established racial hierarchy but lets it operate without a check. In reality, "what people are ultimately avoiding when they say they do not see color, when they overlook differences in power, or avoid 'race words' is racism" (Beeman 2015, 131).

The Era of Black Lives Matter and the Presidential Election of 2016

Thanks to viral videos of police killing unarmed Black people and the Black Lives Matter movement that rose up to highlight and address these acts of racial injustice, the color-blind ideology has been challenged. It is much harder to minimize and evade racism when you can see it before your eyes in the form of a video. Thanks to social scientific research, we can show that these horrifying videos are but extreme examples of present-day racial discrimination. As former President Jimmy Carter describes it, the now widely

The Black Lives Matter movement has helped publicize and challenge racial discrimination in the criminal justice system.

REUTERS/Eric Miller

with other nations, banning Muslims from entering the United States, forcing Mexico to pay for a wall to stop the flow of "rapists" and "criminals" into the United States, and bringing more stop-and-frisk policies to urban minority neighborhoods (Ye Hee Lee 2015; Alcindor 2016; DelReal 2016). Racial and ethnic hate crimes spiked after the election, as some people felt that it was suddenly acceptable to publicly vent their anger on minority group members (Levin 2017).

Ways to Address Racism and Ethnic Discrimination

So, what can you do to address racial and ethnic discrimination? Here are some ways:

- Use your sociological eye to notice patterns of racial inequality around you and in the larger society—and hold the leaders in your community and the larger society accountable for addressing them.

- Make an effort to interact with people of races and ethnicities other than your own. Research shows that such interactions on a level playing field (e.g., among students on campus, coworkers of the same rank, campmates) can reduce racial and ethnic prejudice (Pettigrew and Tropp 2008).

- Call out racism and ethnocentrism when you see or hear it. **Microaggressions**, everyday slights aimed (intentionally or not) at racial and ethnic minority groups, can cause real damage. When you hear one, say something.

- Advocate for and participate in efforts on your campus to recognize systemic racial inequality—and to take steps to dismantle it—such as the preorientation program run by Meghan Burke, the Sociologist in Action featured in this chapter.

known information about current discrimination against Black people has "reawakened" the country to the fact that racism still exists and must be addressed (Goodstein 2016, paragraph 8).

Meanwhile, as noted in Chapter 7, the presidential election of 2016 brought racial resentments to the forefront, as economic frustration among less educated White people led to a desire for radical change and a backlash against minority groups (racial and ethnic, as well as sex and gender minorities) seen as gaining more rights and greater acceptance in recent decades. President Trump ran for office promising to "make America great again" by deregulating big business, tearing up major trade agreements

TEACHING WHITE STUDENTS ABOUT RACISM

MEGHAN BURKE

I often encounter raised eyebrows when I tell people that I codeveloped and direct a diversity program that is only for White students.

I was raised in a small town in Michigan, which at the time consisted mostly of White people, like my family. I never questioned why our community looked the way it did or why some families struggled more than others. If anything, I thought it was a simple matter of hard work and having the right values, like most of the people I knew. I was color-blind.

It was not until college that I learned how so much of our history, along with the many barriers or privileges that stifle or elevate us on otherwise arbitrary categories like race or gender, remains largely hidden from view. I had developed a sociological imagination and a passion for social justice, and I wanted to help others see what had been invisible to me for so long. This is why I became a professor, but I still wanted to do more.

I was in my first year working at my university when a colleague, Kira Banks, approached me with an idea: many U.S. colleges and universities have preorientation (or, as we call them, pre-O) programs for international students and students of color, so that they can assemble a support network and tools for survival on predominantly White campuses. But weren't we missing a key demographic? We realized that if we really want to shift the climate on predominantly White campuses like ours, we have to be intentional in our work with White students, so that they can develop the capacity to work for social and racial justice.

The pre-O that Kira and I developed, and which I continue to direct, brings a voluntary group of about thirty White students onto campus early, creating an intentional space for these students to process hard questions about race and privilege. It's not a totally separate program. We do lots of fun activities and deep discussions with the other pre-O programs, so that students can form friendships and support networks across the color and culture line. That's crucial. But we also do some caucus work on our own, diving deeply into the dynamics of racial inequality and White privilege—that stuff of the sociological imagination that I wasn't able to fully see until I started taking sociology courses.

And it works. Students who go through this program show decreased levels of color-blindness and a heightened awareness of, and ability to challenge, social and racial inequalities in both the short and long term. Efforts like this should always center on the voices and experiences of people of color. But as a White person, I also think that part of my work is to reach out to other White folks, to help us see what too often remains hidden. After all, before we can confront systems of power, we must recognize them. Programs like ours allow White students to recognize a system of racial inequality—and to take steps to challenge it.

Discussion Question: What programs on your campus help White students recognize and challenge racism? Why is it important for White people to challenge a system of racial inequality?

Meghan Burke is an associate professor of sociology at Illinois Wesleyan University.

- Vote and advocate for political candidates who acknowledge and promise to address racism and ethnocentrism.

Check Your Understanding

- What led to the creation of the color-blind perspective on race?

- How has the minimization frame contributed to the increase in interracial marriages?
- How has the minimization frame of the color-blind perspective led to racism evasiveness?
- How have the viral videos of police killing unarmed Black men and the Black Lives Matter movement affected the minimization frame of the color-blind perspective?
- What are some ways you can address racial and ethnic discrimination?

DOING SOCIOLOGY 9.6

A REFUGEE INTEGRATION PLAN FOR YOUR CAMPUS

In this activity, you will work in a group to draft a plan, using the information you have learned about race and racism, to help a group of refugees newly arrived at your school.

Imagine your college or university has agreed to accept refugees from another nation and asked you to design a program to help them adjust to campus life and to ensure that they will be accepted by and integrated into the campus population. You can assume that they all want to come and that their academic abilities match those of the typical student at your school. Your instructor will assign you to a group to develop a plan for a refugee group.

You will be assigned to one of following refugee groups or another that your instructor chooses:

- Fifty students from a college in Dublin, Ireland, that burned to the ground

- One hundred students from a Christian college in Nigeria closed after an attack by a terrorist group

- Twenty Turkish students facing potential arrest by the Turkish government

Now complete the exercise below, being sure to use information and terms (e.g., *stereotypes*, *prejudice*, *discrimination*, *ethnocentrism*) from your text in your answers:

1. Draft an outline of a plan.

2. How was your plan shaped by the refugees' nation of origin, race, religion, language, the number of refugees, and the demographic makeup of students at your school?

3. What challenges might you face in carrying out this plan? Why?

4. How would you overcome those challenges?

5. Which groups on campus would you turn to for help? Why?

6. What do you think are the chances your plan will be successful? Why?

7. Now, using your answers to the questions above, revise and improve your plan and describe what you think are your chances of success (and why).

CONSIDER THIS

President Trump has banned all Syrian refugees from entering the United States for fear that some may be terrorists. Do you support this ban? Why? How does this compare with what President Roosevelt did leading up to World War II?

Conclusion

Learning about race and ethnicity and addressing racism and ethnocentrism can benefit every member of society—and society as a whole. It can make society and the organizations within it stronger, with more people able to fully contribute to them. It can also help individuals succeed in virtually any profession. For example, teachers and social workers need to understand the racial and ethnic-based perspectives and experiences of their students and clients.

Medical professionals must understand how the social realities of their patients can affect their health. Business managers have to recruit and manage diverse workforces to succeed in an increasingly diverse marketplace. Those who hope to succeed in business or the nonprofit world must learn to work effectively with people from other racial and ethnic backgrounds.

Addressing racial and ethnic inequality also connects deeply with the core mission of sociology—to understand how society works and to use that knowledge to improve it. Increasing numbers of people now recognize that racial inequality still exists. Now *you* know how sociological tools can help address it.

To fully address racial and ethnic inequality, we must reform our institutions, as well as our attitudes and behavior on the individual level. In the following chapters, you will learn more about some of the key social institutions in our society: the family, education, religion, health care, and government and the economy. We will look first at government and the economy.

REVIEW

9.1 What are race and ethnicity?

Once thought of as based on biological or genetic differences among humans, race is now widely recognized as a social construction that varies over time and from society to society. Today, sociologists define a race as a group of people *perceived* to be distinct on the basis of physical appearance (not genetic makeup). We tend to categorize people we meet into racial groups on the basis of their skin tone and facial features (Black, American Indian or Alaskan Native, Asian or Pacific Islander, or White).

Members of a particular ethnic group share the same cultural heritage (e.g., language, nation of origin, and religion). There are various ethnic groups in the United States today, including African Americans, Jamaican Americans, Cuban Americans, Italian Americans, Irish Americans, and Chinese Americans.

9.2 What is the difference between prejudice and discrimination?

Prejudice is irrational feelings toward members of a particular group, while discrimination is unfair treatment of people on the basis of their (perceived) group membership. Prejudice can stem from stereotypes, predetermined ideas of particular groups of people (e.g., all Irish are drunks, all Asians are good at math). Discrimination can occur with or without prejudice or intent.

9.3 How is power related to racism?

Racism requires prejudice *and* power. Although everyone is prejudiced to some degree, racists use racial prejudice to create and maintain a racial hierarchy that permeates society and its major social institutions.

9.4 How has racism influenced social policies throughout U.S. history?

The history of the United States is full of examples of blatant racial prejudice and discrimination at both the individual and institutional levels. Indeed, it can be found in the nation's founding documents as well as in legislation and court decisions throughout U.S. history (e.g., the Constitution, the Compromise of 1877, and *Plessy v. Ferguson*).

Racism also influenced immigration legislation throughout the history of the United States, with complete bans on Chinese and Japanese immigration and restrictions on migration from Southern and Eastern Europe. It was not until 1965, at the height of the civil rights movement and in the midst of worldwide pressure to address racial discrimination in the United States, that racist immigration quotas were finally eliminated.

9.5 How can you show that racism and ethnocentrism are key social issues in the United States—and across the world—today?

We can see the impact of historical and present-day racism in the United States by looking at how different racial groups are currently situated in some of the major social institutions in the United States—housing, the economy, education, the criminal justice system, health care, and government. Although much progress has been made in race and ethnic relations in the United States, racial and ethnic inequality persists.

Far from being a problem only in the United States, racism and ethnocentrism exist around the world. Europe's reaction to predominantly Arab and Muslim refugees from Syria provides a powerful example. For people in many European nations, the recent influx of immigrants is their first experience of cultural diversity. In nations across Europe, most people do not see diversity as a net positive experience for their society (Wike, Stokes, and Simmons 2016).

9.6 How can you work to diminish racism and racial discrimination?

Use your sociological eye to notice patterns of racial inequality around you and in the larger society—and hold the leaders in your community and the larger society accountable for addressing them. Make an effort to interact with people of races and ethnicities other than your own. Become aware of the racial and ethnic stereotypes you have and learn to dismiss them (as such) as they arise. Call out racism and ethnocentrism when you see or hear them. Advocate for and participate in efforts on your campus to address racism and promote racial and ethnic diversity.

KEY TERMS

CHAPTER 10

UNDERSTANDING INSTITUTIONS

Politics and the Economy

Richard A. Zdan

Business and government are interrelated components of modern society. Our sociological imagination can help us understand how the pieces fit together.
iStockphoto.com/Andrii Yalanskyi

BUSINESS

GOVERNMENT SUPPORT

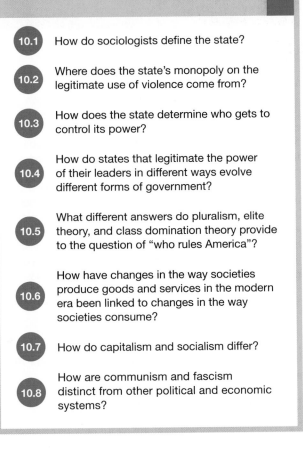

LEARNING QUESTIONS

10.1 How do sociologists define the state?

10.2 Where does the state's monopoly on the legitimate use of violence come from?

10.3 How does the state determine who gets to control its power?

10.4 How do states that legitimate the power of their leaders in different ways evolve different forms of government?

10.5 What different answers do pluralism, elite theory, and class domination theory provide to the question of "who rules America"?

10.6 How have changes in the way societies produce goods and services in the modern era been linked to changes in the way societies consume?

10.7 How do capitalism and socialism differ?

10.8 How are communism and fascism distinct from other political and economic systems?

On the night of August 25, 2006, Todd Upton, a 51-year-old father of three, was killed while driving through Queens, New York, on his way home to his Long Island residence after dropping one of his daughters off at college. He was shot in the neck by 34-year-old Matthew Coletta, who pulled up beside him on the highway and opened fire into Mr. Upton's minivan with a handgun. Before the night was over, Mr. Coletta would injure thirteen more people with a gun that he later told police he had borrowed from the devil. He allegedly told authorities that he was shooting at people in red cars or wearing red clothing because he believed that he was being hunted by members of the Bloods—a street gang known for wearing red. During his trial, it was revealed that Mr. Coletta was a paranoid schizophrenic who was being medicated for his condition at the time of the shootings. None of that mattered to the jury. Five years after his shooting spree, Mr. Coletta was convicted of numerous crimes and sentenced to 384 years to life in prison.

Three months after the death of Mr. Upton, on the night of November 25, 2006, Sean Bell, a twenty-three-year-old father of two, also lost his life to gunfire on the streets of Queens, New York. Mr. Bell had been at a club with some friends celebrating his wedding, which was planned for the following day. As they were leaving, one of Mr. Bell's friends got into an argument with a man outside the club, and a nearby undercover police officer named Gescard Isnora overheard him making reference to having a gun. Officer Isnora followed Mr. Bell and his friends to their nearby car, drew his handgun, and ordered the men to step away from their car. Witness accounts differ as to exactly what happened next—some say that Officer Isnora identified himself as a police officer, others say that he did not—but the end result is not under dispute. Mr. Bell and his friends put the car in gear and tried to escape from the armed man, and Officer Isnora, along with the four other police officers who had arrived to back him up, opened fire on the car. Mr. Bell was killed and his two friends were injured. No gun was found in the car, and although Mr. Bell and his friends all had criminal records, they were not committing any crimes on the night in question. Three of the five officers involved in Mr. Bell's death were indicted for manslaughter and reckless endangerment and eventually stood trial. In April 2008, the three officers were acquitted and cleared of all criminal responsibility for their actions because, according to the judge, their actions were in response to what they perceived to be criminal conduct and, consequently, permissible under the law.

Let us consider the similarities between these two incidents. They took place in the same borough of New York City within three months of each other. Both incidents ended with one innocent man dead—a father in each case—and multiple others wounded. In both cases, the shooters acted in response to what they incorrectly believed at the time to be a threat to their lives.

However, in one case the shooter received a harsh sentence, and in the other the shooters were acquitted. The difference, of course, is that in one case the shooter was a civilian, and in the other, the shooters were police officers. Police officers have the right to do many things in the course of their duties that citizens cannot. They can break traffic laws, they can carry handguns, and, as this example illustrates, they can avoid criminal responsibility for taking a human life because of what would later be revealed as a misunderstanding. This is because being a police officer isn't just a job like any other; to be a police officer is to be a sworn agent of the state.

The State, Power, and Legitimacy

10.1 How do sociologists define the state?

So, what exactly is a state anyhow? Max Weber believed that because states come in so many different forms and pursue so many different tasks, it was impossible to define

HOW I GOT ACTIVE IN SOCIOLOGY

RICHARD A. ZDAN

I have a secret. I have never actually taken a SOC 101 class. As an undergrad at Carnegie Mellon University, I was interested in understanding how the people and culture around us help shape who we are and how those identities, in turn, influence the way we become politically active. Sure sounds like sociology, right? Well, I had never heard of sociology, and CMU did not even have a sociology department! I double majored in psychology and political science and took electives in philosophy and social history—a kind of do-it-yourself sociology program, in hindsight—but I always felt that I was missing some tool I needed to understand the social world as I saw it.

I discovered that tool in an interdisciplinary social science graduate program. I learned that sociology offered a way of combining my interests into a coherent approach that suddenly enabled me to describe the social world. Maybe this is why, as a sociology teacher, I focus so much effort on my SOC 101 classes. Many students enter those classes having no idea what sociology is and certainly no interest in majoring in it—at least not yet. My goal is that these students walk out able to understand how their place in the social world influences who they are and who they will become and how they can influence that world in return—a perspective that will serve them well as both citizens and well-rounded people, regardless of what sort of career their future holds.

---

a state by what it does—by the ends it strives to achieve. States must, therefore, according to Weber, be sociologically defined by the specific and unique means by which they attempt to achieve these ends.

Power and Legitimacy

Weber defined **the state** as "a human community that (successfully) claims the monopoly of the legitimate use of physical force within a given territory" (Weber, Gerth, and Mills 1958). This should not be interpreted to mean that the state is the only entity in a given geographical area that uses physical violence, but rather that it is the only entity that may do so legitimately. **Legitimate power**, also called authority, is power exercised in a manner that is supported by the community. In contrast, **illegitimate power**, or coercion, is power exercised without the support of the community.

Returning to the two vignettes with which we began this chapter, we can now see why the death of Mr. Upton was punished in a way that the death of Mr. Bell was not. The police and the military are the two main ways in which the state exercises its monopoly on physical violence, and the officers who killed Mr. Bell were, at the time, acting in their capacities as agents of the state. As such, they had the authority to use deadly force if they felt that the situation required it. They were wrong, and shortly after their acquittal they were all either fired or forced into retirement, but they did not suffer any criminal penalties. Conversely, Mr. Coletta was not acting as an agent of the state when he killed Mr. Upton. Therefore,

his use of physical violence was considered illegitimate and therefore punishable by law.

Legitimacy and the Right to Punish

Let us consider another example of the difference between legitimate and illegitimate uses of power. On June 20, 2015, a Louisiana man named Robert Noce pleaded "no contest" to charges that he had repeatedly sexually assaulted his then seventeen-year-old stepdaughter, Brittany Monk, when she was a child. Mr. Noce received five years of probation in exchange for his plea. Thirteen days later, Ms. Monk and her boyfriend, Jace Crehan, broke into the trailer where Mr. Noce lived. They beat, strangled, and stabbed him, and stuffed his body into a fifty-five-gallon drum. Ms. Monk, who pled guilty to manslaughter, was sentenced to thirty-five years in prison, while Mr. Crehan, who was found guilty of murder, was sentenced to life in prison.

You might believe, as Ms. Monk and Mr. Crehan obviously did, that five years of probation is not a sufficient punishment for repeated sexually assaulting one's stepdaughter. You might also believe that what Ms. Monk and Mr. Crehan did was right, or at least excusable. But even if we believe that they were right to kill Mr. Noce, they were not granted the right to do so by the state. That is why the state punished Ms. Monk and Mr. Crehan as severely as it did—ironically, much more severely than it had punished Mr. Noce. Their decision to kill Mr. Noce was an exercise of illegitimate power; the state's reciprocal decision to take away their freedom was a necessary exercise of the state's legitimate authority, even if you don't think it was particularly fair.

LEGITIMATE VERSUS ILLEGITIMATE VIOLENCE

In this exercise, you will consider conditions under which violence is legitimate and illegitimate.

What is an example of the use of violence that Weber would consider legitimate? What is an example of the

use of violence that Weber would consider illegitimate? Do you see any problems with Weber's definition? Your instructor may assign you to discuss these questions with a peer.

Check Your Understanding

- Why does Weber feel that the state must not be defined by what it does and must instead be defined by how it pursues those ends?
- What is the difference between authority and coercion?

Origins of the State

> 10.2   Where does the state's monopoly on the legitimate use of violence come from?

But where does the state's monopoly over the legitimate use of physical violence come from, and what, if anything, can we do if we feel that the state is misusing the power granted by that monopoly? After all, it can seem unjust that the killings of some innocent men are excused while others are punished and that child molesters receive probation while their victims receive prison. Thomas Hobbes, a seventeenth-century English political philosopher, attempted to answer these very questions.

Hobbes's State of Nature and the Social Contract

Hobbes started his analysis by first trying to describe what life was like in what he called the **state of nature**, before the development of the state or any other form of civil society. Because laws come from society and our concept of private property is defined by law, neither exists in the state of nature. Might makes right, and property belongs to whoever can hold and keep it. However, even the strongest person must sleep sometime, and even the fastest person must rest. Not only are the weak threatened by the strong, but the strong are in return threatened by groups whose combined might is greater than their own. Hobbes describes the life of people living in this state of nature as "solitary, poor, nasty, brutish, and short" and governed

by "continual fear, and danger of violent death" (Hobbes [1651] 1962).

CONSIDER THIS

Hobbes makes some very big assumptions about what life was like before civil society. What if he is wrong? How would our view of the power wielded by the state change if the natural state of humanity was peaceful coexistence instead of violent competition?

All is not lost, however, for a civil society can emerge out of the state of nature. Because so much of the misery inherent to the state of nature Hobbes describes can be blamed on fear of violence, life would improve dramatically if it were eliminated. This could be accomplished, Hobbes argued, if all people living within a given territory were willing to give up just a few of their rights—specifically, their right to engage in violence against one another. These rights would be vested in the hands of one individual—a sovereign—who would use this monopoly on the legitimate use of violence to protect the people from one another. This agreement by the people to give up certain individual rights in exchange for protection and other benefits is called the **social contract**. As the kingdoms and fiefdoms of feudalism gave way to the rise of modernity, the role by these sovereigns passed to the modern state.

This is why the state will sometimes use its power in ways that appear unjust. The state must sometimes put the safety of all the people ahead of that of any individual person. Police officers must be allowed to make spilt-second decisions to use deadly force in order to protect themselves and others without fear of criminal repercussions for making a mistake; citizens cannot be allowed to seek justice beyond that authorized by the state, even if what the state has decided does not seem particularly fair.

DOING SOCIOLOGY 10.2

WRITING A SOCIAL CONTRACT

In this activity, you will examine how the social contract evolves out of mutual interests of both the sovereign and the citizens.

Imagine for a moment that the classroom exists in a Hobbesian state of nature. The only food that is available is three-foot submarine sandwich that appears every day at exactly noon and is not enough to satisfy the hunger of everyone in the class. After much fighting and bloodshed, your class has decided to elect a sovereign to eliminate the fear of violence and starvation that governs your daily life.

Imagine yourself in the role of the sovereign. How would you use your power? What benefits would you claim for yourself as a reward for the responsibilities of your position? How would you ensure that the rest of the class does not overthrow and replace you? Make note of your answers.

Imagine yourself in the role of a common citizen. What expectations do you have of the sovereign? What privileges are you willing to allow the sovereign to claim as a reward for keeping you safe? Under what circumstances would you choose to overthrow and replace the sovereign? Make note of your answers.

Keeping in mind your answers to these questions, write a simple contract that formally lays out the rights and responsibilities of both the people and the sovereign. Under your contract, who is it that rules whom? Does the sovereign rule the people or do the people rule the sovereign? Or is it some combination of both? Now apply your social contract to twenty-first-century America. What similarities and differences do you see between your social contract and the way the American government relates to the people? Be prepared to discuss your contract and your conclusions with peers. Your instructor may ask you to submit this as a written assignment.

Otherwise, the state would not be able to keep up its end of the social contract.

But what happens if the state abuses this power? What if the state starts using violence to oppress the people instead of protect them? In that case, the people can simply reclaim their individual rights from the state. When Thomas Jefferson wrote in the Declaration of Independence that "Governments are instituted among Men, deriving their just powers from the consent of the governed," he was referring to the social contract described by Hobbes. He went on to say that "whenever any Form of Government becomes destructive of these ends, it is the Right of the People to alter or to abolish it." States (or sovereigns) that do not use their monopoly on the legitimate use of violence wisely to protect the people soon find that they have lost their power and are replaced.

Check Your Understanding

- What does Hobbes mean by the state of nature?
- How does Hobbes describe life in the state of nature?
- What is a social contract?
- What happens when the social contract is broken?

Forms of Legitimate Domination

> 10.3   How does the state determine who gets to control its power?

Now that we understand how the state gets its power, we must consider how it is determined who gets to wield that power. In Hobbes's terms, how do the people choose who gets to be the sovereign? As seen in Figure 10.1, Weber identifies three different ways in which the state can justify its claims to legitimate power.

▼ FIGURE 10.1

Types of Legitimate State Power

Weber's types of legitimate state power
• traditional domination
• rational-legal domination
• charismatic domination

Source: Weber, Max, Hans Gerth and C. Wright Mills. 1946. *From Max Weber: Essays in Sociology.* New York: Oxford University Press.

Traditional Domination

The first type of legitimate domination described by Weber is traditional domination. Weber claims that **traditional domination** is based on "the authority of the 'eternal yesterday'" (Weber, Gerth, and Mills 1958). This means that the legitimacy of an individual's claim to wield power is based on custom or tradition; the leader's authority is accepted because that is the way that things have always been done in the past. Kings and queens who rule for no other reason than that their family has done so for hundreds of years justify their authority through traditional domination. In most cases, the leader's authority is absolute and cannot be questioned or countermanded. There is usually a process in place for appointing a custodian for absolute authority, often called a regent, if the leader is temporarily unable to exercise his power, as well as a time-honored process for replacing him when he dies or otherwise permanently abdicates his position, thus ensuring continuity and stability of the government. This stability is most clearly demonstrated in the phrase used all over the world to acknowledge the passing of a monarch—"The king is dead; long live the king!"

Although traditional domination was much more common in the Western world before the rise of modernity than it is today, there are still some societies that are governed via traditional domination. Several nation-states, such as Saudi Arabia and Qatar, are ruled by monarchs with absolute traditional authority. Similarly, the Pope's rule over the nation-state of the Vatican City, as well as the Roman Catholic Church, is legitimated through traditional domination. Finally, there are any number of tribal or patriarchal groups all over the world—such as Scottish clans—whose leaders inherit and wield power on the basis of traditional domination.

Rational-Legal Domination

The second type of legitimate domination described by Weber is rational-legal domination. Unlike in systems governed through traditional domination, in which power is vested in an individual directly, leaders who use **rational-legal domination** to legitimate their authority draw their power from occupying a legally defined position. Presidents or prime ministers who wield power only as long as they occupy their constitutionally defined positions justify their authority through rational-legal domination.

Whether power is vested in the office that a leader occupies or in the leader himself is the key distinction between systems of rational-legal domination and traditional domination. As president of the United States, Barak Obama wielded great power. He could unilaterally make many important decisions and sign executive orders that became the law of the land. However, once his term of office ended, Obama gave up that power to his successor, Donald Trump. President Trump now wields the same power that President Obama did and, in fact, has used it to undo some of President Obama's decisions and executive orders. Obama is powerless to do anything about this because he no longer occupies the position and thus no longer wields the power. Once Trump leaves the office of the presidency, the power will pass to the next duly elected leader.

Much like systems of traditional domination, rational-legal systems also have time-honored processes in place to ensure the stability of the government when a leader leaves his or her position. In the United States, for example, we hold elections every four years to determine who will serve as president. The current leader may wish to hold on to his position, but if he is defeated by a rival, as happened in 1992 when Bill Clinton defeated George H. W. Bush, who was seeking a second term as president, the loser steps aside after the election and acknowledges the legitimacy of the new occupant of the office. There is also usually a process in place to ensure continuity if a leader dies or is otherwise unable to finish his term in office. When President John F. Kennedy was assassinated in 1963, Vice President Lyndon Johnson assumed the office of president to complete Kennedy's term; similarly, Vice President Gerald Ford assumed the office of president when President Richard Nixon resigned halfway through his second term in 1974.

Charismatic Domination

The third and final type of legitimate domination described by Weber is charismatic domination. Under **charismatic domination**, leaders draw their legitimacy from the devotion of their followers and their belief that the leaders possess some sort of extraordinary personal qualities. Although charismatic domination is similar to traditional domination in that power is intrinsically invested in the leader himself, there is one very important distinction. Under traditional domination, leaders need no outstanding personal characteristics, or even any basic competence, in order to assume power; the fact that tradition dictates that they are next in line is all that they require. Charismatic leaders, however, must actively do something to earn the devotion of their followers by inspiring them to join some sort of movement, group, or campaign.

What makes charismatic domination unique is the fact that charismatic leaders are not beholden to any system.

They are free agents who are subject neither to custom and tradition nor to any legal restraints imposed by the office they hold. They are subject only to their own consciences and to doing whatever is necessary to maintain the allegiance of their devoted followers. In this way, they represent a true threat to the established power structure.

Dr. Martin Luther King Jr.

Consider the example of Dr. Martin Luther King Jr. King is widely considered to have been the leader of the American civil rights movement. But who elected him to that position? What norms constrained his actions? What legally defined rights and responsibilities did he gain when he occupied it? The answers to these questions are, of course, "no one," "none," and "none." Neither elected nor appointed, King's authority came from the legion of followers he inspired with his words and his adherence to the nonviolent doctrine of passive resistance.

The March on Washington led by King and other civil rights leaders in August 1963 shook the established political power structure to such a degree that it led to a Democratic president and a Democratic-controlled Congress passing the Civil Rights Act of 1964, over the forceful objections of the segregationist southern Democrats. It is one of the most significant reasons why most Whites in the South switched political allegiance from Democratic to Republican and still reliably vote for Republican candidates today. This example illustrates just how disruptive charismatic authority can be. Is it any wonder that after his speech during the March on Washington, King was personally named by Federal Bureau of Investigation director J. Edgar Hoover as a "potential troublemaker" whom the bureau ought to endeavor to "expose, disrupt, misdirect, discredit, or otherwise neutralize" (U.S. Senate, Select Committee to Study Governmental Operation with Respect to Intelligence Activities 1976)?

For all the disruptive power inherent in charismatic domination, it is inherently unstable. When King was assassinated in April 1968, who assumed his position as leader of the American civil rights movement? It was not his wife, Coretta Scott King, or his son, Martin Luther King III. It was not Jesse Jackson or John Lewis or any other member of his inner circle. Ralph Abernathy succeeded King as chairman of the Southern Christian Leadership Conference, but not as leader of the civil rights movement. The reality is that no one was able to take King's place. Charismatic domination is based on the ability of an individual to use his or her extraordinary qualities to inspire the devotion of the masses. These qualities cannot be passed on to a successor, and consequently, when charismatic leaders like King either die or are incapacitated, their authority dies with them.

CONSIDER THIS

We usually think of charismatic leaders as being beloved by their followers, like King or Mohandas Ghandi. Is that the only way a charismatic leader can inspire followers? Can you think of a charismatic leader who was able to build a movement and get his followers to fall in line by terrorizing them?

The Routinization of Charisma. It is, however, possible to transfer power from a charismatic leader to a system based on either traditional domination or rational-legal domination. Weber refers to this process, illustrated in Figure 10.2, as the **routinization of charisma**, noting that although "the original charismatic community lived communistically off donations, alms, and the booty of war," eventually, "the organization of authority becomes permanent" (Weber, Gerth, and Mills 1958). This process perfectly describes what Fidel Castro did in Cuba. Castro was a charismatic leader who was able to lead a revolution that overthrew the government of Cuba in 1959. However, upon taking power, Castro was able to establish a permanent basis for his power in a new system of rules and laws so that, when he was ready to step down after ruling Cuba in one capacity or another for almost 50 years, the system of rational-legal domination he had established was able to provide stability and continuity in his absence.

Check Your Understanding

- What is traditional domination?
- What is rational-legal domination?
- What is charismatic domination?
- What can the routinization of charisma accomplish?

▼ FIGURE 10.2

Routinization of Charisma

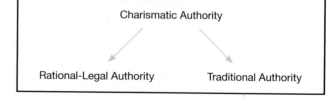

DOING SOCIOLOGY 10.3

LEGITIMATE DOMINATION: 2016

In this exercise, you will apply Weber's forms of legitimate domination to understand a recent presidential election.

The 2016 presidential election between Donald Trump and Hillary Clinton was not just a clash between a Republican and a Democrat but represented a clash between very different styles of campaigning. Trump ran an outsider campaign, built around his celebrity, which challenged the Republican Party establishment, while Clinton's campaign, based around her experience and personal connections, made her the favorite of the Democratic Party establishment.

Watch this webcast from a June 2016 episode of PBS's *Washington Week*: "Trump's Money Machine, Clinton &

Trump Campaign Styles, 'Stop Trump' Standstill and Is Hillary Clinton Too Well Known?" that discusses these differences between the styles of the Trump and Clinton campaigns (https://www.pbs.org/weta/washingtonweek/web-video/trumps-money-machine-clinton-trump-campaign-styles-stop-trump-standstill-and-hillary). As you watch the video, consider the three forms of legitimate domination described by Weber. Take notes.

How can Weber help us understand the stylistic differences between the two campaigns? Which form of domination do you think each candidate was using to legitimate his or her claim on the presidency? What explanation do you think Weber would give for Trump's eventual victory over Clinton?

Types of Government

10.4 How do states that legitimate the power of their leaders in different ways evolve different forms of government?

States that legitimate the authority of their leaders in different ways evolve different governmental systems to support and, if necessary, select those leaders. We compare several different systems below.

Monarchy

As we discussed earlier, states governed through traditional domination are very often **monarchies**. These states are headed by some sort of individual sovereign—such as a king, a queen, a sultan, or an emperor—who inherited his position and will pass it on to his children. In keeping with the ideas of traditional domination, many sovereigns associate their reign with the will of the gods. In medieval Europe, a doctrine called the **divine right of kings** argued that the king was given his power by God, and thus no mortal man could stand in judgment against him. Similarly, the Emperor of Japan was considered to be the direct descendent of the sun goddess, Amaterasu, and although the earliest pharaohs of ancient Egypt were considered to be merely emissaries of the gods, later pharaohs were considered to be gods themselves.

Democracy

Modern rational-legal societies are generally governed through some sort of **democracy**. Democracy is

government by the people, but democratic societies vary in exactly how much control the people have over the workings of their government. The classical Athenian style of democracy developed in the sixth century BCE gave every citizen a vote in the legislative assembly. This assembly, called the Ekklesia, had a role very similar to that of the U.S. Congress and was responsible for passing laws, appointing state officials, and declaring war. This system of **direct democracy**, whereby citizens directly controlled the entire political process and were actively responsible for making all the decisions of the state, was able to work effectively because of the relatively small number of citizens in ancient Athens. But imagine how difficult it would be to enact such a system in the United States, if all 140 million registered voters were also members of Congress.

Given the veritable impossibility of this sort of system working with populations as large as those of most modern states, a different system of democracy has evolved. Under this system of **representative democracy**, citizens do not actively vote on every single issue the government must address but instead vote to elect a group of representatives who then make decisions on behalf of the voters who elected them. These representatives must periodically stand for reelection in order to maintain their positions. These regular elections are intended to ensure that they faithfully represent the interests of their constituents; those who do not may expect to lose their positions and the power that goes

SOCIOLOGISTS IN ACTION

EVALUATING GOVERNMENT-FUNDED PROGRAMS

KRISTIN PITTS

More than ever before, government-funded agencies face pressure to show that their programs are effective and worth funding. Most program managers have a vested interest (their jobs!) in continued funding for their programs. So, government agencies need external evaluators, like me, to provide an unbiased perspective and to gather data about programs so that they can make evidence-based funding decisions.

I use my sociological skills every day in my work as an external program evaluator of government funded training and education programs. I have evaluated a variety of programs, from instructor training programs to programs designed to facilitate online learning. On the basis of my findings, I make recommendations for continued or increased funding or, if a program does not show evidence of effectiveness, withdrawal of funding.

Often, I work as part of a team of evaluators. For example, I was part of a group hired to evaluate the effectiveness of a training course designed to teach new instructors how to incorporate various student-centric strategies in their classrooms. Student-centric strategies shift the focus from the teacher to the student, so students take a more active role in their learning. Supervisors of the instructors attending the course, however, were not convinced of the effectiveness of student-centric strategies and opposed the course. Our team's evaluation revealed that instructors using the student-centric strategies were more effective instructors than the instructors who did not receive the training (including their supervisors). The government agency that funded this program decided to keep it going and to make modifications on the basis of data we collected during the evaluation.

Our team also evaluated a program responsible for creating learning applications for different courses. The program managers thought the applications were wonderful tools and that they helped students learn the material in their courses. Our team collected data from five different courses that used the learning applications. Our findings revealed that students were not using the applications because they either did not know about them or, more important, they did not think they helped them learn the course material. The findings from the second group of students led us to recommend cutting off funding for this ineffective program.

If the agencies had not used external evaluators to measure the effectiveness of these programs, funding outcomes might have been very different. In the past, agencies received money to build and implement programs that were in favor with one political party or another—with no expectation to show that their programs worked. In the current era of limited government spending, those days are over, and professional external evaluators are in demand. Today, more and more sociologists are using their expertise to help design and evaluate government funded programs. In the process, we are increasing program effectiveness and decreasing poor investments of taxpayers' money.

Discussion Question: How can sociologists' work as evaluators of government programs protect or challenge governments' legitimate power?

Kristin Pitts is an evaluation specialist for a private contractor and provides evaluation support for various agencies.

---

along with them. Representatives must be prepared to show their constituents that the policies and programs they have enacted are beneficial and effective. As seen in the Sociologists in Action feature in this chapter, sociologists often play a role in evaluating government programs.

Oligarchy and Plutocracy

Although monarchy and democracy are perhaps the most familiar forms of government, there are alternatives to investing the power of state in the hands of either one person or all the people.

One such system is called an **oligarchy**, a type of government in which power is held by a small group of elites. Any number of factors might serve to distinguish the ruling elites from other members of society. The former Soviet Union and the modern-day People's Republic of China would both be considered oligarchies because the governments of both states were or are controlled by their Communist parties. South Africa under apartheid was also an oligarchy because governmental power rested in the hands of the White minority. A military junta that takes control of a state after a successful coup d'état would be yet another example of an oligarchy. One of the more common types of oligarchy is **plutocracy**, in which power is held by the economic elites.

The Iron Law of Oligarchy

Robert Michels, an early twentieth-century German sociologist, argued that over time, all representative democracies would slowly transform into oligarchies. Michels argued that this process is inevitable, which is why he called it the **iron law of oligarchy**. This happens because in every organization, a divide eventually starts to grow between the leaders of the organization and the members. The reason for this is that different members of the organization have different levels of investment. Some members are able to devote more time or resources to the organization than others. Those who have a greater investment will naturally be more concerned about the direction in which the organization moves and, therefore, more likely to seek leadership positions. The other members are usually happy that someone else is willing to handle that responsibility. The particular organizations that interested Michels were political parties, and he argued that this process explained why so few members of any party actually ran for office.

Imagine for a moment that you are a member of a revolutionary political party that seeks to make radical changes to the American system. Let us also imagine that you have the necessary commitment and resources to run for office, and you are victorious. You now have the power to shape governmental policy. However, as we established earlier, that power lasts only as long as you are able to keep your position. How would you handle a situation in which taking action in pursuit of your agenda might cost you your position? Would you consider not doing the thing you consider to be right in favor of doing the thing that will allow you to keep your power and thus potentially do more good over time?

Michels argued that elected leaders must prioritize decisions that will allow them to hold on to their position because, if they fail to do that, they will not be able to enact any of the policies they were elected to support. "Thus," Michels ([1911] 1966) wrote, "from a means, organization becomes an end. To the institutions and qualities, which at the outset were destined simply to ensure the good working of the party machine . . . a greater importance comes ultimately to be attached than to the productivity of the machine." In other words, politicians start focusing more on keeping their jobs than on enacting the reforms for which they supposedly sought those jobs in the first place.

The United States and the Iron Law of Oligarchy. Considering the high costs of running and winning elections in the United States, it should come as no surprise that politicians tend to pay more attention to individuals and groups that help fund their campaigns than their average constituent. In fact, a study found that "when the preferences of economic elites and the stands of organized interest groups are controlled for, the preferences of the average American appear to have only a minuscule, near-zero, statistically non-significant impact upon public policy" (Gilens and Page 2014). Given these findings, the study's authors questioned whether the United States is now more like an oligarchy than a democracy.

CONSIDER THIS

Do you think the United States is more like an oligarchy or a democracy? How would you support your argument?

Autocracy, Dictatorship, and Totalitarianism

Governments systems based on both traditional and rational-legal domination have internal checks and balances on the exercise of power by leaders. Democracies place constitutional limitations on the powers of all officials, and the sovereigns that rule monarchies are bound by the traditions and customs from which they derive their power. Not all forms of government, however, place such restrictions on their leaders.

Autocracy and Dictatorships. **Autocracy** is a form of government in which absolute power is held by one person whose authority is not restricted in any way by either law or custom. Although it is possible for a monarchy to evolve into an autocracy if the sovereign becomes sufficiently powerful to ignore the constraints of custom and tradition without consequence, most autocratic governments are dictatorships. **Dictatorships** are systems of government in which a leader is able to either overthrow or subvert the existing government and seize absolute power through charismatic domination. Most often, we think of dictators as cruel leaders who are hated by their people but remain in power because of the fear and terror they inspire. Saddam Hussein's iron-fisted rule over the people of Iraq can be described this way, particularly in the years after the first Persian Gulf War, when a combination of crippling economic sanctions and Saddam's need to forcibly put down any threat to his power led to a humanitarian crisis in Iraq.

Other dictators draw their power from the enthusiastic support of their citizens and the cult of personality they construct around themselves. The former president of Haiti, François "Papa Doc" Duvalier, is a good example. Despite overseeing one of the most brutal regimes in the Western Hemisphere during the twentieth century, he was still generally beloved by the poor, rural, Black people who constituted the majority of Haiti's population. They loved Papa Doc for his success destroying the economic and social power of the mixed-race (mulatto) elites that had ruled Haiti since it gained its independence.

Totalitarianism. Autocracy is often confused with **totalitarianism**. Although they are similar, there is an important distinction. An autocratic state is created when an individual consolidates absolute power in the political sphere and then uses repressive tactics to crush potential opposition and retain that power. In contrast, totalitarian states attempt to exercise monopoly control over every aspect of social, political, and economic life. This means not just seizing control over political institutions, but cultural institutions—such as the arts, science, religion, and education—and the economy.

Totalitarian states pursue this total consolidation of power in the name of a movement toward some overarching ideology. The two classic examples of totalitarianism, Nazism and Stalinism, were both driven by race-based identity movements—Pan-Germanism in the case of the former and Pan-Slavism in the case of the latter. The importance of these ideologies is so great that Hannah Arendt (1951), goes so far as to say that "[the] 'totalitarian state' is a state in appearance only, and . . . the Movement by now is above state and people, ready to sacrifice both for the sake of its ideology."

Check Your Understanding

- What is the difference between direct and representative democracy?
- How does oligarchy differ from democracy?
- Explain Michels's iron law of oligarchy.
- What differentiates totalitarianism from autocracy?

Theoretical Approaches to Politics

10.5   What different answers can pluralism, elite theory, and class domination theory provide to the question of "who rules America"?

Now that we have a basic understanding of what the state is, where it comes from, and how it works, we can begin looking at different theories that attempt to explain why it operates the way it does. As we have seen in earlier chapters, theories that fall under the structural functionalist and conflict perspectives offer very different explanations. As we describe them, think about what makes the most sense to you.

Structural Functionalism

Structural functionalism, as you know, sees society as a complex system in which each part serves a purpose in maintaining the stability of the status quo. Political leaders, no matter the type of government, have to deal with the fact that the citizens of their states do not all have the same interests. This means that every action that the leader takes or does not take will please some of the people and displease others. Too much displeasure can lead to instability. This affects all types of governments. For example, although a dictator may not be concerned about being voted out of office, he still must be concerned about being removed from office via coup d'état or assassination if the wrong people—such as military leaders, for example—become too displeased with his decisions.

Pluralism. Political sociologists seeking to understand how leaders attempt to balance the competing demands of their different constituencies often use a structural functionalist theory called pluralism. **Pluralism** sees the political system as a struggle between competing interest groups for power and control of the decision-making process in which no single group is in control all the time. Political leaders may have their own personal views on any number of issues or policies before them and may have their own ideas about what is "best" for the people, but tradition and custom, the bureaucratically defined limits on their power, and the need to maintain the allegiance of their strongest supporters often limit their ability to pursue those preferences.

Consequently, the pluralist perspective sees the state as a neutral forum in which the preferences of different interest groups and individual citizens can be gathered and evaluated in order to provide the policies and services that will please the greatest number of citizens. It might seem as if such a neutral forum would lead to ceaseless, destabilizing conflicts among competing interests, but pluralists do not believe that is true. Instead, they argue that a system of checks and balances that prevents any one faction or individual from consolidating too much power over too long a period of time actually makes the state more stable.

Conflict Theory

In contrast to a structural functionalist theory like pluralism that focuses on stability, conflict theorists see the state, not as a neutral forum for the objective evaluation of policy but as a battleground where a dominant elite is able to consistently advance their own interests over those of the masses. The belief that power is not diffused throughout society but rather consolidated in the hands of a small group of people both inside and outside of government is called **elite theory**.

C. Wright Mills and the Power Elite.
C. Wright Mills refers to this group of influential decision makers as the **power elite**, describing them as the individuals "in positions to make decisions having major consequences" (Mills 1956). Mills argues that the individual members of the power elite are drawn from one of three different spheres of social life. First are the corporate elite. These include both the chief executives and major shareholders of the largest and most important corporations. Their influence is based not just on their wealth but also on the power of the corporations that they control. For example, in March 2019, the leader of Amazon was able to pressure lawmakers in Washington State to change the language in a new labor protection bill in a way that exempted most Amazon workers from those protections.

Second are the political elite. These include not only certain elected officials, such as the president, the congressional leaders of both the Republican and Democratic parties, and the chairs of certain powerful congressional committees, but also various appointed aides, advisers, and agency directors, many of whom have terms of service that span multiple presidential administrations. Have you ever noticed that when there is an important issue about which the Republicans and Democrats in Congress cannot agree—think of the government shutdowns that have occurred fairly regularly in recent years—it is always the same group of political leaders who sit down to try and solve the problem? These leaders reach a compromise agreement and then bring it back to Congress, where the individual congresspersons are able to do little more than vote "yes" or "no." As the ones with the real power to make important decisions, the members of this small group of leaders are part of the political power elite.

The third and final social sphere from which members of the power elite are drawn is the military elite. Referred to by Mills as the "warlords," the military elite consists of high-ranking current and former members of the armed forces. They draw their power from the status and honors afforded to warriors in most societies and use that power to influence decisions in the name of "patriotism" and "security." General Douglas MacArthur, who used the stature he gained from his role in helping the United States

win World War II to directly challenge the authority of President Harry Truman, is an obvious example of a warlord. Today, large corporations that are part of the military industrial complex and ensure that the United States constantly remains on a war footing might be considered a new style of warlord. After all, despite all of the other pressing financial needs and the fact that the United States has not been involved in a declared war since World War II, almost half of the $1.2 trillion dollars of discretionary spending appropriated in the 2018 federal budget were allocated for defense spending.

These three groups do not operate independently, nor do they serve as checks and balances against one another. Instead, they come together to shape the course of human events. This is not because of some deliberate conspiracy. Rather, because of the numerous overlapping relations among the different groups that make up the power elite, its members tend to share common interests. For example, three of the last eight men to serve as secretary of the U.S. Treasury had previously been partners at the investment bank Goldman Sachs. The first, Robert Rubin, oversaw President Bill Clinton's dismantling of the Glass-Steagall banking regulation act and subsequent deregulation of the financial services industry. The second, Henry Paulson, oversaw President George W. Bush's response to the 2007 financial crisis, which was a direct consequence of the banking deregulation. He managed the bailout fund that left many of the investment banks that helped cause the crisis—including Goldman Sachs—in better economic shape than they were before the crisis.

CONSIDER THIS

Changing the way political campaigns are financed is a popular suggestion for limiting the power of the economic elite over American politics. Given what you now know, do you think campaign finance reform would have the desired effect? Explain your position.

G. William Domhoff and Class Domination.
This revolving-door relationship between the economic elite and the political elite has led some theorists to offer a revision to Mills's construction of the power elite. G. William Domhoff offers just such a revision with his class domination theory. The **class domination theory** argues that the economic elite are able to dominate society because of their power over the workings of the economy—what Domhoff calls **distributive power**. Corporate elites'

MEDICARE FOR ALL

In this exercise, you will apply different theoretical approaches to understand a current political issue.

Since the passage of the Patient Protection and Affordable Care Act (also known as "Obamacare") in 2010, access to health care has been one of the issues most frequently discussed by policy makers. Recently, a plan to expand Medicare access to all citizens and create a "single-payer" health care system has been gaining popularity, particularly among Democratic politicians and voters.

Read the *New York Times* article "Medicare for All Would Abolish Private Insurance. 'There's No Precedent in American History'" discussing the possibility of a "Medicare for all" program: https://

www.nytimes.com/2019/03/23/health/private-health-insurance-medicare-for-all-bernie-sanders.html. Think about who would benefit from the passage of a Medicare for all program and who would not. Now consider this policy proposal from each of the three theoretical approaches to politics that we have discussed: pluralism, elite theory, and class domination theory. How can each of these three approaches help us understand the debate over Medicare for all? What would each approach believe would be necessary for Medicare for all to become the law of the land? What reasons would each approach offer for why it might not become law? Your instructor may ask you to write a response and/or be prepared to discuss your analysis with peers.

ability to make financial investments or hire more workers in a particular community gives them influence over political leaders in that area. This is because if those political leaders don't agree to certain terms favored by those corporate elites, they can withdraw their financial investments and downsize their workforce in that community. Do you remember the earlier example of how Amazon was able to influence the final version of a labor protection bill in Washington State? Amazon's ability to get what it wanted over the objections of workers who otherwise would have benefited is exactly the sort of thing Domhoff means when he talks about the distributive power of the elite.

Domhoff agrees with Mills that a power elite exists but believes that instead of just influencing the direction of important political decisions, the power elite actively "work to preserve the governmental rules and regulations that make possible the inequality in the wealth and income distributions" (Domhoff 2014). Consistent with the slightly different role played by the power elite in class domination theory, Domhoff sees the power elite as being composed of slightly different groups than Mills had identified.

Domhoff views the political and military elites as subordinate to the interests of the economic elite. So, he focuses on the economic elite, breaking them into two different categories: the upper class and the corporate community. Domhoff notes that the upper class, in addition to having the same economic status, also share a highly cohesive, status-based culture. The other economic elite group, the **corporate community**, consists of a network

composed of the directors, partners, and managers of various profit-seeking enterprises. These two groups are joined by the **policy-planning network**, nonprofit think tanks, foundations, and policy discussion groups, all funded by the corporate community and the upper class and tasked with developing and advocating social policy reforms that will advance their funders' interests.

Check Your Understanding

- What do pluralists mean when they refer to the state as a "neutral forum"?

- Who are the power elite?

- What groups does Mills believe make up the power elite?

- What groups does Domhoff say make up the power elite?

Politics and the Economy

10.6 How have changes in the way societies produce goods and services in the modern era been linked to changes in the way societies consume?

As described in Chapter 4, societies have evolved and changed throughout human history as technology has advanced and changed. These changes in technology naturally lead to changes in the economy. Karl Marx was particularly interested in the relation between changes in the mode of economic production and social change. He even went so far as to say that "the whole natural structure of the nation itself depends on the stage of development reached by its production" (Marx, Engels, and Arthur 1974). Marx felt that the political system governing a particular state was strongly linked to the nature of that state's economy.

Even today, this strong relationship between politics and the economy described by Marx remains. In 1992, Bill Clinton's successful campaign for the U.S. presidency used "It's the economy, stupid" as an unofficial slogan to remind both campaign workers and voters alike that the most important issue in deciding the election would be the state of the economy. Ironically, failure to remember that slogan contributed to Hillary Clinton's defeat by Donald Trump in the 2016 U.S. presidential election. Trump focused his campaign efforts on the working- and middle-class voters who felt they had not benefited from the economic recovery presided over by President Barack Obama, which Clinton had promised to continue if elected. As these examples indicate, understanding the **economy**—by which we mean a system of producing and consuming goods and services—is essential to understanding the structure and functioning of the state. Key to this understanding is being able to see how the industrial economy evolved over time.

Industrialization

In the late eighteenth century, a series of technological advancements and social changes began the process of industrialization in many areas of the world. **Industrialization** is the systematic transformation of an economy from a focus on agricultural production to one focused on the manufacturing of finished goods. Although manufactured goods were certainly a part of preindustrial societies, they tended to be produced as they were needed, either in small shops by a lone craftsman and his apprentices or at home by the individuals who would use them. Industrialization shifted the locus of production to large factories where hundreds of workers toiled to mass-produce goods in advance of need.

The invention of machines able to produce goods quickly sparked the Industrial Revolution. No longer was it necessary for workers to possess skills honed through long apprenticeships in order to craft things from wood or metal; now the machine did most of the work, and the worker just needed to be able to operate it. Factories were, consequently, able to hire low-skilled and even unskilled workers, to whom they were able to pay very low wages.

However, it is important to remember that economies are not just defined by how goods are produced but also by how they are consumed. The mass production of goods at a standardized level of quality increased their availability and made them accessible to more people. This meant that even working-class families were able to acquire some of the luxuries previously reserved for the elite. Thorstein Veblen argued that this blurring of the distinction between high-status and low-status members of society threatened the social position of the elites, because status is measured, in part, by comparing ourselves with our neighbors. In order to reinforce traditional status differences, elites began to engage in actions to "put [their] opulence in evidence" through "the wasteful consumption of goods" and the "the giving of valuable presents and expensive feasts and entertainments" (Veblen 1899). Veblen refers to this practice of spending money for the purpose of demonstrating or enhancing social prestige as **conspicuous consumption**.

Fordism and Post-Fordism

Industrialization reached a peak in the early twentieth century in the factories of the Ford Motor Company. There, Henry Ford used an assembly line to facilitate the mass production of his automobiles. All the cars that came off the assembly line were identical, put together by unskilled workers trained to perform one simple task over and over again as each partially constructed automobile reached their station on the line. Unlike earlier industrial factory owners who paid their workers barely enough to allow them to survive, Ford paid his workers a wage that allowed them not just to survive but also to afford a few luxuries. This was not generosity on his part; it was a smart business decision. Aware of the economic link between production and consumption, Ford wanted to be sure that all his workers could afford to buy one of the automobiles they were producing. This system of mass production of standardized, relatively inexpensive products by unskilled workers paid wages sufficient to purchase those products is called **Fordism**.

As the twentieth century progressed, however, the economies of scale made possible by the patterns of mass production and mass consumption that defined Fordism became less effective. Markets started to fragment as consumers began to demand less standardized products that were able to meet more specialized needs. Elites sought more luxurious versions of standard products as a way of demonstrating their social status. As variations on standard products became more common, options and features began to become as important to consumers as price in determining whether they would purchase a product. In order to meet the demands of these new patterns of consumption, a new model of economic production was needed.

This model, called **post-Fordism**, was defined by a shift away from mass production of large quantities of identical products toward the production of smaller quantities of products, in wider variety, carefully targeted at specific groups of consumers. As economies of scale were replaced by economies of scope, the nature of factory work began to change as well. Smaller production runs of less standardized products meant that workers not only needed to have more specialized skills but also to have greater flexibility in the sort of work they could perform. Because this sort of worker was difficult to find and expensive to pay, part-time and temporary work became more common as workers with certain necessary skills or knowledge were hired when needed and then let go when they were no longer necessary.

Deindustrialization

As the Fordist mass production model became more obsolete, companies that had invested heavily in manufacturing capacity began to redirect funds toward new products and product development to keep up with changing public tastes or, in some cases, to stockholders as dividends. These stockholders either invested those dividends or spent the income on luxury products and services (as Veblen described the rich doing 100 years before). These new patterns of consumption accelerated the changes in the production of goods. Goods still needed to be produced, of course. However, as the economy became increasingly international in nature through the processes of globalization, it became cheaper for many companies to move production to the Global South, where labor and production costs were lower.

A good illustration of the way the deindustrialization of the United States changed the nation's economy can be found by looking at the *Fortune* 500 list of the most profitable U.S. companies. In 2018, the top ten companies on that list consisted of three financial services companies (Berkshire-Hathaway, JPMorgan Chase, and Wells Fargo), three communications companies (Verizon, AT&T, and Comcast), two technology companies (Apple and Microsoft), one drug company (Pfizer), and one oil company (Exxon Mobil). Contrast that to fifty years earlier, in 1968, when *Fortune*'s list of the top ten most profitable companies included five oil companies (Standard Oil of New Jersey, Texaco, Gulf Oil, Chevron, and Mobil), four technology and manufacturing companies (General Motors, IBM, General Electric, and Eastman Kodak), and one chemical company (DuPont). The oil companies and manufacturing companies have almost completely fallen off the list, replaced by companies that provide services. The chemical company that provided materials to support American industry has been replaced with a drug company that supports the medical service industry. The only company on the 2018 list that actually manufactures anything is Apple, and most of its production takes place in China.

Check Your Understanding

- How did industrialization change the way goods were produced and consumed?

- What does Veblen believe is the nature of the relationship between industrialization and conspicuous consumption?

- How did the economy change as it shifted from a Fordist to a post-Fordist model?

- How did globalization contribute to deindustrialization in the United States?

Modern Economic Systems

10.7   How do capitalism and socialism differ?

The industrial and postindustrial ages have been dominated by two main economic systems: capitalism and socialism. Neither system really exists in practice in a pure form, but most modern states have economies that can be described as capitalist, socialist, or some combination of the two.

Capitalism

Capitalism is an economic system in which the means of production are privately owned, and economic activity is driven by the pursuit of profit in a competitive market. Capitalists believe that profit-motivated economic activity benefits not just themselves but all of society. The desire to realize a profit drives established corporations to develop new products and entrepreneurs to innovate entirely new types of goods and services that might not have otherwise been made available on the market. Competition between capitalists also serves to keep prices low and quality high in an effort to maximize profits by attracting as many customers as possible.

Capitalism assumes that there will be competition between rival capitalists. Think about how fewer and fewer corporations are controlling more and more of today's economic activity. Do you think that meaningful competition still exists in most of the American economy? How would a lack of sufficient competition change the way capitalists behave?

The extent to which any particular capitalist economy matches this definition varies, not just from place to place but over time as well. For example, as discussed in Chapter 2, the unregulated **laissez-faire capitalism** of Marx's time, in which business owners were free to maximize their profits any way they could, no longer exists. Today capitalist economies the world over are, to a greater or lesser extent, subject to various regulations of both their ownership and of the business practices they are permitted to use in pursuit of profit. In the United States, regulation of business has waxed and waned over the years, depending on the politicians in power. Regulations can sometimes stifle economic growth, but they can also prevent businesses from taking risks that might destabilize the economy. For example, lack of regulations led to the stock market collapse of 1929 and the Great Depression, and deregulation of the banking sector in the 1990s led to the banking crisis of 2007 and contributed greatly to the great recession that followed.

Socialism

In almost direct contrast to capitalism, **socialism** is an economic system in which the means of production are collectively owned, and economic activity is driven by a desire to satisfy the needs of the people with no consideration of profit. Socialists believe that the profits realized by capitalists represent a form of theft from workers. This is because profit represents the difference between what it costs capitalists to produce a good or provide a service and what they can charge for it. Because the costs of both raw materials and overhead are fixed, profit must necessarily result from paying workers less than the value that they provide. Socialists also disagree with the idea that the only thing that can motivate creation and innovation is the desire to make a profit. On the contrary, they argue that if people were not forced to labor solely for the purpose of creating profit for capitalists, they would have more time and energy to devote to acts of creation and innovation.

Much as with capitalism, however, socialism in practice looks very different than it does in theory. Most modern nations with socialist economies are examples of democratic socialism. Under **democratic socialism**, the state controls public utilities such as energy, transportation, and communication while leaving the rest of the economy to be governed by heavily regulated capitalism. Democratic socialist economies also have strong taxpayer-supported welfare states that guarantee public access to basic necessities, such as food and housing, as well more complex needs like health care and education. These welfare states reduce the economic inequalities inherent in capitalism by simultaneously providing an economic floor below which no member of the society can fall, while funding that floor through progressive taxation that is more heavily targeted on the upper economic class.

Health care and education provide an excellent way to think about the difference between capitalism and democratic socialism. For example, in the capitalist-dominated economy of United States, the Patient Protection and Affordable Care Act was created not to provide health care but to make it easier and more affordable for citizens to purchase their own health insurance. Similarly, the federal student loan program makes it easier and somewhat more affordable for students to borrow money in order pay their college tuition. In comparison, in a state such as Denmark, with a social democratic economy, both health care and university education are available to all citizens free of charge, as a basic benefit of citizenship.

Certain public services in America are funded by taxpayer dollars on a not-for-profit basis. How would your community be different if the police and fire departments were run as for-profit enterprises that required you to pay a subscription in order to call upon them for help?

The United States has a very complex relationship with the idea of socialism. On the basis of surveys and polls, many Americans seem to like the idea of receiving the benefits provided under a more socialist economy but not to like the idea of socialism. British public historian Tony Judt argued that this seeming paradox is a consequence of the way we talk about these issues. When we talk about hunger or homelessness or sickness as social problems in America,

THE UNITED STATES: A CAPITALIST COUNTRY?

In this exercise, you will consider what is the best way to describe the U.S. economy.

It is often observed that the United States is a capitalist country. But is it really? Go to the official U.S. government benefit web site and investigate the Temporary Assistance for Needy Families (TANF) program (https://www.benefits.gov/benefit/613). You can also find information on TANF in your state by entering "TANF in [your state]" into the search bar.

Look at both the benefits provided by TANF and the requirements to receive those benefits. What features of this program are consistent with a capitalist economy, and which are consistent with a social democratic economy? With which economic system do you think TANF is more consistent?

we "avoid moral considerations [and] restrict ourselves to issues of profit and loss" (Judt 2009). We don't ask whether taking steps to address these social problems is right or wrong but rather whether doing so is economically feasible. Socialists believe that this way of thinking is yet another product of capitalism that, as we discussed in Chapter 7, is intended to fool us into not questioning the normalcy of the inequalities that it creates.

Check Your Understanding

- Why do capitalists think that the ability to make a profit is not only good for themselves but good for society?

- What is laissez-faire capitalism?

- Why do socialists think that profit making is not only unnecessary for the economy to function but also a bad thing?

- How does democratic socialism differ in practice from the more theoretical "ideal type" socialism?

Beyond Politics and Economy: Communism and Fascism

10.8 How are communism and fascism distinct from other political and economic systems?

As we have seen, political systems and economic systems, although distinct, are sometimes difficult to fully separate. The state plays a clear role in dictating the terms under which economies are permitted to function, and in turn, the nature of the economy has a significant influence over the type of government that controls the state. However, in some cases, the roles of politics and the economy are purposefully fully combined. We will examine two examples of such systems—communism and fascism.

Communism

As you will recall, communism is the hybrid economic and political system that Marx believed would eventually evolve out of socialism. The term *communism* is often used interchangeably with *socialism*, but they are distinct concepts in very important ways. Moreover, although many societies over the past hundred years have claimed to be communist in nature, none have come close to living up to the definition laid out by Marx.

Socialism, as you know, is an economic system in which the means of production are collectively owned, and economic activity is driven by the goal of meeting the needs of the people without consideration of profit. Communism, on the other hand, is a system in which private ownership of property is eliminated to create social and economic equality. Contrary to what many people believe, communism is not a totalitarian political system, because the social changes that define the advent of a communist society would not be dictated to the people by the state. In fact, under communism, the state itself would no longer be necessary. Marx believed that by the time human society was able to achieve communism, humanity would be so morally advanced that there would be no need for a sovereign of any sort to protect the people from the danger present in the state of nature as described by Hobbes. All people would contribute to the society to the best of their ability, and in exchange, all their needs would be satisfied.

The idea of abolishing private property horrifies most people who hear it. People think about needing to share their homes, their cars, their clothing, even their toothbrushes with anyone who wants to use them and immediately conclude that communism is a terrible idea. However, Marx intended to abolish just excess property—once hoarded by the bourgeoisie. For example, people would

GOVERNMENT-PROVIDED HEALTH CARE

In 1965, President Johnson and the U.S. Congress created two government-funded health insurance plans: Medicare, health care for the elderly, and Medicaid, health care for the poor. Originally, Medicaid covered only low-income families but has since been expanded to cover children, pregnant women, people with disabilities, and those in need of long-term care.

In this online activity, you will explore how many Americans are enrolled in Medicaid and how that number has changed in recent years using data from the U.S. Department of Health and Human Services.

*Requires the Vantage version of *Sociology in Action*.

▼ FIGURE 10.3

Medicaid Enrollment (State) 2016

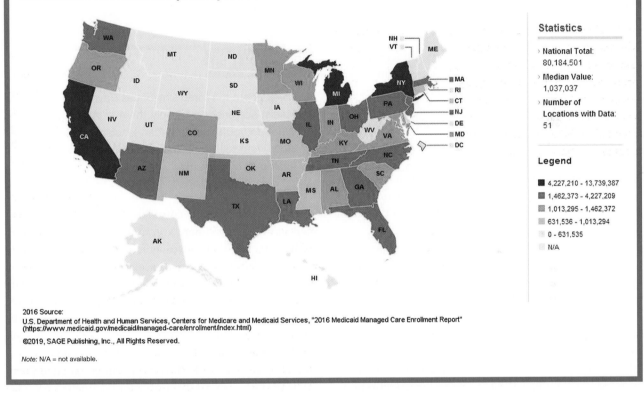

Statistics

› **National Total:**
80,184,501

› **Median Value:**
1,037,037

› **Number of Locations with Data:**
51

Legend

- ■ 4,227,210 - 13,739,387
- ■ 1,462,373 - 4,227,209
- ■ 1,013,295 - 1,462,372
- ■ 631,536 - 1,013,294
- ■ 0 - 631,535
- ■ N/A

2016 Source:
U.S. Department of Health and Human Services, Centers for Medicare and Medicaid Services, "2016 Medicaid Managed Care Enrollment Report" (https://www.medicaid.gov/medicaid/managed-care/enrollment/index.html)

©2019, SAGE Publishing, Inc., All Rights Reserved.

Note: N/A = not available.

own only the homes they lived in; no second (or third or fourth) homes allowed. With a societal guarantee that every individual's needs will be met, there would be no need to hoard excess resources.

CONSIDER THIS

Communist societies are defined by more than just their economy. What broader social changes would be necessary for a society to convert to communism today? What specific norms and values would need to change?

Clearly, the real-world examples of societies that have claimed to be communist never came close to achieving the theoretical "ideal type" communism described by Marx. The Soviet Union, for example, despite being popularly viewed as an archetypal communist society, was really an oligarchy. The "Communist" Party held power legitimated through rational-legal domination and oversaw a **command economy** in which the state determined the type, quantity, and price of goods to be produced.

Fascism

Fascism is a hybrid economic and political system that is, in many ways, the opposite of communism. Whereas communism was defined in exacting detail at the theoretical level, but never really practiced, fascism existed in practice before in theory.

Historian Stanley Payne attempted to develop a definition of fascism by examining the traits that all societies deemed fascist have in common. He noted that every fascist society contained similar negations, goals, and styles (Payne 1980). By negations, Payne meant that fascism is defined as much by what it is not as by what it is. All fascist societies were aggressively antiliberal and anticommunist. Ideologically, they were also anticonservative, as they hoped to eventually replace traditional norms and values with something new; however, in most cases, fascists tended to ally with conservative movements to first defeat liberal and communist factions. Because of this, fascism is considered by most political sociologists to be a right-wing political ideology.

In terms of goals, fascist societies tend to be imperialistic and expansionistic in foreign policy, although exactly how expansionist varies. Militarism is a very important component of fascist societies, with military and paramilitary organizations held in an elevated status. In past fascist societies, parades, drills, and marches were common events, and uniforms, symbols, and rituals were emphasized so as to reinforce feelings of aggressive nationalism. Violence seemed to possess "a certain positive and therapeutic value in and of itself." And "a certain amount of continuing violent struggle . . . was necessary for the health of a national society" (Payne 1980).

The economic policy goals of fascist societies to transform the economy involved taking indirect control of the means of production while reinforcing the existing economic class structure. For example, Nazi Germany privatized many companies previously run by the state, including banks, railways, and steel mills. At the same time, the Nazis deregulated these industries, eliminated labor protections for workers, and outlawed unions. In exchange for this opportunity to generate incredible profits, however, businesses were expected to be loyal to the state and pursue whatever sort of specific production or projects deemed in the national interest. Often these were military projects intended to support the fascist expansionist foreign policy.

Stylistically, fascism tends to be highly authoritarian and often evolves out of a cult of personality surrounding a strong, charismatic leader. Societies created by these movements value the qualities the leader seems to possess (e.g., masculinity and virility) and tend to be dismissive of roles for women, the old, and the infirm.

Having considered these qualities, what sort of definition can we construct for fascism? Based on the above,

fascism can be defined as an authoritarian system of militaristic nationalism in which the means of production are privately owned but regulated by the state to reinforce social stratification and carry out the goals of the state. The one thing that fascism is not is a form of socialism. This common misconception about fascism stems largely from the fact that the Nazi Party in Germany was officially known as the National Socialist German Workers Party. However, as we have seen, fascist ideology has very little overlap with the workings of socialist economic systems. In fact, in an essay titled "The Doctrine of Fascism," Benito Mussolini (1933) directly states that "Fascism is therefore opposed to Socialism" and that "Fascism is likewise opposed to trade unionism."

CONSIDER THIS

Think about the three similarities Payne identified in all fascist societies and apply them to American society. What do you think American fascism would look like? How would it be similar and different from historical examples of fascism?

Fascism is generally considered a uniquely twentieth-century ideology. There are, in fact, no states that currently identify themselves as fascist, nor are there any mainstream self-identified fascist parties that hold any meaningful power. However, that does not necessarily mean that fascism is entirely an artifact of the past. White nationalist and neo-Nazi groups in the United States have strong ideological and stylistic connections to the fascist systems of the past, even if they do not hold power. In the United Kingdom, the UK Independence Party (UKIP)—the party responsible for leading the push for Brexit—is a right-wing populist party with a strong focus on British nationalism that also supports the privatization of government run services and industries. Although this does not match up perfectly with the way we have defined fascism, there are certainly some clear similarities that have been noted by UKIP's critics.

Similarly, some critics of President Trump have observed that the tone of his antiestablishment, charisma-based campaigns for the presidency seems to revel in strength, masculinity, and vitality while being dismissive of women, the infirm, and people of color—particularly refugees and immigrants of color. When that campaign is coupled with the nationalism, militarism, and privatization that have characterized his time in office, it is not surprising that those critics have asked if the United States is embracing fascism under President Trump. Although, much as with UKIP, the definition of fascism does not perfectly characterize the Trump administration, we must also remember that definition was constructed by observing self-proclaimed fascist states from history. Perhaps the definition needs to be revised for the twenty-first century. On the other hand, we may be seeing the first examples of a new hybrid political and economic system unique to the current time in the same way that fascism was unique to the twentieth century.

Check Your Understanding

- What is the difference between socialism and communism?
- What did Marx mean when he said that communists want to abolish excess property?

- What is fascism?
- Where can we see elements of fascism in the United States and the United Kingdom today?

Conclusion

Political and economic systems do much to shape the structure of the societies in which we live. They determine who holds legitimate power, how leaders are chosen, and what, if anything, can be done to replace leaders if the people are not satisfied with their leadership. They determine the sort of goods and services that are made available in society, as well as to whom they are made available. An understanding of exactly how these institutions work is essential to good citizenship, especially in the face of political propaganda—or "fake news"—disseminated by self-interested parties to sway the political opinions we hold. In the next chapter you will learn how these social institutions can affect the institution of the family.

REVIEW

10.1 How do sociologists define the state?

The state, according to Weber, is the community that holds the monopoly on the legitimate use of physical force within a given territory. Force that is used by the state or its agents is considered legitimate and called authority. Force that is used without the consent of the state is considered illegitimate and is called coercion.

10.2 Where does the state's monopoly on the legitimate use of violence come from?

The state's monopoly on the legitimate use of violence comes from the social contract between the sovereign and the people. In exchange for the power that monopoly confers, the state agrees to keep the people safe from one another. This is why the state must always put the safety of all the people ahead of any individual person, even if doing so can sometimes appear unjust.

10.3 How does the state determine who gets to control its power?

Weber identifies three forms of legitimate domination that can be used to lay claim to the power of the state. Traditional domination is based on custom or tradition, and leaders are chosen not on the basis of individual merit but because that is how things have always been done. Rational-legal domination is based on a bureaucratic system of laws and rules. Leaders do not have intrinsic power but instead occupy positions that are vested with power. Charismatic domination is based on the extraordinary personal qualities with which a leader can command the support of the masses. Unless charismatic leaders use their power to create a system of either traditional or rational-legal domination, it's unlikely that that their states or movements will survive their death.

10.4 How do states that legitimate the power of their leaders in different ways evolve different forms of government?

Monarchies are a form a government in which power is legitimated through traditional domination because they are headed by a sovereign who inherited his position and will pass it on to his children. Representative democracies, on the other hand, in which the people elect a group of representatives to make decisions on their behalf, are more compatible with rational-legal forms of domination. Finally, the power of autocratic dictators is generally legitimated through charismatic domination, at least until they can create a new tradition-based or rational-legal system.

10.5 What different answers can pluralism, elite theory, and class domination theory provide to the question of "who rules America"?

Pluralists believe that America is ruled by the people through their elected representatives. These representatives make choices to maximize the greatest benefit for the greatest number of their constituents. Elite theorists believe that a power elite composed of economic, political, and military elites rules America. Class domination theorists agree that America is ruled by a power elite but believe that elite is composed of an elite upper social class connected to one another through the corporate community and supported by a policy-planning network.

10.6 How have changes in the way societies produce goods and services in the modern era been linked to changes in the way societies consume?

With industrialization, many goods formally only available to the elite became available to the working class. To find a new way to demonstrate their high status, the elite began spending money for the sole purpose of enhancing their social prestige. This, in turn, led to a shift away from mass production of large quantities of identical products toward the production of smaller quantities of products, in wider variety, to better cater to elite tastes. This shift contributed to the process of deindustrialization.

10.7 How do capitalism and socialism differ?

Capitalism is an economic system in which the means of production are privately owned, and economic activity is driven by the pursuit of profit in a competitive market. In a socialist economic system, the means of production are collectively owned, and economic activity is driven by a desire to satisfy the needs of the people with no consideration of profit.

10.8 How are communism and fascism distinct from other political and economic systems?

The roles of politics and the economy are so difficult to separate in communism and fascism that we must conclude that they are both simultaneously political and economic in nature. Both systems are based on ideologies that subsume the normal functions of political systems and use the economy to fulfill their goals.

KEY TERMS

autocracy   197

capitalism   202

charismatic domination   193

class domination theory   199

command economy   205

conspicuous consumption   201

corporate community   200

democracy   195

democratic socialism   203

dictatorship   197

direct democracy   195

distributive power   199

divine right of kings   195

economy   201

elite theory   199

fascism   206

Fordism   201

illegitimate power   190

industrialization   201

iron law of oligarchy   197

laissez-faire capitalism   203

legitimate power   190

monarchy   195

oligarchy   196

pluralism   198

plutocracy   197

policy-planning network   200

post-Fordism   202

power elite   199

rational-legal domination   193

representative democracy   195

routinization of charisma   194

social contract   191

socialism   203

the state   190

state of nature   191

totalitarianism   198

traditional domination   193

Introducing…

⑤SAGE vantage™

Course tools done right.

Built to support teaching. Designed to ignite learning.

SAGE vantage is an intuitive digital platform that blends trusted SAGE content with auto-graded assignments, all carefully designed to ignite student engagement and drive critical thinking. Built with you and your students in mind, it offers easy course set-up and enables students to better prepare for class.

SAGE vantage enables students to **engage** with the material you choose, **learn** by applying knowledge, and **soar** with confidence by performing better in your course.

PEDAGOGICAL SCAFFOLDING	**CONFIDENCE BUILDER**	**TIME-SAVING FLEXIBILITY**	**QUALITY CONTENT**	**HONEST VALUE**
Builds on core concepts, moving students from basic understanding to mastery.	Offers frequent knowledge checks, applied-learning multimedia tools, and chapter tests with focused feedback.	Feeds auto-graded assignments to your gradebook, with real-time insight into student and class performance.	Written by expert authors and teachers, content is not sacrificed for technical features.	Affordable access to easy-to-use, quality learning tools students will appreciate.

To learn more about **SAGE vantage**, hover over this QR code with your smartphone camera or visit **sagepub.com/vantage**

CHAPTER 11

UNDERSTANDING INSTITUTIONS

Family

Carissa Froyum

Families are perhaps the most cherished social institution in our society, but they vary more than most of us understand.
iStockphoto.com/kate_sept2004

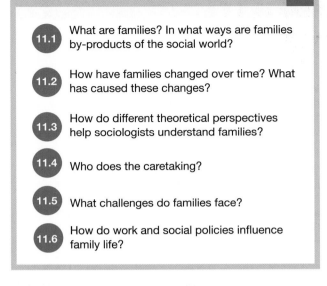

11.1 What are families? In what ways are families by-products of the social world?

11.2 How have families changed over time? What has caused these changes?

11.3 How do different theoretical perspectives help sociologists understand families?

11.4 Who does the caretaking?

11.5 What challenges do families face?

11.6 How do work and social policies influence family life?

What Shapes Families?

11.1   What are families? In what ways are families by-products of the social world?

Imagine a time machine has allowed you to share a holiday dinner with your great-great-grandparents. The conversation turns to courtship and marriage. They tell you how they met and courted, how many children they had and when, what expectations they faced, what challenges threatened family life, and how they divided work, childcare, and caring for the household. Then, the conversation turns to you and your life, particularly your own dating, marital status, and fertility history. How are your experiences similar? How are they different? What economic, technological, and cultural changes have happened across those generations to shape your experiences? For example, how have cell phones shaped dating? How has birth control changed the timing of having children? How have immigration and urbanization influenced how many children people have and the role children play in families?

In its most basic form, a **family** is a group of people who take responsibility for meeting one another's needs. Whom we consider family, the basis for our bonds, and the needs families meet, however, change over time in response to the social environment. Do you think you define family in the same way your great-great-grandparents did? Biological connections, living together, economic responsibility for one another, and the law probably featured prominently in your great-great-grandparents' understanding of family. Their definition even may have emphasized **nuclear family**: parents and their children. Does yours?

You may consider close friends to be family, even though you are not legally tied to them, because they provide you support and are there for you when you need them. Your definition likely emphasizes emotional bonds and the desire to decide who your family is, yourself. And yet, if you are not legally connected to them, your chosen family members cannot make medical decisions for you. They have no legal economic responsibility for you (or you for them). They cannot declare you as a dependent on taxes, you do not report their income when applying for financial aid for college, and you cannot sue them for monetary support. Policy makers and government agencies still hold onto a definition of family that may better resemble families of generations past than your own. According to the U.S. Census Bureau, for example, "a family consists of a householder and one or more other people living in the same household who are related to the householder by birth, marriage or adoption" (Pemberton 2015).

Also, you might be wondering why you must live under the same roof to be considered a family by the Census Bureau. You probably still think you belong to a family, even if you live on your own. The Census Bureau uses this definition because it assigns every person in the United States to one household to avoid counting people more than once.

Socially Constructing Families

As society changes, so do our families and our understanding of what makes a family. A social construction approach suggests that we think of family as a verb—we *do* or *accomplish* family in interaction with one another. Our socially constructed definitions and the needs families meet in society are **institutionalized**, or encoded in laws, policies, and widely accepted practices, that organize our family life. These laws, policies, and practices can change over time, as seen in the legal and popular support for same-sex marriage over the past decade.

Our sociological imaginations push us to consider who most influences and benefits from specific ways of doing family. In 1996, for example, President Clinton signed the Defense of Marriage Act (DOMA). DOMA defined marriage as between one man and one woman, and it allowed states not to recognize same-sex marriages granted by one another. Despite the desire of some same-sex couples to marry, the social legitimacy and benefits afforded to family—visiting each other in the hospital, inheriting property after death, and others—were restricted to heterosexual couples.

As described in Chapter 8, in 2015 the definition of marriage expanded, conferring the benefits of official recognition to families headed by same-sex partners. In the landmark case *Obergefell v. Hodges*, the Supreme Court

HOW I GOT ACTIVE IN SOCIOLOGY

CARISSA FROYUM

Like many of the boys in my small town growing up, my two older brothers played football when they entered fifth grade. I had grown up watching football—the Vikings—alongside my dad and brothers, from whom I absorbed the intricacies of I-formations and cross-blocking. But as my brothers grew older and developed more in the game, the family devotion to football became more intense. My dad coached, so we talked football nonstop and watched game-day tape. My mom knew all the plays and cheered so loudly I could pick out her voice on the videos my family reviewed every week. Football was always central

to what it meant to be a "Froyum." When I entered fifth grade, I remember thinking, "Girls don't get to play football? Well, that's not fair! How can I be a Froyum without playing football?"

By the time I found sociology in college at Concordia College in Moorhead, Minnesota, issues of fairness, justice, and belonging occupied many of my thoughts. I wanted to know why the world was the way it was, and couldn't we make it better for those left behind? Sociology was an entrée to grappling with those questions.

In 1996, President Bill Clinton signed DOMA, the Defense of Marriage Act, which defined marriages as between one man and one woman and allowed states not to recognize same-sex marriages. The Supreme Court ruling *Obergefell v. Hodges* overturned DOMA in 2015.

AP Photo/J. Scott Applewhite

ruled states must issue marriage licenses to same-sex couples and recognize same-sex marriages from other states. The shift to gender-neutral marriage is the most recent in

a long line of legal and moral contests over who should and should not be considered family. In 1967, *Loving v. Virginia* overturned bans on interracial marriages, while 1987's *Turner v. Safley* upheld the right for inmates to marry. These changes help show us that marriage is a social construct which varies over time and place.

CONSIDER THIS

How would you convince someone who has never taken a sociology class that families are socially constructed? Would it be hard or difficult? Why?

Check Your Understanding

- How do historical forces shape families?
- In their most basic form, what are families?
- What is a nuclear family?
- How can you show that family is a social construction?

Changing Families across History

11.2   How have families changed over time? What has caused these changes?

We can use our sociological imaginations to understand the origins of family and how and why families have changed across time. Looking across history, we see how changes in the political and economic institutions of societies influenced the construction and purpose of families.

WHAT IS A FAMILY?

In this activity, you will consider what constitutes a family and draw a representative picture.

What makes someone family? What differentiates "family" from "friend"?

1. Provide a definition of a family.
2. Draw a picture, diagram, or meme that illustrates your definition.

Early Families

According to Stephanie Coontz's (2005, 40) *Marriage, A History*, families and family life changed as human societies changed. In the earliest years of human life, hunting and gathering groups developed marriage and kinship systems as a way to forge bonds and encourage cooperation with one another. "Bands needed to establish friendly relations with others so they could travel more freely and safely in pursuit of game, fish, plants, and water holes or move as the seasons changed" (p. 40). Marriage expanded the group's social network into a group of "in-laws," which facilitated goodwill and access to resources.

With the development of settled agriculture about 11,000 years ago, and later as European cultural influences spread, groups became more concerned about owning land, controlling surplus goods, and maintaining their social status. Accordingly, marriage and lineage systems became increasingly strategic, exclusive, and political (Coontz 2005). Marrying the right person from the right background allowed one to attain or secure wealth and social standing.

Preindustrial U.S. Families. During the sixteenth and seventeenth centuries, "North American native societies used family ties to organize nearly all their political, military, and economic transactions" (Coontz 2010, 33). Native American societies did not have other social institutions, such as police or courts, to resolve conflicts. Nor did they consider land or property to be something that could or should be owned by individual people. Instead, kinship groups administered justice and organized how resources were gathered and shared.

Among European preindustrial families in the colonial United States, there was a "family economy." Families created the goods they consumed (Cherlin 1983), such as food and clothing, rather than buying them at a supermarket or retail store. In a time of short life spans, families also provided ways of passing along land and status to the next generation and forging connections to others. Although

there was much religious diversity within the American colonies, most fell under the Calvinist Protestant umbrella, which emphasized individualism, the importance of marriage, and male headship of families. This set the stage for **coverture**, the legal doctrine in which wives' standing was subsumed into their husbands'. Only men could own property and sign contracts (Cherlin 2009). Although men were heads of households, both women and men carried out essential work and depended on each other to survive.

Slavery and Families. Families were of central importance to slaves, who established and maintained kinship ties, even as slave owners intervened in them. Slaves could not enter legally binding contracts, and slave owners could allow or disrupt informal marriages at their whim. The sale of children and other loved ones regularly ripped apart families (Staples and Johnson 1993).

In 1662, Act XII of Virginia law declared, "All children borne in this country shall be held bond or free only according to the condition of the mother." In other words, whether a child was free or a slave depended on whether his or her mother was free or a slave. This act ensured lifetime servitude on the basis of the mother-child relationship and transformed family relationships into a means of reproducing the labor force. White men increased their own slave holdings by raping Black slave women, who bore legally Black slave children owned by their own White fathers. Nonetheless, slaves coupled, developed broad kinship units for support, searched for sold-off loved ones, and socialized their children to survive the horrors of slavery (Dill 1988).

Industrial U.S. Families

Families are the site of **reproduction**, whereby people create and raise members of the next generation. Prior to industrialization, reproductive labor (creating and raising a family) and productive labor (the creation of goods to trade or sell) took place in the same location—at home. With industrialization during the late 1700s and 1800s, however,

One of the most brutal practices of slavery was selling family members to different owners, including separating mothers from children.

families increasingly moved off farms and into cities, where they worked outside the home, in factories, setting the stage for a "family wage economy" (Cherlin 1983).

Work and family life, for many, separated into public and private spheres, with women specializing in domesticity (**private sphere**) and men in breadwinning (**public sphere**) (Dill 1988). Concentrating on maintaining a home and raising children was possible only for well-off White women, however. They could rely on their husbands' earning capacity and focus on demonstrating their purity and piety through domesticity (Dill 1988). Many poor immigrant and Black women worked in factories or as domestic workers (Kamo and Cohen 1998).

By the mid-1800s, as activists for women's rights gained victories, new laws allowed married women to own property, take legal action, and gain custody of children following divorce (Cherlin 2009, 57). Children became an economic liability for the urban poor and working classes. The use of early forms of birth control spread during this time.

On farms, children were still considered small adults and expected to do their fair share of farm labor. But off farms, childhood for the middle and upper classes came to

occupy a special time marked by innocence and protection (Mintz 2004). More people divorced, although divorce was still uncommon. Affection and emotional intimacy grew in importance (Cherlin 1983). Across the century, family sizes shrank and private life concentrated on the nuclear family. By 1900, these changes gave rise to **companionate marriage**, or a partnership based on romantic love.

The 1900s and Emotion-Based U.S. Families

Emotion-based marriage dominated the 1900s. New technologies, such as the automobile and later the birth control pill, brought couples freedom to date outside of the home and experience sexuality for the sake of intimacy and enjoyment without fear of pregnancy. During World War II, young couples hurriedly married before men left for war, while many women, some for the first time, worked in factories to support the war effort. Divorce rates spiked as men returned from war changed and women were displaced from workplaces.

The end of World War II brought greater economic prosperity and veterans benefits for Whites

The 1950s nuclear family has been romanticized as an ideal family type but is based more on nostalgia than reality.

A. E. French/Archive Photos/Getty Images

Our image of 1950s families is based more on nostalgia than reality.

Diversifying U.S. Families

The 1960s and 1970s were times of social upheaval and rapid change. The feminist, civil rights, and sexual revolution movements drove ideological change, affirming the values, rights, and independence of women, people of color, and gay and lesbian individuals. A wave of civil rights legislation prohibited workplace and housing discrimination on the basis of sex and race, and the Equal Employment Opportunity Commission was created to ensure fair hiring practices. Policies, like affirmative action programs, were enacted to help more Americans of color gain a foothold in the middle class.

During the 1970s and 1980s, however, the U.S. economy deindustrialized, destroying the family wage and pushing many more women into the paid workforce. Manufacturing work shifted out of central cities to the suburbs and then later overseas. Service industries, such as insurance, travel, and retail, grew, creating lower paying, nonunion, less stable jobs.

During these turbulent 1960s and 1970s, family life upended, too. Couples waited to marry until they were older, and rates of premarital sex increased. Divorce rates also rose, as families experienced the **stalled revolution**. Women expected men to more fully share household responsibilities such as cooking and cleaning, while men valued the traditional family in which women were responsible for private life. But as women increasingly worked for pay, few men picked up the slack at home. Many families found themselves overstretched and conflict ridden over who should do what. Stepfamilies and single motherhood became increasingly common, and same-sex couples began to come out of the closet in greater numbers. The idea that the traditional nuclear family should be the norm was starting to fade to the past.

(e.g., the GI Bill and U.S. Department of Veterans Affairs home loans), which fed suburbanization for White families and a national baby boom. The post–World War II economic boom produced a **family wage**, meaning that many men (particularly White men in unions) earned enough to support an entire family, permitting their wives to remain at home. In turn, this supported the separation of the public and private spheres for both White middle- and working-class families during the 1950s. Americans idealized the traditional 1950s nuclear family with a breadwinning husband and homemaking wife (Coontz 1992).

Within the collective U.S. imagination, families of the 1950s occupy a special, overly nostalgic, space. Oftentimes, we imagine 1950s families as perfectly ordered and harmonious, a place of refuge and happiness. Dad supposedly went to work every day and returned to a happy homemaking wife and a well-kept house, filled with the smell of freshly baked cookies. In the decades to follow, many in the United States, especially White, heterosexual, middle-class individuals, looked back to the 1950s as if they were the "good old days." But for many others, the "perfect" family of the 1950s represents, as Stephanie Coontz (1992) shows us, "the way we never were." Same-sex couples were in the closet, and families of color were denied equal rights and many economic opportunities. Domestic violence and economic stress were commonplace, albeit hidden from view.

Making Way for Families of Today

Today, more and more adults in the United States remain single or live with but do not marry their partners. Figure 11.1 shows that the percentage of Americans living alone climbed from 8.6 percent in 1970 to 14.3 percent in 2018. Over the same time period, the number of **cohabiting couples**—those living together but unmarried—rose dramatically from just 0.5 percent to 7.7 percent. Meanwhile, the proportion of Americans living with a spouse plummeted from nearly 70 percent to 51.2 percent.

Marriage has become a class luxury. As discussed in Chapter 7, more and more young adults view marriage as too risky unless they are financially stable, which is too often not possible for poor or working-class couples and increasingly difficult for those in the middle class. Single parenthood—especially single *motherhood*—has become socially accepted, especially for working-class and poor families who value having children but are cautious about the possibilities of divorce (Edin and Kefalas 2005). Today, 40 percent of all babies born in the United States have unmarried mothers. As you can see in Figure 11.2,

▼ FIGURE 11.1

With Whom Do Adults Live?

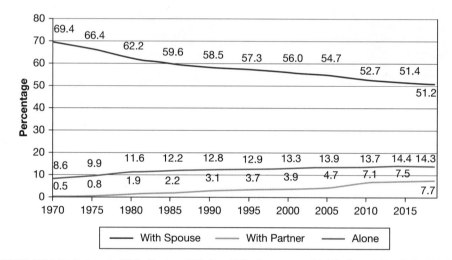

Source: US Census Bureau, 2016. Table AD-3. "Living Arrangements of Adults, 18 and over, 1967 to Present." https://www.census.gov/data/tables/time-series/demo/families/adults.html.

▼ FIGURE 11.2

Births of Unmarried Mothers by Race and Education

| Characteristic | All races and origins[2] | Non-Hispanic, single race[1] | | | | | Hispanic[3] |
		White	Black	American Indian or Alaska Native	Asian	Native Hawaiian or Other Pacific Islander	
Births to unmarried mothers	39.8	28.5	69.5	69.1	11.8	48.7	52.2
Educational attainment of mother:							
High school diploma or higher	86.7	92.8	86.1	78.0	93.2	77.3	72.1
Bachelor's degree or higher	32.3	41.8	17.3	8.4	64.2	9.7	13.5

Source: childtrends.org; 2018 data from US Census Bureau. "Living Arrangements of Adults, 18 and over, 1967 to Present."

Notes: Birth rates are births per 1,000 population. Fertility rates are computed by relating total births, regardless of age of mother, to women aged 15–44. Total fertility rates are sums of birth rates for 5-year age groups multiplied by 5. Unmarried rates are births to unmarried women per 1,000 unmarried women. Populations estimated as of July 1, 2017. Mean age at first birth is the arithmetic average of the age of mothers at the time of birth, computed directly from the frequency of first births by age of mother.

[1]Race and Hispanic origin are reported separately on birth certificates; persons of Hispanic origin may be of any race. In this table, non-Hispanic women are classified by race. Race categories are consistent with the 1997 Office of Management and Budget standards; see Technical Notes in report. Single race is defined as only one race reported on the birth certificate.

[2]Includes births to race and origin groups not shown separately, such as Hispanic single-race white, Hispanic single-race black, and non-Hispanic multiple-race women, and births with origin not stated.

[3]Includes all persons of Hispanic origin of any race; see Technical Notes.

SINGLE MOTHERHOOD IN AMERICA

The composition of American families has undergone rapid change in the past few decades. In 1970, half of all households were headed by married couples, but by 2015, that number had dropped to 29 percent. Meanwhile, in that same period, the number of single parents has climbed from 3 million to more than 10 million.

In this online activity, you will consider which states have the highest rate of single motherhood and how it has changed over time using data from the U.S. Census Bureau's American Community Survey.

_____

*Requires the Vantage version of *Sociology in Action*.

▼ FIGURE 11.3

Percentage of U.S. Households Headed by Single Mothers, 2017

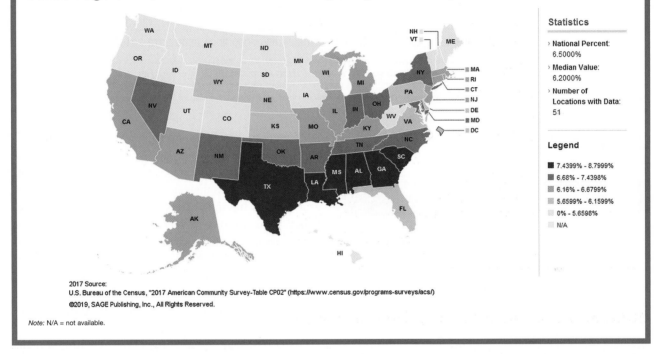

Statistics

› **National Percent:**
6.5000%
› **Median Value:**
6.2000%
› **Number of Locations with Data:**
51

Legend

- ■ 7.4399% – 8.7999%
- ■ 6.68% – 7.4398%
- ■ 6.16% – 6.6799%
- ■ 5.6599% – 6.1599%
- □ 0% – 5.6598%
- ░ N/A

2017 Source:
U.S. Bureau of the Census, "2017 American Community Survey-Table CP02" (https://www.census.gov/programs-surveys/acs/)
©2019, SAGE Publishing, Inc., All Rights Reserved.

Note: N/A = not available.

the rate varies by race and ethnicity, as well as social class. The racial and ethnic groups with higher income levels (Whites and Asian Americans) have fewer births outside of marriage than other groups. Finally, education matters. Those with bachelor's degrees are more likely to get and stay married than those with a high school education or less, and marriage rates have especially declined for those with little education (Martin et al. 2018, 27).

Over the past couple of decades, divorce rates—although still high—have dropped, in part because people delay marriage until they are older and more economically secure. Higher income, better educated families have less stress, can deal with unexpected expenses more readily, and can afford counseling if things go awry. Figure 11.4 (next page) shows us the divorce rate among women. As you can see, after rising

dramatically in the 1970s, it has declined in recent years. In 2015, the divorce rate was at a forty-year low.

Check Your Understanding

- Why do we live in families?
- What social, political, and financial needs did early U.S. families meet? Industrial families? Families in the 1900s and 2000s?
- What social, political, and technological changes have influenced families over the course of U.S. history?
- What role has the economy played in supporting (or not) particular ways of doing family?
- How and why have rates of marriage, births to unmarried mothers, and divorce rates have changed over recent decades?

Women's Divorce Rate, 1960–2016

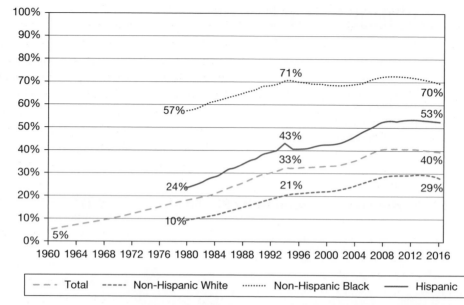

Source: Divorce Rate in the U.S. Geographic Variation, 2015. Lydia R. Anderson. FP-16-21. Reprinted with permission from the National Center for Family and Marriage Research, Bowling Green State University.

Understanding Families through Theory

11.3   How do different theoretical perspectives help sociologists understand families?

As you have seen in earlier chapters, theoretical perspectives provide us with ways to make sense of how society and its institutions operate. We now look at how structural functionalism, feminist theory, intersectionality, and social exchange theory offer different ways of thinking about and understanding families. As you will see, each gives us a unique angle through which to view families.

Structural Functionalism

Recall from Chapter 2 that structural functionalists are concerned primarily with how various social institutions, such as families, create stability in social life and social harmony. This approach to understanding families emphasizes how families serve as a socialization agent that allows society to move, with little disruption, from one generation to the next. Functionalists also focus on the structure of families and which types of family arrangements provide the most stability, especially for children. For example, structural functionalists often worry that replacing traditional nuclear families with other family types creates problems for children and broader society. Functionalists argue that families are important because they regulate sexual behavior, legitimize childbirth, and establish a division of labor.

Functionalists view marriage much like a puzzle: distinct and complementary individual parts that come together to form a stable whole. For example, in the 1950s, structural functionalist Talcott Parsons viewed women and men as having different biological natures and, hence, different roles in the family. He described women as expressive (emotion oriented) and men as instrumental (task oriented). Women were expected to act out their expressive natures by doing housework and care work, while men were supposed to act out their instrumental natures by being the heads of the house and the primary earners (Parsons and Bales 1956).

Although many people may consider functionalist approaches to families old-fashioned and unsupported by empirical evidence, they have nevertheless played an important role in social policies aimed at family life. In 1996, President Clinton's welfare reform legislation included "promoting marriage" among poor families as an explicit goal (Hays 1996). George W. Bush's administration implemented marriage promotion programs as a way to reduce poverty, although they haven't (Cohen 2018), and Supreme Court justice Antonin Scalia cited research conducted in the functionalist tradition in his dissent in the Supreme Court case that legalized same-sex marriage (Pear and Kirkpatrick 2004; Supreme Court of the United States 2014). Marriage promotion programs have continued at the federal and state levels, particularly as a poverty reduction approach (Cohen 2018). One of the four main purposes of the federal Temporary Assistance for Needy Families ("welfare") program, for example, is to "reduce the dependency of needy parents by promoting job preparation, work and marriage" (U.S. Department of Health and Human Services, Office of the Administration for Children & Families, Office of Family Assistance 2019).

Conflict Perspective

Conflict theories have shifted the paradigm within family research away from an emphasis on maintaining family stability through traditional nuclear families and toward understanding families as a site of inequality. Conflict theorists emphasize two things in family research. First, social inequalities affect family life. For example, poor families and families of color have less access to affordable housing, creating strain on family life. Marriage promotion programs are ineffective at reducing poverty (Cohen 2018). Our nostalgia for traditional nuclear families often ignores these realities. Second, family life is an arena for acting out inequalities, particularly gender inequality. Conflict research also notes that marriage is declining around the globe, not just in the United States. Cohen (2018), for example, notes that the "decline in marriage—people spending a smaller portion of their lives married, on average—is part of a larger global transition toward gender equality" (p. 62).

Feminist Perspective. Sociologists who use a feminist perspective illustrate how families tend to create and reinforce gender inequality. Feminists view families as a "gender factory" (Berk 1985). They argue that family relationships are inherently gendered because we expect individuals to learn and act out gendered expectations around caring for others and breadwinning through family life. Many families provide girls and boys with gendered toys that teach girls (through dolls, dress-up, playhouses, etc.) to care take and boys (through sports, weapons, superheroes, etc.) to dominate.

Gender attitudes have grown increasingly egalitarian with successive generations, with two-thirds of Americans now supporting equality at work and home. Still, more than a quarter of Americans support gender equality in work and political life but not at home (Scarborough, Sin, and Risman 2019). Attitudes have grown especially flexible for girls and women, while a new norm toward active fathering has taken hold (Ishizuka 2019; McGill 2014; Kane 2018; Petts, Shafer, and Essig 2018). Ethnic and racial minorities are especially egalitarian about parenting (Acosta and Salcedo 2018).

In adulthood, women continue to face largely unattainable expectations that they devotedly care for children,

spouses, and parents. We also expect them to run an efficient and clean household, which fosters the health and well-being of all family members (Adams 2018). These expectations are true for all women—even career-oriented high-earning women and busy single mothers (Schneider 2011; Elliott, Powell, and Brenton 2015; Hook 2017). Many men, on the other hand, now feel pressure to be involved parents but also to reveal their manhood by being the breadwinner, disciplinarian, and "man of the house" (McGill 2014; Kane 2018; Petts, Shafer, and Essig 2018). The lack of family supports from workplaces, public policies, or extended families strain all types of families (Kane 2018). Despite all the social changes of the past 150 years, economic pressures, lagging social policies, traditional gender ideologies, and racial discrimination still influence families and promote gender inequality.

Intersectionality. As you have seen in previous chapters, intersectionality is a conflict perspective that pushes sociologists to look at multiple forms of inequality, such as sexuality *and* class *and* gender, at the same time (Collins 2000). Intersectionality has encouraged family researchers to ask, for example, if gender expectations shape LGBT families differently from straight ones. Research shows that lesbian couples in particular are more egalitarian than heterosexual ones, yet many LGBT or queer families face the same pressures to perform femininity through housework and childcare and masculinity through breadwinning as straight families (Acosta and Salcedo 2018; Biblarz and Savci 2011; Carrington 1999; Moore 2011). Even the feminist women partners of feminist transgender men in Pfeffer (2011) found themselves engaging in gender-stereotypic divisions of household labor. Intersectionality researchers also examine such issues as how parenthood varies across social classes (Cohen 2018; Hill 2012; Ishizuka 2018; Shows and Gerstel 2009), the challenges of single motherhood in the most fragile families (Edin and Kefalas 2005; Elliott, Powell, and Brenton 2015), and how poverty and racism interact to create hardships for parents (Cardoso et al. 2018; Creighton, Park, and Teruel 2009; Edin and Nelson 2013; Kalmijn 2017; Turney, Schnittker, and Wildeman 2011).

Social Exchange Theory

Sociologists who view family members through the lens of **social exchange theory** presume that they make decisions by weighing the benefits and costs of various actions and then pick the action or arrangement that brings the biggest reward (or least cost). Social exchange theorists note that when contemplating divorce, each marriage partner analyzes the rewards of his or her current arrangement in relation to (1) other marriages and (2) other relationship types. If he or she views either one to be more rewarding than his or her current relationship, marriage satisfaction decreases and motivation for separation increases. The person may still not pursue a divorce, however, if the costs of divorce, such as social disapproval or alimony, seem too high.

The Norm of Reciprocity. Exchange theorists use the **norm of reciprocity**, or the expectation that we give and take with others in relatively equal ways, to help explain how we think and feel about our relationships. The norm of reciprocity is evident when someone does something nice for you and you feel compelled to repay him or her in a relatively commensurate way. For example, if a stranger offers you assistance on the side of the road when your car breaks down, you may offer him or her some money in return or feel compelled to "pay it forward" by performing a similar act of kindness. In relationships, the norm of reciprocity dictates that partners support each other in relatively equal ways, even if the type of support is different, to maintain relationship happiness.

The socialization of children has varied greatly across historical periods and social classes.
©iStockphoto.com/kali9

Check Your Understanding

- What are the functions of families, according to structural functionalists? How do functionalists view gendered roles in families? Why?

- How do feminist theory and intersectionality challenge the approach of structural functionalists?

- What makes family members content, according to social exchange theorists? What makes them discontent?

Families Caring for Each Other

11.4   Who does the caretaking?

One of the primary tasks of families is to meet the needs of family members, especially children. Raising children involves making sure they are safe, well fed, housed, healthy, educated, and loved. The ways we think about childhood and how we meet children's needs, however, have changed dramatically over the past several centuries. As noted earlier, until industrialization, the expansion of the middle class, and the rise in sentimentality during the 1800s, childhood as we know it now did not exist (Mintz 2004).

During the early 1900s, as compulsory public education spread throughout the United States, more children spent much of their time with their peers in school, developing unique peer cultures (Corsaro 2005). Adults considered children to be malleable and believed they required moral training and education to develop their full character. Mothers and teachers turned to science to guide them in proper childrearing techniques (Mintz 2004).

Psychology turned an unprecedented critical eye onto childhood, characterizing stages of development and interrogating the nature of children's relationships with their mothers and siblings (Mintz 2001). The joys and burdens of parenthood shifted from a societal task to an individual one. The result was **intensive mothering** (Hays 1996), an exhausting child-centered style of parenting that requires women to copiously devote emotions, money, and time to raising children.

Intensive mothering is still the standard we measure mothers against today. Intensive mothers (and, increasingly, intensive fathers) research—reading advice books and blogs, scrutinizing social media posts, consulting experts—how best to parent to ensure their children's development—even before their children are born or adopted. They keep an eye on their children at all times. They sign up their children for lessons to ensure they have every opportunity. Intensive parents focus on spending quality time *and* an abundant quantity of time with children. Today, even many single parents who lack the financial or time resources to parent intensively feel pressured to do so, particularly if they interact with parents who have more time and money (Elliott, Powell, and Brenton 2015; Ishizuka 2018; Kane 2018).

INCREASING ACCESS TO HEALTHY FOOD

SINIKKA ELLIOTT

With a group of dedicated and talented colleagues and community members, I was involved in a five-year project that aimed to increase access to healthy food and places to be active in three North Carolina communities—two communities are in rural areas and one is in an urban city. All three communities have high proportions of residents who are low income, and many are food insecure—meaning that they do not have enough food for an active, healthy life. Food insecurity is more prevalent in households with children, especially female-headed households, and is related to the feminization and juvenilization of poverty. Mothers in food-insecure households make personal sacrifices to try to make sure that their children have enough to eat, such as skipping meals themselves.

We wanted our efforts to improve access to healthy food and places to be active to be community driven, so we drew on our relationships with local organizations in each of the three communities to recruit research participants to be a part of a five-year study of food and families.

All participants were low-income mothers or grandmothers of small children from diverse backgrounds, approximately mirroring the racial/ethnic composition of the communities. We focused on women because they are still largely responsible for the work of feeding the family. Along with interviewing participants about their experiences feeding a family, we conducted ethnographic observations of families' food-work inside and outside of their homes (e.g., grocery shopping, going to food pantries, preparing meals, enticing children to eat) to situate food experiences and practices within everyday life.

Listening and learning about each community's unique context and existing resources have helped ensure that our efforts were community led and collaborative. For example, we emphasized throughout how the participants' voices stimulate community change (in fact, the project is called Voices into Action: The Family, Food, and Health Project, or VIA for short). We have shared the research and community outreach with participants through monthly newsletters, social media, and community festivals and held community workshops to strategize ways to build on local resources. We have also drawn broader attention to the often invisible work of feeding families by writing in accessible venues and being interviewed on radio programs. In addition to our work with VIA, a team member conducted interviews with middle- and upper-middle-class Black, White, and Latina mothers of small children. Insights from 168 families from all walks of life inform our book, *Pressure Cooker: Why Home Cooking Won't Solve Our Problems and What We Can Do about It*. The book highlights the work of feeding families and how women disproportionately do this work.

Discussion Question: What do you think Dr. Elliott means when she says that the work of feeding families is often "invisible work"? Do you think it would be more visible if men were largely responsible for the work of feeding the family? Why?

Sinikka Elliott is an associate professor of sociology at the University of British Columbia.

Sinikka Elliott, the Sociologist in Action for this chapter, worked on a project studying nutrition, gender, and the family. She and her partners note that women are largely responsible for making sure that family members are fed.

Parenting and Social Class

Although some financially struggling parents may feel pressure to parent intensively, inspired by images of intensive parenting in television and other media, most working-class families follow child-raising techniques that differ from those of wealthier families. These differences arise because of how they themselves were raised, their occupations, and the stresses working-class families face juggling work and family. Middle-class families tend to adopt a **concerted cultivation** approach to interaction and discipline, through which they proactively engage with and guide their children, preparing them for future success (Calarco 2018; Lareau 2002). They reason and negotiate with their children, exploring their children's feelings and motivations for their behavior. They provide them with various structured, expensive extracurricular experiences and encourage them to negotiate for assistance, accommodation, and attention from teachers (Bernstein 2003; Calarco 2014, 2018; Schneider, Hastings, and LaBriola 2018). Through their experiences, middle-class parents pass on cultural resources so that kids learn to negotiate with authority and secure advantages in school (Jæger and Breen 2016; Calarco 2018).

Working-class and poor parents, too, invest heavily in their children but have fewer resources with which to do so (Schneider, Hastings, and LaBriola 2018).

APPLYING YOUR SOCIOLOGICAL IMAGINATION: WHO TOOK CARE OF YOU?

In this self-reflection activity, you will think back on your own childhood and analyze the social factors that affected your own upbringing.

Think back through your own childhood, how you were raised, and by whom you were raised. Then, apply your sociological imagination to your own circumstances to better understand how social influences shaped your own upbringing.

1. Ask yourself: Who was your primary caretaker(s)? Did it change over time? How so? Who did the housework? Breadwinning? What household tasks were you primarily responsible for, as a child?

2. Pick two sociological ideas to help explain your own childhood circumstances. Fully describe the sociological ideas and then apply them to your life. For example, you may identify the model of caretaking that dominated your childhood (e.g., intensive mothering, concerted cultivation, constraining, something else). Or you may consider the relationship between paid employment and caretaking in your childhood environment. Another option would be to analyze how race or class affected the division of labor in your childhood environment.

They also tend to be more authoritarian, using directives, obedience, and discipline, sometimes including physical punishment, to guide children (Calarco 2014, 2018; Friedson 2016; Kohn 1977). The parents' status as adults establishes their authority over their children. Neither reasoning nor negotiating with their children, working-class and poor parents generally tell kids what to do and demand compliance, and they teach children a "no excuse" approach to problem solving in which seeking help is equated with selfishness (Bernstein 2003; Calarco 2014, 2018). Children raised in working-class families gain an "emerging sense of constraint," which orients them to do as they are told. In other words, working-class kids learn to defer to authority for obedience's sake and problem solve on their own (Calarco 2014, 2018; Lareau 2015).

Caretaking and Changing Gendered Roles

Historically, fathers' most important roles have been as breadwinners and disciplinarians. But with increasing family diversity, high levels of divorce, women's mass employment, and shifting gender attitudes, men increasingly assume caretaking roles, including when they work long hours. As shown in Figure 11.5, over the past three decades, fathers have tripled the number of hours per week they spend doing childcare. As discussed in Chapter 8, fathers, as well as mothers, desire time with their children—and most wish they had more of it!

▼ FIGURE 11.5

Who Does Childcare? Hours per Week Doing Childcare, 1965–2016

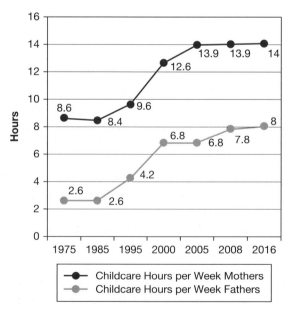

Sources: Adapted from Bianchi (2011), Table 1 and Table 2.

Look back at how you described a "typical" family in the United States earlier in the chapter. If asked the same question now, how would you respond?

The Sandwich Generation. The **sandwich generation** has double caretaking duties. These midlife adults are raising children and caring for aging parents at the same time. Whereas families have always been responsible for caring for aging relatives, especially those who lived with them, extended life spans, working away from home, medical bureaucracies, and diminished social supports often leave the sandwich generation squeezed by competing responsibilities. Working families of today coordinate doctors' appointments and complex medical treatments while juggling daily caregiving duties for both parents and children and the demands of a job. Dealing with the prospect of a parent dying is emotionally difficult, especially if the parent is uncomfortable planning for death. Because families have fewer children and live farther apart from each other than in the past, caretaking of a parent may fall to one adult child, creating extra strain.

Check Your Understanding

- How has parenting changed over time?
- How does parenting vary by social class?
- Describe some factors that have led fathers to take on more caretaking in the family.
- What are some challenges the sandwich generation faces?

Family Problems

11.5   What challenges do families face?

Although most families provide stability, safety, and nurturance in their members' lives, sometimes family life becomes conflict ridden. For example, the stress of work may bleed over into the home or worries about money may cause partners to argue. Partners can have different expectations about who should contribute how much financially, who should do what housework, when to have sex, or how to make family decisions. Or the burdens of dealing with racism or sexism in public life may lead to discord at home.

Violence and Victimization

Some families become sites of violence. **Family violence**, or when someone in a family hurts or controls someone else, takes on many different forms: sexual abuse, financial abuse, emotional mistreatment, and physical violence. The Centers for Disease Control and Prevention (Smith et al. 2015) reports that "over 1 in 3 . . . women experience sexual violence, physical violence, and/or stalking by an intimate partner during their lifetime." More than one in five face severe physical violence, and more than 10 percent are stalked (Smith et al. 2015). Men, too, report high levels of intimate partner violence: one in three experience violence, with nearly 15 percent facing severe physical violence. Psychological aggression by an intimate partner was common: more than one in three men and women experienced it (Smith et al. 2015).

Children are especially harmed by family violence. Nearly 14 percent of children experienced maltreatment in the past year, including physical, sexual, or emotional abuse, neglect, or custodial interference or family abduction (Finkelhor et al. 2015). By fourteen to seventeen years of age, more than 40 percent of children have experienced some type of maltreatment, with emotional abuse by a caregiver being the most common type (Finkelhor et al. 2015). Moreover, those victimized often experience multiple forms of abuse and maltreatment in various social contexts (home, school, neighborhoods), and the negative effects accumulate, especially when children have no safe place (Finkelhor et al. 2015; Turner et al. 2017). Abused children are more likely to become depressed, anxious, and angry (Finkelhor, Ormrod, and Turner 2007; Turner et al. 2012), and those who are abused in multiple ways have fewer psychosocial resources, such as family and friend support and self-esteem (Turner et al. 2017). Finally, each year, approximately 8 percent of children witness family members being assaulted, and one in five see this during their childhood (Finkelhor et al. 2015). The good news is that when safe from the victimization they have experienced, children tend to be resilient and recover their sense of well-being and self-esteem (Turner et al. 2017).

Breaking Apart and Staying Together

Despite popular perceptions, divorce rates are at a forty-year low; they have decreased by 26 percent since 1980 (Hemez 2016). Nonetheless, divorce remains a common experience: 16.1 women divorce for every 1,000 who are married (Payne 2017). Couples who cohabit also break up. As with other aspects of social life, families draw on the resources available to them to create stability and deal with problems when they arise. What may become a crisis leading to stress and conflict in some families may be more readily absorbed in families with more financial and social resources. Take the case of a broken-down car or a health scare such as finding an unexpected lump under an armpit.

Families with savings in the bank and quality health insurance with low copays, for example, may quickly address the problems by taking the car to a repair shop and setting up a doctor's appointment to address the lump. Families without these resources, though, may have to take unpaid time off work to take the car to a friend who knows about cars or choose between paying the doctor's copay or going grocery shopping. What seems like small problems in the first family become big, compounding problems in the second.

Research on divorce and relationship dissolution shows that couples with fewer resources are more at risk for divorcing than others. Marrying young, growing up in a divorced family, being poor, and losing a job, for example, are key risk factors for divorce (Amato and Hohmann-Marriott 2007; Amato 2010; Lehrer and Son 2017). Education especially brings stability to family life because it opens up resources and opportunities to couples: more secure jobs with benefits, financial resources to deal with life challenges, neighborhoods with quality schools and little violence, and social ties with other well-educated people who can help navigate life's difficulties. As discussed in Chapter 7, people tend to marry class-homogamously, to people who share their social class. College-educated couples are more likely to stay together than their non-college-educated peers, and as more couples have gotten college degrees over the past several decades, we have seen the divorce rate drop (Amato 2010; Rotz 2016). Early research shows that same-sex and different-sex couples have similar levels of relationship instability (Manning, Brown, and Sykes 2016).

Effects of Instability on Children.
Sociologists have historically been very concerned about the potential effects of family instability on children. Multiple family transitions, family separation, or the loss of a parent can be hard on children. On the extreme end, for example, children who have had a parent die perform worse academically, internalize their problems (e.g., experience anxiety and loneliness), and struggle to maintain self-control more than other children (Amato and Anthony 2014). Children with divorced parents or disrupted cohabiting parents also tend to have poorer academic performance, lower self-esteem, and more mental health and disciplinary problems than children from intact families (Amato and Anthony 2014; Arkes 2017; Bzostek and Berger 2017; Eriksen, Hvidtfeldt, and Lilleør 2017). They are more likely to divorce or separate themselves (Amato and Patterson 2017).

However, the effects of these events tend to be modest and short-lived because children are remarkably resilient, especially when they have family and economic resources to help them work through tough times. Some children actually fare better after their parents' divorce. Research shows that *most* children experience no negative effects from divorce (Amato and Anthony 2014). About a quarter of children experience negative effects, such as decreased school performance or externalizing problems (Amato and Anthony 2014). About 15 percent experience *positive* effects following divorce because the conflict in their families decreases (Amato and Anthony 2014). However, sociologists see multiple family transitions (e.g., repeated divorces, a divorce and moving the family to a new city) as more detrimental than a single event (Shafer, Jensen, and Holmes 2017).

Other separations are also challenging for families, especially military deployment, migration, incarceration of a parent, or the deportation of a parent (Andersen 2016; Cardoso et al. 2018; Creighton, Park, and Teruel 2009; Gorman, Eide, and Hisle-Gorman 2009; Kalmijn 2017; Turney, Schnittker, and Wildeman 2011). Each physically separates partners from each other and children from their parents, leading to the loss of a caretaker in the household and possibly lost wages (particularly in the case of incarceration). Families also experience added stress as members miss their loved ones, fear they may be hurt or killed, or even deal with the stigma that comes with single parenthood or incarceration. Children, especially, are at risk for negative consequences, such as dropping out of school.

Supporting Children.
Parents can mediate the challenges posed by family disruption (Murry and Lippold 2018). For example, when families experience stressful events, parents can seek couples or family therapy to learn how to help their children cope. Divorced parents can cooperatively coparent by working together to prioritize the needs of their children and help children maintain healthy relationships with both parents. Parents can attempt to minimize other transitions, such as switching schools, to add stability. Finally, parents can seek support from teachers, school counselors, friends, neighbors, and extended family. Accessing community resources and cooperating improve children's resiliency in the face of transitions. Sociologists help families deal with family transitions by researching their effects and positive interventions. They also recommend specific policies that support families.

Check Your Understanding

- What are some typical causes of stress in families?
- Describe the backgrounds of people most likely and least likely to get divorced.
- What are some life experiences that are particularly challenging for children? How can parents mitigate their effects on children?

DOING SOCIOLOGY 11.4

EXAMINING FAMILY-FRIENDLY POLICIES FOR STUDENTS ON YOUR CAMPUS

In this exercise, you will examine how family friendly your campus is by looking at the family-related policies for students and faculty.

You and your classmates are members of a new task force on campus whose charge is to examine how family friendly your campus's policies are for students. Look through university resources online to identify the availability of family-related policies in three areas. First, find policies related to taking leave for caretaking (to miss class to care for a sick family member or to welcome a new family member via birth, adoption, or foster care). Second, find any attendance policies that excuse absences related to caretaking or family-related responsibilities. Third, identify any policies related to bringing students' children to class. When analyzing the policies, consider questions such as these: Is there a policy? Is it easily accessible? Is there an incentive or a disincentive to using the policy? What sort of evidence does the student have to provide to use it? Does the policy apply universally to every student? If not, who might be able to use it most readily? And who gets to decide which students use it?

The task force must present a report to the chief academic officer outlining its findings related to the policies identified by your group. As a key member of the task force, you will summarize your findings by:

1. Describing how family friendly your campus's policies are for students.

2. Describing one or more changes you would recommend to make your campus more family friendly.

How Work and Policy Shape Families

> 11.6   How do work and social policies influence family life?

In *The Second Shift*, originally published in 1989, Arlie Hochschild describes how one married couple, Nancy and Evan Holt, tried to balance work and home responsibilities. Nancy, a social worker, expected her husband, who did not work as much as she did, to contribute to the routine work of the household, such as cooking, cleaning, washing, shopping, and caring for their young child. Despite his promises to do his share of the housework, however, Evan failed to do his share. He resisted doing what he considered women's work around the house. This left Nancy having to do the mundane and time-consuming housework and childcare—after she came home from work, working what Hochschild dubbed the **second shift**. Over time, the marriage became increasingly conflict ridden (Hochschild and Machung 2012).

Nancy and Evan's struggles show how closely family life is tied to the economy. Evan could not adjust to an economy that required two earners in a household and consequent gender role adjustment at home. The result was a resentful, exhausted Nancy—and marital conflict.

CONSIDER THIS

If you could pick your ideal arrangement, how many hours per week would you work for pay and how many hours would you spend doing housework, cooking, and childcare? How would you deal with your competing obligations if you lived alone? How would you deal with your competing obligations if you lived with a partner who didn't want to contribute to housework or childcare?

Addressing Work and Family Challenges Today

Whereas a majority of U.S. households were headed by male breadwinners in 1970, a majority are now headed by dual-earner couples (Jacobs and Gerson 2004; William, Berdahl, and Vandello 2016). The number of single mothers heading households has also grown substantially. As a result, not only do U.S. families *depend* on the earnings of all adults to make their families work, but many U.S. families are also **overworked**, or devoting more time to paid work than ever, leaving less time for leisure (Williams, Berdahl, and Vandello 2016). These work environments, paired with intensive parenting standards and responsibility for caring for the elderly or sick, leave many families stressed and overwhelmed.

Work-family strain experienced by families in the United States is exacerbated by the dearth of workplace policies accommodating family life. Childcare is perhaps the most important benefit workplaces or government agencies could offer, but few employers in the United States do so and the government does not either. Nor does the United States have a federal *paid* family leave policy allowing workers to care for a newly born or adopted baby, sick parent, ill child, injured spouse, or personal illness. The federal Family and Medical Leave Act, passed in 1993, entitles eligible workers up to twelve weeks of

unpaid, job-protected leave—and applies only in workplaces with fifty or more employees. Most U.S. workers, if they even qualify for leave, face great financial hardship if they must take an unpaid leave.

California, New Jersey, Rhode Island, New York, Washington, Massachusetts, and the District of Columbia have created their own state-based paid family leave programs to help fill the gap (Noguchi 2019). Still, however, family life policies in the United States lag far behind other Global North nations (Organisation for Economic Co-operation and Development 2016), despite research showing that families that can use family-friendly work arrangements experience less stress and conflict (Schooreel and Verbruggen 2016). The vast majority (approximately 86 percent) of workers are not eligible for paid leave through their employers. Note how access to paid leave varies among occupations, as seen in Figure 11.6.

Other workplace policies, such as paid vacation, bereavement leave, sick leave, flextime scheduling, or flexible work locations, ease pressure on workers, increase productivity, and reduce the spread of illness but are not available to some or most workers (Bloom and Van Reenen 2006; Council of Economic Advisers 2014; National Conference of State Legislatures 2016; Stearns and White 2018). Workers, furthermore, often fear they will be looked down upon or fired for asking about or using flexible workplace policies. San Francisco and Vermont have adopted "right to request" laws, which protect workers from retaliation from their employers if they request a flexible work arrangement (Council of Economic Advisers 2014).

Using Sociology to Address Family Issues. Being a professional researcher who studies families is just one way to use sociology to support families. Sociology offers many other career opportunities to make life better for families. In the nonprofit sector, for example, family sociologists work as volunteer coordinators in domestic violence shelters, case managers in child

▼ FIGURE 11.6

Getting Paid Family Leave Depends on the Workplace

% of workers with access to paid family leave, by industry, 2016

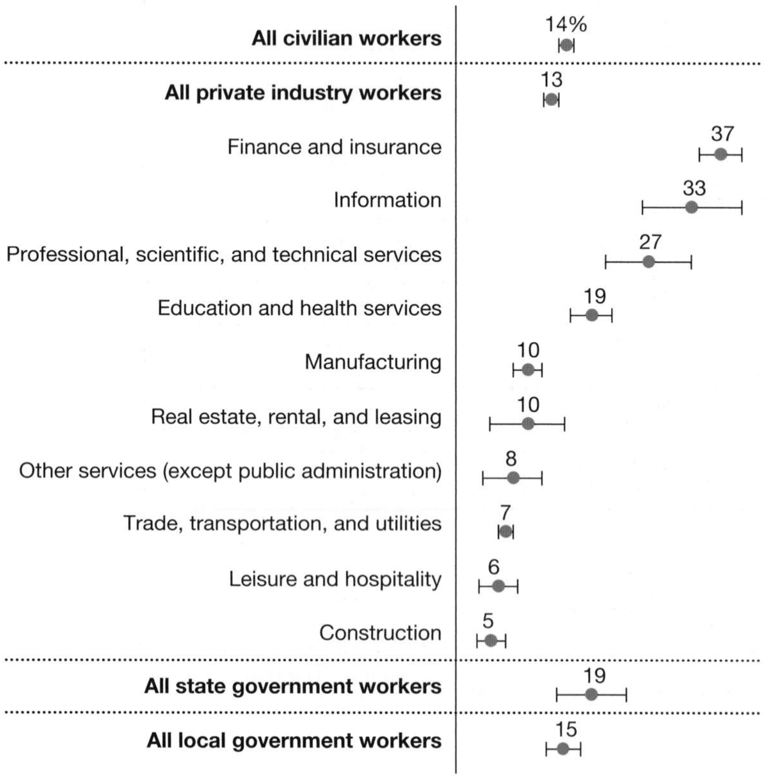

Source: DeSilver, Drew. "Access to paid family leave varies widely across employers, industries." Pew Research Center, Washington, D.C. (March 23, 2017). https://www.pewresearch.org/fact-tank/2017/03/23/access-to-paid-family-leave-varies-widely-across-employers-industries/.

Note: Lines indicate high and low point of the estimated 95% confidence interval. Survey excludes federal government, agricultural, and household workers and the self-employed.

COMPARING PAID LEAVE IN TWENTY-ONE COUNTRIES

In this activity, you will analyze a graph showing leave policies in various countries.

Figure 11.7 presents the number of weeks of paid maternity and paternity leave available to workers in the

▼ FIGURE 11.7

Family Leave: How Does the United States Compare? Paid and Unpaid Leave for Two-Parent Families by Country

Duration of paid maternity leave and the average payment rate[a] across paid maternity leave for an individual on national average earnings

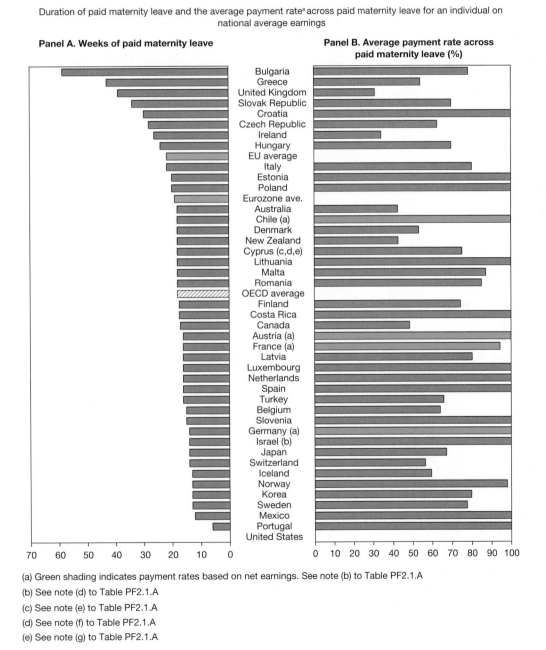

(a) Green shading indicates payment rates based on net earnings. See note (b) to Table PF2.1.A

(b) See note (d) to Table PF2.1.A

(c) See note (e) to Table PF2.1.A

(d) See note (f) to Table PF2.1.A

(e) See note (g) to Table PF2.1.A

(Continued)

(Continued)

Duration of paid paternity leave and paid father-specific parental and home care leave[a] in weeks, and the average payment rate[b] across paid paternity and father-specific leave for an individual no national average earnings

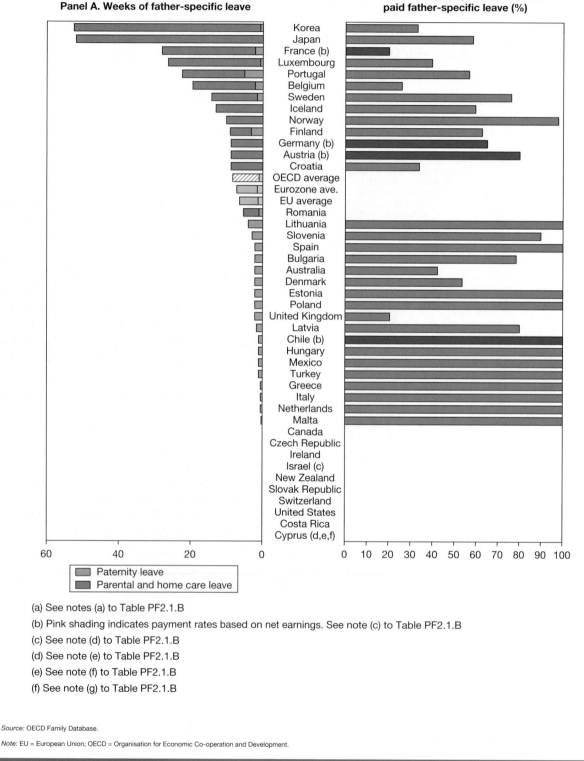

Panel A. Weeks of father-specific leave

Panel B. Average payment rate across paid father-specific leave (%)

Korea, Japan, France (b), Luxembourg, Portugal, Belgium, Sweden, Iceland, Norway, Finland, Germany (b), Austria (b), Croatia, OECD average, Eurozone ave., EU average, Romania, Lithuania, Slovenia, Spain, Bulgaria, Australia, Denmark, Estonia, Poland, United Kingdom, Latvia, Chile (b), Hungary, Mexico, Turkey, Greece, Italy, Netherlands, Malta, Canada, Czech Republic, Ireland, Israel (c), New Zealand, Slovak Republic, Switzerland, United States, Costa Rica, Cyprus (d,e,f)

- Paternity leave
- Parental and home care leave

(a) See notes (a) to Table PF2.1.B

(b) Pink shading indicates payment rates based on net earnings. See note (c) to Table PF2.1.B

(c) See note (d) to Table PF2.1.B

(d) See note (e) to Table PF2.1.B

(e) See note (f) to Table PF2.1.B

(f) See note (g) to Table PF2.1.B

Source: OECD Family Database.

Note: EU = European Union; OECD = Organisation for Economic Co-operation and Development.

United States and those in other countries. Examine the graph and then answer the questions below.

1. How many weeks of paid leave does the United States guarantee its employees who become ill or need to care for someone else? What about unpaid leave for illness or to care for someone?

2. Which countries provide the largest number of weeks of total leave? Which countries provide the most paid leave?

3. Where, in relation to the other nations, does the United States stand?

4. Assume that you are running for political office. Would you make guaranteed time off from work a part of your political platform? Why or why not? If you would campaign for guaranteed leave, would you emphasize paid or unpaid leave? Why?

advocacy organizations, and patient advocates at hospitals. If you are interested in public sector work, family sociology can help you better support families whether you work as a case manager in a department of human services, an advocate with a child protective services agency, a parole officer, a school administrator, or a policy maker. You can also support families through work in the private sector as a business owner, manager, or human resources officer by advocating family-friendly leave policies. Even if your job does not put you directly in charge of some dimension of family life, understanding the role of families in our society will help you better serve your clients and coworkers.

Check Your Understanding

- Why are many parents overworked today?

- How can family friendly policies help reduce stresses on families?

- How does the United States compare with European nations in terms of workplace family policies?

- What is the Family and Medical Leave Act of 1993?

- How can sociological knowledge of the family help professionals in a variety of fields?

Conclusion

Families are a central part of social life. As an institution, the family is flexible and adaptive to changing social conditions. The needs families meet and how they meet them have changed over time. Industrialization, the decline of the family wage, shifting ideologies about gender and sexuality, and technological innovations have transformed families from sites of economic production and political connection building to those of emotional comfort. How we parent has also changed over time and depends on our own socialization and the resources we bring to the task.

Families are where we deal with the stress and strain of life at work and in the public realm. Economic, social, and policy resources affect the well-being and stability of families. Despite all of the changes families have undergone, they remain as vital to our lives as ever. Understanding families in a sociological way leads us to wonder about what new needs families will meet in the next fifty years and what families will look like then.

Many of the social advantages and disadvantages children start off with in their families affect their success in school. The next chapter examines the relationship among education, families, and other institutions in the United States.

REVIEW

11.1 What are families? In what ways are families by-products of the social world?

Families are groups of people who take responsibility for meeting one another's needs. What needs families meet has changed over time; families were once sites of economic production and political connection building but now offer emotional comfort. Our definitions of family are institutionalized through social policy, law, and our shared beliefs.

11.2 How have families changed over time? What has caused these changes?

Our sociological imaginations help us identify social factors that influence family life. Some of the key social factors include slavery, industrialization, social class, technological innovations (such as the car, birth control, and mobile phones), social movements, and gender roles. Since the 1970s, social factors such as deindustrialization, the decline of the family wage, and several social movements have led to change in norms around marriage, cohabitation, and births outside of marriage. Same-sex marriages are now recognized but the overall marriage rate has declined, while cohabitation and births to unmarried mothers have increased.

11.3 How do different theoretical perspectives help sociologists understand families?

Different theories allow us to view families from various angles. Structural functionalists emphasize the socialization functions of families and the structure of families. Conflict theorists focus on how social inequalities affect family life and how families provide an arena for acting out inequalities. Conflict theorists who use a feminist perspective show how families tend to create and reinforce gender inequality. Those who use intersectionality look at multiple forms of inequality, such as sexuality *and* class *and* gender, at the same time within families. Social exchange theorists maintain that people contemplate costs and rewards when making decisions, such as whether to stay married.

11.4 Who does the caretaking?

Families are tasked with taking care of their own, especially children. Intensive parenting invests copious time and resources into raising children and is practiced by middle-class and wealthier families. Mothers still spend more time caretaking, but over the past few decades, fathers have increased the time they spend caring for their children. Many adults take care of their aging parents, as well, as part of the sandwich generation.

11.5 What challenges do families face?

Although families often are places of comfort and security, sometimes they become stressful, distressful, or abusive. Children are especially susceptible to family abuse. Family violence, when someone in a family hurts or controls someone else, takes on many different forms: sexual abuse, financial abuse, emotional mistreatment, and physical violence.

Families may break apart when their members are unhappy and conflictual or have little commitment to each other. Although most kids fare well after divorce, about a quarter of children of divorced parents experience academic or behavioral problems. About 15 percent of kids actually benefit from divorce. Families that experience discrimination have to deal with additional stressors.

11.6 How do work and social policies influence family life?

Family members balance the demands of work life with those of home life. Work demands can cause families stress and strain. The lack of family-friendly workplace policies in the United States leaves most families overburdened. Most other postindustrial nations have far more policies in place to help their citizens balance work and family life.

KEY TERMS

Introducing...

$\circledS$SAGE vantage™

Course tools done right.

Built to support teaching. Designed to ignite learning.

SAGE vantage is an intuitive digital platform that blends trusted SAGE content with auto-graded assignments, all carefully designed to ignite student engagement and drive critical thinking. Built with you and your students in mind, it offers easy course set-up and enables students to better prepare for class.

SAGE vantage enables students to **engage** with the material you choose, **learn** by applying knowledge, and **soar** with confidence by performing better in your course.

PEDAGOGICAL SCAFFOLDING	**CONFIDENCE BUILDER**	**TIME-SAVING FLEXIBILITY**	**QUALITY CONTENT**	**HONEST VALUE**
Builds on core concepts, moving students from basic understanding to mastery.	Offers frequent knowledge checks, applied-learning multimedia tools, and chapter tests with focused feedback.	Feeds auto-graded assignments to your gradebook, with real-time insight into student and class performance.	Written by expert authors and teachers, content is not sacrificed for technical features.	Affordable access to easy-to-use, quality learning tools students will appreciate.

To learn more about **SAGE vantage**, hover over this QR code with your smartphone camera or visit **sagepub.com/vantage**

CHAPTER 12

UNDERSTANDING INSTITUTIONS

Education

Melissa S. Fry

Education plays a major role in all societies. It can train a society's members to be productive citizens, workers, and family members. It can also pass along privilege and inequality from one generation to the next.

iStockphoto.com/benkrut

LEARNING QUESTIONS

12.1 What does it mean to look at education as a social institution?

12.2 How do historical moment, the social structure, and changing systems of production shape the functions of education over time and across place?

12.3 How do functionalism, conflict theory, and symbolic interaction approach and explain education as an institution?

12.4 How does education reproduce social inequality?

12.5 What are the central issues facing global education today?

12.6 How do policy debates surrounding pre-K, K–12, and higher education all revolve around the tension between public education and individual choice and responsibility for accessing opportunities and achieving success?

What Is Education as an Institution?

12.1 What does it mean to look at education as a social institution?

Kadijah Williams, a young woman from California, spent her childhood moving from shelter to shelter, sometimes sleeping on the street or in a bus station. In high school, her evening study sessions were often cut short by "lights out" at the homeless shelter, but she never gave up. From tenth to twelfth grades, she woke at 4:30 a.m., took several buses, and spent two hours each morning commuting to keep herself from having to switch schools for a thirteenth time. She was determined to graduate from Jefferson High, which was a consistent touch point for her (Okura 2013).

The instability of her homeless life affected Kadijah's ability to make friends and perform well in school. She described her experience this way: "Though school was my salvation, my test scores suffered as a result of missing so much school and having no place to study" (Kristof 2016). Still, Kadijah worked hard and applied to Harvard University. Harvard accepted her on a full scholarship. Her university dorm room provided a needed home.

Kadijah credits her mother's high expectations and access to the Los Angeles Public Library for helping her remain focused and envision a different life (Okura 2013;

Harpo Productions 2009). Kadijah graduated from Harvard with a sociology degree and now works for the Washington, D.C., city government helping homeless kids. Kadijah combines her personal experiences with the sociological perspective to understand and address the issue of homelessness.

Kadijah's story is one that many Americans embrace as evidence that the United States is a meritocracy, a society in which one's status, income, and place in the social structure are determined by hard work and ability. In reality, Kadijah's story is a rare exception. Most Americans grow up to have earnings similar to their parents' and occupy the same socioeconomic status as their parents—thanks, in part, to the U.S. educational system (Mitnik, Cumberworth, and Grusky 2016; Witteveen and Attewell 2017; Pfeffer 2018; Pfeffer and Hertel 2015; Hertel and Groh-Samberg 2014).

Education is essential to upward mobility, movement up the class and status structure, and a democratic society. This chapter explores education, its functions, the power dynamics that shape education, and the ways education relates to upward mobility and social inequality. It also examines education's role in socialization and cultural reproduction, as well as current issues in global and domestic education policy and practice.

Institutionalizing Education

Education is the process through which a society transmits its culture and history, as well as teaches social, intellectual, and specific work skills that result in productive workers and citizens. Like the family, education has been institutionalized, encoded in laws, policies, and common practices that organize schools and their support systems. Institutionalization is important to stability. Roles, rules, and routines limit how much individual personalities shape an organization's operation. This allows smooth transitions when people are hired or depart, and it ensures that different organizations within an institution are comparable. Have you ever switched schools? If so, you know that some things were different, but you could also count on many things being basically the same. With a pretty good understanding of how "school" works, kids can readily adapt to a new setting.

As noted in Chapter 11, institutions reflect the time and place in which they exist. In preindustrial societies, adults passed knowledge and skills through modeling and oral tradition. The rise of manufacturing in the industrial age moved parents' work away from the home and family, and it required skills many parents could not teach. Society thus needed a system to prepare workers

HOW I GOT ACTIVE IN SOCIOLOGY

MELISSA S. FRY

I started college as a life sciences and Spanish double major with clear plans for medical school and a future serving the health needs of underserved Latino communities. Then Rodney King was beaten. On video. The four officers we watched beat him on the video were acquitted by an all-White jury. Los Angeles erupted in flames and violence. The irrationality of racism got under my skin, and all I wanted to do was learn about how and why our society divided itself along the lines of race and ethnicity. I wanted to know how the "justice" system could produce such an outcome in a country that embraced ideals of equality.

That was the spring of my first year of college. I enrolled in an urban sociology course the following fall and fell in love with the discipline. I could not read enough, never had trouble writing papers, loved attending classes—my whole approach to learning changed. My interest in race and social movements evolved into an interest in political institutions and public policy. Race fundamentally shapes education policy, as well as the institutions and organizations that constitute our public education system, in ways that reproduce social inequality. The need to understand the social dynamics that produce and reinforce this feedback loop and others like it are what hooked me on sociology.

for the labor force. In addition to particular work skills, the industrial era required a workforce that could be on time, follow directions, conform to a structured work environment, and accept the authority of management. A compulsory public education system emerged to meet these needs.

Check Your Understanding

- From a sociological perspective, why is it important to recognize that Kadijah's story is exceptional?

- What does it mean to see education as a social institution?

- In what ways does institutionalizing education promote stability?

Education and Modes of Production

> 12.2 How do historical moment, the social structure, and changing systems of production shape the functions of education over time and across place?

As societies change, so must their institutions. Education prepares people to fill different roles in relation to the means of production (the methods for producing goods). If the means of production change, education must adapt to reflect those changes, or risk harming the economy and creating instability in society.

Preindustrial Societies

As noted earlier, in preindustrial societies, school as we know it did not exist. Only the wealthy and religious leaders

went to school, where classes focused on philosophy, sacred texts, and the arts.

Most children in preindustrial societies worked alongside their parents, who taught them work skills, life lessons, and values. In agrarian societies, where farming was the means of production, land ownership was the primary source of economic and social power, and it transferred to the next generation through inheritance. The aristocracy held the land, and the peasants worked it with simple tools that did not require education outside the family.

Industrial Manufacturing and Large-Scale Agriculture

Industrialization altered the division of labor and resulted in mass migration to industrial centers and in changes to education (Rauscher 2015). Industrialization created a need for mechanics, welders, factory workers, newspaper writers, bookkeepers, and other skilled workers. The demand for skills like reading, writing, and calculating laid the foundation for a compulsory educational system.

The Postindustrial Knowledge and Service Economy

In the late 1970s and early 1980s, U.S. manufacturing started to decline as lower transportation costs, liberal trade policies, and tax breaks allowed companies to move their factories to places with cheaper labor. At the same time, higher levels of education coupled with new computing technology expanded knowledge-based work. The midcentury baby boom produced the largest and most highly educated generation thus far in U.S.

EXAMINING THE LOCAL SCHOOL BOARD AS AN INSTITUTION

In this activity, you will use the web site of a local school board to examine the policies and processes that make it an institution.

Using a web browser of your choice, search for a local school board web site. Explore the site and jot down your answers to the following questions:

1. What are the vision and mission of the school board? If they do not have both, note what they do have.

2. What is the stated function of the school board? This may be listed as objectives or goals.

3. If agendas and minutes are posted on the web site, review a few of their recent meeting agendas and minutes and describe the routines for these meetings. Is there a regular order and pattern of activity? Describe that pattern in two to four sentences.

4. On the basis of posted agendas and minutes, list three recent topics addressed.

5. Are there any rules for school board membership or for attending meetings? If so, what are they?

6. Why is it important for the school system to have a board with clear roles, rules, and routines that govern its actions? Why might meetings be organized the same way (or nearly the same way) every time?

7. Imagine you are a parent of a child in the school district. What is a policy you would like to see the school board change or implement? On the basis of the agendas, describe how you could use the institutional structure of the school board to bring your idea up for discussion and consideration.

---

history. They created more demand for goods and services, and they made innovation itself a valued commodity.

Since the late 1970s, the numbers of both professional and service jobs have grown dramatically. Securing higher paid work requires more education and/or technical training, while throughout the labor market, work increasingly demands strong social skills. Teaching children to show up on time, conform to a rigid structure, and yield to authority fails to develop either the creativity or knowledge needed to succeed at high income and professional levels in the current economy. These skills may still be important, but alone they cannot ensure social mobility.

Public Education and the Postindustrial Economy

The education system in the United States today reflects the industrial age more than it does the information era that it now serves (Collins and Halverson 2018; Livingstone [1998] 2018). Most public schools do not adequately develop the knowledge, critical thinking, and creativity students need to succeed in today's white-collar professions. Meanwhile, most vocational high schools continue to operate on the assumption that a shop-based high school curriculum will help students attain manufacturing jobs, which now tend to require advanced technological knowledge and training.

CONSIDER THIS

Do you think your K–12 education equipped you with the skills needed in today's workplace? How? Provide examples that support your answer.

Check Your Understanding

- How have changing systems of production shaped education historically?
- What factors led to the emergence of compulsory public education?
- How are the labor needs of the postindustrial service and knowledge economy different from those of the industrial era?

Theorizing Education

12.3   How do functionalism, conflict theory, and symbolic interaction approach and explain education as an institution?

Sociological theories help us examine the structure, functions, power dynamics, and interactions within and among institutions through different lenses. Functionalists point to the ways a compulsory education system contributes to socialization and economic

DOING SOCIOLOGY 12.2

HOW THE INTERSECTION OF BIOGRAPHY AND HISTORY SHAPES EDUCATIONAL EXPERIENCES

In this exercise, you will look at how your educational experience is shaped by the time in which you live and your personal biography.

The fundamental insight of the sociological imagination is that an individual's reality is the product of the intersection of biography and history. Take a few moments to consider how your own experience and understanding of education are shaped by the intersection of your individual biography with the historical moment in which you live and write your answers to the following questions:

1. What year were you born? What year did you begin formal schooling? What year did you graduate from high school?

2. List three to five specific things related to schooling and your education that you think are different for you than they were for your parents or grandparents.

3. What historical changes might be responsible for differences between your experiences and opportunities and your parents' or grandparents'? These may be social, cultural, technological, or political changes. Be specific.

4. If you could implement one policy in all public schools, what would it be? Why?

---

development. Conflict theorists view those same functions as working to create and justify inequality. Symbolic interactionists examine the explicit and implicit curriculum of values and behaviors transmitted through social interactions in schools. All these perspectives will help you notice and understand both the obvious and obscured aspects of education.

The Social Functions of Education

Functionalists point out that the institution of education provides a structure that teaches students about our shared culture and socializes workers and citizens. It trains and sorts workers by strengths and interests, and it provides access to various parts of the labor market while leveling the playing field with universal access. It can also protect democracy by creating an informed and educated electorate capable of electing good leaders.

As noted in earlier chapters, in addition to these manifest functions, a mandatory education system has latent (hidden) functions like providing childcare for working parents and regulating entry into the labor force. The **hidden curriculum** is also responsible for reinforcing elements of social status and order, such as ideas about gender-appropriate roles and behaviors and race and class hierarchies. These messages are delivered through substantive choices in the curriculum and often through the social structure and functioning of the school itself.

Socialization: Cohesion and Control. Although families are the site of primary socialization, functionalists note that schools are essential to **secondary socialization**—teaching us how to behave appropriately in small groups and structured situations. Schooling, for example, teaches children to be punctual, follow rules and directions, obey authority figures, and complete assigned tasks. Whenever you listen quietly to a presentation at work or raise your hand to speak, you are expressing values and norms you learned in the classroom.

Labor Force Preparation. Public schools, from the perspective of functionalists, give everyone an opportunity to succeed in and contribute to society. Education holds out the promise of being a great equalizer in a society in which all children have access to it. Indeed, education does, in some cases, allow people to move up the social class ladder, like Kadijah Williams.

Public schools benefit both individuals and society by helping children develop essential skills while sorting these future workers into appropriate positions in the labor market. From a functionalist perspective, success in the classroom leads to higher level courses and acceptance into highly competitive and elite colleges and graduate schools. Those with the highest abilities receive the most advanced training, earn the highest credentials, and enter the most challenging fields. Likewise, those with less ability receive less training, earn lower level credentials, and

As economic changes create the need for different skills, education must adapt to help workers prepare for changing job requirements.
©iStockphoto.com/FatCamera

enter less demanding (and often less lucrative) areas of work (Davis and Moore 1945).

CONSIDER THIS

What functions do you think your experience of education served? Think about this both at the individual level and at the larger societal level.

Conflict, Power, and Education

While functionalists contend that education promotes **social cohesion** and stability, conflict theorists argue that the power dynamics of society shape schools and student outcomes. Differences in school experiences range from teacher quality and the physical state of school facilities (Ballantine, Hammack, and Stuber 2017; Lavy and Nixon 2017; Kozol 1991) to classroom interactions and school discipline (Calarco 2018; King, Rusoja, and Peguera 2018; Diamond and Lewis 2019; Halberstadt et al. 2018; Kane et al. 2017; Glock 2016; Anyon et al. 2017). These differences are not distributed randomly.

Class, Gender, Race, and School Experiences. In his landmark book *Savage Inequalities*, Jonathan Kozol (1991) takes readers into the very different worlds of America's poorest and richest schools. In America's poorest schools, burned-out teachers struggle to teach, and children struggle to focus in overcrowded classrooms with leaky ceilings,

poor heating, and inadequate school supplies. In contrast, wealthy schools filled with new technology, well-trained and energized teachers, and abundant extracurricular opportunities provide a clear picture of the benefits of wealth in U.S. society. Kozol's work sounded the alarm and posed the question, "Do American schools provide equal opportunities for children?" His answer—they do not.

Beyond the physical aspects of the school environment, sociologists recognize that even within a single classroom, children may have very different experiences on the basis of social characteristics, including race, class, and gender (Calarco 2018). Research in the 1970s and 1980s indicated that boys' voices, even when they were wrong, were more highly valued and sought in the classroom than were girls' (Cherry 1975; BenTsvi-Mayer, Hertz-Lazarowitz, and Safir 1989).

In the spotlight today are the ways racial bias in school discipline may be criminalizing young Black boys in ways that may produce self-fulfilling prophecies (Diamond and Lewis 2019; Halberstadt et al. 2018; King, Rusoja, and Peguera 2018; Kane et al. 2017; Glock 2016; Anyon et al. 2017). Current studies indicate that Black boys are more likely than other students to face criminal consequences for disciplinary infractions in school (Mallett 2017; Debnam, Bottiani, and Bradshaw 2017; Rudd 2014). Some argue this "criminalization" of child and adolescent behavior facilitates the so-called school-to-prison pipeline (Rocque and Snellings 2018; King Rusoja, and Peguera 2018; Mallet 2017; Amurao 2013).

The Curriculum, Ideology, and Inequality. Conflict theorists argue that the school curriculum, the courses and material taught in school, reinforces dominant ideologies and the status quo by presenting only the perspective of those in power (Loewen 2018a; Gibbs 2018; Suh, An, and Forest 2015; Zinn 2015). This version of our history tends to minimize or ignore inequality based on race, class, gender, sexual orientation, and other social characteristics. For example, American children learn a great deal about the prison camps in Europe during World War II but seldom learn about the less violent forced internment of Japanese Americans on U.S. soil during the same period. Most high school history courses jump from the Emancipation Proclamation to celebrating the civil rights movement and fail to acknowledge the more than 4,000 Blacks who were

DOING SOCIOLOGY 12.3

GENDER AND K–12 TEACHING OCCUPATIONS AND SALARIES

In this exercise, you will take on the role of school district human resources consultant.

Imagine you are considering a job mediating a school district dispute over the gender wage gap among teachers in a local K–12 system. Without knowing the details of the case, you decide to do a little basic research on where men and women tend to teach in the school system.

Choose a high school and an elementary school from the same general geographic area. Using the teaching staff portions of the schools' web sites, look at the gender composition of the schools. Create the following table and fill in your count of teachers that go in each cell. Calculate the percentage of all elementary teachers who are male, the percentage who are female, and then do the same for the high school.

	Elementary School		High School	
	Number	Percentage	Number	Percentage
Male				
Female				
Total		100		100
Average salary				

Use salary.com to look up average salaries for teachers at each level in the geographic location where the schools are located.

1. Write one paragraph describing the data and what they tell us about gender and K–12 teaching.

2. Do the data on gender and salary provide support for the assertion that there is likely to

be a gendered wage gap in the school district in question? Explain.

3. What kinds of actions or policies would you suggest to remedy any imbalances that you find in the data on gender composition and salary by school level? What might be the problems with your proposed remedies?

---

lynched in the intervening years. This artificial, sanitized leap provides another example of how school curricula can shade and ignore racial abuse or make inequality seem like a justified reflection of historical contributions (Loewen 2005, 2018a, 2018b; Equal Justice Initiative 2017; Suh, An, and Forest 2015; Zinn 2015). Marx would point out that the school curriculum helps create a false consciousness among students from poor and working-class families, as it encourages them to support, rather than challenge, the political and economic structures of the nation.

CONSIDER THIS

Can you think of at least two ways your social class, gender, or race influenced your school experience? How might your school experience be different if you were a member of a different demographic group? Why?

Tracking and Inequality. Conflict theorists also maintain that schools reproduce social stratification by tracking students toward occupations consistent with their social class. Students' home environments and neighborhoods shape their vocabularies, ways of interacting, and communication skills. Teachers and administrators interpret these behavior patterns and place children in their educational tracks accordingly (van de Werfhorst 2018; Ryan, Procopio, and Taberski 2017; Kane et al. 2017). Children who show up to school less attuned to the social rules around sitting still, quietly awaiting instruction, raising their hands, and taking turns speaking may be seen as less intelligent or less able to manage more challenging work and teachers funnel them into lower tracks. Students who arrive at school with reading time etiquette, listening skills, deference to a teacher's authority, and understanding of hand raising and taking turns may be perceived as more intelligent, and teachers track them into higher level

APPLYING SOCIOLOGICAL THEORY TO EDUCATIONAL ISSUES

In this exercise, you will take on the role of a school principal to analyze and respond to community concerns about your school.

Imagine you are a high school principal. Your teacher will assign you one of the following challenges:

- You receive a series of parent complaints that their daughters have noticed that the high school biology teacher never presents any examples of, or research from, female research scientists.

- An area newspaper publishes an investigative report documenting that students of color at your school are more likely to be placed in lower tracks and appear to have lower average test scores than otherwise similar White students.

- You attend a community meeting at which local employers complain that the past three years of high school graduates have noticeably lower skills in answering phones and interacting in a

professional manner with customers. Employers are concerned they may need to look elsewhere for qualified workers.

Write your responses to the following questions:

1. Why is the issue raised by the parents, reporter, or employers a concern to the people who raised it and/or the students directly affected?

2. Why is it a social problem? How does it affect society, rather than just individuals? Consider the three theoretical perspectives we have discussed.

3. Which theoretical perspective do you find most useful in explaining why the issue is a social problem? Why?

4. On the basis of your analysis of the problem through the lens of your chosen theory, describe two policies you would enact to address the issue.

---

reading groups that will prepare them for more challenging work throughout their school experience.

Symbolic Interaction, Socialization, and Cultural Production in Schools

While functionalists acknowledge that schools socialize individuals into citizenship and worker roles and conflict theorists focus on how education reproduces social inequality, symbolic interactionists examine how social interactions create and reproduce school experiences and educational success or failure. Peer interactions teach kids the norms and values of youth culture, ingroup and outgroup boundaries and meanings, and ultimately their definition of self. They can also make school life fun, miserable, or somewhere in between.

Imagine a high school freshman who enjoys playing chess when he arrives on campus and is happy to hear that the school has a chess club. He soon hears his new peers making jokes about kids who play chess, and now has to contend with a new self-definition placing him outside his peer ingroup. To manage impressions and retain his ingroup status, he decides not to join the chess club.

Interactions with teachers and administrators teach kids about trust in and submission to nonparental authority

as these adults try to socialize students to adult group behavior. A close relationship with a teacher may also provide important mentoring on what it takes to be successful in life. Think about how your teachers influenced your sense of your own competence as a student and your ability to succeed in college and a career.

Socialization, Socioeconomic Status, and School Success. The children of parents with higher levels of education will tend to have greater exposure to books and other reading materials and to be socialized to sit through the reading and discussion of books from an early age. Children in these homes are "coached for the classroom" (Calarco 2018). They are more likely to participate in structured leisure activities like organized sports, music lessons, cultural events, or concerts, where they learn the norms for such activities (Podesta 2014; Lareau 2003, 276–77). Children from blue-collar families do more of their early learning through less structured experiences like free outdoor play with other children, which requires less restrictive behavior (Podesta 2014; Lareau 2003, 276–77). Kindergarten may be the first time they are expected to conform to a more structured environment. Children who have trouble conforming can be labeled troublemakers, face disciplinary action, and ultimately have to deal with the label's effect on their self-concept and future interactions (Marsh and Noguera 2018; King, Rusoja, and Peguero 2018).

> **CONSIDER THIS**
>
> Among the three theoretical perspectives described above, which would you use to make sense of your own K–12 educational experience? Explain your choice.

Check Your Understanding

- What are the functions of compulsory education in the United States?

- According to conflict theorists, how do schools reproduce inequality?

- From the perspective of symbolic interactionists, how do peers and teachers influence students?

- How can socialization within families affect children's success in school?

Education and Social Inequality in the United States

12.4   How does education reproduce social inequality?

Universal access to education is supposed to provide the opportunity for individuals to build their **human capital** (knowledge, skills, habits, and attributes necessary to succeed in work and in life) and realize their full potential. In this way, education produces economic mobility and, ideally, sorts the most talented individuals into the most challenging roles. But is this really how it works? This section uses a sociological lens to explore how American education is both a product and producer of social inequality in the United States.

Class and Family Background

A significant body of research suggests that educational institutions reproduce relations of power and social inequality rather than leveling the playing field. The strongest predictors of educational success are parents' education and income (Calarco 2018; Liu 2018; Cozzolini, Smith, and Crosnoe 2018; Dixon-Roman 2017; Monaghan 2016). Children tend to follow their parents' path in school.

In 1966, the U.S. Department of Education released *Equality of Educational Opportunity* (Coleman et al. 1966). Lead researcher James Coleman, a sociologist, found that the quality of schools and teachers had some impact on student outcomes, but the strongest determinant was the students' socioeconomic status. Parents' education and income begin shaping children's educational readiness, school performance, outcomes, and access to opportunity from birth (Liu 2018; Monaghan 2016; Cozzolini, Smith, and Crosnoe 2018; Dixon-Roman 2017; Hout 2018). In addition, middle-class parents intervene in subtle and not-so-subtle ways to ensure that their children access attention, assistance, accommodations, and key opportunities and to protect their children from ending up on the wrong end of labeling, tracking, and discipline (Calarco 2018).

Leveling the Playing Field with Early Education. The research on early childhood brain development suggests that providing quality care and education from birth to age five can reduce child poverty and increase labor force participation. Quality preschool programs improve nutrition and stimulate brain development, closing the gap between poor and privileged children before they ever walk into a kindergarten classroom. These structured programs also prepare children to interact effectively in school settings (Gorski 2018; Bierman et al. 2017). Unfortunately, only 54 percent of U.S. three- and four-year-olds are enrolled in pre-K programs (National Center for Education Statistics 2018b).

Quality preschool programs are especially crucial for children in poverty.
©iStockphoto.com/FatCamera

During World War II, the U.S. government provided childcare to support women entering the labor force as part of the war effort (Stoltzfus 2000). This was a notable exception, however. Early education and care in the United States have traditionally been the responsibility of individual families.

Low-income and even many middle-income families struggle to access affordable, quality education and care for preschool-age children (National Survey of Early Care and Education Project Team 2016; Madill et al. 2018; Moodie-Dyer 2012; Liu 2015). The federal government recommends that families spend no more than 10 percent of income on childcare. Yet the average cost of quality childcare ranges from $4,800 to more than $21,000 per year per child depending on location and age of child (Tran 2014). A family with two $10 per hour full-time jobs earns a net income of less than $40,000 per year. Even the cheapest childcare will cost that family 12 percent of its income for a single child.

Separate and Unequal: Racial and Economic Segregation in Schools

Imagine two five-year-old girls in the Chicago suburbs: Julie, a White child on the north side in Winnetka, and Denise, an African American child on the south side in Chicago Heights. By age five, the two girls have had very different experiences as a result of their social class positions, and this, in turn, has affected brain development (Kim et al. 2018; Center on the Developing Child at Harvard University 2016). Both girls can take advantage of a free public education, which should be an opportunity to eliminate any differences arising from family resources. In reality, it does not.

Julie will enter a nearly all-White school with the children of educated parents who read to them at home, engage them in stimulating play, and take them to the zoo on a regular basis. Denise will enter a school where a large percentage of the children come from low-income, single-parent households of color where a working mother with a high school education has little time or energy to read, play games, or make trips to the zoo. These very different experiences represent the extremes of the U.S. class hierarchy—wealth with racial

▼ FIGURE 12.1

Per Pupil Expenditures by State, 2013

State	Expenditure
New York	$19,818
Alaska	$18,175
District of Columbia	$17,953
New Jersey	$17,572
Connecticut	$16,631
Vermont	$16,377
Wyoming	$15,700
Massachusetts	$14,515
Rhode Island	$14,415
Pennsylvania	$13,864
Delaware	$13,833
Maryland	$13,829
New Hampshire	$13,721
Illinois	$12,288
Maine	$12,147
North Dakota	$11,980
Hawaii	$11,823
Nebraska	$11,579
Ohio	$11,197
West Virginia	$11,132
Minnesota	$11,089
Wisconsin	$11,071
Virginia	$10,960
Michigan	$10,948
Montana	$10,625
Louisiana	$10,490
Iowa	$10,313
Kansas	$9,828
Washington	$9,672
Missouri	$9,597
Indiana	$9,566
Oregon	$9,543
South Carolina	$9,514
Arkansas	$9,394
Kentucky	$9,316
California	$9,220
Georgia	$9,099
New Mexico	$9,012
Alabama	$8,755
Colorado	$8,647
South Dakota	$8,470
Florida	$8,433
North Carolina	$8,390
Nevada	$8,339
Texas	$8,299
Tennessee	$8,208
Mississippi	$8,130
Oklahoma	$7,672
Arizona	$7,208
Idaho	$6,791
Utah	$6,555

Source: U.S. Census Bureau. 2015. "Table 8: Per Pupil Amounts for Current Spending of Public Elementary-Secondary School Systems by State: Fiscal Year 2013." Public Elementary-Secondary Education Finance Data.

and class privilege for Julie and poverty with racial and class barriers for Denise.

Public schools in the United States receive a combination of local, state, and federal funds. The portion that comes from each level of government is determined by school funding formulas that vary by state (on average, 45 percent comes from the state, 45 percent from local property taxes, and 10 percent from the federal government). Local funding for schools is often tied to property tax revenues. In areas with higher property values, communities have more local funding for public schools. In areas with lower property values, communities have less local school funding (Turner et al. 2016). As you can see in Figure 12.1, funding levels vary widely among states.

How do these funding disparities affect education's capacity to level the playing field? Without resources, it is very difficult for low-income schools to be effective in making up differences in kids' school preparedness related to parents' income and education levels.

Resources also affect teachers' experiences in schools. Teachers in schools where support services for students are readily available, books are up to date, and the physical space is in good repair can devote their energy to developing engaging classroom experiences. Moreover, school funding differences affect teacher pay. Desirable teaching jobs, in terms of the school atmosphere and salary, attract quality teachers. In many well-resourced schools, for example, a majority of teachers hold advanced degrees.

The Supreme Court decision in *Brown v. Board of Education of Topeka* declared school segregation unconstitutional in 1954, but federally mandated desegregation ended in the 1990s, and since then, school segregation has returned to pre-*Brown* levels (Orfield et al. 2016; Gamoran and An 2016; Ravitch 2014; Harper and Reskin 2005, 362; Kozol 2005). The percentage of K–12 public schools in the United States with 75 percent to 100 percent of students who are poor and Black or Hispanic nearly doubled between 2000 and 2014 (U.S. Government Accountability Office 2016; Orfield et al. 2016).

In addition to these stark differences, schools vary in terms of parental engagement, which can affect funding and support for extracurricular activities. Parents in professional occupations have more flexibility in their work schedules and can more easily participate in school activities. Engaged and supportive parents can enhance school offerings through volunteer work and fund-raising.

Reproducing Inequality within Schools

Although Julie and Denise exemplify the ways residential segregation patterns map onto schools, even within more racially and economically diverse schools, race and class segregation often persist. The practice of **tracking** involves placing students in classes on the basis of "ability," often measured by classroom behavior, academic performance, and academic aspiration (i.e., college bound or vocational). High school courses, for example, might be offered at Advanced Placement, honors, regular, and remedial levels. Tracking seems like a logical way to make teaching and learning more efficient. Tracking, however, privileges the education of some students over others and determines future education and career paths from an early age.

Higher class White and Asian students are overrepresented in college-preparatory tracks, while lower class Black and Hispanic students are overrepresented in vocational tracks, suggesting that factors other than ability shape placement (Batruch et al. 2019; Parker et al. 2016; Glock 2016; Dixon-Roman 2017; Kane et al. 2017; van de Werfhorst 2018). As noted earlier, kids who arrive at school with cultural capital (school appropriate behaviors and

Advanced Placement classes are often filled with only White and Asian students. Why is this?
AP Photo/John Davis

large vocabularies) may attract more positive attention from teachers regardless of their intellectual ability. This positive attention may feed positive outcomes. Similarly, teachers may conclude that students who lack cultural capital also lack intellectual ability (Mayer, LeChasseur, and Donaldson 2018; Dixon-Roman 2017; Kane et al. 2017; Glock 2016; Palardy, Rumberger, and Butler 2015).

Parental involvement also affects student tracking. Educated parents who understand the college application process are far more likely to push to place their children into the advanced tracks that look better on college applications and to help their kids get the attention and support to succeed in their classes (Calarco 2018). They are also more likely to recognize that challenging high school courses prepare their children for success in college (Calarco 2018; Dixon-Roman 2017; Gamoran 2001; Worthy 2010; Oakes 1994a, 1994b).

CONSIDER THIS

How did your parents' educational experiences influence your educational aspirations and your chances to get into a competitive college?

The unintended consequences of tracking are not limited to teacher perceptions and parental engagement.

Tracking labels some students as "academic" and others as "vocational," which in turn structures the students' interactions. These interactions in turn determine students' self-concepts and their own perceptions of what they can or cannot achieve. Current tracking also tends to devalue vocational trades—sources of many well-paying jobs.

Education is strongly related to earnings and the likelihood of living in poverty, as you can see in Figures 12.2 and 12.3 (next page). Students who gain neither skills for trades nor preparation for college will face tough futures, with lower earnings and higher levels of poverty.

Check Your Understanding

- How do schools reflect inequality across communities?
- In what ways does tracking within schools reproduce inequality?
- Is education leveling the playing field?

Higher Education

Although controversial at the time, the post–World War II GI Bill changed the face of higher education. The GI Bill democratized higher education, previously accessible only to the wealthy, by making it available to returning soldiers regardless of their parents' social class. By 1947, 49 percent of all college students were veterans, and by the time

▼ FIGURE 12.2

Median Income for Women and Men by Educational Attainment

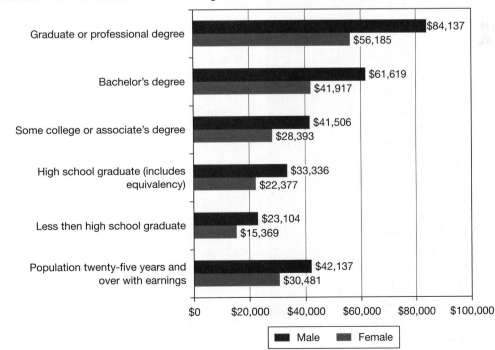

Source: U.S. Census Bureau. 2015. "S1501: Educational Attainment." 2010–2014 American Community Survey 5-Year Estimates.

Poverty Rates by Educational Attainment for Men and Women, 2010–2014

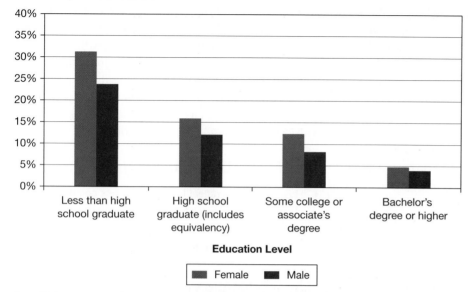

Education Level

Legend: ■ Female ■ Male

Source: U.S. Census Bureau. 2015. "Educational Attainment of the Population 18 Years and Over, by Age, Sex, Race, and Hispanic Origin." American Community Survey 2014, 5 Year Estimates, Tables 01-1 through 01-6. Accessed July 25, 2019. http://www.census.gov.

President Bill Clinton takes part in a ceremony in 1994 marking the 50th anniversary of the signing of the GI Bill. The GI Bill made it possible for many working-class men to attend college.

the GI Bill ended in 1956, 7.8 million World War II veterans had used the bill to fund their educations and job training (U.S. Department of Veterans Affairs 2013). One consequence of the GI Bill was to demonstrate that students from across the social structure could find success and reap the rewards of higher education.

Despite having better access to postsecondary education, lower socioeconomic status students face significant nonacademic barriers to completion. In fact, in 2016, 58 percent of those in the highest family income quartile had achieved a bachelor's degree by age twenty-four, compared with just 12 percent in the lowest family income quartile (Figure 12.4; Cahalan et al. 2018, 98). First-generation college students and low-income students often lack full support from their families. They may have to work to pay bills while in school, reducing available study time and creating scheduling conflicts. When faced with a conflict between keeping their job and succeeding in coursework, they often choose the job. Over time, this role strain takes a toll and many drop out.

Types of Colleges, Student Success, and Tracking. Which college or university students attend and whether they graduate directly affects their adult position in the social structure (Bowles and Gintis 1976). Advanced Placement and honors students who go to public universities are more likely to go to one of the flagship institutions, where they will find research assistantships and enrichment opportunities that give them an edge, from social networks and experience, upon graduation.

The next level in higher education is state (nonflagship) universities. These universities prepare students for roles in local leadership positions and midlevel management. Community colleges may help people access white-collar work or management of low-wage work, such as retail.

Funding for Higher Education. Higher education was once viewed as a public good that was well funded by state governments. States now give far less support to their public universities and colleges, which must therefore rely more

Bachelor's Degree Attainment by Age Twenty-Four by Family Income Quartile, 1970–2015

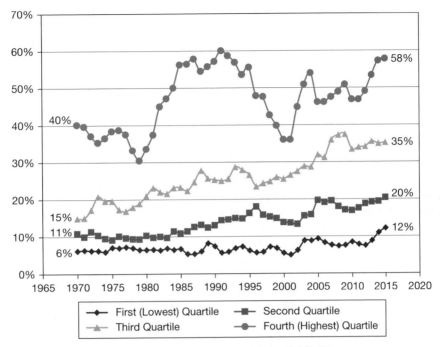

Source: Indicators of High Education Equity in the United States, 2017 Historical Trend Report. Reprinted with permission from The Pell Institute.

on student tuition for funding. As Figure 12.5 indicates, on average, state funding for public higher education has declined by 16 percent since 2008 (Mitchell, Leachman, and Masterson 2016; Seltzer 2018).

Affirmative Action in College Admissions. Higher education officials recognized the value of diversity and the barriers that many racial minority students faced competing on a "level" admissions playing field. In the 1960s and 1970s, selective public and private colleges and universities voluntarily engaged in affirmative action practices to recruit minority students and examine student applications in a more holistic way to identify and admit promising students from underrepresented minority groups (Harper and Reskin 2005, 362). These policies produced more minority college graduates, increased minority representation in graduate and professional programs, and helped corporations diversify their white-collar workforce.

In 1996, California passed a referendum that barred racial preference in admissions. Within a few years, Washington, Florida, Michigan, Nebraska, Arizona, and Oklahoma passed similar legislation. Minority enrollments declined. A series of court decisions determined that it is constitutional to consider race only as part of individualized assessments of each applicant

Affirmative action is a mechanism used to ensure greater racial and ethnic diversity in higher education.

AP Photo/Paul Sakuma

Percentage Change in State Spending per Student, Inflation Adjusted, 2008–2016

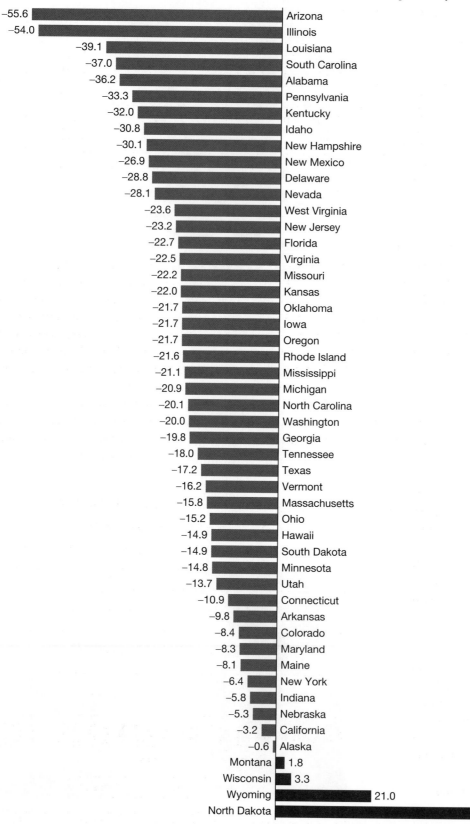

−55.6	Arizona
−54.0	Illinois
−39.1	Louisiana
−37.0	South Carolina
−36.2	Alabama
−33.3	Pennsylvania
−32.0	Kentucky
−30.8	Idaho
−30.1	New Hampshire
−26.9	New Mexico
−28.8	Delaware
−28.1	Nevada
−23.6	West Virginia
−23.2	New Jersey
−22.7	Florida
−22.5	Virginia
−22.2	Missouri
−22.0	Kansas
−21.7	Oklahoma
−21.7	Iowa
−21.7	Oregon
−21.6	Rhode Island
−21.1	Mississippi
−20.9	Michigan
−20.1	North Carolina
−20.0	Washington
−19.8	Georgia
−18.0	Tennessee
−17.2	Texas
−16.2	Vermont
−15.8	Massachusetts
−15.2	Ohio
−14.9	Hawaii
−14.9	South Dakota
−14.8	Minnesota
−13.7	Utah
−10.9	Connecticut
−9.8	Arkansas
−8.4	Colorado
−8.3	Maryland
−8.1	Maine
−6.4	New York
−5.8	Indiana
−5.3	Nebraska
−3.2	California
−0.6	Alaska
Montana	1.8
Wisconsin	3.3
Wyoming	21.0
North Dakota	46.0

Source: Center on Budget and Policy Priorities, "A Lost Decade in Higher Education Funding State Cuts Have Driven Up Tuition and Reduced Quality," Michael Mitchell, Michael Leachman, and Kathleen Masterson, August 23, 2017. Reprinted with permission.

Educational Attainment by Race and Hispanic Origin

	Less Than High School	High School Graduate	Some College but No Degree	Associate's Degree	Bachelor's Degree	Graduate or Professional Degree
Total population	4.1%	28.8%	16.3%	4.3%	21.3%	12.8%
Non-Hispanic White	1.5%	28.3%	16.6%	4.8%	23.7%	14.3%
Asian	5.4%	20.2%	9.4%	2.0%	30.5%	24.3%
Black	3.2%	33.0%	20.1%	4.2%	15.1%	8.8%
Hispanic	16.1%	31.0%	14.4%	3.3%	12.2%	5.0%

Source: U.S. Census Bureau. 2019. "Table 1. Educational Attainment of the Population 18 Years and Over, by Age, Sex, Race, and Hispanic Origin: 2018." Accessed July 26, 2019. https://www.census.gov/data/tables/2018/demo/education-attainment/cps-detailed-tables.html.

(largely impossible for large schools that receive tens of thousands of applicants each year). Schools have used a number of strategies to remain within these rulings while pursuing diversity. Some tried class-based affirmative action strategies. Income-based policies promote social class diversity but do not achieve strong minority representation (Harper and Reskin 2005, 363; Wilson 1999, 97, 99). Table 12.1 shows that Whites and Asians continue to enjoy far higher levels of educational attainment than do Blacks and Hispanics. However, as noted in Chapter 9, the diverse ethnic groups that constitute the Asian population in the United States include a full range of economic and social experiences that, as with all other groups, affect school experiences, performance, access to higher education, and overall attainment.

In addition to court battles in recent years, the transition from President Obama to President Trump brought significant changes to administrative guidance on the implementation of affirmative action policies. Under President Trump's guidelines, institutions that continue race-conscious admissions may be subject to Justice Department investigation or lawsuits or may lose funding from the Education Department (Green, Apuzzo, and Benner 2018).

Gender and Education

Historically, higher education has been the domain of men. As illustrated in Figure 12.6, it was not until the second wave of the women's movement in the 1960s and 1970s that women began entering higher education in significantly larger numbers. Today, however, more women than men attain a college degree. Men who do become educated see a greater return on their education than do women. Women have lower incomes than men. As noted in Chapter 8, men continue to hold an advantage in the labor market and earn higher salaries, even when they hold the same positions. Figure 12.7 illustrates the difference in median earnings for men and women overall and at each level of education.

▼ FIGURE 12.6

Bachelor's Degree or Higher by Sex, 1940–2017

Bachelor's or higher degree

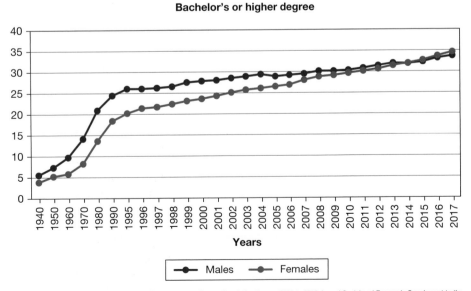

Sources: U.S. Census Bureau. 1947, and 1952 to 2002 March Current Population Survey, 2003 to 2015 Annual Social and Economic Supplement to the Current Population Survey (noninstitutionalized population, excluding members of the Armed Forces living in barracks); 1960 Census of Population, 1950 Census of Population, and 1940 Census of Population (resident population) as presented in Table A-1. "Years of School Completed by People 25 Years and Over, by Age and Sex: Selected Years 1940–2015."

RACIAL REPRESENTATION IN HIGHER EDUCATION

In this exercise, you will locate data from your own institutions and learn to interpret those data in relation to national figures to better understand what it means when a group is over- or underrepresented.

The goal of affirmative action in higher education is to create diverse educational environments, regardless of the composition of the larger population. How well do you think your college or university is doing at creating a diverse environment?

1. Using Microsoft Excel or Google Sheets, create a table just like the one pictured below.

2. Find the fact page of your institution's web site and record reported demographics (percentage of students from each listed racial or ethnic category, to the extent that you can match them to the categories used in the U.S. figures).

3. Compare your own institution with the percentage of eighteen- to twenty-four-year-olds enrolled in college in the United States by subtracting the U.S. figure for each category from the figure for your institution.

4. Positive numbers in the difference column indicate groups that are *overrepresented* on your campus compared with U.S. enrollments overall. A negative number indicates that a group is *underrepresented* on your campus compared with U.S. eighteen- to twenty-four-year-old enrollments.

	Percentage of Students at [Institution Name]	Percentage of 18- to 24-Year-Old College Enrollment in the United States (2016)*	Difference (Institution Percentage – U.S. Percentage)
White alone, not Hispanic		56	
Black or African American alone, not Hispanic		14	
American Indian and Alaska Native alone, not Hispanic		1	
Asian alone, not Hispanic		6	
Native Hawaiian and Other Pacific Islander alone, not Hispanic		< 0.5	
More than one race alone, not Hispanic		4	
Hispanic Origin		19	

a. Describe the racial composition of your institution (who is over- and underrepresented?).

b. What factors might affect the racial and ethnic makeup of the institution you attend?

c. On the basis of this quick look at the data, how would you say your institution is doing in creating a racially and ethnically diverse educational experience?

d. Do you think the school needs to do anything different in this regard? If so, what should they do, and what do you think it would accomplish?

Median Weekly Earnings by Sex and Educational Attainment: Full-Time Workers, Ages 25 and Older

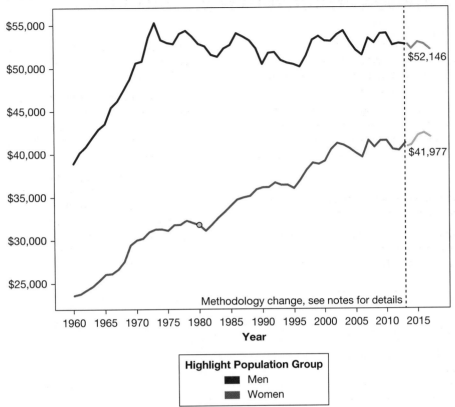

Source: U.S. Department of Labor. 2019. "Median Weekly Earnings by Sex and Educational Attainment: Full-Time Workers, Ages 25 and Older." Accessed July 26, 2019. https://www.dol.gov/wb/stats/earnings.htm.

Check Your Understanding

- How did the post–World War II GI Bill change the face of higher education?

- Why do college completion rates remain below 10 percent for low-income students?

- In what ways do the tiers of higher education reflect the class structure?

- How has public funding for higher education changed in recent decades?

- What is the purpose of affirmative action? What has happened in places where race was removed from consideration in favor of class-based color-blind affirmative action?

- Do men who become educated see a greater return on their education than do women?

Global Education and Global Inequality

12.5 What are the central issues facing global education today?

Today, both individuals and nations compete in a global economy. And educational systems must prepare citizens to work in a global marketplace. To do this, educational institutions must continually adapt to changing economic forces and teach students how to interact effectively with people from other countries and cultures.

Giving U.S. Students a Global Perspective

A global economy demands international knowledge and experience. From March 2017 to March 2018, the Student

THE IMPORTANCE OF A GLOBAL PERSPECTIVE FOR TODAY'S WORKFORCE?

In this exercise, you will explore the potential value of international experiences and perspectives to your own workforce readiness.

1. Write down a response to the following question: How do international experiences and perspectives improve workforce readiness in today's economy?

2. Share your response with the person next to you and combine your answers to make the most thorough response you can.

3. Together, write answers to the following questions that you are prepared to share: Does the average college student (a) in the United States and (b) at your school have the opportunity to have an international experience in college? Why? Given your answers, how will this affect the U.S. economy and socioeconomic inequality in the United States?

and Exchange Visitor Program reported more than 1.2 million foreign students studying in the United States (U.S. Immigration and Customs Enforcement 2018). By contrast, just 332,727 U.S. students (1.6 percent) enrolled at institutions of higher education studied abroad during the 2016–2017 academic year (NAFSA 2019).

A 2016 survey found that six out of ten employers around the world value applicants with international student experience more highly than similar candidates without such experience, and more than 80 percent said that they actively sought applicants who have studied abroad

(Loveland and Morris 2018). Individual workers, companies, and the nation would benefit from more study-abroad experiences for college students (Farrugia and Sanger 2017; Loveland and Morris 2018).

Global Educational Parity Efforts

Like domestic inequality, global inequality affects and is affected by educational attainment. Education and health are essential precursors to economic development and the basis for addressing all other social concerns (Rosling 2007). In 2000, at the World Education Forum in Dakar, Senegal, 164 governments agreed on a plan for meeting some key education goals by 2015. The international effort yielded positive results. They reduced the number of children and adolescents out of school by half, increased school attendance dramatically, and achieved greater gender parity, particularly in primary education. Still, significant gaps remain: 55 million primary school–age children remain out of school globally (International Bank for Reconstruction and Development/The World Bank 2016), about 100 million do not complete primary education, and many leave primary education without basic skills (UNESCO 2015). Continued efforts seek to reach more children and to devote greater attention to improving education quality.

Developing nations are often not able to provide education to all of their children, widening global inequality.

AP Photo/Ton Koene/VWPics

SUPPORTING LIFE CHANCES FOR OUR MOST VULNERABLE POPULATIONS

GABRIELLA C. GONZALEZ

As a sociologist of education and immigration, I learned all about Marx, Weber, and Durkheim; about social capital and the strength of weak ties; about inequality and its effects on children's life chances; and about social stratification and how schools act as organizations to either reproduce the status quo or propel change. I felt empowered by how statistical analysis of large data sets could find objective truth: relationships and correlations that otherwise would be obscured by political rhetoric. I was enraptured by how ethnography and qualitative methods could unearth the meaning and feelings of populations we studied and answer the question of "Why is that?"

But I wanted more. I wanted to roll up my sleeves in schools, with students, with teaching professionals. I wanted to make a difference.

In 2002, I joined a nonpartisan think tank, the RAND Corporation, which enabled me to make a difference through policy-based research. Rather than examining social problems from the sidelines, I now spend my days on interdisciplinary team-based projects (often with psychologists, anthropologists, economists, or political scientists) working directly with countries and school districts to enact change and make a direct impact on the lives of the children in most need of support.

From 2003 through 2007, I helped the country of Qatar develop curriculum standards and assessments for their schoolchildren—using sociologically based understandings of how language, ethnicity, and identity formation could affect students' approach to learning. I am now in the United States applying my sociological training to work in urban school districts. I've worked closely with district officials, principals, and teachers in Pittsburgh, Baltimore, New Haven, Connecticut, and Jackson, Mississippi, to evaluate the effectiveness of new education reform efforts, the rebuilding of school facilities, and programs to improve school climate and safety on students' social and emotional well-being and on their academic achievement and college going.

Each project I lead brings a sociological lens to ensure that the interplay of social structures, family background, peer networks, race, class, and gender is not lost in how school districts develop and implement policies and practices to improve schooling.

What have I learned? Without considering the social context and struggles in which our students live, no policy or practice will make a dent. Without getting full buy-in and support from families and teachers, the shiniest, most innovative, and potentially effective effort will fail—miserably. Not because it wasn't a good idea, but because it wasn't implemented to its full potential. Or worse, no one thought it mattered.

Discussion Question: Why would someone think that efforts to improve schools don't matter? What would be your (sociological) response if someone said that to you?

Gabriella C. Gonzalez is a RAND Corporation senior sociologist with a PhD in sociology from Harvard University.

Security concerns keep many children out of school, and funding for education remains a problem worldwide (UNESCO 2015, i–ii). Lower income children are less likely to attend school than higher income children. Gender disparities in primary education declined significantly between 2000 and 2015, but progress has been slower in secondary schools (UNESCO 2015).

Finland: Global Leader in Quality Education

Finland stands out as a top-performing country on standardized tests of secondary students. Most notable is the consistency of performance across schools and among students within schools (Organisation for Economic Co-operation and Development 2010, 128). The gap between the highest performing and lowest performing schools and students is quite small (p. 128).

The Finnish system is relatively new and is the result of a national effort to establish a single compulsory system that educates all children without tracking (Organisation for Economic Co-operation and Development 2010, 128–31). The upper grades offer a vocational path, but that path also prepares students for higher education in technological fields and is no less rigorous than the academic track (p. 120). The system is learner centered and emphasizes happiness and well-being. Teachers assign little homework, and students do not take a standardized test until they apply to college (Ravitch 2014). These approaches require highly qualified and engaged teachers. All teachers must hold a master's degree, and they are generally drawn from the pool of high academic performers (Organisation for Economic Co-operation and Development 2010, 121; Ravitch 2014, 261).

Finland is a society that has seen its investments in education pay off in significant economic growth tied to a highly qualified and innovative workforce. Although the United States is larger and more diverse, there are lessons in the Finnish experience (e.g., in teacher recruitment and training). Many sociologists, such as Gabriella Gonzalez, featured in the Sociologists in Action box, work to improve the lives of children through designing education policies and curricula.

Check Your Understanding

- Why do U.S. workers need to be internationally competent?

- List three key issues the World Education Forum seeks to address.

- In what ways is Finland's school system different from what you have learned about the U.S. education system? How might this example inform U.S. discussions of school reform?

Leveling the Playing Field: Public Policy and Education in the United States

12.6 How do policy debates surrounding pre-K, K–12, and higher education all revolve around the tension between public education and individual choice and responsibility for accessing opportunities and achieving success?

Recent policy debates about public education in the United States center on a desire to improve the quality and competitiveness of the system. Some argue that market-based models are the best way to achieve these goals (Campi 2019; Ferrare and Setari 2017). Others argue that directing greater attention to equalizing quality within and across public schools is the best way to improve educational outcomes and global competitiveness (Allen and Gawlik 2018; Parker et al. 2018).

Pre-K Education

Proponents of the value of quality early education and care argue for universal access from birth to age five and rigorous education and training for birth-to-five caregivers and teachers. Ninety percent of the brain's architecture develops by age five (Markowitz, Bassok, and Hamre 2017; Romeo et al. 2018; California Newsreel 2014). This means that the experiences of children from birth through age five are vital to later outcomes (Center on the Developing Child at Harvard University 2016).

Research suggests that public investments in quality pre-K education and care can reduce public spending on special education and social welfare programs. When families have access to affordable quality care, more parents work. The rise in employment reduces child poverty and increases tax revenue to help pay for the public provision of care (Whitehurst 2017).

The Abecedarian Project. The Abecedarian Project examined the long-term impacts of quality pre-K education and care. Researchers randomly selected children born between 1972 and 1977 and assigned them to the intervention group or a control group. The intervention group received full-time, high-quality education and childcare from infancy through age five. Educational games and activities supported social, emotional, and cognitive development. Researchers followed up with both groups at ages twelve, fifteen, twenty-one, thirty, and thirty-five, and the results were encouraging: kids enrolled in the Abecedarian pre-K program were four times more likely to attend college than kids in the control group (California Newsreel 2014; Temple and Reynolds 2007).

K–12 Education

In 1983, the National Commission on Excellence in Education released "A Nation at Risk: The Imperative for Educational Reform." The report found that U.S. schools underperformed and failed to produce a globally competitive workforce (National Commission on Excellence in Education 1983; Ravitch 2010, 2014). Concerns about the failure of U.S. schools gave rise to market-based models for improving quality, lowering costs, and increasing accountability culminated in the 2001 No Child Left Behind Act (NCLB) (Ravitch 2014; Ravitch 2016).

NCLB increased standardized assessments, raised penalties for low performance, expanded school choice through charter schools and vouchers, monitored teacher quality through student performance, enacted a "reading first" approach aimed at ensuring that all children read at grade level by the end of third grade, and consolidated bilingual and immigrant education programs (U.S. House of Representatives 2001). The most apparent results of this reform were a dramatic increase in class time spent preparing

WHICH PUBLIC SCHOOLS HAVE THE MOST MONEY TO SPEND?

Public schools in the United States receive their funding through a combination of local, state, and federal sources. Local funding come from property taxes tied to the value of homes in the area. As a result, schools in wealthy neighborhoods, where home values are higher, typically receive more funding.

In this online activity, you will explore how school spending has changed over time and how that has

affected the funding gap among states, using data from the National Education Association's "Rankings and Estimates of School Statistics" report.

*Requires the Vantage version of *Sociology in Action*.

▼ FIGURE 12.8

Estimated per Pupil Public Elementary and Secondary School Expenditures (State)

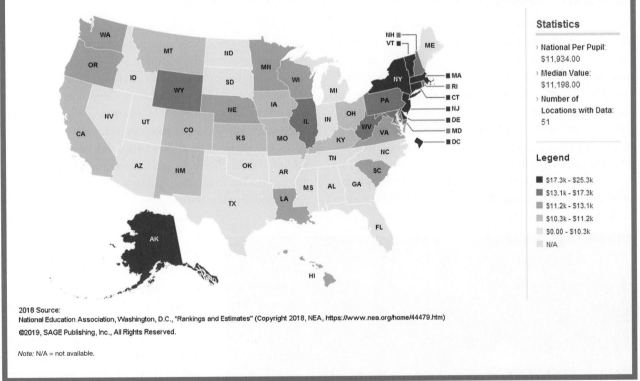

Statistics

› **National Per Pupil:**
$11,934.00

› **Median Value:**
$11,198.00

› **Number of Locations with Data:**
51

Legend

■ $17.3k - $25.3k
■ $13.1k - $17.3k
■ $11.2k - $13.1k
■ $10.3k - $11.2k
□ $0.00 - $10.3k
□ N/A

2018 Source:
National Education Association, Washington, D.C., "Rankings and Estimates" (Copyright 2018, NEA, https://www.nea.org/home/44479.htm)
©2019, SAGE Publishing, Inc., All Rights Reserved.

Note: N/A = not available.

for and administering standardized tests, an increase in **school choice** options, and the rapid growth of charter schools and the use of vouchers. School choice options vary by location but can include the ability to attend the public school of the family's choosing, attend a charter school, or use a voucher to subsidize attendance at a private school.

Charter Schools and Vouchers. Supporters of market models argue that when individuals are free to choose and

to maximize their own benefit, the cumulative enterprise also benefits. Advocates of this movement argue that if a school falls short in providing services, consumer-citizens can opt for higher quality alternatives and generate a virtuous cycle of improvement. The two primary mechanisms for creating a market in public primary and secondary education are charter schools and vouchers.

Beginning in the 1990s, states began passing laws authorizing **charter schools**, publicly funded schools

APPLYING CHOICE OUTSIDE OF SCHOOLS

In this exercise, you will use an analogy to consider the potential impacts of using school choice logic for other public goods.

Your instructor will place the class in small groups to discuss the following brain exercise. Be sure to choose who in your group will report back to the class the issues raised.

Imagine if individual citizens were able to determine where their shares of per capita funding for roads got used. Everyone could choose where their shares

of federal, state, and city and county funds went for interstates, state roads, local roads, or even private roads on their own private property or the private property of businesses and organizations they frequent. If they use their allotments for private roads, they can of course also supplement with their own private funds.

As a group, consider the following questions: What might the unintended consequences be? How might this affect the movement of goods and the provision of services across the country? Record key takeaways from your discussion and be prepared to share them with the class.

---

that are established under a charter and governed by parents, educators, community groups, or private organizations. The "charter" details the school's mission, curriculum or philosophy, students to be served, performance goals, evaluation plans, and commitments. Depending on state law, charter status may free these schools from some of the legal and bureaucratic constraints of the traditional public school structure and thus allow greater innovation. After more than two decades, however, the effects of charter schools on student achievement appear to be mixed. Overall, charter

school students do not necessarily perform better than other public school students on tests such as the SAT or ACT, but more of their students go on to college than those in regular public schools (Berends 2015).

School voucher programs also began in the 1990s. **Vouchers** are certificates of government funding that make each pupil's state funds portable, allowing parents to choose to use their child's funds at a public or private school of their choice. Proponents argue that all students are entitled to their state funding allotment, and where they choose to use it should be up to them. Others argue that states are not funding individuals but a system. When vouchers are used to pay for private education, needed funds are removed from the public schools, and working-class taxpayers subsidize wealthy kids' attendance at private schools.

The market approach assumes that consumers are knowledgeable and engaged. Students whose parents research and discern the best options will benefit from market models, while the children of parents who lack the time, ability, or interest in researching options will be disadvantaged by the market model and left in failing schools. Critics argue that increased use of vouchers will further segregate schools by class as better educated and well-resourced parents will use vouchers to send their children to

The purpose of the No Child Left Behind Act was to improve the quality of education for all children, but the legislation also resulted in increased time spent taking standardized exams.
AP Photo/Charles Dharapak

WHAT COULD IMPROVE PUBLIC EDUCATION?

In this exercise you will discuss changes that could improve the public education system in the United States.

Your instructor will create small groups and ask you to discuss the following question. Be sure to select one person to record your response for the group.

How do you think the United States could change the public education system to level the playing field and produce better outcomes? Be specific about policies, practices, or approaches that could make a difference

---

the best schools, diminishing the resources of the public schools they leave behind and filling those public schools with students whose parents likely have less education and lower incomes. This creates a feedback loop going the wrong direction. Detractors argue that segregating students in this way will exacerbate existing problems in the public school system and further separate the haves from the have-nots.

Nearly twenty years after the implementation of NCLB, concerns about the quality and competitiveness of American schools remain (Ravitch 2014; Porter and Rivkin 2012). Test scores have not improved for disadvantaged groups (Strauss 2015). The emphasis on high-stakes testing has come under fire as physical education, arts, and humanities courses have been cut back to funnel resources to test preparation (Ravitch 2016; Layton 2015; Supovitz 2016).

Responding to this criticism, Congress passed the Every Student Succeeds Act (ESSA) in 2015, in an effort to address some of the unintended negative consequences of NCLB. Notably, ESSA deemphasized punitive responses, such as schools losing funding or being closed down for persistent poor student performance, and emphasized the use of incentives to improve school and teacher quality (U.S. House of Representatives 2015). The act also reduces onerous testing requirements while maintaining a focus on accountability (The White House 2015). With the election of President Donald Trump and his appointment of school choice advocate Betsy DeVos as secretary of education, we see a greater emphasis on market-based approaches to school reform.

CONSIDER THIS

What do you think are the biggest strengths and weaknesses of a market-based approach to school reform?

The Future of Public Education and Democracy

As noted, state governments across the country have cut funding to institutions of higher education. They also have done little to provide opportunities for rigorous high-tech training and higher education outside the traditional college setting to build a qualified workforce for new manufacturing jobs.

Early proponents of public education argued that democratic societies require an educated citizenry capable of making informed and responsible decisions about who will govern (Sadovnik 2007, 5). However, the 2018 edition of *The Nation's Report Card* indicates that only 12 percent of twelfth grade students were proficient or above in U.S. history, 20 percent in geography, and 24 percent in civics (National Center for Education Statistics 2018a). At a time when alternative facts and fake news proliferate, lack of knowledge about key elements of civics and history is dangerous.

For democracy to survive in the United States, the public K–12 and higher education systems must produce critical thinkers and problem solvers who can discern evidence-based facts from propaganda, who understand the role of legitimate institutions in protecting the integrity and relatively smooth functioning of U.S. democracy, and who can demand full discussion of policy options with clear evidence to support decisions. A democratic government only works if its citizens know enough to make informed choices about the policies proposed by candidates for office. An uneducated voter is an easily manipulated voter.

Looking at education from a sociological perspective, the benefits of more educated workers and citizens are clear. Education lays the foundation for progress, economic success, democracy, and quality of life. Our education system should leave no doubt about this in the minds of those who pass through its doors.

How has your education prepared you to be a knowledgeable voter and an active citizen? Now imagine if every other student had a similar experience. What are the ramifications for our democracy?

Check Your Understanding

- What are the arguments in favor of market models (charters and vouchers) for improving public education?

- What are some unintended negative consequences of applying market models to public education?

- Explain the arguments for and against publicly funded childcare, public K–12 schools, and public higher education.

Conclusion

Education is an essential institution in society. It provides the foundation for development and innovation, and it is the centerpiece of the American belief in meritocratic success. Educated people can shape their lives and their society.

A sociological perspective can help us understand and shape the educational institution to more fully reflect the meritocratic and democratic values it serves. Sociology provides a similar opportunity to examine health care as an institution. Good health is important for both individuals and society. However, not everyone has access to healthy environments or health care. The next chapter will explore the power dynamics behind health, healthy environments, and health care systems.

REVIEW

12.1 What does it mean to look at education as a social institution?

Education comprises roles, rules, and routines that provide consistency across time and place and are slow to change. These patterns help individuals—students, staff, and parents—move from one organization to another within the institution and limit the influence of individual personalities on the functioning of organizations.

12.2 How do historical moment, the social structure, and changing systems of production shape the functions of education over time and across place?

Education reflects the mode of production across time and place. In preindustrial societies, parents had their children work alongside them, learning the skills and modeling the behaviors necessary to meet basic needs.

Formal schooling emerged with the industrial system of manufacturing that separated workers from their homes and required new skills to meet the needs of a growing and diverse economic system. Production required basic reading, writing, and math skills and benefited from a system that socialized workers to

show up on time and conform to authority. Compulsory public schooling emerged to meet these needs.

In a service and knowledge economy, soft skills, including communication, depth of knowledge, and problem solving, are essential. Today's economy requires strong critical thinking, collaborative work habits, and creative innovation.

12.3 How do functionalism, conflict theory, and symbolic interaction approach and explain education as an institution?

Functionalists note that education provides children with secondary socialization, which helps young people learn to interact within organizations, with peers, and in nonfamily group settings. Schools play an important role developing a national identity, a qualified workforce, and an educated citizenry. Schools also serve latent functions of providing universal childcare for children ages five to eighteen years and regulating entry into the labor force.

Conflict theorists point out that in the United States, school structures, resources, and the content of the curriculum all reflect larger systems of social inequality. Schools tend to favor middle-class norms and values. Educators perceive and treat children on the basis of elements of behavior that are largely reflective of parents' income and education. From physical structures and course offerings to tracking and discipline, education systems favor those with more power and higher status.

Symbolic interactionists focus on interactions within schools and how they lead to cultural reproduction. Schools transmit a hidden curriculum of cultural values and beliefs. The hidden curriculum supports and promotes dominant ideologies about the economy and system of governance but may also reflect inequalities embedded in stereotypes tied to race, class, gender, and other social characteristics. These messages shape students' perceptions of others, their self-esteem, and their behaviors and thus produce outcomes that reflect the social norms, rules, and stereotypes of the culture.

12.4 How does education reproduce social inequality?

School systems reflect the inequalities of the labor market and race and class segregation in housing. This affects physical aspects of schools, the curriculum offered, parent engagement, and the learning readiness and educational focus of the student population. Schools assess student potential and ability on the basis of measures of performance and behavior that favor children from educated middle-class backgrounds. Schools track students on the basis of these assessments and provide different levels of challenge and rigor, preparing students for distinct education and career paths. More often than not, the system funnels children into the same relative class status as their parents.

12.5 What are the central issues facing global education today?

In an increasingly globalized world, cultural and international competency is essential, making international education more important than ever. Low literacy and school attendance rates in many poor and war-torn nations and neglect for the education of girls leave many areas of the world unable to develop and progress. Meanwhile, among developed nations, Finland provides some of the best education in the world by focusing on equal quality education for all citizens, hiring only highly qualified teachers, and offering a holistic approach that focuses on child happiness and well-being.

12.6 How do policy debates surrounding pre-K, K–12, and higher education all revolve around the tension between public education and individual choice and responsibility for accessing opportunities and achieving success?

Childcare and preschool, a high-quality public school system for all, and publicly supported higher education all work to provide equal opportunity to all citizens. Market-based approaches, such as charter schools and vouchers, rely on citizens to be actively engaged critical consumers, which may leave students with fewer resources behind. Current approaches to pre-K and higher education place quality programs out of reach for many. Current policy debates revolve around how to pay for and hold accountable an education system that needs to meet the changing needs of a diverse population in a knowledge-based economy.

Moves to privatization are counter to traditional understandings of the public goods provided by education, including its role in producing an educated electorate. The U.S. public education system has a vital role to play in teaching citizens to think critically, engage in civil society, and discern between facts and fake news or propaganda. Without a high-quality public education system, the health of democratic institutions is at risk.

KEY TERMS

charter schools   253

education   233

hidden curriculum   236

human capital   240

school choice   253

secondary socialization   236

social cohesion   237

tracking   242

vouchers   254

CHAPTER 13

EXPERIENCING HEALTH, ILLNESS, AND MEDICAL CARE

Amy Irby-Shasanmi

Illness is socially patterned. The water crisis that began in Flint, Michigan, in 2014, which resulted in illnesses due to high levels of lead exposure, disproportionately affected low-income residents and people of color.

©Bill Pugliano/Stringer/Getty Images

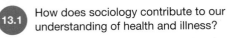
13.1 How does sociology contribute to our understanding of health and illness?

13.2 In what ways are health and illness social experiences and not simply biological phenomena?

13.3 What is medicalization?

13.4 How are an individual's health behaviors (e.g., lack of exercise, unhealthy eating) influenced by social factors?

13.5 How do sex and gender, race and ethnicity, and social class affect health and life expectancy?

13.6 What are the major issues facing the U.S. health care system?

What Does Sociology Have to Do with Health, Illness, and Medical Care?

13.1 How does sociology contribute to our understanding of health and illness?

Have you ever wondered why some groups of people live longer than others? Or have you thought about how your chances of having asthma, or lead poisoning, or many other health problems relate to where you live? A sociological understanding of health and illness can help you find answers to these questions—and many more.

Sociologists study health and illness because illness is socially patterned (recall that one of the core commitments of sociology is to observe social patterns). Who gets sick is not random. Recognizing health patterns allows us to look at why they exist and find ways to address them.

How Sociology Helps Medical Professionals (and Everyone) Understand Health and Illness

Since 2013, the Medical College Admission Test, the admission test for medical school, has included a section that covers the social sciences, including many of the concepts taught in an introductory sociology course. Medical schools encourage students interested in medical school to take an introduction to sociology course, like the one in which you are now enrolled. The Association of American Medical Colleges (AAMC) believes that physicians should recognize societal and culture effects on health as they treat and interact with patients (Warshaw 2017).

A sociology background helps medical professionals understand how social factors such as social relationships, neighborhoods, and socioeconomic status influence health. Darrell Kirch, president of the AAMC, said, "Being a good physician is about more than scientific knowledge. It is about understanding people—how they think, interact, and make decisions" (Kirch 2012). His words, though aimed at future medical students, apply to almost any occupation whose main tasks involve interacting and communicating.

A sociological perspective can help you understand how social factors also affect your own health. Your health is what keeps you alive. Thus, it makes sense to understand as many factors (biological, psychological, social, etc.) that influence this most valuable resource. As the poet Virgil (and the nineteenth-century philosopher Ralph Waldo Emerson) noted, "The greatest wealth is health." This chapter highlights the social factors that shape how sick or well we are.

Sociologists who study health and illness, often called medical sociologists, generally focus on one of the following three broad topics: experiences with illness, health disparities, or the health care system. Sociologists in the

It is important for medical professionals to understand their patients' social relationships.
©Bunlue Nantaprom/EyeEm/Getty Images

AMY IRBY-SHASANMI

As a high school student, I was the editor of my school's newspaper and interned for my county's local newspaper. I had every intention to be a journalist. However, in college, I ended up taking a course in sociology and eventually majored in sociology. For me, sociology helped explain issues of inequality that I saw in my own life and in the lives of others.

My desire to pursue a PhD in sociology happened at the end of my college career. In the first semester of my

senior year, I studied abroad in Brazil. The theme of the trip centered on social justice. Our main assignment was to conduct an independent study project. I chose to carry out a research project on Movimento Sem Terra (the Landless Farmer's Movement). I fell in love with research and decided to pursue a PhD in sociology so that I could conduct sociological research and teach sociology.

---

first category may explore how people cope with a chronic illness (an illness that lasts for months or indefinitely) or mental health issues. Sociologists who focus on health disparities examine social patterns of health and illness, more specifically, how race, ethnicity, sex, gender, and socioeconomic status affect health and disease patterns. They study how this social distribution of health and illness is, in part, rooted in inequality, shaped by social factors such as discrimination, environmental racism, and government policies (e.g., health care, gun control). Sociologists who examine the health care system look at how doctors interact with patients, what it is like to engage with the U.S. health care system, inequalities in medical treatment, and issues related to a lack of health insurance.

CONSIDER THIS

Consider government policies that relate to health (e.g., universal health care coverage vs. private insurance, gun control policies, regulations controlling how much companies can pollute). Now, imagine if the government used a "hands off" approach and did not create rules and regulations regarding these issues. How might that affect society—and your own life?

Check Your Understanding

- Why do sociologists study health and illness?
- Why should medical providers have a sociological perspective?

- What can you gain from studying health and illness through a sociological perspective?
- What are three broad topics of health that medical sociologists typically study?

The Illness Experience

13.2   In what ways are health and illness social experiences and not simply biological phenomena?

Illness affects more than a person's body. It can also affect a person emotionally, economically, and socially. This is particularly common with **chronic illnesses**, diseases that last for several months or years or even persist until death. Chronic illnesses (e.g., cancer, diabetes, heart disease, HIV infection) often have such a profound effect on a person's life that they cause **biographical disruption**, disturbing a person's usual activities and social life (Bury 1982). **Acute illnesses**, on the other hand, come on and generally leave relatively quickly—though they can cause death. Examples include the common cold, influenza, and chicken pox.

We do not experience illness in isolation. Take, for example, a person diagnosed with cancer. How might cancer affect her, her family, and her friends? The treatments for cancer can take an average of eight hours, as many as three times a week, at an outpatient infusion center. In addition, a person who has cancer will need someone to drive her to treatment. That drive may be a long one. If so, it may be impossible for the driver (as well as the patient) to work a full-time job. The cancer experience will also affect her social life, because of exhaustion and feeling sick from

EXPERIENCING ILLNESS

In this exercise you will experiment with what it feels like to have diabetes.

Imagine that suddenly you are diagnosed with diabetes. You are prescribed two pills to be taken three times a day with a nutritious meal. For two days, be sure to eat three nutritious meals a day. Use your imagination. Pretend to take two pills after every meal and write down the date and the time you ate and took the pills. The side effects of the pills include diarrhea, loss of appetite, and nausea (all real symptoms of some medications used to manage diabetes). You are not allowed to drink alcohol while taking this medication.

Write a short (about one page) essay addressing the following questions.

1. How successful were you at remembering to take your medication?

2. How might this physical illness affect your mental health?

3. How might it affect your social relationships and social life?

---

treatment. She may also want to avoid friends who either want to focus on her cancer or act as if it does not exist, because of their own discomfort with it. In this scenario, cancer is experienced biologically but also socially, emotionally, and economically.

CONSIDER THIS

How might the progressive effects of rheumatoid arthritis affect a person's social life, marriage, finances, mental health, and sense of identity?

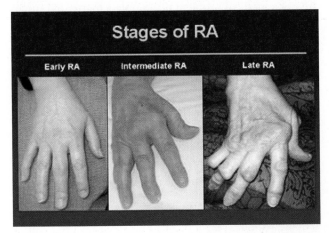

Stages of RA

Early RA · Intermediate RA · Late RA

Stages of rheumatoid arthritis in the hand.
Courtesy of James Heilman, MD, licensed under a Creative Commons Attribution-Share Alike 3.0 Unported license

The Sick Role and the Impact of Illness on Families

Talcott Parsons laid the foundation for understanding people's experience with illness. His theory fits within a structural functionalist approach, which you learned about in Chapter 2. Parsons believed that being a healthy, productive member of society is functional for society and that too many sick people would harm society. Therefore, sick people must behave in certain ways and carry out a "sick role" to have their lack of productivity excused. Fulfilling the sick role requires people who say that they are sick to (a) go to a doctor and (b) adhere to medical recommendations. Those who do so will not be blamed for their illness and lack of productivity (Parsons 1951; Collyer 2018). This theory assumes that physicians know best and does not distinguish among illnesses (e.g., a sexually transmitted infection for which some people might blame the sick person vs. breast cancer).

The sick role focuses on the impact of illness on society. Illnesses, however, also affect families. For example, a child's ear infection requires a parent to take the child to a doctor. This may entail taking time off work—which could mean a reduction in pay. A chronically ill child, partner, or parent may necessitate leaving work to care for and transport the sick person to and from treatments. Other people in the family may feel neglected when care providers spend time and energy on the sick member of the family.

Illness also can lead to financial instability for families. As we discuss later in the chapter, a combination of lack of insurance or underinsurance and high medical costs in the United States can make illness the cause of financial disaster, causing enormous strain on families. Imagine if you suddenly became seriously ill, requiring around-the-clock care. Who would take care of you? How would it affect your family?

Check Your Understanding

- Other than biologically or physiologically, how can illness affect a person?
- What are examples of chronic illnesses?
- What impact can illness have on families?

Medicalization

13.3 What is medicalization?

Medicalization, the process by which conditions become seen as medical conditions, also shapes how people experience illness. As the health institution has grown, more conditions once seen as moral failures or simply bad behavior, such as alcoholism and hyperactivity, have been deemed illnesses. Other medicalized conditions include erectile dysfunction and excessive gambling. Today, people with these conditions can seek medical treatment, and most people perceive them as illness rather than deviance.

In the United States, most people once considered childbirth a natural bodily process that did not usually require medical intervention. In many parts of the world,

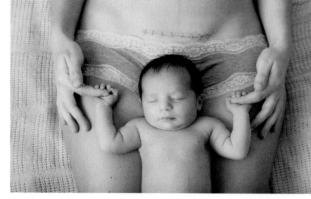

The prevalence of cesarean sections in the United States is one example of how certain conditions become medicalized.
©Westend61/Getty Images

still, it is the norm for women to deliver babies at home with midwives. Today, in the United States, however, most women choose to have a surgeon (usually an obstetric and gynecologic surgeon) oversee delivery in a hospital. One of the results is that far more women undergo surgery (cesarean sections) to deliver their children in the United States than in many other areas of the world. One in three births in the United States involves surgery (Martin et al. 2018). However, the World Health Organization estimates that only 10 percent of births should be performed by cesarean section (Betran et al. 2016).

Medicalization and Marketing

Medicalization has grown more pervasive in the United States over the past several decades, encouraged, in part, by direct-to-consumer advertising by the pharmaceutical industry (Conrad 2007). How many times have you seen commercials for drugs that treat erectile dysfunction, fibromyalgia, psoriasis, or some other illness? Illnesses once rarely discussed (or even treated as illnesses) now bring big drug sales through prescriptions.

Today, the average TV viewer in the United States sees nine prescription drug advertisements each day. Direct-to-consumer advertising substantially increased in the late 1990s, when the Food and Drug Administration (FDA) eased up on a rule that previously required the pharmaceutical industry to provide extensive information about the potential side effects of their drugs. In 2017, drug companies spent $5 billion on advertisements (Parekh and Shrank 2018).

One newly medicalized condition is hypotrichosis, a "less than normal" amount of hair on one's eyelashes (Segre 2018). For many people, short or sparse eyelashes are not a medical problem but simply a matter of human variation, much the same way that some people are born with thin hair while others are born with thicker strands of hair. Short, sparse eyelashes became viewed as a medical problem after a drug was discovered to treat it. Literally, the treatment led to the medicalization of the condition. Some glaucoma patients noticed that their eyelashes became more prominent when they used their glaucoma medication. Now, you can see advertisements for that same drug (Latisse) in beauty magazines such as *Allure*, aimed at those "suffering" from hypotrichosis.

CONSIDER THIS

Should prescription drugs be marketed to the public? Why?

"LONGER, DARKER, FULLER LASHES"

In this activity, you will compare and contrast two types of commercials, both about the length and thickness of eyelashes. One commercial focuses on eyelash length and thickness as a medical concern; the other focuses on eyelash length and thickness as a beautification or aesthetic concern.

Watch this Latisse commercial: https://www.youtube .com/watch?v=QWm4rGjf_38. After you watch the Latisse commercial, watch this mascara commercial: https://www.youtube.com/watch?v=gmF_So5H3wU.

Your instructor may ask you to simply record your answers or write them out in an essay form. You may also be asked to discuss your answers in class or in an online forum.

1. What is hypotrichosis?
2. How are the commercials similar and different?
3. Aside from those who use Latisse, what interest groups benefit from an increase in people being diagnosed with hypotrichosis?
4. What other mundane problems have been medicalized?

CONSIDER THIS

On the basis of this poster and the symptoms and scenarios that are highlighted, does social anxiety disorder seem like a mundane problem that many people experience, like an example of human variation, or like a mental condition? Might a person who is shy incorrectly assume that he or she has social anxiety from the way the poster is worded?

Pros and Cons of Medicalization

There are both positive and negative consequences of medicalization. For those who suffer from a problem that has been medicalized, they likely experience more understanding from friends, family, and the public when their problem is seen as a medical one instead of a moral one. Additionally, they may get access to medical treatment that can alleviate negative symptoms. Medicalization can create new problems, however. For example, once a problem becomes medicalized, treatment tends to be restricted to medical professionals, with an emphasis on medical techniques such as prescribing drugs and performing surgery, rather than on counseling or other treatments.

Another important possible negative consequence of medicalization is that we may overlook other possible causes for a condition. For example, increasing numbers of rambunctious and inattentive children these days receive a medical diagnosis of a chemical imbalance

SOCIAL ANXIETY DISORDER:
More Than Just Shyness

Are you extremely afraid of being judged by others?

Are you very self-conscious in everyday social situations?

Do you avoid meeting new people?

If you have been feeling this way for at least six months and these feelings make it hard for you to do everyday tasks—such as talking to people at work or school—you may have a **social anxiety disorder.**

A poster describing some aspects of social anxiety disorder.
NIH National Institute of Mental Health

ADHD Diagnoses through the Years

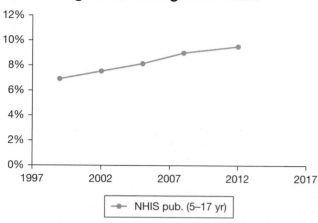

Source: CDC 2018b NHIS: National Health Interview Survey. Accessed October 1, 2018. https://www.cdc .gov/ncbddd/adhd/timeline.html.

(attention-deficit/hyperactivity disorder [ADHD]). As Figure 13.1 shows, the increase in diagnoses of ADHD has led some to question if these behaviors have become *over-medicalized* because of the increased numbers of ADHD medications approved by the FDA in the 1990s (Centers for Disease Control and Prevention 2018a). In medicalizing the problem, we fail to consider the social context, which may be at the root of the problem. For example, it could be the structure of the school day, such as too little recess time, that causes the child's behavior.

Check Your Understanding

- What is medicalization?

- What are some conditions that have been medicalized?

- Which industry is the driving force behind medicalization?

- What are some advantages of direct-to-consumer advertising? What are some disadvantages of direct-to-consumer advertising?

- What are some advantages of medicalization? What are some disadvantages of medicalization?

Explaining Health Disparities and Social Determinants of Health

13.4 How are an individual's health behaviors (e.g., lack of exercise, unhealthy eating) influenced by social factors?

Now we'll look into why some groups are healthier than others. If someone asked you, "What affects your health?" what would you say? Would you mention how much you

exercise? Whether you smoke? What you eat? How much stress you are under? What else? Now think about how your society and your place in it affect those aspects of your life.

Let's take exercise. A sociologist interested in health inequality would be interested in comparing rates of exercise across communities and looking at why some groups of people might exercise more than others. To do this, a sociologist might record the features of the neighborhood, such as whether there is access to sidewalks, walking trails, and (affordable) gyms and whether residents feel safe in their neighborhood. Crime rates affect exercise. Imagine that you live a neighborhood with high rates of gun and drug activity. You may very well feel uncomfortable walking or jogging in such a neighborhood. Furthermore, if you have children, you may prefer that they stay inside and play video games as opposed to playing outside and exercising, because of safety concerns. The Sociologists in Action feature in this chapter describes how one sociology student has tackled this issue.

Fundamental Cause Theory

Fundamental cause theory argues that socioeconomic status is the most important factor that explains disparities in health. Income constrains or expands access to resources that promote health (Link and Phelan 1995; Link et al. 2017). To illustrate this point, consider that a doctor asks two individuals who work for the same company to reduce their risk for heart disease. One of the individuals is the store manager of the company and is middle class; the other is a cashier who is part of the working class. To lower their risk for heart disease, the physician recommends that they exercise, eat healthy foods, and reduce stress.

The theory of fundamental cause predicts that the manager will be more likely (and able) to reduce her risk

Many Americans live in food deserts, where fast food may be the only accessible or affordable option.
©David McNew/Getty Images

IMPROVING COMMUNITY HEALTH THROUGH TRANSFORMING A PARK

TYESHA CRAWFORD

Sociology has helped me understand how society works and develop relationships with individuals and organizations to create change in society. Throughout my time in college, I've used my sociological skills to affect both my school, William Paterson University, and the larger community. In the process, I have met a wide variety of people and gained social capital that I have used to positively affect society and my own life.

In the summer of 2017, my EOF (Educational Opportunities Fund—an organization that provides support for students from educationally and economically disadvantaged backgrounds) counselor let me know of a job opening at the New Jersey Community Development Corporation (NJCDC) located in Paterson. I looked at what NJCDC does in Paterson, a city dealing with high poverty and crime rates, and was impressed. I had an interview and landed the job!

At NJCDC, I learned firsthand how environments affect the health of both communities and the individuals living in them. As part of a NJCDC project funded by New Jersey Health Initiatives, I conducted participant research with fifteen Paterson youth ages sixteen to twenty-one whom I recruited. Throughout the course of the year, we met with residents to learn about the area and how they thought it could be improved. One consistent theme in our findings revealed that residents needed a place where they felt safe to take their children to play outside. Residents said that they no longer felt safe at their neighborhood park. In part because of its decrepit condition, only homeless people used it. Many of the homeless people were drug users, and parents didn't feel that their children would be safe around them or the many needles they left on the grounds of the park. They wanted to retake their park and provide their children with a safe place to play outside of their apartments.

In the summer of 2018, we put our research findings into action and focused on making Lou Costello Park in Paterson more attractive, to encourage more families to bring their children to the park to play and send a message that the park is for children, rather than for adults to take drugs. As a Youth Cares coach, I guided the youth as they created their beautification plan and helped them make their vision a reality. We scraped, sanded, and repainted the lamp posts and the gazebo in the park—making them look brand new. The youth also turned all the park benches so that they faced the park rather than

the road. This provided parents a place to sit and watch their children play. Finally, we planted flowers around the entranceways to welcome people into the renovated park.

Working in Paterson with these youth, who share my drive and passion to change the world, has made me more aware of how I can put sociological research findings into action and make a career out of doing so. I look forward to starting my own nonprofit organization and dedicating my life to helping community members make their neighborhoods safer and healthier.

Discussion Question: When you were growing up, did you have a safe place to play outside? Why? How can a safe public park make a difference in the physical and mental health of a community?

Tyesha Crawford is a student at William Paterson University majoring in sociology and criminology and criminal justice.

Tyesha Crawford
Provided by Tyesha Crawford

FOOD INSECURITY

In this exercise you will examine food insecurity in your state and the nation as a whole.

Jot down your answers to the following questions.

1. Look at Figure 13.2. Does your state have more, less, or an average amount of food insecurity?

2. Now examine Figure 13.3. Which groups are most at risk for food insecurity? Using the information in this figure, propose possible explanations for the degree of food insecurity experienced in your state. Or, if your state does not experience food insecurity, choose one that does and pose potential explanations.

▼ FIGURE 13.2

Prevalence of Food Insecurity in the United States, Average by State, 2012–2017

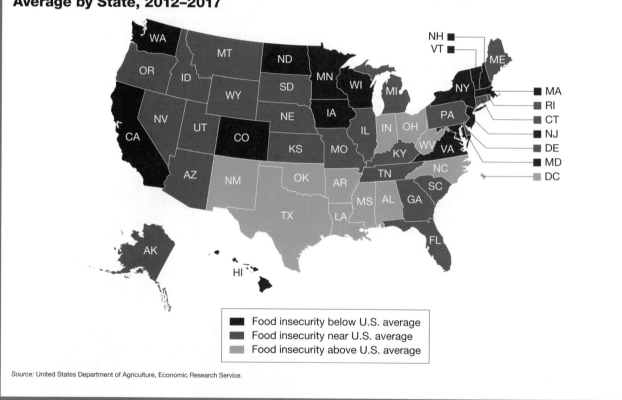

Food insecurity below U.S. average
Food insecurity near U.S. average
Food insecurity above U.S. average

Source: United States Department of Agriculture, Economic Research Service.

for heart disease because her income allows her to purchase healthy foods and live in a neighborhood that is safe for walking and jogging and contains grocery stores with fresh food options. Her level of education helps her understand and evaluate information related to health and disease. The people in her social network are of a similar socioeconomic status and recommend additional wellness programs she can use to carry out the doctor's recommendation. Although stress exists in her life, she can manage it through regularly exercising and going on vacation a couple times a year. With this example, you can see how the manager's middle-class status expands her resources to improve her health and lower her risk for heart disease.

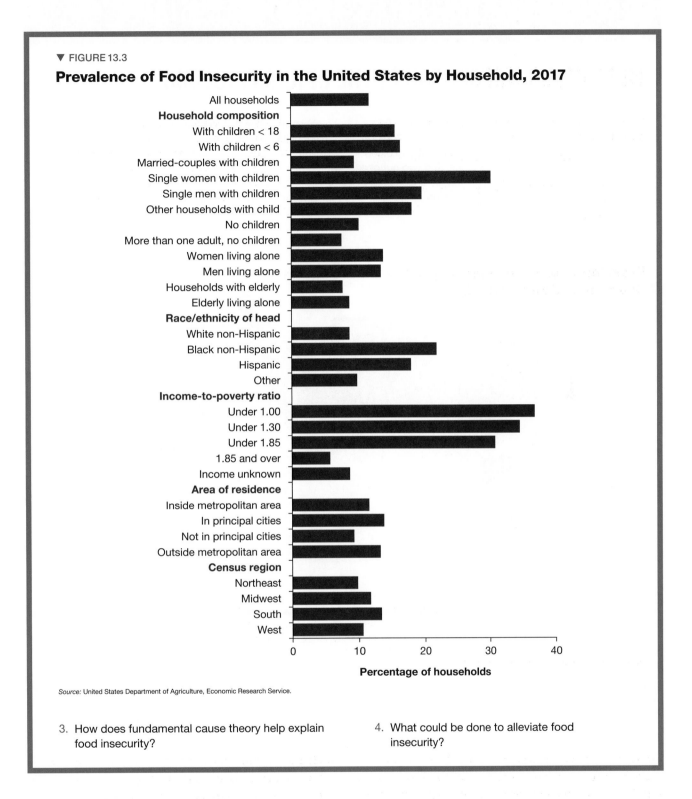

▼ FIGURE 13.3

Prevalence of Food Insecurity in the United States by Household, 2017

Percentage of households

Source: United States Department of Agriculture, Economic Research Service.

3. How does fundamental cause theory help explain food insecurity?

4. What could be done to alleviate food insecurity?

On the other hand, the working-class cashier rents a home in a rough area of town because that is the only area she can afford the rent. The neighborhood is in a **food desert**, an area with limited access to healthy and affordable food. There are more fast food restaurants than stores with reasonably priced healthy foods. She does not feel safe walking to the bus stop and would not dream of walking or jogging in her neighborhood for

MEASURING THE SPREAD OF THE OPIOID EPIDEMIC

The Centers for Disease Control and Prevention (CDC) reports that between 1999 and 2017, more than 700,000 Americans died from drug overdoses. More than 70,000 of those deaths occurred in 2017 alone, and two out of three involved opioids. On average, 130 Americans die every day from opioid-related drug overdoses. In this online activity, you will explore which states have the highest opioid death rates and how quickly rates have risen, using data from the CDC's National Center for Health Statistics.

*Requires the Vantage version of *Sociology in Action*.

▼ FIGURE 13.4

Opioid Overdose Death Rate (State)

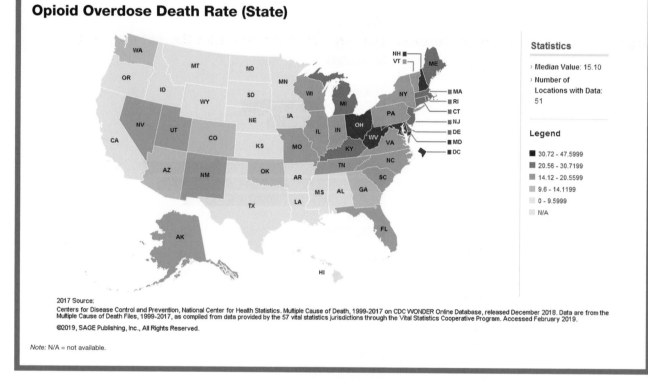

Statistics

› Median Value: 15.10
› Number of Locations with Data: 51

Legend

■ 30.72 – 47.5999
■ 20.56 – 30.7199
■ 14.12 – 20.5599
■ 9.6 – 14.1199
■ 0 – 9.5999
■ N/A

2017 Source:
Centers for Disease Control and Prevention, National Center for Health Statistics. Multiple Cause of Death, 1999-2017 on CDC WONDER Online Database, released December 2018. Data are from the Multiple Cause of Death Files, 1999-2017, as compiled from data provided by the 57 vital statistics jurisdictions through the Vital Statistics Cooperative Program. Accessed February 2019.

©2019, SAGE Publishing, Inc., All Rights Reserved.

Note: N/A = not available.

exercise. Her anxiety rises at the end of every month when she must find funds to pay her rent. Vacations are not an option. Her time relaxing consists of watching TV when she can find the time and eating a half a carton of ice cream. Because of the features of her neighborhood and her low income, the cashier is less able to reduce her risk for heart disease.

Stress at work also affects our health. Our jobs shape how much autonomy and flexibility we have over our work. Low-paying jobs tend to have little autonomy and flexibility. Workers in these sorts of occupations tend to have rigid schedules and little room for creativity or decision making. This can lead to higher levels of stress and increased likelihood of death (Gonzalez-Mule and Cockburn 2017).

Check Your Understanding

- How does the fundamental cause theory explain health disparities?

- What are some social factors that affect health?

- What is a food desert?

- How can your job influence your health?

Social Distribution of Illness

13.5 How do sex and gender, race and ethnicity, and social class affect health and life expectancy?

Social scientists use two primary variables to assess how well a country is doing in terms of keeping its citizens healthy. The first measure is **life expectancy**, the average number of years a person is expected to live. The other measure is **infant mortality**, the number of deaths of children under thirteen months of age for every 1,000 live births. Figures 13.5 and 13.6 show how the United States compares with other Global North nations on these indicators of national health. These low rankings exist despite the fact that the United States spends more than any other country on health care. Surprised?

Distributions of Physical Illnesses and Life Expectancy

Health disparities exist by sex and gender, race and ethnicity, and socioeconomic status. As Table 13.1 indicates, women (regardless of the racial group to which they belong) have a longer life expectancy than men (by as much as ten years). In other words, women have a lower **mortality** (the death rate for a population).

▼ FIGURE 13.5

Organisation for Economic Co-operation and Development Life Expectancy Rates

Source: Organisation for Economic Co-operation and Development. 2018. "Life Expectancy at Birth." Accessed October 1, 2018. https://www.oecd-ilibrary.org/social-issues-migration-health/life-expectancy-at-birth/indicator/english_27e0fc9d-en.

Organisation for Economic Co-operation and Development Infant Mortality Rates

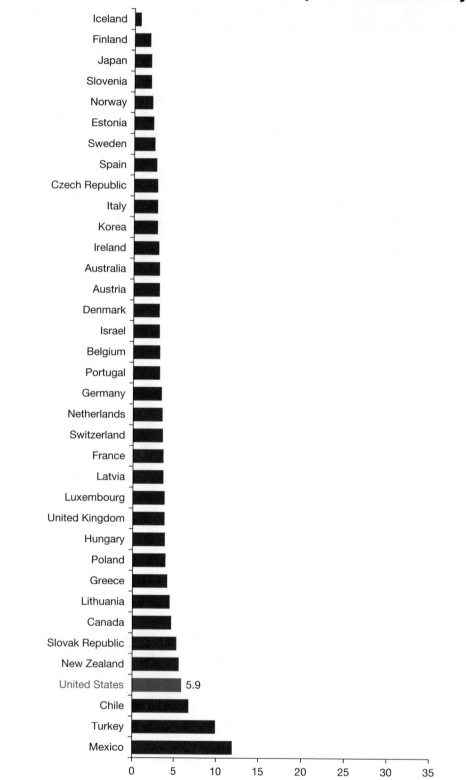

Source: Organisation for Economic Co-operation and Development. 2018. "Infant Mortality Rates." Accessed October 1, 2018. https://www.oecd-ilibrary.org/social-issues-migration-health/infant-mortality-rates/indicator/english_83dea506-en.

However, women also have higher **morbidity** (rates of illness, injury, disease, or other unhealthy states) than men.

This biological phenomenon is also a sociological one. As you will recall from Chapter 8, the differences in mortality and morbidity rates relate to the different gender scripts assigned to men and women. Women tend to go to the doctor more (as they are more likely to ask for help, in general, than men) and have more and higher quality social relationships. The gender script that men are assigned tends to condone unhealthy behaviors and life-threatening acts like reckless driving, unhealthy eating, violent behavior, and inability to show need (and thus go to the doctor), which all contribute to men having a shorter life expectancy than women. Although women live longer than men, they are generally sicker than men, because of their roles as caregivers (Manandhar et al. 2018).

Life expectancy also varies by race and ethnicity, as seen in Table 13.2. Asian, White, and Hispanic Americans tend to live longer than Blacks and American Indians in the United States. Fundamental cause theory explains much of these differences. As Figure 9.3 in Chapter 9 and Table 12.1 in Chapter 12 show, income and educational attainment vary by race and ethnicity in the United States. The relatively long life expectancy of Hispanic Americans, despite their relatively low levels of income and education, results from the relatively good health of immigrant Hispanics, which tends to decline the more time they reside in the United States (Riosmena, Kuhn, and Jochem 2017).

The chronically underfunded and understaffed Indian Health Services provides health care for American Indians residing on or around reservations. It spends just $3,332 per capita on each patient, about one-third the medical funds spent on the typical U.S. resident (Laughland and Silverston 2017; Leston 2018; National Congress of American Indians 2018). Life expectancy among American Indians can vary dramatically. For example, life expectancy for the Lakota on the Pine Ridge reservation in South Dakota is only 66.6 years.

There are also differences in the health status of Latinos and Asian Americans according to nationality. For example, on average, Cubans have better health than Mexicans. Chinese Americans tend to do better overall on health measures than Hmong and Vietnamese Americans. There is also evidence that African-born Blacks do better on some measures of health than Blacks whose families have been in the United States for generations. For example, U.S.-born Black women are more likely to have low-birth-weight infants than African-born Blacks who live in the United States (Elo, Vang, and Culhane 2014; Novoa and Taylor 2018). In sum, sex and gender, race and ethnicity, nation of origin, and length of time in the United States affect health. The latter factor indicates that people of color are more at risk for poorer health the longer they stay in the United States.

The Distribution of Mental Illnesses

When looking at issues related to health and health care, it is important to include mental health and mental illness. **Mental illnesses**, as defined by the American Psychiatric Association (2018), are "health conditions

▼ TABLE 13.1

Life Expectancy by Sex, 1950–2015

Year	Male	Female
1950	65.6	71.1
1960	66.6	73.1
1970	67.1	74.7
1980	70.0	77.4
1990	71.8	78.8
2000	74.1	79.3
2010	76.2	81.0
2015	76.3	81.2

Source: National Center for Health Statistics. 2017. "Health, United States, 2016: With Chartbook on Long-Term Trends in Health." Hyattsville, MD: National Center for Health Statistics.

▼ TABLE 13.2

Life Expectancy at Birth by Sex, Race, and Hispanic Origin, 2015

	All	White	Black	Hispanic
All	78.8	79.0	75.5	82.0
Male	76.3	76.6	72.2	79.3
Female	81.2	81.3	78.5	84.3

Source: National Center for Health Statistics. 2017. "Health, United States, 2016: With Chartbook on Long-Term Trends in Health." National Center for Health Statistics. Accessed July 26, 2019. https://www.cdc.gov/nchs/data/hus/hus16.pdf.

TOP TEN CAUSES OF DEATH

In this activity, you will examine the major causes of death in the United States.

These are the top ten causes of death, not in order: diabetes, heart disease, cancer, chronic lower respiratory diseases, accidents (unintentional injuries), stroke (cerebrovascular diseases), Alzheimer's disease, influenza and pneumonia, kidney disease (nephritis, nephrotic syndrome, and nephrosis), and intentional self-harm (suicide).

1. List the top ten causes of death in order of most to least prevalent on the basis of your current information or assumptions.

2. Now go to the CDC's web site to check your answer: "Leading Causes of Death" (https://www.cdc.gov/nchs/fastats/leading-causes-of-death.htm).

3. Write a short explanation of how the messages we receive from society shape which causes of death you thought were numbers one and two.

involving changes in emotion, thinking or behavior (or a combination of these) . . . associated with distress and/or problems functioning in social, work or family activities." One in five people in the United States live with some type of mental illness.

As with physical health, there is a strong relationship between social class and mental health. People of lower socioeconomic status have a greater likelihood of having a mental disorder. The types of disorders people experience also tend to differ depending on their social class. People of lower socioeconomic status are more likely to be diagnosed with schizophrenia and personality disorders. Those who are upper and middle class are more likely to be diagnosed with anxiety and depression (Eaton and Muntaner 2017).

Check Your Understanding

- Explain how the United States compares with other Global North countries on life expectancy and infant mortality.

- What two primary variables do social scientists use to assess how well a country is doing in terms of keeping its citizens healthy?

- How do sex and gender, race and ethnicity, nation of origin, and years spent in the United States affect life expectancy?

- What is the difference between mortality and morbidity?

- What is mental illness?

People of lower socioeconomic status, such as those who are homeless, have a greater likelihood of having a mental disorder.
©istockPhoto.com/coldsnowstorm

The U.S. Health Care System

13.6 What are the major issues facing the U.S. health care system?

People in most Global North countries do not have to worry about health coverage, as you can see in Figure 13.9. In nations with **universal coverage**, the government guarantees that all citizens can receive health care. Some countries, like France, Japan, and Switzerland, follow a multipayer health insurance model, with citizens required to have health insurance, private companies offering health care, and prices regulated by the government. In other systems, as in Italy and the United Kingdom, the government pays for and provides health services to its citizens (the National Health Service model). A third system can be found in Canada and Australia. They follow a national health insurance model. Under this model, private health care providers provide health care for which the government pays.

Cost of and Access to Health Care

Because of the high cost of drugs and medical procedures and, to a lesser extent, the greater use of services, the United States spends much more on health care than other Global North nations (Kamal and Cox 2018). As Figure 13.7 shows, the United States spends about double the amount comparable nations spend, per person, on health care.

Access to health providers can also be an issue in the United States. Again, compared with other Global North nations, the United States has fewer doctors (Kamal and Cox 2018). Figure 13.8 reveals where the United States stands among other comparable countries in terms of number of physician visits per 1,000 people. To make matters worse, most physicians cluster in urban areas, leaving many people in the rural United States far from available medical care.

Health Insurance

As you can see in Figure 13.9, the United States does not have universal health care. Instead, it includes a patchwork of different ways of getting health insurance coverage that leaves some without access to health care. The majority of those with health insurance (and 49 percent of all U.S. residents) obtain it through their employers (Kaiser Family Foundation 2018). Two government programs, **Medicaid**, which covers disabled people and those within a certain percentage of the poverty line, and **Medicare**, which gives some health insurance to people older than sixty-five, cover 19 percent and 14 percent, respectively, of people in the United States (Kaiser Family Foundation 2018). (Here's a tip to remember the difference between Medicaid and Medicare: we aid the poor—Medicaid—and care for the elderly—Medicare.)

Those not insured through an employee or a government program have the option to buy private insurance, but most plans are prohibitively expensive. Also, before passage of the Patient Protection and Affordable Care Act in 2010, insurance carriers could deny coverage to people who had preexisting conditions. These facts led to many people being uninsured.

The Patient Protection and Affordable Care Act. The 2010 Patient Protection and Affordable Care Act (ACA), also known as Obamacare, was created to remedy some

▼ FIGURE 13.7

Total Health Expenditures per Capita, U.S. Dollars

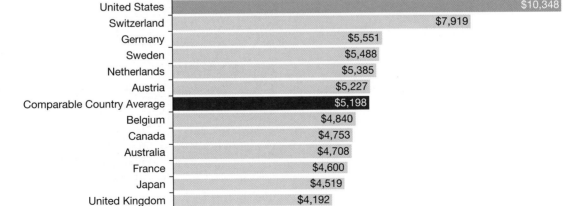

United States	$10,348
Switzerland	$7,919
Germany	$5,551
Sweden	$5,488
Netherlands	$5,385
Austria	$5,227
Comparable Country Average	$5,198
Belgium	$4,840
Canada	$4,753
Australia	$4,708
France	$4,600
Japan	$4,519
United Kingdom	$4,192

Source: Peterson-Kaiser Health System Tracker 2018.

Physician Consultations per Capita

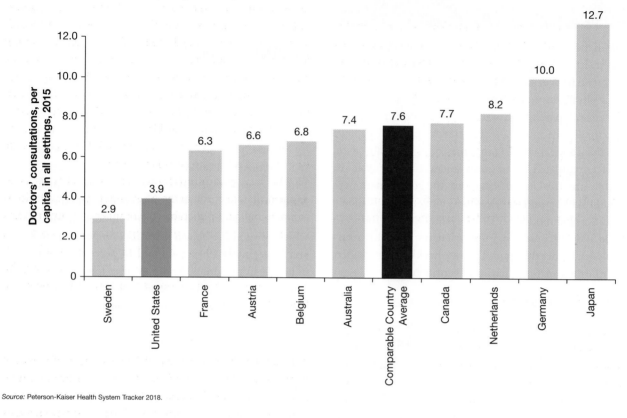

Source: Peterson-Kaiser Health System Tracker 2018.

Nations with Universal Health Care

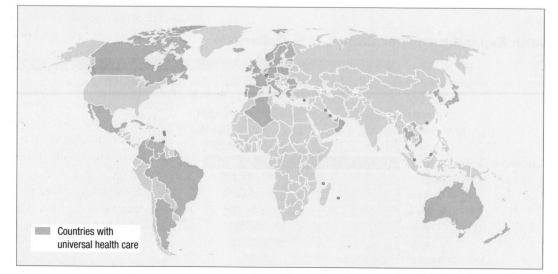

Source: Data from WorldAtlas.com.

problems with the U.S. health care system. The ACA includes the following provisions:

- It requires insurance companies to cover individuals, no matter the cost of their health care needs. In the past, insurance companies could drop people from coverage if they met a maximum year or lifetime expense for health care services.

- It allows young adults to be covered by their parents' insurance plans until they are twenty-six years old (in the past, young adults were dropped at nineteen years of age).

- It prohibits insurance companies from turning people down for coverage because their health needs are extensive and/or expensive.

- It requires that preventive health services be free of charge (e.g., screenings for cancer, vaccinations, testing for diabetes).

The ACA also offers states funds to expand Medicaid programs and, until recent changes made by the Trump administration, mandated that everyone obtain health insurance. Similar to the reasoning for having all drivers buy car insurance, the goal of the mandate was to decrease the cost of health insurance by having healthy as well as ill people contribute to the system. The ACA reduced the number of people without insurance, as seen in Figure 13.10. However, more progress would have been made in increasing access to health care and lowering the cost of health services if more states had expanded Medicaid coverage. Expanding Medicaid coverage under the ACA meant that more people with financial constraints would have been eligible for Medicaid and that lower income adults without children also could have been eligible for Medicaid. Medicaid before the ACA was generally available only to select groups such as children, pregnant women, parents with children, and people with disabilities who had very little income.

The Trump administration cut funding for advertising opportunities to enroll in the ACA and rolled back the individual mandate. Predictably, the number of uninsured has started to climb again, increasing among adults between sixteen and sixty-four years old from 12.7 percent in 2016 to 15.5 percent in 2018 (Collins et al. 2018). Therefore, the number of uninsured continues to be a serious issue in the United States.

The Underinsured

Today, medical debt is the number one cause of personal bankruptcy filings in the United States (Backman 2017). An illness can be financially devastating even for those with insurance. A common problem is **underinsurance**, when a person has health insurance, but, even with the insurance, health services are not affordable. For example, at one university, the cost of insurance for one of the most popular health plans is $75.12 a month for an individual (for the premium). In addition to the premium a person pays for the insurance plan, there is the cost of health services. The individual first must pay a $2,000 deductible before the insurance company will pay for any medical fees associated with the health plan and then an additional 20 percent of the medical fees charged.

Heart disease is the leading cause of death in the United States for both men and women. The lowest cost of a coronary artery bypass graft surgery, a common procedure for those who have experienced a heart attack, is about $31,000 without insurance. That means that if the cost of treating the heart attack is $31,000, the sick person might have a copay

▼ FIGURE 13.10

Percentage of People in the United States without Health Insurance Coverage, 1997–2016

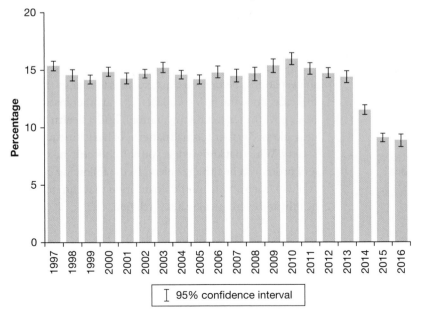

Source: Clarke TC, Norris T, Schiller JS. Early release of selected estimates based on data from 2016 National Health Interview Survey. National Center for Health Statistics. May 2017.

MEDICAID EXPANSION

In this activity, you will learn which states extended Medicaid coverage and which states did not and discuss the causes and consequences of this choice.

Go to the Kaiser Family Foundation's web page "Status of State Action on the Medicaid Expansion Decision" (https://www.kff.org/health-reform/state-indicator/state-activity-around-expanding-medicaid-under-the-affordable-care-act). Write your answers to the following questions.

Did the state you live in expand Medicaid coverage? Compare your state with one in another region of the country. (The regions of the country are Northeast, Midwest, South, and West.) Why might some states choose to expand Medicaid while others do not? Who is most affected by a state's choice to expand Medicaid coverage?

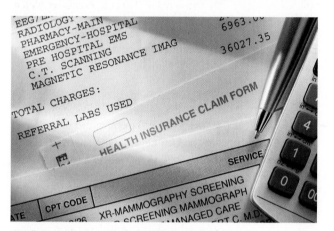

Even with insurance, the cost of medical treatment for individuals suffering from an illness can be unaffordable.
©iStockphoto.com/DNY59

of $20, a deductible of $2,000, and a charge of $6,200 for the $31,000 fee. This does not include follow-up visits and laboratory tests. Do you see how costly one health problem can be—even with insurance?

Check Your Understanding

- How does health coverage in the United States compare with that provided in other Global North nations?
- How did the Affordable Care Act affect health care coverage for people in the United States?

- How has the Trump administration supported or not supported the ACA?
- Why can even people with insurance have trouble paying for medical bills?

Conclusion

Sociology helps us see the social patterns of health and illness. Health is as much a social experience as it is a biological one. Those with higher socioeconomic status tend to live longer lives than those with lower socioeconomic status. Whether you are healthy or ill is, in part, shaped by the social environment and social conditions to which you are, or have been, exposed. We all have some options as to the lifestyles we lead, but they are limited by social factors such as the cost of health care, racial and ethnic discrimination, income level, location, and gender scripts.

As we pointed out in Chapter 1, you have to notice social patterns before you can take steps to change them. In this case, knowing how social factors and other institutions (e.g., government, economy, family) affect health and illness allows you to recognize patterns of health inequality in society. With that knowledge, you can choose to take action and promote a healthier society. In the following chapter, you will learn about another institution that can influence health, and even suicide rates—religion.

REVIEW

13.1 How does sociology contribute to our understanding of health and illness?

Sociology helps us understand how social factors shape health and illness. Both health care professionals and the general public can benefit from understanding how the social environment and social conditions affect health and illness.

13.2 In what ways are health and illness social experiences and not simply biological phenomena?

Health and illnesses are social experiences because they affect more than our physical bodies. They also help shape the way we see ourselves and the way others see us. Illness can change the kinds of activities we can do, affect our social relationships, and put strains on our finances and families.

13.3 What is medicalization?

Medicalization is the process by which conditions become perceived as medical conditions. Some conditions once seen as moral failures, such as excessive gambling and alcoholism, are now considered illnesses. As the health institution grows, medicalization increases.

13.4 How are an individual's health behaviors (e.g., lack of exercise, unhealthy eating) influenced by social factors?

Individual health behaviors (just like non-health-related behaviors) are shaped by society and social conditions. People may want to eat healthy foods, but if they live in a food desert or their utilities are turned off, they might make a reasonable decision to eat packaged and processed foods. The decision is shaped by their social circumstances, including their income and neighborhood.

13.5 How do sex and gender, race and ethnicity, and social class affect health and life expectancy?

On average, Asian Americans have the longest life expectancy, followed by Latinos, Whites, American Indians, and then African Americans. The main factors shaping the shorter life expectancy of American Indians and African Americans are low socioeconomic status and racial discrimination. Asians Americans and Latinos have a long life expectancy in part because immigrants tend to have better health than those born in the United States. Relatively high percentages of both Asian Americans and Latinos are first-generation U.S. residents.

Men die more quickly, but women are sicker. This is due in part to gender scripts. Women are more likely than men to ask for help and go to the doctor, have more social relationships, and have safer jobs. Women are also more likely to act as care-takers for ill family and friends, thus exposing them to more illnesses.

As the fundamental cause theory notes, social class is the biggest predictor of health. Those with higher socioeconomic status tend to live longer than those with lower socioeconomic status. Social class shapes health and life expectancy because people's income, education, and occupations expand or constrain the choices they have to improve or harm their health.

13.6 What are the major issues facing the U.S. health care system?

Two of the major issues in the U.S. health care system are access to health care and the cost of health care. In the United States, health care is not universal. A significant segment of the population does not have health insurance; this was true both before and after the passing of the Affordable Care Act. This means that many people go without needed services because they do not have health insurance. Those between twenty-five and thirty-four years of age are most likely to be uninsured and thus have no or limited access to health care.

There are several out-of-pocket costs associated with obtaining health services. In addition to paying for health insurance through premiums, consumers are usually responsible for copay and deductible charges. The high cost of health care means that people may delay treatment, making their illness worse when they finally do obtain care.

KEY TERMS

acute illnesses   260

biographical disruption   260

chronic illnesses   260

food desert   267

fundamental cause theory   264

infant mortality   269

life expectancy   269

Medicaid   273

medicalization   262

Medicare   273

mental illnesses   271

morbidity   271

mortality   269

underinsurance   275

universal coverage   273

CHAPTER 14

UNDERSTANDING INSTITUTIONS

Religion

Andrea N. Hunt

The concept of the sacred is a powerful social idea that guides the lives of millions of people.
REUTERS/Tarmizy Harva

LEARNING QUESTIONS

14.1 How do sociologists define religion, religiosity, and spirituality?

14.2 What are pluralism and secularization?

14.3 What is fundamentalism?

14.4 What are the current trends in religious affiliation and participation in the United States?

14.5 How does the process of global diffusion apply to religion?

14.6 How does each of the major theoretical paradigms in sociology explain religion?

14.7 What are some recent examples of how religion has fostered social change efforts?

Defining Religion Sociologically

14.1 How do sociologists define religion, religiosity, and spirituality?

In *The Elementary Forms of Religious Life*, Émile Durkheim ([1912] 1995) distinguished between the **profane**, a sphere of everyday life, and the **sacred**, that which inspires reverence and devotion. Although it may be difficult to distinguish between the sacred and profane within some religions (such as Hinduism), the notion of the sacred serves as the basis for most *general* definitions of religion. Sociologists define **religion** as a social institution that involves the beliefs and practices of what has been socially constructed as sacred in a given society. "Religion is a social institution that bonds communities through a shared meaning system; a set of beliefs, practices, and symbols that reflect the shared meaning system; a sense of belonging; ethics that guide the lives of the members; and routinized social expectations" (Roberts and Yamane 2016, 21).

CONSIDER THIS

How can we determine how religious people are or to what extent they practice their religion?

These elements do not describe a certain religious affiliation but rather capture the broad characteristics of religion in general. Different religious traditions, such as Islam, Christianity, Buddhism, Confucianism, Hinduism, Buddhism, Judaism, and many others, share these traits. Despite some very general similarities, however, each of these religions has unique beliefs and practices that differentiate them from one another.

We can measure religiousness or **religiosity** by looking at a range of religious beliefs, activities, and practices in which people participate. Looking at just one can be misleading, however. For example, some people participate in religious ceremonies and church, temple, or synagogue attendance to celebrate and practice their faith as a member of a larger community. Their attendance at a religious ceremony reflects their belief system. For others, attending a religious ceremony might just be a public display of adherence to a religion, while their actions in everyday life do not reflect faith-based practices. Relying on rituals and practices alone as a measure of religiosity can be problematic.

What is the difference between religion and spirituality? **Spirituality** is the search for the sacred, which involves finding meaning or purpose in your life and trusting in some higher power. This implies more of a journey or process rather than being defined by the boundaries of specific religions (Roberts and Yamane 2016). Spirituality is fluid rather than constant with clearly defined practices, which means that it is not always compatible with organized religions. Some people consider themselves spiritual but not religious and may reject organized religion while embracing more individualized forms of spiritual practice, such as prayer, meditation, and yoga. However, spirituality does not stand in direct opposition to organized religion, as both include practices orientated toward the sacred (Roberts and Yamane 2016).

CONSIDER THIS

How are religion and spirituality related and how are they different? Some people say they are spiritual but not religious, but is it also possible to be religious but not spiritual?

Religion Is More Than a Private Matter

Our sociological imagination gives us the ability to see how outside forces affect our individual lives and the connections among different parts of society. For example, we can see how religion operates as an individual belief system but also as a social institution that creates a shared meaning system and defines acceptable behavior for a group of

ANDREA N. HUNT

I was originally a psychology major and planned to pursue marriage and family therapy for a career. I didn't have an engaging experience in introduction to sociology, so my first real aha moment came in a course on juvenile delinquency. I was fascinated by the role of the family in shaping the life course of youth and was even more intrigued by juvenile programming. This led to a research assistantship during my master's program, evaluating juvenile aftercare programs, and to the beginning of a life as a public sociologist. As a doctoral student, I discovered the scholarship of teaching and learning and came to more fully understand the importance of the introduction to sociology course as the key to bringing students into the discipline. Today, I regularly teach introduction to sociology. Another of my favorite topics to teach about is religion. It's a great way to show students how to apply the major theoretical perspectives in sociology, understand how inequality is reproduced in our society, and assess how positive social change occurs.

people. The sociological imagination also allows us to see how religion intersects with other major social institutions, such as the family and government. Recall the discussion in Chapter 11 of how Calvinist religious beliefs about marriage shaped legal doctrine around who could own property and become the head of a household. For many people, a wedding ceremony is both a civil contract that joins two people legally and a religious rite that includes religious symbols, practices, and rituals. At one time, interracial marriage in the United States was prohibited. The U.S. Supreme Court struck down individual state laws prohibiting interracial marriage in the landmark case *Loving v. Virginia* (1967). The Virginia judge who originally heard the case cited biblical passages justifying racial segregation in his decision. Prayer in school continues to be debated today, even after the Supreme Court prohibited school- or state-sanctioned prayer in 1962. Some schools have adopted "moments of silence" to reflect the level of religious pluralism in the United States today.

Check Your Understanding

- How do sociologists define religion?
- What is the difference between religion and spirituality?
- How do you know if someone is religious?
- How is religion more than a private matter?

Religious Pluralism and Secularization

14.2 What are pluralism and secularization?

Social changes in society, including changes in the economic system, political and social movements, and immigration,

can affect religiosity. This helps explain current trends in the United States that show more diversity in religious affiliation and participation than in previous decades.

Changing Demographics and Pluralism

In large part because of changing demographics of new immigrants, we have seen increases in non-Christian faiths in the United States (Chaves 2017). Figure 14.1 shows that from 1992 to 2012, the percentage of immigrants identifying with non-Christian religions grew by 6 percent. Historically, immigrants to the United States originated primarily from European countries and brought with them Christian (mostly Roman Catholic) and Jewish religious traditions. Today, there are still many immigrants to the United States who identify as Christian, and they tend to arrive from Central and South America. However, there are also an increasing number of immigrants from Asian and African countries who are more likely to be Muslim, Hindu, or Buddhist. Note that there are also many more "unaffiliated" immigrants, with the percentage steady until 2012 but jumping to 20 percent by 2014.

Religious pluralism arises when different religious belief systems coexist within a society. Immigration can lead to more religious diversity and, in some cases, create a religiously pluralistic society with increasing numbers of interreligious marriages, one of the best indicators of religious acceptance (Chaves 2017). The Pew Research Center's (2015a) Religious Landscape Study shows that 39 percent of Americans who have married since 2010 are in interreligious marriages. This is up from 19 percent of those who got married before 1960. Although pluralism suggests a degree of diversity and more religious and spiritual choices, religious pluralism does not necessarily lead to more religious participation (Berger 2014).

DOING SOCIOLOGY 14.1

CLARIFYING YOUR UNDERSTANDING OF RELIGION

In this activity, you will use the SEE-I method to think clearly about religion.

Religion can seem like a difficult concept to describe in the abstract, although it touches many of our lives in profound and intimate ways. Use the SEE-I (state, elaborate, exemplify, illustrate) critical thinking method (Nosich 2009, 33–38) to clarify and understand the concept of religion.

1. *State* a basic definition of religion in one sentence.

2. *Elaborate* on the concept of religion in your own words and describe the difference between sacred and profane.

3. *Exemplify* the concept of religion by giving concrete examples of the different components of the definition of religion provided in the text, and describe how these components might be reflected in public policy decisions.

4. *Illustrate* the concept of religion with a picture or diagram that shows the difference between religion and spirituality.

▼ FIGURE 14.1

A Growing Share of Legal Immigrants Belong to Religious Minorities

Religious composition of legal permanent residents in the United States

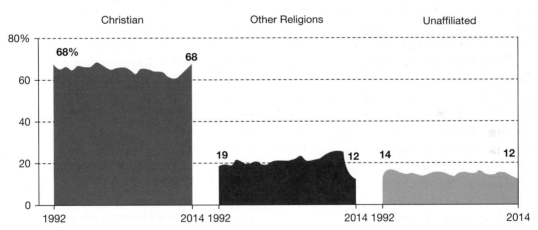

Source: "America's Changing Religious Landscape, "Pew Research Center, Washington, D.C. (May 12, 2015) http://www.pewforum.org/2015/05/12/americas-changing-religious-landscape/; updated with data from: https://www.pewforum.org/religious-landscape-study/immigrant-status/immigrants/.

Secularization

Secularization occurs when a society moves away from identification with religious values and institutions. Data in Figures 14.2 and 14.3 from the Public Religion Research Institute (Jones and Cox 2017) indicate an increase in the percentage of people in the United States indicating no religious affiliation, with a higher percentage of unaffiliated in the eighteen to twenty-nine age range. Although many people who are religiously unaffiliated still have a belief in a god, a rising number of people do not share this belief. This includes **atheists**, who do not believe in a god, and **agnostics**, who maintain that nothing is known or can be known about god(s). Agnosticism differs from atheism in that agnostics do not disbelieve in a god, but they also do not claim a particular faith-based belief system. Humanists can be either agnostics or atheists. **Secular humanists** believe that humans have the capability of being moral and just without adhering to religious rules or believing in a divine god.

IDENTIFYING COMMON BELIEFS AND PRACTICES ACROSS RELIGIONS

Many surveys of religion group respondents by the religions with which they identify. Although helpful in many ways, these categories may ignore similarities between and differences within religious groups. The Pew Research Center (2018b) developed the following new categories on the basis of religious and spiritual characteristics that extend beyond religious affiliation.

- **Sunday stalwarts** are the most religious group. They actively practice their faith, are deeply involved in their religious congregations, and lean right politically.

- **God-and-country believers** are less active in church groups or other religious organizations, but like Sunday Stalwarts, they hold many traditional religious beliefs and tilt right on social and political issues. They are the most likely of any group to see immigrants as a threat.

- Racial and ethnic minorities make up a relatively large share of the **diversely devout**, who are diverse not only demographically but also in their beliefs. It is the only group in which solid majorities say they believe in God "as described in the Bible" *and* in psychics, reincarnation, and spiritual energy located in physical things.

- Seven in ten **relaxed religious** say that they believe in the God of the Bible, and four in ten pray daily. But relatively few attend religious services or read scripture, and they almost unanimously say that it is not necessary to believe in God to be a moral person.

- All **spiritually awake** Americans hold at least some new-age beliefs (views rejected by most of the relaxed religious, such as belief in psychics, astrology, reincarnation, and spiritual energy in physical objects like trees, mountains, and crystals) and believe in God or some higher power, though many do not believe in the biblical God, and relatively few attend religious services on a weekly basis.

- The **solidly secular** are the least religious of the seven groups. These relatively affluent, highly educated U.S. adults—mostly White and male—tend to be neither religious nor spiritual and to reject all new-age beliefs as well as belief in the God of the Bible. Many do not believe in a higher power at all. They tend to be liberal and Democratic in their political views.

- **Religion resisters**, on the other hand, largely do believe in some higher power or spiritual force (but not the God of the Bible), and many have some new-age beliefs and consider themselves spiritual but not religious. At the same time, members of this group express strongly negative views of organized religion, saying that churches have too much influence in politics and that, overall, religion does more harm than good. They are generally liberal and Democratic in their political views (paraphrased from Pew Research Center 2018b).

Write your answers to the following questions:

1. Why might it be helpful for sociologists to use religious and spiritual characteristics that extend beyond religious affiliation?

2. How do these new categories help you understand the relationship between religious beliefs and practices and current political issues focused on immigration, same-sex marriage, and abortion?

3. Do you see yourself represented in this typology? Why or why not?

There are several possible explanations for this increase in people who identify as religiously unaffiliated. As noted earlier religious ideologies have influenced many governmental practices. However, the influence of religion in governmental matters declines with urbanization, migration, developments in science and technology, and mass participation in the political process. Even with these changes, though, there are still connections between some religious affiliations and conservative political ideologies (Djupe, Neiheisel, and Sokhey 2018). For example, Mormons and evangelical Protestants are more likely to identify as both religiously and politically conservative and agree that religion is an essential part of the political process (Pew Research Center 2015a). This connection between religion

Growth of the Religiously Unaffiliated, 1976–2016

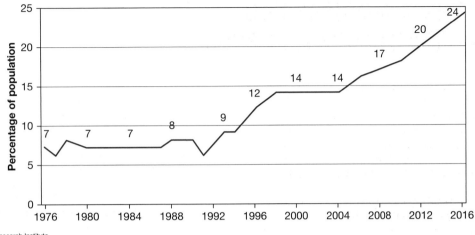

Source: Public Religion Research Institute.

Percentage Unaffiliated by Age

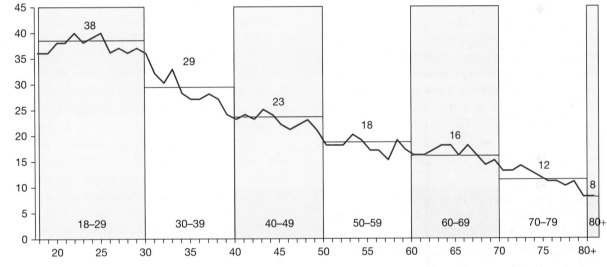

Source: Public Religion Research Institute.

and politics leads some people to turn away from organized religion and identifying with a particular, or any, religious affiliation. As Figure 14.4 illustrates, just as fewer people in the United States are identifying with a religion, fewer are also identifying with a political party. Growing numbers of Americans, particularly younger Americans, are rejecting both traditional political parties and organized religions.

Second, religious involvement in youth is one of the best predictors of involvement in adulthood. Recent cohorts are more likely to be born into nonreligious households, which creates a cohort effect in religious affiliation. As Table 14.1

shows, Millennials are less likely to report a Christian affiliation and more likely to say that they are unaffiliated with any religion compared with previous generations. This means, in turn, that their children are less likely to be born into religiously affiliated households than they were.

Third, **secularization theory** (Berger 1992) suggests that modernization encourages the demystifying of the world and undermines the influence of religion. **Modernization** happens as countries undergo the process of industrialization and decisions become based more on reason and logic than tradition. As a result, organized

U.S. Party Identification, Yearly Averages, 1988–2018

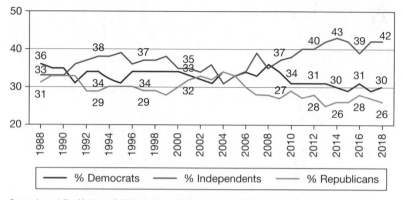

Source: Jones, Jeffrey M. January 7, 2019. "Americans Continue to Embrace Political Independence." Gallup.

Note: Based on multiple-day polls conducted by telephone.

religion takes on a less significant role in people's lives, faith becomes more individualized, and the prominence of religion as a social institution decreases, which can be seen in the large percentage of religiously unaffiliated in North America and most of Europe.

Critics of secularization theory suggest that modernization is not the cause of a decline in the influence of religion in society. Instead, modernization leads to pluralization, with different religions existing within the same society. They point to the fact that religion plays an important role in many areas of the world. However, unlike in premodern societies, in which people tended to take their membership in the one dominant religion for granted, in religiously pluralistic

Today, many more Americans marry someone from a different religion than in the past, reflecting the religious pluralism of our society.

Paul Quayle/Alamy Stock Photo

societies, individuals can choose their religions. As a conscious choice, religion could, perhaps, have an even greater influence in the lives of individuals—and in society. For example, even as the percentage of Americans who identify as unaffiliated is growing, most people still choose to identify with religious organizations, with increasing numbers choosing to move from one religion to another when they become adults (Pew Research Center 2015a).

Sects, Cults, and New Religious Movements.

Some people, not satisfied with established religions, form counter religious movements that reject the beliefs and practices of dominant religions. These include sects, cults, and new religious movements. **Sects** are subgroups of larger religions and have some of their own distinct beliefs and practices. They are often critical of their larger religion or denomination and branch off as a way to return to what they view as the legitimate or proper way to seek salvation. Sects are often closed off to outsiders, whom they see as nonbelievers. All religions have different sects. For example, Sthavira nikāya is one of the earliest schools of Buddhist thought and consists of eleven different sects. Likewise, the Community of the Lady of All Nations is one of the many sects within Catholicism. Tensions can arise between sects, as can be seen in the long-standing divide between Sunni and Shia, who both claim to follow the one true Islam.

What comes to mind when you hear the word *cult*? You might think about groups that have charismatic leaders that use force or conversion methods such as brainwashing to keep members, such as the Charles Manson family, Heaven's Gate, the Branch Davidians, and Jonestown. In each of these cases, the religious leaders had total control over their members to the extent that followers harmed others or themselves in the name of their beliefs. The extensive media coverage of these cases has shaped the way the public thinks about cults.

Generational Replacement Helping Drive the Growth of Unaffiliated and the Decline of Mainline Protestantism and Catholicism

	Silent Generation (b. 1928–1945) (%)	Baby Boomers (b. 1946–1964) (%)	Generation X (b. 1965–1980) (%)	Older Millennials (b. 1981–1989) (%)	Younger Millennials (b. 1990–1996) (%)
Christian	85	78	70	57	56
Protestant	57	52	45	38	36
Evangelical	30	28	25	22	19
Mainline	22	17	13	10	11
Historically Black	5	7	7	6	6
Catholic	24	23	21	16	16
Other Christian groups	3	3	4	3	3
Other faiths	4	5	6	8	8
Unaffiliated	11	17	23	34	36
Don't know/refused	a	1	1	1	1

Source: America's Changing Religious Landscape, Pew Research Center, May 12, 2015. http://www.pewforum.org/2015/05/12/americas-changing-religious-landscape/.

a. No one in this column responded "don't know" or refused to answer.

However, **cults** are simply unorthodox sects, and violence is not a necessary component. In sociology, cults are also called newly formed religious movements (NRMs). At one point in time, every established religion (including Catholicism, Calvinism, and Islam) was an NRM. Sects want to preserve traditional beliefs, whereas cults or NRMs intend to establish new religions. Many NRMs are countercultural and are founded by charismatic leaders who develop their own rituals, beliefs, and practices. For example, the Church of Scientology was founded in 1953 by L. Ron Hubbard and has followers around the world.

Live-streaming worship services provide ways to participate in religion in an informal way.
Ed Simons/Alamy Stock Photo

CONSIDER THIS

Do you see religious pluralism or secularization in your hometown or college campus? What factors in your hometown or college campus contribute to this? Do you agree with secularization theory or its critics? Why?

Check Your Understanding

- How can religious pluralism affect religious participation?
- What are some explanations offered for the increase in secularization in the United States?
- How are secularization and modernization related?
- What do sociologists refer to when they use the words *sect* and *cult*?

Religious Fundamentalism

Fundamentalism does not exist without modernization and secularization (Emerson and Hartman 2006). **Fundamentalists** resist such societal changes and hold on to idealized, conservative, traditional religious practices. Table 14.2 provides a list of ideological and organizational characteristics that can be found within fundamentalist groups and movements regardless of their religious affiliation. As you will see, strict ideological and organizational guidelines for followers control most aspects of their lives.

Although fundamentalism was originally associated with conservative Protestants beginning in the late 1800s, it is now a global phenomenon (Emerson and Hartman 2006). Fundamentalist groups have strong ideological and organizational beliefs and practices that shape their worldview. They believe that their religion is the one true religion and is without flaws (Altemeyer and Hunsberger 2004). Some fundamentalist groups use their beliefs to justify harmful and violent actions toward others. For example, the 9/11 attacks in 2001, the ISIS attacks at the Ariana Grande concert in Manchester, England, in 2017, and the Christchurch attacks in New Zealand in 2019 are examples of the type of violence perpetrated by some fundamentalist groups that practice religious extremism and strict conformity to religious scriptures, in the belief that they have the absolute truth. Domestic hate groups within the United States such as neo-Confederates and the Ku Klux Klan also intertwine religious beliefs with political ideologies. Both these groups identify as Christian organizations and use Christianity to support their beliefs and actions.

It is important to note that not all fundamentalist groups use violence or force, and some groups that do use violence are not fundamentalist. The Fundamentalist Church of Jesus Christ of Latter-Day Saints is one of the largest Mormon fundamentalist religious groups today. They have strong core religious beliefs and practices around marriage, dress, schooling, and property ownership that members must adhere to. The Westboro Baptist Church provides another example of a modern fundamentalist group. They are well known for their anti-LGBT beliefs and protests at the funerals of U.S. soldiers killed in action. Both the Fundamentalist Church of Jesus Christ of Latter-day Saints and the Westboro Baptist Church have the ideological and organizational characteristics of fundamentalist groups described in Table 14.2 but do not practice or promote violence. Moreover, responses and solutions to terrorist attacks and hate crimes also often draw upon religious teachings and traditions. Religion not only defines the sacred but also serves as a lens through which people view the world and make decisions within their everyday lives—including about how they should act toward those who hold different religious beliefs.

▼ TABLE 14.2

Characteristics of Fundamentalist Groups and Movements

Ideological Characteristics (Roberts and Yamane 2016)	
Radicalism	Focused on returning to an idealized cultural version of the past
Scripturalism	The belief that the scriptures are the literal word of their deity
Traditionalism	Traditions of the past are still relevant and applicable to today
Oppositionism	Hostility to modernization or secularization
Totalism	Religion regulates all aspects of life without any possible compromises
Puritanism	The search for internal purity and militant opposition to an impure world
Organizational Characteristics (Emerson and Hartman 2006, 134)	
Chosen	Members see themselves as selected to defend religious tradition
Sharp boundaries	Either you are a believer or not, a defender of religious tradition or not
Authoritarian	Typically have charismatic leaders who are seen as chosen by their deity
Behavioral restrictions	Regulate speech, dress, sexuality, drinking, eating, family, children, etc.

Sources: Ideological Characteristics (Roberts and Yamane 2016); Organizational Characteristics (Emerson and Hartman 2006:134).

Fundamentalists believe that their belief system is the only legitimate religion.
Al Drago/CQ-Roll Call Group/Getty Images

Extreme and Violent Fundamentalism

If we know that not all fundamentalist groups are violent, then what factors can lead some of these religious groups to violence? First, fundamentalists may be threatened by pluralism and use violence to as a way to keep groups segregated. Second, fundamentalists may use violence in reaction to the fear of economic dependence on different, alien others and a desire to retain autonomy from those they deem impure (Roberts and Yamane 2016). Last, fundamentalists may resort to violence as a reaction against modernization, a separation of social institutions from religion, and religious reforms. Religious groups that turn to violence tend to be influenced by patriarchy, ethnocentrism, nationalism, and homophobia (Roberts and Yamane 2016; Zwissler 2012). In sum, some fundamentalists use violence as a means to protect a certain way of life, as seen with 9/11 and the recent attack on mosques in Christchurch. After the 9/11 terrorist attacks, news and other media portrayals of Muslims and Arabs increased, often framing them as violent fundamentalists. These portrayals contribute to **Islamophobia**, the fear or dislike of all or most Muslims, and help shape the way we think about violence, religions, and fundamentalism.

CONSIDER THIS

How do news and other media portray terrorism? Identify some examples to support your answer.

Check Your Understanding

- What is fundamentalism?
- What are some of the characteristics of fundamentalist movements?
- What factors may lead to the use of violence among some religious fundamentalist groups?

Changing Religious Life in the United States

14.4   What are the current trends in religious affiliation and participation in the United States?

Many factors affect religious affiliation and participation in the United States, including race, ethnicity, gender, and sexual orientation. There are signs of increased racial and ethnic diversity among U.S. congregations, and more women now hold leadership roles within congregations. In the United States and globally, we can also see growing acceptance of lesbian, gay, bisexual, and transgender (LGBT) clergy and more religious organizations now sanctioning same-sex marriages.

Religious Affiliation and Race

Standing on the steps of the National Cathedral in Washington, D.C., on March 31, 1968, Dr. Martin Luther King Jr. said that Sunday at 11 a.m. was the most segregated hour in America. He was referring to the widespread racial segregation in American churches. Today, many people still worship in racially segregated congregations. However, research suggests a growing trend toward greater racial and ethnic diversity within Christian religions in the United States (Chaves 2017) (see Figure 14.5). This change can be attributed to the growing racial and ethnic diversity in the United States and the increasing number of immigrants and refugees today who have strong Christian affiliations. For example, immigrants from Latin American countries tend to be Catholic (Chaves 2017). As secularization increases, churches become more dependent on new immigrants to keep their congregations going. Many Catholic, mainline Protestant, and Episcopal leaders have publicly criticized restrictive immigration policies. This public support of immigrants may be a part of what is drawing members of color to their churches and congregations.

New members from different cultures bring change to religious organizations. Religious leaders and their

Increasing Racial and Ethnic Diversity within Christianity in the United States

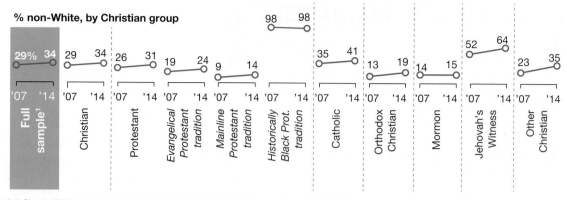

% non-White, by Christian group

Source: America's Changing Religious Landscape, Pew Research Center, May 12, 2015. http://www.pewforum.org/2015/05/12/americas-changing-religious-landscape/.

congregations must find ways to both welcome and serve new and old members of their religious communities. For example, they will need to work with people who speak various languages and are used to different styles of worship, types of food, and community fellowship activities. Sustaining a multicultural religious community takes effort and commitment.

Religious Affiliation and Gender

Religion and gender have a complicated relationship. Feminist theorists draw attention to how social institutions, such as religion, and the practices associated with those institutions promote social inequality, patriarchy, and gender stratification. Most of the dominant religious figures throughout history, such as Jesus of Nazareth, the Prophet Mohammad, Confucius, and the Dalai Lama, have been men. Many

Although most religions continue to oppose same-sex marriage, more and more Christian denominations and branches of Judaism have started to support marriage equality. The reluctance of some religions to accept same-sex marriage may help explain why fewer young people attend religious services today.

Marc Piscotty/Getty Images News/Getty Images

religious groups, such as Roman Catholics, Orthodox Jews, and some evangelical Protestant denominations, still allow only men to serve as clergy. Many of the major world religions have supported patriarchy through their teachings, and many holy texts define appropriate gender roles for their followers. Many religious teachings reinforce women's subordinate status to men and include guidelines for women's dress and behaviors. Yet women, especially Christian women, are more likely to report a religious affiliation and engage in worship services than men (Pew Research Center 2016). Among Muslims and Orthodox Jews, on the other hand, men are more likely to attend religious services than women because of their strong cultural norms and traditions that emphasize male religious attendance.

People on both sides of debates regarding female veiling, birth control, abortion, and same-sex relationships use religion to support their views. As we have seen, some religions mandate violence against nonbelievers and religious rule breakers. Some also teach followers to commit violence against women, such as honor killings, and female genital cutting—acts that reinforce the subordination of women. Yet many religions promote greater gender equality, and many rabbis and ministers are women. Whereas in 1970, only 3 percent of clergy in the United States were women, by 2014, women composed 16 percent of clergy in the United States. Women who do become clergy, however, tend to work for men who run the congregation or synagogue (just 11 percent of head clergy are women; Chaves 2017). Feminists, including

PERSONAL CONCEPTIONS OF GOD

In this exercise, you will consider the physical appearance you ascribe to God and the consequences for society of that image.

The way people imagine God to look varies dramatically depending on the religion of the people doing the imagining and their personal beliefs. Consider what image appears in your head when you think of God and answer the following questions:

1. Write a paragraph describing your image of God. What does God look like? In your image, is God a masculine or feminine figure? Old or young? Large or small?

2. How did you come to have this kind of image of God? Think of all the socializing agents that encouraged you to view God this way.

3. How does this image of God affect our understanding of gender?

4. How might our society change if most people had a different vision of God?

Muslim, Christian, and Jewish feminists, have worked for greater human rights for women and argued that gender equality should be at the center of religion and faith.

Religious Affiliation and Sexual Orientation

Many LGBT individuals continue to seek a "church home" and want to remain active in religious communities after they come out, despite the stigma and marginalization they face (Roberts and Yamane 2016). More than half of the LGBT sample surveyed in the Religious Landscape Study reported religious affiliation, with 48 percent identifying as Christian (see Figure 14.6). In 2017, B. T. Harmon launched his podcast *Blue Babies Pink* to share his coming-out story and his experiences growing up in north Alabama as a son of a Southern Baptist minister. *Blue Babies Pink* was number one on the iTunes "Religion/Spirituality" podcast chart and

▼ FIGURE 14.6

Religious Composition by Self-Reported Sexual Identity

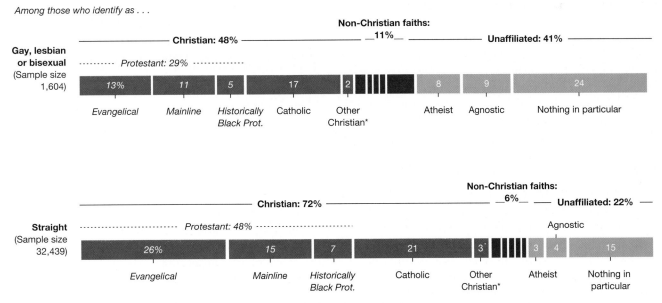

Among those who identify as . . .

Gay, lesbian or bisexual (Sample size 1,604)

Christian: 48% — Non-Christian faiths: 11% — Unaffiliated: 41%

Protestant: 29%

| 13% | 11 | 5 | 17 | 2 | | 8 | 9 | 24 |

Evangelical | Mainline | Historically Black Prot. | Catholic | Other Christian* | | Atheist | Agnostic | Nothing in particular

Straight (Sample size 32,439)

Christian: 72% — Non-Christian faiths: 6% — Unaffiliated: 22%

Agnostic

Protestant: 48%

| 26% | 15 | 7 | 21 | 3 | | 3 | 4 | 15 |

Evangelical | Mainline | Historically Black Prot. | Catholic | Other Christian* | Atheist | | Nothing in particular

Source: Lesbian, gay and bisexual Americans differ from general public in their religious affiliations, Pew Research, May 26, 2015. https://www.pewresearch.org/fact-tank/2015/05/26/lesbian-gay-and-bisexual-americans-differ-from-general-public-in-their-religious-affiliations/.

*Other Christian groups include Orthodox Christians, Mormons, Jehovah's Witnesses, and a number of smaller Christian groups. Don't know/refused answers are omitted.

Where Major Religions Officially Stand on Same-Sex Marriage

Sanctions Same-Sex Marriage	Prohibits Same-Sex Marriage	No Clear Position
Conservative Jewish Movement	American Baptist Churches	Buddhism
Episcopal Church	Assemblies of God	Hinduism
Evangelical Lutheran Church in America	Church of Jesus Christ of Latter-Day Saints (Mormons)	
Presbyterian Church (USA)	Islam	
Reform Jewish Movement	Lutheran Church – Missouri Synod	
Society of Friends (Quaker)	National Baptist Convention	
Unitarian Universalist Association of Churches	Orthodox Jewish Movement	
United Church of Christ	Roman Catholic Church	
	Southern Baptist Convention	
	United Methodist Church	

Source: David Masci and Michael Lipka, Where Christian churches, other religions stand on gay marriage. Pew Research Center, December 21, 2015. https://www.pewresearch.org/fact-tank/2015/12/21/where-christian-churches-stand-on-gay-marriage/.

in the top fifty of all podcasts worldwide. In his podcast, Harmon describes how he reconciles these different parts of his life and maintains his faith as an openly gay man.

LGBT rights and religion remain a frequent topic of debate, with people on both sides holding strong convictions. Most religious institutions continue to oppose same-sex marriage, citing scripture as the basis for definitions of sexual contact and marriage. In 2019, a special session of the general conference of the United Methodist Church met to discuss its official stance on same-sex marriage. After highly contentious discussions, with people across the world watching televised coverage of the meetings, the United Methodist Church voted to uphold its opposition to same-sex marriage and gay clergy. This vote and the opposition to this vote will reshape the denomination. Over the past two decades, though, more Christian denominations and some branches of Judaism (see Table 14.3 for a more complete list) have begun to support marriage equality and equal rights for LGBT members of society (Pew Research Center 2015a). Individual congregations often signify their support by identifying as "open and affirming." Numerous Christian denominations, such as the United Church of Christ, the Evangelical Lutheran Church in America, the Presbyterian Church (USA), and the Episcopal Church, now ordain LGBT clergy, signaling institutional, as well as local, support for LGBT rights.

Check Your Understanding

- How has Christianity in the United States become more racially and ethnically diverse?
- How are religious affiliation and religious activities related to gender?
- How are some congregations changing to become more inclusive of sexual orientation?

Global Diffusion of Religion

14.5 How does the process of global diffusion apply to religion?

Globally, the most common religions today are Christianity, Islam, Buddhism, Hinduism, Judaism, and folk religions (African traditional religions, Chinese folk religions, Native American religions, and Australian Aboriginal religions). Other religions are practiced worldwide, such as Bahá'í and Sikhism, but they are not as common as the others. As shown in Figure 14.7, Christianity is currently the most widely practiced religion and can be found almost everywhere in the world. Islam is the second most common religion, with most Muslims living in the Asia-Pacific region, the Middle East, and northern Africa. Most Buddhists, Hindus, and followers of folk religions reside in the Asia-Pacific region, while the vast majority of Jews live in either Israel or the United States.

Largest Religious Group, by Country

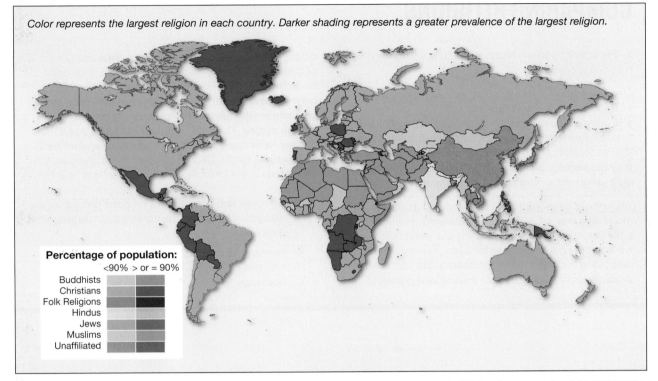

Color represents the largest religion in each country. Darker shading represents a greater prevalence of the largest religion.

Percentage of population:
<90% > or = 90%
- Buddhists
- Christians
- Folk Religions
- Hindus
- Jews
- Muslims
- Unaffiliated

Source: Conrad Hackett and Timmy Huynh, What is each country's second-largest religious group? Pew Research Center, June 22, 2015. https://www.pewresearch.org/fact-tank/2015/06/22/what-is-each-countrys-second-largest-religious-group/.

Note: Estimates are for 2010. Followers of other religions do not make up the largest religion in any country.

The Pew Research Center (2015b) projects that the distribution of people following the major world religions will remain steady over the next several decades, with the exceptions of Buddhism losing and Islam gaining adherents. The Muslim population is expected to reach parity with the Christian population by 2050 (see Figure 14.8, next page). Although religious conversion (e.g., unaffiliated converting to Islam) explains some of this trend, the projected change primarily reflects the age of followers and fertility rates. Muslims tend to be younger than Christians and to have more children.

Cultural Diffusion

Cultural attributes, like religion, can spread throughout the world through a process known as **cultural diffusion**. The global diffusion of religion is part of a larger globalization process (Roberts and Yamane 2016). As elements of one culture spread to another through modernization and migration, two other processes emerge: pluralism and assimilation. In a pluralistic society, smaller groups within a larger society maintain their unique cultural and religious identities, and their values and practices are accepted by others. When smaller groups adopt the cultural and religious practices of the dominant group, we call it assimilation.

Although some immigrants assimilate to the dominant religious practices in their new countries, others maintain the cultural and religious practices of their countries of origin. The fact that some people maintain traditional religious practices after moving to other nations results in transnational religious connections whereby religion spans societal borders (Kurien 2014). It can also help lead to the formation of ethnic enclaves in new countries with a strong religious commitment among recent immigrants. Ethnic enclaves help immigrants maintain a shared identity and a sense of belonging.

DOING SOCIOLOGY 14.4

COMPARING RELIGIONS

In this activity, you will analyze and compare data on religious groups.

The Association of Religion Data Archives created an interactive data analysis tool that allows you to analyze and compare data.. Start by accessing their web site at http://www.thearda.com. Click on "Religious Groups" in the red tool bar. Next, click "Compare Members" in the gray tab section. Select two religious groups from the drop-down menu, and click "Run Comparison."

You will see data on the following areas: demographics, moral attitudes, other beliefs and attitudes, political attitudes, religious beliefs, and religious practices. You will compute the differences between your chosen two religious groups and report the items within each of the six sections with the greatest similarity and greatest

difference. For example, examine Buddhist and Church of Christ. Within the demographics section, they both have similar levels of members who are of Hispanic origin or descent but show the greatest difference in the percentage who have a BA, a BS, or another four-year college degree. The data on Buddhists show that 61 percent have four-year college degrees compared with 28.5 percent for the Church of Christ. Next compute the differences in the other five sections. Now, it is your turn.

1. Compare and contrast two religious groups on six categories by noting their greatest similarities and differences.

2. How would you classify both of your chosen religious groups using the typology in the Doing Sociology 14.2 exercise?

▼ FIGURE 14.8

Projected Change in Global Population

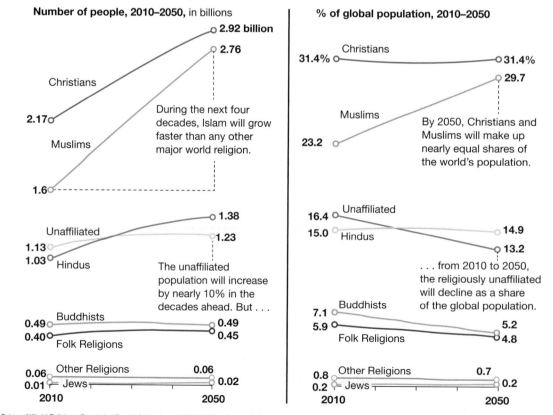

Source: The Future of World Religions: Population Growth Projections, 2010–2050, Pew Research Center, April 2, 2015. http://www.pewforum.org/2015/04/02/religious-projections-2010-2050.

MEASURING THE GROWTH OF ISLAM IN THE UNITED STATES

Globally, Islam is the fastest growing religion. It's projected to nearly double in size from 1.6 billion followers in 2010 to 2.76 billion in 2050. How does the growth of Islam in the United States compare with that in the rest of the world? In this online activity, you will address this question by examining the rate of Islamic followers in the United States between 2000 and 2010, using data from the Religious Congregations and Membership Study.

*Requires the Vantage version of *Sociology in Action*.

▼ FIGURE 14.9

Islamic Adherence Rate per 1,000 People (County)

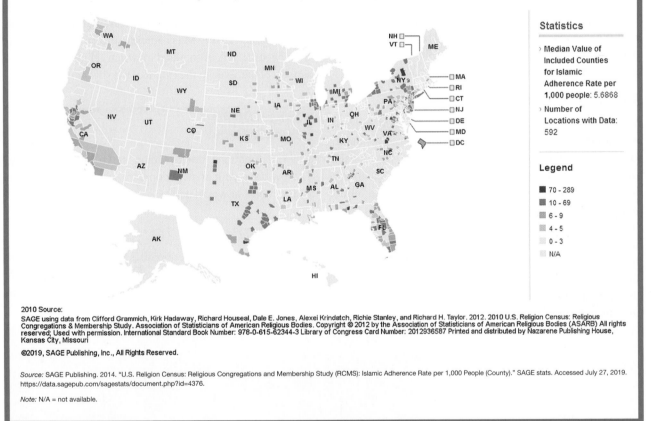

Statistics

› Median Value of Included Counties for Islamic Adherence Rate per 1,000 people: 5.6868

› Number of Locations with Data: 592

Legend

■ 70 - 289
■ 10 - 69
■ 6 - 9
■ 4 - 5
□ 0 - 3
■ N/A

2010 Source:

SAGE using data from Clifford Grammich, Kirk Hadaway, Richard Houseal, Dale E. Jones, Alexei Krindatch, Richie Stanley, and Richard H. Taylor. 2012. 2010 U.S. Religion Census: Religious Congregations & Membership Study. Association of Statisticians of American Religious Bodies. Copyright © 2012 by the Association of Statisticians of American Religious Bodies (ASARB) All rights reserved; Used with permission. International Standard Book Number: 978-0-615-62344-3 Library of Congress Card Number: 2012936587 Printed and distributed by Nazarene Publishing House, Kansas City, Missouri

©2019, SAGE Publishing, Inc., All Rights Reserved.

Source: SAGE Publishing. 2014. "U.S. Religion Census: Religious Congregations and Membership Study (RCMS): Islamic Adherence Rate per 1,000 People (County)." SAGE stats. Accessed July 27, 2019. https://data.sagepub.com/sagestats/document.php?id=4376.

Note: N/A = not available.

The experiences of second-generation immigrants illustrates the intersection of religious, cultural, and national identities. Although ethnic and religious identities are intertwined for recent immigrants, second-generation immigrants may practice their parents' religion but within a different cultural context. Second-generation immigrants often weave together the religious traditions of parents and family while incorporating religious practices common in the nations where they grew up, creating a new way of practicing religion in the process (Byng 2017).

CONSIDER THIS

Imagine you just told your neighbors that you are Catholic. How do you think they would respond? How would their own immigration status, ethnicity, race, economic status, religious affiliation, sexual orientation, and so on influence their response? Now, imagine you just told your neighbors that you are Muslim. How do you think they would respond? Why?

Check Your Understanding

- What changes are projected in religious affiliation in the global population?

- How does the process of cultural diffusion apply to religion?

- How can ethnic enclaves and religious practices support immigrants and affect religious pluralism?

Applying Sociological Theory to Religion

14.6 How does each of the major theoretical paradigms in sociology explain religion?

Theoretical perspectives are frameworks that help us make sense of the world around us. When applying the major sociological theories to religion, we can see the role of religion in our larger society and how religion shapes individual lives.

Structural Functionalism

As you recall from Chapter 2, structural functionalism assumes that all parts of society work together to promote solidarity and stability. According to structural functionalists, social institutions such as religion have a specific function or purpose in our society. Religion works with other major social institutions to create norms, customs, and practices that maintain social order. Faith-based organizations also provide many social services, addressing social problems such as poverty and homelessness. For example, the Episcopal Church has more than 600 ministries in the United States that specifically address poverty and community development. Most of these efforts consist of local antihunger programs, such as food banks and soup kitchens. On a global scale, the World Bank, one of the largest funders of efforts to reduce extreme poverty, partnered with thirty leaders from major world religions to issue a call for action to end poverty by 2030. In doing so, it acknowledged that faith-based organizations serve vital roles in addressing poverty and creating sustainable solutions to global poverty.

For Durkheim and other structural functionalists, religion provides a strong common morality that guides and constrains our actions. This can be seen in religious teachings, doctrines, and the rules that prescribe certain behaviors. Religion also creates a sense of social order and social cohesion through shared symbolism and rituals. Last, it provides people with a sense of purpose and meaning even in times of despair. In his research on suicide, Durkheim ([1897] 1951) found that lower suicide rates were connected to integration within a social group and the guidance they offered. Close-knit religious groups had lower levels of suicide. Durkheim pointed out that religion provided these strong integration functions, which lowered suicide rates; however, he also cautioned that religion can create an extreme amount of social integration and conformity that can also result in suicide, for instance, mass suicide or religious suicide bombers. In such cases, the religious groups that support these actions have many of the ideological and organizational characteristics of fundamentalism. Mass suicide and suicide bombing then become acts of totalism in which religion dictates all aspects of life, even to the extent of who lives and who dies.

CONSIDER THIS

What functions does religion serve in U.S. society? How does your answer compare with what a structural functionalist would say?

Conflict Theory

Whereas structural functionalists focus on the interrelatedness of social institutions, conflict theorists highlight how economic, societal, religious, and political systems

Rituals are centerpieces of all religions.
imageBROKER/Alamy Stock Photo

create a system of social stratification. Conflict theorists point to the unequal distribution of power and resources across society. Those with more power and prestige are invested in maintaining the status quo and use religion to oppress and exploit subordinate groups.

Karl Marx. Karl Marx ([1843] 1970) referred to religion as the opiate of the masses. He believed that the people in power (those who own the means of production) use religion to distract the workers. He argued that religious leaders, whose salaries tend to be based on donations from the wealthy, encourage workers to focus on gaining rewards in the afterlife rather than on demanding present-day justice and overthrowing the capitalist system.

Some symbols, such as the pentagram, are used by different religions to mean different things.
©iStockphoto.com/zager

CONSIDER THIS

Do you agree with Marx that religion is the "opiate of the masses"? Why or why not?

Max Weber. Max Weber spent much of his life studying religion. In *The Protestant Ethic and the Spirit of Capitalism*, Weber ([1904] 1958) connected the spread of certain religious ideas with the rise of a capitalist economic system. He maintained that the Protestant Reformation and the rise of Calvinism encouraged industrial capitalism. Calvinists believe in predestination, the idea that people are destined for heaven or hell from birth. Financial success became seen as evidence that one was preordained to go to heaven. This, combined with the Calvinist emphasis on simple lifestyles, encouraged people to work hard and to rationally invest their money into new technology and other aspects of their business—the perfect recipe for capitalism. Those who did *not* succeed financially were clearly deserving of their poverty, as they were destined to go to hell. Together, predestination and rationalization created the "Protestant work ethic."

Symbolic Interaction

Structural functionalists and conflict theorists provide a macro analysis of religion, whereas symbolic interactionists focus on the micro aspects. From a symbolic interactionist perspective, religion is characterized by having a set of symbols, **rituals** (or ceremonial behaviors), and a shared understanding among a group of people. Individuals actively create religions as they construct their social environments on the basis of the meanings they attribute to their actions and interactions (Blumer 1969).

Religion consists of socially constructed sets of practices based on what members of the religion define and accept as sacred. For example, fasting rituals associated with the Islamic Ramadan, Jewish Yom Kippur, and Christian Lenten season all have symbolic meanings to those who take part in these practices. Likewise, practices in other religions also serve symbolic purposes. For example, during the Catholic ceremony of the Eucharist, bread and wine become sacred as they are transformed, in the eyes of believers, into the literal body and blood of Christ.

Religious practices and the meaning of religious symbols can change over time. We can also see how religions alter their gender-related practices as the societies around them change. The acceptance of the ordination of women in many Western Christian congregations provides a prime example of how religions can adjust to changing gender roles. As societies change, so do their institutions—including religion.

Symbols mean something when groups ascribe a meaning to them. For example, the pentagram, a five-pointed star, is a symbol used across religions but with different meanings attached to it. In Christianity, the pentagram is a symbol of the five wounds of Jesus. In the Bahá'í faith, a religious movement dating to the nineteenth century, a pentagram is known as a *haykal*, meaning "temple" in Arabic. Wiccans see the pentagram as a symbol of the goddess Morgan and of the five elements of life.

Table 14.4 summarizes how each of the major sociological perspectives contributes to our understanding of religion.

Applying Sociological Theory to Religion

	Structural Functionalist Perspective	Conflict Perspective	Symbolic Interactionist Perspective
Level of analysis	**Macro**	**Macro**	**Micro**
Contributions to understanding religion	Establishes cohesion and social solidarity Provides a sense of purpose and meaning	Connected to the growth of industrial capitalism Used to oppress and exploit subordinate groups	Socially constructed set of practices Contains symbols, rituals, and shared understanding of the sacred

CONSIDER THIS

What are some examples of religious symbols and rituals?

Check Your Understanding

- What are the major functions of religion?
- Why did Marx call religion the "opiate" of the people?
- How did Calvinism help create capitalism?
- What is the relationship between religion and gender inequality?
- What role do rituals play in religious practice?

Religion and Social Issues, Social Change, and Everyday Life

14.7 What are some recent examples of how religion has fostered social change efforts?

Although religions must adjust to changes in society, they can also influence followers' perspectives on social issues and help create social change. Many of the roots of both violence and positive social change throughout history can be found in religion. Religions have been used to enforce hierarchies and to mobilize efforts to dismantle such oppressive structures.

Religious Affiliation and Attitudes toward Social Issues

The **subcultural identity theory** (Smith et al. 1998) is particularly helpful in explaining the relationship between religious affiliation and attitudes toward social issues. This theory suggests that individuals seek a collective identity that helps provide them with a strong moral code. The group identity becomes stronger when there is an ingroup/outgroup distinction. Religious groups and organizations strive to create a moral commitment on the behalf of followers, which leads to complying with the larger group norms and values. This includes defining what is sacred and what behavior is sinful. Observance of these beliefs signifies ingroup membership and loyalty to the religious organization.

Charitable giving and volunteer service provide ways members of a religious group can demonstrate their moral commitment to the religion. In the United States, people who identify as highly religious are more likely to volunteer than others. Not surprisingly, they tend to volunteer primarily in religious settings versus **secular** (nonreligious) settings (Taniguchi and Thomas 2011). Many religious organizations provide ample opportunities for their members to volunteer and act out their faith through good works.

CONSIDER THIS

On your campus, do you think volunteerism is affected by religious affiliation? On what would you base that opinion? What other factors encourage volunteerism on your campus?

Religion and Social Change

While the Ku Klux Klan used Christianity to justify their violence, African American churches fostered and became symbols of the civil rights movement. Religious leaders such as Dr. Martin Luther King Jr. and many others played a large role in the leadership of the civil rights movement. Dr. King's "I Have a Dream" speech remains a powerful symbol of racial equality. Recall that Dr. King was a Baptist minister who saw Christianity as a powerful force in creating social change. Black clergy became spokespersons and strategists for the movement. Church organizations, mostly run by women, provided food and help to those in need, while church buildings became meeting places to organize protests and boycotts and receive spiritual and emotional strength in the face of danger.

The Taliban, an Islamic terrorist group that now controls territory in Afghanistan and Pakistan, has forbidden

Malala Yousafzai was the youngest person to ever receive the Nobel Prize. She is helping establish the right to education for all girls, in defiance of the Taliban.

CORNELIUS POPPE/AFP/Getty Images

girls from attending schools. Taliban leaders claim that they cannot allow cross-gender contact between boys and girls. Malala Yousafzai also uses her Islamic faith, but to counter the ways the Taliban uses Islam. Along with her father, Malala promotes education for girls while showing how some groups, like the Taliban, misuse religion to pursue their own agendas (https://www.malala.org). She defied the Taliban by writing blogs about the treatment of girls in Pakistan and by attending a school for girls that was founded by her father. As a result, Malala and her family received threats, even some printed in the newspaper! On October 9, 2012, as she was heading to school, a gunman boarded her school bus and shot her in the head (and wounded two of her friends). Malala was fifteen years old at the time of her shooting. Her message about faith and social change had become a threat to the Taliban. The attempt on her life was intended to silence her forever, but the shooting (and her miraculous survival) led to widespread fame and helped her spread her message of girls' access to education across the globe. Soon after, Pakistan passed its Right to Education Bill, guaranteeing (at least on paper) the right to a free education for all children ages five to sixteen. In 2014, Malala became the youngest person to ever receive the Nobel Prize.

Meanwhile, Pope Francis has called for a rethinking of the world's problems as human problems and urged all people—of all religions—to help each member of the human family. Pope Francis has challenged other world leaders and advocated on the behalf of refugees, those in poverty, and for the health of our polluted planet. In 2016,

he urged world leaders not to think of refugees as numbers but as people with names and stories. In his speech for the 52nd World Day of Peace, Pope Francis spoke on the "great project of peace" that is "grounded in the mutual responsibility and interdependence of human beings" and that "entails a conversion of heart and soul" and includes a peace with oneself, a peace with others, and peace with all creatures (Vatican Press Office 2018). He urges people to think about religion as a force for good that can heal the wounds of human tragedy.

Indigenous religions, such as those practiced by many Native Americans, have long stressed the importance of the spiritual relationship between the Earth and its inhabitants. As the dangers of climate change and environmental degradation have become more widely known over the past several decades, many religions have infused their religious teachings with environmentalism. **Religious environmentalism** refers to the environmental actions of religious leaders and communities within organized religion as well as more general environmentalism grounded in spirituality (Jenkins and Chapple 2011). Many religious leaders from across the religious spectrum—most notably Pope Francis—proclaim that addressing environmental degradation and climate change is a religious imperative.

CONSIDER THIS

How has religion been used in your own hometown to address social problems? Are there any faith-based organizations that work toward ending poverty and feeding the hungry? Are any churches in your hometown involved in advocacy for different populations?

The Continuing Influence of Religion in Everyday Life

Even with changing religious affiliation and participation, faith-based practices remain an integral part of U.S. society and many people's individual identities. Using the sociological imagination, we see how religion can contribute to *and* counter patriarchy, racism, homophobia, nationalism, ethnocentrism, violence, and other social issues. An understanding of the sociology of religion is helpful in any job that requires interacting with others, particularly

RELIGION AND END-OF-LIFE CARE

HEATHER GRIGSBY

I majored in sociology and minored in religious studies while in college and sought for a way to incorporate both into a future career. My experience interning with hospice gave me a new outlook on how important sociology is in the medical field, especially in cancer care, palliative care, and end-of-life care. I was overwhelmed at the opportunities that arose for me to put my textbook information into action. My experiences interning with hospice helped me to make connections in the community, which allowed me to make relationships with people of different races and different belief systems.

While interning at Keller Hospice in Tuscumbia, Alabama (the birthplace of Helen Keller), I learned the functions that hospice serves for families. I was surprised to discover that Keller Hospice as well as other hospices offer chaplain services. This means that there is a chaplain in each workplace, whose main job is to connect with the patients and their families. This was highly appealing to me, as I have always been passionate about talking to people about religion. I learned that the most important service that chaplains can provide is to listen to the thoughts, concerns, and feelings of the patients and families. Their work is not about forcing patients to believe what they believe but about connecting on their level and providing comfort.

I shadowed a chaplain doing home visits with patients and was able to see how the patients would open up about their feelings related to religion and spiritual topics. The chaplain was Christian and had different religious beliefs than most of the patients he served, but he was able to offer some sort of prayer or scripture reading that meant something special to each patient. He asked them questions about life and death, provided them with advice or prayer, and gave them spiritual comfort. No matter their religion, the patients had a special bond with the chaplain because he was able to bring peace to the situation by being a friend and offering respect for their beliefs. I saw that feeling heard and having a sense of belonging, meaning, and peace is important patients at the end of their life.

While on home visits with the social worker, patients and families would ask us spiritual questions and express their concerns related to the afterlife. With my knowledge of different religions from my sociology classes, I felt prepared to answer their basic questions and to be respectful of their cultural and religious beliefs—whether that was to offer a prayer, to take off my shoes when I entered their home, or to not mention funeral plans or afterlife. I strongly believe that we are better equipped to provide services when we know more about the religious beliefs of others.

Through interning with hospice, my eyes were opened on how important it is to listen and to be respectful of culture and religion even when it is different from your own and how important sociology is to understanding people's end-of-life needs. I will never forget the wonderful patients who shared their beliefs with me and allowed me to have an impact on their final days. I look forward continuing my work in hospice.

Discussion Question: Heather notes how her education in the sociology of religion helped her act appropriately and effectively during her internship with hospice. How can a background in the sociology of religion be helpful in other settings, such as schools, hospitals, and counseling centers?

for those in volunteer or outreach coordinator positions, religiously affiliated nonprofit organizations, campus ministry, childcare, bereavement, adoption, and foster care settings. Heather Grigsby, the sociologist in action featured in this chapter, provides an example of this as she relays how her sociological training helped her during her internship with a hospice provider.

CONSIDER THIS

Consider again the question from the beginning of the chapter: how can we determine how religious people are or to what extent they practice their religion? Has your answer changed after reading this chapter?

Check Your Understanding

- How does religious affiliation affect attitudes toward social issues?

- What role did religion play in the civil rights movement?

- How is Malala Yousafzai using her religion to advocate for girls and women?

- According to Pope Francis, how does religion help us take action when displaced groups need assistance?

Conclusion

As you have seen, religions both reflect society and work to change it. In the next chapter, you will learn how environmental issues relate to and influence changes in social behavior. Chapter 15 describes why we need to work on changing social behavior to alleviate injustice, stem global climate change, and save society.

REVIEW

14.1 How do sociologists define religion, religiosity, and spirituality?

Religion is a social institution that involves the beliefs and practices of what has been socially constructed as sacred in a given society. Religiosity is the level of religiousness of an individual and includes religious activities, practices, and beliefs. Spirituality is the search for the sacred that may occur outside of doctrinal boundaries.

14.2 What are pluralism and secularization?

Pluralism is a diversity and coexistence of different religions. Secularization is a society's movement away from identification with religious values and institutions and can be seen in the growing number of people who identify as nonreligious.

14.3 What is fundamentalism?

Fundamentalism is a response to modernization and secularization. Fundamentalists resist such societal changes by holding onto idealized, conservative, traditional religious practices; strict conformity to religious scriptures; and a belief in one true religion.

14.4 What are the current trends in religious affiliation and participation in the United States?

The current trends in religious participation in the Unites States suggest an increase in non-Christian faiths, which can be attributed to changing demographics and more acceptance of religious diversity. As the percentage of nonreligiously affiliated Americans continues to increase, many religious groups have become more racially and ethnically diverse, more accepting of female leadership, and more supportive of LGBT people and same-sex marriage.

14.5 How does the process of global diffusion apply to religion?

The Pew Research Center (2015b) describes contemporary global trends in religion and projects that Christian affiliation will decline while adherents of Islam will grow, resulting in equal shares of Christians and Muslims among the world population. The expansion of religion across spatial boundaries is part of the globalization process and the global diffusion of religion. Globalization also affects the spread of secularization and fundamentalism.

14.6 How does each of the major theoretical paradigms in sociology explain religion?

From a structural-functional perspective, religion works with other major social institutions to create norms and practices that maintain stability and social order. The functions religion serves in a given society include establishing social cohesion, creating social integration, promoting social control, and providing people with a sense of purpose and meaning. Conflict theory focuses on the unequal distribution of power and resources across society. From this perspective, those with more power and prestige are invested in maintaining the status quo and use religion to oppress and exploit subordinate groups. Symbolic interactionists see individuals as actively constructing their social environments as they interact. They use symbols, practices, and shared understanding to create religions. Like other parts of society, most religions change over time, as they respond to social forces within and outside their organizations.

14.7 What are some recent examples of how religion has fostered social change efforts?

Although religion has been used as the basis for violence throughout history, it is also a driving force in positive social change. The American civil rights movement shows how churches can become a safe haven from violence. Malala Yousafzai demonstrates how young people today are using their faith to counter messages of hatred. Pope Francis is an example of the role of religious leaders in advocating for displaced and disadvantaged groups.

KEY TERMS

agnostics 281

atheists 281

cults 285

cultural diffusion 291

fundamentalists 286

Islamophobia 287

modernization 283

profane 279

religion 279

religiosity 279

religious environmentalism 297

religious pluralism 280

rituals 295

sacred 279

sects 284

secular 296

secular humanists 281

secularization 281

secularization theory 283

spirituality 279

subcultural identity theory 296

CHAPTER 15

SAVING THE ENVIRONMENT

John Chung-En Liu

Environmental problems are social problems.
AP Photo/Erik McGregor

15.1 Why are environmental problems social problems?

15.2 How do sociologists study environmental issues?

15.3 How would eco-Marxists and ecological modernization theorists define and discuss environmental problems and their solutions?

15.4 What are the promises and constraints of green consumption?

15.5 What is environmental justice?

15.6 What are social solutions to environmental problems?

Facing Our Environmental Challenges

15.1 Why are environmental problems social problems?

We now face serious environmental challenges. Air and water pollution, soil erosion, ocean acidification, biodiversity loss, species extinction, cancer villages, food safety, and so on—this unnerving list can go on. And there is global warming. At the time we updated this textbook in mid-2019, we learned that the years 2014, 2015, 2016, 2017, and 2018 were the five hottest years in history (Borunda 2019). According to the Fourth National Climate Assessment, without immediate steps to mitigate it, the effect of climate change will continue to drain economies across the world, with hundreds of billions of dollars of economic losses. Changing water availability will lead to both floods and droughts, as well as loss of hydropower production. The changing climate will increase the numbers of heat-related deaths and species extinctions and will expose people to new diseases. Many communities are already vulnerable to rising waters and actively attempting or considering relocating (U.S. Global Change Research Program 2018). Some scholars argue that we have entered the "Anthropocene" period—a new geological era characterized by human impacts on the planet (National Centers for Environmental Information 2016).

As citizens of the Earth, what should we do? Some students respond to this question by emphasizing the importance of technological development:

"Install solar panels!"

"Drive electric cars!"

"How about we try geoengineering or carbon storage and capture?"

Others talk about the small steps everyone can take in their everyday lives:

"I always make sure that I recycle diligently."

"Turn off the lights when you leave the room."

"Bike or take public transportation, minimize driving your car!"

Indeed, technology can be our friend—solar panels, in most cases, are more environmentally friendly than burning coal. We probably will rely heavily on various technological breakthroughs in our pursuit of a cleaner future. In addition, individual actions are certainly laudable—we all want to do something to help save the planet, right? When asked, however, "Do you really believe we can solve all the environmental problems by developing new technologies, recycling, planting trees, and riding bikes?" a few students are optimistic, but many more are uncertain.

As you will learn from this chapter, sociologists go beyond the common technocratic and individualistic framework when examining environmental problems. Sociologists, first and foremost, consider environmental problems as social problems. Environmental problems are problems for society, threatening our current forms of social organization. In other words, the environment is not something to be "saved" by us—we're really saving ourselves by addressing environmental degradation.

Environmental problems are also problems of society. This means that the problems are not the result of bad intentions or ineffective leaders; instead, they are the consequences of larger social forces and social organizations. To fundamentally deal with environmental problems, we need to address the ways we collectively structure our lives (Bell and Ashwood 2015). With this sociological perspective in mind, let's turn to the physical reality of environmental problems. Are things really as bad as many environmental activists claim?

CONSIDER THIS

Think of all the things we can do to help save the environment. Which do you think are the most important? Why?

JOHN CHUNG-EN LIU

I was a latecomer to sociology. In college, I was a chemical engineering major; in my master's program, I focused on economics and environmental policy. My intellectual journey made me realize that environmental problems—the challenges I've been seeking to address—are ultimately social problems.

That was the moment I found my love of sociology. At the University of Wisconsin, I was nurtured by a tradition that specifically focuses on communities and the environment. The training allowed me to rigorously examine the origins of environmental problems and, at the same time, boldly imagine solutions. In my own work,

I use sociology to come up with policy insights that can contribute to solving urgent environmental issues such as climate change. Recently, my work on climate change skepticism was featured in *Foreign Policy* and on Public Radio International.

Besides research, I also have a passion for teaching sociology. I especially like to use various hands-on projects to connect sociological knowledge with our everyday lives. My goal is to help students create a sense of sociological imagination with ecological consciousness.

The Physical Reality of Environmental Problems

When looking at the state of the environment, it is useful to start with the concept of **sustainability**. A sustainable social-economic system can function within the earth's ecological constraints. In 1987, the United Nations (UN) World Commission on Environment and Development published "Our Common Future" (also known as the Brundtland report), in which it defined **sustainable development** as "development that meets the needs of the present without compromising the ability of future generations to meet their own needs." How we achieve this ideal remains a subject of heated discussions. How can we continue to live the way we have been living indefinitely? Sociology, especially its subfield of **environmental sociology**, which focuses on the interaction between the social and the natural systems, provides many useful insights to guide us toward sustainability.

Some researchers developed the **ecological footprint** indicator as a yardstick to assess sustainability (Wackernagel and Rees 1998). The ecological footprint represents the productive area—expressed in number of "planet Earths"—required to provide the resources humanity is using and to absorb its waste. According to the calculation, on the basis of our food consumption, energy use, transportation, and so on, we need 1.5 Earths to sustain our current consumption level. Moreover, if everybody lived like an average U.S. resident, we would need 5 Earths. Obviously, one is all we have! Footprint analysis

scholars argue that we are in an unsustainable **overshoot** situation—using resources at a pace more than the earth's regenerative capacity.

On the basis of the concept of the ecological footprint, others have developed similar measures, such as "carbon footprint" and "water footprint," to illustrate our environmental impacts. These indicators certainly are not without their flaws. The data sources are not perfect, and the calculation is often difficult; more important, they do not directly tell us who or what is driving these environmental impacts. Yet, the central take-home message is clear: we cannot continue consuming resources at our current pace forever!

Footprint analysis has shown another important result: individual consumption is only a small part of overall resource use. A major portion of our economic activities happens in the "background"—infrastructure, power generation, agriculture—the things usually beyond individual control. No matter how "green" you try to be, there are activities at the collective level that you, alone, cannot control. We are all in this unsustainable system together, willingly or reluctantly. This lesson illustrates the need to think and act sociologically to respond to environmental problems. The quest toward sustainability is a team sport. It is not enough to confine our thinking to individual attitudes and behaviors. We need to be thinking about larger social forces that shape environmental outcomes and facilitating changes in our communities (on our campus, city, state, nation, and world), as well as changing our individual behavior.

CALCULATE YOUR OWN ECOLOGICAL FOOTPRINT

In this activity, you will use an online tool to calculate the ecological footprint of your lifestyle.

Ecological footprint analysis is one approach to gauging our environmental impacts on the planet. Use the online tool developed by the Global Footprint Network to calculate your own ecological footprint (http://www .footprintnetwork.org/en/index.php/GFN/page/calculators/). After you are done, answer the following questions and be prepared to discuss them with your class:

1. How much is your ecological footprint? How many planets would we need to support humanity if everyone maintained your lifestyle?

2. What factors are the largest contributors to your footprint? Food? Shelter? Services?

3. What are some possible steps you could take to decrease your footprint?

4. How would your footprint change if you changed your dietary habits or transportation modes in the tool?

5. Now, answer the questions in the tool again as if you lived in a different country. What do you see as the cause of any difference in the size of ecological footprint?

6. Imagine you are an urban planner working for a city council. What would you recommend the city council do to reduce residents' ecological footprints?

Check Your Understanding

- What is sustainability?

- What is an ecological footprint? What does it measure?

- What do scientists mean when they say we are in an ecological overshoot?

- On what does the subfield of environmental sociology focus?

- Why must we think and act sociologically to respond to environmental problems?

How Do Sociologists Study Environmental Issues?

15.2   How do sociologists study environmental issues?

Before sociologists tackle environmental degradation, we step back to reflect deeply, sometimes even philosophically, on our understanding of environmental issues. We ask questions such as the following:

- What is nature?

- Where does our environmental knowledge come from?

- What shapes our understanding of a particular environmental issue?

- Does everyone perceive environmental problems in the same way? If not, what explains the variation?

Answering these questions helps ensure that our actions are sociologically grounded and not biased by individualistic or ethnocentric perspectives. In this section, we look at the social construction of nature and environmental problems.

Social Construction of Nature

To protect the environment, conventional wisdom is that we should use "natural" products instead of artificial ones. Sounds great, right? But what exactly do we mean when we say that something is "natural"? What about germs, viruses, and diseases? They are part of "nature," too. Also, are humans part of nature? If yes, what makes artificial things "unnatural" if humans make them? The more you think about this, the more you'll see the difficulty in drawing a clear boundary between the "artificial" and the "natural" components. This conundrum gets to the concept of what sociologists called social construction—an idea you have already encountered in other chapters of this book. It means that a category (e.g., natural or artificial) or a phenomenon (e.g., climate change or biodiversity loss) is understood to have certain characteristics because we agree they do.

American Wilderness. A **constructivist analysis of the environment** focuses on the role of ideology and knowledge in understanding our environmental conditions. For example, environmental historian Bill Cronon has famously traced the concept of "**wilderness**." We

HOW MUCH OF OUR ELECTRICITY COMES FROM BURNING COAL?

Despite the growth of alternative energy sources like wind and solar, most of America's electricity is still produced by burning fossil fuels (coal, natural gas, and petroleum). In this online activity, you will consider which states are most reliant on coal and whether that reliance is increasing or decreasing, using data from the U.S. Department of Energy.

*Requires the Vantage version of *Sociology in Action*.

▼ FIGURE 15.1

Percentage of Electricity Generation from Coal (State)

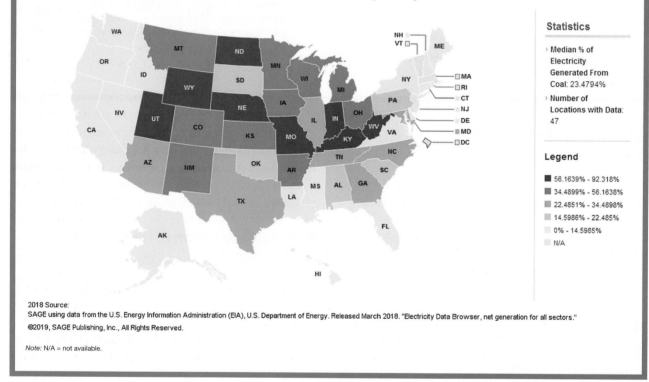

Statistics

› Median % of Electricity Generated From Coal: 23.4794%

› Number of Locations with Data: 47

Legend

■ 56.1639% - 92.318%
■ 34.4899% - 56.1638%
■ 22.4851% - 34.4898%
■ 14.5986% - 22.485%
□ 0% - 14.5985%
□ N/A

2018 Source:
SAGE using data from the U.S. Energy Information Administration (EIA), U.S. Department of Energy. Released March 2018. "Electricity Data Browser, net generation for all sectors."
©2019, SAGE Publishing, Inc., All Rights Reserved.

Note: N/A = not available.

tend to think of wilderness as the highest ideal of nature: pristine, pure, and untouched by humans. Cronon demonstrates that the concept of wilderness is a product of America's frontier mentality, in which people romanticized the vast and supposedly untrammeled landscape (Cronon 1996). Such an understanding of nature is a social construction and a product of North American cultural and historical contexts.

Outside the Western world, many cultures do not distinguish the "wild" from the "nonwild" environment. In some cases, they do not even have an equivalent term for wilderness or pristine nature in their languages! For example, in classical Chinese, the closest word to "nature" is *tiandi* (meaning heaven and earth) or *wanwu* (literally, ten thousand things), neither of which applies to the categorical distinction between humans and their environment (Weller 2006).

"So what?" you might wonder. We care about the social construction process because it often leads to tangible political and social implications. For example, seeing "wilderness" as the truest exemplar of nature, the United States and many countries following its lead have established national parks to protect nature from human development. The process sometimes has led to forced removal

What does the term *wilderness* mean to you?

of local people from their homes, strangled the ecological relationships between indigenous communities and wildlife, and distracted us from attending to the mundane non-pristine environments around us. The creation of national parks is a human intervention based on a very particular cultural construct of nature.

China's Great Leap Forward. Another example of the social construction of nature can be found in the environmental disasters that occurred in revolutionary China during the 1950s. Threatened by Western powers and driven by Marxist ideology, Chinese leader Mao Zedong took an adversarial and extreme stance toward the natural world. He viewed humans as distinctly separated from nature. In his words, humans must "conquer" and "defeat" nature to achieve the modernist ideal. This philosophy represented a sharp break from the traditional Chinese emphasis on harmony between humans and nature and moderation in resource consumption. The consequence was large-scale environmental and social disasters (Shapiro 2001).

During the Great Leap Forward—a political, economic, and social campaign to catch up with the West—Mao encouraged every commune or neighborhood to build small furnaces in their backyards to produce steel. Finding fuel to work these backyard furnaces led to massive deforestation. Mao also championed unscientific agricultural practices, including eradicating sparrows—birds that eat grains—and overusing fertilizers, resulting in the largest famine in human history and irreversible ecological damage to Chinese soil (Shapiro 2001).

As you can see from these examples, the social construction of nature has material consequences. How we think about nature influences how we act toward it. To think sociologically is to be mindful of how our thoughts about nature can influence our actions and, in the process, our society.

Constructing Environmental Problems

A social constructivist approach also examines how we come to perceive and define certain issues—such as air pollution, the ozone hole, and climate change—as environmental problems. You must have heard of the "ozone hole," but have you wondered what kind of "hole" it is? It turns out the hole is not an area with zero ozone in the atmosphere—just that the ozone layer is a lot thinner there. The more scientific term for the ozone hole would be *ozone thinning* or *ozone depletion*.

The hole metaphor is a particular (and powerful) representation of the problem—that hydrofluorocarbons from aerosol sprays, refrigerants, and so on were severely thinning the ozone layer that protects us from the sun's harmful ultraviolet rays. "Ozone hole" caught many people's attention and led to the establishment of the Montreal Protocol to limit ozone-depleting substances. The Montreal Protocol, subsequently, was widely recognized as the most successful international environmental agreement and effectively phased out the ozone-depleting substances.

Under the 2015 UN Paris Agreement on climate change, nations across the globe agreed to work to limit further warming of the world to within 2 degrees Celsius. (In 2017 President Trump said that he would pull the United States out of the agreement.) Why 2 degrees? Why not 1.5 to make it safer? How about 3, 4, or 5? We collectively, under the guidance of scientists, construct the extent of change (in this case, global warming) that we deem alarming.

Although the idea of social construction we've discussed in other chapters (of gender, for instance) appears to happen organically or unconsciously, the social construction of an environmental problem—defining the problem and its solutions—can be quite direct and contentious. By now, you have probably figured out that environmental problems relate to people's interests. Different groups can try to shape them for their own benefit. For example, as efforts to address climate change threaten the fossil fuel industry, some fossil fuel companies have used misinformation campaigns to create confusion among the public about the realities of climate change. Scholars call them

HUMAN-NATURE PHOTO CONTEST

Take a photo of human-nature interaction around your campus or local communities. Is the relationship harmonious, contentious, intertwined, or separated? How did you conceptualize "nature" when you took the photo?

Write a few sentences to describe the human nature interactions in your photo and how you conceptualized nature when you took the photo. Submit your photo and response to your instructor.

"Backyard furnaces" in China led to large-scale environmental disasters as people chopped down trees to provide fuel for them.

environmental concerns evolve over time, and why some problems are prioritized over others.

Environmental Awareness and Concern

Why are some of your friends tree-huggers while others couldn't care less about the environment? Our interactions with the environment depend on social experiences. Nature is often a symbolic environment for humans to confer meanings. For example, Émile Durkheim, one of sociology's founding figures, found that some aboriginal people worship particular types of plants or animals—the totem—as part of a ritual that increases social solidarity (Jerolmack and Tavory 2014). A study of male Turkish immigrants in Berlin, Germany, revealed that they experience a connection to their homeland and express their ethnic identity through keeping domestic pigeons, as they had in Turkey (Jerolmack 2007). In England, rural villagers who self-identify as "country people" believe that they live a more authentic and wholesome life than city dwellers—whom they see as removed from nature. Villagers believe that their proximity to nature offers them an escape from urban societal ills such as greed and alienation (Bell 1994).

To make sense of the rise of contemporary environmental concern, sociologists Riley Dunlap, William Catton, and their colleagues have come up with the **paradigm shift theory** (Catton and Dunlap 1978). They distinguish two sets of worldviews—the old "human exemptionalist paradigm" (HEP) and the "new environmental

the "merchants of doubt," delaying critical actions through attacking the social construction that climate change is happening and/or is a problem that threatens the well-being of humans (Oreskes and Conway 2010; Union of Concerned Scientists 2018).

To be clear, saying that climate change is socially constructed does not negate the physical reality that the world is warming. It does, however, help us see how our views toward it are shaped by social forces. It enables us to recognize where our environmental knowledge comes from, how paradigm" (NEP). The former reflects an anthropocentric, or human-centered, relationship with the environment. Nature is to be mastered by humans. Humans are meant to dominate the earth, without concern for their impact on it. The NEP views humans as only part of the complex ecosystem and subject to ecological limits. The paradigm shift theory suggests that environmental concerns arise as people gradually adopt a more environmentally aware worldview—shifting from the HEP to the NEP.

Our likelihood to make the shift from HEP to NEP relates to our social positions. Environmental issues, contrary to the stereotype, tend not to be an elite concern. Women and minority groups rate environmental problems a higher concern than other demographic groups (Macias 2016; McCright 2010). People in more dominant positions tend to have better resources to protect themselves from environmental risk and thus may care less about the environment.

Environmental concern is also influenced by **risk perception**—the tendency to evaluate the danger of a situation not in purely rational terms but through the lens of individual biases and cultures. For example, the physical risks of traveling in cars far outweigh the risks of flying in airplanes. According to the National Transportation Safety Board, the probability of dying in an airplane accident is 1 in 1.2 million, while the odds of being killed in a car crash are 1 in 5,000. But people usually fear flying more than driving. Similarly, the chance of dying in a terrorist

attack is negligible in the United States, roughly equal to the chance of being killed by unstable furniture or televisions at home. It is hard to avoid hearing about the threat of terrorism. When is the last time you heard someone speak about being afraid of their furniture or their TV?

Recognizing environmental risks is based on more than having the best information and exercising rational calculations. Values also matter. As our values often come from the communities in which we live, group identities also come into play in our concerns regarding the environment. The debate about climate change in the United States provides a good example. Research has shown that the persistent disagreement over its existence and the danger it poses to humans has, to a large extent, become an us-versus-them issue rather than primarily a scientific matter. As Figure 15.2 reveals, 95 percent of liberal Democrats think that global warming is happening, and

▼ FIGURE 15.2

Americans' Divided Attitudes on Climate Change

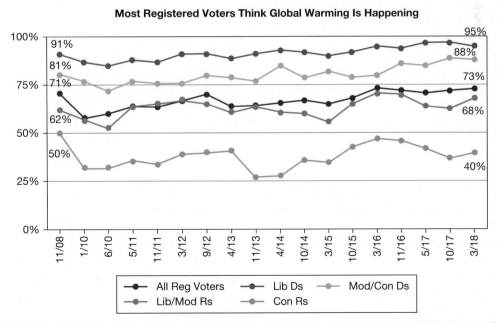

Most Registered Voters Think Global Warming Is Happening

Source: Leiserowitz, A., Maibach, E., Rosenthal, S., Kotcher, J., Goldberg, M., Ballew, M., Gustafson, A., & Bergquist, P. (2019). Politics & Global Warming, December 2018. Yale University and George Mason University. New Haven, CT: Yale Program on Climate Change Communication.

Note: D = Democrat; R = Republican.

CLIMATE CHANGE CAMPAIGNER FOR A DAY

In this activity, you will consider the ways in which you would tailor a message promoting efforts to combat climate change depending on your audience.

Suppose you are trying to persuade people to take action on climate change. As we have learned, values matter in how people understand and respond to environmental problems. Brainstorm different ways to present climate change that will resonate with different individuals or groups of people.

Write a few sentences explaining how you would make the case for climate change actions to each of the following people:

1. The president of the United States
2. The president of China
3. Executives in oil companies
4. Low-income households in an inner-city neighborhood
5. Regular churchgoers
6. Your local Parent-Teacher Association

---

88 percent of them are worried; on the contrary, only 40 percent of conservative Republicans believe that it is happening, and 30 percent are worried. The partisan gap is stark (Leiserowitz et al. 2018). This divide is a result of the long-term politicization of science in the public sphere. Although overall public attitudes toward science have not changed much since the 1970s, conservatives and regular churchgoers have shown an abrupt drop in their trust in science (Gauchat 2012; Pew Research Center 2017).

We often assume that if we only let people know about the importance of saving the environment, things will improve. But this idea that inaction is caused by a lack of information is wrong or at least incomplete. Environmental education is certainly useful. And raising awareness is among the most common missions of environmental organizations. Yet it is essential to understand that it is not only a lack of awareness or scientific knowledge that keeps people from taking environmental action.

Maybe you are too busy to recycle; maybe you do not have the financial resources to shop green—even if you know you should for the environment. The **attitude-behavior split**, when we think one way and act another, does not mean that we are hypocrites. It does, though, reveal that we live in a society and do not have complete control over the everyday choices we are offered. Many environmentally significant decisions, such as fuel economy standards, food safety regulations, and city planning, happen at the societal level. As individuals, we can only control a small part of our environmental impacts. Responding to environmental challenges is also about reflecting on how we should live as a society and designing a more sustainable social system.

Check Your Understanding

- How do people in the United States describe the concept "wilderness"? Why do sociologists say that it is socially constructed, and what are the consequences?

- What do we mean when we say that the ozone hole problem is socially constructed?

- Explain the attitude-behavior split. What determines whether our attitude toward the environment corresponds with our behavior?

How Did We Mess Up? Theories of Environmental Change

15.3 How would eco-Marxists and ecological modernization theorists define and discuss environmental problems and their solutions?

So far, we have discussed how our current levels of economic development and consumption are not sustainable. We also learned how we form our understanding of environmental issues. For sociologists, the next big issue is to diagnose the drivers of environmental destruction and ways to address them.

Population and the Environment

Are there just too many people on the planet? Linking population with environmental degradation is not a new argument. We can trace this school of thought all the way back to *An Essay on the Principle of Population*, by English philosopher Thomas Robert Malthus. Malthus ([1798] 2007) noted that populations tend to grow exponentially—that is, more and more rapidly—while food supply only increases linearly—that is, at a steady rate. If population growth is left unchecked, he predicted that society will end up with misery, starvation, and resource scarcity. This is the so-called Malthusian catastrophe.

Malthus's prediction was proved largely incorrect. Yet his ideas never faded away completely. As the ecological economist Herman Daly said, "Malthus has been buried many times…anyone who has been buried so often cannot be entirely dead" (Daly 1991, 43). Modern-day neo-Malthusian works, such as Paul Ehrlich's (1968) *Population Bomb* and the Club of Rome's "The Limits to Growth" (Meadows et al. 1972), still argue that overpopulation is the main driver of environmental degradation, despite the absence of the large-scale famine and food shortages that their theories would predict.

What's wrong with Malthus's prophecy? The blind spot of Malthusianism lies in its overly deterministic view on population and the environment. Human interaction with the environment is mediated through technologies that change constantly. Malthus failed to foresee the tremendous productivity growth in agriculture that supports an ever growing number of people. Also, linking famine to the food supply is too simplistic. The problem lies in access to food, not the availability of food. For example, Amartya Sen—a

Nobel Prize–winning economist and philosopher—examined four major famines and discovered that there was enough food for everyone, but the food did not reach the people who needed it (Sen 1981). Famines typically happen when systems of food distribution, rather than production, break down.

Malthus's argument that population growth causes poverty is also off base. Experiences from many developing countries tell us that the causal effect works the other way around. People in poverty tend to have more, rather than fewer, children. Children are economic assets in agrarian societies, as they can help with farm work. High death rates due to poverty, therefore, lead poor agricultural households to have more children, not fewer.

Finally, Malthusians overlook the **demographic transition** associated with modernization (see Figure 15.3). Looking at population growth trends, demographers have noticed that in traditional societies, the birth rate (number of births per 1,000 people per year) and death rate (number of deaths per 1,000 people per year) are both high, causing the population to stay in a stable state. As societies go through industrialization, the death rate tends to drop before the birth rate because of improvements in health and increases in food supply. Because the birth rate is higher than the death rate, the population increases. In the last stage of economic development, social

▼ FIGURE 15.3

Demographic Transitions Associated with Modernization

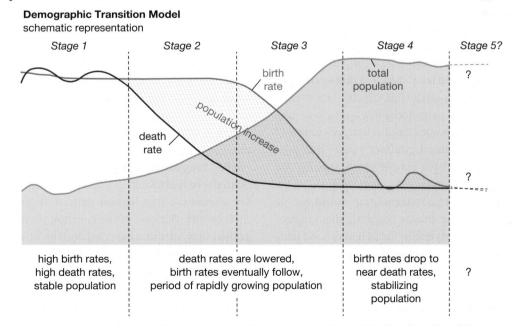

Demographic Transition Model
schematic representation

Source: One Small Planet, Seven Billion People by Year's End and 10.1 Billion by Century's End. UNEP Global Environmental Alert Service (GEAS). With permission from UN Environment.

norms finally catch up with the improved standard of living, causing the birth rate to drop to a level similar to the death rate. The population thus stabilizes again. Some scholars optimistically predict that the global population will cease growing by 2050.

The demographic transition theory is a simplified model. We have seen countries follow somewhat different paths through the transition. The process very often involves frantic political projects—sometimes violent ones—such as China's one-child policy (which came to an end in 2015) and India's sterilization campaign in the 1970s. One lesson is particularly worth mentioning: scholars consistently find that the status of women is the best predictor of the fertility rate. The more power women have in society, the fewer children they tend to have. Therefore, women's empowerment is not only a gender issue but also an environmental issue.

Just because Malthus's predictions did not come to pass does not mean that population does not affect the environment. More people on the planet requires more food on the table and affects our ecological footprint. Calculations of that footprint, covered earlier in this chapter, take population into account in the analysis. Yet having more people living in McMansions has a much larger environmental impact than an increase in the number of people struggling to stay above the poverty line. We need to consider a population's production and consumption of resources rather than merely its size.

Production and the Environment

To sociologists, environmental degradation is not a result of too many people in the world, nor is it due to individuals' bad intentions or technological failures. Instead, it is a product of our unsustainable economic system.

What leads to an unsustainable economic system? Understanding **externalities** is the key to answering this question. Externalities are all the side effects—things people fail to incorporate in their decision making—of economic activities. Externalities can be both positive and negative, and by definition, they affect a party that does not choose to incur the cost or benefit (that's why they are "external").

An example of positive externalities would be the flowers in your front yard: maybe you plant them to decorate your house, but everyone in the neighborhood benefits from them. They are beautiful to look at and give the impression of a well-cared for home and neighborhood, increasing property values for all. Pollution, on the other hand, is a classic example of negative externalities. Industries produce goods we all use and need, but when they emit pollutants as by-products, the dirty air or water harms plants, animals, and people not involved in the production or consumption of the goods being created. In modern societies, economic exchanges are rarely, if ever, strictly between buyers and sellers. They also affect other parties. Thus, both positive and negative externalities are common features in our economy.

Many scholars are quick to point out that **capitalism**, defined by private properties, markets, and profits, has an ecologically destructive tendency. In the capitalist system, firms do not simply produce goods and services; they try to maximize profits. To do so, they have incentives to externalize the costs.

Imagine that you own a company. Your profits come from the difference between the price that you sell your merchandise for on the market (your revenue) and what you paid to produce it, including raw materials, labor costs, and environmental management (your cost). Under intense competition, which required you to set your prices low, your company barely made any profit last year. Your instinct tells you to cut costs to increase profits. Earlier this week, your best employee enthusiastically proposed buying a new device to install at the end of your smokestacks to control pollution. Seeing the balance sheet, you decide to postpone buying the new devices. You try to justify your decision: "Dirty air won't kill people immediately." And you can't remember the last time your local government sent someone to audit the pollution numbers—you're not going to get caught anyway.

Now imagine a year has gone by and you find yourself in the same situation: no profit, company barely surviving. You now consider sourcing raw materials from a new Chinese company whose price is 30 percent cheaper than the partner you've worked with for twenty years. Maybe the Chinese company has very low labor and environmental protocol, but that is really the last thing you can worry about now. And the cycle goes on. . . .

Getting Off the Treadmill of Production. The scenario above reflects the Marxist-inspired conflict theory of the "**treadmill of production**" (Schnaiberg 1980; Schnaiberg and Gould 2000). On the capitalist treadmill, firms must use and degrade natural resources to sustain their profits. Because of the constant pressure to expand profits, they are forced to compete with others by running faster and faster, producing more and more, and drawing ever more resources. If they don't, they will go bankrupt and "fall off the treadmill." In this process, firms face no choice but to externalize environmental and social costs or lose out to firms that do.

THE STORY OF STUFF

In this activity, you will watch a brief video, "The Story of Solutions" (https://youtu.be/cpkRvc-sOKk) to understand where consumer goods come from and end up, as well as the ways to make our economic system more sustainable and just.

After watching the video, summarize Leonard's view on the causes of the environmental crisis in our society by writing your answers to the e following questions:

1. In the video, Leonard describes the current system as a "game of more"—cheering for more roads, more malls, more stuff! How does this point relate to the "treadmill of production"?

2. Are there statements or assertions that make you uncomfortable? If so, which ones? Why?

3. What are the solutions offered by this video? What are some other solutions you can think of?

Many other schools of Marxist-inspired analysis have reached the same overall conclusion—capitalism is the ultimate cause of our ecological crisis. According to capitalist logic, the system must continue to grow, seeking to secure raw materials, cheap labor, and new markets. The mantra of growth and accumulation inevitably will run into the physical limit of finite natural resources (Magdoff and Foster 2011). Eco-Marxists (Marxists who focus on the environment) argue that if we do not steer our societies toward an alternative economic system, they will collapse. Their solution is a massive radical movement toward a system that focuses on communal needs and the balance between human and nature.

The eco-Marxist analysis of the roots of our environmental problems paints a very grim picture. Indeed, the challenge is daunting. But is overthrowing capitalism our only way out? Some people disagree.

Ecological Modernization Theory. **Ecological modernization** theorists, unlike eco-Marxists, maintain that societies have the potential to develop "ecological rationality"—decision making that incorporates ecological concerns—to replace the old model of modernization, which focuses only on economic growth and industrial development. The proponents of ecological modernization argue that humans are smart enough to internalize the negative externalities—to shoulder the costs of conducting their business in ecologically friendly ways—through new technologies, social innovations, and better management. Researchers found that some European countries, such as Germany and the Netherlands, have successfully achieved economic growth while lowering environmental impact through better product design, clean technology, and government incentives for innovation. For example, there is a regulation in the European Union requiring car

manufacturers to take back vehicles that have reached the end of their product life span, resulting in a reduction of hazardous substances and better reuse of car components. Ecological modernization proponents argue that a different modernization is possible for the United States and the rest of the world—without having to overthrow capitalism (Spaargaren and Mol 1992; Mol, Spaargaren, and Sonnenfeld 2014).

CONSIDER THIS

Eco-Marxists and ecological modernization theorists see the world through drastically different lenses. Which do you think is most helpful? Why?

Check Your Understanding

- What is the Malthusians' view on population and the environment? What is the weakness of this theory?
- What are positive and negative externalities?
- According to eco-Marxists, what is the root of environmental problems?
- How do ecological modernization theorists view environmental issues?

Consumption and the Environment

15.4 What are the promises and constraints of green consumption?

The previous section mainly considers environmental degradation as a result of production. What about the other side of the equation—consumption? After all, people have to buy things to complete the economic transaction.

Weddings provide an opportunity for conspicuous consumption during which families can display their wealth.

Xinhua/Xinhua News Agency/Getty Images

Consumption does not happen in a vacuum. There are many factors going into what you buy, why you buy, and how you buy. For sociologists, the central tenet is that consumption is not an individual but a social process. This perspective traces back to Thorstein Veblen's (1899) book *The Theory of the Leisure Class*. Veblen came up with the concept of conspicuous consumption: the practice of spending money for the purpose of demonstrating or enhancing social prestige.

The items that symbolize social status change over time and place. For example, not long ago, in all parts of the world, any kind of smartphone was considered a piece of conspicuous consumption. Today, in many communities, only the latest version of the iPhone—and only in the first days of its release—elevates a person's status. Even though status objects may change constantly, the bottom line remains the same: we always have other people's reactions on our mind when buying stuff!

Conspicuous consumption has ecological implications. To be conspicuous, you have to do better than the community average. The process is inherently competitive. This creates momentum to constantly elevate the consumption level, leading to increasing environmental degradation. Every time people buy a new smartphone, they necessitate the production of that phone, with all the ecological impacts that implies. They also usually get rid of an older phone, which had similar environmental costs to produce and now must be thrown into a landfill or broken down into its component parts in another environmentally costly process.

Green Consumption

You might be wondering by now whether all consumption is bad. What about organic, local, and fair-trade goods? Those created through renewable energy?

Indeed, we have seen in recent years a growing trend of green consumption. **Green consumption** allows consumers to "vote with their pockets" and to engage in social change through the marketplace. Its logic goes like this: if you care about the environment, you should shop accordingly.

Producers use various ecolabels to indicate the superior environmental standards for their product (Hatanaka, Bain, and Busch 2005; Bartley 2007). Nowadays, you can find sustainability certification for a wide variety of foods and material goods. For example, you can purchase organic bananas, fair-trade coffee, Marine Stewardship Council–certified salmon, paper towels that contain paper certified by the Forest Stewardship Council, and a brand-new flat-screen TV with an Energy Star label on it.

Ecolabels sound like a good idea. Some people, however, say that the green certification process privileges larger producers. If you run an organic family farm, the cost associated with being certified as "organic" can become a real financial burden.

Another important problem lies in credibility. According to the Ecolabel Index, a global clearinghouse of green labeling, as of early 2019, there were 463 ecolabels in 199 countries and twenty-five industry sectors. There are almost always multiple labels within one product sector. Who oversees their claims?

For consumers, labeling does not always provide useful information but sometimes gives us an illusion that we're choosing something environmentally friendly. Do you know the difference between Rainforest Alliance certified and U.S. Department of Agriculture organic? Even worse, the standard may be so loose that the ecolabel does not mean anything. Ecolabels might become a tool for **greenwashing**—a public relations campaign that promotes an environmentally friendly, positive image of an organization whose environmental practices are not in line with the image (Delma and Burbano 2011, Scheer and Moss 2019). Smart consumers should use caution when using ecolabels to determine their purchases.

DOING SOCIOLOGY 15.6

GREENWASHING PRODUCT REVIEW

In this exercise, you will search for an example of a greenwashing product and write a product review. Search for products on Amazon.com or other online shopping web sites. Pay special attention to terms such as *eco-friendly*, *pure*, *green*, *vegan*, *nontoxic*, and *100 percent natural*, as they all lack legal definitions and thus can be used in whatever products the companies want.

Write a short product review to expose the greenwashing tactics you observe. You can learn about the different

forms of greenwashing from the web site Sins of Greenwashing (http://sinsofgreenwashing.com). In the review, you can use a playful tone to challenge these consumption-oriented messages. You should also think about alternatives to purchasing this product. If your instructor asks you to work in a group, include your review and a photo of your product in a single slide. Be prepared to discuss your work.

Inverted Quarantines. Focusing our environmental efforts on our purchases can also distract us from addressing the causes of environmental degradation (Maniates 2001). In his book, *Shopping Our Way to Safety: How We Changed from Protecting the Environment to Protecting Ourselves*, Andrew Szasz (2007) uses the term "inverted quarantine" to illustrate this idea. Normally, we quarantine bad things from our clean environment, but as our environment is increasingly polluted, many of us have started to quarantine ourselves from the unsafe environment. For example, people worried about the chemicals in the municipal water supply protect themselves from it by buying bottled water.

Szasz argues that such individual efforts distract us from carrying out necessary political actions (not to mention that some bottled water is just tap water put into bottles or the environmental harm created through producing, packaging, and distributing bottled water). He points out that we could be using our resources more effectively by pressuring elected officials to pass legislation to improve the quality and infrastructure of public water supply systems. People ought to question and address why the water is contaminated and unsafe to drink in the first place!

Check Your Understanding

- What is conspicuous consumption? How does it relate to the environment?
- What is green consumption?
- How can ecolabels promote "greenwashing"?
- In what ways do people carry out environmental inverted quarantines? What are the negative effects?

Who Suffers Most from Environmental Problems?

15.5   What is environmental justice?

Flint, Michigan, is a predominantly African American and low-income community. In mid-2014, the city switched its municipal water source from the Detroit water system to the Flint River. Before long, local citizens started to complain about the strange color and foul smell of the tap water. A few months later, people began to report rashes, hair loss, and vision problems. It turns out the water is seriously contaminated with lead—a persistent pollutant that can accumulate in the body over time and have devastating effects. The Environmental Protection Agency has set a goal to eliminate lead in drinking water and takes action if it is higher than 15 parts per billion. In some homes in Flint, the lead level was as high as 10,000 parts per billion.

Government officials did not, at first, take the concerns of Flint's residents seriously. They allowed residents to continue to drink lead-tainted water. It was not until researchers from outside the community verified the lead poisoning—and held a news conference about it—that government officials began to acknowledge and address the issue (Hohn 2016). Finally, in early January 2016, the state of Michigan declared a state of emergency to address the crisis, and the federal government followed suit a week later, freeing up $5 million in federal relief. As of early 2019, lead levels in the Flint water were at acceptable levels, but the process of replacing lead-leaching pipes was still ongoing (Fonger 2019).

Would the Flint River disaster have been as likely to occur if Flint were a wealthy city?

AP Photo/Carlos Osorio

Would the drinking water problem in Flint have been handled differently if it had taken place in a White suburb of Detroit? The answer seems to be "yes." The Flint Water Advisory Task Force commissioned by the state government of Michigan found that

> the facts of the Flint water crisis lead us to the inescapable conclusion that this is a case of environmental injustice. Flint residents, who are majority Black or African American and among the most impoverished of any metropolitan area in the United States, did not enjoy the same degree of protection from environmental and health hazards as that provided to other communities. . . . Flint residents were not provided equal access to, and meaningful involvement in, the government decision-making process. (Flint Water Advisory Task Force 2016, 54)

Environmental Racism

Flint is no isolated case. Across the United States and the world, low-income and minority communities do not receive the same level of environmental protection as Whiter, wealthier communities. As in the case of Flint, Michigan, they often bear disproportionate burdens of environmental harm. Sociologists who focus on **environmental justice** work to document the social inequality in the environmental realm and promote more just environmental policies and laws (Mohai, Pellow, and Roberts 2009).

Sociological research on environmental justice issues was sparked by recognition of **environmental racism**—when environmental hazards are disproportionally borne by racial and ethnic minority groups (Bullard 1990, 1993). In the early 1980s, the U.S. General Accountability Office found that four major landfill sites in the South were situated near a disproportionately high percentage of African American communities. In 1987, the United Church of Christ published a landmark study, "Toxic Wastes and Race in the United States" (United Church of Christ, Commission for Racial Justice 1987), showing that African Americans are two to three times more likely than Whites to live close to a hazardous landfill. A third classic study, by the sociologist Robert Bullard, found that twenty-one of Houston's twenty-five waste facilities were placed in African American neighborhoods. These cases show that rather than the ordinary "not in my backyard" politics, many waste-siting decisions follow the route of "put in Blacks' backyard." Bullard (1990) explains that governments and private industries seek the "path of least resistance" to distribute pollutants. Because African American and other minority groups are less represented in the political processes and have less power to defend themselves, they are more likely to end up with these pollutants near their homes.

The Environmental Justice Movement. This research on environmental racism helped create a vibrant **environmental justice movement**, with the goal of ending the practice of using poor and racial and ethnic minority areas as dumping grounds for environmental hazards. In the fall of 1982, a group of roughly 500 people participated in a six-week protest to stop the placement of 32,000 cubic yards of PCB-contaminated soil in a mostly African American rural community in Warren County, North Carolina. The protest did not achieve its goal, and the landfill was completed. Yet as one of the first fights against environmental racism that gained national attention, the Warren County protest became a transformative event. Many other communities also formed organizations and coalitions to fight for environmental justice (McGurty 2000).

The environmental justice movement is a reminder of how our social status and experiences shape our interaction with the environment. While an upper-middle-class White man tries to preserve a natural habitat for his birding interest, the local minority community might be going through a fight against groundwater contamination poisoning their drinking water. Same environment, but very different interests and experiences. As a result, the environmental justice movement, since its inception, has had an uneasy relationship with the mainstream environmental movement—represented predominantly by Whites and the middle class (Taylor 2000; Martinez-Alier 2003). The environmental justice activists have criticized the mainstream environmental organizations as "lost in the woods" and focusing too much on preserving nature—often in the form of wilderness we discussed early in this chapter—rather than fighting environmental injustice.

CONSIDER THIS

Think back to how you answered the first Consider This question in this chapter (What are the most important things we can do to help save the environment?). Given what you have learned, would you change your list of the most important things we can do to save our environment? Why?

The environmental justice movement has made substantial and positive impacts. For example, the federal government officially recognized the principle of environmental justice in 1994. Executive Order 12898, signed by President Bill Clinton, mandates "fair treatment and meaningful involvement of all people regardless of race, color, national origin, or income with respect to the development, implementation, and enforcement of environmental laws." The recognition of environmental justice issues has led mainstream environmental groups to make greater efforts to diversify their membership and goals.

Dorceta Taylor, an environmental science professor and expert on diversity issues in the field, advises both environmental organizations and students of color interested in working in the field. She tells environmental groups that they should "stop being so afraid of people of color. Meet them, interact with them, cultivate them, identify students early, and start recruiting them. . . . [These students] are excited, they know it's a challenge [to work in a field that needs to diversify], but they want to be a part of that challenge" (Taylor 2015; Toomey 2018).

Meanwhile, environmental justice scholars and activists have broadened their efforts from their initial focus on racism to include issues of social class as well. There has been a long-lasting debate on whether race or class better predicts the distribution of environmental harms (Ringquist 2005; Mohai, Pellow, and Roberts 2009). There are also ongoing efforts to tease out the causes of environmental injustice—whether it is a product of intentional political targeting or the result of economic sorting whereby disadvantaged groups move closer to pollution because of lower housing prices. These are complicated questions to answer. In general, we have learned about the importance of looking beyond the simple perpetrator-victim framework to pay more attention to history and local contexts that produce the inequality (Pellow 2000).

Three decades after the early protests, we have gradually seen environmental justice enter the mainstream. The gap in environmental conditions remains huge, but

E-waste is more likely to be disposed in developing countries such as Nigeria. Olusosun is the largest waste dump in Africa and is a major hub for e-waste disposal where hundreds of thousands of scavengers work to dismantle electronic junk, endangering their health and their community in the process.

FINBARR O"REILLY/REUTERS/Newscom

initiatives to mitigate these problems are under way. For example, California, through its Senate Bill 535, has allocated 25 percent of the funds generated by its cap-and-trade system for use in disadvantaged communities. On the federal level, the Environmental Protection Agency established an "EJ 2020 Action Agenda" to further institutionalize environmental justice concerns in its decision making and improve on-the-ground results.

Sacrifice Zones. In recent years, environmental justice has increasingly become a global concern and a global movement (Pellow 2007). In many cases, when a company appears to make progress in its environmental practices in developed countries, it just moves the dirty parts to developing countries, where the costs of pollution are cheaper. These **sacrifice zones** are defined by more than race and class; they also relate to countries of origin.

Olususun landfill in Nigeria is one sacrifice zone. The largest waste dumpsite in Africa, it is located right in the heart of Lagos, the largest city in Africa. Approximately 500 container ships, each carrying about 500,000 used computers and other electronic equipment, enter the port of Lagos every month from the United States, Europe, and Asia. Workers, very often with their bare hands, strip down discarded electronic devices to recover the lead, gold, copper, and other metals they contain. During the process, they are exposed to harmful metals like lead and mercury, and the nearby soil and water bodies are all contaminated, too (Lawal 2019). You can find places like Olususun in India, Malaysia, Ghana, and China. The high costs of end-of-life treatment of electronic products are invisible to consumers in the developed nations.

Global environmental injustice goes far beyond the e-waste case mentioned above. The online data collection and visualization platform *Environmental Justice Atlas* currently lists more than 2,700 cases of environmental injustice incidents around the world, ranging from land grabbing and mega-mining to biodiversity and conservation conflicts. Environmental issues are essentially a problem of global inequality, with lower income people burdened with more environmental hazards than others.

Climate Justice. Climate change can also be viewed through an environmental justice lens. To sociologists, **climate justice** highlights the fact that climate change relates to global inequality, in its creation and its impact (Roberts and Parks 2006, 2009). Countries have made vastly different contributions to the problem. The per capita carbon emission of the average person in the United States is about ten times that of the average Indian! Furthermore, if we look at the greenhouse gases in the atmosphere, most were released by Western countries over the history of industrialization, while the contribution from most developing countries is negligible.

The impacts of climate change will also not be distributed equally. For example, Charleston, South Carolina, is projected to face nearly 180 tidal floods per year in 2045, compared with 11 floods per year in 2014; in the southern Great Plains, extreme heat could cause thousands of premature deaths and billions in lost work hours by the end of the century. The Fourth National Climate Assessment points out that "people who are already vulnerable, including lower-income and other marginalized communities, have lower capacity to prepare for and cope with extreme weather and climate-related events and are expected to experience greater impacts" (U.S. Global Change Research Program 2018).

Moreover, across the globe, the people who contributed the least to climate change suffer the most from it. Many citizens in low-lying Bangladesh and in island countries are facing an existential threat. Current research predicts that much of their homeland will be under water well within this century. And they have no way to turn the tides, literally. Using the environmental/climate justice framework, researchers now use the concept of "climate debt" or "development rights" to describe the disproportionate atmospheric space developed countries have taken and demand they take stronger actions to mitigate the impact of climate change and to help developing nations to prepare for it (Warlenius 2018). Sociologists, such as Professor Timmons Robert in the Sociologists in Action box, have made contributions to climate justice through capacity building, action research, and policy advisement.

CONSIDER THIS

Look at the electronic gadgets you own. Think about the whole "chain" between the birth and death of a product—from mining, to manufacturing, to waste disposal. What are some of the environmental impacts these devices create? Who bears the burden of these gadgets?

Check Your Understanding

- What is environmental racism?
- Why is there tension between the environmental justice movement and mainstream environmentalism?

SOCIOLOGISTS IN ACTION

CREATING ENGAGED CLIMATE JUSTICE SCHOLARSHIP

TIMMONS ROBERTS

I founded the Climate and Development Lab (CDL) when I came to Brown University in 2010. The CDL is an experiment in engaged learning and scholarship, whose mission is to contribute timely, accessible, and influential research that informs more just and effective climate policy. The lab has two very different groups running under very different models—one working on international climate justice and the other on local and state issues and legislation.

Since 2010, the international part of the CDL has brought more than fifty Brown students to the annual UN climate change negotiations, in Cancun, Durban, Warsaw, Lima, Bonn, and Paris. That group's research focuses on how equity, justice, and finance have an impact on the UN climate change negotiations. We focus on providing research support to the least developed countries group—the world's forty-eight poorest nations—through collaborating with leading international research institutes, environmental nongovernmental organizations, and negotiating groups.

My students and I provide "capacity" to the neediest countries and to the most effective civil society organizations in the UN climate negotiations by conducting research that meets their interest to which they would otherwise not have access. We usually seek to first publish streamlined core research findings as policy briefing papers, whose impact is tied to their originality and their timeliness. We release those widely and target them to climate experts. These experts and participants in the tussle of climate politics provide immediate feedback, help publicize our findings, and use them in social policy change efforts. We also put our research on our web sites (www.climatedevlab.brown.edu and AdaptationWatch.org), and we write blogs and tweet about them and many other timely issues of climate and equity. We then sometimes turn our research findings into peer-reviewed scholarly articles and incorporate the findings into our books.

In a fall semester seminar called "Engaged Climate Policy," students first receive "boot camp" training of the essential parts of global climate governance. They participate in small team-based climate policy research groups, preparing briefing papers with experts around the world. Students are then "embedded" with organizations prior to and during the UN climate change talks, which allows them to develop and use their academic knowledge of global climate governance in practical and meaningful ways. During this time, students prepare op-eds, blogs, and individual presentations on key areas of climate policy.

The domestic part of CDL has focused on climate change legislation in Rhode Island and in Providence. In talking to local officials, we learned we could work with state legislators to develop and help introduce bills. The first bill we worked on created a permanent standing committee to study the issue of climate change. In 2014, we helped draft the first state legislation addressing adaptation to climate change that included targets for reducing emissions by 80 percent by 2050. Most recently, we have been working on carbon pricing legislation.

Discussion Question: If you had the opportunity to write legislation to affect climate change, what would your law mandate? Why?

Timmons Roberts is Ittleson Professor of Environmental Studies and Sociology at Brown University.

- How is environmental justice a global issue?
- What does the term *climate justice* highlight?

Social Solutions to Environmental Problems

> **15.6** What are social solutions to environmental problems?

The environment does not exist outside of our social life. Sociology is concerned with the social consequences of environmental issues, as well as the social causes of them. Environmental problems are intertwined with social inequality.

Social problems require collective solutions. It is not enough to put bottled water containers into the recycling bin correctly. It may give you a warm moral glow, but it, alone, does little to lower the environmental impact of bottled water. A more sociological approach is to think about how bottled water becomes an acceptable commodity and the actors involved in the process. Why don't we install more drinking water fountains so that people don't

ENVIRONMENTAL INEQUALITIES AND SOCIAL SOLUTIONS

This exercise asks you to review and speculate about who suffers the most from environmental problems and some solutions for addressing environmental challenges.

Draw a concept map linking two ideas in your text, "who suffers most from environmental problems" and "social solutions to environmental problems." Draw two circles and write "Suffers" in one circle and "Solutions" in the other. Now, think of as many examples of each as you can come up with and draw arrows to link "Suffers" to "Solutions" to indicate the relationship between the two. Use information from your text and your own ideas. If you need more information about how to draw a concept map, this YouTube video will give you the basic idea: https://www.youtube.com/watch?v=sZJj6DwCqSU.

Creating safe conditions for bikers would encourage more people to bike and reduce car emissions.
©iStockphoto.com/olaser

need to buy bottled water? Or, more radically, how about simply banning the sale of bottled water, as the city of San Francisco does on its city-owned properties?

The sociological approach also seeks to create social conditions that lead people to help preserve the environment without thinking much about it. Examples include building a public transportation system that becomes the most convenient and affordable way to move around, creating bike lanes so that biking is safe and enjoyable, and revamping agricultural regulations so that the food always comes from sustainable farms. There are many more examples. Rather than focusing on enlightening individuals, this form of environmentalism aims to cultivate sustainable communities.

Creating sustainable communities is a team effort. It requires us to be active citizens. It demands that we build social capital and work with others to achieve our goals. It also reminds us to be always conscious of the environmental consequences of our consumption. The good news is that such change is already happening. People have started to realize the negative impacts, both socially and environmentally, of fast food, fast fashion, and the throwaway society. The burgeoning sharing economy, maker culture, local food movement, and open-source models all point to the potential to slow down the economic treadmill and connect more with others in our communities. While we create a more enjoyable and connected society, we will also slow down pollution and reduce climate change (Schor 2011).

Check Your Understanding

- Why is individual action not enough to solve environmental problems?
- What are some examples of how we can create social conditions that lead people to help preserve the environment without thinking much about it?

Conclusion

In this chapter, we showed how environmental problems are social problems and require social solutions.

Sociology, through social constructivist analysis, offers us insights on how environmental problems are defined and understood by the public, as well as how individuals may perceive the environment differently on the basis their social experiences. Sociology also highlights that environmental degradation is mainly a systematic problem of our unsustainable economic system. In addition, negative environmental impacts often fall unequally onto low-income and minority groups. Environmental issues are social justice issues, too.

We can all agree that society cannot exist without the environment. If you care about society, you have to care about the environment. The environmental movement has become one of the most vibrant realms of social activism today. You can learn more about it and what it takes to create a successful social movement in the next chapter.

REVIEW

15.1 Why are environmental problems social problems?

Environmental problems are problems *for* society, as they threaten our current social order; they are also problems *of* society, as they are the results of our current unsustainable social practices. To address these problems and search for sustainability, we need to use our sociological imagination to think beyond individual behaviors (e.g., recycling, changing light bulbs, turning off lights) and focus on the social constraints that shape our everyday choices.

15.2 How do sociologists study environmental issues?

Before sociologists tackle environmental degradation, we ask questions such as the following: What is nature? Where does our environmental knowledge come from? What shapes our understanding of a particular environmental issue? Does everyone perceive environmental problems in the same way? If not, what explains the variation?

Sociologists view both nature and environmental problems as social constructions with social solutions.

15.3 How would eco-Marxists and ecological modernization theorists define and discuss environmental problems and their solutions?

Eco-Marxists believe that environmental problems are based in the roots of capitalism. On the capitalist "treadmill," businesses must use and degrade natural resources to sustain their profits. In this process, firms face no choice but to externalize environmental and social costs. Their solution is a radical transformation to a new economic system.

Ecological modernization theorists argue that the challenges of sustainability can lead us to reshape our social institutions to adapt to environmental changes. Societies have the potential to incorporate *ecological rationality*—considering environmental consequences in decision making—to replace the old model of modernization. Humans are smart enough to internalize the negative externalities through new technologies, social innovations, and better management. Their solution is reformist, focusing on technological development and innovations in existing institutions.

15.4 What are the promises and constraints of green consumption?

Green consumption allows consumers to protect the environment through buying environmentally friendly products marked with "green" labels. These labels are not always accurate, however, and consumers should use them with caution. Ecolabels might become a tool for greenwashing—a green public relations campaign that promotes an environmentally friendly, positive image of an organization that does not accurately reflect its practices.

15.5 What is environmental justice?

Sociologists have come to use the term *environmental justice* to document the social inequality in the environmental realm. Across the United States and the world, low-income and minority communities do not receive the same level of environmental protection as Whiter, wealthier communities. As in the case of Flint, Michigan, they often bear disproportionate burdens of environmental harm.

The environmental justice movement seeks to equalize the exposure of environmental problems, as well as involve disadvantaged communities in the decision-making processes.

15.6 ▪ What are social solutions to environmental problems?

Social problems, like climate change and other environmental problems, require collective solutions. Individual behavior, alone, cannot adequately address them. The sociological approach aims to cultivate sustainable communities rather than focusing on changing individuals. For example, rather than just encouraging people to recycle their water bottles, we can work to create policies requiring drinking fountains in public buildings or banning the sale of bottled water. Creating social solutions to environmental problems is a team effort that requires us to work with others to develop sustainable communities. Joining an environmental social movement is one way to do this. In the next chapter you will learn about the power of organized people and how to create an effective social movement.

KEY TERMS

attitude-behavior split   310

capitalism   312

climate justice   318

constructivist analysis of the environment   305

demographic transition   311

ecological footprint   304

ecological modernization   313

environmental justice   316

environmental justice movement   316

environmental racism   316

environmental sociology   304

externalities   312

green consumption   314

greenwashing   314

overshoot   304

paradigm shift theory   308

risk perception   309

sacrifice zones   318

sustainability   304

sustainable development   304

treadmill of production   312

wilderness   305

Introducing…

SAGE vantage™

Course tools done right.

Built to support teaching. Designed to ignite learning.

SAGE vantage is an intuitive digital platform that blends trusted SAGE content with auto-graded assignments, all carefully designed to ignite student engagement and drive critical thinking. Built with you and your students in mind, it offers easy course set-up and enables students to better prepare for class.

SAGE vantage enables students to **engage** with the material you choose, **learn** by applying knowledge, and **soar** with confidence by performing better in your course.

PEDAGOGICAL SCAFFOLDING	**CONFIDENCE BUILDER**	**TIME-SAVING FLEXIBILITY**	**QUALITY CONTENT**	**HONEST VALUE**
Builds on core concepts, moving students from basic understanding to mastery.	Offers frequent knowledge checks, applied-learning multimedia tools, and chapter tests with focused feedback.	Feeds auto-graded assignments to your gradebook, with real-time insight into student and class performance.	Written by expert authors and teachers, content is not sacrificed for technical features.	Affordable access to easy-to-use, quality learning tools students will appreciate.

CHAPTER 16

CHANGING SOCIETY THROUGH SOCIAL MOVEMENTS

Wendy M. Christensen

Social movements work to promote social change. In March 2018, survivors of the shooting at Marjory Stoneman Douglas High School in Parkland, Florida, organized protests in Washington, D.C., and across the United States to lobby for tighter gun control laws. An estimated 800,000 students and supporters protested in Washington alone.

Visions of America/Universal Images Group via Getty Images

What Is a Social Movement?

16.1 What is a social movement?

Five people are gathered outside city hall after a city council meeting. Each had attended the meeting to demand that the city address the rapidly multiplying feral cat population. Each was involved in helping reduce the feral cat population on their own, spending their own time and money to trap and spay or neuter cats. Noting the dangers faced by the cats and the smell and noise of the growing feral cat population, these five residents came to the meeting to press the city council to adopt what is known as a TNR (trap-neuter-return) program. A coordinated, citywide program could reduce the population and would get cats fixed and adopted.

Despite the impassioned pleas of the five concerned residents, the council members did not promise to address the feral cat problem. The five are agitated as they talk about the council's disinterested response to their requests. One suggests that they join together to form a new organization, "Friends of Cats," to raise awareness and push the city council to act. They exchange numbers and promises to find each other on Facebook before heading home.

Two days later, the fledging social movement has a Facebook page with more than 100 followers. Soon after, membership in the movement grows from the original five to fifteen individuals. Meeting at a local coffee shop to plan their next steps, they decide to make informational flyers to distribute around town and start a petition demanding the city council adopt their proposed policies.

The next time the city council meets, Friends of Cats has thirty-five people in attendance, all with signs demanding that the council take action. They present a petition with 1,500 signatures of local residents and introduce experts on TNR policy from the Animal Protection League to speak to the council. At that meeting, the council agrees to form a committee with Friends of Cats members on animal control. A few months later, it drafts and passes a TNR policy for the city.

Components of a Social Movement

The formation of the social movement organization Friends of Cats is typical of social movements. A **social movement** forms when people who want social change create an organization that is collective, organized, and sustained and challenges authorities, powerholders, or cultural beliefs and practices.

Friends of Cats is a *collective*, made up of a group of people cooperating as they work toward a shared goal. Its members discovered they cared about the same issue (feral cats) and had the same goal as the city council (humanely reducing the feral cat population). They decided that joining forces and working with city council members would make them more powerful.

CONSIDER THIS

When you think of a social movement or protest, what comes to mind? Have you ever participated in a protest? Why?

Friends of Cats is also *organized*; its members coordinate their efforts. They started organizing through email, Facebook, and face-to-face planning meetings soon after they met. As with many social movements today, social media tools facilitated their organizing efforts.

The movement members *sustained* their efforts until their goals were met. Their sustained efforts included passing around a petition, distributing literature, recruiting experts to research and present their case, attending city council meetings, and making themselves visible at those meetings. Their close work with the council led to the council's turning to them when it selected people to place on the city's Animal Control Committee.

HOW I GOT ACTIVE IN SOCIOLOGY

WENDY M. CHRISTENSEN

I often joke that I began thinking sociologically when I listened to Pink Floyd's album *Animals* nonstop as a teenager (*Animals* is a rock album about economic inequality, borrowing from George Orwell's *Animal Farm*). But I was a sociologist long before that. From the time I could read, I devoured books that focused on women's rights, racism, and social inequality.

I started college as a technical theater major. I took a sociology course as part of my general requirements. I enjoyed the material, and the professor suggested that I switch majors. But it took a couple years, including transferring and taking a year off, to finally switch to sociology. For the first time, I loved my college courses.

I wrote an undergrad thesis on masculinity and school shootings. My advisors encouraged me to apply to graduate school.

Since earning my PhD, I feel like I have the best job possible. I study what interests me, which right now is community-based political activism. My favorite courses to teach are Social Movements and Social Stratification. My work allows me to be active in my community and contribute to social justice movements. I love teaching social activism in nonacademic settings to carry the lessons of past movements into today's social movement community.

Together, the Friends of Cats members challenged powerholders within city government with the goal of changing city policy. To be successful, social movements must target the institution or authority figure with the power to make the changes they seek. Such target institutions or figures could be a city council, a mayor, a member of Congress, a school principal, or any other group or individual in a position of power.

Protests: The Most Visible Part of Social Movements. When you think of a social movement, what images come to mind? You might picture groups of individuals demonstrating out in the street with signs, yelling; individuals sitting with their arms linked, blocking the access to a building; or tens of thousands of people flooding a public space, singing and chanting for social change. These are all examples of a **protest**, an individual or group act of challenging, resisting, or making demands toward social change. Protests are often the most visible part of social movements, while the behind-the-scenes work of organizing and mobilizing is often unnoticed but will be covered in this chapter.

Some movements use **civil disobedience** in their protests, purposely breaking social customs or laws to make their point. Lunch counter sit-ins during the 1960s civil rights movement are an example of civil disobedience. The 1999 protests against the World Trade Organization (WTO) in Seattle, Washington, provide another example. Protestors disrupted the 1999 WTO meeting by taking over street intersections and preventing delegates from getting to their hotels.

Check Your Understanding

- What is a social movement?
- Why is organization important for a social movement?
- Why do social movements work outside institutions?
- Who are some of the powerholders that social movements might target for social change?
- How do sociologists define a protest?

Participating in Social Movements

16.2 Why do people participate in social movements?

Social movement organizing takes considerable time and resources. Not everyone has time to spend passing out petitions, marching in demonstrations, and organizing meetings and protests. Individuals who participate in social movements may face other costs, as well. If a demonstration becomes heated or disrupts the routines of others (e.g., by blocking traffic), demonstrators risk confrontations with nonparticipants and police, as well as possibly arrest.

So why do individuals become involved in social movements? Members of the Friends of Cats organization are all individuals committed to improving the lives of feral cats. They have volunteered their own time and often their own money to rescue feral cats. As individuals, they stand to benefit if the city adopts a TNR program. Their individual efforts and expenses will be replaced by the city's animal control department. These members are **beneficiary constituents**, people who stand to benefit directly from the social change being sought. Other individuals who are

PLANNING DIRECT ACTION

In this exercise you will begin to think like a social movement organizer, planning actions that have a high impact toward a specific goal.

Imagine that you just found out your school will significantly increase student activity fees to make up for a budget shortfall. Financial aid will not cover the increase, and the fee will be difficult for some students at your school to pay. Working with a group of other students, use the handout "198 Methods of Nonviolent Action" (https://www.aeinstein.org/nonviolentaction/198-methods-of-nonviolent-action/) to answer the following questions:

1. Select three methods of action you believe would be successful in stopping the student activity fee increase.

2. For each method of action you selected, describe in one or two sentences why you selected it, whom it targets, and why you believe it will be successful.

---

not involved in animal rescue may join the social movement organization because they believe the city would benefit from helping animals. These members would be **conscience constituents**, people who care about the cause but do not benefit directly from the changes.

Power and Inequality Issues in Social Movements

Although there are social movements focused on animal rights, many social movements fight for people's rights. In the Black Lives Matter movement, Black Americans experiencing discrimination are the beneficiaries of the movement. But consider for a minute the role White people play in the Black Lives Matter movement. They are not beneficiary constituents who stand to directly benefit from the movement's efforts but instead join as allies, morally committed to the cause as conscience constituents.

The roles conscience constituents take in social movements raise issues of power and inequality in social movement organizations. Some social movement organizers argue that the voices of the marginalized—those the movement is fighting for—must be centered in the movement. If the voices of the marginalized are not centered, the movement risks forming goals or mobilizing actions that

do not actually help the individuals they want to help. For example, members of an impoverished community may need better access to affordable grocery stores, instead of another food pantry. White people can be strong allies in civil rights movements, but addressing racism requires listening to the experiences of people of color who confront racism on a daily basis. By the same token, men can be important allies in the feminist movement, but women must be the ones to decide how the movement addresses sexism. Participating in a social movement can be empowering for community members when they are encouraged to take part in their own mobilization.

In this picture, MoveOn.org leaders present petitions calling for a ban on assault weapons. Through this effort, they hope to gain the attention and support of members of Congress.

Jim Watson/AFP/Getty Images

Socioeconomic Status and Ability. Participation in social movements can be limited by socioeconomic status and ability. Demonstrations, protests, and marches require physical stamina, leaving some less able-bodied individuals out. Not every student has the financial support to take off a summer from work and volunteer, as some students did during the Freedom Summer campaign to register Black voters in Mississippi in 1964. Likewise, students at Marjory Stoneman Douglas High School were largely from middle-class backgrounds and had more time to organize a movement than less privileged students. Some chose to take a year off before college to campaign for changes in gun laws. Attending meetings and demonstrations can be difficult for lower income workers who often have multiple jobs, inflexible hours, and no childcare. Participating in a social movement can be empowering, but not everyone has the economic or social security required to take some of the risks associated with participation. The potential for confrontation with powerholders or with the police is also not a gamble everyone can take. Many individuals cannot risk their jobs, children, public assistance, or education with an arrest record.

Mobilizing and Organizing

The process of organizing a social movement begins when people who share the same grievance begin to mobilize by getting together and finding others who support their goals. **Mobilizing** means spreading the word and bringing people together to support the goal of the social movement. The Internet, particularly social media, makes social movement participation easier for a wider variety of people. Online communication also makes mobilizing a social movement easier. Mobilizing efforts can be facilitated by social networking sites like Instagram and Twitter.

The next stage is when people come together more formally toward a shared goal. Organizing includes coordinating the regular operations of the social movement, which is another key part of social movements. Successful social change efforts require both. Social media campaigns can be very powerful for organizing, and popular hashtags become cultural markers of a movement. For example, the #BlackLivesMatter hashtag was first used in 2013 by activists Alicia Garza and Patrisse Cullors, after George Zimmerman was acquitted of killing Trayvon Martin. The hashtag quickly took off on Twitter, galvanizing a multifaceted international movement for Black lives. Activist Tarana Burke created the "Me Too" movement in 2006 to support survivors of sexual assault and harassment. The #MeToo hashtag took off in 2017 as survivors came forward with allegations against powerful men in entertainment and politics. After the school shooting in Parkland, Florida, students used the hashtags #NeverAgain, #GunSenseNow, and #MarchForOurLives to build support for gun control.

Community-Based Organizing. Social movements can grow nationally or internationally around an issue that affects people's lives at any level. Amnesty International, for example, is an organization focused on issues of human rights around the world. Other social movements are located and organized within communities. Through **community-based organizing**, individual activists become involved in a movement because of an issue directly affecting their community. Friends of Cats is an example of a community-based organization.

The Industrial Areas Foundation (IAF) is one of the oldest national community organizations in the United States. Founded in 1940 by activist Saul Alinsky, the IAF was developed to foster and support community-based groups, by training local-level leaders and organizers so that they can make change in their local communities. Some of the organization's work includes successfully advocating for a living wage for workers in Baltimore and New York City. West and Southwest IAF advocate to bring people out of poverty-level jobs and to provide education opportunities for workers. The IAF often works through local religious organizations, as does People Improving Communities through Organizing, a national network of faith-based community organizations.

Some sociologists also work with organizations to make social change. See, for example, sociologist Professor Alicia Swords's activism against poverty in her community described in the following Sociologists in Action box.

Check Your Understanding

- Who are beneficiary constituents?
- Who are conscience constituents?
- How can someone's economic status affect his or her ability to participate in a social movement?
- What is community-based organizing?

Types of Social Movements

16.3   What are the different types of social movements?

Many people think of social movements as progressive, but in fact, you can find social movements all over the ideological map. Some of the most extreme conservative

SOCIOLOGISTS IN ACTION

PARTICIPATING IN THE MOVEMENT TO END POVERTY

ALICIA SWORDS

My teaching and scholarship are grounded in the experiences and knowledge of the people most affected by the inequalities I study. For years, leaders of the University of the Poor, a national network of poor people's organizations committed to building a movement to end poverty, mentored me. They helped me answer questions like the following: Why are people poor in a land of plenty? What can be done to unite people across racial and religious lines? Their answers resonated with what I knew and with the sociologists I was studying. They challenged me to ask questions that deeply matter and develop my accountability as a scholar and a sociologist with the tools to help change society.

My involvement in the University of the Poor gives me evidence of the realities of poverty I share with my students at Ithaca College. When we study the history of the organized poor in the United States, students in my classes often say, "Why did I never learn about this before?" We analyze "projects of survival"—homeless people organizing tent cities and housing takeovers in Philadelphia, low-wage workers uniting for decent pay in Baltimore, and rural people resisting mountaintop removal mining in West Virginia. My students take part in immersion programs in which they learn firsthand from those engaged in struggles against hydraulic fracking and mountaintop removal. They also participate in action research by interviewing people who get food from food pantries and pantry volunteers to learn about their experiences and explanations for poverty and hunger.

There are enough resources in the world to end poverty, but it will take political will—a massive social movement—to change the fundamentals of our economic system and make it happen. Today it's clear such a movement to end poverty must be global. I was part of a University of the Poor delegation of homeless people that met with the Landless Workers movement in Brazil. It was remarkable to realize the common struggles of the poor around the world and the power of connecting the poor transnationally.

Willie Baptist, an organizer, scholar, and formerly homeless father, has been a key part of building this global movement. He has traveled tirelessly, meeting and cultivating local leaders, listening to their stories, and helping them see they aren't alone and their struggles are interconnected. Baptist insists that solving the problem of poverty requires combining poor people's life experiences with rigorous study. "Never in the history of the world has a dumb force risen up and overthrown a smart force," he says. That's one place where the work of sociologists is so important! We can bring perspectives from history and from all over the world to efforts for social change. Although the movement to end poverty will have to be led by the poor, it also requires engaged intellectuals, young people, students, and people from all segments of society. I love getting to be a part of this effort every day through my teaching and sociological research.

Discussion Question: What do you think would happen if poor people all over the world worked with sociologists to form a movement to end poverty? Would you want to be part of such an effort? Why?

Alicia Swords is an associate professor of sociology at Ithaca College. She conducts research with social movements in the United States and Latin America and enjoys supporting student engagement with grassroots efforts for social change.

---

social movements are racist hate organizations like neo-Nazi groups and the Ku Klux Klan. Although some social movements push for massive social change, others press for limited changes to society. There are four different types of movements: alternative, redemptive, reformative, and revolutionary.

Alternative social movements advocate for limited societal change but do not ask individuals to change their personal beliefs. They often target a narrow group of people and focus on a single concern. Friends of Cats is an example of an alternative social movement. Their goal was to change animal control policy in their city. Another alternative social movement, the DREAMers movement, advocates for a pathway to citizenship for children of undocumented immigrants. Many environmental movements—like the antifracking movement—provide more examples of alternative social movements. Mothers Against Drunk Driving (MADD) and Mothers for Gun Control are both examples of movements advocating for changes to specific policies and laws. MADD advocates for harsher laws against drunk driving, and Mothers for Gun Control lobbies for stricter gun control laws and gun safety.

THE USE AND EFFECTIVENESS OF "SLACKTIVISM"

In this activity, you will find and examine the effectiveness of examples of "slacktivism."

Slacktivism is a term used to describe activism that requires very little time or effort. Usually slacktivism is online (changing a profile picture, posting a link or a tweet) but could also be offline (signing a petition, wearing a T-shirt). Write your answers to the following questions and be prepared to discuss them in class.

1. Go online and find at least five examples of slacktivism. Where did you search and what search terms did you use to find these examples?

2. Describe the kinds of images and words these examples use. What do they have in common?

3. Have you ever changed your Facebook or Twitter picture to make a political statement? Does this count as social activism?

4. Can online protest actions like "slacktivism" be effective? When and how?

Some social movements can fall into multiple categories. MADD is also an example of a redemptive social movement as they ask individuals to change their behavior and not drive while intoxicated. **Redemptive social movements** seek radical change in individual behavior. For example, the temperance movement in the 1800s advocated for individuals to stop drinking alcohol. Although People for the Ethical Treatment of Animals is an alternative social movement in that they advocate against animal abuse, they are also a redemptive movement with the goal of convincing individuals to adopt a vegan diet and lifestyle.

Whereas alternative social movements are focused on social change for a narrow portion of society, **reformative social movements** work for specific change across society. In working for an end to racism and racial injustice, the civil rights movement and the more recent Black Lives Matter movement fit this type of movement. The marriage equality movement is another example of a reformative social movement; it aimed to change one aspect of society—the ability for same-sex couples to marry. Reformative social movements can also be conservative, aiming to restore traditional ways of behavior or maintain the status quo. For example, conservative movements like the anti–marriage equality movement try to keep traditional gendered family roles. Another movement, the Texas Minutemen, deployed to the border of the United States and Mexico in 2018 in response to what President Trump called a crisis in illegal immigration. Attempts to stop illegal immigration may be driven, in part, by fear and status anxiety. Illegal immigration spurs fear that immigrants will monopolize limited employment opportunities, take advantage of welfare resources, and bring crime to the United States.

CONSIDER THIS

What type of social movement would be the easiest to organize, one that focuses on a changing a limited part of society or one that seeks broader social change? Which would you rather join? Why?

The goal of **revolutionary social movements** is a radical reorganization of society. The American Revolution is an example of a revolutionary social movement. The Communist Party in the United States and around the world challenges capitalism and government policies that exploit workers. It advocates for environmental protection, living wages for workers, the rights of labor unions, and shared ownership of resources. U.S. militia organizations (like the Militia of Montana) are paramilitary groups that seek to end the federal government's power in areas like the economy, trade, and business, in favor of individual and business rights.

Check Your Understanding

- What are the different kinds of social movements?
- Which type of social movement seeks the most limited kind of change?
- Which type of social movement advocates for the most radical social change?

Social Movement Theory

16.4 How would you use the conflict and symbolic interaction theories to explain social movements?

Sociological theories help us understand how social movements form, how they act, and whether they are successful. Theories about social movements highlight the different aspects of social movement mobilization, from how they function to the symbolism they use.

Conflict Theory

Conflict theorists focus on how social movements develop out of systematic inequality. According to conflict theorists, social movements arise when goods and services are distributed unevenly. One of the most well-known conflict theories used in the arena of social movements is resource mobilization.

Resource mobilization theory focuses on the resources needed to mobilize and sustain a social movement. The presence of resources—followers, money, political connections, and so on—predicts whether a movement will be successful. Resource mobilization theorists believe all social movements need resources to mobilize, and without these resources, mobilization is much more difficult, if not impossible (McCarthy and Zald 1977). However, focusing on resources does not help us understand how individuals and groups with little to no resources (poor people, marginalized people) form a successful social movement (Piven 2006; Cress and Snow 1996). For example, undocumented migrant farm workers have relatively little power to protest their working conditions. They do not have access to typical resources like money, politicians, the media, or food distribution companies. However, even without these resources, migrant workers ran a five-year strike against Delano grapes and, by withholding their labor, gained the media coverage needed to spark a consumer boycott. Despite their relative powerlessness, the farm workers were successful in improving their working conditions and pay.

Symbolic Interactionist Theory

As you know, symbolic interactionists focus on how people interactively construct meaning through shared symbols and language. The peace sign, for example, is a shared social movement symbol calling for an end to war. Symbolic interactionists theorize that collective behavior develops when established institutions no longer provide meaning that aligns with the views of a majority of its constituents (Benford and Hunt 1992). For example, if the state defines *marriage* as an institution only male-female couples can participate in, but society is largely open and accepting of same-sex couples, a social movement will organize to redefine the meaning of *marriage* to include same-sex couples.

Symbolic interactionists look at how people create meaning, goals, and shared culture within their collective action. The powerful use of symbols during the collective actions carried out after Trayvon Martin, a seventeen-year-old African American, was killed in 2012 in Sanford, Florida, by neighborhood watchman George Zimmerman provides an example. Martin was walking home from a local convenience store, but Zimmerman was suspicious of what the teen was doing in the neighborhood and followed him. Zimmerman and Martin got into an altercation, and Martin was shot. Zimmerman claimed self-defense, but Martin was unarmed (Blow 2012). The killing started nationwide protests against racism and the perception that young Black men are dangerous.

When Zimmerman confronted him, Martin was wearing a hoodie and carrying Skittles candy and an Arizona iced tea. These items became symbols of Martin's innocence at the time of the shooting, and the innocence of all

Pastor Thirkel Freeman wears a hoodie and carries bags of Skittles, two symbols used to counter the image of Treyvon Martin and other young Black men as dangerous, at a memorial for Martin in Washington, D.C., on March 23, 2012.

Keith Lane/Tribune News Service/Getty Images

FRAMING THE GAY RIGHTS MOVEMENT

In this exercise, you will apply the idea of framing to slogans associated with the gay rights movement over the past several decades.

Go online and find images from the gay rights movement (1970s to the present). Look for images of signs, buttons, and T-shirts activists use to advocate for equality. If you are not working on your computer in class, print at least three of these images and bring them to class.

Individually or with a group of other students, compare framing in early slogans like "Come out," "We're here,

we're queer, get used to it," and "queer pride," with more recent slogans like "love is love," and "freedom to marry," and "love makes a family."

1. What master frames are being used?

2. What do these changing frames tell you about shifts in the strategy of the gay rights movement?

3. How did this framing shift lead to marriage equality in 2015?

---

young Black men stereotyped as dangerous. To make this point at antiracism demonstrations, protesters held up Skittles and iced tea. Protesters wore hoodies to mock the idea that a hoodie makes a Black teenager look dangerous.

CONSIDER THIS

What symbols, objects, and phrases can you think of that have helped mobilize people for social action? Why do you think they were so powerful?

Social Movement Framing. The framing approach is another way to understand social movements under the symbolic interactionist umbrella. Sociologists who use the framing approach focus on how social movements use images and language to frame their causes. Through **framing**, leaders influence how people think about an issue by highlighting certain facts and themes, while making others invisible (Snow et al. 1986). For example, when making their pitch to the city council, the Friends of Cats organization would frame the issue around how the city could save money with a TNR program. In their meeting with other organization members, however, they would use the frame of love for animals to make a case for TNR policy. Context matters for framing. The same frame that works in one context will not necessarily be successful in another.

In U.S. culture, there are frames that appeal nearly universally. These **master frames** include ideas like "freedom," "democracy," "love," and "choice" and can be used by movements with different goals. Think about both sides of the abortion rights debate. The "pro-life" movement

chose that name to center the issue on a master frame everyone values: life. The "pro-choice" movement similarly framed their movement around the universally valued idea of choice. But on bumper stickers, the "pro-life" movement evokes the same master frame to declare "fetuses don't have a choice." This is an example of **frame competition**, when an organization uses another group's frames to discredit or ridicule its position (Oliver and Johnston 2000).

Identity-Based Social Movements. Before the 1950s, social movements tended to focus on economic concerns and workers' rights. Identity-based social movements, however, tend to mobilize around issues of rights and collective social identities. For example, the civil rights movement organized around a shared racial identity and experience. The **women's movement** brought women together *as women* to fight for rights and equality.

Organizing around a shared identity can be empowering for movement members, especially when that identity has been marginalized. But collective mobilization around a shared identity can also exclude individuals who do not fully fit that identity. For example, the women's movement of the 1960s and 1970s is often criticized for mobilizing around the collective identity of White, heterosexual, middle-class women, whose experiences of oppression are not the same as those of other women.

When Betty Friedan's book *The Feminine Mystique* came out in 1963, it helped start this new women's movement in the United States. But her book spoke largely to middle-class, straight, White women and excluded low-income women, lesbian and bisexual women, and women of color. Concerned the movement would be perceived as "antimale" and that lesbian women would

The cover of the first edition of Betty Friedan's book *The Feminine Mystique* (1963), which helped spark the second wave of the women's movement.

threaten the image of feminists, Friedan described lesbian women within the movement as the "Lavender Menace." Although the term was meant to be derogatory, lesbians in the movement made "Lavender Menace" T-shirts and wore them to a protest—which showed just how many lesbians were a part of the movement.

CONSIDER THIS

Is it possible to mobilize around a shared identity *and* be inclusive of differences?

Check Your Understanding

- According to conflict theorists, why do social movements arise?

- What do symbolic interactionists tend to focus on when studying social movements?

- What is a master frame? Provide an example of a master frame.

- What does it mean to organize around a shared identity?

The Six Steps of Social Movement Success

16.5 What are the steps a social movement must take to become successful?

Social movements tend to be successful when they can identify a goal they can rally others around, form a group, create an effective strategy, mobilize enough resources, organize effective actions, and build power. Those that can't do all of these will not reach their goals. Much also depends on the social and historical context and the forces that muster for or against the movement. Social movements are more likely to develop in political climates in which people have the freedom to organize and mobilize for their cause.

Social movements occur in every country all over the world. This section covers primarily U.S.-based social movements, with an emphasis on activism and organizing in the twentieth- and twenty-first-century civil rights and women's movements.

Identify an Issue

The first task of any social movement is to identify an issue that needs to be addressed. This could be a widespread change in culture or a specific change to policy or an institutional practice. The goal must be described as necessary to improve people's lives or make the world and/or community a better place. The context leading up to a social movement matters a great deal.

The Women's Movement. Identifying an issue to organize around also means making a case for why change should occur. The women's movement in the United States follows four distinct waves of collective action—1848 to 1920, the 1960s and 1970s, the 1990s, and from 2000 on. Each wave had its own goals. The first wave, the suffrage movement, focused on women gaining the right to vote. In arguing for this right, suffragists asserted that women were fundamentally different from men and would bring their unique qualities to government if they could participate. This argument of **difference feminism** used images of women as caring, nurturing mothers to argue that women would bring an end to war and poverty if they could vote and serve in office (Fox-Genovese 1994).

The first wave of the women's movement focused on attaining the right to vote for women. It began in 1848 and culminated with the ratification of the Nineteenth Amendment in 1920.

The antisuffrage movement also emphasized gender differences by arguing that women would be taking on men's roles in public, at the expense of taking care of the household. Antisuffrage postcards depicted women in pants, demonstrating on street corners, while husbands suffered at home trying to take care of crying children. Despite opposition, the suffrage movement won women the right to vote throughout the United States with the ratification of the Nineteenth Amendment in 1920.

The second wave of the feminist movement started in the 1960s and peaked in the 1970s. After working in factories during World War II, women were expected to go back to being full-time wives and mothers once the war ended. During this time, women had few rights and were expected to become wives, mothers, and full-time homemakers. In 1963, Betty Friedan released her book *The Feminine Mystique*, in which she criticized the 1950s image of the modern, suburban housewife. The book recognized the discontent housewives felt and became widely popular

as a result, sparking the second wave of the feminist movement, which advocated for an end to gender discrimination in the workplace and reproductive rights for women. Some feminist leaders established the National Organization for Women to lobby Congress for women's rights.

Form a Group

The next step in a successful social movement is to form an organization of both beneficiary and consciousness constituents who will work toward the movement's goals. Beneficiary constituents and consciousness constituents must believe the change is necessary.

The Civil Rights Movement. The civil rights movement consisted of individuals joining together to fight racial injustice. You have probably heard of the importance of Black churches during the civil rights movement, but did you know that students played an important role in the civil rights movement? From participating in the Student

National Rally for Equal Rights

On May 16, 1976, approximately 10,000 supporters of the Equal Rights Amendment marched to the state capitol building in Springfield, Illinois.

AP Photo/Anonymous

Nonviolent Coordinating Committee to planning large-scale actions like Freedom Summer in 1964, students were essential to the movement's success. During that summer of 1964, college students and other young people—Black and White—from all over the United States volunteered to join groups traveling to Mississippi to register Black voters. Because of various means of racial discrimination, only 7 percent of the state's eligible Black voters were registered. Although many participants were beneficiary constituents, White students participated as consciousness constituents. Partly because some of these students were White, they were able to gain national media attention as they traveled through the South (McAdam 1990).

The Women's Movement. By title, it would seem that the women's movement comprises entirely women. But movement membership has varied over the years. When you think of a feminist, what kind of person comes to mind? Do you think of a young woman burning her bra in the 1970s, demanding equal pay for equal work? A radical lesbian, refusing to shave her legs and screaming against the patriarchy? A member of a men's antirape group? A college woman marching in a Take Back the Night event on her campus, advocating for women's safety?

A **feminist** is someone committed to gender equality. A **feminist organization** is an organization working to end women's oppression.

As noted earlier, the women's movement has not always been inclusive of all women. The needs of poor women and women of color were largely excluded from the second wave of the movement as activists focused on issues such as professional opportunities and salary equity—and largely ignored issues related to classism and racism (hooks 1984). During the 1980s, feminists faced a backlash, with headlines like the *Time* cover asking "Is feminism dead?" (Faludi 1994).

By the 1990s, however, a new, third wave of feminism was well under way. Instead of assuming that all women experienced oppression in the same ways as White, middle-class women, the third wave focused on inclusiveness and intersectionality. Third-wave feminists drew from a diverse group of women to advocate around various issues, including sexual violence, gay rights, and reproductive justice. One of the most visible groups in third-wave feminism were the riot grrrls. The riot grrrls movement developed out of the feminist hardcore punk music scene, and activists published and sold self-made zines (magazines) on feminist issues. Activists, musicians, and writers in the movement covered everything from body-positive messages to surviving sexual violence. Zines used images and commentary to empower young women to feel good about themselves and speak up against patriarchy (Rosenberg and Garofalo 1998).

Challenges to Forming a Group

Convincing beneficiary constituents and consciousness constituents to join a group is not without challenges, however. Beneficiary constituents must believe that their situations will improve as a result of their participation. Consciousness constituents must be willing to see something as a problem even when it does not directly affect them. Social movements also face issues such as keeping participants engaged over long periods of time, especially when there are stretches without clear victories. Social movement organizations must keep beneficiary and consciousness constituents engaged by fostering a shared sense of purpose and achievable small goals.

Marginalization of Members. Social movements can limit participation by marginalizing some members within the organization. For example, despite playing important roles in civil rights efforts, women were marginalized in the civil rights movement (Barnett 1993). Women in organizations like the National Association for the Advancement of Colored People, Student Nonviolent Coordinating Committee, and the Southern Christian Leadership Conference found that they were often assigned clerical work instead of on-the-ground organizing work. While male leaders placed themselves on the front lines of demonstrations and marches, women like Diane Nash and Ella Baker did much of the back-stage work of organizing.

Cultural Differences. Organizing becomes more difficult when social movements are global and cross-cultural. The women's movement, for example, ran into a problem trying to alleviate the perceived oppression of women in other countries (Rupp 1997). The 1984 U.S. book *Sisterhood Is Global: The International Women's Movement Anthology* by Robin Morgan is an example of how some movements can have a culturally biased perspective. The phrase "sisterhood is global" implies that all women experience oppression in the same way and that they are equal to one another in oppression, as sisters. The book was criticized for glossing over the different ways women are oppressed and for not addressing how oppression and empowerment may mean different things in different contexts. For example, wearing a hijab might seem like oppression from a Western perspective, when in fact a woman may see her hijab as a personally empowering choice to honor her religion (Read and Bartkowski 2000).

The idea that "sisterhood is global" also ignores inequalities among women. Now global feminist movement organizations strive to understand that not all women face the same types and extent of oppression and that some women (poor women, women of color) are more vulnerable than others. These organizations must consider how oppression and empowerment look different across contexts as they strive to create groups that can work together effectively.

Create a Strategy

To be successful, social movements must identify a strategy for making social change. Doing this requires consulting with experts and with the affected community to find solutions to the problem. Often the best strategies for social change are the result of careful research into what the problems are and what the best solutions might be. While creating a strategy, social movements must also identify the powerholders they need to target. These powerholders are people, institutions, voters, or lawmakers who have the power to enact the change the movement members want to see happen.

The Civil Rights Movement. Strategic research and planning was a key part of the civil rights movement. For example, before they began sit-ins at lunch counters in Nashville, Tennessee, activists collected data on how the lunch counters were run and how customers and employees responded to incidents of integration. Using this information, civil rights organizer James Lawson trained student activists to use nonviolent responses to the open aggression and hostility they expected to receive. They carefully rehearsed and prepared for their actions. In 1960, after their four-month campaign, Nashville became the first city to desegregate department store lunch counters (Morris 1981). This successful campaign to desegregate lunch counters through sit-ins became a model, and activists in many other the cities carried out similar actions.

Mobilize Resources

A successful social movement needs resources. Constituents are every social movement's most important resource. Other resources include

Joan Jett plays with singer Kathleen Hanna and drummer Tobi Vailfrom of Bikini Kill at Irving Plaza in New York on July 14, 1994. Jett's collaboration with Bikini Kill helped bring the punk extension of the third wave, riot grrrl, into the mainstream media.
Ebet Roberts/Redferns/Getty Images

MEDIA COVERAGE OF PROTESTS

In this exercise you will examine how different media sources vary in their coverage of a protest march.

Select a recent large-scale protest march (e.g., one of the Women's Marches, the March for Our Lives, a Black Lives Matter protest, or a March for Life). Using a news search engine such as Google News, find five different news articles about the protest, all from different news sources. Individually or with a group of other students, compare and contrast the articles to answer the following questions.

1. How do the articles describe the goals of the march?

2. How do they describe who was in attendance? What kinds of words do they use to describe participants?

3. Do the articles vary in their estimations of crowd size?

4. Does each article portray the protest and protesters positively or negatively? How do you know?

---

money, access to media, and supplies. Organizations must assess what resources they have and organize to gain those they need.

The Women's Movement. Women are a key resource for the women's movement. To mobilize women to join, women's organizations during the second wave of the women's movement in the 1960s and 1970s held consciousness-raising circles where women could share their experiences of oppression in a safe space. This helped connect more women to the movement.

As noted earlier, third-wave feminists used zines and music as resources to distribute their message. The Internet is a vital resource for the fourth wave of the women's movement (post-2000). Today, feminists use blogging and social media (Facebook, Instagram, and Twitter) to organize protests and rallies and to raise awareness about issues of rape culture, consumerism, beauty standards, and sexuality. Hashtag campaigns like "#EverydaySexism" and "#RapeCultureIsWhen" spread across the globe, generating conversations about key feminist issues (Clark 2014). The #MeToo hashtag has been used more than 20 million times on Twitter, spiking in use during events connected to the movement, such as when Supreme Court nominee Brett Kavanaugh, and the woman who accused him of attempted sexual assault, Dr. Christine Blasey Ford, testified before Congress in November 2018 (Pew Research Center 2018).

Organize Actions

Social action is the lifeblood of social movements. Specific actions, or tactics, might include protesting, marching, boycotting, and so on. Goals of actions include raising awareness, building constituents, and/or directly asking for change. As symbolic interactionists argue, shared cultural symbols and language are powerful parts of social movement action and used by movement leaders to organize and inspire followers. It is also important to remember that actions, no matter how well planned, organized, or eloquently inspired, come with risks.

The Civil Rights Movement. Before going to Mississippi in 1964, the Freedom Summer activists were taught how to talk to people about voting and how to register voters. They planned summer-long Freedom Schools to educate Black Mississippians on voting, politics, Black history, and other topics. All their preparation could not always keep them safe, however. When they went to Mississippi, the activists were threatened and lived with families who faced hostility for hosting the volunteers. One of their buses was burned, and many endured beatings and jail time. Three activists were abducted and brutally killed in Neshoba County, Mississippi. The murders of James Earl Chaney, Andrew Goodman, and Michael Schwerner symbolized the connection between brutality and racism and brought national attention to Freedom Summer (McAdam 1990).

Not everyone in the civil rights movement agreed on which tactics were best for the movement. We frequently learn about peaceful civil rights protests and marches but do not learn that some participants in the movement broke the law (through civil disobedience) and used violence to fight for civil rights. The Black Panther Party, for example, rejected the nonviolence of Martin Luther King's followers, believing instead that Black people needed to defend

Diane Nash, a key but often unsung civil rights leader, was a creator and chair of the Student Nonviolent Coordinating Committee.

The Civil Rights Movement. The successes of the civil rights movement included the following:

- the Civil Rights Act of 1964, which forbids discrimination based on race, color, religion, sex, or national origin;

- the Voting Rights Act of 1965, which made it illegal for states and local governments to block individuals from voting and created a system to monitor states and counties with low voter turnout among minorities; and

- the Civil Rights Act of 1968, which prohibits discrimination in renting, selling, or financing housing based on race, color, religion, sex, or national origin.

Thanks to the civil rights movement, the United States largely dismantled Jim Crow legislation that enforced racial segregation and other forms of discrimination (such as in employment and housing) and prevented millions of Black Americans from voting.

themselves against state-sanctioned violence (Bloom and Martin 2013). They often went to protests and events openly armed, to symbolize the seriousness of their intent to defend their community.

Gaining Power and Success

Every social movement must gain power to be successful. If they successfully complete the steps above, movements will gain power and the subsequent ability to achieve their goals. Both the civil rights movement and the women's movement were able to reach many of their key goals. Movement success arrives when the problem is solved or the goal achieved.

CONSIDER THIS

Under what conditions is violence (against property or people) ever justifiable in a social movement? If never, why not?

The Women's Movement. The women's movement won victories like the Equal Pay Act of 1963 and the 1973 Supreme Court decision in *Roe v. Wade*, granting women legal access to abortion. The women's movement also became an influential part of mainstream political institutions. Started as an organization targeting politicians for social change, the National Organization for Women now has hundreds of thousands of members, chapters in every state (including on many college campuses), and a strong lobbying presence in Washington, D.C.

Why Social Movements Fail

Social movements may fail to reach their goals for a variety of reasons. Failure may come from organizational issues (disagreements and infighting), a lack of resources, or an inability to mobilize supporters. Social movements may also be repressed. **Repression** takes place when people and/or institutions with power use that power to control or destroy a movement. Countries that ban any form of public protest include Russia, the Ukraine, and Egypt. Making

A sit-in at a Whites-only, racially segregated lunch counter in Nashville, Tennessee, in 1960. These successful protests sparked others across the South.

a social movement's activities—like distributing flyers—illegal is another example of repression. In 2018, the Center for Human Rights in Iran reported that the Iranian government blocked access to critical social media sites used to organize protests against the government's economic policies. Cutting access to social media also made it difficult for the protests to rally international support.

Social movements can also be co-opted. **Co-optation** can happen when the leadership of the movement begins to identify with the targets of social change and starts to work more for them than for the original movement goals. Social movements can also end up taking on the values and actions they are trying to change. For example, the environmental movement seeking corporate responsibility in growing and selling coffee found its language of "fair trade" co-opted by some coffee sellers to appeal to a high-end niche consumer, without much concern about whether the coffee was actually fairly traded. Social movement goals—like fair-trade coffee—may become watered down or changed to accommodate the corporation's needs.

Check Your Understanding

- List the steps social movements must take to become successful.

- What kinds of strategies did the civil rights movement use in planning actions?

- Who is a feminist?

- What is the most important resource for all social movements?

- What are some of the key achievements of the civil rights movement and the women's movement?

Success Can Bring Backlash: The Marriage Equality Movement

16.6 What tactics do social movements use to achieve their goals, and what kind of backlash do they face?

The marriage equality movement is one of the most successful movements in recent history. As Figure 16.1 indicates, public approval for same-sex marriage rose dramatically in a single decade, with 35 percent supporting it in 2006 compared with 55 percent in favor in 2016 (a year after the Supreme Court ruling legalizing it).

Successful Tactics of the Marriage Equality Movement

The movement used a variety of tactics to achieve marriage equality, including increasing numbers of gay and lesbian public figures coming out. By the late 1990s, there were openly gay and lesbian main characters on primetime

▼ FIGURE 16.1

Percentage of Opposition and Support for Same-Sex Marriage, 2006–2016

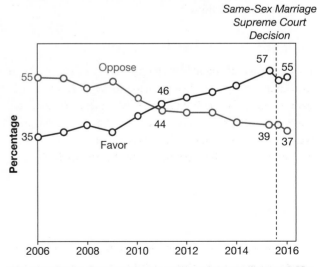

Source: Hannah Fingerhut, "Support steady for same-sex marriage and acceptance of homosexuality," Pew Research Center, Washington, D.C. (May 12, 2016) https://www.pewresearch.org/fact-tank/2016/05/12/support-steady-for-same-sex-marriage-and-acceptance-of-homosexuality/.

television shows like *Ellen*, starring Ellen DeGeneres. Today, television shows with gay characters and gay married couples are commonplace. This changed public perception of gays and lesbians and of same-sex couples, paving the way for marriage equality (Fetner 2016).

Direct action and protests were other tactics that helped the movement become successful. The gay rights movement in the United States, of which the marriage equality movement was an offshoot, began with the Stonewall riots on June 28, 1969. During the 1950s and 1960s, it was illegal for bars to serve gays and lesbians, and they could lose their liquor licenses for letting gay people congregate. The riots broke out in the Stonewall Inn, a bar in New York City frequented by gay men and lesbians. Police raids on known gay and lesbian bars were commonplace, but when police raided the Stonewall Inn, patrons decided they had enough and fought back (Carter 2005). The riots served to galvanize the gay and lesbian community to organize into activist groups and push for equal treatment. The following year, to commemorate the anniversary of the riots, gay and lesbian rights activists held a march in New York City running from Greenwich Village up Fifth Avenue to Central Park. This was the first Pride March, now an annual event held on the last Sunday of June in New York.

Beginning in 2000, the marriage equality movement turned to the court system to advocate for equality, strategically suing states for the right of same-sex couples to marry. In 2004, they enjoyed their first major victory. As the result of a discrimination case brought to the Massachusetts Supreme Court, gay and lesbian couples won the right to marry in Massachusetts.

After Massachusetts, individual states passed either marriage equality laws or "marriage protection" laws (defining marriage between a man and a woman). Each state presented a challenge for activists. For example, in early 2009, Maine's legislature passed a marriage equality law. People around the state then organized against marriage equality and were able to get the issue on the ballot. In November 2009, Mainers voted to keep marriage "between one man and one woman." In response, the marriage equality movement changed its organizing strategy. Activists surveyed people around the state, particularly in rural areas, to discuss the importance of marriage and family. When marriage equality was put on Maine's ballot again in 2012, activists went door to door explaining that gays and lesbians in Maine wanted the same things everyone else did—lifelong love and commitment. Commercials by organizations like Maine Equality depicted very few actual gay individuals, instead depicting families and loved ones who believed love and marriage should be accessible to everyone. In 2012, marriage equality won in Maine.

By 2015, all but fourteen states had marriage equality laws. Then, the Supreme Court decided that the Fourteenth Amendment requires states to issue marriage licenses to couples, regardless of sex. Marriage equality became the law of the land. Individuals and institutions used social media to show their support of the ruling. Facebook made it possible for people to superimpose a rainbow flag over their profile picture—some 26 million users showed their support (Dewey 2015).

With Success Comes Backlash. Sometimes successful movements face backlash. As support for a movement grows, fear and resentment of this change among those most ardently opposed to the movement also grow. This can lead to increased acts of discrimination. Same-sex couples seeking marriage licenses after the *Obergefell v. Hodges* (2015) decision have sometimes faced local officials who refuse to follow the law. Interracial couples trying to get married shortly after the *Loving v. Virginia* (1967) decision, which made interracial marriages legal, faced similar obstacles. Also, as noted in Chapter 8, in a majority of states in the United States, employers still have the legal right to fire employees simply for being gay, lesbian, or transgender. Most horrifyingly, LGBT

The first Gay Pride Day (then known as Gay Liberation Day) parade in New York City, June 28, 1970.
Fred W. McDarrah/Premium Archive/Getty Images

HAS THE MARRIAGE EQUALITY MOVEMENT LED TO MORE SAME-SEX MARRIAGE?

The marriage equality movement is one of the most successful social movements in modern times. In 2007, only 37 percent of Americans supported same-sex marriage, but by 2017, that number had grown to 62 percent. In 2013, the Supreme Court struck down the Defense of Marriage Act prohibiting same-sex marriage, and in 2015 the Court made same-sex marriage legal nationwide.

In this online activity, you will examine how same-sex marriage rates have changed since 2013, using data from the U.S. Census Bureau's American Community Survey.

*Requires the Vantage version of *Sociology in Action*.

▼ FIGURE 16.2

Percentage of Same-Sex U.S. Household Couples Who Are Married

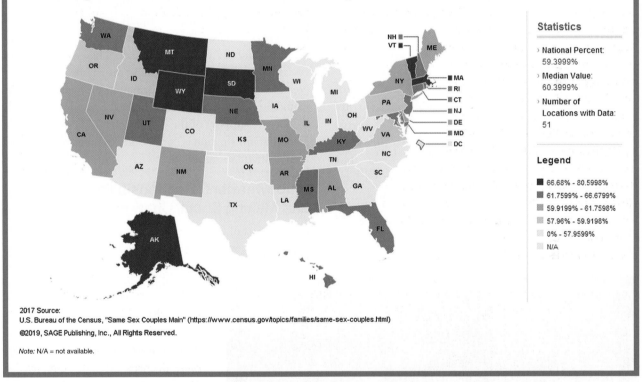

Statistics

› **National Percent:**
59.3999%

› **Median Value:**
60.3999%

› **Number of Locations with Data:**
51

Legend

- 66.68% – 80.5998%
- 61.7599% – 66.6799%
- 59.9199% – 61.7598%
- 57.96% – 59.9198%
- 0% – 57.9599%
- N/A

2017 Source:
U.S. Bureau of the Census, "Same Sex Couples Main" (https://www.census.gov/topics/families/same-sex-couples.html)
©2019, SAGE Publishing, Inc., All Rights Reserved.

Note: N/A = not available.

people have also faced violent attacks. When gay and lesbian people gain equality through policies, social acceptance increases and hate crimes also decrease overall. But we also see an increase in the more extreme and violent hate crimes (Levy and Levy 2017).

Check Your Understanding

- What were the tactics of the marriage equality movement?
- Why can successful movements face backlash?
- What are some examples of discrimination the LGBT community still faces?

How Can We Create Social Change?

16.7   How can we create social change?

The success of a social movement depends on everything from the number and commitment of activists, the kinds of actions planned, the resources available to the movement, to the symbolic power of the movement to grab media and public attention. Money certainly makes it easier to exert influence. But civil rights protesters who changed Jim Crow laws did not have large amounts of money behind them. Instead, they had large numbers of people and careful planning. Their power came from organizing effectively and successfully mobilizing people and influencing public opinion through their carefully planned actions.

Francis Fox Piven's (2006) concept of **interdependent power** helps explain how social change can come from the organized efforts of relatively poor and powerless individuals because of the ties that bind institutions and individuals together. Individuals are connected to one another through institutions that organize our lives. Teachers rely on having students in their classrooms, just as students rely on access to a teacher for their educations. These same institutions depend on the actions of their members—teaching, learning—to survive. Take, for example, the growing problem of student loan debt. Individuals who owe student loans can do little alone to change the system of financing higher education. They relied on the loan company to pay for school, and the loan company relies on them to pay that loan back. As individuals, they would face negative consequences for not paying their student loans back. But, as part of a large group (44 million Americans), they have power. If all 44 million people stopped paying their loans, they would be exercising interdependent power and affecting all the players. That kind of mass action would be difficult to organize, but the concept of interdependent power does explain some of the ways social change can happen from below.

Participatory Action Research

Sociological research skills can help foster social change and organize social movements effectively. **Participatory action research** (PAR) starts with the idea that people are the experts in their own lives and can participate in the research process. Instead of the typical model of a researcher coming into a community to study it, the people who live in that community participate in the research process and help produce the knowledge collectively (Greenwood and Levin 2006).

PAR is an especially useful technique in disadvantaged communities where members may not trust outsider researchers and are more likely to talk to one another. Take, for example, the Friends of Cats organization described at the beginning of this chapter. If Friends of Cats found that the community was reluctant to support outside solutions for the feral cat problem, PAR could be a solution. Using PAR, sociology researchers might work with Friends of Cats and community leaders to better understand the community members' views on the issue. They would design a research plan together. They might distribute a survey they created together. With the information they gathered, they would be able to construct an animal control policy likely to gain the support of the community. In PAR, the act of gathering information is community building and can lead to meaningful social action.

Empowerment, Responsibility, and Making Social Change

Being a part of a social movement can be very empowering. Social movements bring individuals together in a kind of **collective solidarity**, or sense of social bonding, that strengthens our ties to one another (Oliver 1993). When social movements bring victories—no matter how small—members are empowered to see that they can take part in social change. For this reason, individuals who take part in social movements are more likely to take part in other protests and to be politically active.

Being a part of collective efforts for social change is also a responsibility. Many of the social movements you have read about in this chapter have struggled with issues of inclusion. Organizing around a shared identity can be a powerful experience but can leave others out. Feminist organizations

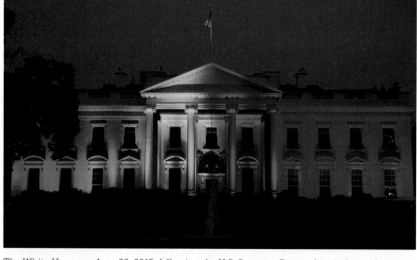

The White House on June 26, 2015, following the U.S. Supreme Court ruling in favor of same-sex marriage.

AP Photo/Drew Angerer

BOOKS AND DOCUMENTARIES ABOUT SOCIAL MOVEMENTS

BOOKS ABOUT SOCIAL MOVEMENTS

Poor People's Movements: Why They Succeed, How They Fail, by Frances Fox Piven

Bringing the War Home: The Weather Underground, the Red Army Faction, and Revolutionary Violence in the Sixties and Seventies, by Jeremy Varon

The Autobiography of Malcolm X, by Malcolm X

The Next American Revolution: Sustainable Activism for the Twenty-First Century, by Grace Lee Boggs

Democracy in the Making: How Activist Groups Form, by Kathleen Blee

This Is an Uprising, by Mark and Paul Engler

Beautiful Uprising: A Toolbox for Revolution, by Andrew Boyd and Dave Oswald Mitchell

Freedom Is a Constant Struggle: Ferguson, Palestine, and the Foundations of a Movement, by Angela Davis

The World Split Open: How the Modern Women's Movement Changed America, by Ruth Rosen

How Change Happens, by Duncan Greene

Freedom's Daughters: The Unsung Heroines of the Civil Rights Movement from 1830–1970, by Lynne Olsen

SOCIAL MOVEMENT DOCUMENTARIES

Eyes on the Prize (PBS, 1987)

Berkeley in the Sixties (Kitchell Films, 1990)

Freedom on My Mind (Clarity Films, 1994)

This Is What Democracy Looks Like (Big Noise Films, 2000)

Brother Outsider: The Life of Bayard Rustin (PBS, 2003)

This Black Soil: A Story of Resistance and Rebirth (Bullfrog Films, 2004)

The Billionaire's Tea Party (Larrikin Films, 2011)

The Black Power Mixtape 1967–1975 (Story AB, 2011)

The Square (Noujaim Films, 2013)

How to Change the World (Met Film, 2015)

The Hand That Feeds (Jubilee Films, 2014)

Delores (PBS, 2017)

How to Survive a Plague (Independent Lens, 2012)

American Revolutionary: Grace Lee Boggs (PBS, 2013)

Disruption: Climate Change (PF Pictures, 2016)

She's Beautiful When She's Angry (Music Box Films, 2016)

Stay Woke: The Black Lives Matter Movement (BET, 2016)

---

committed to intersectionality work to make sure that all voices within the organization are heard, especially the voices and needs of those women who are most vulnerable.

Men in the feminist movement and White people in the Black Lives Matter movement have also raised questions of how to be a good ally. An **ally** is a conscience constituent who is committed to the cause (Porta and Diani 2008). Although allies can be important parts of a movement, they need to make sure they do not speak for those they are fighting for or take advantage of their own privilege by being in the spotlight or taking credit for activism. Being a good ally means listening to the needs of beneficiaries and working together to plan a course of action that will bring about change.

How You Can Help Bring about Social Change

- Be aware of inequalities and oppression. Find out which groups are the most marginalized in our society and why. Learn about their marginalization from their perspective.

- Learn the history of social movements. There are fantastic books and documentaries about social movements. Find causes that matter to you and learn the history of that movement.

- Examine inequality and oppression from an intersectional perspective. Race, class, gender, sexuality, age, and ethnicity are all intertwined. Consider how your activism may include some while excluding others.

- Raise awareness. Share links and news on Facebook, Instagram, and Twitter. Follow social movements you care about online. Sign online petitions. Engage in discussions with friends and family. But do not stop at "slacktivism." Think about how you can become a more active activist.

- Engage in the political process. Learn who your representatives are and communicate with them through letter writing and social media. Follow political campaigns at the local, state and national levels. Vote.

- Go to a local political meeting. Attend city council or school board meetings in your community. Find out what issues matter and what decisions are being made.

- Work to not make assumptions about oppression and privilege. What might look like oppression to you may mean freedom to someone else. Listen to people's experiences and goals.

- Speak out about issues that matter to you. Sometimes speaking out means taking risks, and only you can decide what risks you are comfortable with.

- Work with others who share your concerns. Organized people have more power.

CONSIDER THIS

What social or political issue are you concerned about? How would sociology and sociological theory help you to understand this issue? Brainstorm some ways you could become involved in addressing this issue.

Check Your Understanding

- What is interdependent power and how can it help individuals without much power alone effect change?

- What is participatory action research?

- What can you do to help bring about social change?

- Why should you work with others when seeking social change?

Conclusion

Studying social movements helps us understand what matters in our society and where we might be heading. Sociological tools can also help social movements work more effectively. For example, being able to conduct surveys and interviews with community members about their needs and goals is an essential skill for mobilizing and organizing people. Understanding how to gain power and effect change are invaluable assets for social movement leaders.

Knowledge of social movements can also come in handy in a variety of careers. Knowing how to mobilize people to action can help anyone who works with people—in any field. Professionals in fields from community organizing to nonprofit management to education to marketing use these skills. Think of how you can use them in your chosen career.

As we have seen in this chapter, social change can come from the top (from people with resources and influence) or from the bottom (from community action and exercising interdependent power). Social change can also come through education—informing people about activism, equality, and independence. Although social movements usually begin outside of established institutions, participating in the political process (by voting, campaigning, etc.) can also bring about social change. Individuals, like you, can use all these avenues to help create social change and make an impact on society.

$SAGE edge™

Want a better grade? Get the tools you need to sharpen your study skills. Access practice quizzes, eFlashcards, video, and multimedia at **edge.sagepub.com/korgen2e**

REVIEW

16.1 What is a social movement?

A social movement is a collective, organized, sustained effort to make social change.

16.2 Why do people participate in social movements?

People participate in social movements when they feel passionately about an issue. They may participate as beneficiary constituents, who will directly benefit from the goals of the social movement (i.e., same-sex couples who would like marriage equality). Or they may participate as conscience constituents, who will not benefit directly but feel strongly about the cause.

16.3 What are the different types of social movements?

While some social movements push for massive social change, others press for limited changes to society. There are four different types of movements: alternative, redemptive, reformative, and revolutionary. Alternative social movements advocate for limited societal change. Redemptive social movements seek more radical change in individual behavior. Reformative social movements work for specific change across society. The goal of revolutionary social movements is a radical reorganization of society.

16.4 How would you use the conflict and symbolic interaction theories to explain social movements?

Sociologists use theories to understand different aspects of how social movements work. Conflict theorists look at how social movements develop from inequality. When a group of people feels deprived of something they believe they should have access to (rights, money, power, etc.), they will protest. Symbolic interactionists are interested in the shared language and symbolism—like the peace sign—that hold social movements together and help spread their message.

16.5 What are the steps a social movement must take to become successful?

Social movements that succeed follow the following steps:

1. Identify a social change goal
2. Form a group of likeminded people committed to the goal

3. Create a strategy (a plan of action to achieve the goal)
4. Mobilize resources
5. Organize actions
6. Build power

Movement success arrives when the problem is solved or the goal achieved.

16.6 What tactics do social movements use to achieve their goals, and what kind of backlash do they face?

Some organizations stay within the limits of the law, protesting with permits and cooperating with police and officials. Other organizations may decide to participate in civil disobedience—blocking roads or buildings—to make their point heard. Other more radical organizations might break into buildings, destroy property, and further disrupt people's lives. Each of these tactics has positive and negative aspects the movement must consider. Organizations often do research and work with communities to find the best tactics for social change. Effective tactics build support for a movement, but this growth in support can inspire fear and resentment of change among those most ardently opposed to the movement. This can lead to increased acts of discrimination.

16.7 How can we create social change?

Social change can come from the top or the bottom, but it requires getting involved. Examine inequality and discrimination from an intersectional perspective. Raise awareness about the things that matter to you and engage in the political process. Speak up when you disagree with what you see around you, but be sure to listen to people with other perspectives and consider their views.

KEY TERMS

ally 343

alternative social movements 329

beneficiary constituents 326

civil disobedience 326

collective solidarity 342

co-optation 339

community-based organizing 328

conscience constituents 327

difference feminism 333

feminist 335

feminist organization 335

frame competition 332

framing 332

interdependent power 342

master frames 332

mobilizing 328

participatory action research 342

protest 326

redemptive social movements 330

reformative social movements 330

repression 338

resource mobilization theory 331

revolutionary social movements 330

social movement 325

women's movement 332

GLOSSARY

Absolutist perspective: States that some behaviors, conditions, and beliefs are inherently, objectively deviant.

Acute illnesses: Illnesses that come on and generally leave relatively quickly—though they can cause death.

Agency: The ability to act and think independently of social constraints.

Agents of socialization: People, groups, institutions, and social contexts that contribute to our socialization.

Agnostics: Maintain that nothing is known or can be known about god(s).

Alienation: A theoretical concept to describe isolating, dehumanizing, and disenchanting effects of working within a capitalist system of production.

Ally: A conscience constituent who is committed to the cause.

Alternative social movements: Advocate for limited societal change but do not ask individuals to change their personal beliefs. They often target a narrow group of people and focus on a single concern.

Anomie: A state in which a society's norms fail to regulate behavior.

Appearance: Consists of everything from dress to age, sex, and race to ethnicity, to nonverbal forms of communication like body language and gestures.

Applied research: Research designed to produce results that are immediately useful in relation to some real-world situation.

Atheists: Do not believe in a god.

Attitude-behavior split: When we think one way and act another.

Autocracy: A form of government in which absolute power is held by one person whose authority is not restricted in any way by either law or custom.

Back stage: Where one prepares for an interaction.

Basic research: Research directed at gaining fundamental knowledge about some issue.

Beliefs: What we deem to be true.

Beneficiary constituents: People who stand to benefit directly from the social change being sought.

Biographical disruption: When a person's usual activities and social life are disturbed.

Capitalism: An economic system in which the means of production are privately owned, and economic activity is driven by the pursuit of profit in a competitive market.

Caste: Rigid systems that confine individuals to social groups for their lifetimes, assigning them specific roles in a society with tight rules over the relationships among castes.

Causation: Whether a change in one variable causes a change in another variable.

Charismatic domination: Authority based on the extraordinary personal qualities of a leader and the resulting devotion of his or her followers.

Charter schools: Publicly funded schools, established under a charter, and governed by parents, educators, community groups, or private organizations. The charter details the school's mission, curriculum, or philosophy; students to be served; performance goals; evaluation plans; and commitments.

Chinese Exclusion Act of 1882: Halted Chinese immigration.

Chronic illnesses: Diseases that last for several months or years or even persist until death.

Cisgender: Identifying gender consistent with the sex assigned at birth.

Civil disobedience: Purposely breaking social customs or laws to make a point about a cause.

Class-based: In these systems, members of a given social class share common economic statuses and lifestyles and have social mobility.

Class domination theory: A conflict theory perspective that argues that the economic elite are able to dominate society because of their power over the workings of the economy.

Climate justice: Highlights the fact that climate change relates to global inequality, in its creation and its impact.

Coding: Applying descriptive labels to sections of text or images so they can be classified into categories or themes.

Cohabitating couples: Couples living together without being married to each other.

Collective solidarity: A sense of social bonding that strengthens our ties to one another.

Color-blind ideology: A way of viewing race that maintains that if we ignore race and racial issues, racism will not exist.

Command economy: An economic system in which the state determines the type, quantity, and price of goods to be produced.

Communism: Under Karl Marx's conceptualization of communism, all citizens would be equal and able to fulfill their unique potential to imagine and create what we imagine.

Community-based organizing: Individual activists become involved in a movement because of an issue directly affecting their community.

Companionate marriage: Partnership based on romantic love.

Compensatory strategies: When individuals attempt to offset the deviance that is ascribed to them or make others more comfortable with their stigma.

Concerted cultivation: An approach to interaction and discipline through which parents proactively engage with and guide their children.

Conflict theory/conflict perspective: Tensions and conflicts arise when resources, status, and power are not distributed equitably; these conflicts then become the driving force for social change.

Conscience constituents: People who care about a cause but do not benefit directly from the changes.

Conspicuous consumption: The practice of spending money for the purpose of demonstrating or enhancing social prestige.

Constructivist analysis of the environment: Focuses on the role of ideology and knowledge in understanding our environmental conditions.

Content analysis: When researchers use texts and systematically categorize elements of those texts on the basis of a set of rules.

Control group: A group that does not experience the treatment or manipulation in a study.

Co-optation: Happens when the leadership of the movement begins to identify with the targets of social change and starts to work more for them than for the original movement goals.

Core commitments: The first core commitment of sociology is to *use the sociological eye* to observe social patterns. The second requires noticing patterns of injustice and *taking action* to challenge those patterns.

Corporate community: A network composed of the directors, partners, and managers of various profit-seeking enterprises.

Counterculture: Cases in which one group in a society espouses rules, values, or beliefs that conflict with the mainstream culture.

Coverture: The legal doctrine in which wives' standing was subsumed into their husbands'.

Cults: Unorthodox sects; violence is not a necessary component. Cults are also called newly formed religious movements.

Cultural capital: A type of capital related to education, style, appearance, and dress that promotes social mobility.

Cultural diffusion: How cultural attributes can spread throughout the world.

Cultural relativism: The idea that cultures cannot be ranked as better or worse than others.

Cultural universals: Cultural practices that exist in most or all societies, such as social structures, tool making, art, song, dance, religious beliefs, rituals, families, a division of labor, and politics.

Culture: The characteristics of a group or society that make it distinct from other groups and society or the way of life of a particular group of people.

Culture of poverty: The beliefs, attitudes, and values that characterize those living in poverty; the poor are blamed for their poverty.

Data: Pieces of information, including facts, statistics, quotations, images, or any other kind of information.

Data analysis: The process of reducing the mass of raw data researchers have collected to a set of findings that provide the basis for making conclusions.

Define the situation: Making meaning of what is going on by using cues and clues from the individuals and objects around us.

Democracy: Government by the people.

Democratic socialism: A form of socialism in which the state controls public utilities such as energy, transportation, and communication while leaving the rest of the economy to be governed by heavily regulated capitalism.

Demographic transition: When societies begin to have lower birth and death rates after industrialization.

Dictatorship: A type of government in which a leader is able to either overthrow or subvert the existing government and seize absolute power.

Difference feminism: Holds that men and woman are different but no value judgment can be placed on these differences.

Direct democracy: A type of government in which citizens directly control the entire political process and are actively responsible for making all the decisions of the state.

Discrimination: Unfair treatment of groups of people.

Distributive power: The ability of a group or an individual to overcome the opposition of others in order to achieve his or her goals.

Divine right of kings: The idea that the king was given his power by God, and thus no mortal man could stand in judgment against him.

Downward mobility: When one loses a class position.

Dysfunctions: Unintended consequences of behavioral patterns.

Ecological footprint: The productive area required to provide the resources humanity is using and to absorb its waste.

Ecological modernization: The idea that material conditions—the challenges of sustainability—have led us to reshape our social institutions and to adapt to environmental changes.

Economic inequality: Unequal distribution of economic resources.

Economy: A system of producing and consuming goods and services.

Education: The process through which a society transmits its culture and history and teaches social, intellectual, and specific work skills that result in productive works and citizens.

Elite theory: A conflict theory perspective that sees power as consolidated in the hands of a small group of people both inside and outside of government.

Empirical: Empirical statements are those that could hypothetically be proved true or false.

Environmental justice: A term used to document social inequality in the environmental realm.

Environmental justice movement: Has the goal of ending the practice of using poor and racial and ethnic minority areas as dumping grounds for environmental hazards.

Environmental racism: When environmental hazards are disproportionally borne by racial and ethnic minority groups.

Environmental sociology: Focuses on the interaction between social and natural systems.

Estates: In an estate system, there is very limited social mobility, but those with the lowest standing have more freedom than slaves. In this system, laws distribute power and rights on the basis of social standing.

Ethnic group: Consists of those who share the same cultural heritage, including languages, nation or origin, and religion.

Ethnocentrism: The belief that one's own culture is superior to others.

Ethnography: Research that systematically studies how groups of people live and make meaning by understanding the group from its own point of view.

Ethnomethodology: The study of the "ethno" (meaning ordinary or everyday) methods people use to make sense of their social interactions.

Experiment: Used to find out how people are likely to act in particular and potentially controlled situations.

Externalities: All the side effects—things people fail to incorporate in their decision making—of economic activities.

False consciousness: Marx's theory that the proletariat did not understand how they were being mistreated and misled by the owners of the means of production.

Family: A group of people who take responsibility for meeting one another's needs.

Family violence: When someone in a family hurts or controls someone else. It can take on many forms, such as sexual abuse, financial abuse, emotional mistreatment, and physical violence.

Family wage: Earnings that are enough to support an entire family.

Fascism: An authoritarian system of militaristic nationalism in which the means of production are privately owned but regulated by the state to reinforce social stratification and carry out the goals of the state.

Feminist: Someone who is committed to gender equality.

Feminist organization: An organization working to end women's oppression.

Field experiments: Experiments conducted in the real world, not in a laboratory setting.

Folk devils: Those blamed for the collapse of public morality and therefore treated as threats to the social order.

Folkways: Rules of behavior for common and routine interactions.

Food desert: An area with limited access to healthy and affordable food.

Fordism: The system of mass production of standardized, relatively inexpensive products by unskilled workers paid wages sufficient to purchase those products.

Formal organization: A planned secondary group created to achieve a goal.

Frame competition: When an organization uses another group's frames to discredit or ridicule its position.

Framing: How leaders influence how people think about an issue by highlighting certain facts and themes while making others invisible.

Front: The "expressive equipment" an individual uses to define the situation and convince others of the sincerity of his or her performance.

Front stage: Where an interaction actually takes place.

Fundamental cause theory: Argues that socioeconomic status is the most important factor that explains disparities in health.

Fundamentalists: Those who resist societal changes and hold on to idealized, conservative, traditional religious practices.

Gender: A social concept associated with being male or female that is taught to us and continually created by us through interactions with others.

Gender as social structure: Emphasizes that gender incorporates socialization, social interactions, and organizational structures and that these are all dimensions of every society's gender structure.

Gender scripts: Expectations for behavior appropriate for our assigned genders.

Gender segregation in the workplace: The practice of labeling certain fields of employment as for *either* men or women, which has led to relatively few women in high-paying jobs.

Gender socialization: The process by which we learn to be a man or woman in our particular place and time.

Gender wage gap: The gap between the wages women and men earn.

Generalizability: Whether it is possible to assume that the patterns and relationships observed among the sample in the research study would also hold true for the broader population.

Generalizations: Statements used to describe groups of people or things in general terms, with the understanding that there can always be exceptions.

Generalized other: Our perceptions of the attitudes of a whole community.

Gentlemen's Agreement of 1907: Halted Japanese immigration.

Glass ceiling: The unofficial barrier women and minorities face when trying to advance to the upper levels of an organization.

Green consumption: Allows consumers to "vote with their pockets" and to engage in social change through the marketplace.

Greenwashing: A public relations campaign that promotes an environmentally friendly, positive image of an organization whose environmental practices are not line with the image.

Group: Any set of two or more people with whom you share a sense of belonging, purpose, and identity.

Hayes-Tilden Compromise of 1877: An agreement between the presidential candidates of 1877 whereby Hayes, the northern candidate, won the Electoral College, but Tilden, the southern candidate, won more of the popular vote. The compromise, whereby Hayes would become president, was reached provided that federal troops were withdrawn from the former confederacy and that Whites were once again able to dominate political power in the South. After this, Jim Crow laws began to be established in the South.

Hidden curriculum: Implicit messages learned in school.

High culture: The culture of elites.

Hooking up: Generally means getting together at the end of an evening for the purposes of an intimate, no-strings-attached encounter.

Human capital: Knowledge, skills, habits, and attributes necessary to succeed in work and in life.

Hypotheses: Predictions about the expected findings of research, typically about the relationships between specific phenomena under study in the research project.

Ideal bureaucracy: A formal organization designed to complete complex tasks rationally and with maximum efficiency.

Identity: The characteristics by which we are known.

Illegitimate power: Power exercised without the support of the community, which is also called coercion.

Immigration Act of 1924: Established 2 percent immigration quotas per nation, on the basis of the 1890 U.S. census (when relatively few Southern and Eastern Europeans were in the United States); this was done because Southern and Eastern Europeans were considered "less than White" at the time.

Immigration Act of 1965: Abolished national quotes, replacing them with quotas for the Eastern and Western Hemispheres, and aimed to increase immigration and alter the racial makeup of the United States during the civil rights movement and worldwide pressure to address racial discrimination in the United States.

Income: Earnings from employment, government programs, investments, or inheritances.

Industrialization: The systematic transformation of an economy from a focus on agricultural production to one focused on the manufacturing of finished goods.

Infant mortality: The number of deaths of children under thirteen months of age for every 1,000 live births.

Informed consent: Requires that participants be told the purpose of research, what they will be asked to do, and any risks of harm prior to participating. They must be given the chance to withdraw their participation at any time.

Institutional discrimination: Happens as a result of how institutions operate.

Institutional review board: Reviews experiments and was established to protect human subjects.

Institutionalized: Encoded in laws, policies, and widely accepted practices.

Intensive mothering: An exhausting child-centered style of parenting that requires women to copiously devote emotions, money, and time to raising children.

Interdependent power: The ties that bind institutions and individuals together and help explain how social change can come from poor or powerless individuals.

Intergenerational mobility: Moving from the social class in which one was born.

Internal colonialism: Results from one ethnic or racial group (White Americans) subordinating and exploiting the resources of other racial and ethnic groups.

Intersex: Not clearly biologically male or female.

Interviews: A research design in which the researcher talks to the participant (in person, over the phone, through video chat), using an interview guide (a list of questions or topics to cover).

Iron law of oligarchy: The theory that over time, all representative democracies slowly transform into oligarchies.

Islamophobia: The fear or dislike of all or most Muslims.

Labeling: How certain individuals or groups come to be regarded as deviant; who is defined or labeled as deviant is the result of a social process in which others react as though the person is deviant.

Laissez-faire capitalism: A form of capitalism in which markets are not subject to regulation by the state.

Language: A series of symbols used to communicate meaning among people.

Latent functions: Unintended consequences of an institution.

Legalistic approach: Deviance defined as violation of the law.

Legitimate power: Power exercised in a manner that is supported by the community, which is also called authority.

Life expectancy: The average number of years an individual is expected to live.

Literature review: Finding out what is already known about a topic by reading prior scholarly literature.

Macro level of analysis (macro): Focuses on the overall social structure of society and large-scale societal forces.

Manifest functions: Obvious and stated reasons that a social institution exists.

Manner: The attitude conveyed by an individual in his or her particular social role.

Master frames: Frames that have near universal appeal.

Master status: The primary status by which others interact with a person.

Material culture: Consists of artifacts ranging from tools to products designed for leisure. Reflects the values and beliefs of the people who live in a culture.

Means of production: The technology and materials needed to produce products.

Medicaid: A government program that covers disabled people and those within a certain percentage of the poverty line.

Medicalization: The process by which conditions become seen as medical conditions.

Medicalization of deviance: The transition from viewing behaviors, conditions, and beliefs as attributed to the deviant's evil character, or "badness," due to a pathology of the mind, or "madness."

Medicare: A government program that gives some health insurance to people older than sixty-five.

Mental illnesses: According to the American Psychiatric Association, "health conditions involving changes in emotion, thinking or behavior (or a combination of these) . . . associated with distress and/or problems functioning in social, work or family activities."

Meritocracy: A society in which those with the most talent rise to the top and are appropriately rewarded for their contributions.

Microaggressions: Everyday slights aimed, intentionally or unintentionally, at racial and ethnic minority groups.

Micro level of analysis (micro): Focuses on either an individual or small groups.

Mobilizing: Spreading the word and bringing people together to support the goal of a social movement.

Modernization: Occurs as countries undergo the process of industrialization and decisions begin to be based more on reason and logic than tradition.

Monarchy: A type of government in which the state is headed by some sort of individual sovereign who inherited his position on the basis of custom or tradition and will pass the position on to his children.

Moral entrepreneurs: Individuals or groups who actively seek to change norms to align with their own moral worldview, often while taking part in social movements.

Moral panic: An exaggerated, widespread fear regarding the collapse of public morality.

Morbidity: Rates of illness, injury, disease, or other unhealthy states.

Mores: Widely held beliefs about what is considered moral and just behavior in society.

Mortality: The death rate for a population.

Multiculturalism: The ideal of multiculturalism is that people respect differing cultures in a society and honor their unique contributions to a larger, "umbrella" culture that incorporates multiple subcultures.

Nature: Biology, how we are born.

Nonmaterial culture: Concepts such as norms, values, beliefs, symbols, and language.

Norm of reciprocity: The expectation that we give and take with others in relatively equal ways.

Normative: Commonly accepted as appropriate.

Normative approach: Deviance defined as evoking disapproval from others.

Norms: Expectations about the appropriate thoughts, feelings, and behaviors of people in a variety of situations.

Nuclear family: Parents and their children.

Nurture: Our cultural and social learning.

Observation: Studying a phenomenon as a spectator.

Oligarchy: A type of government in which power is held by a small group of elites.

Overshoot: Using resources at a pace more than the earth's regenerative capacity.

Overworked: Devoting more time to paid work, leaving less time for leisure and home life.

Paradigm shift theory: The shift in views toward the environment from the human exemptionalist paradigm, which reflects an anthropocentric relationship, to the new environmental paradigm, which views humans as only part of the complex ecosystem.

Participant-observation: Observing action and interaction while participating as part of the social context being studied.

Participatory action research: Starts with the idea that people are the experts in their own lives and can participate in the research process. The people who live in a community participate in the research process and help produce the knowledge collectively.

Peer pressure: Pressure to conform to the norms of one's peers.

Peers: Others in one's age group.

Pluralism: A structural functionalist theoretical perspective that sees the political system as a struggle between competing interest groups for power and control of the decision-making process in which no single group is in control all the time.

Plutocracy: A type of oligarchic government in which power is held by the economic elites.

Policy-planning network: A network of individuals and institutions that develop and advocate for social policy reforms that will advance their funders' interests.

Popular culture: Culture that exists among common people in a society.

Population: All the people or things that meet the criteria for participation in a study from which researchers select a sample.

Post-Fordism: The shift away from mass production of large quantities of identical products toward the production of smaller quantities of products, in wider variety, carefully targeted at specific groups of consumers.

Power elite: Individuals from the corporate, political, and military elite whose decisions have major consequences for society.

Prejudice: Irrational feelings toward members of a particular group.

Presentation of self: Efforts to shape the physical, verbal, visual, and gestural messages we give to others to achieve impression management.

Primary deviance: Rule breaking individuals engage in without a deviant label.

Primary groups: Small collections of people of which a person is a member, usually for life, and in which deep emotional ties develop.

Primary socialization: Socialization that occurs in childhood, the most intense time for socialization.

Private sphere: The nonexposed sphere, an example being how wives stay at home to specialize in domesticity, staying in the private sphere.

Profane: A sphere of everyday life, not sacred.

Protest: An individual or group act of challenging, resisting, or making demands toward social change.

Public sphere: The exposed sphere, an example being how men left the home to work and be the family breadwinner, leaving the private sphere of the home for the public sphere.

Qualitative methods: Methods that rely primarily on information that is not numerical, such as words or images.

Quantitative methods: Methods that rely on numerical information.

Race: A group of people perceived to be distinct on the basis of physical appearance.

Racism: Belief in the superiority of one or more racial groups that creates and maintains a racial hierarchy.

Racism evasiveness: Ignoring issues of racism.

Random: A sample in which everyone who meets the criteria for participation in a study has an equal chance of being selected.

Rational-legal domination: Authority based on occupying a legally defined position.

Redemptive social movements: Seek radical change in individual behavior.

Reformative social movements: Work for specific change across society.

Relativist perspective: Behaviors, conditions, and beliefs are deviant only to the extent that cultures regard them as deviant.

Reliability: The extent to which research results are consistent.

Religion: A social institution that involves the beliefs and practices of what has been socially constructed as sacred in a given society.

Religiosity: Religiousness, measured by looking at a range of religious beliefs, activities, and practices in which people participate.

Religious environmentalism: The environmental actions of religious leaders and communities within organized religion as well as more general environmentalism grounded in spirituality.

Religious pluralism: Arises when different religious belief systems coexist within a society.

Representative: The people in a sample have characteristics typical of people in the broader population.

Representative democracy: A type of government in which citizens vote to elect a group of representatives who make decisions on behalf of the voters who elected them.

Repression: Takes place when people and/or institutions with power use that power to control or destroy a movement.

Reproduction: People creating and raising members of the next generation.

Research: The systematic process of data collection for the purpose of producing knowledge.

Resocialization: Learning to adapt to new social norms and values.

Resource mobilization theory: Looks to the resources needed to mobilize and sustain a social movement. The presence of resources, such as followers and money, predicts whether or not a movement will be successful.

Revolutionary social movements: Aim to achieve a radical reorganization of society.

Risk perception: The tendency to evaluate the danger of a situation not in purely rational terms but through the lens of individual biases and cultures.

Rituals: Ceremonial behaviors.

Role conflict: When one's different social roles conflict with one another.

Role engulfment: Occurs when the deviant role takes over people's other social roles because others relate to them in response to their spoiled identities.

Role strain: Competing demands within a particular social role and status.

Routinization of charisma: A process by which power is transferred from a charismatic leader to a system based on either traditional domination or rational-legal domination.

Sacred: That which inspires reverence and devotion.

Sacrifice zones: The areas in developing countries where companies have moved the dirty parts of their business to appear to be making progress in developed countries.

Sampling: The process of selecting respondents for inclusion in a research project.

Sanctions: Punishments or penalties.

Sandwich generation: Those with double caretaking duties: raising children and caring for aging parents at the same time.

Sapir-Whorf hypothesis: Also known as linguistic relativism, notes that language influences our understanding of reality above and beyond the meaning of its symbols.

School choice: Can include the ability to attend the public school of the family's choosing, attend a charter school, or use a voucher to subsidize attendance at a private school.

Scientific method: A systematic process of steps that takes researchers from the development of a research question through the collection and analysis of data.

Second shift: The phenomenon wherein women return from their jobs to then begin their "second shift," when they do the housework and childcare.

Secondary deviance: Rule-breaking behavior that occurs as a result of a deviant label.

Secondary socialization: Teaching us how to behave appropriately in small groups and structured situations.

Sects: Subgroups of larger religions that have some of their own distinct beliefs and practices.

Secular: Nonreligious.

Secular humanists: Believe that humans have the capability of being just without religion or a divine god.

Secularization: A society's movement away from identification with religious values and institutions.

Secularization theory: Suggests that modernization encourages the demystifying of the world and undermines the influence of religion.

Self: Sense of self, the knowledge that one is unique, separate from every other human.

Self-consciousness: An individual's awareness of how others see her or him.

Self-identity: Our own understanding of who we are that is shaped by our interactions with others.

Setting: Location of the "performance" or social interaction.

Sex: A biological construct that is defined by external genitalia, chromosomes, and internal reproductive organs.

Sexual harassment: Verbal or physical harassment of a sexual nature when the harassment creates a hostile work environment or when the victim's advancement at work is affected.

Sexuality: Our emotional and physical attraction to a particular sex.

Social class: Distinctions among groups of people in terms of income, education, and occupation or access to means of success.

Social class reproduction: How members of the upper class ensure that their children maintain their status.

Social cohesion: The willingness of members of a society to work together to survive and prosper.

Social constructionism: Holds that every society creates norms, values, objects, and symbols it finds meaningful and useful.

Social contract: Agreement by the people to give up certain individual rights to the state in exchange for protection and other benefits.

Social exchange theory: Presumes that individual family members, as rational actors, make decisions by weighing the benefits and costs of various actions and then pick the action or arrangement with the biggest reward or least cost.

Social institutions: Sets of statuses and roles that focus on one central aspect of society.

Social intelligence: Our ability to understand social relationships and get along with others.

Social interactions: The way individuals behave and interact with other people.

Socialism: An economic system in which the means of production are collectively owned, and economic activity is driven by a desire to satisfy the needs of the people with no consideration of profit.

Socialization: Learning through social interaction how to follow the social norms and expectations of your society.

Social movement: Forms when people who want social change create an organization that is collective, organized, and sustained and challenges authorities, powerholders, or cultural beliefs and practices in noninstitutional ways.

Social reproduction: The continuation of society's culture across generations.

Social stratification: The way valuable goods and desired intangibles are distributed in society.

Socioeconomic status: Status determined by class, status or prestige, and power.

Sociological eye: Enables you to see what others may not notice. It allows you to peer beneath the surface of a situation and discern social patterns.

Sociological imagination: The ability to connect what is happening in your own life and in the lives of other individuals to social patterns in the larger society.

Sociology: The scientific study of society, including how individuals both *shape* and *are shaped by* society.

Spirituality: The search for the sacred, which involves finding meaning or purpose in your life and trusting in some higher power.

Stalled revolution: The period during the 1960s and 1970s when divorce rates rose as women began to work at home and men had differing expectations about household responsibilities and earning income.

The state: A human community that successfully claims the monopoly of the legitimate use of physical force within a given territory.

State of nature: The conditions of life that existed before the development of the state or any other form of civil society.

Statistical approach: Treats anything that is statistically unusual, or anything that has a low probability or likelihood, as deviant.

Stereotypes: Predetermined ideas about particular groups of people that are passed on through hearsay or small samples and held regardless of evidence.

Stigma: A mark of disgrace and interactions that communicate that one is disgraced, dishonorable, or otherwise deviant.

Structural functionalism: A view of modern societies as consisting of interdependent parts of working together for the good of the whole.

Structural mobility: Occurs when changes in the economy create or destroy jobs for workers.

Structured inequalities: Advantages and disadvantages built into social institutions.

Subcultural identity theory: Suggests that individuals seek a collective identity that helps provide them with a strong moral code.

Subcultures: Cultural groups that exist within another, larger culture.

Surveys: A set of prewritten questions respondents are asked to answer.

Sustainability: A social-economic system that can function within the earth's ecological constraints.

Sustainable development: Development that meets the needs of the present without compromising the ability of future generations to meet their own needs.

Symbol: Anything that has the same meaning for two or more people.

Symbolic interaction: Viewing society as a social construction, continually constructed and reconstructed by individuals through their use of shared symbols.

Taking the role of the other: Imitating those around them.

Techniques of neutralization: Strategies deviants use to maintain a positive self-concept.

Theoretical perspective: Groups of theories that share certain common ways of "seeing" how society works.

Theory: A set of ideas used to explain how or why certain social patterns occur.

Three-Fifths Compromise: Treated slaves as three-fifths of a person for the purposes of representation in the House of Representatives and taxation.

Total institution: An institution that is closed to external influences in which a group of people live together, following a strictly structured routine.

Totalitarianism: A type of government that exercises monopoly control over every aspect of social, political, and economic life in the name of a movement toward some overarching ideology.

Tracking: Involves placing students in classes based on "ability," which is usually measured by classroom behavior, academic performance, and academic aspiration.

Traditional domination: Authority based on custom or tradition

Transgender: People who identify as a gender other than the one assigned to them at birth.

Treadmill of production: On the capitalist treadmill, firms must use and degrade natural resources to sustain their profits. Because of the constant pressure to expand profits, they are forced to compete with others by running faster and faster, producing more and more, and drawing ever more resources. If they don't, they will go bankrupt and "fall off the treadmill."

True consciousness: When the proletariat are no longer in false consciousness and are aware of how they are being mistreated and misled.

Underinsurance: When a person has health insurance, but, even with the insurance, health services are not affordable.

Universal coverage: A health system in which the government guarantees that all citizens can receive health care.

Upward mobility: When one climbs up the economic ladder.

Validity: Whether research results accurately reflect the phenomena being studied.

Values: What a society holds to be desirable, good, and important.

Vouchers: Certificates of government funding that make each pupil's state funds portable, allowing parents to choose to use their child's fund at a public or private school of their choice.

Wealth: Assets one owns minus debts.

Wilderness: The highest ideal of nature, a product of America's frontier mentality.

Women's movement: Brought women together as women to fight for rights and equality.

REFERENCES

CHAPTER 1

Association of American Colleges and Universities. 2018. "Fulfilling the American Dream: Liberal Education and the Future of Work." Accessed January 18, 2019. https://www.aacu.org/sites/default/files/files/LEAP/2018EmployerResearchReport.pdf.

Bank, Justin, Liam Stack, and Daniel Victor. 2018. "What Is QAnon: Explaining the Internet Conspiracy Theory That Showed Up at a Trump Rally." *The New York Times*, August 1. Accessed August 2, 2018. https://www.nytimes.com/2018/08/01/us/politics/what-is-qanon.html.

Brooks, Anthony. 2018. "Trump Labels News Media 'Enemy of the American People.'" WBUR, July 31. Accessed August 2, 2018. http://www.wbur.org/onpoint/2018/07/31/trump-labels-news-media-enemy-of-the-american-people.

Collins, Randall. 1998. "The Sociological Eye and Its Blinders." *Contemporary Sociology* 27 (1): 2–7.

Deegan, Mary Jo. 1988. "W.E.B. Du Bois and the Women of Hull-House, 1895–1899." *American Sociologist* 19 (4): 301–11.

Fisher, Marc, John Woodrow Cox, and Peter Hermann. 2016. "Pizzagate: From Rumor, to Hash-Tag, to Gunfire in D.C." *The Washington Post*, December 6. Accessed May 16, 2017. https://www.washingtonpost.com/local/pizzagate-from-rumor-to-hashtag-to-gunfire-in-dc/2016/12/06/4c7def50-bbd4-11e6-94ac-3d324840106c_story.html?utm_term=.3002952c77d1.

Gamble, Teri, and Michael Gamble. 2015. *The Gender Communication Connection*. New York: Routledge.

Kantrowitz, Mark. 2018. "Growth in Student Loan Debt at Graduation Slows as Borrowers Hit Loan Limits." Accessed May 21, 2019. https://www.savingforcollege.com/article/growth-in-student-loan-debt-at-graduation-slows-as-borrowers-hit-loan-limits.

Mills, Wright C. 1959. *The Sociological Imagination*. Oxford, UK: Oxford University Press.

Morris, Aldion. 2015. *The Scholar Denied: W.E.B. Du Bois and the Birth of Modern Sociology*. Oakland: University of California Press.

Shane, Scott. 2017. "From Headline to Photograph, a Fake News Masterpiece." *The New York Times*, January 18. Accessed May 16, 2017. https://www.nytimes.com/2017/01/18/us/fake-news-hillary-clinton-cameron-harris.html?hp&action=click&pgtype=Homepage&clickSource=story-heading&module=b-lede-package-region&region=top-news&WT.nav=top-news&_r=0.

Small, Albion W. 1896. "Scholarship and Social Agitation." *American Journal of Sociology* 1 (March): 564–82.

CHAPTER 2

Best, Joel. 2012. *Social Problems*. 2nd ed. New York: W. W. Norton.

CBS News. 2014. "S.C. Mom's Arrest over Daughter Alone in Park Sparks Debate." CBS News, July 28. Accessed July 11, 2017. http://www.cbsnews.com/news/south-carolina-moms-arrest-over-daughter-alone-in-park-sparks-debate/.

Friedersdorf, Conor. 2014. "Working Mom Arrested for Letting Her 9-Year-Old Play Alone at Park." *The Atlantic*, July 15. Accessed May 28, 2017. https://www.theatlantic.com/national/archive/2014/07/arrested-for-letting-a-9-year-old-play-at-the-park-alone/374436/.

Goffman, Erving. 1959. *The Presentation of Self in Everyday Life*. New York: Anchor.

Meitiv, Danielle. 2015. "When Letting Your Kids Out of Your Sight Becomes a Crime." *The Washington Post*, February 13. Accessed December 27, 2015. https://www.washingtonpost.com/opinions/raising-children-on-fear/2015/02/13/9d9db67e-b2e7-11e4-827f-93f454140e2b_story.html.

Reese, Diana. 2014. "South Carolina Mom Who Left Daughter at Park Sues Station." *The Washington Post*, August 14. Accessed July 11, 2017. https://www.washingtonpost.com/blogs/she-the-people/wp/2014/08/14/south-carolina-mom-who-left-daughter-at-park-sues-tv-station/?utm_term=.3d4b2c482243.

St. George, Donna. 2015a. "'Free Range' Parents Cleared in Second Neglect Case after Kids Walked Alone." *Washington Post*, June 22. Accessed December 27, 2015. https://www.washingtonpost.com/local/education/free-range-parents-cleared-in-second-neglect-case-after-children-walked-alone/2015/06/22/82283c24-188c-11e5-bd7f-4611a60dd8e5_story.html.

St. George, Donna. 2015b. "Parents Investigated for Neglect after Letting Kids Walk Home Alone." *The Washington Post*, January 14. Accessed December 27, 2015. https://www.washingtonpost.com/local/education/maryland-couple-want-free-range-kids-but-not-all-do/2015/01/14/d406c0be-9c0f-11e4-bcfb-059ec7a93ddc_story.html.

St. George, Donna. 2015c. "'Unsubstantiated' Child Neglect Finding for Free-Range Parents." *Washington Post*, March 2. Accessed December 27, 2015. https://www.washingtonpost.com/local/education/decision-in-free-range-case-does-not-end-debate-about-parenting-and-safety/2015/03/02/5a919454-c04d-11e4-ad5c-3b8ce89f1b89_story.html.

Utah State Legislature. 2018. "Child Neglect Amendments." Retrieved July 18, 2018. https://le.utah.gov/~2018/bills/sbillenr/SB0065.pdf.

CHAPTER 3

Adelman, Robert, Lesley Williams Reid, Gail Markle, Saskia Weiss, and Charles Jaret. 2017. "Urban Crime Rates and the Changing Face of Immigration: Evidence across Four Decades." *Journal of Ethnicity in Criminal Justice* 15 (1): 52–77.

Andrews, Michelle. 2018. "For Many College Students, Hunger 'Makes It Hard to Focus.'" National Public Radio, July 31. Accessed March 15, 2019. https://www.npr.org/sections/health-shots/2018/07/31/634052183/for-many-college-students-hunger-makes-it-hard-to-focus.

Arum, Richard, and Josipa Roksa. 2011. *Academically Adrift: Limited Learning on College Campuses*. Chicago: University of Chicago Press.

Bennett, Joan W., and King-Thom Chung. 2001. "Alexander Fleming and the Discovery of Penicillin." In *Advances in Applied Microbiology*, Vol. 49, edited by Allen I. Laskin, Joan W. Bennett, and Geoffrey M. Gadd, 163–84. San Diego, CA: Academic Press.

Broton, Katharine, and Sara Goldrick-Rab. 2018. "Going Without: An Exploration of Food and Housing Insecurity among Undergraduates." *Educational Researcher* 47 (2): 121–133.

Desmond, Matthew. 2016. *Evicted: Poverty and Profit in the American City*. New York: Crown.

Ewing, Walter A., Daniel E. Martínez, and Rubén G. Rumbaut. 2015. "The Criminalization of Immigration in the United States." American Immigration Council, Washington, D.C. Accessed July 12, 2019. http://immigrationpolicy.org/sites/default/files/docs/the_criminalization_of_immigration_in_the_united_states_final.pdf.

Gallup. 2019. "Immigration." Accessed July 14, 2019. https://news.gallup.com/poll/1660/immigration.aspx.

Goldrick-Rab, Sara, Vanessa Coco, Christine Baker-Smith, and Elizabeth Looker. 2019. "City University of New York RealCollege Survey." Accessed March 20, 2019. https://hope4college.com/wp-content/uploads/2019/03/HOPE_realcollege_CUNY_report_final_webversion.pdf.

Murphy, Sherry L., Jiaquan Xu, Kenneth D. Kochanek, Sally C. Curtin, Elizabeth Arias. 2017. "Deaths: Final Data for 2015." *National Vital Statistics Reports* 66 (6): 1–75.

Pager, Deva. 2003. "The Mark of a Criminal Record." *American Journal of Sociology* 108 (5): 937–75.

Porter, J. R. 1976. "Antony van Leeuwenhoek: Tercentenary of his Discovery of Bacteria." *Bacteriological Reviews* 40 (2): 260–69.

Sampson, Robert J. 2008. "Rethinking Crime and Immigration." *Contexts* 7 (1): 28–33.

Senter, Mary, Roberta Spalter-Roth, and Nicole Van Vooren. 2015. "Jobs, Careers, and Sociological Skills: The Early Employment Experiences of 2012 Sociology Majors." Washington, DC: American Sociological Association.

Wineburg, Sam, Sarah McGrew, Joel Breakstone, and Teresa Ortega. 2016. "Evaluating Information: The Cornerstones of Civic Online Reasoning." Stanford Digital Repository. Accessed December 30, 2018. https://purl.stanford.edu/fv751yt5934.

CHAPTER 4

Berger, Peter L., and Thomas Luckmann. 1966. *The Social Construction of Reality: A Treatise in the Sociology of Knowledge*. Garden City, NY: Doubleday.

Bourdieu, Pierre. 1984. *Distinction: A Social Critique of the Subject of Taste*. Cambridge, MA: Harvard University Press.

Bourdieu, Pierre, and Jean Claude Passeron. 1990. *Reproduction in Education, Society and Culture*. Thousand Oaks, CA: Sage.

Brown, Donald. 1991. *Human Universals*. Philadelphia: Temple University Press.

CNN. 2019. "Deadliest Mass Shootings in Modern US History Fast Facts." June 12. Accessed July 14, 2019. https://www.cnn.com/2013/09/16/us/20-deadliest-mass-shootings-in-u-s-history-fast-facts/index.html.

Cottle, Michelle. 2018. "How Parkland Students Changed the Gun Debate." *The Atlantic*. Accessed January 4, 2019. https://www.theatlantic.com/politics/archive/2018/02/parkland-students-power/554399/.

Faucher, Kane X. 2018. *Alienation and Accumulation*. London: University of Westminster Press.

Goleman, Daniel. 2006. *Social Intelligence: The New Science of Human Relationships*. New York: Bantam.

Hahl, Oliver, Ezra W. Zuckerman, and Minjae Kim. 2017. "Why Elites Love Authentic Lowbrow Culture: Overcoming High-Status Denigration with Outsider Art." *American Sociological Review* 82 (4): 828–56.

Healy, Andrew, and Neil Malhotra. 2013. "Childhood Socialization and Political Attitudes: Evidence from a Natural Experiment." *Journal of Politics* 75 (4): 1023–37.

Kamenetz, Kayla, Anya Lattimore, and Julie Depenbrock. 2017. "Harvard Rescinds Admission of 10 Students over Obscene Facebook Messages." NPR. Retrieved January 11, 2019. https://www.npr.org/sections/ed/2017/06/06/531591202/harvard-rescinds-admission-of-10-students-over-obscene-facebook-messages.

Kregting, Joris, Peer Scheepers, Paul Vermeer, and Chris Hermans. 2018. "Why God Has Left the Netherlands: Explanations for the Decline of Institutional Christianity in the Netherlands between 1966 and 2015." *Journal for the Scientific Study of Religion* 57 (1): 58–79.

Leming, Laura M. 2007. "Sociological Explorations: What Is Religious Agency?" *Sociological Quarterly* 48:73–92.

Lichtblau, Eric. 2016. "Orlando Gunman Told Police that U.S. Should 'Stop Bombing' Syria and Iraq." *The New York Times*, June 20. Accessed June 20, 2016. http://www.nytimes.com/2016/06/21/us/fbi-transcripts-orlando-shooting-omar-mateen.html?rref=collection%2Fnewseventcollection%2F2016-orlando-shooting&action=click&contentCollection=us&region=stream&module=stream_nit&version=latest&contentPlacement=2&pgtype=collection.

Mark, Noah P. 2003. "Culture and Competition: Homophily and Distancing Explanations for Cultural Niches." *American Sociological Review* 68 (3): 319–45.

Mead, George Herbert. 1934. *Mind, Self, and Society from the Standpoint of a Social Behaviorist*. Chicago: Chicago University Press.

Murdock, George P. 1945. "The Common Denominator of Culture." In *The Science of Man in the World Crisis*, edited by Ralph Linton. New York: Columbia University Press.

Musolf, Gil Richard. 2003. "The Chicago School." In *Handbook of Symbolic Interactionism*, edited by L. T. Reynolds and N. J. Herman-Kinney, 91–118. Lanham, MD: Rowman & Littlefield.

National Public Radio. 2018. "NRA 2017 Tax Records Reveal Decline in Income." November 29. Accessed January 11, 2019. https://www.npr.org/2018/11/29/671799992/nra-2017-tax-records-reveal-decline-in-income.

Nolan, Patrick, and Gerhard Lenski. 2010. *Human Societies: An Introduction to Macrosociology*. 11th ed. Boulder, CO: Paradigm.

O'Brien, John. 2015. "Individualism as a Discursive Strategy of Action: Autonomy, Agency, and Reflexivity among Religious Americans." *Sociological Theory* 33 (2): 173–99.

Sapir, Edward. 1958. *Culture, Language and Personality*. Berkeley: University of California Press.

Swidler, Ann. 1986. "Culture in Action: Symbols and Strategies." *American Sociological Review* 51:273–86.

U.S. Census Bureau. 2017. "CP02: Comparative Social Characteristics in the United States: 2017 American Community Survey 1-Year Estimates." Accessed July 14, 2019. https://factfinder.census.gov/faces/tableservices/jsf/pages/productview.xhtml?src=bkmk.

Varkey GEMS Foundation. 2018. "Global Teacher Status Index 2018." Accessed July 13, 2019. https://www.varkeyfoundation.org/media/4790/gts-index-9-11-2018.pdf.

Vasilogambros, Matt. 2018. "After Parkland, States Pass 50 New Gun-Control Laws." Pew, August 2. Accessed January 11, 2019. https://www.pewtrusts.org/en/research-and-analysis/blogs/stateline/2018/08/02/after-parkland-states-pass-50-new-gun-control-laws.

Wetzler, Rachel. 2018. "How Modern Art Serves the Rich: More Art Is Being Produced and Sold Than Ever Before, at Ever Higher Prices." *The New Republic*. Accessed January 4, 2019. https://newrepublic.com/article/147192/modern-art-serves-rich.

Williams, Robin M., Jr. 1970. *American Society: A Sociological Interpretation*. 3rd ed. New York: Knopf.

World Bank. 2018. "Rural Population (% of Total Population)." Accessed July 14, 2019. http://data.worldbank.org/indicator/SP.RUR.TOTL.ZS.

CHAPTER 5

Adachi, Paul J. C., Gordon Hodson, Teena Willoughby, Carolyn Blank, and Alexandra Ha. 2016. "From Outgroups to Allied Forces: Effect of Intergroup Cooperation in Violent and Nonviolent Video Games on Boosting Favorable Outgroup Attitudes." *Journal of Experimental Psychology: General* 145 (3): 259–65.

Anderson, Monica, and Jingjing Jiang. 2018. "Teens, Social Media and Technology 2018." Pew Research Center. Accessed July 16, 2019. http://www.pewinternet.org/2018/05/31/teens-social-media-technology-2018/.

Blake, Jamilla J., Verna M. Keith, Wen Luo, Huong Le, and Phia Salter. 2017. "The Role of Colorism in Explaining African American Females' Suspension Risk." *School Psychology Quarterly* 32 (1): 118–30.

Bowles, Nellie. 2018. "The Digital Gap between Rich and Poor Kids Is Not What We Expected." *The New York Times*, October 26. Accessed July 16, 2019. https://www.nytimes.com/2018/10/26/style/digital-divide-screens-schools.html.

Calvert, Sandra L., Mark Appelbaum, Kenneth A. Dodge, Sandra Graham, Gordon C. Nagayama Hall, Sherry Hamby, Lauren G. Fasig-Caldwell, Martyna Citkowicz, Daniel P. Galloway, and Larry V. Hedges. 2017. "The American Psychological Association Task Force Assessment of Violent Video Games: Science in the Service of Public Interest." *American Psychologist* 72 (2): 126–43.

Caron, Christina. 2018. "Students Who Made Apparent Nazi Salute in Photo Won't Be Punished." *The New York Times*, November 24. Accessed July 16, 2019. https://www.nytimes.com/2018/11/24/us/baraboo-wisconsin-nazi-salute-photo.html.

Carson, E. Ann. 2018. "Prisoners in 2016." Bureau of Justice Statistics, January 9, 2018. Accessed July 16, 2017. https://www.bjs.gov/index.cfm?ty=pbdetail&iid=6187.

Chatterjee, Rhitu. 2018. "More Screen Time for Teens Linked to ADHD Symptoms." National Public Radio, July 17. Accessed July 17, 2019. ©https://www.npr.org/sections/health-shots/2018/07/17/629517464/more-screen-time-for-teens-may-fuel-adhd-symptoms.

Cho, Sujung, and Jeoung Min Lee. 2018. "Explaining Physical, Verbal, and Social Bullying among Bullies, Victims of Bullying, and Bully-Victims: Assessing the Integrated Approach between Social Control and Lifestyles-Routine Activities Theories." *Children and Youth Services Review* 91:372–82.

Common Sense Media. 2018. "The Common Sense Census: Media Use by Teens and Tweens." Accessed July 16, 2019. https://www.commonsensemedia.org/sites/default/files/uploads/research/census_executivesummary.pdf.

Gabbiadini, Alessandro, Paolo Riva, Luca Andrighetto, Chiara Volpato, and Brad J. Bushman. 2016. "Acting Like a Tough Guy: Violent-Sexist Video Games, Identification with Game Characters, Masculine Beliefs, & Empathy for Female Violence Victims." *PLoS ONE* 11 (4): e0152121.

Garfinkel, Harold. 1967. *Studies in Ethnomethodology*. Cambridge, UK: Polity.

Gatto, John Taylor. 2017. *Dumbing Us Down: The Hidden Curriculum of Compulsory Schooling*. Gabriola Island, CA: New Society.

Goffman, Erving. 1959. *The Presentation of Self in Everyday Life*. New York: Anchor.

Goffman, Erving. 1961. "Asylums: Essays on the Social Situation of Mental Patients and Other Inmates." Garden City, NY: Anchor.

Goldberg, Shoshana K., and Kerith J. Conron. 2018. "How Many Same-Sex Couples in the US Are Raising Children?" The Williams Institute, UCLA School of Law. Accessed July 16, 2019. https://williamsinstitute.law.ucla.edu/wp-content/uploads/Parenting-Among-Same-Sex-Couples.pdf.

Halpern, Hillary Paul, and Maureen Perry-Jenkins. 2016. "Parents' Gender Ideology and Gendered Behavior as Predictors of Children's Gender-Role Attitudes: A Longitudinal Exploration." *Sex Roles* 11–12 (74): 527–42.

Harrington, Brian, and Michael O'Connell. 2016. "Video Games as Virtual Teachers: Prosocial Video Game Use by Children and Adolescents from Different Socioeconomic Groups Is Associated with Increased Empathy and Prosocial Behavior." *Computers in Human Behavior* 63:650–58.

Hasan, Youssef, Laurent Bègue, Michael Scharkow, and Brad J. Bushman. 2018. "Corrigendum to: 'The More You Play, the More Aggressive You Become: A Long-Term Experimental Study of Cumulative Violent Video Game Effects on Hostile Expectations and Aggressive Behavior.'" *Journal of Experimental Social Psychology* 74:328.

Heid, Markham. 2018. There's Worrying New Research about Kids' Screen Time and Their Mental Health." *Time*, October 29. Accessed July 16, 2019. http://time.com/5437607/smartphones-teens-mental-health/.

Jackson, Philip W. 1968. *Life in Classrooms*. New York: Teachers College Press.

Lareau, Annette. 2002. *Unequal Childhoods: Class, Race and Family Life*. Oakland: University of California Press.

Livingston, Gretchen. 2018. "About One-Third of US Children Are Living with an Unmarried Parent." *Pew Research Center*, April 27. Accessed July 16, 2019. http://www.pewresearch.org/fact-tank/2018/04/27/about-one-third-of-u-s-children-are-living-with-an-unmarried-parent/.

Mead, George Herbert. 1964. *On Social Psychology*. Chicago: University of Chicago Press.

Merrin, Gabriel J., Kayla de la Haye, Dorothy L. Espelage, Brett Ewing, Joan S. Tucker, Matthew Hoover, and Harold D. Green, Jr. 2017. "The Co-evolution of Bullying Perpetration,

Homophobic Teasing, and a School Friendship Network." *Journal of Youth and Adolescence* 47 (3): 601–18.

Mervosh, Sarah. 2018. "School District Apologizes for Costumes of Mexican Stereotypes and Border Wall Prop." *The New York Times*, November 3. Accessed July 16, 2019. https://www.nytimes.com/2018/11/03/us/idaho-school-mexican-costumes.html?module=inline.

Movement Advancement Project. 2019. "Nondiscrimination Laws." Accessed July 16, 2019. http://www.lgbtmap.org/equality-maps/non_discrimination_laws.

Nielsen. 2018. "The Nielsen Total Audience Report: Q2 2018." Accessed July 16, 2019. https://www.nielsen.com/us/en/insights/reports/2018/q2-2018-total-audience-report.html.

Parsons, Talcott. 1959. "The School Class as a Social System: Some of Its Functions in American Society." *Harvard Educational Review* 29 (4): 297–318.

Pew Research Center. 2017. "Changing Attitudes on Gay Marriage." Accessed July 16, 2019. http://www.pewforum.org/fact-sheet/changing-attitudes-on-gay-marriage/.

SAGE Publishing. 2018. "Grandchildren Living with Grandparent Responsible for Their Care (Metro)." SAGE stats. Accessed July 16, 2019. http://data.sagepub.com/sagestats/document.php?id=6924.

Scharrer, Erica. 2018. "Teaching about Media Violence." In *The International Encyclopedia of Media Literacy*. Hoboken, NJ: John Wiley and Sons. Accessed July 16, 2019. https://doi.org/10.1002/9781118978238.ieml0231.

Thompson, Maxine S., and Steve McDonald. 2016. "Race, Skin Tone, and Educational Achievement." *Sociological Perspectives* 59 (1): 91–111.

Weber, Max. (1947) 2012. *The Theory of Social and Economic Organization*. Eastford, CT: Martino Fine Books.

Wentzel, Kathryn R. 2005. "Peer Relationships, Motivation, and Academic Performance at School." In *Handbook of Competence and Motivation*, edited by A. Elliot and C. Dweck, 279–96. New York: Guilford.

Wentzel, Kathryn R., and Katherine Muenks. 2016. "Peer Influence on Students' Motivation, Academic Achievement and Social Behavior." In *Handbook of Social Influences in School Contexts: Social-Emotional Motivation and Cognitive Outcomes*, edited by K. R. Wentzel and G. B. Ramani, 13–20. New York: Routledge.

Will, Jerri Ann, Patricia A. Self, and Nancy Datan. 1976. "Maternal Behavior and Perceived Sex of Infant." *American Journal of Orthopsychiatry* 46 (1): 135–39.

Wun, Connie. 2016. "Unaccounted Foundations: Black Girls, Anti-Black Racism, and Punishment in Schools." *Critical Sociology* 42 (4–5): 737–50.

CHAPTER 6

Becker, Howard. (1963) 1973. *Outsiders*. New York: Free Press.

Carson, E. Ann. 2018. "Prisoners in 2016." Bureau of Justice Statistics, January 9, 2018. Accessed July 16, 2017. https://www.bjs.gov/index.cfm?ty=pbdetail&iid=6187.

Centers for Disease Control and Prevention. 2000. "CDC Growth Charts: United States." Accessed December 15, 2015. http://www.cdc.gov/growthcharts/data/set2/chart-08.pdf.

Cohen, Stanley. 1972. *Folk Devils and Moral Panics: The Creation of the Mods and the Rockers*. London: MacGibbon & Kee.

Contreras, Randol. 2012. *The Stickup Kids: Race, Drugs, Violence, and the American Dream*. Berkeley: University of California Press.

Copes, Heith, and Lynne Vieraitis. 2012. *Identity Thieves: Motives and Methods*. Boston: Northeastern University Press.

Curtin, Sally C., Margaret Warner, and Holly Hedegaard. 2016. "Suicide Rates for Females and Males by Race and Ethnicity: United States, 1999 and 2014." Centers for Disease Control and Prevention. Accessed July 17, 2019. https://www.cdc.gov/nchs/data/hestat/suicide/rates_1999_2014.pdf.

Durkheim, Émile. (1897) 1951. *Suicide*. New York: Free Press.

Durkheim, Émile. (1895) 1964. *The Rules of Sociological Method*, edited by George E. G. Catlin, translated by Sarah A. Solovay and John H. Mueller. New York: The Free Press of Glencoe.

Goffman, Erving. 1963. *Stigma: Notes on the Management of Spoiled Identity*. Englewood Cliffs, NJ: Prentice Hall.

Jacques, Scott, and Richard Wright. 2015. *Code of the Suburb: Inside the World of Young, Middle-Class Drug Dealers*. Chicago: University of Chicago Press.

Kershaw, Sarah. 2009. "Shaking Off the Shame." *The New York Times*, November 25.

Lemert, Edwin. 1951. *Social Pathology: A Systematic Approach to the Theory of Sociopathic Behavior*. New York: McGraw-Hill.

Levey, Tania, and Dina Pinsky. (2015). "A Constellation of Stigmas: Intersectional Stigma Management and the Professional Dominatrix." *Deviant Behavior* 36:347–67.

Lombroso, Cesare. 1876. *On Criminal Man*. Milan, Italy: Hoepli.

Matza, David. 2010. *Becoming Deviant*. New York: Routledge.

Ousey, Graham C., and Charis E. Kubrin. 2018. "Immigration and Crime: Assessing a Contentious Issue." *Annual Review of Criminology* 1:63–84.

Panfil, Vanessa. 2017. *The Gang's All Queer: The Lives of Gay Gang Members*. New York: NYU Press.

Reiman, Jeffrey, and Paul Leighton. 2017. *The Rich Get Richer and the Poor Get Prison: Ideology, Class, and Criminal Justice*. 11th ed. New York: Routledge.

Reinarman, Craig. 1994. "The Social Construction of Drug Scares." In *Constructions of Deviance: Social Power, Context, and Interaction*, edited by P. Adler and P. Adler, 92–105. Belmont, CA: Wadsworth.

Rios, Victor. 2012. *Punished: Policing the Lives of Black and Latino Boys*. New York: NYU Press.

Smith, Alexander, and Harriet Pollack. 1976. "Deviance as a Method of Coping." *Crime and Delinquency* 22 (1): 3–16.

Spector, Malcolm, and John Kitsuse. 1977. *Constructing Social Problems*. Menlo Park, CA: Cummings.

Sumner, William G. 1907. *Folkways: A Study of the Sociological Importance of Usages, Manners, Customs, Mores, and Morals*. Boston: Ginn & Company.

Sykes, Gresham, and David Matza. 1957. "Techniques of Neutralization: A Theory of Delinquency." *American Sociological Review* 22:664–70.

Tannenbaum, Franklin. 1938. *Crime and Community*. New York: Columbia University Press.

Thomas, W. I., and Dorothy Thomas. 1928. *The Child in America: Behavior Problems and Programs*. New York: Knopf.

Wolf, Brian, and Phil Zuckerman. 2012. "Deviant Heroes: Nonconformists as Agents of Justice and Social Change." *Deviant Behavior* 33:639–54.

CHAPTER 7

Alvaredo, Facundo, Lucas Chancel, Thomas Piketty, Emmanuel Saez, and Gabriel Zucman. 2018. "World Inequality Report 2018." World Inequality Lab. Accessed December 12, 2018. https://wir2018.wid.world/files/download/wir2018-full-report-english.pdf.

Badger, Emily, and Quoctrung Bui. 2018. "Detailed New National Maps Show How Neighborhoods Shape Children for Life." *The New York Times*, October 1. Accessed October 15, 2018. https://www.nytimes.com/2018/10/01/upshot/maps-neighborhoods-shape-child-poverty.html.

Board of Governors of the Federal Reserve System. 2018. "Report on the economic Well-Being of U.S. Households in 2017." Accessed December 10, 2018. https://www.federalreserve.gov/publications/files/2017-report-economic-well-being-us-households-201805.pdf.

Bower, Joseph L., and Lynn S. Paine. 2017. "The Error at the Heart of Corporate Leadership." *Harvard Business Review*. Accessed January 3, 2019. https://hbr.org/2017/05/managing-for-the-long-termthe-error-at-the-heart-of-corporate-leadership.

Carter, Shawn, M. 2018. "Here's the Big Reason So Many Young People Need Mom and Dad to Pay Their Rent." CNBC, May 24. Accessed January 3, 2019. https://www.cnbc.com/2018/05/24/high-housing-costs-mean-young-people-need-family-help-with-rent.html.

Chetty, Raj, John Friedman, Nathaniel Hendren, Maggie Jones, and Sonya Porter. 2018. "The Opportunity Atlas: Mapping the Childhood Roots of Social Mobility." U.S. Census Bureau Opportunity Insights. Accessed December 20, 2018. https://opportunityinsights.org/wp-content/uploads/2018/10/atlas_paper.pdf.

Chetty, Raj, Maximilian Hell, Nathaniel Hendren, Robert Manduca, and Jimmy Narang. 2016. "The Fading American Dream: Trends in Absolute Income Mobility since 1940." December 2016. Accessed September 10, 2018. http://www.nber.org/papers/w22910.pdf.

Chyn, Eric. 2016. "Moved to Opportunity: The Long-Run Effects of Public Housing Demolition on Labor Market Outcomes of Children." Accessed April 20, 2016. http://www-personal.umich.edu/~ericchyn/Chyn_Moved-to_Opportunity.pdf.

Collins, Chuck, and Josh Hoxie. 2018. "Billionaire Bonanza 2018: Inherited Wealth Dynasties of the United States." Institute for Policy Studies. Accessed December 1, 2018. https://inequality.org/great-divide/billionaire-bonanza-2018-inherited-wealth-dynasties-in-the-21st-century-u-s/.

Credit Suisse. 2018. "Global Wealth Report 2018." Accessed December 8, 2018. http://publications.credit-suisse.com/tasks/render/file/index.cfm?fileid=B4A3FC6E-942D-C103-3D14B98BA7FD0BCC.

Davis, Kingsley, and Wilbert Moore. 1945. "Some Principles of Stratification." *American Sociological Review* 10 (2): 242–49.

DeSilver, Drew. 2018. "For Most of U.S. Workers, Real Wages Have Barely Budged for Decades." Pew Research Center, August 17. Accessed October 10, 2018. http://www.pewresearch.org/fact-tank/2018/08/07/for-most-us-workers-real-wages-have-barely-budged-for-decades/.

Desmond, Matthew. 2018. "Heavy Is the House: Rent Burden among the American Urban Poor." *International Journal of Urban and Regional Research* 42 (1): 160–70.

Domhoff, G. William. 2018. *Studying the Power Elite: Fifty Years of Who Rules America.* New York: Routledge.

Dunn, Amina. October 4, 2018. "Partisans Are Divided over the Fairness of the U.S. Economy—And Why People Are Rich or Poor." Pew Research Center. Accessed January 3, 2019. https://www.pewresearch.org/fact-tank/2018/10/04/partisans-are-divided-over-the-fairness-of-the-u-s-economy-and-why-people-are-rich-or-poor/.

Fontenot, Kayla, Jessica Semega, and Melissa Kollar. 2018. "Income and Poverty in the United States, 2017." Current Population Reports, P60-263. U.S. Government Printing Office, 2018. Accessed October 10, 2018. https://www.census.gov/content/dam/Census/library/publications/2018/demo/p60-263.pdf.

Free the Slaves. 2019. "Home Page." Accessed July 19, 2019. https://www.freetheslaves.net.

Friedman, Zack. 2018. "Student Loan Debt Statistics in 2018: A Trillion Dollar Crisis." *Forbes.* Accessed December 26, 2018. https://www.forbes.com/sites/zackfriedman/2018/06/13/student-loan-debt-statistics-2018/56869eb37310.

Goldrick-Rab, Sara, Christine Baker-Smith, Vanessa Coca, Elizabeth Looker, and Tiffani Williams. 2019. "College and University Basic Needs Insecurity: A National RealCollege Survey Report." Accessed at May 5, 2019. https://hope4college.com/wp-content/uploads/2019/04/HOPE_realcollege_National_report_digital.pdf.

Ingraham, Christopher. 2017. "The Richest 1 Percent Now Owns More of the Country's Wealth Than at Any Time in the Past 50 Years." *The Washington Post*, November 17. Accessed January 22, 2019. https://www.washingtonpost.com/news/wonk/wp/2017/12/06/the-richest-1-percent-now-owns-more-of-the-countrys-wealth-than-at-any-time-in-the-past-50-years/?utm_term=.c9a3a5110a84.

Internal Revenue Service. 2018. "Individual Income Tax Shares." Accessed July 19, 2019. https://www.irs.gov/statistics/soi-tax-stats-individual-income-tax-rates-and-tax-shares.

Jackson, David, and Doug Stanglin. 2017. "Trump Is Now President: 'The Forgotten . . . Will Be Forgotten No Longer.'" *USA Today*, January 20. Accessed January 13, 2019. https://www.usatoday.com/story/news/politics/2017/01/20/donald-trump-inauguration-day-president-white-house/96782700/.

Kochkar, Rakesh, and Anthony Cilluffo. 2018. "Income Inequality in the U.S. Is Rising Most Rapidly among Asians." Pew Research Center. Accessed October 30, 2018. http://www.pewsocialtrends.org/2018/07/12/income-inequality-in-the-u-s-is-rising-most-rapidly-among-asians/.

Marcus, Jon. 2018. "Embattled Colleges Focus on an Obvious Fix: Helping Students Graduate on Time." Hechinger Report. May 14. Accessed September 4, 2018. https://hechingerreport.org/embattled-colleges-focus-on-an-obvious-fix-helping-students-graduate-on-time/.

Marx, Karl, Frederich Engels, and Frederic L. Bender. 1988. *The Communist Manifesto: Annotated Text.* New York: W. W. Norton.

Mishel, Lawrence, and Jessica Schieder. 2018. "CEO Compensation Surged in 2017." Economic Policy Institute. Accessed October 18, 2018. https://www.epi.org/files/pdf/152123.pdf.

Murphy, Devin, Michelle Boyd, and Debby Bielak. 2016. "Overview of Estimated Returns on Six Big Investments and Their Impacts on Lifetime Earnings: 'Billion Dollar Bets' to Create Economic Opportunity for Every American." The Bridgespan Group. Accessed October 5, 2018. https://www.bridgespan.org/bridgespan/Images/articles/billion-dollar-bets-to-create-economic-opportunity/bridgespan-social-mobility-2016-impact-estimates.pdf.

Organisation for Economic Co-operation and Development. 2018. "A Broken Social Elevator? How to Promote Social Mobility." Accessed October 15, 2018. http://www.oecd.org/social/broken-elevator-how-to-promote-social-mobility-9789264301085-en.htm.

Owens, Ann. 2018. "Income Segregation between School Districts and Inequality in Students' Achievement." *Sociology of Education* 91 (1): 1–27.

Pearlstein. Steven. 2018. *Can American Capitalism Survive? Why Greed Is Not Good, Opportunity Is Not Equal, and Fairness Won't Make Us Poor.* New York: St. Martin's.

Reynolds, Matt. 2018. "No, Finland Isn't Scrapping Its Universal Basic Income Experiment." *Wired*, April 26. Accessed January 4, 2019. https://www.wired.co.uk/article/finland-universal-basic-income-results-trial-cancelled.

Segarra, Maryellen. 2018. "When It Comes to the New Tax Cut, Lots of People Are Just Not Feelin' It." Marketplace Radio, October 17. Accessed September 5, 2018. https://www.marketplace.org/2018/10/17/economy/new-tax-law-people-arent-feeling.

Steele, James B., and Lance Williams. 2016. "Who Got Rich off the Student Debt Crisis." Reveal, June 28. Accessed June 2, 2017. https://www.revealnews.org/article/who-got-rich-off-the-student-debt-crisis/.

Stewart, Matthew. 2018. "The 9.9 Percent Is the New American Aristocracy." *The Atlantic*, June 2018. Accessed October 17, 2018. https://www.theatlantic.com/magazine/archive/2018/06/the-birth-of-a-new-american-aristocracy/559130/.

Stolberg, Sheryl Gay, and Jeanna Smialek. 2019. "House Passes Bill to Raise Minimum Wage to $15, a Victory for Liberals." *The New York Times*, July 18. Accessed July 21, 2019. https://www.nytimes.com/2019/07/18/us/politics/minimum-wage.html.

Tax Policy Center. 2017. "Distributional Analysis of the Conference Agreement for the Tax Cuts and Jobs Act." Urban Institute and Brookings Institution. Accessed October 17, 2018. https://www.taxpolicycenter.org/sites/default/files/publication/150816/2001641_distributional_analysis_of_the_conference_agreement_for_the_tax_cuts_and_jobs_act_0.pdf.

U.S. Census Bureau. N.d. "Table B19083: Gini Index of Income Inequality." Accessed July 19, 2019. https://censusreporter.org/tables/B19083/.

Weber, Max, Hans Gerth, and C. Wright Mills. 1958. *From Max Weber: Essays in Sociology.* New York: Oxford University Press.

Wolff, Edward N. 2017. "Household Wealth Trends in the United States, 1962 to 2016: Has Middle Class Wealth Recovered?" National Bureau of Economic Research, November 2017. Accessed January 22, 2019. https://www.nber.org/papers/w24085.

World Bank. 2018a. "GNI per Capita, Atlas Method (Current US$)." Accessed October 17, 2018. https://data.worldbank.org/indicator/NY.GNP.PCAP.CD?locations=XM-XD-XT-XN.

World Bank. 2018b. "World Bank Country and Lending Groups 2019." Accessed October 17, 2018. https://datahelpdesk.worldbank.org/knowledgebase/articles/906519-world-bank-country-and-lending-groups.

World Inequality Lab. 2018. "World Inequality Report 2018." Accessed July 19, 2019. https://wir2018.wid.world/files/download/wir2018-full-report-english.pdf.

CHAPTER 8

American Psychological Association. N.d. "Answers to Your Questions about Individuals with Intersex Conditions." Accessed October 12, 2017. http://www.apa.org/topics/lgbt/intersex.pdf.

Bailey, Beth. 2004. "From Front Porch to Back Seat: A History of the Date." *OAH Magazine of History* 18 (4): 23–26.

Baker, Michael, and Kirsten Cornelson. 2018. "Gender-Based Occupational Segregation and Sex Differences in Sensory, Motor, and Spatial Aptitudes." *Demography* 55 (5): 1749–75.

Bonos, Lisa, and Emily Guskin. 2019. "It's Not Just You: New Data Shows More Than Half of Young People in America Don't Have a Romantic Partner." *The Washington Post*, March 21.

Accessed April 29, 2018. https://www.washingtonpost.com/lifestyle/2019/03/21/its-not-just-you-new-data-shows-more-than-half-young-people-america-dont-have-romantic-partner/?utm_term=.0bb34d4f67a3.

Bridges, Tristan. 2017. "Shifts in the U.S. LGBT Population." Accessed September 4, 2017. https://thesocietypages.org/socimages/2017/01/16/shifts-in-the-us-lgbt-population.

Brown, Anna, and Eileen Patten. 2017. "The Narrowing, but Persistent, Gender Gap in Pay." Accessed July 19, 2019. http://www.pewresearch.org/fact-tank/2017/04/03/gender-pay-gap-facts/.

Bureau of Labor Statistics. 2018a. "Labor Force Statistics from the Current Population Survey, Household Data Annual Averages, Employed Persons by Detailed Occupation, Sex, Race and Hispanic or Latino Ethnicity." Accessed March 19, 2019. https://www.bls.gov/cps/cpsaat11.htm.

Bureau of Labor Statistics. 2018b. "Labor Force Statistics from the Current Population Survey, U.S. Bureau of Labor Statistics, Household Data Annual Averages, Employment Status of the Civilian Noninstitutional Population 16 Years and Over by Sex, 1978 to Date." Accessed January 20, 2019. http://www.bls.gov/cps/cpsaat02.htm.

Bureau of Labor Statistics. 2019. "Usual Weekly Earnings of Wage and Salary Workers: Second Quarter 2019." Accessed May 22, 2019. http://www.bls.gov/news.release/pdf/wkyeng.pdf.

Carlsen, Audrey, Maya Salam, Claire Cain Miller, Denise Lu, Ash Ngu, Jugal K. Patel, and Zach Wichter. 2018. "Powerful Men: Nearly Half of Their Replacements Are Women." *The New York Times*, October 23. Accessed March 2019. https://www.nytimes.com/interactive/2018/10/23/us/metoo-replacements.html.

Council of Foreign Relations. 2019. "Same Sex Marriage: Global Comparisons." Accessed May 3, 2019. https://www.cfr.org/backgrounder/same-sex-marriage-global-comparisons.

DeSilver, Drew. 2018. "A Record Number of Women Will Be Serving in the New Congress." Accessed May 8, 2019. https://www.pewresearch.org/fact-tank/2018/12/18/record-number-women-in-congress/.

Deutsch, Francine M. 2007. "Undoing Gender." *Gender & Society* 2 (1): 106–27.

Dill, Kathryn. 2015. "The Best Paying Jobs for Doctors in 2015." *Forbes.* Accessed June 15, 2016. http://www.forbes.com/sites/kathryndill/2015/07/22/the-best-paying-in-demand-jobs-for-doctors-in-2015/1da4a08b7da3.

England, Paula. 2015. "Online College Social Life Survey." Accessed May 1, 2016. http://www.nyu.edu/projects/england/ocsls/.

Equal Employment Opportunity Commission. N.d. "Sexual Harassment." Accessed July 24, 2019. https://www.eeoc.gov/laws/types/sexual_harassment.cfm.

Fausto-Sterling, Anne. 2000. *Sexing the Body: Gender Politics and the Construction of Sexuality.* New York: Basic Books.

Ferguson, Donna. 2018. "Must Monsters Always Be Male? Huge Gender Bias in Children's Books." *The Guardian*, January 21. Accessed March 1, 2019. https://www.theguardian.com/books/2018/jan/21/childrens-books-sexism-monster-in-your-kids-book-is-male.

Fernandez, Roberto M., and Brian Rubineau. 2019. "Network Recruitment and the Glass Ceiling: Evidence from Two Firms." *Journal of the Social Sciences* 5 (3): 88–102.

Ferrante, Mary Beth. 2018. "Before Breaking the Glass Ceiling, Women Must Climb the Maternal Wall." Accessed May 8, 2019. https://www.forbes.com/sites/marybethferrante/2018/10/31/before-breaking-the-glass-ceiling-women-must-climb-the-maternal-wall/3a4ff519c519.

Freedom for All Americans. 2018. "LGBTQ Americans Aren't Fully Protected from Discrimination in 30 States." Accessed February 16, 2019. https://www.freedomforallamericans.org/states/.

Frisby, Cynthia M., and Elizabeth Behm-Morawitz. 2019. "Undressing the Words: Prevalence of Profanity, Misogyny, Violence, and Gender Role References in Popular Music 2006–2016." *Media Watch* 10 (1): 5–21.

Gamble, Hilary. 2019. "Acquiescing to the Script: A Panel Study of College Students' Sexual Media Habits, Endorsement of Heteronormative Scripts, and Their Hesitance toward Resisting Unwanted Hookups." *Sex Roles* 80 (11–12): 707–23.

Gansen, Heidi, and Karin Martin. 2018. "Not Just Kid Stuff: Becoming Gendered." Council on Contemporary Families. Accessed January 12, 2019. https://contemporaryfamilies.org/becoming-gendered/.

Godbeer, Richard. 2004. "Courtship and Sexual Freedom in Eighteenth-Century America." *OAH Magazine of History* 18 (4): 9–13.

Gordon, Allergra R., Keirth J. Conron, Jerel P. Calzo, Matthew T. White, Sari Reisner, and S. Bryn Austin. 2018. "Gender Expression, Violence, and Bullying Victimization: Findings from Probability Samples of High School Students in 4 US School Districts." *Journal of School Health* 88 (4): 306–14.

Graham-McLay, Charlotte 2018. "A 4-Day Workweek? A Test Run Shows a Surprising Result." *The New York Times*, July 19. Accessed April 5, 2019. https://www.nytimes.com/2018/07/19/world/asia/four-day-workweek-new-zealand.html?smprod=nytcore-ipad&smid=nytcore-ipad-share.

Hidreley. 2019. "Budweiser Adapts Its Sexist Ads from the 1950s and 60s to 2019." Accessed March 12, 2019. https://www.boredpanda.com/modernized-vintage-sexist-beer-advertisements-budweiser/.

Human Rights Campaign. 2018. "New FBI Statistics Show Alarming Increase in Number of Reported Hate Crimes." Accessed May 8, 2019. https://www.hrc.org/blog/new-fbi-statistics-show-alarming-increase-in-number-of-reported-hate-crimes.

Hussar, William J., and Tabitha M. Bailey. 2018. "Projections of Education Statistics to 2026." NCES 2018-019. U.S. Department of Education, National Center for Education Statistics. Accessed July 22, 2019. https://nces.ed.gov/pubs2018/2018019.pdf.

Ingraham, Christopher. 2019. "The Share of Americans Not Having Sex Has Reached a Record High." *The Washington Post*, March 29. Accessed April 29, 2019. https://www.washingtonpost.com/business/2019/03/29/share-americans-not-having-sex-has-reached-record-high/?utm_term=.230f6a88b1ce.

Kuperberg, Arielle, and Rachel Allison. 2018. "Gender and Hooking Up." In *Handbook of the Sociology of Gender*, 2nd ed., edited by Barbara J. Risman, Carissa M. Froyum, and William J. Scarborough, 315–28. New York: Springer.

Kuperberg, Arielle, and Alicia M. Walker. 2018. "Heterosexual College Students Who Hookup with Same-Sex Partners." *Archives of Sexual Behavior* 47:1387–1403.

La Bella, Jaimie, and Kevin Downey, Jr. 2019. "The GilletterMeToo Ad Is Dishonest, Insulting to Men." Accessed February 14, 2019. https://video.foxnews.com/v/5989784514001/sp=show-clips.

Laber-Warren, Emily. 2018. "New Office Hours Aim for Well-Rested, More Productive Workers." *The New York Times*, December 24. Accessed April 5, 2019. https://www.nytimes.com/2018/12/24/well/mind/work-schedule-hours-sleep-productivity-chronotype-night-owls.html?smid=nytcore-ios-share.

Livingston, Gretchen, and Kristen Bialik. 2018. "7 Facts about U.S. Moms." Pew Research Center, May 10. Accessed February 2, 2019. http://www.pewresearch.org/fact-tank/2018/05/10/facts-about-u-s-mothers/.

Masci, David, and Drew DeSilver. 2017. "A Global Snapshot of Same-Sex Marriage." Accessed March 1, 2019. https://www.pewresearch.org/fact-tank/2017/12/08/global-snapshot-sex-marriage/.

McAneny, Barbara L. 2018. "Challenging Gender Bias in the House of Medicine." Accessed April 5, 2019. https://www.ama-assn.org/practice-management/physician-diversity/challenging-gender-bias-house-medicine.

McCann, Carly, Donald Tomaskovic-Devey, and M.V. Lee Badgett. 2018. "Employers' Responses to Sexual Harassment." Center for Employment Equity, University of Massachusetts. Accessed February 24, 2019. https://www.umass.edu/employmentequity/diversity-reports 2018.

Meisner, Jason. 2019. "R. Kelly to Be Taken in Custody to New York to Face Racketeering Charges There." *Chicago Tribune*, July 19. Retrieved July 21, 2019. https://www.chicagotribune.com/news/criminal-justice/ct-r-kelly-new-york-arraignment-20190719-styfdsqlh5birldnqqwffvlgfa-story.html.

Mendos, Lucas Ramon. 2019. "State Sponsored Homophobia." Accessed April 19, 2019. https://ilga.org/downloads/ILGA_State_Sponsored_Homophobia_2019.pdf.

Moss-Racusin, Corinne A., John F. Dovidio, Victoria L. Brescoll, Mark J. Graham, and Jo Handelsman. 2012. "Science Faculty's Subtle Gender Biases Favor Male Students." *Proceedings of the National Academy of Sciences* 109 (41): 16474–79.

National Science Board. 2018. "Science and Engineering Indicators 2018." Arlington, VA: National Science Foundation.

Newport, Frank. 2018. "In U.S., Estimate of LGBT Population Rises to 4.5%." Accessed March 1, 2019. https://news.gallup.com/poll/234863/estimate-lgbt-population-rises.aspx.

Pascoe, C. J. 2007. *Dude, You're a Fag: Masculinity and Sexuality in High School*. Berkeley: University of California Press.

Pascoe, C. J. 2011. *Dude, You're a Fag: Masculinity and Sexuality in High School*. 2nd ed. Berkeley: University of California Press.

Pew Research Center. 2013. "Growing Support for Gay Marriage: Changed Minds and Changing Demographics." Accessed April 7, 2014. http://www.people-press.org/2013/03/20/growing-support-for-gay-marriage-changed-minds-and-changing-demographics.

Pew Research Center. 2017. "Changing Attitudes on Gay Marriage." Accessed July 16, 2019. http://www.pewforum.org/fact-sheet/changing-attitudes-on-gay-marriage/.

Pew Research Center. 2018. "Women CEOs in Fortune 500 Companies, 1995–2018." Accessed March 1, 2019. https://www.pewsocialtrends.org/chart/women-ceos-in-fortune-500-companies-1995-2014/.

Pham, Janelle M. 2019. "Campus Sex in Context: Organizational Cultures and Women's Engagement in Sexual Relationships on Two American College Campuses." *Sociological Forum* 34 (1): 138–57.

Rainey, James. 2018. "Women Introduce Powerful #MeToo Video at the Academy Awards." Accessed March 20, 2019. https://www.nbcnews.com/storyline/harvey-weinstein-scandal/women-introduce-powerful-metoo-video-academy-awards-n853461.

Risman, Barbara J. 2004. "Gender as a Social Structure: Theory Wrestling with Activism." *Gender & Society* 18 (4): 429–51.

Risman, Barbara J. 2019. "Is Recreational Sex a Social Problem? Or, What's Wrong with Kids Today?" *Contemporary Sociology* 48 (2): 123–29.

Risman, Barbara J., and Georgiann Davis. 2012. "From Sex Roles to Gender Structure." *Current Sociology* 61 (5–6).

Romano, Nick. 2018. "The Prom Celebrates 'First LGBTQ Kiss' in Macy's Thanksgiving Day Parade History." Accessed March 12, 2019. https://ew.com/theater/2018/11/22/the-prom-macys-thanksgiving-day-parade-first-same-sex-kiss/.

Rousseau, Ann, Rachel F. Rodgers, and Steven Eggermont. 2019. "A Short-Term Longitudinal Exploration of the Impact of TV Exposure on Objectifying Attitudes toward Women in Early Adolescent Boys." *Sex Roles* 80:186–99.

Rugheimer, Sarah. 2018. "Women in STEM Resources." Accessed July 19, 2019. https://www.cfa.harvard.edu/~srugheimer/Women_in_STEM_Resources.html.

Schwartz, Pepper, and Virginia Rutter. 1998. *Gender of Sexuality.* Thousand Oaks, CA: Pine Forge.

Smith, Stacy L., Marc Choueiti, Katherine Pieper, Ariana Case, and Angel Choi. 2018. "Inequality in 1,100 Popular Films: LGBT & Disability From 2007 to 2017." Annenberg Foundation, USC Anneberg Inclusion Initiative. Accessed April 6, 2019. http://assets.uscannenberg.org/docs/inequality-in-1100-popular-films.pdf.

Suggett, Paul. 2019. "The Objectification of Women in Advertising." Accessed February 1, 2019. https://www.thebalancecareers.com/advertising-women-and-objectification-38754.

Taie, Soheyla, and Rebecca Goldring. 2017. "Characteristics of Public Elementary and Secondary School Principals in the United States: Results from the 2015–16 National Teacher and Principal Survey." U.S. Department of Education. Accessed March 13, 2019. https://nces.ed.gov/pubs2017/2017070.pdf.

Tramontana, Mary Katherine. 2017. "What Trans Men Know about Gender in the Workplace." Citylab. Accessed March 23, 2019. https://www.citylab.com/life/2017/01/what-trans-men-know-about-gender-in-the-workplace/512501/

U.S. Department of Education. 2018. "Fast Facts: Race/Ethnicity of College Faculty." Accessed July 21, 2019. https://nces.ed.gov/fastfacts/display.asp?id= 61.

Wade, Lisa. 2017. *American Hookup: The New Culture of Sex on Campus.* New York: W. W. Norton.

West, Candace, and Don H. Zimmerman. 1987. "Doing Gender." *Gender & Society* 1 (2): 125–51.

Wetcher, Barry. 2018. "*Ocean's 8, Ghostbusters,* and Franchises Taken Over by Women." Accessed March 20, 2019. https://variety.com/gallery/oceans-8-ghostbusters-reboots-starring-women/.

Williams, Christine L. 2013. "The Glass Escalator, Revisited." *Gender & Society* 27 (5): 609–29.

Williams Institute. 2019. "LGBT People in the U.S. Not Protected by State Nondiscrimination Statutes." UCLA School of Law. Accessed July 21, 2019. https://williamsinstitute.law.ucla.edu/wp-content/uploads/Equality-Act-March-2019.pdf.

Women's Media Center. 2019. "Divided 2019: The Media Gap." Accessed April 6, 2019. http://www.womensmediacenter.com/reports/divided-2019-the-media-gender-gap.

Wynn, Alison, and Shelley J. Correll. 2018. "Combating Gender Bias in Modern Workplaces." In *Handbook of the Sociology of Gender*, 2nd ed., edited by Barbara J. Risman, Carissa M. Froyum, and William J. Scarborough, 509–22. New York: Springer.

Zraick, Karen. 2018. "Lawyers Say They Face Persistent Racial and Gender Bias at Work." *The New York Times*, September 6. Accessed April 5, 2019. https://www.nytimes.com/2018/09/06/us/lawyers-bias-racial-gender.html?smid=nytcore-ios-share.

CHAPTER 9

Ajunwa, Ifeoma, and Angela Onwuachi-Willig. 2018. "Combating Discrimination against the Formerly Incarcerated in the Labor Market." *Northwestern University Law Review* 112 (1385).

Alcindor, Yamiche. 2016. "Minorities Worry What a 'Law and Order' Donald Trump Presidency Will Mean." *The New York Times*, November 11. Accessed January 9, 2017. http://www.nytimes.com/2016/11/12/us/politics/minorities-worry-what-a-law-and-order-donald-trump-presidency-will-mean.html.

Beeman, Angie. 2015. "Walk the Walk but Don't Talk the Talk: The Strategic Use of Color-Blind Ideology in an Interracial Social Movement Organization." *Sociological Forum* 30 (1): 127–47.

Bialik, Kristen. 2017. "Key Facts about Race and Marriage, 50 Years after *Loving v. Virginia.*" *Pew Research Center*, June 12. Accessed January 6, 2019. http://www.pewresearch.org/fact-tank/2017/06/12/key-facts-about-race-and-marriage-50-years-after-loving-v-virginia/.

Blauner, Robert. 1972. *Racial Oppression in America.* New York: Harper & Row.

Botsford, Jon D., Dwight L. Hamilton, Randall E. Mehrberg, and Deanne E. Maynard. 2000. "Amicus Brief in the United States District Court for the Eastern District of Michigan." Accessed July 21, 2019. http://www.umich.edu/~bhlumrec/a/admissions/legal/gratz/amici.html.

Bradner, Eric, and Ted Barrett. 2015. "Republicans to Obama: Keep Syrian Refugees Out." CNN, November 16. Accessed June 1, 2017. http://www.cnn.com/2015/11/16/politics/republicans-syrian-refugees-2016-elections-obama/.

Bureau of Labor Statistics. 2017. "Labor Force Statistics from the Current Population Survey: Household Data, Not Seasonally Adjusted, Quarterly Averages: E-16. Unemployment Rates by Age, Sex, Race, and Hispanic or Latino Ethnicity." Accessed September 6, 2017. https://www.bls.gov/web/empsit/cpsee_e16.htm.

Bureau of Labor Statistics. 2018. "Table 5. Median Usual Weekly Earnings of Full-Time Wage and Salary Workers for the Foreign Born and Native Born by Selected Characteristics, 2016–2017 Annual Averages." Accessed February 18, 2019. https://www.bls.gov/news.release/forbrn.t05.htm.

Crenshaw, Kimberlé, Neil T. Gotanda, Gary Peller, and Kendall Thomas, ed. 1995. *Critical Race Theory: The Key Writings That Formed the Movement.* New York: Free Press.

Davis, Julie Hirschfeld. 2016. "U.S. Could Exceed Goal of Accepting 10,000 Syrian Refugees." *The New York Times*, August 5. Accessed September 6, 2016. https://www.nytimes.com/2016/08/06/us/politics/us-could-exceed-goal-of-accepting-10000-syrian-refugees.html.

DelReal, Jose A. 2016. "Trump Campaign Staff Redirects, Then Restores, Mention of Muslim Ban from Website." *The Washington Post*, November 10. Accessed January 9, 2017. https://www.washingtonpost.com/news/post-politics/wp/2016/11/10/trump-campaign-staff-deletes-mention-of-muslim-ban-from-website/?utm_term=.6fa81b24e3b6.

Desmond, Matthew, and Mustafa Emirbayer. 2009. *Racial Domination, Racial Progress.* New York: McGraw-Hill.

de Vogue, Ariane. 2018. "Supreme Court Finally Rejects Infamous Korematsu Decision on Japanese-American Internment." *CNN*, June 26. Accessed February 21, 2019. https://www.cnn.com/2018/06/26/politics/korematsu-supreme-court-travel-ban-roberts-sotomayor/index.html.

Diamant, Jeff. 2018. "Q&A: Measuring Attitudes toward Muslims and Jews in Western Europe." Pew Research Center, June 1. Accessed February 18, 2019. http://www.pewresearch

.org/fact-tank/2018/06/01/qa-measuring-attitudes-toward-muslims-and-jews-in-western-europe/.

Dobbin, Frank, and Alexandra Kalev. 2016. "Why Diversity Programs Fail." *Harvard Business Review*, July/August 2016. Accessed May 14, 2018. https://hbr.org/2016/07/why-diversity-programs-fail.

Domonoske, Camila. 2016. "Denying Housing over Criminal Record May Be Discrimination, Feds Say." NPR, April 4, 2016. Accessed May 30, 2019. http://www.npr.org/sections/thetwo-way/2016/04/04/472878724/denying-housing-over-criminal-record-may-be-discrimination-feds-say.

Douglass, Frederick. 1857. "If There Is No Struggle, There Is No Progress." Accessed January 9, 2017. http://www.blackpast.org/1857-frederick-douglass-if-there-no-struggle-there-no-progress.

Dovey, Dana. 2016. "Healthcare on Native American Reservations Is 'Horrifying': In the US, Who You Are Affects How You're Treated." *Medical Daily*. Accessed September 5, 2016. http://www.medicaldaily.com/native-american-reservations-healthcare-terrible-372442.

Du Bois, W. E. B. 1948. "Is Man Free?" *Scientific Monthly* 66: 432–33.

Du Bois, W. E. B. 1961. "Application for Membership in the Communist Party by W. E. B. Du Bois." Accessed September 8, 2016. http://www.cpusa.org/party_info/application-to-join-the-cpusa-by-w-e-b-du-bois-1961.

Durkheim, Émile. (1892) 1997. *The Division of Labor in Society*. New York: Simon & Schuster.

Federal Bureau of Investigation. 2016. "Table 43. Arrests by Race and Ethnicity, 2015." 2015 Crime in the United States. Accessed February 18, 2019. https://ucr.fbi.gov/crime-in-the-u.s/2015/crime-in-the-u.s.-2015/tables/table-43_.

Federal Reserve Bank of St. Louis. 2019. "Unemployment Rate: Black or African American (LNS14000006)." Accessed April 4, 2019. https://fred.stlouisfed.org/series/LNS14000006.

FindLaw.com. 2016. "Fair Housing: Race Discrimination." Accessed September 3, 2016. http://civilrights.findlaw.com/discrimination/fair-housing-race-discrimination.html.

Flake, Dallan F. 2015. "When Any Sentence is a Life Sentence: Employment Discrimination against Ex-offenders." *Washington University Law Review* 93 (1): 45–102.

Gee, Buck, and Denise Peck. 2017. "The Illusion of Asian Success: Scant Progress for Minorities in Cracking the Glass Ceiling from 2007–2015." Ascend Foundation. Accessed February 18, 2019. https://c.ymcdn.com/sites/www.ascendleadership.org/resource/resmgr/research/TheIllusionofAsianSuccess.pdf.

Geiger, Abigail, and Gretchen Livingston. 2019. "8 Facts about Love and Marriage in America." Pew Research Center, February 13. Accessed February 19, 2019. http://www.pewresearch.org/fact-tank/2019/02/13/8-facts-about-love-and-marriage/.

Gibson, Campbell J., and Emily Lennon. 1999. "Historical Census Statistics on the Foreign-Born Population of the United States: 1850–1990." Washington, DC: U.S. Census Bureau.

Glantz, Aaron, and Emmanuel Martinez. 2018. "Modern-Day Redlining: How Banks Block People of Color from Homeownership." *Chicago Tribune*, February 17. Accessed December 17, 2018. https://www.chicagotribune.com/business/ct-biz-modern-day-redlining-20180215-story.html.

Goodstein, Laurie. 2016. "Jimmy Carter, Seeing Resurgence of Racism, Plans Baptist Conference for Unity." *The New York Times*, May 23. Accessed September 5, 2016. http://www.nytimes.com/2016/05/24/us/jimmy-carter-racism-baptist-conference-unity-donald-trump.html).

Gramlich, John. 2018. "The Gap between the Number of Blacks and Whites in Prison Is Shrinking." Pew Research Center, January 12. Accessed February 21, 2019. http://www.pewresearch.org/fact-tank/2018/01/12/shrinking-gap-between-number-of-blacks-and-whites-in-prison/.

Green, Erica L., and Annie Waldman. 2018. "'I Feel Invisible': Native Students Languish in Public Schools." *The New York Times*, December 28. Retrieved December 29, 2018. https://www.nytimes.com/2018/12/28/us/native-american-education.html.

Griffin, John D. 2014. "When and Why Minority Legislators Matter." *Annual Review of Political Science* 17:327–36.

Gross, Daniel A. 2015. "The U.S. Government Turned Away Thousands of Jewish Refugees, Fearing That They Were Nazi Spies." Smithsonian Magazine, November 18. Accessed January 9, 2017. http://www.smithsonianmag.com/history/us-government-turned-away-thousands-jewish-refugees-fearing-they-were-nazi-spies-180957324/.

Harris, Art. 1983. "Louisiana Court Sees no Shades of Gray in Woman's Request." *The Washington Post*, May 21. Accessed August 28, 2016. https://www.washingtonpost.com/archive/politics/1983/05/21/louisiana-court-sees-no-shades-of-gray-in-womans-request/ddb0f1df-ba5d-4141-9aa0-6347e60ce52d/.

Hewes, Hilary A., Mengtao Dai, N. Clay Mann, Tanya Baca, and Peter Taillac. 2018. "Prehospital Pain Management: Disparity by Age and Race." *Prehospital Emergency Care* 22 (2): 189–97.

Ignatiev, Noel. 1995. *How the Irish Became White*. New York: Routledge.

Jaynes, Gregory. 1982. "Suit on Race Recalls Lines Drawn under Slavery." *The New York Times*, September 30. Accessed August 28, 2016. http://www.nytimes.com/1982/09/30/us/suit-on-race-recalls-lines-drawn-under-slavery.html?pagewanted=all.

Johnson, Shauna. N.d. "Historical Primer." Accessed July 21, 2019. https://native-land.ca/teachers-guide/.

Jorde, Lynn B., and Stephen P. Wooding. 2004. "Genetic Variation, Classification, and Race." *Nature Genetics* 36:S28–33.

Kahn, Andrew, and Chris Kirk. 2015. "There's Blatant Inequality at Nearly Every Phase of the Criminal Justice System." *Business Insider*, August 9. Accessed July 21, 2019. http://www.businessinsider.com/theres-blatant-inequality-at-nearly-every-phase-of-the-criminal-justice-system-2015-8.

Kennel, Jamie. May 31, 2018. "Investigating EMS Treatment Disparities by Patient Race/Ethnicity for Traumatic and Painful Emergencies." Accessed February 18, 2019. http://opb-imgserve-production.s3-website-us-west-2.amazonaws.com/original/oha_ems_pain_study_full_053118_1544116167731.pdf.

Khanna, Nikki. 2013. *Biracial in America: Forming and Performing Racial Identity*. Lanham, MD: Lexington.

King, Gilbert. 2012. "The Ugliest, Most Contentious Election Ever." *Smithsonian Magazine*, September 7. Accessed September 1, 2016. http://www.smithsonianmag.com/history/the-ugliest-most-contentious-presidential-election-ever-28429530/?no-ist.

Kochkar, Rakesh, and Anthony Cilluffo. 2018. "Income Inequality in the U.S. Is Rising Most Rapidly among Asians." Pew Research Center. Accessed October 30, 2018. http://www.pewsocialtrends.org/2018/07/12/income-inequality-in-the-u-s-is-rising-most-rapidly-among-asians/.

Korgen, Kathleen Odell, ed. 2010. *Multiracial Americans and Social Class*. Abingdon, UK: Routledge.

Korgen, Kathleen Odell, ed. 2016. *Race Policy and Multiracial Americans*. Bristol, UK: Policy.

Korver-Glenn, E. 2018. "Compounding Inequalities: How Racial Stereotypes and Discrimination Accumulate across the Stages of Housing Exchange." *American Sociological Review* 83 (4): 627–56.

Krogstad, Jens Manuel, Antonio Flores, and Mark Hugo Lopes. 2018. "Key Takeaways about Latino Voters in the 2018 Midterm Elections." Pew Research Center, November 9. Accessed February 2, 2019. http://www.pewresearch.org/fact-tank/2018/11/09/how-latinos-voted-in-2018-midterms/.

Krogstad, Jens Manuel, and Mark Hugo Lopez. 2017. "Black Voter Turnout Fell in 2016, Even as a Record Number of Americans Cast Ballots." Accessed September 4, 2017. http://www.pewresearch.org/fact-tank/2017/05/12/black-voter-turnout-fell-in-2016-even-as-a-record-number-of-americans-cast-ballots.

Krogstad, Jens Manuel, and Jynnah Radford. 2018. "Education Levels of U.S. Immigrants Are on the Rise." Pew Research Center, September 14. Accessed February 18, 2019. http://www.pewresearch.org/fact-tank/2018/09/14/education-levels-of-u-s-immigrants-are-on-the-rise/.

Kytle, Ethan J., and Blain Roberts. 2018. *Denmark Vesey's Garden: Slavery and Memory in the Heart of the Confederacy.* New York: The New Press.

LaBarrie, Theressa L. 2017. "Multiracial Identity Development Factors: Illuminating Influential Factors." *Clinical Science Insights,* October. Accessed February 17, 2019. https://www.family-institute.org/sites/default/files/pdfs/multiracial_identity_development.pdf.

Levin, Brian H. 2017. "Hate Crimes Rise in Major American Localities in 2016." Center for the Study of Hate and Extremism, California State University, San Bernardino. Accessed September 4, 2017. https://csbs.csusb.edu/sites/csusb_csbs/files/Levin%20DOJ%20Summit%202.pdf.

Livingston, Gretchen. 2017. "The Rise of Multiracial and Multiethnic Babies in the U.S." Pew Research Center, June 6. Accessed February 17, 2019. http://www.pewresearch.org/fact-tank/2017/06/06/the-rise-of-multiracial-and-multiethnic-babies-in-the-u-s/.

Looney, Adam, and Nicholas Turner. 2018. "Work and Opportunity before and after Incarceration." The Brookings Institution. Accessed December 18, 2018. https://www.brookings.edu/wp-content/uploads/2018/03/es_20180314_looneyincarceration_final.pdf.

López, Gustavo, Kristen Bialik, and Jynnah Radford. 2018. "Key Findings about U.S. Immigrants." Pew Research Center, November 30. Accessed February 17, 2019. http://www.pewresearch.org/fact-tank/2018/11/30/key-findings-about-u-s-immigrants/.

Lopez, Mark Hugo, Ana Gonzalez-Barrera, and Jans Manuel Krogstad. 2018. "More Latinos Have Serious Concerns about Their Place in America Under Trump." Pew Research Center, October 25. Accessed February 17, 2019. http://www.pewhispanic.org/2018/10/25/more-latinos-have-serious-concerns-about-their-place-in-america-under-trump/.

Marte, Janelle. 2017. "Wells Fargo Steered Blacks and Latinos toward Costlier Mortgages, Philadelphia Lawsuit Alleges." *The Los Angeles Times,* May 16. Accessed May 30, 2017. http://www.latimes.com/business/la-fi-wells-fargo-philadelphia-20170516-story.html.

Marx, Karl, and Friedrich Engels. (1845) 1970. *The German Ideology, Part I.* New York: International Publishers.

"The Most Racist Countries in the World." 2016. BusinessTech, March 21. Accessed July 21, 2019. http://businesstech.co.za/news/lifestyle/116644/the-most-racist-countries.

National Center for Education Statistics. 2018. "Table 104.10. Rates of High School Completion and Bachelor's Degree Attainment among Persons Age 25 and Over, by Race/Ethnicity and Sex: Selected Years, 1910 through 2017." Accessed February 18, 2019. https://nces.ed.gov/programs/digest/d17/tables/dt17_104.10.asp?referrer=report.

National Center for Education Statistics. 2019. "Public High School 4-Year Adjusted Cohort Graduation Rate (ACGR), by Race/Ethnicity and Selected Demographic Characteristics for the United States, the 50 States, and the District of Columbia: School Year 2016–17." Accessed February 18, 2019. https://nces.ed.gov/ccd/tables/ACGR_RE_and_characteristics_2016-17.asp.

National Center for Health Statistics. 2018. "Health Insurance Coverage: Early Release of Estimates from the National Health Interview Survey, January–March 2018." Accessed December 18, 2018. https://www.cdc.gov/nchs/data/nhis/earlyrelease/Insur201808.pdf.

National Conference of State Legislatures. 2016. "Felon Voting Rights." Accessed May 30, 2017. http://www.ncsl.org/research/elections-and-campaigns/felon-voting-rights.aspx.

National Geographic. 2019. "Map of Human Migration." Accessed July 21, 2019. https://genographic.nationalgeographic.com/human-journey.

Panetta, Grace, and Samantha Lee. 2019. "This Graphic Shows How Much More Diverse the House of Representatives Is Getting." *Business Insider,* January 12. Accessed February 2, 2019. https://www.businessinsider.com/changes-in-gender-racial-diversity-between-the-115th-and-116th-house-2018-12.

Peter G. Peterson Foundation. 2018. "Income and Wealth in the United States: An Overview of Recent Data." Accessed July 21, 2019. https://www.pgpf.org/blog/2018/09/income-and-wealth-in-the-united-states-an-overview-of-data.

Pettigrew, Thomas F., and Linda R. Tropp. 2008. "How Does Intergroup Contact Reduce Prejudice? Meta-Analytic Tests of Three Mediators. *European Journal of Social Psychology* 38:922–34.

Pew Research Center. 2018. "Being Christian in Western Europe." Accessed February 18, 2019. http://www.pewforum.org/2018/05/29/being-christian-in-western-europe/.

Quillian, Lincoln, Devah Pager, Ole Hexel, and Arnfinn H. Midtbøen. 2017. "Meta-analysis of Field Experiments Shows No Change in Racial Discrimination in Hiring over Time." *Proceedings of the National Academy of Sciences* 114 (41): 10870–75.

Rockquemore, Kerry, and David L. Brunsma. 2008. *Beyond Black: Biracial Identity in America.* Lanham, MD: Rowman & Littlefield.

Rodriguez, Clara E. 2000. *Changing Race: Latinos, the Census and the History of Ethnicity.* New York: NYU Press.

Rutherford, Adam. 2015. "Why Racism Is Not Backed by Science." *The Guardian,* March 1. Accessed August 28, 2016. https://www.theguardian.com/science/2015/mar/01/racism-science-human-genomes-darwin.

Shear, Michael D. 2017. "New Order Indefinitely Bars Almost All Travel from Seven Countries." *The New York Times,* September 24. Accessed December 17, 2018. https://www.nytimes.com/2017/09/24/us/politics/new-order-bars-almost-all-travel-from-seven-countries.html?module=inline.

Siddons, Andrew. 2018. "The Never-Ending Crisis at the Indian Health Service." *Roll Call,* March 5. Accessed December 18, 2018. https://www.rollcall.com/news/policy/never-ending-crisis-indian-health-service.

Singhal Astha, Yu Yu Tien, and Renee Y. Hsia. 2016. "Racial-Ethnic Disparities in Opioid Prescriptions at Emergency Department Visits for Conditions Commonly Associated with Prescription Drug Abuse." *PLoS ONE* 11 (8).

Smithsonian Institute. 2016. "Genetics." Accessed September 8, 2016. http://humanorigins.si.edu/evidence/genetics.

Spickard, Paul. 2009. *Japanese Americans: The Formation and Transformations of an Ethnic Group.* Piscataway, NJ: Rutgers University Press.

Stanford Open Policing Project. 2019. "Findings." Accessed March 15, 2019. https://openpolicing.stanford.edu/findings/.

Swarns, Rachel L. 2015. "Biased Lending Evolves, and Blacks Face Trouble Getting Mortgages." *The New York Times*, October 30. Accessed September 3, 2016. http://www.nytimes.com/2015/10/31/nyregion/hudson-city-bank-settlement.html.

Syrianrefugees.eu. 2016. "Syrian Refugees: A Snapshot of the Crisis—In the Middle East and Europe." Accessed September 6, 2016. http://syrianrefugees.eu.

Torimoto, Ikuko. 2017. *Okina Kyūin and the Politics of Early Japanese Immigration to the United States 1868–1924.* Jefferson, NC: McFarland.

Ueda, Michiko. 2008. "Does Minority Representation Matter for Policy Outcomes? Evidence from the U.S. States." California Institute of Technology, Working Paper. Accessed May 31, 2017. http://s3-us-west-1.amazonaws.com/hss-prod-storage.cloud.caltech.edu/hss_working_papers/sswp1284.pdf.

U.S. Census Bureau. 2018. "Census Bureau Statement on 2020 Census Race and Ethnicity Questions." Accessed February 2, 2019. https://www.census.gov/newsroom/press-releases/2018/2020-race-questions.html.

Valverde, Miriam. 2017. "For Trump, No Signal Yet Refugee Policy Will Change after U.S. Airstrike in Syria." Politifact, April 7. Accessed June 1, 2017. http://www.politifact.com/truth-o-meter/article/2017/apr/07/after-syrian-missile-airstrikes-will-trump-change-/.

Wike, Richard, Bruce Stokes, and Katie Simmons. 2016. "Europeans Fear Wave of Refugees Will Mean More Terrorism, Fewer Jobs." Accessed September 6, 2016. http://www.pewglobal.org/2016/07/11/europeans-fear-wave-of-refugees-will-mean-more-terrorism-fewer-jobs.

Wiltz, Teresa. 2015. "Legislative Boundaries, Lack of Connections Lead to Few Minority Lawmakers." The Pew Charitable Trusts, September 12. Accessed August 30, 2016. http://www.pewtrusts.org/en/research-and-analysis/blogs/stateline/2015/12/09/legislative-boundaries-lack-of-connections-lead-to-few-minority-lawmakers.

Ye Hee Lee, Michelle. 2015. "Donald Trump's False Comments Connecting Mexican Immigrants and Crime." *The Washington Post*, July 8. Accessed January 9, 2017. https://www.washingtonpost.com/news/fact-checker/wp/2015/07/08/donald-trumps-false-comments-connecting-mexican-immigrants-and-crime/?utm_term=.70b090b9add6.

Zucchino, David. 2016. "'I've Become a Racist': Migrant Wave Unleashes Danish Tensions over Identity." *The New York Times*, September 5. Accessed September 6, 2016. http://www.nytimes.com/2016/09/06/world/europe/denmark-migrants-refugees-racism.html.

Zweigenhaft, Richie. 2018. "The 116th Congress Has More Women and People of Color Than Ever—But There's Still Room to Improve." The Conversation, November 8. Accessed February 2, 2019. http://theconversation.com/the-116th-congress-has-more-women-and-people-of-color-than-ever-but-theres-still-room-to-improve-105930.

CHAPTER 10

Arendt, Hannah. 1951. *The Origins of Totalitarianism.* New York: Schocken.

Domhoff, G. William. 2014. *Who Rules America? The Triumph of the Corporate Rich.* New York: McGraw-Hill.

Gilens, Martin, and Benjamin I. Page. 2014. "Testing Theories of American Politics: Elites, Interest Groups, and the Average Citizens." *Perspectives on Politics* 12 (3): 564–81.

Hobbes, Thomas. (1651) 1962. *Leviathan.* New York: Simon & Schuster.

Judt, Tony. 2009. "What is Living and What Is Dead in Social Democracy?" *The New York Review of Books* 56 (20).

Marx, Karl, Friedrich Engels, and C. J. Arthur. 1974. *The German Ideology.* London: Lawrence & Wishart.

Michels, Robert. (1911) 1966. *Political Parties: A Sociological Study of the Oligarchical Tendencies of Modern Democracy.* New York: Free Press.

Mills, C. Wright. 1956. *The Power Elite.* New York: Oxford University Press.

Mussolini, Benito. 1933. "The Doctrine of Fascism." Accessed May 17, 2019. http://www.gutenberg.org/files/14058/14058-h/14058-h.htmTHE_DOCTRINE_OF_FASCISM.

Payne, Stanley G. 1980. *Fascism: Comparison and Definition.* Madison: University of Wisconsin Press.

U.S. Senate, Select Committee to Study Governmental Operation with Respect to Intelligence Activities. 1976. "Intelligence Activities and the Rights of Americans: Book II." Final Report. Accessed May 17, 2019. https://www.intelligence.senate.gov/sites/default/files/94755_II.pdf.

Veblen, Thorstein. 1899. *The Theory of the Leisure Class.* New York: Viking Penguin.

Weber, Max, Hans Gerth, and C. Wright Mills. 1958. *From Max Weber: Essays in Sociology.* New York: Oxford University Press.

CHAPTER 11

Acosta, Katie L., and Veronica B. Salcedo. "Gender (Non) Conformity in the Family." In *Handbook of the Sociology of Gender*, 2nd ed., edited by Barbara J. Risman, Carissa M. Froyum, and William J. Scarborough, 365–75. New York: Springer.

Adams, Michele. 2018. "Gender Inequality in Families." In *Handbook of the Sociology of Gender*, 2nd ed., edited by Barbara J. Risman, Carissa M. Froyum, and William J. Scarborough, 351–64. New York: Springer.

Amato, Paul R. 2010. "Research on Divorce: Continuing Trends and New Developments." *Journal of Marriage and Family* 72 (3): 650–66.

Amato, Paul R., and Christopher J. Anthony. 2014. "Estimating the Effects of Parental Divorce and Death with Fixed Effects Models." *Journal of Marriage and Family* 76 (2): 370–86.

Amato, Paul R., and Bryndl Hohmann-Marriott. 2007. "A Comparison of High- and Low-Distress Marriages That End in Divorce." *Journal of Marriage and Family* 69 (3): 621–38.

Amato, Paul R., and Sarah E. Patterson. 2017. "The Intergenerational Transmission of Union Instability in Early Adulthood." *Journal of Marriage and Family* 79 (3): 723–38.

Andersen, Lars H. 2016. "How Children's Educational Outcomes and Criminality Vary by Duration and Frequency of Paternal Incarceration." *Annals of the American Academy of Political and Social Science* 665 (1): 149–70.

Arkes, Jeremy. 2017. "Separating the Harmful versus Beneficial Effects of Marital Disruptions on Children." *Journal of Divorce & Remarriage* 58 (7): 526–41.

Berk, Sarah Fenstermaker. 1985. *The Gender Factory: The Apportionment of Work in American Households*. New York: Plenum.

Bernstein, Basil. 2003. *Class, Codes, and Control: Towards a Theory of Educational Transmission*. New York: Routledge & Kegan Paul.

Bianchi, Suzanne M. 2011. "Family Change and Time Allocation in American Families." *Annals of the American Academy of Political and Social Science* 638:21–44.

Biblarz, Timothy J., and Evren Savci. 2010. "Lesbian, Gay, Bisexual, and Transgender Families." *Journal of Marriage and Family* 72 (3): 480–97.

Bloom, Nick, and John Van Reenen. 2006. *Measuring and Explaining Management Practices across Firms and Countries*. Cambridge, MA: National Bureau of Economic Research.

Bzostek, Sharon H., and Lawrence M. Berger. 2017. "Family Structure Experiences and Child Socioemotional Development during the First Nine Years of Life: Examining Heterogeneity by Family Structure at Birth." *Demography* 54 (2): 513–40.

Calarco, Jessica McCrory. 2014. "Coached for the Classroom: Parents' Cultural Transmission and Children's Reproduction of Educational Inequalities" *American Sociological Review* 79 (5): 1115–37.

Calarco, Jessica McCrory. 2018. *Negotiating Opportunities: How the Middle Class Secures Advantages in School*. New York: Oxford University Press.

Cardoso, Jodi Berger, Jennifer L. Scott, Monica Faulkner, and Liza Barros Lane. 2018. "Parenting in the Context of Deportation Risk." *Journal of Marriage and Family* 80 (2): 301–16.

Carrington, Christopher. 1999. *No Place Like Home: Relationships and Family Life among Lesbians and Gay Men*. Chicago: University of Chicago Press.

Cherlin, Andrew. 1983. "Changing Family and Household: Contemporary Lessons from Historical Research." *Annual Review of Sociology* 9:51–66.

Cherlin, Andrew J. 2009. *The Marriage-Go-Round*. New York: Knopf.

ChildTrends. 2019. "Births to Unmarried Women." Accessed July 23, 2019. https://www.childtrends.org/indicators/births-to-unmarried-women.

Cohen, Philip N. 2018. *Enduring Bonds: Inequality, Marriage, Parenting, and Everything Else That Makes Families Great and Terrible*. Berkeley: University of California Press.

Collins, Patricia Hill. 2000. *Black Feminist Thought: Knowledge, Consciousness, and the Politics of Empowerment*. New York: Routledge.

Coontz, Stephanie. 1992. *The Way We Never Were: American Families and the Nostalgia Trap*. New York: Basic Books.

Coontz, Stephanie. 2005. *Marriage, A History: How Love Conquered Marriage*. New York: Viking.

Coontz, Stephanie. 2010. "The Evolution of American Families." In *Families as They Really Are*, edited by B. Risman. New York: W. W. Norton.

Corsaro, William A. 2005. *The Sociology of Childhood*. Thousand Oaks, CA: Pine Forge.

Council of Economic Advisers. 2014. "Work-Life Balance and the Economics of Workplace Flexibility." Accessed July 23, 2019. https://obamawhitehouse.archives.gov/sites/default/files/docs/updated_workplace_flex_report_final_0.pdf.

Creighton, Mathew J., Hyunjoon Park, and Graciela M. Teruel. 2009. "The Role of Migration and Single Motherhood in Upper Secondary Education in Mexico." *Journal of Marriage and Family* 71 (5): 1325–39.

DeSilver, Drew. 2017. "Access to Paid Family Leave Varies Widely across Employers, Industries." Pew Research Center, March 23. Accessed May 30, 2019. Accessed July 23, 2019. https://www.pewresearch.org/fact-tank/2017/03/23/access-to-paid-family-leave-varies-widely-across-employers-industries/.

Dill, Bonnie Thornton. 1988. "Our Mothers' Grief: Racial Ethnic Women and the Maintenance of Families." *Journal of Family History* 13 (4): 415–31.

Edin, Kathryn, and Maria Kefalas. 2005. *Promises I Can Keep: Why Poor Women Put Motherhood before Marriage*. Berkeley: University of California Press.

Edin, Kathryn, and Timothy J. Nelson. 2013. *Doing the Best I Can: Fatherhood in the Inner City*. Berkeley: University of California Press.

Elliott, Sinikka, Rachel Powell, and Joslyn Brenton. 2015. "Being a Good Mom." *Journal of Family Issues* 36 (3): 351–70.

Eriksen, Hanne-Lise Falgreen, Camilla Hvidtfeldt, and Helene Bie Lilleør. 2017. "Family Disruption and Social, Emotional and Behavioral Functioning in Middle Childhood." *Journal of Child and Family Studies* 26 (4): 1177–89.

Finkelhor, David, Richard K. Ormrod, and Heather A. Turner. 2007. "Poly-victimization: A Neglected Component in Child Victimization." *Child Abuse & Neglect* 31 (1): 7–26.

Finkelhor, David, Heather Turner, Anne Shattuck, Sherry Hamby, and Kristen Kracke. 2015. "Children's Exposure to Violence, Crime, and Abuse: An Update." *Juvenile Justice Bulletin*. Laurel, MD: U.S. Department of Justice.

Friedson, Michael. 2016. "Authoritarian Parenting Attitudes and Social Origin: The Multigenerational Relationship of Socioeconomic Position to Childrearing Values." *Child Abuse & Neglect* 51:263–75.

Gorman, Gregory H., Matilda Eide, and Elizabeth Hisle-Gorman. 2009. "Wartime Military Deployment and Increased Pediatric Mental and Behavioral Health Complaints." *Pediatrics* 136 (6): 1058–66.

Hays, Sharon. 1996. *The Cultural Contradictions of Motherhood*. New Haven, CT: Yale University Press.

Hemez, Paul. 2016. "Divorce Rate in the U.S.: Geographic Variation." National Center for Family and Marriage Research, Bowling Green State University. Accessed July 23, 2019. https://www.bgsu.edu/ncfmr/resources/data/family-profiles/hemez-divorce-rate-2016-fp-17-24.html.

Hill, Shirley A. 2012. *Families: A Social Class Perspective*. Thousand Oaks, CA: Pine Forge.

Hochschild, Arlie, and Anne Machung. 2012. *The Second Shift: Working Families and the Revolution at Home*. New York: Penguin.

Hook, Jennifer L. 2017. "Women's Housework: New Tests of Time and Money." *Journal of Marriage and Family* 79:179–98.

Ishizuka, Patrick. 2019. "Social Class, Gender, and Contemporary Parenting Standards in the United States: Evidence from a National Survey Experiment." *Social Forces* 98 (1): 31–58.

Jacobs, Jerry A., and Kathleen Gerson. 2004. *The Time Divide*. Cambridge, MA: Harvard University Press.

Jæger, Mads Meier, and Richard Breen. 2016. "A Dynamic Model of Cultural Reproduction." *American Journal of Sociology* 111 (4): 1079–1115.

Kalmijn, Matthijs. 2017. "Family Structure and the Well-Being of Immigrant Children in Four European Countries." *International Migration Review* 51 (4): 927–63.

Kamo, Yoshinori, and Ellen L. Cohen. 1998. "Division of Household Work between Partners: A Comparison of Black and White Couples." *Journal of Comparative Family Studies* 29:131–45.

Kane, Emily W. 2018. "Parenting and Gender." In *Handbook of the Sociology of Gender*, 2nd ed., edited by Barbara J. Risman, Carissa M. Froyum, and William J. Scarborough, 393–404. New York: Springer.

Kohn, Melvin L. 1977. *Class and Conformity: A Study in Values.* Chicago: University of Chicago Press.

Lareau, Annette. 2002. "Invisible Inequality: Social Class and Childrearing in Black Families and White Families." *American Sociological Review* 67 (3): 747–76.

Lareau, Annette. 2015. "Cultural Knowledge and Social Inequality." *American Sociological Review* 80 (1): 1–27.

Lehrer, Evelyn L., and Yeon Jeong Son. 2017. "Women's Age at First Marriage and Marital Instability in the United States: Differences by Race and Ethnicity." *Demographic Research* 37:229–50.

Livingston, Gretchen, and Kristen Bialik. 2018. "7 Facts about U.S. Moms." Pew Research Center, May 11. Accessed July 23, 2019. http://www.pewresearch.org/fact-tank/2018/05/11/facts-about-u-s-mothers/.

Loving v. Virginia, 388 U.S. 1 (1967).

Manning, Wendy D., Susan L. Brown, and J. Bart Stykes. 2016. "Same-Sex and Different-Sex Cohabiting Couple Relationship Stability." *Demography* 53 (4): 937–53.

Martin, Joyce A., Brady E. Hamilton, Michelle J. K. Osterman, Anne K. Driscoll, and Patrick Drake. 2018. "Table 11. Selected Demographic Characteristics of Births, by Race and Hispanic Origin of Mother: United States, 2017." *National Vital Statistics Reports* 67 (8). Accessed July 24, 2019. https://www.cdc.gov/nchs/data/nvsr/nvsr67/nvsr67_08-508.pdf.

McGill, Brittany S. 2014. "Navigating New Norms of Involved Fatherhood: Employment, Fathering Attitudes, and Father Involvement." *Journal of Family Issues* 35:1189–1216.

Mintz, Steven. 2001. "Introduction: Does the American Family Have a History? Family Images and Realities." *OAH Magazine of History* 15 (4): 4–10.

Mintz, Steven. 2004. *Huck's Raft: A History of American Childhood.* Cambridge, MA: Harvard University Press.

Moore, Mignon. 2011. *Invisible Families: Gay Identities, Relationships, and Motherhood among Black Women.* Berkeley: University of California Press.

Murry, Velma McBride, and Melissa A. Lippold. 2018. "Parenting Practices in Diverse Family Structures: Examination of Adolescents' Development and Adjustment." *Journal of Research on Adolescence* 28 (3): 650–64.

National Conference of State Legislatures. 2016. "State Family and Medical Leave Laws." Accessed July 23, 2019. http://www.ncsl.org/research/labor-and-employment/state-family-and-medical-leave-laws.aspx.

Noguchi, Yuki. 2019. "Paid Family Leave Gains Momentum in States as Bipartisan Support Grows." NPR Morning Edition, March 5. Accessed May 30, 2019. https://www.npr.org/2019/03/05/698336019/paid-family-leave-gains-momentum-in-states-as-bipartisan-support-grows.

Obergefell v. Hodges, 576 U.S. ___ (2015).

Organisation for Economic Co-operation and Development. 2016. "PF2.1 Key Characteristics of Parental Leave Systems." Family Database. Accessed July 23, 2019. http://www.oecd.org/els/soc/PF2_1_Parental_leave_systems.pdf.

Parsons, Talcott, and Robert F. Bales. 1956. *Family Socialization and Interaction Processes.* London: Routledge & Kegan Paul.

Payne, Krista K. 2017. "Charting Marriage & Divorce in the U.S.: The Adjusted Divorce Rate." National Center for Family and Marriage Research, Bowling Green State University. Accessed July 23, 2019. https://www.bgsu.edu/ncfmr/resources/data/resources-by-topic/marriage-divorce-rates/payne-us-adjusted-divorce-rate-2008-2017.html.

Pear, Robert, and David D. Kirkpatrick. 2004. "Bush Plans 1.5 Billion Drive for Promotion of Marriage." *The New York Times*, January 14. Accessed September 10, 2017. http://www.nytimes.com/2004/01/14/us/bush-plans-1.5-billion-drive-for-promotion-of-marriage.html.

Pemberton, David. 2015. "Statistical Definition of 'Family' Unchanged Since 1930." U.S. Census Bureau, January. Accessed September 10, 2017. https://www.census.gov/newsroom/blogs/random-samplings/2015/01/statistical-definition-of-family-unchanged-since-1930.html.

Petts, Richard J., Kevin M. Shafer, and Lee Essig. 2018. "Does Adherence to Masculine Norms Shape Fathering Behavior?" *Journal of Marriage and Family* 80:704–20.

Pfeffer, Carla A. 2011. "'Women's Work'? Women Partners of Transgender Men Doing Housework and Emotion Work." *Journal of Marriage and Family* 72 (1): 165–83.

Rotz, Dana. 2016. "Why Have Divorce Rates Fallen? The Role of Women's Age at Marriage." *Journal of Human Resources* 51 (4): 961–1002.

Scarborough, William J., Ray Sin, and Barbara Risman. 2019. "Attitudes and the Stalled Gender Revolution: Egalitarianism, Traditionalism, and Ambivalence from 1977 through 2016." *Gender & Society* 33 (2): 173–200.

Schneider, Daniel. 2011. "Market Earnings and Household Work: New Tests of Gender Performance Theory." *Journal of Marriage and Family* 73 (4): 845–60.

Schneider, Daniel, Orestes P. Hastings, and Joe LaBriola. 2018. "Income Inequality and Class Divides in Parental Investments." *American Sociological Review* 83 (3): 475–507.

Schooreel, Tess, and Marijke Verbruggen. 2016. "Use of Family-Friendly Work Arrangements and Work-Family Conflict: Crossover Effects in Dual-Earner Couples." *Journal of Occupational Health Psychology* 21 (1): 119–32.

Shafer, Kevin, Todd M. Jensen, and Erin K. Holmes. 2017. "Divorce Stress, Stepfamily Stress, and Depression among Emerging Adult Stepchildren." *Journal of Child and Family Studies* 26 (3): 851–62.

Shows, Carla, and Naomi Gerstel. 2009. "Fathering, Class, and Gender: A Comparison of Physicians and Emergency Medical Technicians." *Gender & Society* 23 (2): 161–87.

Smith, Sharon G., Xinjian Zhang, Kathleen C. Basile, Melissa T. Merrick, Jing Wang, Marcie-Jo Kresnow, and Jieru Chen. 2015. "National Intimate Partner and Sexual Violence Survey: 2015 Data Brief." Centers for Disease Control and Prevention. Accessed December 27, 2018. https://www.cdc.gov/violenceprevention/nisvs/2015NISVSdatabrief.html.

Staples, Robert, and Leanor Boulin Johnson. 1993. *Black Families at the Crossroads: Challenges and Prospects.* San Francisco, CA: Jossey-Bass.

Stearns, Jenna, and Corey White. 2018. "Can Paid Sick Leave Mandates Reduce Leave-Taking?" *Labour Economics* 51: 227–46.

Supreme Court of the United States. 2014. *Obergefell et al. v. Hodges, Director, Ohio Department of Health, et al.*, Syllabus. Accessed September 10, 2017. https://www.supremecourt.gov/opinions/14pdf/14-556_3204.pdf.

Turner, Heather A., David Finkelhor, Richard Ormrod, Sherry Hamby, Rebecca T. Leeb, James A. Mercy, and Melissa Holt. 2012. "Family Context, Victimization, and Child Trauma Symptoms: Variations in Safe, Stable, and Nurturing Relationships during Early and Middle Childhood." *American Journal of Orthopsychiatry* 82 (2): 209–19.

Turner, Heather A., Anne Shattuck, David Finkelhor, and Sherry Hamby. 2017. "Effects of Poly-victimization on Adolescent Social Support, Self-Concept, and Psychological Distress." *Journal of Interpersonal Violence* 32 (5): 755–80.

Turner v. Safley, 482 U.S. 78 (1987).

Turney, Kristin, Jason Schnittker, and Christopher Wildeman. 2012. "Those They Leave Behind: Paternal Incarceration and Maternal Instrumental Support." *Journal of Marriage and Family* 74 (5): 1149–65.

U.S. Census Bureau. 2017. "CP02: Comparative Social Characteristics in the United States: 2017 American Community Survey 1-Year Estimates." Accessed July 14, 2019. https://factfinder.census.gov/faces/tableservices/jsf/pages/productview.xhtml?src=bkmk.

U.S. Census Bureau. 2018. "Historical Living Arrangements of Adults: Table AD-3. Living Arrangements of Adults 18 and Over, 1967 to Present." Accessed July 23, 2019. https://www2.census.gov/programs-surveys/demo/tables/families/time-series/adults/ad3.xlsx.

U.S. Department of Health and Human Services, Office of the Administration for Children & Families, Office of Family Assistance. 2019. "About TANF." Accessed July 23, 2019. https://www.acf.hhs.gov/ofa/programs/tanf/about.

Williams, Joan C., Jennifer L. Berdahl, and Joseph A. Vandello. 2016. "Beyond Work-Life 'Integration.'" *Annual Review of Psychology* 67 (1): 515–39.

CHAPTER 12

Allen, Ann, and Marytza Gawlik. 2018. "Changing the Landscape: A Look at a Market District as an Emerging Model of K–12 Schooling." *Educational Policy*. Accessed July 25, 2019. https://journals.sagepub.com/doi/10.1177/0895904818813297.

Amurao, Carla. 2013. "Fact Sheet: How Bad Is the School-to-Prison Pipeline?" Accessed March 31, 2016. http://www.pbs.org/wnet/tavissmiley/tsr/education-under-arrest/school-to-prison-pipeline-fact-sheet.

Anyon, Yolanda, Chalane Lechuga, Debora Ortega, Barbara Downing, Eldridge Greer, and John Simmons. 2017. "An Exploration of the Relationships between Student Racial Background and the School Sub-contexts of Office Discipline Referrals: A Critical Race Theory Analysis." *Race, Ethnicity and Education* 21 (3): 390–406.

Ballantine, Jeanne H., Floyd M. Hammack, and Jenny Stuber. 2017. *The Sociology of Education: A Systematic Analysis*. 8th ed. New York: Routledge.

Batruch, Anatolia, Frederique Autin, Fabienne Bataillard, and Fabrizio Butera. 2019. "School Selection and the Social Class Divide: How Tracking Contributes to the Reproduction of Inequalities." *Personality and Social Psychology Bulletin* 45 (3): 477–90.

BenTsvi-Mayer, Shoshanna, Rachel Hertz-Lazarowitz, and Marilyn Safir. 1989. "Teachers' Selections of Boys and Girls as Prominent Pupils." *Sex Roles* 21 (3/4): 231–46.

Berends, Mark. 2015. "Sociology and School Choice: What We Know after Two Decades of Charter Schools." *Annual Review of Sociology* 41:159–80.

Bierman, Karen L., Brenda S. Heinrichs, Janet A. Welsh, Robert L. Nix, and Scott D. Gest. 2017. "Enriching Preschool Classrooms and Home Visits with Evidence-Based Programming: Sustained Benefits for Low-Income Children." *Journal of Child Psychology and Psychiatry* 58 (2): 129–37.

Bowles, Samuel, and Herbert Gintis. 1976. *Schooling in Capitalist America*. New York: Basic Books.

Brookfield, Stephen D., and Stephen Preskill. 2016. *The Discussion Book: 50 Great Ways to Get People Talking*. San Francisco, CA: Jossey-Bass.

Cahalan, Margaret, Laura Perna, Mika Yamashita, Jeremy Wright, and Sureima I. Santillan. 2017. "Indicators of Higher Education Equity in the United States: 2017 Historical Trend Report." Accessed July 25, 2019. http://pellinstitute.org/downloads/publications-Indicators_of_Higher_Education_Equity_in_the_US_2017_Historical_Trend_Report.pdf.

Calarco, Jessica McCrory. 2018. *Negotiating Opportunities: How the Middle Class Secures Advantages in School*. New York: Oxford University Press.

California Newsreel. 2014. "Are We Crazy about Our Kids?" *The Raising of America*. Accessed July 25, 2019. http://www.raisingofamerica.org/are-we-crazy-about-our-kids.

Campi, Ashleigh. 2019. "Preemptive Criminalization: Neoliberalism and the School-to-Prison Pipeline." Social Science Research Council, February 5. Accessed July 26, 2019. https://items.ssrc.org/race-capitalism/preemptive-criminalization-neoliberalism-and-the-school-to-prison-pipeline/.

Center on the Developing Child at Harvard University. 2016. "From Best Practices to Breakthrough Impacts: A Science-Based Approach to Building a More Promising Future for Young Children and Families." Accessed July 25, 2019. https://developingchild.harvard.edu/resources/from-best-practices-to-breakthrough-impacts/.

Cherry, Louise. 1975. "The Preschool Teacher-Child Dyad: Sex Differences in Verbal Interaction." *Child Development* 46 (2): 532–35.

Coleman, James S., Ernest Q. Campbell, Carol J. Hobson, James McPartland, Alexander M. Mood, Frederic D. Weinfeld, and Robert L. York. 1966. *Equality of Educational Opportunity*. Washington, DC: U.S. Department of Health, Education, and Welfare.

Collins, Allan, and Richard Halverson. 2018. *Rethinking Education in the Age of Technology: The Digital Revolution and Schooling in America*. New York: Teachers College Press.

Cozzolini, Elizabeth, Chelsea Smith, and Robert L. Crosnoe. 2018. "Family-Related Disparities in College Enrollment across the Great Recession." *Sociological Perspectives* 61 (5): 689–710.

Davis, Kingsley, and Wilbert Moore. 1945. "Some Principles of Stratification." *American Sociological Review* 10:242–49.

Debnam, Katrina J., Jessika H. Bottiani, and Catherine P. Bradshaw. 2017. "Promoting Culturally Responsive Practice to Reduce Disparities in School Discipline among African American Students." In *Linking Health and Education for African American Students' Success*, 97–124. New York: Routledge.

Diamond, John B., and Amanda E. Lewis. 2019. "Race and Discipline at a Racially Mixed High School: Status, Capital, and the Practice of Organizational Routines." *Urban Education* 54 (6): 831–59.

Dixon-Roman, Ezekiel J. 2017. *Inheriting Possibility: Social Reproduction & Quantification in Education*. Minneapolis: University of Minnesota Press.

Equal Justice Initiative. 2017. "Lynching in America: Confronting the Legacy of Racial Terror. Equal Justice Initiative Reports. Accessed June 5, 2017. http://eji.org/reports/lynching-in-america.

Farrugia, Christine, and Jodi Sanger. 2017. "Gaining an Employment Edge: The Impact of Study Abroad on 21st Century Skills and Career Prospects in the United States." Institute for International Education, Center for Academic

Mobility Research and Impact. Accessed July 25, 2019. https://www.iie.org/Research-and-Insights/Publications/ Gaining-an-Employment-Edge---The-Impact-of-Study-Abroad.

Ferrare, Joseph, and R. Renee Setari. 2017. "Converging on Choice: The Interstate Flow of Foundation Dollars to Charter School Organizations." *Educational Researcher* 47 (1): 34–45.

Gamoran, Adam. 2001. "American Schooling and Educational Inequality: A Forecast for the 21st Century." *Sociology of Education* 74:135–53.

Gamoran, Adam, and Brian P. An. 2016. "Effects of School Segregation and School Resources in a Changing Policy Context." *Educational Evaluation and Policy* 38 (1): 43–64.

Gibbs, Brian. 2018. "The Bending of History Made Straight." In *Re(Imagining Elementary Social Studies: A Controversial Issues Reader*, edited by Sarah B. Shear, Christina M. Tschida, Elizabeth Bellows, Lisa Brown Buchanan, and Elizabeth Saylor, 219–33. Charlotte, NC: Information Age.

Glock, Sabine. 2016. "Stop Talking Out of Turn: The Influence of Students' Gender and Ethnicity on Preservice Teachers' Intervention Strategies for Student Misbehavior." *Teaching and Teacher Education* 56:106–24.

Gorski, P. 2018. *Reaching and Teaching Students in Poverty: Strategies for Erasing the Opportunity Gap*. 2nd ed. New York: Teachers College Press.

Green, Erica L., Matt Apuzzo, and Katie Benner. 2018. "Trump Officials Reverse Obama's Policy on Affirmative Action in Schools." *The New York Times*, July 3. Accessed October 18, 2018. https://www.nytimes.com/2018/07/03/us/politics/trump-affirmative-action-race-schools.html.

Halberstadt, Amy G., Vanessa L. Castro, Qiao Chu, Fantasy T. Lozada, and Calvin M. Sims. 2018. "Preservice Teachers' Racialized Emotion Recognition, Anger Bias, and Hostility Attributions." *Contemporary Educational Psychology* 54:125–38.

Harper, Shannon, and Barbara Reskin. 2005. "Affirmative Action at School and on the Job." *Annual Review of Sociology* 31:357–79.

Harpo Productions. 2011. "Khadija Williams' Story." *Oprah's Lifeclass*, November 11. Accessed February 22, 2016. http://www.oprah.com/oprahs-lifeclass/Khadijah-Williams-Story-Video.

Hertel, Florian R., and Olaf Groh-Samberg. 2014. "Class Mobility across Three Generations in the U.S. and Germany." *Research in Social Stratification and Mobility* 35:35–52.

Hout, Michael. 2018. "Americans' Occupational Status Reflects the Status of Both of Their Parents." *Proceedings of the National Academy of Sciences* 115 (38): 9527–32.

International Bank for Reconstruction and Development/The World Bank. 2016. "Global Monitoring Report 2015/2016: Development Goals in an Era of Demographic Change." Accessed October 18, 2018. http://pubdocs.worldbank.org/ en/503001444058224597/Global-Monitoring-Report-2015. pdf.

Kane, Meissel, Frauke Meyer, Esther S. Yao, and Christine M. Rubie-Davies. 2017. "Subjectivity of Teacher Judgments: Exploring Student Characteristics That Influence Teacher Judgments of Student Ability." *Teaching and Teacher Education* 65:48–60.

Kim, Pilyoung, Gary W. Evans, Edith Chen, Gregory Miller, and Teresa Seeman. 2018. "How Socioeconomic Disadvantages Get under the Skin and into the Brain to Influence Health Development across the Lifespan." In *Handbook of Life Course Health Development*, edited by Neal Halfon, Christopher B. Forrest, Richard M. Lerner, and Elaine M. Faustman, 463–97. Cham, Switzerland: Springer.

King, Sanna, Alicia Rusoja, and Anthony A. Peguera. 2018. "The School-to-Prison Pipeline." In *The Palgrave International Handbook of School Discipline, Surveillance, and Social Control*, edited by Jo Deakin, Emmeline Taylor, and Arron Kupchik, 269–90. New York: Palgrave Macmillan.

Kozol, Jonathan. 1991. *Savage Inequalities*. New York: Crown.

Kozol, Jonathan. 2005. *Shame of a Nation: The Restoration of Apartheid Schooling in America*. New York: Three Rivers.

Kristof, Nicholas. 2016. "So Little to Ask For: A Home." *The New York Times*, April 7. Accessed April 7, 2016. http://www.nytimes.com/2016/04/07/opinion/so-little-to-ask-for-a-home.html?_r=0.

Lareau, Annette. 2003. *Unequal Childhoods: Class, Race, and Family Life*. Berkeley: University of California Press.

Lavy, Sarel, and Jerri L. Nixon. 2017. "Applications, Enrollment, Attendance, and Student Performance in Rebuilt School Facilities: A Case Study." *International Journal of Construction Education and Research* 13 (2): 135–41.

Layton, Lindsey. 2015. "U.S. Schools Are Too Focused on Standardized Tests, Poll Says." *The Washington Post*, August 23. Accessed July 25, 2019. https://www.washingtonpost.com/ local/education/us-schools-are-too-focused-on-standardized-tests-poll-finds/2015/08/22/4a954396-47b3-11e5-8e7d-9c033e6745d8_story.html.

Liu, Hexuan. 2018. "Social and Genetic Pathways in Multigenerational Transmission of Educational Attainment." *American Sociological Review* 83 (2): 278–304.

Liu, Meirong. 2015. "An Ecological Review of Literature on Factors Influencing Working Mothers' Child Care Arrangements." *Journal of Child and Family Studies* 24:161–71.

Livingstone, D. W. (1998) 2018. *The Education-Jobs Gap: Underemployment or Economic Democracy*. New York: Routledge.

Loewen, James. 2005. *Sundown Towns: A Hidden Dimension of American Racism*. New York: The New Press.

Loewen, James. 2018a. *Lies My Teacher Told Me: Everything Your American History Textbook Got Wrong*. 2nd ed. New York: The New Press.

Loewen, James. 2018b. *Teaching What Really Happened: How to Avoid the Tyranny of Textbooks and Get Students Excited about Doing History*. 2nd ed. New York: Teachers College Press.

Loveland, Elaina, and Catherine Morris. 2018. "Study Abroad Matters: Linking Higher Education to the Contemporary Workplace through International Experience." Institute for International Education. Accessed July 25, 2019. https://www.iie.org/Research-and-Insights/Publications.

Madill, Rebecca, Van-Kim Lin, Sarah Friese, and Katherine Paschall. 2018. "Access to Early Care and Education for Disadvantaged Families: Do Levels of Access Reflect States' Child Care Subsidy Policies?" Bethesda, MD: Child Trends.

Mallett, Christopher. 2017. "The School-to-Prison Pipeline: Disproportionate Impact on Vulnerable Children and Adolescents." *Education and Urban Society* 49 (6): 563–92.

Markowitz, Anna J., Daphna Bassok, and Bridget Hamre. 2017. "Leveraging Developmental Insights to Improve Early Childhood Education." *Child Development Perspectives* 12 (2): 87–92.

Marsh, L. Trenton S., and Pedro A. Noguera. 2018. "Beyond Stigma and Stereotypes: An Ethnographic Study on the Effects of School-Imposed Labeling on Black Males in an Urban Charter School." *Urban Review* 50 (3): 447–77.

Mayer, Anysia, Kimberly LeChasseur, and Morgaen Donaldson. 2018. "The Structure of Tracking: Instructional Practices of Teachers Leading Low- and High-Track Classes." *American Journal of Education* 124 (4): 445–77.

Mitchell, Michael, Michael Leachman, and Kathleen Masterson. 2016. "Funding Down, Tuition Up: State Cuts to Higher Education Threaten Quality and Affordability at Public Colleges." Center on Budget and Policy Priorities, August 15. Accessed July 25, 2019. http://www.cbpp.org/research/state-budget-and-tax/funding-down-tuition-up_ftn1.

Mitchell, Michael, Michael Leachman, and Kathleen Masterson. 2017. "A Lost Decade in Higher Education Funding: State Cuts Have Driven Up Tuition and Reduced Quality." Center on Budget and Policy Priorities, August 23. Accessed July 25, 2019. https://www.cbpp.org/research/state-budget-and-tax/a-lost-decade-in-higher-education-funding.

Mitnik, Pablo A., Erin Cumberworth, and David B. Grusky. "Social Mobility in a High-Inequality Regime." *Annals of the American Academy of Political and Social Science* 663 (1): 140–84.

Monaghan, David. 2016. "Does College Enrollment and Bachelor's Completion by Mothers Impact Children's Educational Outcomes?" *Sociology of Education* 90 (1): 3–24.

Moodie-Dyer, Amber. 2011. "A Policy Analysis of Child Care Subsidies: Increasing Quality, Access, and Affordability." *Children & Schools* 33 (1): 37–45.

NAFSA. 2019. "Trends in U.S. Study Abroad." Accessed July 25, 2019. https://www.nafsa.org/Policy_and_Advocacy/Policy_Resources/Policy_Trends_and_Data/Trends_in_U_S__Study_Abroad/.

National Center for Education Statistics. 2018a. "The Nation's Report Card." Accessed July 25, 2019. https://www.nationsreportcard.gov.

National Center for Education Statistics. 2018b. "Preschool and Kindergarten Enrollment." In *The Condition of Education*. Washington, DC: National Center for Education Statistics. Accessed July 25, 2019. https://nces.ed.gov/programs/coe/pdf/coe_cfa.pdf.

National Commission on Excellence in Education. 1983. "A Nation at Risk: The Imperative for Educational Reform." Accessed October 2, 2011. http://www2.ed.gov/pubs/NatAtRisk/index.html.

National Survey of Early Care and Education Project Team. 2016. "Early Care and Education Usage and Households' Out-of-Pocket Costs: Tabulations from the National Survey of Early Care and Education (NSECE)." OPRE Report 2016-09. Washington, DC: Office of Planning, Research and Evaluation, Administration for Children and Families, U.S. Department of Health and Human Services.

Oakes, Jeannie. 1994a. "More Than Misapplied Technology: A Normative and Political Response to Hallinan on Tracking." *Sociology of Education* 67:84–89.

Oakes, Jeannie. 1994b. "One More Thought." *Sociology of Education* 67:91.

Okura, Lynn. 2013. "From Homeless to Harvard (and Beyond): Khadijah Williams Starts New Life in NYC." *The Huffington Post*, December 24. Accessed February 22, 2016. http://www.huffingtonpost.com/2013/12/24/khadijah-williams-homeless-harvard_n_4493490.html.

Orfield, Gary, Jongyeon Ee, Erica Brankenberg, and Genevieve Siegel-Hawley. 2016. *Brown at 62: School Segregation by Race, Poverty, and State*. Los Angeles: Civil Rights Project/Proyecto Derechos Civiles, University of California, Los Angeles.

Organisation for Economic Co-operation and Development. 2010. "Finland: Slow and Steady Reform for Consistently High Results." Accessed July 25, 2019. https://www.oecd.org/pisa/pisaproducts/46581035.pdf.

Palardy, Gregory, Russell Rumberger, and Truman Butler. 2015. "The Effect of High School Socioeconomic, Racial, and Linguistic Segregation on Academic Performance and School Behaviors." *Teachers College Record* 117 (12): 1–52.

Parker, Philip D., John P. Jerrim, Ingrid Schoon, and Herbert W. Marsh. 2016. "A Multination Study of Socioeconomic Inequality in Expectations for Progression to Higher Education: The Role of Between-School Tracking and Ability Stratification." *American Educational Research Journal* 53 (1): 6–32.

Parker, Philip D., Herbert W. Marsh, John P. Jerrim, Jiesi Guo, and Theresa Dicke. 2018. "Inequity and Excellence in Academic Performance: Evidence from 27 Countries." *American Educational Research Journal* 55 (4): 836–58.

Pfeffer, Fabian T. 2018. "Growing Wealth Gaps in Education." *Demography* 55 (3): 1033–68.

Pfeffer, Fabian T., and Florian R. Hertel. 2015. "How Has Educational Expansion Shaped Social Mobility Trends in the United States?" *Social Forces* 94 (1): 143–80.

Podesta, Jennifer. 2014. "Habitus and the Accomplishment of Natural Growth: Maternal Parenting Practices and the Achievement Of 'School-Readiness.'" *Australasian Journal of Early Childhood* 39 (4): Online Annex.

Porter, Michael E., and Jan W. Rivkin. 2012. "The Looming Challenge to U.S. Competitiveness." *Harvard Business Review*, March. Accessed July 25, 2019. https://hbr.org/2012/03/the-looming-challenge-to-us-competitiveness.

Rauscher, Emily. 2015. "Educational Expansion and Occupational Change: US Compulsory Schooling Laws and the Occupational Structure 1850–1930." *Social Forces* 93 (4): 1397–1422.

Ravitch, Diane. 2010. *The Death and Life of the Great American School System: How Testing and Choice Are Undermining Education*. Philadelphia: Basic Books.

Ravitch, Diane. 2014. *Reign of Error: The Hoax of the Privatization Movement and the Danger to America's Public Schools*. New York: Vintage.

Ravitch, Diane. 2016. *The Death and Life of the Great American School System: How Testing and Choice Are Undermining Education*. 3rd ed. Philadelphia: Basic Books.

Rocque, Michael, and Quincy Snellings. 2018. "The New Disciplinology: Research, Theory, and Remaining Puzzles on the School-to-Prison Pipeline." *Journal of Criminal Justice* 59 (November-December): 3–12.

Romeo, Rachel R., Julia A. Leonard, Sydney T. Robinson, Martin R. West, Allyson P. Mackey, Meredith L. Rowe, and John D. E, Gabrieli. 2018. "Beyond the 30-Million-Word Gap: Children's Conversational Exposure Is Associated with Language-Related Brain Function." *Psychological Science* 29 (5): 700–10.

Rosling, Hans. 2007. "New Insights on Poverty." TED: Ideas Worth Spreading. Accessed October 13, 2015. https://www.ted.com/talks/hans_rosling_reveals_new_insights_on_poverty?language=en.

Rudd, Tom. 2014. *Racial Disproportionality in School Discipline: Implicit Bias Is Heavily Implicated*. Columbus: Kirwan Institute for the Study of Race and Ethnicity, The Ohio State University.

Ryan, Colin, Sam Procopio, and Brian Taberski. 2017. "On Track for Success: Detracking Classes within a Middle School as an Exercise of Organizational Culture and Change." ProQuest Dissertations Publishing.

Sadovnik, Alan R. 2007. "Theory and Research in the Sociology of Education." In *Sociology of Education: A Critical Reader*, 2nd ed., edited by Alan R. Sadovnik, 3–21. New York: Routledge.

Seltzer, Rick. 2018. "'Anemic' State Funding Growth." Inside Higher Education, January 22. Accessed July 26, 2019. https://

www.insidehighered.com/news/2018/01/22/state-support-higher-ed-grows-16-percent-2018.

Stoltzfus, Emilie. 2000. *Child Care: The Federal Role during World War II*. Washington, DC: U.S. Congressional Research Service.

Strauss, Valerie. 2015. "No Child Left Behind: What Standardized Test Scores Reveal about Its Legacy." *The Washington Post*, March 10. Accessed August 20, 2016. https://www.washingtonpost.com/news/answer-sheet/wp/2015/03/10/no-child-left-behind-what-standardized-test-scores-reveal-about-its-legacy.

Suh, Yonghee, Sohyun An, and Danielle Forest. 2015. "Immigration, Imagined Communities, and Collective Memories of Asian American Experiences: A Content Analysis of Asian American Experiences in Virginia U.S. History Textbooks." *Journal of Social Studies Research* 39 (1): 39–51.

Supovitz, Jonathan. 2016. "Is High-Stakes Testing Working?" University of Pennsylvania Graduate School of Education. Accessed July 25, 2019. https://www.gse.upenn.edu/review/feature/supovitz.

Temple, Judy A., and Arthur J. Reynolds. 2007. "Benefits and Costs of Investments in Preschool Education: Evidence from the Child-Parent Centers and Related Programs." *Economics of Education Review* 26:126–44.

Tran, Andrew Ba. 2014. "Map: The Average Cost for Child Care by State." The Boston Globe, July 2. Accessed July 25, 2019. https://www.bostonglobe.com/2014/07/02/map-the-average-cost-for-child-care-state/LN65rSHXKNjr4eypyxT0WM/story.html.

Turner, Corey, Reema Khrais, Tim Lloyd, Alexandra Olgin, Laura Isensee, Beckey Vevea, and Ben Carson. 2016. "Why America's Schools Have a Money Problem." *NPR*, April 18. Accessed September 14, 2016. http://www.npr.org/2016/04/18/474256366/why-americas-schools-have-a-money-problem.

UNESCO. 2015. "Education for All 2000–2015: Achievements and Challenges; EFA Global Monitoring Report, 2015." Paris: UNESCO.

U.S. Census Bureau. 2015a. "Educational Attainment of the Population 18 Years and Over, by Age, Sex, Race, and Hispanic Origin." American Community Survey 2014, 5 Year Estimates, Tables 01-1 through 01-6. Accessed July 25, 2019. http://www.census.gov.

U.S. Census Bureau. 2015b. "Table 8: Per Pupil Amounts for Current Spending of Public Elementary-Secondary School Systems by State: Fiscal Year 2013." Public Elementary-Secondary Education Finance Data. Accessed July 25, 2019. https://www.census.gov/content/dam/Census/library/publications/2015/econ/g13-aspef.pdf.

U.S. Census Bureau. 2019. "Table 1. Educational Attainment of the Population 18 Years and Over, by Age, Sex, Race, and Hispanic Origin: 2018." Accessed July 26, 2019. https://www.census.gov/data/tables/2018/demo/education-attainment/cps-detailed-tables.html.

U.S. Department of Labor. 2019. "Median Weekly Earnings by Sex and Educational Attainment: Full-Time Workers, Ages 25 and Older." Accessed July 26, 2019. https://www.dol.gov/wb/stats/earnings.htm.

U.S. Department of Veterans Affairs. 2013. "History and Timeline. Veterans Benefits Administration Education and Training." Accessed March 27, 2016. http://www.benefits.va.gov/gibill/history.asp.

U.S. Government Accountability Office. 2016. "Better Use of Information Could Help Agencies Identify Disparities and Address Racial Discrimination." Accessed August 18, 2016. http://www.gao.gov/assets/680/676744.pdf.

U.S. House of Representatives. 2001. "H.R. 1—No Child Left Behind Act of 2001." Accessed March 15, 2016. https://www.gpo.gov/fdsys/pkg/CRPT-107hrpt334/pdf/CRPT-107hrpt334.pdf.

U.S. House of Representatives. 2015. "ESEA Conference Report Summary: S. 1177, the Every Student Succeeds Act." Accessed March 15, 2016. http://edworkforce.house.gov/uploadedfiles/esea_conference_report_summary.pdf.

U.S. Immigration and Customs Enforcement. 2016. "Student and Exchange Visitor Program: ICE Releases Quarterly International Student Data." Accessed September 10, 2017. https://www.ice.gov/news/releases/ice-releases-quarterly-international-student-data.

van de Werfhorst, H. G. 2018. "Early Tracking and Socioeconomic Inequality in Academic Achievement: Studying Reforms in Nine Countries." *Research in Social Stratification and Mobility* 58:22–32.

The White House. 2015. "Fact Sheet: Congress Acts to Fix No Child Left Behind." Briefing Room Statements and Releases. Accessed March 15, 2016. https://www.whitehouse.gov/the-press-office/2015/12/03/fact-sheet-congress-acts-fix-no-child-left-behind.

Whitehurst, Grover J. "Russ." 2017. "Why the Federal Government Should Subsidize Childcare and How to Pay for It." The Brookings Institution, March 9. Accessed July 26, 2019. https://www.brookings.edu/research/why-the-federal-government-should-subsidize-childcare-and-how-to-pay-for-it/.

Wilson, William Julius. 1999. *Bridge over the Racial Divide*. Berkeley: University of California Press.

Witteveen, Dirk, and Paul Attewell. 2017. "Family Background and Earnings Inequality among College Graduates." *Social Forces* 95 (4): 1539–76.

Worthy, Jo. 2010. "Only the Names Have Been Changed: Ability Grouping Revisited." *Urban Review* 42:271–95.

Zinn, Howard. 2015. *A People's History of the United States*. New York: Harper Perennial Modern Classics.

CHAPTER 13

American Psychiatric Association. 2018. "What is Mental Illness?" Accessed September 27, 2018. https://www.psychiatry.org/patients-families/what-is-mental-illness.

Backman, Maurie. 2017. "This is the No. 1 Reason Americans File for Bankruptcy." *USA Today*, May 5. Accessed September 23, 2018. https://www.usatoday.com/story/money/personalfinance/2017/05/05/this-is-the-no-1-reason-americans-file-for-bankruptcy/101148136/.

Betran, A. P., M. R. Torloni, J. J. Zhang, and A. M. Gulmezoglu, for the WHO Working Group on Caesarean Section. 2016. "WHO Statement on Caesarean Section Rates." *BJOG* 123 (5): 667–70.

Bury, Michael. 1982. "Chronic Illness as Biographical Disruption." *Sociology of Health and Illness* 4:167–82.

Centers for Disease Control and Prevention. 2018a. "ADHD throughout the Years." Accessed October 1, 2018. https://www.cdc.gov/ncbddd/adhd/timeline.html.

Centers for Disease Control and Prevention. 2018b. "National Health Interview Survey." Accessed October 1, 2018. https://www.cdc.gov/nchs/nhis/index.htm.

Collins, Sarah R., Munira Z. Gunja, Michelle M. Doty, and Herman K. Bhupal. 2018. "First Look at Health Insurance

Coverage in 2018 Finds ACA Gains Beginning to Reverse." New York: The Commonwealth Fund.

Collyer, Fran. 2018. "Envisaging the Healthcare Sector as a Field: Moving from Talcott Parsons to Pierre Bourdieu." *Social Theory & Health* 16 (2): 111–36.

Conrad, Peter. 2007. *The Medicalization of Society: On the Transformation of Human Conditions into Treatable Disease.* Baltimore, MD: Johns Hopkins University Press.

Eaton, William, and Carles Muntaner. 2017. "Socioeconomic Stratification and Mental Disorder." In *A Handbook for the Study of Mental Health: Social Contexts, Theories, and Systems,* 3rd ed., edited by T. L. Scheid and E. R. Wright, 281–304. New York: Cambridge University Press.

Elo, Irma T., Zoua Vang, and Jennifer F. Culhane. 2014 "Variation in Birth Outcomes by Mother's Country of Birth among Non-Hispanic Black Women in the United States." *Maternal and Child Health Journal* 18 (10): 2371–81.

Gonzalez-Mule, Erik, and Bethany Cockburn. 2017. "Worked to Death: The Relationships of Job Demands and Job Control with Mortality." *Personnel Psychology* 70:73–113.

Kaiser Family Foundation. 2018. "Health Insurance Coverage of the Total Population." San Francisco: Accessed September 23, 2018. https://www.kff.org/other/state-indicator/total-population/?currentTimeframe=0&selectedRows=%7B%22wrapups%22:%7B%22united-states%22:%7B%7D%7D%7D&sortModel=%7B%22colId%22:%22Location%22,%22sort%22:%22asc%22%7D.

Kamal, Rabah, and Cynthia Cox. 2018. "How Do Healthcare Prices and Use in the U.S. Compare to Other Countries?" Peterson-Kaiser Health System Tracker, May 8. Accessed October 1, 2018. https://www.healthsystemtracker.org/chart-collection/how-do-healthcare-prices-and-use-in-the-u-s-compare-to-other-countries/item-start.

Kirch, Darrell G. 2012. "A Word from the President: MCAT 2015: An Open Letter to Pre-med Students." *AAMC Reporter,* March. Accessed July 26, 2019. https://www.aamc.org/about/leadership/kirch-word-from-president/276772/word.html.

Laughland, Oliver, and Tom Silverstone. 2017. "Liquid Genocide: Alcohol Destroyed Pine Ridge Reservation—Then They Fought Back." *The Guardian,* September 29. Accessed October 1, 2018. https://www.theguardian.com/society/2017/sep/29/pine-ridge-indian-reservation-south-dakota.

Leston, Jessica. 2018. "Proposed Budget for Indian Health Services Won't Treat Native American Patients Equally." *The Hill,* March 13. Accessed October 1, 2018. https://thehill.com/opinion/healthcare/378658-proposed-budget-for-indian-health-services-wont-treat-native-american.

Link, Bruce, and Jo Phelan. 1995. "Social Conditions as Fundamental Causes of Disease." *Journal of Health and Social Behavior* 1:80–94.

Link, Bruce G., Ezra S. Susser, Pam Factor-Litvak, Dana March, Katrina L. Kezios, Gina S. Lovasi, Andrew G. Rundle, Shakira F. Suglia, Kim M. Fader, Howard F. Andrews, Eileen Johnson, Piera M. Cirillo, and Barbara A. Cohn. 2017. "Disparities in Self-Rated Health across Generations and through the Life Course." *Social Science & Medicine* 174:17–25.

Manandhar, Mary, Sarah Hawkes, Kent Buse, Elias Nosrati, and Veronica Magar. 2018. "Gender, Health and the 2030 Agenda for Sustainable Development." *Bulletin of the World Health Organization* 96 (9): 644–53.

Martin, Joyce, Brady Hamilton, Michelle Osterman, Anne Driscoll, and Patrick Drake. 2018. "Births: Final Data for 2016." *National Vital Statistics Reports* 67 (1). National Center for Health Statistics. Accessed September 27, 2018. https://www.cdc.gov/nchs/data/hus/hus16.pdf.

National Center for Health Statistics. 2017. "Health, United States, 2016: With Chartbook on Long-Term Trends in Health." National Center for Health Statistics. Accessed July 26, 2019. https://www.cdc.gov/nchs/data/hus/hus16.pdf.

National Congress of American Indians. 2018. "Fiscal Year 2018 Indian Country Budget Request: Investing in Indian Country for a Stronger America." Accessed October 1, 2018. http://www.ncai.org/1_FY2018-NCAI-Budget-Request2-Exec_Summary.pdf.

Novoa, Cristina, and Jamila Taylor. 2018 "Exploring African Americans' High Maternal and Infant Death Rates." Center for American Progress, February 1. Accessed October 1, 2018. https://www.americanprogress.org/issues/early-childhood/reports/2018/02/01/445576/exploring-african-americans-high-maternal-infant-death-rates/.

Organisation for Economic Co-operation and Development. 2018a. "Infant Mortality Rates." Accessed October 1, 2018. https://www.oecd-ilibrary.org/social-issues-migration-health/infant-mortality-rates/indicator/english_83dea506-en.

Organisation for Economic Co-operation and Development. 2018b. "Life Expectancy at Birth." Accessed October 1, 2018. https://www.oecd-ilibrary.org/social-issues-migration-health/life-expectancy-at-birth/indicator/english_27e0fc9d-en.

Parekh, Natasha, and William Shrank. 2018. "Danger and Opportunities of Direct-to-Consumer Advertising." *Journal of General Internal Medicine* 33:586–87.

Parsons, Talcott. 1951. *The Social System.* New York: Free Press.

Riosmena, Fernando, Randall Kuhn, and Warren C. Jochem, "Explaining the Immigrant Health Advantage: Self-Selection and Protection in Health-Related Factors among Five Major National-Origin Immigrant Groups in the United States." *Demography* 54 (1): 175–200.

Segre, Liz. 2018. "Latisse for Longer Eyelashes: Is It Safe for Your Eyes?" All About Vision, August 20. Accessed October 1, 2018. https://www.allaboutvision.com/buysmart/latisse.htm.

Warshaw, Robin. 2017. "Raising the Profile of Social Science in Medical Education." AAMCNews, January 31. Accessed October 3, 2018. https://news.aamc.org/medical-education/article/social-science-medical-education/.

CHAPTER 14

Altemeyer, Bob, and Bruce Hunsberger. 2004. "A Revised Religious Fundamentalism Scale: The Short and Sweet of It." *International Journal for the Psychology of Religion* 14 (1): 47–54.

Berger, Peter. 1992. *A Far Glory: The Quest for Faith in the Age of Credulity.* New York: Free Press.

Berger, Peter. 2014. *The Many Altars of Modernity: Toward a Paradigm for Religion in a Pluralist Age.* Boston: Aldine de Gruyter.

Blumer, Herbert. 1969. *Symbolic Interaction: Perspective and Method.* Englewood Cliffs, NJ: Prentice Hall.

Byng, Michelle. 2017. "Transnationalism among Second-Generation Muslim Americans: Being and Belonging in their Transnational Social Field." *Social Sciences* 6 (4): 141–50.

Chaves, Mark. 2017. *American Religion: Contemporary Trends.* 2nd ed. Princeton, NJ: Princeton University Press.

Djupe, Paul A., Jacob R. Neiheisel, and Anand E. Sokhey. 2018. "Reconsidering the Role of Politics in Leaving Religion: The Importance of Affiliation." *American Journal of Political Science* 62 (1): 161–75.

Durkheim, Émile. (1897) 1951. *Suicide.* New York: Free Press.

Durkheim, Émile. (1912) 1995. *The Elementary Forms of Religious Life*. Translated by K. E. Fields. New York: Free Press.

Emerson, Michael O., and David Hartman. 2006. "The Rise of Religious Fundamentalism." *Annual Review of Sociology* 32:127–44.

Hackett, Conrad, and Timothy Huynh. 2015. "What Is Each Country's Second-Largest Religious Group?" Pew Research Center, June 22. Accessed July 27, 2019. https://www.pewresearch.org/fact-tank/2015/06/22/what-is-each-countrys-second-largest-religious-group/.

Jenkins, Willis, and Christopher Key Chapple. 2011. "Religion and Environment." *Annual Review of Environment and Resources* 36:441–63.

Jones, Jeffrey M. 2019. "Americans Continue to Embrace Political Independence." Gallup, January 7. Accessed July 27, 2019. https://news.gallup.com/poll/245801/americans-continue-embrace-political-independence.aspx.

Jones, Robert P., and Daniel Cox. 2017. "America's Changing Religious Identity: Findings from the 2016 American Values Atlas." Washington, DC: Public Religion Research Institute.

Kurien, Prema. 2014. "The Impact of International Migration on Home Churches: The Mar Thoma Syrian Christian Church in India." *Journal for the Scientific Study of Religion* 53 (1): 109–29.

Marx, Karl. (1843) 1970. "A Contribution to the Critique of Hegel's Philosophy of Right." In *Marx/Engels Collected Works*, Vol. 3, 3–129. New York: International Publishers.

Masci, David, and Michael Lipka. 2015. "Where Christian Churches, Other Religions Stand on Gay Marriage." Pew Research Center, December 21. Accessed July 27, 2019. https://www.pewresearch.org/fact-tank/2015/12/21/where-christian-churches-stand-on-gay-marriage/.

Murphy, Caryle. 2015. "Lesbian, Gay and Bisexual Americans Differ from General Public in Their Religious Affiliations." Pew Research Center, May 16. Accessed July 27, 2019. https://www.pewresearch.org/fact-tank/2015/05/26/lesbian-gay-and-bisexual-americans-differ-from-general-public-in-their-religious-affiliations/.

Nosich, Gerald M. 2009. *Learning to Think Things Through: A Guide to Critical Thinking across the Curriculum*. 3rd ed. Upper Saddle River, NJ: Pearson.

Pew Research Center. 2012. "The Global Religious Landscape." Accessed April 10, 2016. http://www.pewforum.org/global-religious-landscape.aspx.

Pew Research Center. 2013. "The Religious Affiliation of U.S. Immigrants: Majority Christian, Rising Share of Other Faiths." Accessed July 27, 2019. https://www.pewforum.org/2013/05/17/the-religious-affiliation-of-us-immigrants/.

Pew Research Center. 2015a[b]. "America's Changing Religious Landscape." Accessed April 10, 2016. http://www.pewforum.org/files/2015/05/RLS-08-26-full-report.pdf.

Pew Research Center. 2015b[a]. "The Future of World Religions: Population Growth Projections, 2010–2050." Accessed April 20, 2016. http://www.pewforum.org/2015/04/02/religious-projections-2010-2050.

Pew Research Center. 2016. "The Gender Gap in Religion around the World." Accessed September 10, 2017. http://www.pewforum.org/2016/03/22/the-gender-gap-in-religion-around-the-world.

Pew Research Center. 2018a[b]. "Eastern and Western Europeans Differ on Importance of Religion, Views of Minorities, and Key Social Issues." Accessed January 20, 2019. http://www.pewforum.org/2018/10/29/eastern-and-western-europeans-differ-on-importance-of-religion-views-of-minorities-and-key-social-issues/.

Pew Research Center. 2018b[a]. "The Religious Typology." Accessed December 28, 2018. http://www.pewforum.org/2018/08/29/the-religious-typology/.

Pew Research Center. 2019. "Religious Landscape Study: Immigrants: Religious Composition of Immigrants." Accessed May 5, 2019. https://www.pewforum.org/religious-landscape-study/immigrant-status/immigrants/.

Roberts, Keith A., and David Yamane. 2016. *Religion in Sociological Perspective*. 6th ed. Thousand Oaks, CA: Sage.

SAGE Publishing. 2014. "U.S. Religion Census: Religious Congregations and Membership Study (RCMS): Islamic Adherence Rate per 1,000 People (County)." SAGE stats. Accessed July 27, 2019. https://data.sagepub.com/sagestats/document.php?id=4376.

Smith, Christian, Michael Emerson, Sally Gallagher, Paul Kennedy, and David Sikkink. 1998. *American Evangelicalism: Embattled and Thriving*. Chicago: Chicago University Press.

Taniguchi, Hiromi, and Leonard D. Thomas. 2011. "The Influences of Religious Attitudes on Volunteering." *Voluntas* 22:335–55.

Vatican Press Office. 2018. "Message of His Holiness Pope Francis for the Celebration of the 52nd World Day of Peace." Accessed January 2, 2019. http://w2.vatican.va/content/francesco/en/messages/peace/documents/papa-francesco_20181408_messaggio-52giornatamondiale-pace2019.html.

Weber, Max. (1904) 1958. *The Protestant Ethic and the Spirit of Capitalism*. New York: Scribner's.

Zwissler, Laurel. 2012. "Feminism and Religion: Intersections between Western Activism, Theology and Theory." *Religion Compass* 6 (7): 354–68.

CHAPTER 15

Bartley, Tim. 2007. "Institutional Emergence in an Era of Globalization: The Rise of Transnational Private Regulation of Labor and Environmental Conditions." *American Journal of Sociology* 113 (2): 297–351.

Bell, Michael Mayerfeld. 1994. *Childerley: Nature and Mortality in a Country Village*. Chicago: University of Chicago Press.

Bell, Michael Mayerfeld, and Loka Ashwood. 2015. *An Invitation to Environmental Sociology*. Thousand Oaks, CA: Sage.

Borunda, Alejandra. 2019. "The Last Five Years Were the Hottest Ever Recorded." *National Geographic*, February 6. Accessed February 10, 2019. https://www.nationalgeographic.com/environment/2019/02/2018-fourth-warmest-year-ever-noaa-nasa-reports/.

Bullard, Robert D. 1990. *Dumping in Dixie: Race, Class, and Environmental Quality*. Vol. 3. Boulder, CO: Westview.

Bullard, Robert D. 1993. *Confronting Environmental Racism: Voices from the Grassroots*. New York: South End.

Catton, Willian R., Jr., and Riley E. Dunlap. 1978. "Environmental Sociology: A New Paradigm." *American Sociologist* 13:41–49.

Cronon, William. 1996. "The Trouble with Wilderness: Or, Getting Back to the Wrong Nature." *Environmental History* 1 (1): 7–28.

Daly, Herman E. 1991. *Steady-State Economics: With New Essays*. New York: Island.

Delmas, Magali A., and Vanessa Cuerel Burbano. 2011. "The Drivers of Greenwashing." *California Management Review* 54 (1): 64–87.

Ehrlich, Paul R. 1968. *The Population Bomb*. Cutchogue, NY: Buccaneer.

Flint Water Advisory Task Force. 2016. "Flint Water Advisory Task Force Final Report." Accessed October 8, 2016. http://mediad.publicbroadcasting.net/p/michigan/files/201603/taskforce_report.pdf?_ga=1.147700144.609033213.1458749402.

Fonger, Ron. 2019. "Newest Testing Shows Lead in Flint Water at Lowest Level Since Water Crisis Started." Mlive.com, January 16. Accessed February 10, 2019. https://www.mlive.com/news/flint/2019/01/newest-testing-shows-lead-in-flint-water-at-lowest-level-since-water-crisis-started.html.

Gauchat, Gordon. 2012. "Politicization of Science in the Public Sphere: A Study of Public Trust in the United States, 1974 to 2010." *American Sociological Review* 77 (2): 167–87.

Hatanaka, Maki, Carmen Bain, and Lawrence Busch. 2005. "Third-Party Certification in the Global Agrifood System." *Food Policy* 30 (3): 354–69.

Hohn, Donovan. 2016. "Flint's Water Crisis and the 'Troublemaker' Scientist." *The New York Times*, August 16. Accessed October 8, 2018. http://www.nytimes.com/2016/08/21/magazine/flints-water-crisis-and-the-troublemaker-scientist.html.

Jerolmack, Colin. 2007. "Animal Practices, Ethnicity, and Community: The Turkish Pigeon Handlers of Berlin." *American Sociological Review* 72 (6): 874–94.

Jerolmack, Colin, and Iddo Tavory. 2014. "Molds and Totems Nonhumans and the Constitution of the Social Self." *Sociological Theory* 32 (1): 64–77.

Lawal, Shola. 2019. "Nigeria Has Become an e-Waste Dumpsite for Europe, US and Asia." TRT World, February 15. Accessed March 8, 2019. https://www.trtworld.com/magazine/nigeria-has-become-an-e-waste-dumpsite-for-europe-us-and-asia-24197.

Leiserowitz, Anthony, Edward Maibach, Connie Roser-Renouf, Seth Rosenthal, Matthew Cutler, and John Kotcher. 2018. "Politics & Global Warming, March 2018." Yale Program on Climate Change Communication. Accessed July 28, 2019. https://climatecommunication.yale.edu/publications/politics-global-warming-march-2018/2/.

Macias, Thomas. 2016. "Environmental Risk Perception among Race and Ethnic Groups in the United States." *Ethnicities* 16 (1): 111–29.

Magdoff, Fred, and John Bellamy Foster. 2011. *What Every Environmentalist Needs to Know about Capitalism: A Citizen's Guide to Capitalism and the Environment.* New York: NYU Press.

Malthus, T. R. (1798) 2007. *An Essay on the Principle of Population.* Mineola, NY: Dover.

Maniates, Micahel F. 2001. "Individualization: Plant a Tree, Buy a Bike, Save the World?" *Global Environmental Politics* 1 (3): 31–52.

Martinez-Alier, Joan. 2003. *The Environmentalism of the Poor: A Study of Ecological Conflicts and Valuation.* Cheltenham, UK: Edward Elgar.

McCright, Aaron M. 2010. "The Effects of Gender on Climate Change Knowledge and Concern in the American Public." *Population and Environment* 32 (1): 66–87.

McGurty, Eileen Maura. 2000. "Warren County, NC, and the Emergence of the Environmental Justice Movement: Unlikely Coalitions and Shared Meanings in Local Collective Action." *Society & Natural Resources* 13 (4): 373–87.

Meadows, Donella H., Dennis L. Meadows, Jorgen Randers, and William W. Behrens III. 1972. "The Limits to Growth: A Report for the Club of Rome's Project on the Predicament of Mankind." Accessed July 28, 2019. https://www.clubofrome.org/report/the-limits-to-growth.

Mohai, Paul, David Pellow, and J. Timmons Roberts. 2009. "Environmental Justice." *Annual Review of Environment and Resources* 34:405–30.

Mol, Arthur P. J., Gert Spaargaren, and David A. Sonnenfeld. 2014. "Ecological Modernisation Theory: Taking Stock, Moving Forward." In *Routledge International Handbook on Social and Environmental Change*, edited by Stewart Lockie, David A. Sonnenfeld, and Dana R. Fisher, 15–30. New York: Routledge.

National Centers for Environmental Information. 2016. "Global Climate Report—December 2016." Accessed January 28, 2017. https://www.ncdc.noaa.gov/sotc/global/201612.

Oreskes, Naomi, and Eric M. Conway. 2010. *Merchants of Doubt: How a Handful of Scientists Obscured the Truth on Issues from Tobacco Smoke to Global Warming.* New York: Bloomsbury.

Pellow, David N. 2000. "Environmental Inequality Formation: Toward a Theory of Environmental Injustice." *American Behavioral Scientist* 43 (4): 581–601.

Pellow, David N. 2007. *Resisting Global Toxics: Transnational Movements for Environmental Justice.* Cambridge, MA: MIT Press.

Pew Research Center. 2017. "Mixed Messages about Public Trust in Science." Accessed February 10, 2019. http://www.pewresearch.org/science/2017/12/08/mixed-messages-about-public-trust-in-science/.

Ringquist, Evan J. 2005. "Assessing Evidence of Environmental Inequities: A Meta-analysis." *Journal of Policy Analysis and Management* 24 (2): 223–47.

Roberts, J. Timmons, and Bradley Parks. 2006. *A Climate of Injustice: Global Inequality, North-South Politics, and Climate Policy.* Cambridge: MIT Press.

Roberts, J. Timmons, and Bradley Parks. 2009. "Ecologically Unequal Exchange, Ecological Debt, and Climate Justice: The History and Implications of Three Related Ideas for a New Social Movement." *International Journal of Comparative Sociology* 50 (3–4): 385–409.

Scheer, Roddy, and Doug Moss. 2019. "How Can Consumers Find Out if a Corporation Is 'Greenwashing' Environmentally Unsavory Practices?" *Scientific American.* Accessed February 9, 2019. https://www.scientificamerican.com/article/greenwashing/.

Schnaiberg, Allan. 1980. *Environment: From Surplus to Scarcity.* Oxford, UK: Oxford University Press.

Schnaiberg, Allan, and Kenneth A. Gould. 2000. *Environment and Society: The Enduring Conflict.* Caldwell, NJ: Blackburn.

Schor, Juliet B. 2011. *True Wealth: How and Why Millions of Americans Are Creating a Time-Rich, Ecologically Light, Small-Scale, High-Satisfaction Economy.* New York: Penguin.

Sen, Amartya. 1981. *Poverty and Famines: An Essay on Entitlement and Deprivation.* Oxford, UK: Oxford University Press.

Shapiro, Judith. 2001. *Mao's War against Nature: Politics and the Environment in Revolutionary China.* Cambridge, UK: Cambridge University Press.

Spaargaren, Gert, and Arthur P. Mol. 1992. "Sociology, Environment, and Modernity: Ecological Modernization as a Theory of Social Change." *Society & Natural Resources* 5 (4): 323–44.

Szasz, Andrew. 2007. *Shopping Our Way to Safety: How We Changed from Protecting the Environment to Protecting Ourselves.* Minneapolis: University of Minnesota Press.

Taylor, Dorceta E. 2000. "The Rise of the Environmental Justice Paradigm: Injustice Framing and The Social Construction of Environmental Discourses." *American Behavioral Scientist* 43 (4): 508–80.

Taylor, Dorceta E. 2015. "Gender and Racial Diversity in Environmental Organizations: Uneven Accomplishments and Cause for Concern." *Environmental Justice* 8 (5): 165–80.

Toomey, Diane. 2018. "How Green Groups Became So White and What to Do about It." YaleEnvironment360, June 21.

Accessed February 9, 2019. https://e360.yale.edu/features/how-green-groups-became-so-white-and-what-to-do-about-it.

UNEP Global Environment Alert Service. 2011. "One Small Planet, Seven Billion People by Year's End and 10.1 Billion by Century's End." Accessed July 28, 2019. https://na.unep.net/geas/archive/pdfs/Jun_11_Population.pdf.

Union of Concerned Scientists. 2018. "The 2018 Climate Accountability Scorecard." Accessed February 10, 2019. https://www.ucsusa.org/sites/default/files/attach/2018/10/gw-accountability-scorecard18-report.pdf.

United Church of Christ, Commission for Racial Justice. 1987. "Toxic Wastes and Race in the United States: A National Report on the Racial and Socio-economic Characteristics of Communities with Hazardous Waste Sites." New York: United Church of Christ, Commission for Racial Justice.

United Nations World Commission on Environment and Development. 1987. "Chapter 2: Towards Sustainable Development." In "Our Common Future." Accessed January 28, 2017. http://www.un-documents.net/ocf-02.htmI.

U.S. Global Change Research Program. 2018. "Fourth National Climate Assessment, Volume II: Impacts, Risks, and Adaptation in the United States." Accessed July 28, 2019. https://nca2018.globalchange.gov/downloads/NCA4_2018_FullReport.pdf.

Veblen, Thorstein. 1899. *The Theory of the Leisure Class*. New York: Viking Penguin.

Wackernagel, Mathis, and William Rees. 1998. "Our Ecological Footprint: Reducing Human Impact on the Earth (No. 9)." Gabriola Island, Canada: New Society Publishers.

Warlenius, Rikard. 2018. "Decolonizing the Atmosphere: The Climate Justice Movement on Climate Debt." *Journal of Environment & Development* 27 (2): 151–55.

Weller, Robert P. 2006. *Discovering Nature: Globalization and Environmental Culture in China and Taiwan*. Cambridge, UK: Cambridge University Press.

CHAPTER 16

Barnett, Bernice McNair. 1993. "Invisible Southern Black Women Leaders in the Civil Rights Movement: The Triple Constraints of Gender, Race, and Class." *Gender & Society* 7 (2): 162–82.

Benford, Robert D., and Scott A. Hunt. 1992. "Dramaturgy and Social Movements: The Social Construction and Communication of Power." *Sociological Inquiry* 62 (1): 36–55.

Bloom, Joshua, and Waldo E. Martin Jr. 2013. *Black against Empire: The History and Politics of the Black Panther Party*. Berkeley: University of California Press.

Blow, Charles M. 2012. "The Curious Case of Trayvon Martin." *The New York Times*, March 16.

Carter, David. 2005. *Stonewall: The Riots That Sparked the Gay Revolution*. New York: Macmillan.

Clark, Rosemary. 2014. "NotBuyingIt: Hashtag Feminists Expand the Commercial Media Conversation." *Feminist Media Studies* 14 (6): 1108–10.

Cress, Daniel M., and David A. Snow. 1996. "Mobilization at the Margins: Resources, Benefactors, and the Viability of Homeless Social Movement Organizations." *American Sociological Review* 61 (6): 1089–1109.

Dewey, Caitlin. 2015. "More Than 26 Million People Have Changed Their Facebook Picture to a Rainbow Flag. Here's Why That Matters." *The Washington Post*, June 29.

Faludi, Susan. 1994. *Backlash: The Undeclared War against American Women*. New York: Crown/Archetype.

Fetner, Tina. 2016. "U.S. Attitudes toward Lesbian and Gay People Are Better Than Ever." *Contexts* 15 (2): 20–27.

Fingerhut, Hannah. 2016. "Support Steady for Same-Sex Marriage and Acceptance of Homosexuality." Pew Research Center, May 12. Accessed July 30, 2019. https://www.pewresearch.org/fact-tank/2016/05/12/support-steady-for-same-sex-marriage-and-acceptance-of-homosexuality/.

Fox-Genovese, Elizabeth. 1994. "Difference, Diversity, and Divisions in an Agenda for the Women's Movement." In *Color, Class & Country: Experiences of Gender*, edited by G. Young and B. Dickerson. London: Zed.

Friedan, Betty. 1963. *The Feminine Mystique*. New York: W. W. Norton.

Greenwood, Davydd J., and Morten Levin. 2006. *Introduction to Action Research: Social Research for Social Change*. Thousand Oaks, CA: Sage.

hooks, bell. 1984. *Feminist Theory from Margin to Center*. Boston: South End.

Levy, Brian L., and Denise L. Levy. 2017. "When Love Meets Hate: The Relationship between State Policies on Gay and Lesbian Rights and Hate Crime Incidence." *Social Science Research* 61:142–59.

McAdam, Doug. 1990. *Freedom Summer*. Oxford, UK: Oxford University Press.

McCarthy, John D., and Mayer N. Zald. 1977. "Resource Mobilization and Social Movements: A Partial Theory." *American Journal of Sociology* 82 (6): 1212–41.

Morgan, Robin. 1984. *Sisterhood Is Global: The International Women's Movement Anthology*. New York: Feminist Press at City University of New York.

Morris, Aldon. 1981. "Black Southern Student Sit-In Movement: An Analysis of Internal Organization." *American Sociological Review* 46 (6): 744–67.

Obergefell v. Hodges, 576 U.S. ___ (2015).

Oliver, Pam, and Hank Johnston. 2000. "What a Good Idea: Frames and Ideology in Social Movement Research." *Mobilization* 5:37–54.

Oliver, Pamela E. 1993. "Formal Models of Collective Action." *Annual Review of Sociology* 19:271–300.

Pew Research Center. 2018. "The #MeToo Hashtag Has Been Used Roughly 19 Million Times on Twitter in the Past Year, and Usage Often Surges around News Events." Accessed July 31, 2019. https://www.pewresearch.org/fact-tank/2018/10/11/how-social-media-users-have-discussed-sexual-harassment-since-metoo-went-viral/ft_18-10-11_metooanniversary_hashtag-used-19m_times/.

Piven, Frances Fox. 2006. *Challenging Authority: How Ordinary People Change America*. Lanham, MD: Rowman & Littlefield.

Porta, Donatella Della, and Mario Diani. 2008. *Social Movements: An Introduction*. 2nd ed. New York: Wiley-Blackwell.

Read, Jen'Nan Ghazal, and John P. Bartkowski. 2000. "To Veil or Not to Veil? A Case Study of Identity Negotiation among Muslim Women in Austin, Texas." *Gender & Society* 14 (3): 395–417.

Rosenberg, Jessica, and Gitana Garofalo. 1998. "Riot Grrrl: Revolutions from Within." *Signs* 23 (3): 809–41.

Rupp, Leila J. 1997. *Worlds of Women: The Making of an International Women's Movement*. Princeton, NJ: Princeton University Press.

Snow, David A., E. B. Rochford Jr., S. K. Worden, and R. D. Benford. 1986. "Frame Alignment Processes, Micromobilization, and Movement Participation." *American Sociological Review* 51 (4): 464–81.

INDEX

Oligarchy, 196–197
One-drop rule, 163–164
Organic solidarity, 17
Organizing, 328
Overshoot, 304
Overworked, 226
Ozone-depleting substances, 307

Pager, Devah, 44
Pakistan, 297–298
Panfil, Vanessa, 100
Paradigm shift theory, 308–309
Parenting
    discipline approaches, 221, 222
    "free range parenting" case,
        21–23, 25–26, 27, 30–31
    intensive mothering, 220
    single parenthood, 216f–217, 225
    social class, 221–222, 240
Paris Agreement on climate change
    (2015), 307
Park, Robert, 167
Parsons, Talcott, 218, 261
Participant-observation, 44
Participatory action research (PAR), 342
Pascoe, C. J., 142
Passing, 112
Patient Protection and Affordable Care
    Act, 203, 273, 275
Paulson, Henry, 199
Payne, Stanley, 206
Peer pressure, 83
Peers, as agents of socialization, 81, 83
People for the Ethical Treatment of
    Animals (PETA), 330
Performance of social roles, 90–91
Pfeffer, Carla A., 219
Phipps, Susie Guillory, 163–164
Pinsky, Dina, 112
Pitts, Kristin, 196
Piven, Francis Fox, 342
Play and socialization, 79–80
Plessy v. Ferguson (1896), 166
Pluralism
    political, 198
    religious, 280–281f
Plutocracy, 197
Police violence, 182–183, 340
Policy
    economic, of Donald Trump, 130–131
    education, 251, 252–255
    families and work, 215, 225–229
    family, 226, 227t–228t
Policy-planning network, 200
Politics
    economy and, 200–207
    party affiliation trends, 283, 284f
    theoretical approaches to, 198–200
Polls, 40, 203
Popular culture, 65
Population, sampling, 49
Population and the environment, 310–312
Post-Fordism, 202
Postindustrial economy and
    education, 235

Postindustrial knowledge,
    education and, 234–235
Poverty
    culture of poverty theory, 124–125f
    educational consequences, 127
    housing issues, 127–128
    population growth and, 311
    social constructionism, 29–30
    University of the Poor, 329
    War on Poverty, 131
    See also Economic inequality
Power
    charismatic domination, 193–194f
    determinants of socioeconomic
        status, 120
    distributive power, 199–200
    government, types of, 195–200
    legitimate *vs.* illegitimate uses of, 190
    rational-legal domination, 193
    rewriting of history and, 168
    social movement success and, 327
    traditional domination, 193
    See also Politics; State, the
Power elite, 199
Prayer in school, 280
Preindustrial societies, education in, 234
Prejudice, 164
Preschool programs, 240–241
Presentation of self skills, 28–29
Primary deviance, 107
Primary groups, 28, 89
Primary socialization, 28
Private sphere, 214
Privatization, 206, 207
Production and environmental
    change, 312–313
Profane, 279
Program evaluation, 133, 196
Prohibition, 104, 105f
Proletariat, 23–24, 62, 120
Property tax, 242
Props, 28, 90–91
Protestant work ethic, 295
Protestantism, decline of, 285t
Protests, 326
Public education. *See* Education
Public housing, 117
Public morality, creating, 104
Public policy and education,
    252–255
Public sociology, 72, 73, 154
Public sphere, 214
Punishment, 19–20, 102, 190
Push/pull factors, 167

QAnon, 14
Qatar, 146, 193, 251
Qualitative methods, 46
Quantitative data analysis, 46

Race, definition, 161
Race and ethnicity
    color-blind ideology, 182
    conflict theory, 237–238
    defining, 161–162

distinguishing, 161
government office and, 173–176f,
    174f, 175f
hate crimes, 183
interracial marriage, 166, 182f
one-drop rule, 163–164
religious affiliation and, 287–288f
social construction of, 30, 162–164
suicide rates, 103f
symbolic interactionism, 331–332
See also Immigrants
Racial/ethnic inequality
    conflict theory, 237–238
    criminal justice system, 171–173f
    discrimination, 164
    education, 81–82, 165, 237–238,
        241–242
    environmental racism, 316–318
    global considerations, 176–178t
    government office, 173–176f,
        174f, 175f
    health care, 173
    higher education, 171f, 245, 247t
    housing, 128, 169–170
    immigration legislation, 166–167
    institutional discrimination, 165
    Jim Crow laws, 101, 166
    labeling perspective of
        deviance, 106–109
    life expectancy, 271t
    negative consequences for
        society, 178–179
    prejudice and stereotypes, 9, 164
    school experiences, 237
    school segregation, 241–242
    voting, 165–166, 174f, 335, 337
    wage gap, 149, 150t
    ways to address, 183–184
    wealth gap, 117f–118, 122
    See also Civil rights movement
Racism
    color-blind ideology, 182
    defining, 164
    diversity training programs,
        179–181t, 180t
    environmental, 316–318
    global considerations, 176–178t
    hate crimes, 145, 183, 340–341
    police and Black people, 171–172
    police violence, 182–183
    teaching white students about, 184
    See also Discrimination;
        Racial/ethnic inequality
Racism evasiveness, 182
Random samples, 50
Rank, Mark, 124
Rational-legal domination, 193
Reciprocity norm, 220
Redemptive social movements, 330
Redlining, 169–170
Reformative social movements, 330
Refugees, 176–177
Reiman, Jeffrey, 100
Reinarman, Craig, 105, 106t
Relativist perspective of deviance, 99